FOURTH EDITION

CLOSE RELATIONS

An Introduction to the Sociology of Families

Susan A. McDANIEL
University of Lethbridge

Lorne TEPPERMAN
University of Toronto

Pearson Canada
Toronto

For my many friends who see me through the good times,
and bad—SM
To Sandra, my partner and closest relation—LT

Library and Archives Canada Cataloguing in Publication

McDaniel, Susan A., 1946–

    Close relations : an introduction to the sociology of families / Susan A. McDaniel,
Lorne Tepperman.—4th ed.

Includes bibliographical references and index.
ISBN 978-0-13-703171-9

1. Family—Canada—Textbooks.   I. Tepperman, Lorne, 1943–   II. Title.

HQ560.M28 2010   306.850971   C2009-907353-6

ISBN 978-0-13-703171-9

Vice-President, Editorial Director: Gary Bennett
Editor-in-Chief: Ky Pruesse
Editor, Humanities and Social Sciences: Joel Gladstone
Marketing Manager: Arthur Gee
Associate Editor: Brian Simons
Production Editors: Heather Sangster, Avivah Wargon
Copy Editor: Heather Sangster
Proofreader: Suzanne Needs

Production Coordinator: Sarah Lukaweski
Compositor: Aptara® Inc.
Photo Research: Rachel Irwin
Permissions Research: Roxana Chis
Art Director: Julia Hall
Cover Designer: Miriam Blier
Cover Image: Simon Marcus/Corbis

For permission to reproduce copyrighted material, the publisher gratefully acknowledges the copyright holders listed on pages throughout the text and on page 403, which are considered an extension of this copyright page.

Statistics Canada information is used with the permission of Statistics Canada. Users are forbidden to copy the data and redisseminate them, in an original or modified form, for commercial purposes, without permission from Statistics Canada. Information on the availability of the wide range of data from Statistics Canada can be obtained from Statistics Canada's Regional Offices, its World Wide Web site at **www.statcan.gc.ca**, and its toll-free access number 1-800-263-1136.

3 4 5   14 13 12 11

Printed and bound in the United States of America.

Brief Contents

Contents

Preface

As in previous editions, anonymous reviewers have suggested ways to improve the book and we have, in almost every instance, followed their helpful suggestions. This meant that first the book got very long, then we brought it down to size again—a process of editing somewhat like playing the accordion. In particular, reviewers asked us to talk more about the variety of Canadian families: about poor families and prosperous ones, rural families and urban ones, immigrant families and native-born—also, Aboriginal families, single-parent families, same-sex couples and opposite sex couples, single-earner couples and dual-earner couples, and so on. As you can imagine, talking about the general features of Canadian family life and the variations has proven a challenge.

That said, our book has remained the same in its essentials. Readers have agreed with our approach, which is to stress family process over structure, diversity over uniformity, and reality over myth. This is a Canadian book, rooted in sociological research from around the world, and reflecting concerns of the twenty-first century. It continues to cover all the most important topics in the family literature and, as before, ends with a look at the future of families.

THE APPROACH OF THIS BOOK

As recently as 30 years ago, books on the family were often simple "how-to" guides to family life. Sometimes called "matching, hatching, and dispatching" books, they often had chapters such as "Dating and Courtship" and "Family and You." This approach seemed reasonable a few decades ago since the ways in which people lived in families tended to be less diverse than now, and the diversity that did exist was neither portrayed nor celebrated in family texts. There are still books like this today, which tend to "sell" the traditional family way of life. But, of course, shifting patterns and demands of work in post-modern societies create new kinds of family relations and forms, as we explore in this fourth edition.

Far more interesting than the regularities in close relations are the variations in family processes, forms, and structures. Twenty-first-century families are remarkably diverse. It is largely in response to this reality that we wrote the first edition of this book, and then revised it substantially with updated data and new insights about families in the second and third editions, and again in this edition. This book sets itself the task of being different from other family books in use today. Its focus is on applications and theory: what works for families, for us as individuals, and for society. Several themes characterize our book:

- Families are immensely varied and characterized more by processes than by the forms they take.

- Family is becoming more, not less, important to us as individuals and to society as a whole. Recent research and theory have clearly shown that family health affects individual health and longevity and the population health of entire countries.

- Old expectations about family may no longer work. New solutions to family problems, based on what is known from family research, are offered here.

- There is a constantly changing interplay among families, school, and work. Family is both part of the problem and part of the solution, as shown in this book in a variety of ways.

- Historical changes and cross-national comparisons help us to better understand and interpret families today.

Throughout this book, we look at families as plural and diverse. We focus on families in terms of what they do rather than the shape they take.

CANADIAN CONTENT

Speaking of diversity, this is a Canadian book intended primarily for Canadian students and classrooms. While some generalizations based on American, European, or Asian data apply to Canadian situations, others do not. Our laws and policies are different, as are our histories, traditions, values, norms, and customs relating to family and marriage. At the same time, it is difficult to write a text based entirely on the findings of Canadian research. It must be noted, however, that both the volume of research on families in Canada and the scope of the topics covered have expanded enormously in recent years. A Canadian text, to be useful, should rely on the Canadian research and then incorporate findings from abroad. Thus, we attempt here a careful triangulation, using research from Canada, the United States, and the world. We try to offer international comparisons wherever we feel they are important. On the other hand, we do not draw attention to the nationality of a finding if we think that doing so adds nothing to understanding the research on families.

BRIEF OVERVIEW

Chapter 1 begins with an exploration of the variety of interesting shapes and processes of families and family-like relationships. We explore competing definitions of family, and how families are seen through theoretical lenses. We also consider different research approaches to family work, and what they enable us to see.

From here, we move on to Chapter 2, which opens the door to what we now know about families in the past. It offers an exciting glimpse of family diversity from a historical perspective. This discussion provides context for today's debates.

Chapter 3 then explores how families begin by taking a look at dating and mating. A renewed emphasis on ethnic and other cultural differences is offered here; attention is also paid to same-sex dating.

In Chapter 4 we examine the different ways couples form and live, including cohabitation, marriage patterns, and same-sex partnerships.

There follows in Chapter 5 a discussion of ways of being close in which we consider points of satisfaction and dissatisfaction, particularly in relation to communication, trust, and sex.

People sometimes think of real family life as beginning with the entry into parenthood—a time fraught with many new changes and challenges. That is the subject of Chapter 6. In this chapter we also propose several approaches to parenting that are supported by research, and offer some solutions to parenting problems.

In Chapter 7 we discuss work and family life, including the division of both domestic work and paid work. Domestic work is a known source of family conflict, while paid work in relation to the family is a topic of strong interest, as most adult members of families must balance family life with paid employment.

An understanding of violence and stress in families, the topic of Chapter 8, is crucial if we are to solve or even ameliorate these problems. We describe some of the contexts in which stresses occur for families, including poverty, racism, alcoholism, and the particular challenges faced by First Nations families. We also give attention to policies that attempt to reduce the negative situations with which families must cope.

In Chapter 9, the trends, myths, causes, and consequences of relationship dissolution and divorce are considered.

If couples divorce, some people remarry, and some experience step-parenthood. Other families, over the life course, go through the stages of children growing up and leaving home. Second (or subsequent) families, in all their diversity, are the topic of Chapter 10.

Chapter 11 takes a glimpse at families of the future, emphasizing how families create their own futures, influenced by both the opportunities and the constraints of society.

CHAPTER FEATURES

Each chapter of the text begins with a chapter outline.

Throughout the chapters, figures, tables, and boxes cover key current data on the topics, erroneous beliefs, international findings, major Canadian findings, and key statistics. The most important new feature is a series of boxes in each chapter that contain interesting facts and observations drawn from other studies.

Study tools at the end of each chapter include a chapter summary, key terms with definitions, critical thinking questions, and an annotated list of relevant internet sites.

SUPPLEMENTS

Instructor's Manual. An instructor's manual is available with this fourth edition. Its features include chapter outlines, key terms and concepts, motivational activities, answers to critical thinking questions in the text, critical thinking exercises, debate suggestions, group activities, project suggestions, and film and video suggestions.

Test Item File. This carefully prepared test item file contains over 600 multiple-choice questions that correspond to the text. Designed to test students' comprehension of the material, this supplement contains the relevant page numbers from the textbook along with the correct answer for each question.

Both the Instructor's Manual and Test Item File can be downloaded by instructors from a password-protected section of Pearson Education Canada's on-line catalogue (**http://vig.pearsoned.ca**). Navigate to the catalogue page for your textbook to view the list of those supplements that are available. Contact your local sales representative for further information.

ACKNOWLEDGMENTS

The decision to prepare a new edition of this book, though welcome, came when both authors were deeply involved in other projects and, in one case, changing her job and home to Canada from the United States. So, spring and summer of 2009 were not the relaxed, refreshing seasons we might have imagined or hoped for. Instead, they demanded fast, intense work on the book, for we resolved to improve the book significantly even though our time was limited. (The alternatives—to leave the book mostly unchanged or delay revising for another full year—were both unsatisfactory.)

In this edition, we wanted to improve the book in ways both small and not so small. We wanted to include much more discussion of poor families, immigrant families, Aboriginal families, and same-sex couples, for example—in general, to extend the variety of families we discuss in this book and the sensitivity with which we discuss them.

To achieve this goal we relied on a team of research assistants to help; and we were lucky to get excellent support from them. So, our first thanks go to five outstanding undergraduate assistants at the University of Toronto—Natalie Alfano, Roxy Chis, Ekaterina Dolganova, Nina Gheihman, and Rebecca Young—who helped us update and upgrade the third edition by collecting and reviewing new materials for inclusion. Additionally, Roxy Chis compiled the permissions for this edition of the book. Finally, thanks go to undergraduate Marika Dabek for photo suggestions. These fine assistants gave us a huge leg-up in the revision and we thank them for helping so enthusiastically.

Second, we want to thank the people at Pearson for their wonderful support from beginning to end. This includes Joel Gladstone, who encouraged us to revise the book; Brian Simons, who helped develop the changes; and Avivah Wargon, who shepherded the book through production. Important among the professional helpers is Heather Sangster from Strong Finish, who edited the copy and got it print-ready. Heather, a real professional, made the final stages of the publishing process easy and quick. We thank you, Heather, for ensuring that the revision that began inauspiciously would nonetheless finish strongly.

The authors are grateful to those colleagues who acted as reviewers for this edition, including: Ayalah Aylyn, the University of Alberta; Richard Haigh, Grant MacEwan University; Kate Krug, Cape Breton University; and Ann Wagner, Nippissing University.

We hope our readers, new and old, will enjoy this version of the book. Please let us know what you think about it.

Susan McDaniel, University of Lethbridge
Lorne Tepperman, University of Toronto

PEARSON mysearchlab

MySearchLab offers students extensive help with their writing and research project and provides round-the-clock access to credible and reliable source material.

Research

Content on MySearchLab includes immediate access to thousands of full-text articles from leading Canadian and international academic journals, and daily news feeds from The Associated Press. Articles contain the full downloadable text—including abstract and citation information—and can be cut, pasted, emailed, or saved for later use.

Writing

MySearchLab also includes a step-by-step tutorial on writing a research paper. Included are sections on planning a research assignment, finding a topic, creating effective notes, and finding source material. Our exclusive online handbook provides grammar and usage support. Pearson SourceCheck™ offers an easy way to detect accidental plagiarism issues, and our exclusive tutorials teach how to avoid them in the future. And MySearchLab also contains AutoCite, which helps to correctly cite sources using MLA, APA, CMS, and CBE documentation styles for both endnotes and bibliographies.

To order this book with MySearchLab access at no extra charge, use ISBN 978-0-13-208852-7.

Take a tour at **www.mysearchlab.com**.

COURSESMART FOR INSTRUCTORS

CourseSmart goes beyond traditional expectations—providing instant, online access to the textbooks and course materials you need at a lower cost for students. And even as students save money, you can save time and hassle with a digital eTextbook that allows you to search for the most relevant content at the very moment you need it. Whether it's evaluating textbooks or creating lecture notes to help students with difficult concepts, CourseSmart can make life a little easier. See how when you visit **www.coursesmart.com/instructors**.

COURSESMART FOR STUDENTS

CourseSmart goes beyond traditional expectations—providing instant, online access to the textbooks and course materials you need at an average saving of 50%. With instant access from any computer and the ability to search your text, you'll find the content you need quickly, no matter where you are. And with online tools like highlighting and note-taking, you can save time and study efficiently. See all the benefits at **www.coursesmart. com/students**.

Chapter 1
Families and Family-Like Relationships
Definitions, Theories, and Research

Chapter Outline

INTRODUCTION

Among our deepest and most enduring human needs is to have someone close who understands and loves us and in whom we can confide and trust. In an uncertain and insecure world, we seek solace and hope in close relations.

Families belong to a group of relationships we would characterize as "close," including intense friendships, love affairs, and long-term work relationships. These relationships are characterized by a strong attachment or bonding between the partners. Of course, not all family members feel strongly attached or bonded to each other. However, what people commonly imagine when they think of the word "family"—what the word "family" evokes in our culture—is attachment, sentiment, and emotional intensity. For most of us, families provide our most important relationships, our first connection to the social world, and one that remains important throughout our lives.

This book explores the changing dimensions of family relations and the ways in which they affect and are affected by school, work, society, and, perhaps most importantly, social changes. We examine the diversity of close relations and consider how families may be becoming more rather than less important in our lives.

THE IMPORTANCE OF FAMILY

Some people point to the upsurge in single-parent households, increases in the number of children born outside legal marriage (Statistics Canada, 2002b), and high divorce rates (Statistics Canada, 2002d) as evidence that the family is in trouble. At the same time, public opinion polls consistently find that family life is important to Canadians (Angus Reid, 1999; Vanier Institute of the Family, 2004)—perhaps increasingly important. In fact, despite negative trends in marriages, nearly 90 percent of Canadians still consider having children an important aspect of their lives, and about 70 percent consider getting married at some point in their lifetime important (Bibby, 2004c).

People continue to value families because they provide emotional support and economic benefits. Perhaps most importantly, families give us grounding in an otherwise uncertain and chaotic world. The familiarity of family can be reassuring and, throughout our lives, gives us the confidence to explore new things.

WHAT IS FAMILY?

Most people think of families as groups of people related through marriage, blood, or adoption. But is that description specific enough? Is it inclusive enough?

To some people, the answer seems obvious. They argue that the word "families" should be used only to describe "traditional families." Fifty-eight percent of Canadians feel that a traditional family—with one husband, one wife, and children—is the ideal (Bibby, 2004c). But families have varied in form throughout history, still vary from one society to another, and are very different within societies like Canada and the United States. There is, in this sense, no traditional family.

In this text we shall examine the ways in which families are now viewed. We will see that these changes are closely tied to events in society and to what is seen as a social problem or concern.

DEFINING THE FAMILY

People tend to think when they talk about family that everyone is talking about the same thing. "How's the family?" someone might ask, referring perhaps to one's spouse and possibly children. "I'm taking time now to have a family," says a woman to her co-worker. "My family came from the Ukraine," says another. An HIV/AIDs survivor says, "My family are

---

What Is the Family?

Other things may change us, but we start and end with family.

> —Anthony Brandt

Families are like fudge—mostly sweet with a few nuts.

> —Author Unknown

To us, family means putting your arms around each other and being there.

> —Barbara Bush

We cannot destroy kindred: our chains stretch a little sometimes, but they never break.

> —Marquise de Sévigné

The family. We were a strange little band of characters trudging through life sharing diseases and toothpaste, coveting one another's desserts, hiding shampoo, borrowing money, locking each other out of our rooms, inflicting pain and kissing to heal it in the same instant, loving, laughing, defending, and trying to figure out the common thread that bound us all together.

> —Erma Bombeck

Family life is a bit like a runny peach pie—not perfect but who's complaining?

> —Robert Brault

What greater thing is there for two human souls than to feel that they are joined—to strengthen each other—to be at one with each other in silent unspeakable memories.

> —George Eliot

A family is a unit composed not only of children but of men, women, an occasional animal, and the common cold.

> —Ogden Nash

Source: www.quotegarden.com/family.html.

those around me now who support me." Immigration policy refers to "family reunification," where the concept of family has shrunk recently to include only close blood relatives and spouses. What do these images of family have in common? How differently do we see family?

The answers to these questions about family are not merely academic. How family and other close relations are defined matters to us personally—to our values, our dreams, our hopes as individuals, and our identities.

These definitions are important for our rights under the law and to our claims to pensions, schools, and many other social resources.

Debates rage about common-law spouses having the same rights as married spouses, about spousal rights for gays and lesbians, and about the financial responsibilities and the rights (to custody, access, and so on) of divorced people. Let's look now at some definitions of family.

MURDOCK: THREE RELATIONSHIPS

For many years, sociologists used as a benchmark George Murdock's (1949: 1) definition of family as

> a social group characterized by a common residence, economic cooperation and reproduction [including] adults of both sexes, at least two of whom maintain a socially approved sexual relationship, and one or more children, own or adopted, of the sexually cohabiting adults.

Note that by this definition, three basic relationships—co-residence, economic co-operation, and reproduction—must all be present to qualify a social group as a family. Murdock's definition excludes many groups that most of us would consider families: childless married couples, for example, and single parents and their children. Same-sex unions would be excluded, as would be married couples who are separated. Celibate couples, according to Murdock, cannot be a family even if they have children, live together, and share other kinds of intimacy. (This means questioning a couple about their sex life to find out whether they and their children make up a family.) Two sisters who live together cannot be a family, according to Murdock. Thus, Murdock's definition does not seem to allow for the variability that exists among families living in Canada today.

Census Family

Because the approach to defining family discussed previously is so limiting, Statistics Canada (2006a), the official census and survey agency for Canada, takes a much more inclusive approach. Statistics Canada defines family, for the Census, as comprising a married or a common-law couple (a couple can be opposite sex or same sex) with or without children, or a lone parent living with at least one child in the same dwelling. Married or common-law couple families with children refer to a family with at least one child aged 24 and younger who is present in the home. This definition also includes children from either a current or previous union, but excludes children who might have a permanent residence other than that of their parents at the time of the Census.

This definition is better, since it includes a wider variety of people. However, it still misses many groups that would consider themselves to be families, and would be considered families by others outside of their household. This being so, many researchers have changed their focus to households for practical purposes.

Household versus Family

Market researchers and census-takers often try to sidestep difficulties of definition by focusing on "households" as though they were "families." Doing so allows us to talk about changes in households and imply changes in close relations without necessarily addressing changes in families or family life. But this approach also presents problems. As pointed out clearly by Eichler (1997), many families live in separate households but maintain ongoing family relationships. The prime example is divorced families in which custody is joint or shared (Smart and Neale, 1999); the divorced parents and their child(ren) form at least one family and maybe more. For other trends in Canadian families such as this, see "Six Trends for Canadian Families."

A "household" may contain only one person or many unrelated members—roommates, boarders, or residents in a group home. Or it may contain a **nuclear family**, an **extended family**, or multiple families (for example, communes or families sharing living space to save money). Sharing living accommodations among generations is, as we shall see, a growing trend in Canada. Sometimes, these arrangements involve multiple families—parents, for example, with their parents or with their adult children's families. Conversely, a family may spread across many households, even households located in different countries. However, usually families and households coincide, resulting in "family households."

In the United States, family households are officially defined by the Bureau of the Census as married couples with or without children younger than 18 years or one-parent families with children younger than 18. Family households also comprise other households of related individuals (for example, two sisters sharing a household or a parent living with a child older than 17). Non-family households contain unrelated individuals or people who live alone. Canadian definitions from Statistics Canada and other official data-gathering organizations are similar.

Process-Based Definitions

The United Nations (1991) prefers to define family by the important **socio-economic functions** it performs, such as emotional, financial, and material support to its members, care of each other, transmission of cultural values, and personal development. In doing so, the UN is defining families in terms of their main shared processes, rather than in terms of structural features that they may not—and increasingly do not—share. The Vanier Institute of the Family (2000) uses this function- or process-based definition of family in Canada.

In Canada, serious consideration has been given to the question of what family is and what families are. The question has been taken up by family researchers, the Vanier Institute of the Family, and the Canada Committee for the International Year of the Family on which one of the authors of this book (McDaniel) served. The conclusion is that ultimately families are defined not by the shape they take but by what they do (Vanier Institute of the Family 2004: xii). As Moore Lappé (1985: 8) puts it:

> Families are not marriages or homes or rules. Families are people who develop intimacy because they . . . share experiences that come . . . to make up their uniqueness—the mundane, even silly, traditions that emerge in a group of people who know each other . . . It is this intimacy that provides the ground for our lives.

Over the past two decades, a broad process-based definition of family has become generally accepted by most Canadians (see Angus Reid, 1999; Vanier Institute of the Family, 2000, 2004). Much of current Canadian family law and policy reflects the move toward inclusion of families that are diverse but similar in their processes, if not their structures (Vanier Institute of the Family, 2004).

For example, on June 1, 2003, Alberta passed the Adult Interdependent Relationships Act. The law redefines relationship as "a range of personal relationships that fall outside of the traditional institution of marriage" (Alberta Justice, 2002). By doing so, it amends several statutes as they relate to people in non-conjugal relationships and recognizes financial and property benefits and responsibilities attached to these relationships.

Clearly, governments as well as various bodies are trying to keep up with societal changes in the family. However, some groups continue to oppose inclusive definitions. The diversity of families is controversial and has become a highly political issue, with some "family values" groups pushing to have these issues placed at the forefront of the national agenda or some provincial agendas (see Baker, 2005a; Stacey, 1996, for examples). Gay and lesbian families, for example, have become a touchstone in many contemporary debates about what is and is not a family and what rights and entitlements those who are deemed family ought to have. Remember that Statistics Canada, in its recently modified definition of Census family mentioned earlier, includes same-sex families. Similarly, immigration and growing ethnic diversity have challenged the ways we define, form, maintain, and connect in close relations. Definitions of what is family matter greatly when it comes to bringing family members to Canada. And, of course, these definitions may differ by cultural group.

How family is defined and thought about is a weathervane for social ideas and ideologies, and the kind of research done on families reflects the concerns of the day. We shall explore this idea in more detail later on in this chapter.

Six Trends for Canadian Families

- The number of common-law couple families increased 18.9 percent between 2001 and 2006, which is more than five times the increase for married-couple families.

- In 2006, there were more census families that consisted of couples without children (42.7 percent) than with children (41.4 percent).

- Lone-parent families headed by men increased by 14.6 percent since 2001.

- In 2006, young children aged four and younger were more likely to have a mother in her 40s than in 2001.

- More children aged 14 and younger are living in homes with common-law parents (14.6 percent).

- More young adults aged 20 to 29 are living in the parental home compared to 2001.

Source: Statistics Canada. 2007. *Family Portrait: Continuity and Change in Canadian Families and Households in 2006.* Ottawa: Statistics Canada. Catalogue Number 97-553-XIE.

COMMON ELEMENTS OF FAMILY LIFE

The social groups we think of as families typically share many features, and that commonality can help us begin to understand the nature of families. Because families are extraordinarily diverse, it is difficult to generalize about them. However, it is possible to focus our attention on their common processes.

Dependency and Intimacy

All close relations have in common attachment and some dependency or interdependency. This is not unique to families; most close friendships and work relationships also include some degree of emotional dependency, based on familiarity and expectations of reciprocity. However, family relations are special in that they tend to include long-term commitments, both to each other and to the shared family.

Sexuality

Adult partners within families typically have, or are expected to have, a long-term, exclusive sexual relationship, whereas among co-workers and among friends, sexual relations are either absent or of short duration. In families, sexual relations are allowed and expected between certain members (for example, spouses) but banned between other members (for example, parents and children). Norms of sexual propriety are much stronger in families than they are in friendship or work groups. Taboos against sexual exploitation of children exist to prevent sexual relations with a family member other than a spouse. Nevertheless, sexual abuse of children and elders does occur within families.

Protection

Effective families keep their members under guard against all kinds of internal and external dangers. There is a clear cultural expectation that families will try to protect their members. Parents and relatives are supposed to keep children safe from accidents and household dangers, and away from drugs, alcohol, predators, and other forms of harm. As well, spouses are supposed to protect one another, and adult children are supposed to protect and help their parents. All this is an ideal, of course. In reality, family members often fail to protect each other enough, and worse, some people neglect, exploit, or abuse family members. However, those who break the cultural rules face criticism and disapproval.

Power

Households and families are small social groups whose members spend time together and depend on each other to fill both economic and social needs. There are large differences in power, strength, age, and social resources among members. Ideally, the more powerful family members protect the less powerful ones. However, it is this imbalance in power that makes **patriarchy**—control of the family by a dominant male (typically, the father)—a central fact in the history of family life in most known societies. Simply put, men have dominated because they possessed and controlled more of the resources. And, in much of family law and policy, this domination over family by men was seen as a right, sometimes even a duty.

Violence

Likewise, families—though ideally peaceful and loving—are also marked by violence, perhaps to a higher degree than any other groups based on "close relations." Although violence has always existed in families, in the last few decades there have been growing reports of violence within families. Some estimate that one woman in ten will be assaulted at some time in her life. Usually the assailant is a spouse or boyfriend. As well, researchers estimate that one girl in four and one boy in ten is sexually abused before the age of 16, often by friends or relatives. Perhaps violence is more common in families than in other close relations precisely because for many, the family is a place of intense emotions. Also, proximity simply makes it more convenient for violence to be inflicted. Besides, some family members are young or otherwise vulnerable and cannot easily escape.

KINSHIP, CLAN, AND COMMUNITY

So far we have focused on families as they exist normatively in our own dominant culture. However, families vary from one society to another, just as they vary within our own society. In many societies families exist within larger social networks—within kinship groups and clans—and we cannot really understand how these families function unless we also understand their place in these larger networks, and in the community at large. The members of the household—the husband and wife, parent and child, brother and sister—are thoroughly integrated into a larger web of kin—uncles, aunts, cousins, grandparents, grandchildren—and their lives cannot be understood without reference to this larger web.

A **kinship group** is a group of people who share a relationship through blood and/or marriage and have positions in a hierarchy of rights over the property. The definition of a kin relationship varies between societies; kin relationships may also influence where the members must live, whom they can marry, and even their life opportunities.

Some societies count relationships through the male line, so that any individual's relationships are determined by his or her father's relationships; we call such kinship systems **patrilineal**. Others count relationships through the female line; these are **matrilineal** systems. Still others count relationships through both lines; they are **bilateral kinship systems**.

The Canadian system is mildly patrilineal. For example, a woman has historically taken her husband's family name, not the reverse, and this name is the one that passes to the children. It should be noted, however, that this is not the case everywhere in the West. In Quebec, for example, the law prevents women from taking their husband's name on marriage.

Our family system follows the Western pattern, in which property is also typically inherited along the male line. Where families settle down is traditionally determined by the husband's job, not the wife's, although this too is changing. However, our society also has certain matrifocal characteristics. Because women have been defined as the primary **kin-keepers**—the people who maintain family contacts—children tend to have stronger ties with their mother's kin than with their father's kin (Rosenthal, 1985; Thomson and Li, 1992: 15). Children also preserve closer contacts with their mothers when the parents grow old (Connidis, 2001). When parents of grown children live separately, fathers are less often visited, called, and relied on than are mothers.

NEW WAYS TO UNDERSTAND FAMILY DIVERSITY

In this book, we will argue repeatedly that some of the older ways of understanding family life do not serve us well in a diverse and fluid society. As a result, we have adopted some new approaches to studying family life. We did not invent all these new approaches, however; they enjoy wide currency among many sociologists.

The life course approach is one new way of studying family change. This approach follows the variety of social and interpersonal dynamics of close relations and how these change throughout our lifetimes (Elder, 1992; Klein and White, 1996; Kohli, 1986). Over time, families change—they have to change—to meet new needs, such as the arrival, care, or departure of children. These changes have effects on the entire family system: on relations between spouses, parents and children, and siblings; and on the family's relations with the "outside world," such as parents' changing relations with their employers and their careers (Kruger and Levy, 2001; McDaniel, 2001, 2002).

Another "new" approach is to look at family relations from the perspectives of different family members. This approach recognizes that within any given family, different family members have different interests and experiences. Smart and Neale (1999) use this approach, for example, to study post-divorce families. Because different family members often have different interests, it is often inappropriate to speak of "the family" as though it has a single interest and acts in a unified way.

Much family research until the 1970s was done from a male perspective (Eichler, 2001; Giddens, 1992; Luxton, 1997). A popular phrase of the time that has stuck is "bedroom communities," which describes suburban communities in which families lived and women often worked at home. These were living communities and could be seen as bedrooms only from the point of view of men who worked elsewhere. Many other examples exist. What do family life and changes in close relations among adults look like from the viewpoint of children, for example? They look markedly different, as we are now discovering (Marcil-Gratton, 1993; Mason, Skolnick, and Sugarman, 2003). Children live in many and varied kinds of families while still dependent, and changes in family are happening earlier in their lives than those of children in times past. Looking at the changes in close relations among adults from the viewpoint of children gives us a new and important vantage point on families.

Another way to study family diversity is by exploring different groups in society in order to better understand the ways in which families function. This book, for instance, examines the way rural, Aboriginal, and gay and lesbian families work and the way historical and societal changes have shaped and influenced their family life. Consider Aboriginal families. Because of changes imposed on them by the Canadian government, many Aboriginal children were separated from their families and shipped off to boarding schools or to live with other Canadian families in an effort to integrate them into mainstream society. In doing so, many parents were unable to pass on important Aboriginal traditions to their children or be the loving and caring parents they would have liked to be. This, as it will be seen in the following chapters, has had lasting negative effects for Aboriginal families.

By studying differences in families, we learn that although families may look different, it is essentially the process of family life that is important to the health of its members. For one, gay and lesbian families may not be structured like the "typical" heterosexual family, but research shows that usually they provide security, love, and other fundamental family tasks to their children and partner.

Yet another "new" approach is to collect data in new ways so family diversity can be studied over time. One example is Statistics Canada's Survey of Labour and Income Dynamics (SLID) (Statistics Canada, 1996a), which builds a picture of the changes in people's work and family lives over time. Cheal (1997), for example, relies on SLID to examine the longer-term effects of being in a financially dependent family while young or at various life course stages. He finds the effects of both dependence and poverty of youth increase intergenerational inequities over time. Thus, families have different "life histories," and as these histories develop and change over time, they shape the prospects of their members, especially the youngest members.

Another example is Statistics Canada's Longitudinal Survey of Children and Youth (Willms, 2002). This survey follows individual children as they grow up, interviewing them and their families every two years. Data are collected on family changes, schooling, health, and a whole range of variables that affect children's lives. A wealth of new insights is emerging about children's lives and how families and society can best benefit from these insights in the long run. Findings from this survey have already taught us that the effect on children of living with a single parent is more than the result of the low incomes often faced by such families. The good news from this longitudinal research is that good parenting can, largely, overcome these harmful effects. Much more is to be learned by following the same people (children or adults) over time and seeing whether they can, eventually, escape the disadvantages of a low-income childhood and, if so, how.

Of course, all families change, and the times change families. For example, Whitehead (1990: 1) reminds us that "Today's stay-at-home mother is tomorrow's working mother." Or, as Swedish social policy sees it, every married woman with children today is potentially a divorced or separated lone mother tomorrow. Whitehead (1990: 1) points out that families change with the times: "One day, the Ozzie and Harriet couple is eating a family meal at the dining room table; the next day, they are working out a joint custody agreement in a law office." Studying families in a context of change reminds us to stay away from any simple definitions of family, or theories about family life that assume that all families are the same, and stay the same, regardless of their historical context.

THEORETICAL APPROACHES TO UNDERSTANDING FAMILIES

A theory simply puts things together in an orderly fashion, helping us to see and understand the social world. Theories are ways of seeing that help us to focus. Each theoretical approach is different, and each one may have a different insight to contribute to our understanding. Here, we will look at two things. First, we discuss how the thinking about families and the research on families has changed over time. These changes in thinking are closely tied to the events and climate in society at the time. Second, we highlight some basic theoretical approaches to understanding families; however, these are not all the theoretical approaches that exist. Each one of the approaches presented will, we hope, allow you to begin to see aspects of families that you might not be able to see without the use of the theoretical lens.

Theories of Family over Time

Thinking about families over time is challenging for sociologists for three linked reasons. First, there is new information, not only about families now but also about families in the past and how they lived. This new information challenges our understandings and shakes our beliefs about families and family change. Second, new ways to view families, socially and politically, are connected to new theories about families. If you think theories are only academic, think again! Feminist and gay/lesbian theories of family have been hotly contested by society's interest groups and by some politicians. And the debate goes beyond family theory. New sociological and cultural studies theories and their proponents were blamed in part for the lack of simple political agreement on the causes of the September 11, 2001, events. Americans, and at times Canadians too, were asked not only to denounce terrorists and terrorism but also to avoid postmodern social theorizing— theorizing which suggested that societies are complex, with many factors leading to the taking up of terrorism. Theories are very much alive and part of public debate. Third, changing family lives and changing ways to see families have risks and concerns that make us constantly question and revise our theories. Keep these challenges in mind as we out- line how families have been viewed over time.

Family, as such, is a surprisingly recent social idea. Before the eighteenth century in Europe, for example, the term "family" was not used at all (Flandrin, 1979), even when people lived in groups that we would today see as nuclear families—parents with their children. More important then was the larger social grouping or the community. The focus, for example, lay in how people lived to survive, how they produced food and shared it. Therefore much of the study of communities, and indirectly of families, has focused on sustaining life.

Anthropological, close-up studies of small, simply organized communities have found that in foraging societies—which gathered food such as roots and berries—child-bearing was more likely to be postponed to later in life than in early agricultural societies (Fox and Luxton, 2001). Since there were few assets to inherit in societies that foraged, it was argued in theory that there were fewer restrictions on how children were viewed in relation to their parents. Families per se may not have been seen to "own children."

A well-known theory developed by Friedrich Engels ([1884] 1972), the theoretical collaborator of Karl Marx, in the late nineteenth century paints a picture of people living in a group without giving much importance to whose spouse was whose or which children belonged to which parents. The children were "parented" by the entire community, Engels suggests. All children were welcomed, and even though their biological parents may have been known, it didn't change how people lived. There was some evidence that communities like this did, in fact, exist. Some still live much like this, even in urban neighbourhoods (see Stacey, 1990), with entire communities raising children with little focus on nuclear family structures as such.

Once agricultural development began to yield a food surplus, people no longer consumed their food immediately but could save and store it. This led to the idea of "private property" and new ideas about family life. Then, Engels says, it mattered much more who a child's parents were as inheritance was to follow bloodlines. How these bloodlines were decided is unclear, according to Engels' theory. Men began to control the food surplus, it was theorized. Women were expected to be sexually faithful to their husbands, to ensure the children they had were, in fact, their husband's. Monogamy was born not because it was more moral than any other system of family or because living in families was a natural way to live. Monogamy was related, according to Engels' theory, to the economics of life at the time.

In part, some contemporary controversies and debates about family life are efforts to wrest the family away from the effects of economic factors and forces. For example, some conservative groups argue that the family is more natural and fundamental than any economic change. Families, they argue, should respond to economic pressures and shifts by *not* changing. In this way, we are still engaging the theories about family from the late nineteenth century.

Another theory of family and family change parallels Engels' theory but follows a different thread at a different historical moment. The theory of Le Play in the nineteenth century suggests that families in feudal times were large and extended, with blood relatives and members of the community of the castle largely undifferentiated from each other. Large, extended families were not always happy families. Some, for example, had many children not because they wanted them or could afford them. As a result, some large families lived in poverty with a mother worn down by child-bearing. However, with the development of towns and trades and markets, this kind of community "family" became awkward. It was not easily mobile. So, the smaller "stem family" emerged, a family that runs the farm, or small shop, while the rest of the family moves on. In fact, it was this development that led, in large part, to a massive out-migration from Europe to North America in the nineteenth and the early twentieth century, as more people without access to family enterprises sought opportunities in the "new world" of North America.

Prior to the 1850s, sociology was only in its infancy, as was thinking about family. Family theory consisted, largely, of Judeo-Christian religious belief. The Biblical "begats" of the Old Testament characterized a patriarchal theory that saw an elder male as head of a community, clan, extended family, or even a realm. In many ways, monarchies are remnants of this system. It is only rarely, in the absence of a male heir, that women become the heads of state and spiritual leaders of the realm. The system of male headship was more than familial and private; it was a system of governing before public systems of law and democracy were invented. In fact, the parliamentary system of government in Canada still parallels democracy with a ruling monarch who is Head of State. The extended kin, headship system was presumed to be natural and unchanging in both theory and practice. It was also, theoretically at least, presumed as a model for the emerging, urban working class to follow.

With colonial rule in many parts of the world, this family system and the theory supporting it was exported. Many countries today in Africa and in other parts of the world that were part of the British Empire retain aspects of this family headship system, sometimes mixed with traditional cultural practices. Sociologists who study post-colonial societies work to sort out what is inherited from this system in today's policies and family practices and what is unique to that society. The study by Baker (2001) of Australia, New Zealand, and Canada is one example. She describes these three societies as "settler societies," in which we "can discuss the impact of colonial concepts of family on indigenous people, whose ideas about family structure and relationships differed from those of the colonizers in all three societies" (Baker, 2001: 3).

In the middle of the nineteenth century, debates in society started to challenge old religion-based theories about family. This, of course, does not mean that religious beliefs or religious theories about family disappeared. They did not. In fact, they have continued to this day, some say even more actively as the twentieth century closed and the twenty-first century began.

The emerging debate in the 1850s occurred as societies were changing rapidly with industrialization and the beginning of capitalism. Social unrest was apparent, as were social movements that challenged prevailing beliefs. One belief actively challenged at that time was the role of women in family and in society. New kinds of societies were springing up, based not on patriarchal authority, but on communal living arrangements where women and men were more equal and children could be raised collectively (Luxton, 2001: 34). This experimental approach continued with the kibbutz or collective farming settlement in Israel; many there are still communal. Elsewhere, people lobbied for women's rights in both marriage and society. Married women at that time were not entitled to own property or to vote, or to have many other citizenship rights that women today take for granted.

Paralleling these changing social attitudes were changing sociological theories. Émile Durkheim, known as one of the founders of sociology, saw family as a social creation, not as something given by nature or religion. His theories about family had two aspects, and the two did not fit together well. First, he argued in favour of "the law of contraction," or that families were, in the middle of the nineteenth century, being reduced in size at the same time as family ties were being intensified. Second, he then theorized that relations between husbands and wives were organized by society as monogamous and "near perfect" (Sydie, 1987: 19–20). The marriage relationship was seen by Durkheim as permanent, un-equal, highly regulated by society, and, crucially, the means of moral organization of all of society. Family was theorized as both less and more important than in earlier times. It was less important in that family sizes were reduced, but more important in that families' ties were strengthened. Key to Durkheim's contribution was his understanding of family as a social creation, not as something given by nature or religion.

As industrialization continued in the nineteenth century, family and work became more separate. Work, which had been an integral part of family life, was moved out of the family and into the marketplace. As work became separated from family, specialization of men in work and women in family began to emerge, creating the notion of separate spheres in which women were seen as being naturally suited to home life and raising chil-dren (private sphere) and men to the outside world (public sphere). Social theorists like Durkheim saw the bond between husband and wife as strengthened by this increasing spe-cialization (Sydie, 1987: 22). The search began for biological differences between men and women that would parallel the growing social differences in family and in society. In hindsight, some of these searches were rather amusing. A Dr. Lebon is quoted by Durkheim as reporting, "The volume of the crania of men and women, even when we compare subjects of equal age, of equal height and equal weight, show differences in favour of man . . ." (quoted in Sydie, 1987: 22). We now know that this difference does not exist (McGlone, 1980), and in fact, many historians and sociologists are now recog-nizing that even during this period of separate spheres and biological determinism, women still held a great amount of independence and autonomy in running their own households, employing and managing servants, and being involved in charity work. Regardless, that social theories about family were linked to presumed biological differences between men and women was significant to later theories. It is also important to observe that sociological theories of the day were in response to the push in society for social change.

Most of the sociological theorists of the nineteenth century were white, middle-class men. Many, it has been argued since, were keen to defend or promote the new capitalism and the new way to view marriage and family (Luxton, 2001). Some insisted that the birth rate would fall if marriage were changed, and if women were more equal to men. This way of thinking persists into the twenty-first century in some conservative circles. The argument is further made that the gender-unequal marriage is natural and based on both biology and God's will. Other theorists such as Herbert Spencer see this kind of family as a social construction that supports (and should support) capitalism. The patriarchal family was seen as the peak of social evolution (Luxton, 2001; Sydie, 1987). Had these social theorists been women, or working-class or Aboriginal or ethnic minorities, they might have viewed family very differently. Writings from some social movements of that time seem less content with the patriarchal family (Dua, 1999; Eichler, 2001; Luxton, 2001; Sydie, 1987).

The 1950s are seen as the "golden age" of the nuclear family when suburbs were settled and the standard North American family (SNAF) was born.

As society changed, so did the preoccupations of family researchers. For instance, in the 1920s when the Roaring Twenties overtook the Victorian era, sociologists turned their attention to dating and courtship. Women, previously so guarded in their appearance, dress, and behaviour, were dancing the Charleston in public, no longer wearing corsets, and showing not only ankles but also knees as they kicked up their heels! Speakeasy clubs became popular, where men and women could drink, socialize, dance, and listen to music and entertainers. Society, caught up as always in concerns about social and family change, worried. So, sociologists studied these changes by looking at relations among young people and changed dating practices.

The 1950s saw what many still consider the "golden age" of the nuclear family. The suburbs were created and nuclear families thrived, or at least seemed to. Moms did the child rearing and Dads commuted to work. Television programs such as *Father Knows Best, Leave It to Beaver,* and *The Adventures of Ozzie and Harriet* reflected the ideal in family life. The standard North American family (SNAF) was born. As in previous eras, this kind of family had the support of family theory. Patterns of thinking sociologically not only about families but also about all of society were formed at that time and continue into the twenty-first century. Although the theory of the day, structural functionalism (which we will discuss in more detail in the next section), was largely an American creation, it was widely used in various parts of the world. This coincided with a high period of American prestige in the post–World War II period when everything American was seen as good. The 1950s can be better seen as a response to a time of political insecurity and uncertainty after World War II that was, in general, an unusual decade in the twentieth century. This will be further discussed in Chapter 2.

In terms of family theory, the basic concept was that the family was an essential social institution, well adapted to fit into society. Further, the nuclear family differentiated by gender was seen as a universal, something good for everyone. Earlier work by Malinowski among the Australian Aborigines lent a credibility to the North American nuclear family form (Luxton, 2001). His views and assumptions about biological differences between men and women found their way into later theories of structural functionalists such as Talcott Parsons, a giant of twentieth-century sociology. Key to Malinowski's theory was that the nuclear family specialized by gender was essential for societies to function smoothly.

The advent of the structural functional theory led to research on men as breadwinners and less so on women as housewives. Research viewed families with a resolutely happy face. Until the late 1960s, there was nothing in the sociology of the family on family violence or on women's dissatisfaction with their families or their family roles. This is surprising, given what we know now of the "mad housewife" of the 1950s, the very high teen pregnancy rate, and the unhappiness of many men with the breadwinner role of that time. But, so it was.

Structural functional theories of family were not used only to study families; the same theories shaped workplace policies. If women, for example, were theorized to specialize in family, and men in work, then women were presumed not to be good workers. Married women, for example, were often fired from paid employment upon marriage since it was thought that they were now to be housewives and dependent economically on their husbands. Women, who were, according to family theory at the time, emotional and centred on caring, were not thought to be appropriate candidates for jobs that required judgment or supervision. They were also excluded from jobs that involved risk, such as pilots, miners, soldiers, and much blue-collar work. That women had done a lot of this kind of work during World War II while the men who usually worked in these jobs were at war didn't seem to matter. Women were thought to be family specialists and unsuited by nature to working for pay, and certainly not suited to working for pay in high-paying jobs!

Research using this theoretical approach was intensely focused on family dynamics and interactions and on how families around the world were becoming more similar and more like the U.S. ideal. Not surprisingly, other theories developed that let us look at these aspects of family more clearly. One of these was *symbolic interactionism*. While not fully disputing structural-functionalist theory, symbolic interactionists looked at how individuals interpret social organization and expectations. They focused on how we change our behaviours depending on how others behave and treat us. This is an "in the face" look at family interactions. Mothers' interaction with children was a favourite subject of research.

The concept of "roles" became a central part of the vocabulary of sociology of family. Society assigned the roles, but all the roles were not the same in all aspects of our lives. So, a woman could play the mother role with her kids, and then the wife role with her husband. Increasingly, both were "scripted" by self-styled marriage and parenting experts who based the expertise they marketed on social theories of family. The role of the mother, for example, was scripted as caring, selfless, unassertive, always there for the child. It became an ideal, something to be carefully worked toward by women, no matter what their individual inclinations might be. In its demands, the mother role also overshadowed everything else.

Beginning in the 1970s and then in the 1980s, there was what Cheal (1991) and others have called a "big bang" in sociological theories on families. So big was this "bang," argue Cheal (2002), Giddens (1992), Fox and Luxton (2001), among others, that there was no turning back to previous ways of viewing families. All subsequent theories, states Cheal (2002), can be traced to this "big bang"—the feminist theories of families.

There is no single feminist sociological theory of family or of any other aspect of society. There are many. What is so different about feminist sociological theories of family is the opening of fresh new ways to regard families. Feminist theories, like family theories before them, grew out of the times. After the 1960s, there was increased political unrest in women's lives. The political push for daycare, for reproductive rights, for equal access to jobs, promotions, and benefits, for rights in marriage, for rights *not* to marry, for gays and lesbians, for older women, for the disabled, for children, and for the poor and disenfranchised led to the posing of "why" questions. Why are all of these groups disadvantaged relative to straight, white, middle-class men with jobs? The answers called for new ways to see, new lenses through which to view the social and political landscape.

Feminist theories have several dimensions in common. For example, they all note discrimination and unequal advantage: even in families, we find gendered social inequalities.

They agree that no particular family form is God's will or written into our biology. There is a feeling that things we create, we can uncreate and recreate. Family, argues much of feminist theory, is an ideology as much as a way to live. We owe concern and respect to the larger community, as well as to the members of our household. So, the nuclear family should not—cannot—be the extent of our social responsibility and affection.

A key insight of feminist theories of family is that the family is not private, but a very important public social institution. Feminist theories reveal how families are power-based. There are hierarchies of who has the money, who gets listened to, who is more likely to be abused. Gulfs of silences in families are suddenly given voices: abuse survivors, the fact of family as work, the lack of equitable distribution of resources within families. The list is a long one, and we will explore many of these as we continue in this book.

Perhaps most fundamentally, feminist sociology opened new ways of thinking about sociological research on families. As a result, researchers now look through the feminist lens at the multiple ways to live in families, for example. Gay and lesbian families were studied for the first time as families, whereas previously they had been studied only by the sociology of deviance. Families were seen not as given but as in constant change. The ways in which the ideology of the nuclear family and the denial of other ways to live may compel heterosexuality could be explored. It is easy to see why so many see this theorizing as a "big bang."

For Canadian sociologists especially, immigration theories have become popular and an important part of understanding a large segment of our society. Every year, more than 250 000 immigrants and refugees come to Canada, seeking a new home and a new life (Tang and Oatley, 2002: 149). Most research on the topic of immigrant families is concerned with acculturation—the "process by which ethnic and racial groups learn and begin to participate in the cultural traditions, values, beliefs, assumptions, and practices of the dominant or host culture" (Buddington, 2002: 447), or simply the adoption of a foreign culture. Most importantly, acculturation is a gradual process that often occurs more quickly for immigrant children than parents, since immigrant youth must adopt the language and culture of their new country quickly in order to succeed in school and social relations among peers. Moreover, children have an easier time learning languages and cultural habits than do older people.

Meanwhile immigrant parents, facing considerable pressure to integrate successfully into the new country, often turn to their own cultural communities in search of knowledge about ways to start life anew, and for financial and emotional support. Also, many immigrants live in extended family households and rely on kinship ties to face life challenges (Bastida, 2001). Therefore, immigrant parents often fall behind their children in the acculturation due to various factors, including unwillingness to adopt a new culture, or inability to do so successfully, language barriers, and social networks in the new country consisting of other immigrants, usually of the same cultural background.

As a result, over time an **acculturation gap** often emerges within immigrant families, meaning that there is distance between immigrant children and their parents in their language ability and cultural values, in which parents tend to rely more heavily to their former cultural views. According to Hwang (2006), this situation increases the risk for family dysfunction and potential health problems (see also Boyce and Fuligni, 2007).

Since immigrant families are increasingly becoming part of the Canadian population, their challenges and experiences are of essential importance to our society. The effects of acculturation and related topics on immigrant families will be further discussed throughout this book.

Lastly, in the latter part of the twentieth century and now in the twenty-first century, *postmodern* and *post-structural* theories of families have emerged (Cheal, 2002; Klein and White, 1996). With globalization, the spread of international capitalism, and the development of new, more controlling technologies, new theories of the family were needed. A central dimension of postmodernism and post-structuralism is the notion of flux or constant change. Families today may live in multiple families and households that change in response to the changing circumstances around them. But, we also change our families and households and our ways of being women and men, in ways that relate to big changes such as world changes or economic changes. Topics researched from the point of view of this set of theories include sexualities, body images, cultural images, and representations, including theories and ideologies of families.

BASIC THEORETICAL APPROACHES TO THE FAMILY
Structural Functionalism

Structural functionalism proposes that everything in society has a structure and a purpose. It is up to us to see and understand what those purposes might be. Structural functionalism is a theoretical approach developed in the first half of the twentieth century and applied to families by a variety of North American sociologists.

This approach directs us to view families in the light of how they benefit society, and how each member of a family fits in with the purposes that families serve. Why have nuclear families? From this standpoint, nuclear families are seen as useful because they are small, versatile, and mobile; when social change occurs, families can change easily. What purpose is served by a gender division of labour at home where women nurture children and men work for pay? Well, again the answer is simple and compelling. Women specialize in family and emotional relationships, while men specialize in work and relationships based on order and merit. That the two meet in family makes the family stronger, argue structural functionalists, since women and men complement each other. Competition between women and men, it is thought, would not be beneficial to families or to work.

The theoretical approach of structural functionalism has dominated family research for decades. Although much criticized in recent times, structural functionalism is and has remained the dominant theoretical approach to understanding families in North

America. Its semblance of common sense captivates even those who criticize it. Everything about families has a structure and a function. Family relations is orderly and neat. This approach inspires us to find out how and why families act the ways they do.

The trouble with this theoretical approach is that it may be too captivating. It doesn't really allow for conflict and social change. When women work in the paid labour market like men, what then for families? Do they fall apart because there are no longer complementary roles in family and in society? Some might respond, "Yes, this could be a problem." Others would say, "Wait a minute. Societies change. Women and men change. Where is that change allowed for in structural functionalism?"

This theoretical approach dominated family research through much of the twentieth century and is still important today because it tries to answer one important question: Why is gendering so common throughout the world?

Symbolic Interactionism

This theoretical approach to understanding families depends not on structure or function but on sharing. The key to understanding families, this theory argues, is that family members share symbols and meanings. So, for example, the word "Dad" is not something that you alone understand, but is a symbol shared by others. That the meaning is shared makes family experience more universal, and more understood by others whose experience may be a little different than yours.

Individuals are not passive recipients of social meanings, but work to make those meanings their own. They then interact with others on the basis of their own meanings. For example, the meaning of "Dad" is changing. Children, Dads, and Moms are all changing the meanings they give to what a "Dad" is in our society and in our lives. In this way, meanings become new realities in families.

Marxist Theory of Family

Many readers know of Karl Marx as a political theorist or activist. In fact, Marx was a great thinker, a sociological theorist who conceptualized family in relation to economic systems. His thinking led him to see the nuclear family as specialized so that women would have to be faithful to their husbands to benefit economically. Originally, Marx and his collaborator, Friedrich Engels, imagined women and men living together freely in groups. They would have sex and children but would not worry much about whose children they were. Then, as noted earlier, with agricultural surpluses the notion of private property developed. Men had to know who their own children were so that only those children could inherit their rightful surplus of food (dried root crops, dried animal meat, and so on). The only way men could know who their own children were was to demand sexual faithfulness from women. Thus, it is theorized, women traded free and open sexual relations for economic benefit for themselves and their children. The notion of women's sexual faithfulness to men in monogamous marriage was born in this way. Notably, it was not individual preference or religion or anything else that created this system, but the economic system.

Feminist Theory

Feminist sociological approaches view family as a place of discussion and negotiation. Men and women come to family with different resources and power. Therefore, they negotiate from those different places.

Women, feminist theorists argue, do not enter family with full resources comparable to men's. They therefore suffer inequality in close relations and, if the relationship breaks down, are more likely to be in poverty. In fact, single mothers with children have the highest family poverty rate in Canada (52.5 percent) (Russell, Harris, and Gockel, 2008). The following chapters will describe in more detail the major issues that mothers confront in negotiating the relationships among employment, domestic work, child care, and family life. Important to these discussions will be the idea that women's decision-making processes in each of these domains are not isolated to an individual family but, rather, are embedded in a social context and a political ideology.

Feminist theory suggests that women are taught to see family work as based on love and expectation. It may, in fact, be based as much or more on the need of society and of men for cheap labour to keep the society and men going. So, women take on the major responsibilities for child care and for housework, thus freeing men to focus more fully on paid work. Similarly, women's preoccupation with child rearing and unpaid housework compromises their capacity to work for pay outside the home.

With respect to housework, as an example, feminist theory reveals how women's lower pay at work is linked to the domestic division of labour: why they do more work at home and men do less. Recognition of the unpaid work done largely by women in families has led to inclusion of unpaid work on the Census of Canada, and policies that increasingly recognize the importance of this work.

Postmodern Theory

Postmodernists see that numerous ways of understanding and viewing family coexist. The new social, economic, and political dimensions of a globalized world reveal new identities (active disabled, transgendered, immigrant, and so on) and new ways to live in families. This is not a crisis in any way, but something natural and vital to understanding life and society in the early twenty-first century.

Key to the postmodernist theoretical approach to family is that nothing can be taken for granted. Instead, all must be subject to being taken apart (deconstructed) in order to be explained. Families and men's and women's relations to families are seen as social creations, subject to constant change and re-examination. Family members become part of the process. They re-create themselves and their ways to relate as they examine and re-examine what they are doing and why. Their senses of self form in response to this constant process of reflecting, responding, and re-examining.

When applied to the study of families, postmodern theories look at the meanings of mothering, both individual and social. They look at body images and at sexuality in relation to family. Nothing is taken as given by postmodern theory.

VARIATION DESPITE CONVERGENCE

As we have seen throughout this chapter, changing economies and societies, as well as changing approaches to seeing family, play a major role in changing the form and content of family life, both in countries just becoming industrialized and in the Western world, where economic change continues. Many social scientists perceive these changes as part of an inevitable and universal progress toward a single worldwide culture of modernity, in which families have a distinct and different form, compared to traditional families. This approach has several pitfalls. First, it assumes that all modern families are similar to one another and different from all traditional families. Second, and equally important, it assumes that all modern families "choose" their new forms, and that these forms are necessarily better.

Convergence theory presents a rosy picture of family modernization, as though families and individuals are choosing to change and are all changing effectively. In fact, however, modernization forces families to change. William Goode (1982: 57–58), a structural functionalist, argues that families change when societies industrialize precisely because industrialism "fails to give support to the family": He gives several reasons for this conclusion:

1. The industrial system fires, lays off, and demands geographical mobility by reference to the individual, ignoring the family strains these actions may cause.

2. The economy increasingly uses women in the labour force, and thus puts a still larger work burden on them; but few corporations have developed programs for helping women with child care, or making it easier for men to share in these tasks.

3. The industrial system has little place for the elderly, and the neolocal, independent household with its accompanying values in favour of separate lives for each couple, leaves older parents and kin in an ambiguous position.

4. The family is relatively fragile because of separation and divorce, but the larger system offers little help in these crises for adults and their children.

Industrialization produces not only great opportunities but also great perils for families and family life. Some societies, and some families, respond better than others. Some industrial states provide much more support for the family than others. By its laws and policies, a state influences the costs to individuals and to society associated with marriage, divorce, child-bearing, child rearing, and elder care. In this way, the state influences the patterns of family life in that society. That is, in part, why industrial societies do not have identical family forms.

Major forces of change like industrialization, urbanization, and education certainly affect family life; yet the relationships are not simple, nor are the outcomes predictable. Indeed, in two of the most industrialized countries, Japan and Sweden, we find very different family forms. In Japan, traditional family and gender norms persist. In Sweden, by contrast, there are very high rates of cohabitation and of women working in the paid work force (although mostly in traditional female sectors). Throughout this book we argue that many family forms are not only possible but also desirable and, indeed, work well—in Canada and throughout the world.

No simple conclusions can be drawn about what a family is, what causes families to change, or whether family life is getting better or worse. Those who want simple answers may find this ambiguity disappointing. Those who want to understand the modern family will find that the many open questions make for an exciting and intellectually challenging area of sociology.

LIFE COURSE THEORY

The life course perspective is commonly used to understand families and family change. This was not always the case, however. Life histories and connections between individuals and history used to be neglected in studies of family.

The life course perspective consists of five principles. First, human development is seen as occurring throughout life. In families, this matters because adults as well as children are part of family change. Second, individuals construct their own lives through choices and actions. In families, choices matter greatly to outcomes and happiness. Third, individuals' life courses are shaped by the times in which they live. Good economic times shape us and our families, as do wars and tough times. Fourth, the same events affect individuals and families differently depending on when they occur in the life course. For example, having a baby at age 18 is very different in terms of the rest of a woman's life than having a baby at age 28 or 38. Fifth, and very importantly for the understanding of family lives, is that lives are linked. Nowhere is this truer than in families. Transitions in one person's life in a family can affect all members of the family, as well as the family itself. These five principles of the life course perspective, taken together, lead to a focus in family studies on social contexts as well as life change and choice (Elder, Johnson, and Crosnoe, 2004). It is a powerful theoretical lens.

Table 1.1 Sociological Theories on the Family

Structural Functionalism

Elements in society have a structure and function (or purpose)

Study of the family examines how family members fit together, given the purpose families have within a society

Gender division in the family is universal and probably inevitable

Symbolic Interactionism

Society is a product of face-to-face interactions between people

Understanding of the family requires studying the symbols and meanings shared among members

People depend on the labels of their roles to guide them

Marxist

The family exists in relation to economic systems

The family is a way to ensure inheritance is passed down to the proper persons, namely rightful children

Feminist

Men and women negotiate with the resources and power they have

Women suffer more because they have fewer resources when they enter the family

Women take responsibility at home because society needs their unpaid labour while men focus their efforts on paid work

Postmodern

Family is a social creation and changes are expected

Examination of family requires teasing apart the various components

Family members are aware of, and reflect on, family changes

Convergence (a branch of Structural Functionalism)

Changes in society are part of a universal progress that will result in a single worldwide culture of modernity

Economic development requires specific kinds of families and family roles

Life Course

Human development is lifelong

Individuals construct their life courses

History shapes lives

Timing of events matters

Lives are linked, particularly in families

CONCLUDING REMARKS

It seems that everywhere, family relationships are in flux. Around the world, industrialization and urbanization are destroying extended kinship networks and drastically changing the nature of family obligations. In North America, people value family life, but they are spending a smaller fraction of their lives in anything resembling a traditional family. North American families today show signs of stress and conflict. How are these observable realities connected to one another?

Current family trends are the result of long-term worldwide changes in social life. New laws and new contraceptive technology have given rise to new sexual permissiveness. Fertility has continued to fall for more than a century. Divorce rates have reached historically high levels everywhere, while marriage rates have continued to drop. These long-term trends have been boosted by rapid increases in the labour force participation of mothers of young children. In turn, women's behaviour is the culmination of a struggle for equality with men that began in earnest almost two centuries ago.

As we will see, the process of industrialization has set in motion irresistible, irreversible social forces that transform the content of close relations in everyday life. These social forces include the development of a consumer culture, market economy, welfare states, and a mobile, urban social structure. As well, new technology prolongs life, prevents unwanted births, and creates life outside the womb. In future, many scientists expect that it will even create new sentient creatures through genetic engineering and artificial intelligence.

The sociological study of family life offers a good illustration of the relationship between social structures and social processes, between choices and constraints, similarity and diversity. Some aspects of family life—for example, the norm of marital fidelity—are slow to change. The family as a cultural ideal exists outside and beyond individual people, in the ways that people of a particular society think about love, marriage, parenthood, the domestic division of labour, and so on. What is amazing about family life today is the contrast between people's idealization of family life "in the old days" and people's never-ending creativity in the face of a rapidly changing everyday reality.

Family life is constantly being constructed, and every family bears the unique stamp of its members. No two families enact love, marriage, parenthood, or domestic work in precisely the same way. If anything, the study of families makes clear that social life is a process of continued uncertainty, variety, and negotiation. We get the families we struggle for, although some family members have more power than others do in the struggle.

Families *have* changed dramatically in the last 30 years. Accepted ways of thinking, speaking, and behaving have changed because dozens, then thousands, then millions of family members have changed their way of relating closely. We should not conclude that we are in the midst of a breakdown of the family, in which a mate is no more than erotic property and a child no more than a consumer durable. The way most people continue to struggle and sacrifice for their spouses, children, parents, and siblings suggests that the family means a great deal more.

CHAPTER SUMMARY

In this chapter, we have discussed what families are and how they are viewed. We have explored how defining families is a challenge because both families and how they are seen are constantly changing. Families, for most of us, are our most important social relationships, defining who we are and providing us with emotional attachment.

This chapter examines the complexity of what families are, why they are interesting to study sociologically, and how they have changed and are still changing. Family is as important to people as ever, but it has changed. Even the Census of Canada has, as the twenty-first century began, broadened its definition of family to include common-law unions, including same-sex unions, and adult children living with parents.

We have seen that sociologists are moving away from defining families by the shape they take. This is a returning theme throughout the book, as we will see when we explore the ways Aboriginals, gays and lesbians, and immigrant families, to name a few, function and care for their family members. In doing so, it will be clear that families are more often now defined by what they do for us and for society. The common elements of family living—dependency and intimacy, sexuality, protection, and power—are explored.

The key to understanding families is how families are theorized. In this chapter, we take a brief journey through the major changes in theorizing families from the early days of human living to postmodern media imagery.

This chapter sets the stage for an in-depth examination of family change and family diversity in subsequent chapters.

Key Terms

acculturation gap The gap between immigrant children and their parents in regards to language ability and cultural values. Parents tend to rely more heavily on their former cultural views, while immigrant children adapt more easily to the values of the new country.

bilateral kinship system Kinship through both the male and female lines.

extended family A family system in which three or more generations of family members live together and have social rights and obligations.

kin-keeper The family member who maintains and nurtures family contacts.

kinship group A set of people who share a relationship through blood and/or marriage and have positions in a hierarchy of rights over property.

matrilineal kinship system Kinship through the female line.

nuclear family A family group that consists only of spouses, or spouses and their children.

patriarchy A system in which family decision-making is dominated by males, most typically by fathers.

patrilineal kinship system Kinship through the male line.

socio-economic functions Functions that offer emotional, financial, and material support to members of a group.

Critical Thinking Questions

1. Why is studying the family so complicated in our society today?

2. What are the benefits of a function-based definition of the family and a structural-based definition? What are the drawbacks of each?

3. In this chapter we have discussed what the Canadian Census defines as a family. What would you have added or removed from this definition and why?

4. Why have feminist theories become so prominent in recent decades? Do feminist theories improve our understanding of family life?

5. Predict some future changes that will likely occur for Canadian families in the next five years.

6. We have discussed some theoretical approaches to family in this chapter. Which theoretical approach do you think is the most useful for studying the family today? Which do you think is the least useful?

7. Why are gay and lesbian families of particular interest for sociologists studying family?

8. People often refer to the increase in divorce, delaying marriage, and common-law unions as proof that the value of family is decreasing in our society. Do you think that these trends prove that the family is becoming less important, or even unimportant?

Weblinks

The Vanier Institute of the Family
www.vifamily.ca
This Ottawa-based independent organization has a wealth of information, new studies, and data on families in Canada. The site has many links to other sources of information on families.

Institute of Marriage and Family Canada
www.imfcanada.org
This site offers a variety of resources about family life, including some interesting articles and press releases on recent debates such as same-sex marriage, the "value" of marriage today, and issues facing aging families, to name a few.

Childcare Resource and Research Unit
www.childcarecanada.org
This site focuses on providing up-to date resources that deal specifically with child-care issues and family policy in Canada and internationally.

First Nations Child and Family Caring Society of Canada
www.fncfcs.com
This is an incredible site for academic information regarding the issues facing Aboriginal families today. It provides links to community projects that focus specifically on Aboriginal youth and children's rights, along with numerous volunteer opportunities for anyone interested in getting involved.

Citizenship and Immigration Canada
www.cic.gc.ca
This site provides new Canadian immigrants with a location-specific list of resources to assist in settling into Canada and information such as how to set up a business.

Aboriginal Canadian Portal
www.aboriginalcanada.gc.ca
The Canadian government set up this portal to provide access to government programs and services geared for Aboriginals. The site also offers specific information for the older adults, women, and children and youth.

Status of Women Canada
www.swc-cfc.gc.ca
This government-run site supports various women's issues, such as increasing women's economic position, and offers up-to-date information about changes in women's political and economic status in Canada.

www.youth.gc.ca
This site focuses on a variety of youth issues facing Canadian teenagers. One of the best features of the site is that it targets unemployed, immigrant, and disabled youth issues and provides easy-to-understand tips on how to find jobs and earn an education.

Chapter 2
Historical Perspectives on Canadian Families
Demographic, Social, and Economic Origins and Trends

Chapter Outline

In this chapter, we look at families through a sociological lens. We emphasize the big changes in society, such as contact and ongoing relations between Aboriginals and settlers, industrialization, large-scale immigration waves, and wars. We consider how families in the past connect to some of today's patterns, and how contemporary socio-economic changes have altered families and our views of them. We also focus on the multicultural families that have been part of Canada since its beginnings. Historical dimensions of families are explored more specifically in the chapters that follow.

A HISTORICAL, CROSS-CULTURAL PERSPECTIVE
Aboriginals and Settlers: Contact and Conflict

Aboriginal families in what was to become Canada have always been diverse. First contacts between Aboriginal peoples and foreigners were with male explorers, followed by fur traders and missionaries, and lastly women and families who settled in Canada. Such contacts changed Aboriginal family practices, as they did the family practices of some of the settlers. Early settlers in Canada developed strong relationships of mutual aid with their Aboriginal neighbours. Blood First Nation women helped homesteading women on the prairies with childbirth and with building houses that would help them stay warm and survive the harsh winters. The settlement of New France (now Quebec) and Upper Canada (now Ontario) brought together the families of the Aboriginal groups and the colonists. In the early days, children born to unmarried settler women were often adopted by Aboriginal families.

The relationships in those days between settlers and Aboriginals cannot be characterized as simply good or bad. Some explorers and fur traders married or cohabited with Aboriginal women (Van Kirk, 1980). Some of these relationships were committed and long-lasting, while others were short-term and exploitative, with men from afar taking advantage of differences in culture and status between themselves and the local women

(Brown, 1980). This is a common story of colonialism, occurring throughout the world and leaving a legacy of combined racism and sexism toward indigenous women.

Relations between the men from afar and the local women were not sanctioned by the church or society. Missionaries believed the "souls" of the Europeans were endangered by "going native," a term used in the period to describe men who converted to Aboriginal ways of life.

The unions were also disapproved of by fur trading companies, notably the Hudson's Bay Company, which banned these men from taking their country wives and families back home with them upon retirement (Van Kirk, 1980). Some of the men simply abandoned their Canadian families and returned to their original European wives or married European women at home. Others, however, remained in Canada with their families, adapting to Aboriginal societies. One couple, William Hemmings Cook and his wife, Agatha, made a fresh start by marrying after living together according to the "custom of the country" for years (Van Kirk, 1992: 79). Still others provided for their "country wives" in their wills, or organized to find them new husbands to ensure that they would be provided for.

Unlike the Europeans, relatives of the Aboriginal women often did support the relationships. The Huron, for example, saw ties between French men and Huron women as a way to develop kinship alliances, cementing trust and goodwill through family connections. Many thousands of Canadians today can trace their ancestry to the British and French fur traders and Aboriginal women of the seventeenth to nineteenth centuries.

However, the children of unions between European men and Aboriginal women suffered a significant strain. Some, especially boys, left their familiar lives at a young age, sometimes going abroad to their father's relatives to be educated. Daughters more often stayed with their mothers and the mother's culture (Brown, 1992). Efforts were made at various times, notably in the 1820s, to organize and to "civilize" what were seen as mixed-race families and communities. This resulted in officials making new laws, and in missionaries working to sanction relationships. One outcome was a sense of *in loco parentis*, whereby family life was controlled by others who regulated and governed the Aboriginals as children who needed discipline and order.

Other family issues that arose with early contact between Aboriginal peoples and Europeans have to do with kinship ties. For hundreds of years, Aboriginal cultural beliefs and practices around family and family issues had been developing and changing, and were widely divergent throughout Canada. Aboriginals viewed kinship, the basis for assigning rights and duties, more flexibly than did European settlers. For example, their kinship rules included adopted children and adults, friends and people engaged in mutual aid. Furthermore, kinship regulated relations with others without courts and states per se. Decisions about justice and about compensation were often filtered through kinship rules, with different outcomes than might have resulted from following European rules. Some of the conflicts that resulted are continuing to this day.

Another large difference between the early Europeans and Aboriginals was in gender roles. Though societies always seem to organize rights and responsibilities by gender, they differ significantly in the way gender is employed. Bradbury notes that "[i]n most Aboriginal societies women appear to have been able to exercise greater power than their European counterparts . . . " (2001: 72). This system led some European observers to shocked reactions.

Finally, Aboriginal peoples and early Europeans had divergent views on the relationship of family to its community, and of both to property. To the colonial settlers, property, whether it was land, money, or goods, was private and to be traded in a market economy. Assets belonged to individuals and nuclear families. This was not the case with Aboriginal groups, whose extended kinship groups often determined who would be eligible for the benefits of a hunt, for example. These different viewpoints created a clash of values, posing some difficulty in the fur trade. The concept of furs for sale was a new one to many Aboriginal peoples at that time. Ritual exchanges among Aboriginal family groups such as the potlatches of the peoples of the West coast were seen as dangerous by the colonials, both to their economic values and to their sense of righteousness. In fact, potlatches were outlawed by authorities, and in some villages all the goods to be exchanged were symbolically burned (Dickason, 2002).

English and French Settlers

Interestingly, the conflicts between colonists and Aboriginal peoples over family and kinship relations parallel the conflicts between British and French settlers. English Common Law, from which many of the modern understandings of marriage, family, inheritance, and property rights came, tended to concentrate power, authority, and property in male heads of households. For women, marriage meant the "suspension of independent existence" (Bradbury, 2001: 74).

For a long time (until the early part of the twentieth century), married women could not own property, sign a contract, or sue. Like children, they had no rights under law. In contrast, in New France, which became Quebec, rules governing marriage and family were guided by the Custom of Paris (Bradbury, 2001: 75). This set of legal codes was much more egalitarian than English Common Law. Property was seen as shared between husbands and wives, even if controlled by husbands. And children, regardless of gender, could share inheritances.

After the Battle of the Plains of Abraham in 1760, known in Quebec as the Conquest, the English tried to impose their version of family law and practice on the French. This attempt failed immediately and has never succeeded for political reasons. As early as 1774, it was agreed that Quebec would have its own legal code regarding family matters, though all criminal law would follow the English practice. Even today, in Quebec we see different approaches to family than in the rest of Canada. One major family difference is that the Québécois/Québécoise (Quebec men and women) are significantly more likely to live in common-law unions than other Canadians. Another difference is that Québécoise do not take their husband's name on marriage. Both of these points will be discussed in the chapters that follow.

Also after the Conquest, there was a significant gender imbalance in New France, with a much higher proportion of men than women. The low birth rate in the new colony threatened the success of territorial expansion. In response, about 770 young women were imported to New France from the streets of Paris between 1663 and 1673 (Landry, 1992). These women were called *les filles du roi* (daughters of the King). Many were orphans, some were illiterate, all were poor, and, despite their name, none were even remotely related to royalty. Most agreed to be sent to the new colony because of poverty and lack of other options.

The *filles du roi* were expected to find marriage partners quickly, and most did. Out of the whole group, only 15 percent of the marriages were annulled, the equivalent of divorce in Catholic New France at the time (Huck, 2001: 14). Of those, most remarried, and seven even married for a third time. Many Quebeckers today can trace their ancestry to the unions of original French settlers and the *filles du roi*.

The Transition to Industrialism

Before Canada industrialized and urbanized, families were the primary unit of production. Most families were rural, and work and family were found in the same space. Therefore, the two were inseparable. Even children helped to operate the family business and keep the home running smoothly. Each person, old or young, had a role to play, and society defined each person's role.

In this way, agricultural work depended on the formation of extended families. Farmwork—based on land and animals—could not be moved, so people mostly stayed in one place. Exceptions were non-inheriting children, who often migrated or emigrated in search of their own land. People who stayed formed strong bonds among neighbours and generations. This led to the formation of a **gemeinschaft** type of community typical of pre-industrial rural life: that is, one in which everyone knows everyone else and people share common values. Since limited social safety nets existed, families largely had to create their own. Aging grandparents helped busy parents to care for the many children and often provided housing and money when needed (McDaniel and Lewis, 1998).

Moreover, rural life was characterized by a different division of labour between men and women than was typical in Europe at this time. Thus, when many of the Europeans migrated to Canada and established an agricultural way of life, the conventional division of labour was altered. Even though most early settlers to Canada preferred a strict division of labour at home (as in their native countries), they often could not manage this divide. As a result, land was sometimes owned and worked by unmarried women, for example, a practice unheard of in the "old country." This change was motivated less by an interest in gender equality than by a desire to increase agricultural output. At the same time, men's and women's work was still largely separate in pre-industrial times. The husband was usually responsible for representing the family in public. However, men also had domestic responsibilities such as farmwork, child discipline, and some provisioning. The wife, on the other hand, was mainly responsible for the private domain. Besides doing housework and taking responsibility for child care, women at this time also took care of farm animals, manufactured needed household items, and provided social services to those in their community (Cross and Szostak, 1995). When, often, men had to leave their farms and shops to work at other jobs, women would often supplement household income with home-based businesses.

This provided a small source of income for women, which contributed to the family and to their pride. It also gave some women considerable power and autonomy both in their families' enterprises and in the wider society. However, with industrialization many women could not continue such work. For instance, zoning bylaws might prohibit non-family establishments in some neighbourhoods, and in this way they would prevent separated, divorced, and widowed women from taking in boarders to make ends meet (Bradbury, 1984).

With the advent of industrialization, the agricultural family and way of life drastically changed. First, industrialization drove many individuals and families out of the countryside and into the new towns and cities. Some families became migratory, moving where work was available. Since this was almost impossible to do with an extended family, the nuclear family became the more common family form. This type of family was smaller and more compact, thus easier to move. It was also more specialized. Everyone had a role to fill, although the roles were different from those in an extended family.

However, many nuclear families could not survive with only one or two members of the family working for pay. Typically, children worked in factories or on the streets, selling papers, shining shoes, picking rags, or they took care of the younger children so the mothers could work (Parr, 1990). In the early industrial period, a significant portion of family income came from the work of children. However, factory work posed new problems for families. For example, children who were working in the factories often did not want to give their entire wages to their parents. Some even chose to move out. In doing so, children gained control over their own wages, even though they remained poor. Clearly, children in an industrializing society had more independence from their parents than those in an agricultural one. Thus, a significant change occurred in relations between older and younger generations, and a new image of childhood emerged. Increasingly, children became a liability. So, parents started to have fewer children.

As well, the Industrial Revolution, which only began in Canada in the mid-1850s, moved the productive activity of men outside the household. Increasingly, people began to work *with* strangers and *for* strangers. Family life was their own private business, and work life was, if they wished, outside the family's purview. A clear line between work and family life, in the way that we perceive them today, only appeared with the coming of industrialization.

Then, in the beginning of the twentieth century, industrialization of household technology brought new and unexpected dimensions to family life, especially changing what families expected of women. Vacuum cleaners, for example, brought the possibility of cleaning a house more readily than by sweeping or taking heavy area rugs out to the yard to be beaten with brooms or paddles. Yet expectations about cleanliness also rose, so there was no reduction in the housework to be done. Similarly, refrigerators replaced wells, cold storage areas, and iceboxes. Fridges saved the worry and the trouble of food storage in homes but created the necessity to shop longer and with greater care because meals were expected to be more complex and elegant than they had been before.

Thus, the growing availability of new "labour-saving devices" raised standards of living and increased the time women spent shopping. Homes quickly shifted from small-scale production units into showplaces of consumer goods. In the new domestic division of labour, women were no longer producers of goods to sell on the market, but rather specialists in the consumption of goods aimed at making houses "homey." This shift sharpened the domestic division of labour by gender. It was the precursor to the modern "domestic goddess" movement, spearheaded by Martha Stewart.

Campaigns to promote new household technologies stressed the "love" part of housework out of fear that women might abandon their domestic work with the **"mechanization" of housework** (Fox, 1993: 151). Home economists worked to raise the esteem of homemakers by promoting the idea that the new home technologies required skilled operators. Health came to be associated with extreme standards of cleanliness. Homemakers were therefore expected to master household technology and promote family health—complex but unrewarded increases in responsibility. The scientization of housework was complete, and women were cast into the role of preserving the home as their central life work, with limited access through their homemaking skills to the markets they had enjoyed before industrialization. They had been transformed into domestic engineers, responsible for all things related to family and the household.

The History of Immigration in Relation to the Family

People often think of family change and family transitions as recent occurrences. In reality, family changes are nothing new. Immigration has been a significant part of Canada since before Confederation. Early immigrants, mainly from the colonizing countries Britain and France, arrived in search of opportunities for work, land ownership, and a new life. These goals were pursued, in part, as the means to start or support a family. Despite the notable change in other aspects of recent immigration—such as changed countries of origin—many immigrants continue to see economic advancement as a means to ensuring family welfare.

In the eighteenth century, the American Revolution brought to Canada the United Empire Loyalists, including significant numbers of African Americans. The latter settled largely in Nova Scotia and in southern Ontario. Many black families did not fit the expected family model. For instance, black women often worked outside the home to earn enough money to get by. "[F]or African-Nova Scotian men in the early 1800s, many families practised gender interdependence and reversals of traditional gender roles in the division of labour" (Calliste, 2001: 402). This reflects, in part, need that resulted from discrimination. But it is also reflective of the West African cultural tradition where women are both more economically and sexually independent of men and of families.

Later, in the early twentieth century, African American families settled as homesteaders in central Alberta. In *The Keystone Legacy: Recollections of a Black Settler* (1997), author Gwen Hooks, daughter of original homesteaders in that area, describes how settlers banded together in families and communities to make a new and happy life on the prairies. Hooks also states that homesteaders of all ethnic origins banded together to build community facilities such as schools. Later immigrants to the West of Canada have included people from all regions of the world, seeking a better life and bringing along rich family traditions and strong values and beliefs. With time, some of these family practices have changed or even disappeared, while others influenced the practices of other people with whom they came in contact.

Immigration from Europe has also had a long history in Canada, beginning with colonialism and expansion. Canada continued to receive European immigrants from strife-torn, and sometimes poverty-stricken, countries throughout the first half of the twentieth century. Immigrants and refugees from Europe are still coming, as strife and economic difficulties recur, and have now been joined by people from Africa, Asia, and Latin America fleeing an old life or seeking new opportunities.

Today, South Asian families form the largest portion of immigrants in Canada. As such, they experience unique difficulties in their immigration experiences. South Asian women in particular face significant problems in adjusting after immigration because of the rigid gender roles in their home countries. A study by Ahmad, Shik, Vanza, Cheung, and Stewart (2004) found that South Asian women faced stress-inducing factors that include the loss of social support, economic uncertainties, downward social mobility, and health problems associated with climatic and food changes. Equally important, these women feel they cannot turn to professional health workers for help with these concerns. This inability to seek help is aggravated by the fact that immigrant women already faced a lack of resources with the loss of family and friends.

The isolating experience of South Asian women migrants highlights the need for health-care professionals to provide and understand the specific challenges and needs of recent immigrants in order to offer necessary support and care for this vulnerable population. Inevitably, life in the new country forces families—both parents and children—to live in new ways. These family changes are demanded by the process of immigration and the contact with new ways of living in close relations.

The History of Immigration Policies

As Canadians, we like to imagine that our country helps people in need, and occasionally these imaginings prove justified. However, Canada's past immigration policies undermine this idealistic point of view. For example, during the early periods of Chinese immigration to Canada, racially discriminatory laws such as the head tax were imposed in the period of 1885–1923 (Man, 2001). As well, the Chinese Exclusionary Act strictly prohibited Chinese workers (including those who built the railroads and worked in the early mines) from bringing in their wives and children. In this way, their harsh, impoverished lives were made even harder by Canadian immigration laws.

This example reminds us that Canadian immigration laws were not primarily philanthropic: they were intended to supply needed labour power and little more (Green and Green, 2004). The labourers were admitted into Canada specifically to build the Canadian Pacific Railway (Comeau and Allahar, 2001). Then, in the 1920s and again in the 1950s, immigration was used to meet demands for labour resource sectors; in the 1960s and 1970s, to increase skill level among occupational workers; and in the 1980s to compensate for the large population of aging baby boomers in the native-born population. The large inflows of immigrants at these times were permitted mainly to fill shortages of specific people.

At other times, immigration inflows were significantly cut back, and entry restrictions ensured that groups that were not needed were turned away (McLean, 2004). This method of controlling immigration reflected a concern with Canada's as absorptive capacity—that is "only accepting the number of immigrants that the Canadian economy [can] easily absorb" (Green and Green, 2004: 135). Yet over the last 20 years, this short-term focus on demand and fulfillment shifted to a long-term one that considers immigration as essential to future economic growth and prosperity. This policy allows for immigration inflow even during economic hardships, which has inevitably helped immigrant families to start new lives in our country.

Along with changes in policy, the source countries of Canada's immigrants have changed. Between 1981 and 1996, when Canada was actively accepting new immigrants, the visible minority (that is, non-white) population of Toronto, known as the gateway for immigrants into Canada (Raj, 2004), more than doubled from 14 percent to 32 percent (Myles and Hou, 2004). For several years, China provided the most immigrants; it has been recently surpassed by India (see Walton-Roberts, 2003, and Ahmad et al., 2004, for more detail on South Asian immigrants in Canada).

With the development of feminist theory in the 1970s to 1990s, an effort has been made to understand the unique experience of migration on women. This has signalled a shift away from a more male-focused experience of migration that initially deemed women's motives invisible and their experiences the same as those of men. Previously, when women's motives for immigration were taken into account, they were seen as based on family responsibilities, rather than on independent choice. Today, scholars are more likely to examine female migration as a complex and gender-specific experience based on several factors, including the gendered restrictions that often exist in a women's home country and either encourage or inhibit immigration (Boyd and Grieco, 2003).

The immigration policy of a home country can affect migrants in various ways. For one, migration policies sometimes assume a "dependent" status for women and an "independent" status for men (Boyd and Grieco, 2003: 4). Women, therefore, are more likely to be classified in relation to their family and husbands, rather than independently. Secondly, the differences between a dependent and independent status can automatically

The mid-1850s created a paradigm shift from agriculture to industrialism. Families were driven into urban settings, where men left the house to go to work in factories.

place women within a family role and men in a market role. This can reinforce patriarchal relations between spouses, and also shut women out of important economic roles and a chance for bargaining power within the home. More importantly, this power imbalance accounts for much of the social vulnerability of migrant women. Thus, although immigration policy may be seen as "gender neutral," the entry status of men and women can have important implications for the experience of new immigrants in the country.

Wars

The two world wars of the twentieth century had profound impacts on families. They also had an influence on women's social roles and responsibilities. World War II brought an influx of women into the labour force, as men were sent away to fight. Women were employed in jobs that they had previously been excluded from due to their gender, such as work involving manual labour (Coontz, 2005: 221). More importantly, the government supported and encouraged both single and married women to join the labour force, and many women even earned men's wages.

However, upon the return of the men, women had to give up their jobs and resume a domestic way of life, leading to a dip in age at first birth following both wars, as seen in Table 2.1. But families did not effortlessly pick up where they left off before the outbreak of war. For one, marriage experts worried that women had become too independent during wartime and would subsequently demand more autonomy and authority within the household (Ravanera, Rajulton, and Burch, 1998: 223). This would threaten the male breadwinner model of the nuclear family.

Moreover, the experience of families during the 1950s was not as simple or happy as has been previously believed. Although some women willingly embraced domesticity and were pleased to revert back to more traditional gender roles within the household, others resented their exclusion from the labour force and missed the independence they enjoyed during the war years (LaRossa, 2004: 50).

For men, the changing role of the father came to emphasize children's socialization more than in the past. Popular sitcoms such as *Leave It to Beaver* and *Father Knows Best* also reflected the role of the father within the household and as a participant in raising children. However, the role of "father" that was popularly promoted during the 1950s was a traditional, patriarchal version of the role and demanded clear gender lines. In fact, the popular image of a nuclear family during this time—particularly rigid and stereotypical— reflected the need many people felt for stability and clarity during an insecure, fearful Cold War period.

World War II had profound effects on Canadian families who had come from Axis power countries (that is, Germany, Italy, and Japan), Canada's opponents during combat. For instance, between 1941 and 1949, approximately 27 000 Japanese Canadians were forced to leave their homes, deprived of possessions and civil rights, such as the right to vote. Some were even deported to Japan, regardless of their status as Canadian citizens (Kobayashi, 1992). The Canadian government committed these acts under the pretense that Japanese Canadians posed a threat to national security during World War II, despite claims to the contrary by the military and the RCMP (Sunahara, 1981). The geographic dispersal of these people was meant to distribute them across the land in such a way that they could be easily assimilated into Canadian culture, undermining the likeliness that they would retain traces of their own traditions and culture (Sugiman, 1983). These actions had a deep impact on the attitudes of Japanese Canadians growing up in those times, and the effects of World War II policies continue to be felt by the older generations today.

The effect of these actions is shown in a study by Sugiman and Nishio (1983), which examined the attitudes of aging (51 to 67 years old) Japanese Canadians in Toronto toward old age and dependency of the aged. In traditional Japanese culture, care of the elderly by their children or grandchildren is viewed positively as it is considered a repayment of the older individual's life work. Yet, though it is the norm in traditional Japanese culture, Japanese Canadian aging persons prefer not to rely on younger generations for care. In their study, Sugiman and Nishio find the values of aging Japanese Canadians somewhat ambiguous. They report detecting traces of the Japanese upbringing in the participants, but also attitudes that coincide with Anglo Canadian views. Much like their Anglo Canadian counterparts, the Japanese Canadian respondents dislike the prospect of growing dependent on their children and demonstrate a preference for living alone in old age (Sugiman and Nishio, 1983).

Wars and the experiences associated with them directly affect entire generations and their families, but also future generations indirectly, by influencing beliefs and attitudes. Currently, there are more than 2100 Canadians in the Canadian Forces serving overseas in military roles, with another 8000 preparing for, engaged in, or returning from overseas missions (Canada, Department of National Defence, 2006). Large numbers of Canadian families are affected by this military service, even though Canada does not see itself as a military power.

VARIATION IN THE FAMILY LIFE COURSE

In the past century, families have changed significantly, as we can see by examining changes in the timing and sequencing of major life course events. People born between the two world wars married younger, and most married over a narrowed spread of ages. For these cohorts, the transition to adulthood was compressed into a relatively short period of completing formal education, entering the labour force, leaving home, setting up a nuclear household, and having a first child.

In contrast, later cohorts have experienced a lengthening of this time sequence. In addition, the events themselves are less clearly defined and their sequencing is more diverse. This timing of transitions involves trade-offs. Waiting longer to have children allows greater investment in oneself before investing in reproduction. However, delay may mean having no children at all. Later transitions enable more transfers from parents to children, allowing recipients to benefit more from resources, but this may reduce the potential for the parents to invest in their own retirement. Thus these children enter work life later but better equipped. As well, couples in the past spent a much longer period of time having and raising children than they do now, as shown in Table 2.1.

The scale of changes in the timing and duration of family life events is vivid in Table 2.1, which compares cohorts of women born in different periods. Information about several life events is given for women born in the mid-nineteenth century, the 1930s, the 1950s, and the 1970s. Dates of widowhood and death for the latter are projections. Later cohorts (women born in the early 1960s, the late 1960s, and the early 1970s) are added for comparison. However, for these cohorts, only first marriage and first birth are given. Women born in 1975 are now only in their 30s and have likely not yet completed child-bearing, let alone being widowed and experiencing empty nests. Age at first marriage dipped from the first to the second cohort, and only recently rose significantly. The prevailing attitude during the times of the second cohort (parents of the baby boom) was that

Table 2.1 Median Age at Life Course Events and Years Spent in Life States, Canada

Birth Cohort	1841–50	1931–40	1951–60	1961–65	1966–70	1971–75
Median age at event:						
1st marriage	26.0	21.1	22.5	22.7	22.9	27.6
1st birth	28.0	22.9	24.5	27.8	27.8	
Last birth	40.0	29.1	26.3			
"Empty nest"	60.1	49.1	46.3			
Widowhood	59.5	67.2	69.9			
Death	64.3	79.4	82.2			
Median years spent:						
Raising children	32.1	26.2	21.8			
Married; no child at home	0	18.1	23.6			
In widowhood	4.8	12.2	12.3			

Source: Gee, Ellen M. "The Life Course of Canadian Women: An Historical and Demographic Analysis." *Social Indicators Research*, 1986, vol. 18, Table VI, p. 273, Abridged. With kind permission from Springer Science and Business Media; 1971–75 data: Ravanera, Rajulton, and Burch, 1998.

home was women's proper place. Age at first birth is slightly lower for the cohort born most recently than for the first cohort, which may be surprising, since we sometimes think that in the past couples had children earlier than today.

When we look at a woman's age during last birth across **cohorts**, we see a fundamental change in family lives. Women having children in the 1950s had their last birth at the same age as women a hundred years before had their first birth! Even more striking is the huge difference in the timing of last births: at age 40 in the mid-nineteenth century compared with age 26 one hundred years later. Over a hundred-year period, families reduced the time they spent having and raising children by over 10 years! Recall that this happened at a time when life expectancy was increasing substantially. The result is that the portion of life spent as a parent with dependent children has been sharply reduced. By contrast, the portion of life spent married with no children at home, or at least no juvenile children, has sharply increased from 0 to almost a quarter of a century. (We shall see in Chapter 10 that in the early 2000s there is a significant difference between when children become adults and when they leave home).

Given these trends, it may not be surprising that having second or even third families was more characteristic of families in the past than we sometimes admit today. In some ways, widows in the past were similar to single mothers today, both in the economic vulnerability they and their children faced and in the social challenges they experienced (Gordon and McLanahan, 1991). Widows often fell into poverty and had to rely on charity or the generosity of the state or family members to survive. In Chapter 9, we will see the differences in children's lives between the loss of a parent to death and the loss of a parent to divorce.

In the past, people expected a certain sequencing of family-related events. They expected, for example, young people to complete their education before marrying, to marry before having children, to get old before becoming a grandparent, and so on. So predictable was the pattern that sociologists spoke confidently about a normal life cycle of family events. Today, the timing and sequencing of events are too varied to be easily categorized. A woman can be a grandmother and a mid-career professional at the same time, or a new mother at midlife while starting a career. Patterns of family life have evidently become more complex—even "individualized."

The Impact of Modernization on Family Changes, in Canada and Worldwide

Many changes in close relations accompany modernization. Struggles to define and redefine families continue throughout the industrialized world (Baker, 1995). Indeed, industrialization, as we have seen, has had a huge impact on family living. In addition to industrialization, urbanization has also had a great effect on family life (see Finlay, Velsor, and Hilker, 1982). That is mainly because households—or who lives with whom—are determined by property ownership arrangements, which vary between urban and rural areas. Typically, households are larger (that is, extended) and family life is more psychologically important to people in rural than in urban areas—or so we usually think. In many parts of the world, people still spend substantial parts of their lives in extended households, though they increasingly spend significant parts of their lives in nuclear families.

Along with industrialization and modernization, women's roles and responsibilities are changing. Most significantly, women increasingly seek higher education and careers (Divale and Seda, 2001). This trend is occurring throughout the world. In Brazil, for example, there are more women than men seeking job opportunities in cities rather than living the traditional rural life. This is in part because of patriarchical norms still in place that prevent women from inheriting land. Because they have fewer job prospects at home, many women move to urbanized centres (Brumer, 2008).

By means of their higher education and job participation, women are now more able to control their child-bearing and to support themselves economically. Thus, families have changed dramatically since the 1960s, notably in North America but elsewhere as well. These changes have mainly stemmed from changing patterns of intimacy. This trend parallels delayed marriage and delayed (as well as restricted) child-bearing. Men today increasingly tend to value and seek more educated wives who are closer to them in age. In general, marriages now are somewhat more egalitarian than in the past, meaning that family power is shared between spouses more equally. This is not to say that all marriages have become equal and fair; they have not. But marriages in the past were even less equal and fair than they are today, on average.

As in the Brazil example, these and other societal changes can be observed in other parts of the world, wherever modernization has affected social and cultural life. In many modern Arab societies, modernization is associated with smaller family sizes, a higher literacy rate, and better economy (El-Ghannam, 2001). Moreover, Milikian and Al-Easa (1981) have noted that in Qatar (in the Persian Gulf), a modern industrial economy means that young people, even women, earn wages that their families cannot control. Young people today rely on schooling and the media for more of their knowledge and information than generations before them, and they learn to value a high material standard of living. These changes may conflict with traditional family norms, values, and expectations. They certainly have the potential to cause conflicts between the parental generation and their children and, often, between religious and state institutions. These changes may be especially challenging in countries where the state and religion are not separate, such as Iran or Israel. Yet outcomes are not preordained; there is no certainty, for example, that the family in a modernizing Muslim region will be identical to the modern Christian, Hindu, or Jewish family.

Some of the impacts of modernization on other cultures can be predicted, since along with industrialization and individualism, modernization alters traditional customs and norms in foreseeable ways. For instance, in Asian countries where filial piety is a traditional value, massive and sudden modernization in recent years (Quach and Anderson, 2008) has also resulted in negative experiences for families with older relatives (Ding, 2004). The family remains the main support for aging relatives, but providing for them is becoming increasingly difficult, especially because children are pursuing higher education and are influenced by individualistic notions of the West. According to Cha (2004), families in Korea are experiencing similar problems.

These patterns are also occurring in other parts of the world. In Trinidad and Turkey, for example, where modernization is resulting in better education and work opportunities, adult children (especially women who have traditionally taken on the caregiver role) are now less likely to stay at home and help out with the care of family members (Grahame, 2006; Gündüz-Hosgör and Smits, 2008). The profound shifts in family, social, and gender roles that come with modernization often create family conflict, which is undoubtedly distressing to family relations.

As another example, consider the effects of modernization in India. Here, modernization has arguably had the most significant impact on society, and therefore family, than any other social and political shift. Before modernization, even over its expansive history and countless societal changes, the family as a unit in India has remained fairly stable. With industrialization and urbanization, however, as well as the growing influence of Western ideologies, the traditional customs of marriage, family, and kinship have changed significantly. Some of the changes are viewed as positive, yet this is so only for a small percentage of the population. Many more people have been marginalized as a result of modernization and experience suffering (Kashyap, 2004).

Another factor that changes family life is political will and ideology. China, for example, has tried to mobilize families in support of social development. State planning of family life has gone hand in hand with economic and political change. In research by Kejing (1990), both hardship and progress as a result of this are apparent. Many conditions of life in China remain difficult, yet there are indications that family life is improving, especially for women. Despite a lack of prosperity, state efforts to regulate marriage, fertility, and the rights of women are starting to pay off with smaller families and increased gender equality, though at the expense of personal liberty.

Moreover, even in the smaller, more isolated rural areas of the world, where traditional family forms persist most strongly, parent–child relations are changing with modernization (Caldwell, Reddy, and Caldwell, 1984). Children, on average, are gaining more autonomy and power in interactions with parents. These changes show the pervasive influence of Western cultural notions, specifically notions about childhood and adolescence, but also, more generally, notions about the life cycle. They also show the growing importance of education and media even in rural areas, and the socialization of new generations in preparation for an urban, industrial lifestyle.

Changes in Sexual Attitudes and Courtship

Before the nineteenth century, sex was strongly associated with the wedding night and virginity was hugely valued. Then, newlyweds had no privacy. They were accompanied into the matrimonial bedroom by relatives and friends and, of course, rude jokes. In some cultures, the bloodied sheets of a virgin "deflowered" would be tossed from the window to the cheers of crowds of relatives and friends below. However, in the nineteenth century, the Victorians "de-sexed" the honeymoon. Isobel March, a newly married young woman in 1871 in Niagara Falls, cited by Dubinsky (2001: 30), "did all she could to avoid the horror of being an 'evident bride.'"

In the Victorian era, the banishing of sex from public view reached its peak. Legs on tables were covered for fear that, in their naked state, they would make people think of sex! Pregnancy was disguised, hidden, or denied. Women were not expected to be seen in public while pregnant, certainly not naked on magazine covers as occurred in the early 1990s. Feminine ankles were thought too alluring for men to see. Nonetheless, during this period a world of men's pubs, clubs, and male occasions such as hunting and fishing flourished, as did a thriving prostitution trade as well as lurid romance novels. Sex did not cease to exist.

By the late nineteenth century, sex began to be seen as a central part of marriage and sexual attraction a crucial part of courtship. Sex is considered to have "come out" in the 1920s (Dubinsky, 1999)—heterosexuality in a married relationship, that is. Soon, sex experts and romance filmmakers invented the sexual honeymoon. Having culturally sanctioned "sexual papers" allowed a married couple to experience this interlude, filled with expectations about supreme sexual bliss (Dubinsky, 1999). Sexuality and sexual attraction began to occupy a more central place in modern ideas of personality and identity, and sexual happiness came to the fore as a primary purpose of marriage (Dubinsky, 2001).

Identities, personalities, and family beginnings had their origins in this emergence. Honeymoons became a rite of passage into adulthood and, importantly, consumerism. What was (and remains to be) consumed were not only sexual holidays but also a lifestyle with promises of lifetime sexual fulfillment.

At the beginning of the twenty-first century, images remain of pure, virtuous women who search for knights in shining armour. As a result, marriage is seldom considered rationally by sentimental youth, who are often engaged not in planning lives together, but in planning romantic—and increasingly costly—white weddings. Interestingly, in weddings today, all but the most ultra-modern brides still look like fairy princesses and grooms remain one step short of riding in on white horses (but, of course, in some ethnic groups, that is exactly what grooms still do.). Brides are still "given away" by their fathers (or both parents) to their husbands. And the important ritual of uniting the couple sexually as well as socially is shared by families brought together for the wedding.

Changes in Attitudes toward Marriage

Traditionally, marriage was viewed largely in terms of rights, duties, and obligations to each other's families. Throughout the West, a major attitude shift has placed greater emphasis on the personal or emotional side of close relations.

Why, then, do so many people still keep up the old forms? Why do so many still get married, many of them in churches or religious places, dressed in hugely expensive white bridal gowns and formal black tuxedos, or in all the glitter and gold of the Hindu wedding? We shall discuss these questions in detail in Chapter 4. In short, formal weddings and the legal ceremony have more to do with marking a life transition or gaining social approval than with emotional commitment. Many people still find the idea of legal marriage compelling, despite what they know about the realities of marriage and divorce (Vanier Institute of the Family, 2004). Enormous numbers of North Americans are neither rejecting the family or other long-lasting, close relationships nor accepting family in a traditional form. Most are hoping to revitalize and reinterpret family (Scanzoni, 2000; Vanier Institute of the Family, 2004), making families suited to themselves and their needs.

Although many people still get married, one significant change in family life in the Western world has been an increase in cohabitation—people living together without being legally married. Cohabitation, or the "common-law union" as it is also called, used to be more prevalent among working-class people. It also used to be seen as a lesser form of relationship than marriage—the practice was sometimes referred to as "living in sin" or "shacking up." Now, however, cohabitation has lost some of its stigma and is much more accepted. In Quebec, cohabitation has become the norm for younger couples, while legal marriage is decidedly less preferred (Vanier Institute of the Family, 2004). These trends are discussed further in Chapter 4.

It may be coincidental that the growth in cohabitation has coincided with later marriage (since the 1960s and 1970s), higher divorce rates, and lower rates of child-bearing. More and more often, people think of spousal relations as being about love and sexual attraction, not about child-bearing and creating family alliances. People have come to expect more satisfaction of their emotional and psychological needs in their close relationships. Women, particularly, are less economically dependent on their partners

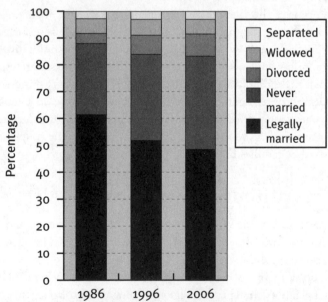

Figure 2.1 For the first time, legally married population aged 15 and over falls below 50%

Source: Statistics Canada website. Retrieved April 2009 from www12.statcan.ca/english/census06/analysis/famhouse/charts/chart7.htm.

Changes in the Marriage Rate over the Twentieth Century

- In 1986, with amendment to the divorce law, the percentage of those married over age 15 decreased to 61.4 percent. Married couples made up 80.2 percent of all census families. Lone-parent families accounted for 12.7 percent and cohabiting couple families for only 7.2 percent, rates that both increased substantially in 2006 (Statistics Canada, 2006a).

- For the first time in 2006, the number of unmarried people (meaning never married, divorced, separated, or widowed) over age 15 surpassed the number of married people, at 51.5 percent (Statistics Canada, 2006a). See Figure 2.1.

- Canada's declining marriage rate is similar to that in other Western countries, including the United Kingdom, Australia, and the United States. In the United States in 2001, the number of married-couple families was down to 70 percent from 83 percent in 1981, and common-law families increased from 6 percent to 14 percent in the same period (Statistics Canada, 2006a).

than they used to be. These shifting norms, opportunities, and expectations have all contributed to a decline in the stability of married and cohabiting life. But both continue, and for the majority seem to work and work happily.

DECLINING FERTILITY AND THE VALUE OF PARENTHOOD

One of the most marked changes in family life has been a change in family size over the last century or so. Since the 1870s, fertility in the West has declined steadily. Birth rates in Canada hit a record low in 2000, after 10 straight years of decline. A total of 327 882 babies were born in 2000, down 2.8 percent from 1999 and the lowest number since 1946 (Statistics Canada, 2002e). Today, most European and North American countries are at, or just below, population replacement levels. While Canada is still showing some population growth, it is steadily decreasing, and growth is due more to immigration than to births. This means that unless there is a radical shift in fertility or immigration in the future, Western populations will get smaller and older during the next century. This process is already well underway in Sweden, France, and Japan. Whether this is a problem—for families and for societies—depends on who is deciding and how the situation is defined. It is a topic to which we will return.

A significant blip on this downward fertility curve was the post-war "baby boom." The baby boom, however, was only a temporary reversal of the long-term trend and was largely confined to North America. The "boom" was also misnamed. Higher birth rates were the result not of increasing family size alone but also of compressing two decades of births into a decade and a half (roughly 1947–1962). In other words, while fertility did increase somewhat, the boom was more the result of postponed fertility due to World War II. Several different age groups then had their desired number of children within a short time frame, leading to a dramatic increase in birth rate for those years. Largely, however, the long-term downward trend in fertility over the course of the twentieth century never really ceased.

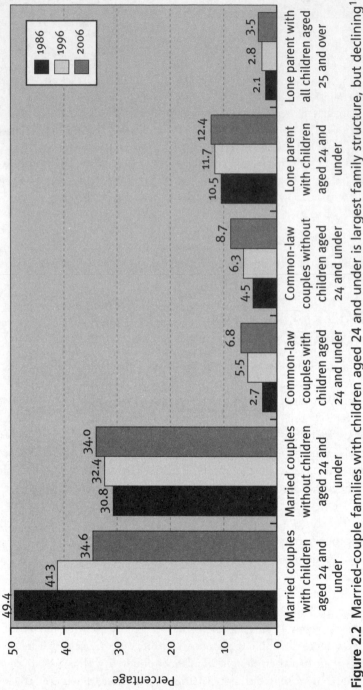

Figure 2.2 Married-couple families with children aged 24 and under is largest family structure, but declining[1]

[1]Historical comparisons for census families, particularly lone-parent families, must be interpreted with caution due to conceptual changes in 2001.

Source: Statistics Canada, censuses of population, 1986, 1996, and 2006. Retrieved April 2009 from www12.statcan.ca/english/census06/analysis/famhouse/charts/chart1.htm.

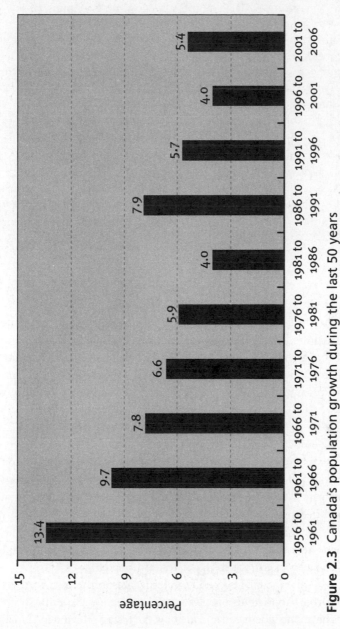

Figure 2.3 Canada's population growth during the last 50 years

Source: Statistics Canada censuses of population, 1956 to 2006. Retrieved April 2009 from www12.statcan.ca/census-recensement/2006/as-sa/97-550/figures/c1-eng.cfm.

Changes in the Birth Rate and Age of First-Time Mothers

- At the start of the Great Depression (1931), women were having fewer than three children. During the baby boom of 1946 to 1965, however, alongside a higher percentage of married people, the number of children born increased to three children per woman on average. Most of these children were born to young mothers (in their early 20s) (Statistics Canada, 2006a).

- With the legalization of contraception devices in 1969, the number of children born decreased, and has continued its decline over the last half-century. In fact, 1971 marked the last year during which the birth rate was at replacement level (Statistics Canada, 2006a).

- There are now more couples without children than with children. It must be noted though that it is only about 2 percent more (43 percent and 41 percent respectively). Couples with children who have left home are included in the "couples without children" category (Statistics Canada, 2006a).

- Women today are having children at increasingly older ages. Number of births by women in their 30s rose from 23 percent in 1982 to 44.8 percent in 2002 (Statistics Canada, 2004b). Whereas in 2001 7.8 percent of children aged 4 and younger had a mother aged 40 to 49, in 2006 this percentage has increased to 9.4 percent (Statistics Canada, 2006a).

Family size and birth rates in Canada have always been political issues, as we mentioned earlier. The term used to describe Quebec's historically high birth rates (before they fell sharply from the late 1950s on) was "the **revenge of the cradle**," an image reflecting the belief that Quebec's long-standing sense of political injustice might be countered by having more Quebec (French-speaking) citizens (see Henripin and Peron, 1971). Early birth-control promoters, such as A.R. Kaufman of Kitchener, Ontario, were concerned about the French in Canada "outbreeding" the English (see McLaren and McLaren, 1986: 124).

The Quebec government awarded prizes in the 1930s and 1940s to women who bore many children. Their photos would appear in newspapers. Both the church and the government encouraged families to have more children. This policy was formalized with baby bonuses, which increase with each extra child born. The shift from large to small families in Quebec has occurred rapidly indeed, leaving many Quebec families with older and younger generations of vastly different sizes. Quebec's birth rate remains a political issue in the 2000s. Family researchers who study birth rates—known as **demographers**—are household names to Quebeckers; not so in the rest of Canada.

Aboriginal peoples in Canada also had high birth rates in the past. In the 1970s and into the 1980s, births to Aboriginals peoples started to decline. Recently, however, First Nations birth rates have since increased and are now the fastest growing in Canada (Vanier Institute of the Family, 2004). The current fertility rate among Aboriginals is around 1.5 times the overall rate among Canadians (Statistics Canada, 2005d), with 10.5 percent of the Aboriginal population being in the youngest age group (0–4 years old) compared to only 5.3 percent of the Canadian population at large (Statistics Canada, 2005c).

Recent Statistical Trends in the Aboriginal Population

- The number of Aboriginal peoples in Canada—including the First Nations, Métis, and Inuit—is now more than one million. Aboriginal peoples make up about 4 percent of Canada's total population. The population has been increasing significantly for the past two decades and grew by 45 percent from 1996 to 2006. The non-Aboriginal population only increased by 8 percent during this time period (Statistics Canada, 2006a).

- Eight in ten Aboriginal people live in either Ontario, British Columbia, or the Prairies (Statistics Canada, 2006a).

- By 2017, the number of Aboriginal young adults aged from 20 to 29 years ready to enter the labour market is projected to increase by more than 40 percent, compared to the 9 percent of the same age group from the general population (Statistics Canada, 2005b).

- The percentage of Aboriginal peoples in Canada is similar to that of New Zealand, Australia, and the United States. Canada's Aboriginal population is second to New Zealand's, where the Maori population accounts for about 15 percent of the total population (Statistics Canada, 2006a).

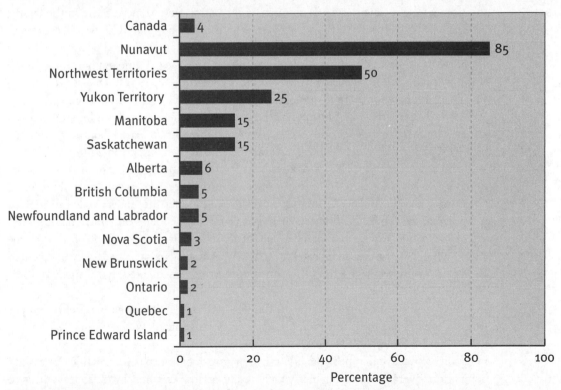

Figure 2.4 Percentage of Aboriginal peoples in the population, Canada, provinces and territories, 2006

Source: Statistics Canada, Census of Population, 2006. Retrieved April 2009 from www12.statcan.ca/english/census06/analysis/aboriginal/charts/chart1.htm.

Although Canadians are having fewer children than before, expectations of marrying and having children remain strong. When asked by family researchers, most young people say that they expect to get married and have children (Vanier Institute of the Family, 2004). Interestingly, few expect ever to be divorced, despite the high divorce rate in modern society. Moreover, in the late nineteenth century and the early part of the twentieth century, many more people than now never married at all, a fact contrary to the common assumption that everyone in the past got married. For example, Gee (1986: 266) finds from historical records that in 1911, 12 percent of Canadians never married. This compares with only 5.8 percent in 1981. Today, fewer than 2 percent of Canadians are likely to remain single their whole lives (neither marrying nor cohabiting). Not marrying in the past generally meant not entering parenthood. So, in fact, parenthood in the past was not part of as many people's lives as it is now. In the past, a lower percentage of the population got married, but those who did had many more children, on average, than couples do today.

The First and Second Demographic Transitions

The **demographic transition** from high mortality and fertility to low mortality and fertility transformed the social meaning of children, child rearing, and women's place in the family. The transition to low fertility in the West, which began around 1870, is called the *first demographic transition*. It brought births into line with a sharply reduced death rate. Since 1965, we have seen a new force for lower fertility in the West. Demographers have called this new phase the *second demographic transition* (Van de Kaa, 1987). This contemporary transition brought birth rates into line with new lifestyle goals and family practices. Wherever we find the second demographic transition well advanced, we find a profusion of new ("non-traditional") family styles, women working in the paid labour force in large numbers, and people seeking autonomy and fulfillment in their personal lives.

The second demographic transition is especially advanced in Northern and Western Europe. Renewed concerns have been expressed in these regions about depopulation and a shortage of young people in the future. In Europe, the fertility rates needed to replace the population—about 2.1 lifetime births per woman—are found only in Ireland, Malta, Poland, Albania, Turkey, and some new countries in Eastern Europe. None of these countries is a highly industrialized, Protestant country. All of them have made a virtue of large family size or limited access to birth control. It must be remembered that Canada did this as well until recently.

In most Protestant industrial countries, fertility rates hover around 1.5 children per woman. Japan's fertility rate has dropped too, from an annual level of 2.1 in 1973 to 1.29 in 2004 (BBC News, 2005, June 1), the lowest ever recorded there. A continuing decline in fertility will leave Europe's population with a growth of only 6 percent while the world's population overall nearly doubles. As a result of low fertility, by 2025 one in five Europeans will be 65 or older.

The effects of this transition are both profound and subtle. A long decline in fertility, together with increased life expectancy, has led to an aging population. On the other hand, people today are much more likely to have many generations alive at once than at any previous time in history, with some families having as many as five or even six living generations (McDaniel, 1996a). Remarried, step, and blended families also expand our kin networks into stepchildren and stepgrandchildren, as well as larger extended families. And, largely because of urbanization and industrialization, more people today live alone or outside conventional families than their parents or grandparents would have done. Domestic lives are becoming more varied and complex.

Several explanations exist for these recent fertility declines. For one, women have been taking advantage of more access to education and employment. Another factor is that couples have delayed marrying. When people delay marriage, they are likely to have fewer children. At the same time, the costs of raising children, both economic and social/personal, rose dramatically during the twentieth century. Children are especially expensive if they need daycare by someone other than the mother (whose child care in the past was presumed to be costless), or if caring for them means forgoing a parent's income and career aspirations for several years. Moreover, parents usually spend increasing amounts of money on children's lessons, camps, and education. As well, children today remain in a state of economic dependency for longer than in the past, sometimes for surprisingly long times, as we shall see in later chapters. Finally, children often contribute less to the family economy than they used to in pre-industrial times and in the early part of the twentieth century. We will discuss these issues further in Chapter 6.

Contraception, Child-bearing Choice, and Abortion

In the past, women found a major source of identity in having children and being mothers. This was the case in such different situations as urban Quebec in the seventeenth century,

Table 2.2 Selected Trend Data, 2006, 2001, and 1996 Censuses

	Census Year		
	2006	**2001**	**1996**
% of couples (married and common-law) with children (of any age)	54.3	56.7	59.3
% of couples (married and common-law) with at least one child under 25 years of age	49.2	51.7	54.7
% of one-person households	26.8	25.7	24.2
% of households containing a couple with children	28.5	30.5	32.9
% of households containing a couple without children	29.0	28.0	26.8
Average household size	2.5	2.6	2.6

Source: Statistics Canada website. *Census Trends for Canada, Provinces and Territories. Statistics Canada Catalogue* No. 92-596-XWE. Retrieved April 15, 2009, from www12.statcan.ca/english/census06/data/trends/Index.cfm.

and the early frontier societies in the West of Canada. Silverman (1984: 59) explains that giving birth and raising children was the answer often given to the question "What are women for?"—an answer given by women as well as by men (also see Mitchinson, 2002). Until recently, both women and men agreed that child-bearing and child rearing gave women's lives meaning. Entering parenthood was also vital to populate Canada, especially in settling the West and, as we have seen, in the earliest settlements in Quebec.

However, there have always been attempts, some of them successful, to regulate pregnancy and births. Although officially illegal in Canada until 1969, some couples tried to use birth control to choose how many children they would have and when they would have them. Among the most common birth control methods in the past were abstinence and prolonged breast-feeding. Other popular birth control methods used in the past include barrier methods, timing or rhythm approaches, withdrawal, abortion, and, as one wise adviser to young married women suggested in her 1908 marriage manual, "twin beds" (McLaren and McLaren, 1986: 19–20).

Abortion was also common in previous centuries, with methods of "bringing down the menses" routinely advertised in daily newspapers and early magazines (McLaren and McLaren, 1986: 33–35). It is only in recent decades that abortion has come to be seen as an important public and moral issue. Interestingly, several of the well-known nineteenth-century **abortifacients** (herbs or potions that brought on a miscarriage) are still in use today for inducing labour.

During the 1960s, however, safe, reliable, and easily available contraception methods were invented. This technological shift significantly changed the concept of birth control, and so contributed to the decline in fertility rate. Therefore, the first demographic transition was accomplished through a combination of strategies including late marriage, abstinence from sex, awkward methods of birth control, and dangerous, illegal abortion. The second demographic transition has occurred in the midst of a liberalizing sexual revolution and new, accessible means of contraception. The pill and other relatively readily available forms of contraception—including IUDs (intrauterine devices), spermicidal gels and foams, and higher-quality condoms—allow women and couples to choose if and when to become pregnant.

Contraceptive devices, for example, were generally scarce in Eastern Europe under Communism. As a result, the average woman in the former Soviet Union and Romania in the mid-1960s would have had seven abortions during her lifetime. Van de Kaa (1987) notes the dramatic rise in third and higher-order births after the repeal of legal abortion legislation in Romania, while the Ceauşescu regime maintained an iron-fisted stance against birth control in a deliberate effort to increase the birth rate. What this shows is that before the ruling of abortion, this method had been playing a large role in controlling fertility where other means of birth control were unavailable. Consequently, many people abandoned their babies to the care of the state. The net result was a huge number of Romanian babies and children crammed into orphanages under appalling conditions.

Up to the 1890s, abortion was tolerated in many jurisdictions, including Canada. Women who wanted to end their pregnancies could do so with the assistance of surgeons, herbalists, or midwives. Abortion was in fact legal in most North American states until the 1890s. Then it became illegal for 70 years, as a result of pressure exerted by social purity movements. Legalizing abortion once again made the process safer and more medically controlled. The (legal) abortion rate rose briefly after the mid-1960s, with a more liberal interpretation of the laws, but the rate soon tapered off (McLaren and McLaren, 1997). The most important factor promoting a decline in the incidence of abortion is the use of contraception, which enables avoidance of unwanted pregnancies. As contraceptive knowledge and use have spread, abortion has become a less often relied-upon means of limiting fertility. These changes have also influenced people's ideas about love, sex, and intimacy in ways that would have been hard to imagine then.

Family and Household Size

As fertility has declined, the number of people in the average household has become smaller. The average Canadian household has shrunk by 50 percent, from around six people in 1681 to now two or even one today. What's more, complex family households, containing a variety of people who are not part of a nuclear family, have almost vanished.

At the same time, a major change in family life has been a rise in the proportion of single-person households (Statistics Canada, 2006b)—the proportion has more than tripled since 1931, while the proportion of people overall living in families declined since 1981 (Vanier Institute of the Family, 1994: 29). In 2006, for example, there were more than three times as many one-person households as those with five or more people (Statistics Canada, 2006b). Curiously, while households have been growing smaller, houses have been growing bigger. Victorian-era houses were intended to serve as single-family homes with space for one or two live-in servants. When immigration was at a peak, as many as 15 people occupied these houses (Iacovetta, 1992). Today, most single-family houses are occupied by couples with fewer than three children, or none at all.

Decrease in Family Size

- The size of families in Canada is continually decreasing. Whereas in 1961, 16 percent of all families were made up of six or more persons, half a century later the percentage is only at 2.6 percent (Statistics Canada, 2006b).

- Along with the size of families, the size of households has been declining over the last half-century. The average size of the Canadian family decreased from 3.9 people in 1961 to 2.5 in 2006 (Statistics Canada, 2006b).

- One-person households are on the rise. The percentage rose from 9 percent in 1961 to 26 percent in 2001. In 2006, it was at 27 percent. This percentage is three times that of those households consisting of five or more people (Statistics Canada, 2006b).

SOCIAL SUPPORT AND REGULATION: THE ROLE OF THE STATE IN FAMILIES

As families have changed and evolved with respect to meeting people's needs for support, state support also developed, changed, and has now shrunk. For example, state support in Canada for lone mothers changed from being largely supportive of widows with dependent children, enabling them to be "stay-at-home" mothers, to encouraging today's lone mothers (who are more often never married, divorced, or separated) to work for pay while their children are young (Baker, 2005b). In the early part of the twenty-first century, there is little doubt that Canada has become less supportive of families overall (Vanier Institute of the Family, 2006). Major cycles of change in state support for families have occurred through recent times, with sharp reductions occurring at the present.

Child Support and Welfare Reforms in Canada

At the beginning of the twentieth century and especially during the Great Depression, child poverty and support for low-income mothers remained a low priority on the political agenda. Instead, legislation of the 1930s tended to reverse earlier progress toward a universally protected childhood (Strong-Boag, 2000). Change began after World War II under the Mackenzie King government, which recognized the state's role in supporting its young citizens and introduced **family allowances**. These monthly payments, based on the number of children at home, went to all women with children—but only to women, never to men. For many women who worked solely at home, this was their only independent income. In a way, family allowances were given to women as a way to compensate for and recognize their child rearing.

During the 1980s, the publication of Lenore Weitzman's book *The Divorce Revolution* sparked widespread concern that rising divorce rates together with inadequate child support were responsible for poverty among single mothers and their children. One of the most notable findings was that "a woman's standard of living decreases by 73% after divorce, while a man's increases by 42% on average" (Millar and Gauthier, 2002: 140). This led to a re-evaluation of child support guidelines in Canada and the United States. In 1989, the Canadian government announced its mandate to erase child poverty by the year 2000 (Crossley and Curtis, 2006).

What followed was a number of tax and benefit policy changes. In 1990, parental benefits were added to the unemployment insurance (UI) benefits. The federal program of family allowances was discontinued in 1992 and was replaced by the Child Tax Benefit program, which aimed to provide relief for low- and middle-income families in Canada (although Quebec adopted its own guidelines) (Millar and Gauthier, 2002). Finally, the National Child Benefit program was established in 1998 to support low-income families that move from welfare into the labour market (National Child Benefit, 2009). Despite these state interventions, child poverty has increased from about one in seven in 1989 to one in five in 1999 (Strong-Boag, 2000).

Critics argue that these reforms do little to relieve child and women's poverty (Williamson and Salkie, 2005; Gazso and McDaniel, 2009). Rather, they fuel the privatization of social benefits, increase economic stratification, and are not responsive enough to changing family circumstances (Millar and Gauthier, 2002). Today, only Quebec continues with some form of family allowances in Canada (LeBourdais and Marcil-Gratton, 1996). The Quebec program of baby bonuses is intended both to increase the numbers of births and to provide support for women raising children. The amounts paid, however, in no way compensate for the costs involved in raising a child.

It is important to note, however, that child poverty is not equally distributed in society. Poverty rates are consistently higher among young, single-parent, immigrant, and Aboriginal families (Prentice, 2007). For example, in 1997 only 13.7 percent of *all* children lived with a single mother compared to 41 percent of *income poor children* and 49.8 percent of children in *deep poverty* who lived in this family type (Kerr and Beaujot, 2003: 327). The rates among Aboriginal populations are as high as 52 percent, and roughly 43 percent of visible minority children experience child poverty (Strong-Boag, 2000: 125).

The rise in lone-parent households, neoliberal economic reforms, and the retrenchment in the welfare state may contribute to the persistence of child poverty (Kerr and Beaujot, 2003). Finally, debates on how to define and measure child poverty make it difficult to evaluate the efficacy and success of government policies.

"Welfare-to-work" initiatives of the 1990s add a new dimension to the plight of low-income families and their children. Prior to the 1990s, single mothers across Canada "could provide full-time care to their children and receive social assistance until their youngest child was at least school age" (Williamson and Salkie, 2005: 56). However, in the mid-1990s, Canadian policy makers sought to reduce the proportion of welfare recipients by mandating them to find work or take part in employment-related programs (for example, job training). Contrary to original goals, these welfare reforms did not improve children's well-being.

Instead, impoverished children are now more likely than before to have parents who are trying to balance work with employment, and they are more likely to live in families that secure income from the labour market rather than social assistance. Unfortunately, most families that move from welfare to employment continue to live below the poverty line and their income tends to decline after supplements end. Therefore, elimination of child poverty will likely entail the integration of several carefully planned and evaluated social policies—not only child support benefits and welfare-to-work initiatives, but also those associated with social assistance incomes, higher minimum wages, affordable housing, and more accessible and universal child care (Lloyd, 2008).

Changing Nature of Elder Support by the State and the Family

Traditionally, support of older individuals was provided by what is sometimes referred to as the "three-legged stool" of responsibility, namely government, employers, and families (Salisbury, 1997). However, efforts to reduce government spending, the precarious nature of employment markets, as well as changes in family life have altered the support received by the elderly (Kemp and Denton, 2003).

The Canadian welfare state began to develop during and immediately after World War II. State intervention in the provision of health care, social services, and economic support underwent a progressive expansion, culminating into a full-blown Canadian social security system in the 1970s (Li, 1996). Given its supply of economic, medical, and social assistance, the system was especially important for older people, who were now supported by the government.

Two other main sources of support were available in later life—the market and the family (Esping-Andersen, 1999). The financial services market provided plans such as life insurance and private pension policies, while the family, often mainly through the efforts of women, provided care for infirm older adults.

The post-industrial society, however, brought with it changes to the traditional sources of support for the aging portion of society. Due to changes in the labour market and demographic transformations, the state, the market, and the family started limiting their provision of welfare compared to their contribution in the past (Esping-Andersen, 1999). Beginning in the 1980s, a concern with the overextension of the welfare state and with the public expenditure implications of an aging population took over in the political realm. This lead to decreased spending, terminated social programs, and streamlining of services (Baines, Evans, and Neysmith, 1998; Brotman, 1998). Such changes caused a greater responsibility for late-life provisions to fall on the shoulders of the family and the market.

However, high levels of unemployment that have characterized the last two decades have forced many into early retirement or unemployment, often with not enough financial resources (Kohli, Rein, Guillemar, and Van Gunsteren, 1991). Further, the new face of the labour market, which included interrupted employment patterns, contract work, and part-time employment, also began limiting the support of employers through private pension plans and insurance programs (McDaniel, 1997).

Besides, the socio-demographic changes during this time, mentioned earlier in the chapter, reduced the availability of relatives able to provide support for older family members. Such changes included a rise in single-parent families, substantially increasing female participation in the labour force, as well as the geographical dispersion of family members. Thus, overall, the post-industrial society and the changes it brought with it have translated into a shift in responsibility for the care of the elderly from the state, market, and family to the elderly trying to take care of themselves.

These circumstances become evident when examining the attitudes and beliefs of today's middle- and old-age population. In a study by Kemp and Denton (2003) that investigated the way in which mid- and late-life Canadians discuss and allocate responsibility for the provision of social, financial, and medical supports in later life, the answer was clear—care for the elderly is the responsibility of the elderly. Recall the example of the Japanese Canadian and Canadian seniors discussed previously. Their reports were similar to those of the participants in this study. Most respondents in this study assumed personal responsibility for later life, citing individual planning and preparation as necessary tasks to secure against the perceived risks associated with becoming or being old. Furthermore, most participants rejected the notion that family members should provide housing, financial support, or personal care and were generally seen as a source of emotional support (Kemp and Denton, 2003).

Even though studies have shown the senior population is not responsible for escalating health-care costs or depletions of the Canadian pension fund (see Barer, Evans, and Hertzman, 1995), the shift to greater individual responsibility for societal and personal social security remains significant today. It has been argued that this can lead to increased social and financial risks in old age (e.g., Esping-Andersen, 1999).

The Regulation of Divorce

Marriage dissolution is of great interest to the state. In fact, at the turn of the twentieth century, divorce in Canada could only be granted by an Act of Parliament. Marriage was considered a crucial part of the social fabric, not to be tampered with by the parties involved.

However, marriage failure and divorce did not, as some might think, begin recently. There have always been men who deserted their families (some women deserted too), and couples who agreed mutually to separate (Gordon and McLanahan, 1991). Some Canadians went to the United States to seek divorce when it was not attainable in Canada (Bradbury, 1996: 72–73). In some provinces, such as Quebec, where divorce was almost impossible to obtain until well into the mid-twentieth century (and was frowned upon strongly), some women slipped into Ontario and declared themselves widows.

In 1968, greater access to divorce was made possible under the Divorce Act. This led to a fivefold increase in divorce between the late 1960s and the mid-1980s. Immediately following the revised 1985 Act, divorces again rose sharply, but much of this increase appears to have been accounted for by people who put off divorcing in 1984 and 1985, in anticipation of the revised legislation, and then initiated proceedings once the new law was enacted. By the late 1980s, the rate was declining.

These changes did not come to all parts of the Western world at the same time. For example, divorce remained illegal in Ireland until 1995. A referendum on the topic in that year defeated existing laws by a narrow margin. The pressure to liberalize Irish divorce laws contributed to a wide-ranging discussion of **secularization** (a move away from religion as an organizing principle of society) and the nature of social and familial change. People have also begun to reconsider the connection between moral and constitutional matters, or the church and state. Ireland is not yet a secular society (Wills, 2001). However, it is more pluralistic and tolerant than it was a decade ago. Individual Catholics, in Ireland as elsewhere, no longer completely embrace all the doctrines of the Church (though it may well be that, in practice, they never did so entirely).

CONCLUDING REMARKS

A long and complex process has marked efforts to reform government policies concerned with family life. One reason that government policies often do not meet the needs of Canadians is that most are based on the outdated assumption that all families are alike.

Canadian sociologist Margrit Eichler (1997) argues that there are increasingly complex ways to live in families and for family life to connect with work life. Thus, her starting point is to recognize the fact that families and work–family relationships vary widely. So must models of the family and state responses to family life.

Further, the Canadian family is not a static entity; rather, it is a product of a unique history of ethnic relations, transition to industrialism, wars, and demographic changes. The historical analysis outlined in this chapter showed how broad cultural, social, and economic changes can redefine traditional notions of courtship, marriage, family, parenthood, and gender relations. Informed by the successes and oversights of the past, we may begin to develop more effective policies and interventions to suit the changing nature of families in modern society. No doubt, the changing social and political landscape of the twenty-first century will have its own influence on the future of the family. The following chapters will discuss in detail the trends in our modern understanding of family norms, structures, and processes.

What the reader should take away from this chapter is the sense that family forms and structures have always varied. They have varied throughout history and they vary today, cross-nationally and cross-culturally. They vary because different circumstances call on families to perform different social tasks, often with different kinds and amounts of support. As a result, families have always had to adapt—to be almost infinitely flexible and resourceful. Keep this in mind when, in the chapters that follow, we examine the ways that different "kinds" of families—legally married and cohabiting, one-parent and two-parent, single-earner and dual-earner, same-sex and opposite-sex, and so on—try to grapple with their changing circumstances.

CHAPTER SUMMARY

Historically, families have been important bases for identity and for resource allocation. In many cultures, broader family structures such as kinship groups and clans have played a large role in determining relationships and social positions.

We have seen in this chapter that families are always, and have always been, changing in response to societal shifts, changing attitudes and expectations of women and men, and altering roles and views of and toward children. We have seen that contact with new cultures, either through colonization or immigration, brings about inevitable change that has both micro and macro implications.

Immigration has been part of Canada since its beginning, and changing immigration policies reflected Canada's position toward new people coming to live in this country, positions that, as we saw, were not always admirable. We have also seen how politics, economic circumstances, state regulations and reforms, wars, and consumerism shape families and family change, and the long-term impacts of these changes. We will explore the effects and significance of such changes in more detail in later chapters.

Key Terms

abortifacients Herbs or potions that bring on a miscarriage.

cohort A group of people who experience some major demographic event, typically birth, migration, or marriage, within the same year or period.

demographic transition The transition to low fertility in the West, which began around 1870, is called the first demographic transition. This brought births into line with a sharply reduced death rate. A second demographic transition, more contemporary, has brought birth rates to a low level and, it is theorized, into line with new lifestyle goals and family practices.

demographers Those who study population changes such as births, deaths, and migrations.

family allowances Monthly payments started in Canada after World War II as a way to give women compensation as well as recognition for child rearing.

They are based on the number of children at home and went to all women with children, but not to men.

gemeinschaft A type of community typical of pre-industrial rural life; that is, one in which everyone knows everyone else and people share common values.

"mechanization" of housework The introduction of new home technologies. Home economists worked to elevate the esteem of homemakers by promoting the idea that the new home technologies required skilled operators.

revenge of the cradle An expression reflecting the belief that Quebec's long-standing sense of political injustice might be countered by having more (French-speaking) citizens.

secularization A move away from religion as an organizing principle of society.

Critical Thinking Questions

1. What is the significance of the original contact and conflict between English and French colonizers and the Aboriginal peoples of Canada on today's society?

2. As the "mechanization" of housework occurred, the standards for cleanliness and material goods in the family home increased, adding pressure for women, especially in the 1950s. Now that many more women engage in the job market and have increasingly less time to spend doing housework, have these standards declined? If not, what are the implications? Consider the challenge, especially for women, to balance work and family responsibilities.

3. In the past, the primary reason for lone motherhood was widowhood. At the present, it is divorce. Why is this so? Why is this important when considering the nature of social support?

4. As we have seen, immigration has been a part of Canada since its foundation. Undoubtedly, immigration is still an important aspect of our country. What will be the impact of increasing immigration for Canada's future?

5. Some of Canada's past immigration policies do not cast our country in a favourable light. In recent years, these policies have improved, shifting to a long-term perspective that considers future growth and prosperity. Is it likely that future circumstances can alter this new perspective? Do you think it is possible that Canada will resort to its traditional viewpoint?

6. As baby boomers age, Canada enters a phase in which a large portion of its population will be made up of seniors. What changes is our society already experiencing as a result of this situation, and what can it expect to experience in the future?

7. Now that the typical life course of an individual is less predictable than in the past, what are the implications for sociologists? What must be considered when forming definitions, generalizations, and predictions?

8. How does modernization impact non-Western cultures? What is its significance for women and older individuals in particular? What conflicts are likely to result between men and women, different generations, and families as a whole?

Weblinks

Library and Archives Canada
www.collectionscanada.gc.ca/index-e.html
Library and Archives Canada has an incredible amount of resources, primary and secondary, about the history of Canada and its people. It features publications, photographs and other images, audio, and internet resources. It provides links to other Canadian government websites. Also visit www.archivescanada.ca for the Archives Canada portal, "your gateway to Canada's past."

Our Roots
www.ourroots.ca
This site features a search system on information about local communities and the histories of specific Canadian families. It also provides a search engine for Canadian books that is frequently updated with new and rare material. For students, several interactive educational resources are available. The collection has both French and English information and documents.

The Peopling of Canada 1946–1976
www.ucalgary.ca/applied_history/tutor/canada1946/index.html
This site is a research project by the Applied History Research Group at the University of Calgary. It provides information about the history of Canada's demographic changes, government and policy changes, and other topics significant to families in the past. It covers history from after World War II to the mid-1970s.

Multicultural Canada
www.multiculturalcanada.ca
This site contains a wealth of information about the history of immigration to Canada and how it has affected people from diverse backgrounds. It includes newspapers, photographs, book references, legal documents, audio files, pamphlets, and other materials, most of which are in languages other than English.

Multicultural History Society of Ontario (MHSO)
www.mhso.ca
MHSO is a "not-for-profit educational institution and heritage centre" founded by Professor Robert F. Harney in 1976. Ontario has had a rich history of multiculturalism, and this site provides information about cultural issues and links to publications and exhibit information at the Oral History Museum in Toronto.

Quebec History
http://faculty.marianopolis.edu/c.belanger/QuebecHistory/index.htm
This site is intended for a post-secondary school course in Montreal. It covers the history of Quebec people and culture from the mid-eighteenth century (after the fall of New France) to the present. It includes supplementary sections on important issues, biographies, statistics, documents, and images. It is also updated on a regular basis.

Global Gathering Place
www.mhso.ca/ggp
Related to the MHSO, Global Gathering Place is an interactive site with an aim to educate Canadians about the diversity of Canadian people through documents, images, videos, and audio material. It has information about immigration, ethnicity, community and family life, labour, and Canadian citizenship.

First People's Heritage Language and Cultural Council (FPHLCC)
www.fphlcc.ca
FPHLCC is an organization based in British Columbia that works to promote Aboriginal culture and language and improve the well-being of Aboriginal peoples. It works in conjunction with the First Peoples Cultural Foundation as well as First Voices, organizations that "raise awareness and funding for Aboriginal language revitalization." Both also have interactive and informative sites. Visit www.fpcf.ca and www.firstvoices.com for more information.

Chapter 3
How Families Begin
Dating and Mating

Chapter Outline

Curiously, love and sociology are linked almost as closely as love and marriage are (or at least were) thought to be. Émile Durkheim, one of the founders of sociology, discovered in the earliest sociological research that close social ties make a difference to survival (married people are less likely to commit suicide, for example). In this context, ceremonies and symbols (such as weddings and wedding rings, for example) bring communities together for common purposes (Durkheim, 1951[1915]). We will talk more about the importance of symbols and rituals in the following chapters when we focus on the effects of close relations on well-being, both individual and social.

Max Weber, another founder of sociology, reveals the centrality of marriage in his exploration of feudalism (Sydie, 1987: 73–77). The chivalry of knighthood required personal bonds and unity among knights. Women of feudal nobility were often the managers of estates and huge feudal households in partnerships with their husbands. Marriages were the means to cement clans or family groups, so that sometimes a man who married a woman who owned a fiefdom took the woman's name on marriage.

Friedrich Engels, who with Karl Marx is also a father of sociology, outlines a theory of marriage (Sydie, 1987: 96). With more resources, Engels argues, women and men became **monogamous** (married to only one partner for life). The link between economic production and marriage is that men would be able to pass their wealth to their offspring with some certainty about their role in fatherhood. Women's faithfulness in marriage then becomes part of an economic system. Here, argues Engels, is found the origin of modern marriage. This is also one basis of inequality between men and women in marriage, and one way in which marriage gives men power over their wives.

LOVE: A RECENT INVENTION?

The idea of romantic love is a social construction, the product of a particular culture in a particular historical period, although some argue that it has a biological basis (Fisher, 1992). Although many people today think that love and marriage have always gone together, there is nothing natural about this connection. In fact, traditionally, most people in the world have thought the purpose of marriage was to benefit the family group, not the individual spouses. So, marriages were arranged that were mutually profitable to the families. Historically, this has mattered more than whether the couple loved each other romantically in the way that we think of love today. But, as we shall see, neither marriage for love nor marriage by arrangement is certain to produce happiness and a durable union.

Morton (1992) tells how the idea of love as a basis for marriage grew out of questioning the traditional social and economic grounds for marriage. As feudalism ended and the market economy began to grow around the fifteenth century, Western European households, which had previously included many unrelated people, began to shrink. The number of family-only households increased rapidly, and people came to question the traditional basis of marriage: the melding of households for economic or political reasons. Finally, marriage as it was then known was transformed. Love came to be the basis on which families began. Divisions of labour emerged between the marriage partners, including different standards for sexual behaviours and for sharing and passing along family resources. Power differentials sharpened between men and women on the domestic front, since they were no longer equal partners in work.

The emergence of the idea of romantic love changed social roles, especially for women. Women had to transform themselves from workers into love objects. In this role, adornment and looks mattered more than their contributions to the family's overall well-being. Women went from being partners in work to being weaker, passive decorations (Abu-Laban and McDaniel, 2004). The differences between men and women became more exaggerated, as social and economic power in society and in marriage shifted more to men—a process that reached its peak with industrialization in the nineteenth and twentieth centuries.

Courtly love, the likely origin of romantic love as we know it today, emerged in Europe in the Middle Ages. Many images of romantic love in the late twentieth century still preserve aspects of this period. Courtly love affairs were not simple. With the emergence of courtly love the woman, as the object of male affections, was placed on a pedestal. She was to be won, though she remained, in a fundamental sense, unattainable. These ideas persist in present-day thinking about love and sex. With them goes the well-entrenched idea of a **sexual double standard**, which places a high value on women's limited sexual experience before marriage and their fidelity afterwards. Men's sexual experience before marriage and fidelity afterwards is seen as less important. Although sexual attitudes have changed, remnants of the double standard persist.

We can see this in the language used to describe sexually experienced males and females. The many terms used to describe women who have had many sexual partners all tend to have negative connotations. For example, "slut," "promiscuous," "loose," "easy." Comparing these to terms used for men who have had many sexual partners ("stud," "stallion," "playboy"), we see that more positive connotations are associated with male sexual promiscuity. Attitudes toward female chastity are not limited to North American men and women. For example, among Sunni and Shiite Muslim American families, the need for Muslim women to preserve modesty in their interactions is highly valued (Carolan, 1999).

THEORIES OF MATE SELECTION

Whether we are examining heterosexual or same-sex couples, a central feature of couple relationships in Canada is commitment to the ideals of romantic love. In our society the arrangements—geographic and economic—of marriage are framed through the ideological rhetoric of romance. Though practical concerns always play some part, more in some relationships than in others, most people marry because they believe they love each other. And often people feel they have discovered the best—even the perfect—mate. Various theories have been suggested to explain mate selection. We discuss some of these.

Complementary Needs Theory

Robert Winch (1962) suggests that a person is drawn to someone whose needs are opposite or complementary to his or her own. This is commonly referred to as the "opposites attract" phenomenon. For example, a person who wants to provide care would be attracted to someone who needs care. Needs are also complementary if the partners have the same needs but at different intensities—for example, if one partner has a stronger need for physical intimacy than the other (Knox, 2005). People may choose a mate different from themselves in hopes of filling in the "missing pieces" in their own lives or personalities.

Exchange Theory

"Exchange" refers to a process of continuing interaction between partners. The exchange perspective sees marriage as give-and-take, where each partner both gives and gets. The stability and well-being of a relationship is thought to depend on how well a balance is struck and maintained in exchanges between partners.

Expressive exchanges in marriage are exchanges of emotion between spouses. They include hugs and kisses, sexual pleasure, friendship, a shoulder to lean on, empathy, and understanding. Expressive exchanges affirm the affection and love each spouse has for the other. By contrast, **instrumental exchanges** involve tangible or material support (Muncer, Burrows, Pleace, Loader, and Nettleton, 2000). The couple typically shares a household and tends to practical matters such as housework, paying the bills, and looking after the children.

Evolutionary Perspective

Developed from Darwin's theory on the evolution of species, this perspective sees humans as guided by principles that maximize survival advantages. Cues differ for men and women because their reproductive potential differs. Men, who can easily father many children, seek women who appear to be fertile, represented by youth and sexual attractiveness. Because giving birth to each child represents a major investment for a woman, women are more interested in the social and economic advantages that men can offer and pass on to their children. Therefore women, in the evolutionary perspective, are thought to base their preference for mates on men's social and economic status (Doosje, Rojahn, and Fischer, 1999).

Social Role Theory

Over the last few hundred years of Western society, traditional roles of men have differed from those of women. Men's roles were more related to the public domain and women's roles to the private. According to social role theory, men and women are thus socialized to prefer partners whose attributes are congruent with those stereotypic roles (Doosje et al., 1999). The mate selection process is guided by these preferences.

In our society, we hold the ideal that people should marry someone they love, not someone who would help them in practical ways. Yet marriage involves more than romance, and likely always will. It involves practical matters and economic concerns. Romantic love may be central to our ideal of married life, and traditional role expectations may be a part of mate selection. But in the last three decades, most families have needed two incomes to support a middle-class lifestyle that one income would have supported in the past. The persistence of beliefs in traditional social roles and expectations has created stressful situations for many women in society. The term "double day" is used to describe women who work all day but are still expected to come home and care for their husband and children because that is their social role as women. While there have been huge increases in proportions of working women, there has been a lag in adjustments to household work and child care. Although men's contributions in the home have increased, there is still inequality in dual-earner families (Hook, 2006). This will be explored more extensively in later chapters.

So, modern marriage continues to struggle with traditional social roles. It also has both instrumental and expressive (emotional) functions, but in our minds' ideal, marriage is mainly expressive, directed to fulfilling emotional and psychological needs. In large part, it is this idealization of marriage and the roles involved that leads to conflict between ideal and real family lives, and high rates of frustration, divorce, and sometimes violence.

MEETING AND MATING

With love as a goal—for better or worse—Canadians of all ages look for intimate partners. Meeting a potential mate is not what it used to be. Yet some older traditions remain, and some new traditions emerge. The range of ways to meet one's life partner has widened in recent years. Many couples meet in the usual places of shared activities—schools and universities, workplaces, religious places, neighbourhoods, sporting groups, or events. Others meet through common friends or relatives. Cyberspace is an immensely popular venue for singles in search of partners. Others are still put together by relatives in arranged marriages or semi-arranged marriages.

Arranged Marriages and Love Matches

A society that practises "arranged marriage" puts parents or kin in the centre of making matches between people. In most societies for most of history, marriages have been arranged in this sense, based not on love but on the needs, beliefs, or desires of the couple's relatives. In Western Canada, for example, there were a large number of arranged marriages in the period between 1860 and 1945 (Millar, 1999), when partners were scarce. And today in Canada, there are arranged marriages among some ethnic groups. Arranged marriages, however, are most common in societies where we find close extended families. In support of this, studies have found that individuals whose daily lives are organized outside of the family before marriage are more likely to choose their own partners. This includes experiences at school or in the workplace, whether in Japan, China, Europe, or India. An emerging influence is exposure to media from outside one's ethnicity, which often involve themes of romantic love and dating (Ghimire, Dirgha, Axinn, Yabiku, and Thornton, 2006).

Reasons for arranged marriages vary from culture to culture. For many, those involved have strong interests in ensuring religion is carried on through generations. In some, rights to land are typically passed from one generation to the next (from father to son). Since marriage is an arrangement between families, it makes sense to arrange marriages in a way that protects family assets such as land, grazing rights, or animals. Parents also want to minimize potential conflict between the families that will be joined by the marriage. For these reasons, the choice of marriage partners is considered far too important to be left to the whims of youth. Spouses are chosen because the union is economically advantageous or because of friendship or kinship obligations.

International Snapshot

- In some cultures, bride kidnapping is a traditional practice that still exists in regions of the Caucasus, areas in the Middle East, Southeast Asia, and Africa. In recent years, this practice has become especially prevalent in Kyrgyzstan, a country in Central Asia formally part of the Soviet Union, following the fall of the communist government (Handrahan, 2004; Grant, 2005; Harris, 2006).

- In addition to bride kidnapping, other forms of violence against women in Asian and African countries include rampant sexual assault, wife battering, bride burning, kidnapping for sale into prostitution, "honour killings," and trafficking of brides (Niaz, 2003; Plambech, 2005; Blanchet, 2005).

- Among children of immigrants to Canada, both South Asian Canadians and Chinese Canadians show a greater preference for chastity in a mate than their European Canadian peers. The views of South Asian Canadians fall in between what they believe their South Asian parents perceive as appropriate and what they believe their Canadian peers perceive as appropriate, showing that young adults from some Eastern cultures are caught between local and traditional norms about sexuality and marriage choices (Lalonde and Giguere, 2008).

- In Western cultures, physical attractiveness and passionate love are valued characteristics in partners. On the other hand, in Eastern cultures, family values and wishes have more significant influence on mate selection (Zhang and Kline, 2009).

In Chinese cultures, Confucian ideology stresses the importance of family perseverance. This meant that arranged marriages were prevalent in China, with two-thirds of marriages arranged in urban areas and even more in rural areas. However, recent trends show steep declines in arranged marriages in China. Friends and colleagues have taken over the matchmaker role that parents used to play. This is consistent with what we said before about the connection between close extended families and arranged marriages. Chinese families used to be known for close-knit, three-generation households. While family remains the main pillar of the support network, the nuclear family has become more popular. As well, consistent with findings that will be discussed later in the chapter, a high value on a partner's education has replaced the value on a partner's family background among the educated in China (Xu, Xie, Liu, Xia, and Liu, 2007).

Among South Asians, arranged marriage remains prevalent. The key characteristics to be considered in a marriage include language, caste, religion, and fairness or lightness of skin (Ternikar, 2004). In Japan, so called *go-betweens*, matchmakers that help out informally, are sought because of their networks. With their familiarity and knowledge of both parties, go-betweens can bring suitable couples together (Abe, 2005).

Sometimes people still marry people they have never met. Today, however, few marriages are "arranged" in the traditional sense. Arranged marriage candidates are becoming more active participants and have more say in the process (see "Dating and Mating Trends"). In multicultural Canada, arranged marriages remain popular among several ethnic communities, for example, some South Asians and some Orthodox Jews (see Howell, with Albanese and Obosu-Mensah, 2001; Weinfeld, 2001). A 1995 study of urban Japanese young people (Applbaum, 1995) finds that 25 percent to 30 percent of all marriages are arranged. Thus, arranged marriages are much present in industrial cultures. We do not know how common this practice is in North America as statistics have yet to be compiled.

Personal Ads and Internet Dating

Personal ads have grown both in popularity and acceptability in the latter part of the twentieth century. What used to be called "lonely hearts ads" for the desperate are now mainstream, appearing in respectable newspapers and used by respectable people. Lavalife.com, Perfectmatch.com, and Matchmaker.com are only a few of the many available on-line dating services. A simple Google search can pull up millions of results. For those who do not want to take the time to get to know a person, ads provide people the convenience of viewing overall profiles with one quick read. People seek this type of service as an easier and quicker avenue to find a partner with the desired qualities. In the United Kingdom, the internet ranks as the third most popular method of getting a date (Nielsen//NetRatings, 2005).

Brym and Lenton (2001) find the following main reasons for the growing use of internet dating:

> As career and time pressure increase, people look for more efficient ways of meeting potential intimate partners.

Growing sensitivity about workplace sexual harassment has led to decline in workplace romance.

Due to job market demands, single people are becoming more mobile, making it harder to meet dating partners.

Much research has focused on the gender differences surrounding the types of language used by men and women in their ads. A recent study found that in general, men and women both prefer ads that describe intrinsic values of the writer such as emotional intimacy, helping others, and personal growth. Less preferred are ads that proclaim extrinsic values such as attractiveness, recognition/fame, and financial success. Not surprisingly, it has been found that people seek out others who have the same values as they hold for themselves. However, consistent with other studies on the topic, research finds that while women do focus more on intrinsic values, financial success remains a strong preference (Sheldon, 2007).

While men also prefer ads where women claim intrinsic values, they also tend to stress looks and physical features (weight, height, ethnicity, even eye and hair colour) more than women do. For example, terms such as "attractive," "slender," "petite," or "sexy" are used much more often by men in their ads to describe the person they seek (Coltrane, 1998: 47; Smith, Waldorf, and Tremblath, 1990). It may even be that in this method of mate-seeking, gender stereotypes matter more than in more conventional mate markets. Sev'er (1990: 76) concludes, "Even in this unconventional market, the rules of the mating game have remained traditional. Women (especially older women) are at a disadvantage, both as choosers and as potential chosen. The personal ads market seems to be a traditional market in disguise, a new bottle for the same old wine." Or it could be that people placing personal ads are especially "consumer"-oriented: they want a good "product."

Interestingly, one study that found that men value physical attractiveness more than women and women value earning prospects more than men as their ideal romantic partner followed up with their participants to find whether these were the characteristics of the people they dated. The study found the participants' ideal preferences did not predict their actual desire—the people they met and went on dates with (Eastwick and Finkel, 2008).

Personal ads have also become a popular method for gays, lesbians, and bisexuals to connect. Due to their smaller total population, these groups use the internet as a meeting space. A 2008 study found that gays, lesbians, and bisexuals are more likely than heterosexuals to meet in person, have sex with, and have a long-term relationship with someone they meet on-line (Lever, Grov, Royce, and Gillespie, 2008). Of course, this does not mean that mate selection is any more random than it ever was. It means only that the pools of potential mates within socially preferred categories have been enlarged by reducing the factor of distance, via the internet and advertising. Maybe this is yet another dimension of globalization!

Older couples are more likely to view their partner negatively, since they have lived together for a longer period of time and are well past the infatuation stage of the first few years of a romantic relationship.

■ Older couples are more likely to view their partners positively and seem to develop an automatic response to handle negative traits in their partner. Older adults are therefore biased toward the positive aspects of their partner and their intimate relationship (Story, Berg, Smith, Beveridge, Henry, and Pearce, 2007; Perunovic and Holmes, 2008).

Even in on-line dating, honesty is the best policy.

■ Although being honest is undoubtedly preferable, studies show that doing so while dating on-line has a negative effect on success (Gibbs, Ellison, and Heino, 2006; Couch and Liamputtong, 2008). This does not mean necessarily that if one intends to date on-line they should be dishonest, since later dating someone face to face will likely reveal previous deception (Barraket and Millsom, 2008; Rosen, Cheever, Cummings, and Felt, 2008).

With arranged marriages, couples meet their spouse for the first time on the wedding day.

■ Arranged marriages have shifted in degrees of "traditionalism." In traditional arranged marriages, spouses may meet each other for the first time on the wedding day. In semi-arranged marriages, couples can date first and decide whether to get married later (Ternikar, 2004).

SOCIAL ASPECTS OF FINDING A MATE

The term "marriage market" may seem too rational or cold-blooded a description of a process we tend to view as largely emotional. And yet, there is much that is market-like about finding a mate. For example, we can think about mating in terms of exchanges, as discussed earlier. Each potential partner brings to the potential relationship something that is of value to the other: personality, skills, physical attractiveness, earnings potential, and so on.

Whether participants admit it or not, rating and ranking is part of the mate market. Meeting, mating, and marrying involve a giant sorting process whereby our "market values" are matched with the market values of others. It can be a cold calculation, as when, for example, a man seeks a wife who will "look good on his arm." We even have a name for such wives, although interestingly not for the men who seek them. "Trophy wives" are typically sought by men climbing the rungs of success in business or politics. These wives are visible at country clubs and in some elite social circles, beautiful and well-groomed, well-coiffed, and well-dressed. Sometimes their husbands match them well in terms of appearance and style, but sometimes they do not. The husband's allure is his earning power, not his good looks. We can all bring to mind many examples of these kinds of couples.

A central part of the mate market is the politics of attractiveness. Good looks make a difference, for men and women, heterosexuals and gays, in getting attention in the mate market. For women, attractiveness is often a life's project (Abu-Laban and McDaniel, 2004). Immense amounts of time, effort, and money go into the construction of female attractiveness. Women pluck, wax, and shave unwanted hair and carefully groom the wanted hair. Through workouts and/or other unnatural processes, they shape and flatten unwanted bulges and enhance wanted ones. Of course, men increasingly focus on their appearance as well. The recently coined term "metrosexual" denotes this increased focus of heterosexual men on their appearance. The metrosexual label is used to describe a straight young man with money, typically living in a city, who takes great interest in his image. Interestingly, the term was coined by advertisers looking to motivate men with money to shop, but has increased in popularity and become part of pop culture and a self-identification of many males who take pride in grooming.

Aspects of the dating script contribute to the decorative potential of women. Often, gifts from the adoring man are decorative to the woman. Certainly, engagement rings have this decorative purpose. A woman wears the ring as a symbol with dual meanings: she is desirable on the mate market, her intended mate makes sufficient money (or comes from sufficient family money), and she can be decorated well. This suggests that she will be "kept well" during their married life and announces to all who see her ring that she has made a "good catch." This idea is supported by research on the amount men spend on engagement rings. A study found that men marrying younger women spent more on rings. The same was true for men who earned more money and whose fiancées earned more money (Cronk and Dunham, 2007). This is consistent with the theory that the engagement ring is a symbol of mate quality.

In the mate market, flirting matters. It is still an important part of the meeting and mating scenario. Women are expected to flirt with a blend of innocence and interest; the mix must be exact so as not to convey unintended messages. However, the flirting script, like the dating market, has been considerably updated. Flirting prior to the 1990s was heavy on the innocence, light on the sexual innuendo. Now, the content is reversed, with women expected to be sexual in flirting, though not too aggressive (Coltrane, 1998: 34). Men tend to report that women display more sexual interest in cross-sex interactions than women admit to displaying. This has been explained by findings that behaviour which men perceive to be sexually motivated is attributed different motivations by women (Henningsen, Dryden, Braz, and Davies, 2008). So, it seems that flirting has a lot to do with perceptions that are not always agreed upon by everyone involved.

With greater equality between men and women in the present, the image of the woman waiting for the man to ask her out is outdated, although some women still wait for men to initiate dating. Patterns of meeting and dating change over time. Lampard (2007) studied trends in the settings in which couples report they met. He notes that a decreasing number of couples report having met in settings such as restaurants, bars, and clubs, while an increasing number of couples report having met at places of work and education (Lampard, 2007). However, in any setting, the cues of who likes whom are hard to read for any but the initiated. It is the special look, the holding of the door only for you, the talking to you more than the others that must be read like tea leaves for signs of interest beyond friendship. At times, the reading of the signs is so complex that both women and men ask others to help them interpret what meanings lurk in behaviours.

The question remains whether wooing is more equal. In some ways it is, since both sexes take initiative in singling out the person they especially like. However, a gender imbalance remains. Several studies of first-date initiation find that men are more likely than women to perceive a woman who asks a man out as showing sexual interest (Mongeau and Carey, 1996; Serewicz and Gale, 2008). Women who initiate dates are seen by a group of impartial observers as being more sociable, more liberal, but less physically attractive than the person being asked. Despite a welcome tendency toward more equality in dating initiatives, it could still be that women who initiate dates are viewed differently from men, who are expected to do so.

Dating Scripts, the Double Standard, and Sexual Practices

A traditional sexual double standard was the premise for dating rituals (or "scripts") that existed in North America from about the 1920s through the 1950s and most of the 1960s (despite popular images of that decade as the era of "free love"). **Sexual scripts** saw boys as initiators, calling girls for dates and often paying for the date. These expectations persist today. The man is still expected to pick up the woman and pay for the date (Serewicz and Gale, 2008). This persistent expectation is part of a traditional dating script. Those same scripts once expected girls to be chaste and virginal until marriage. Schwartz and Rutter (1998: 79) note that girls were cast as "good" if they were chaste and "bad" ("loose," "easy," and worse) if they followed masculine rules of sexuality. While chaste and virginal as virtues are not as explicitly stated today, as mentioned earlier, these labels endure.

The sexual double standard is shifting dramatically as patterns of behaviour of males and females are converging. Sexuality is, however, still seen differently by women than by men. Some of these differences are apparent in approaches to contraception. Women tend to take contraception more seriously, for example.

The age of a young person's first sexual experience depends on cultural as well as social factors. Belgrave, Van Oss Marin, and Chambers (2000) determined that among African American girls aged 10 to 13, girls with higher school interest, family cohesion, religiosity, and behavioural self-esteem engage in less risky sexual behaviour. In addition, ethnic identity and gender role orientations contribute to explaining differences in sexual behaviour. Higher levels of ethnic identity were associated with less risky sexual behaviour (Belgrave et al., 2000). Similar findings were found in Espiritu (2001) with Filipino American girls. These girls considered Anglo Americans to be morally inferior to Filipino Americans and immigrants. Filipino wives and daughters were represented as models of morality. Espiritu concluded that immigrant communities constrain women's lives in order to combat racial discrimination, but these restraints also create generational conflict (Espiritu, 2001).

The media is also included in cultural factors that may play a role in the age of sexual activity. There is constant alarm of the increasingly sexually overt nature of all types of media, specifically women in the media. A recent longitudinal study found that media consumption does matter when it comes to adolescent sex. The study found that, controlling for other factors, white teens who watched the most television when they were ages 12 to 14 were more than twice as likely to have had sex when they were ages 14 to 16 than those who watched the least television. This relationship was not significant for blacks. This was explained by more parental disapproval of teen sex and perceived permissive peer sexual norms (Brown, Bulanda, and Lee, 2005). While media seems to influence sexual attitudes and behaviours among adolescents, parents may act to mediate that connection.

It is clear that the family has an important influence on sexual behaviour. In a study of black and Hispanic families, structural variables such as family income, parental education, and maternal marital status do not determine age of sexuality as much as process variables such as maternal monitoring, mother–adolescent general and sexual communication, and maternal attitudes about adolescent sexual behaviour (Miller, Forehand, and Kotchick, 1999). A longitudinal study of 5041 Scottish teenagers also finds that family processes have a wider influence on young people's sexual behaviour than family structure. The most important variable is parental monitoring. Low parental monitoring actions—that is, too-little tracking, limit setting, and parental surveillance—predicts early sexual activity for both boys and girls, in addition to also predicting more sexual partners and less contraception use for girls (Wight, Williamson, and Henderson, 2006).

Fingerson (2000) also discovered that parents do affect their teens' sexual behaviour, but in terms of the teens' perceptions of parental beliefs about sexual behaviour, not parents' own reported beliefs. In addition, having a good relationship and communication with their mothers is associated with a lower likelihood of teens having sex and fewer partners if they choose to have it. On the contrary, Regnerus (2006) finds that among adolescents in intact, two-parent biological families, closeness of daughters to fathers rather than mothers postpones coital debut and reduces risky sexual behaviour. However, the findings support the notion that parental monitoring, adolescents' *perception* of their parents' disapproval, and adolescent sexual attitudes (mediated by parent–child communication) are important predictors of later age of sexual initiation (Regnerus, 2006). Overall, teens still report that their parents are the biggest influence on their decisions about sex.

Men and women often also differ on how they view sexual activity. These differing views, in turn, may affect how couples engage in sexual behaviour, with important implications during dating. A study by Knox, Zusman, and McNeely (2008) conducted surveys of undergraduate students in the United States. For one thing, men and women disagreed about whether oral sex was sex, with men less likely to think so and women thinking the opposite. These findings were consistent with opinions of Canadian youth indicating that (only) 25 percent considered oral genital behaviour to be sex (Bersamin, Fisher, Walker, Hill, and Grube, 2007: 182).

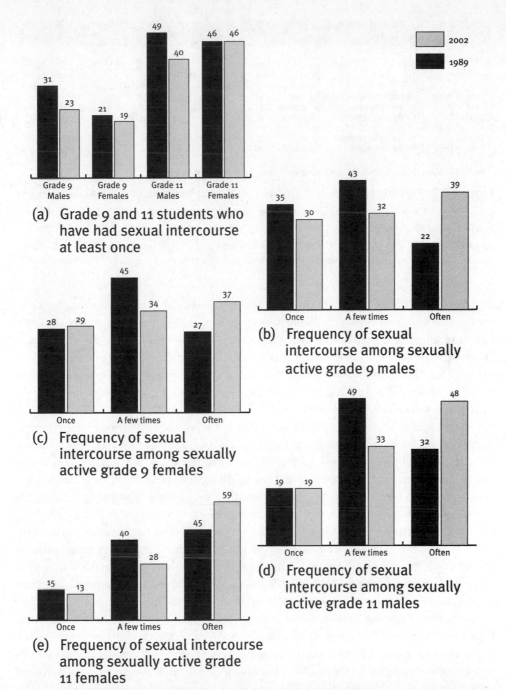

(a) Grade 9 and 11 students who have had sexual intercourse at least once

(b) Frequency of sexual intercourse among sexually active grade 9 males

(c) Frequency of sexual intercourse among sexually active grade 9 females

(d) Frequency of sexual intercourse among sexually active grade 11 males

(e) Frequency of sexual intercourse among sexually active grade 11 females

Figure 3.1 Frequency of sexual intercourse among grade 9 and 11 students (percentages, by year of survey)

Source: William Boyce, Maryanne Doherty, Christian Fortin, and David MacKinnon. 2003. *Canadian youth, sexual health and HIV/AIDS study: Factors influencing knowledge, attitudes and behaviours.* Ottawa: Council of Ministers of Education, Canada. Retrieved November 4, 2004, from www.cmec.ca/publications/aids/CYSHHAS_2002_EN.pdf.

Group	Responses (percentage reporting)								
	Parents	Friends	Teachers, sex educators	Religious leaders	The media	Siblings	Yourself	Someone else	Don't know/ refused
Teens 12 to 14	59	13	5	5	2	5	1	7	
Teens 15 to 19	39	21	4	8	4	4	7	12	
Teens 12 to 19	47	18	4	7	3	5	10	4	3
Girls 12 to 19	50	18	4	7	3	5	3	7	
Boys 12 to 19	43	18	5	6	3	4	6	12	

NOTE: The percentages, as reported in *With One Voice 2007*, do not total 100 percent.

Figure 3.2 Parents remain influential regarding teens' decision about sex

When asked, "When it comes to your decisions about sex, who is the most influential?" about half of high schoolers surveyed indicated their parents. Older teens were more likely to be influenced by their friends.

Source: Bill Albert. 2007. *With One Voice 2007: America's Adults and Teens Sound Off About Teen Pregnancy.* Washington, D.C.: The National Campaign to Prevent Teen Pregnancy. Retrieved www.thenationalcampaign.org/resources/pdf/pubs/WOV2007_fulltext.pdf.

Particularly relevant to youth today is the issue of cybersex. In a study by Knox et al. (2008), women were more likely to see cybersex as cheating on your partner, while men were more likely to believe that it did not constitute cheating (183). Women saw cybersex as just as emotionally painful as an off-line affair. The beliefs of both men and women, and how they view particular sexual acts, are important for understanding conflicts about trust and happiness within relationships; they should therefore be stated in the intimate partnership.

A counter to sexual intimacy in uncommitted relationships has been the threat of AIDS and venereal diseases. In the latter part of the twentieth century, sexually transmitted diseases (STDs) were widely known and reported to be a serious threat. The importance of using protection was emphasized during this period. However, the threat has been controversial and misinformation abounds; many young people mistakenly believe that heterosexuals are not vulnerable to AIDS. Nonetheless, this lethal threat dampened the enthusiasm of some young people for sexual intimacy, at least unprotected sexual intimacy. However, a new wave of adolescents in the twenty-first century has been contracting HIV/AIDs at increasing rates. While the overall number of new AIDs diagnoses declined 4 percent between 2000 and 2006 in the United States, it increased 21 percent among youth ages 13 to 24 (Spiegal and Futterman, 2009). This may signal the need for new vigilance about the prevalence of risky sexual behaviour and the need for stronger prevention. On the other hand, in some quarters, celibacy outside marriage, even including pledges of virginity, has become a popular option (Richer, 2002).

Certain social groups (for example, low-income African American and Puerto Rican young adults in the United States) continue to engage in risky sexual behaviour despite the high prevalence of HIV/AIDS and STDs in their population (Singer, Erickson, Badiane, Diaz, Ortiz, Abraham, and Nicolaysen, 2006). Interviews with a sample of these young adults uncover an underlying cultural logic being followed in their dating and mating lives. In particular, participants said their assessment of risk for STDs, and therefore their perceived need to use condoms, was based on beliefs about "who is safe" rather than "which behaviors are risky." (Singer et al., 2006: 1018). Also, because of living in poverty, and fear and doubt about the future, women value having a relationship with a man that can provide access to essential resources more than they value being risk-free. So, the decision not to ask the partner to use a condom is a rational choice in their economic and cultural context. Yet sexual behaviour cannot be reduced to individual decision-making based solely on health risks. Rather, economic conditions, aspects of the social environment (neighbourhood disadvantage, class or ethnic inequality), and psychosocial factors (internalized racism, living in fear) all play an important role in shaping group behaviour.

Dating in a Multicultural Society

As Canada and other countries become increasingly diverse, any discussion of meeting and mating must recognize the different habits of the cultures within a country. Especially in Canada, since immigrants make up a large part of modern Canadian society, and children of immigrants, whether born in Canada or in their home country, are one of the fastest-growing populations. According to King and Harris (2007), since this demographic shift is so recent, researchers today know little about the social development of these youth during the critical life stage when dating and mating occur. Most of the sociological research on ethnic romantic interactions focuses on sexual behaviour (Raffaelli and Ontai, 2001, for example).

Many factors are associated with the dating practices of immigrants in their new country. To date people of a different culture, language competence is a precondition. Other factors include the interrelationship of a person's cultural background, their family beliefs and values, and the expectations of peers in their school or community in shaping romantic relationships. This is because norms of the cultural tradition may be at odds with the pressures of Canadian society for young people to date and to select their own partners (Howell et al., 2001: 135).

Research also shows that first-generation adolescents are less likely to enter romantic relationships than adolescents in native-born families (King and Harris, 2007). However, those immigrant adolescents that decide to engage in romantic relationships do so as readily as host-country youth, most likely because they are more integrated in the culture of their new country.

Many immigrants come from cultures in which youth have little say in choosing their dating partners and long-term mates. Even if their families are not as traditional as others in the same culture, they are likely to still be more rigid in their beliefs than are families of North American adolescents. For many immigrants, attitudes toward women and dating are seen as indicators of a successful transmission of culture (Dasgupta, 1998). Therefore, many young women, such as those in the study by Espiritu (2001) of Filipino immigrants, believe that abstaining from casual intercourse is declarative of their moral superiority over the dominant culture of the West. However, this study also shows that this outlook may be enforced by a patriarchal society to restrain girls from seeking autonomy.

Further, it is a widely held notion that the parenting style of many immigrant cultures restricts the social opportunities for youth, thus limiting their opportunities for romantic experience. This is true to an extent, with many parents trying to foster a sense of cultural identity early in their children through home activities and organized events. This varies a great deal from culture to culture. In one study, groups of Chinese and European Canadians were asked to respond to a scenario in which a young adult was having a conflict with their parents over interracial dating. In reviewing this scenario, Chinese Canadian respondents gave much more support to the parents than European Canadians, who gave more support to the choice of the young adult (Uskul, Lalonde, and Cheng, 2007).

Parenting style and culture are strongly interconnected and exert different impacts on children from one culture to another. Research shows that some parents who control or oversee their children may be increasing the likelihood that they will go against their family's wishes and engage in unwanted romantic relations (King and Harris, 2007). Besides, if immigrants have close friends that date they are also more likely to do so. One study found that Russian immigrant girls in Israel with many immigrant friends were more likely to date Israeli boys (Eisikovits, 2000). Another study found the same for girls with Israeli friends (Remennick, 2005).

At the same time, there are many other reasons immigrant youth do not date as often as their peers. Many new immigrant families have less money, many dependent relatives, and are isolated from society for linguistic reasons (King and Harris, 2007). All these factors increase the likelihood that an immigrant teenager will have more responsibilities than his or her peers and therefore less time and opportunity for dating.

Increased immigration and ethnic diversity in Canada and other countries predicts that we will see even greater shifts in dating and mating practices in the future (Zhenchao and Lichter, 2007). One effect of growing up in a multicultural society and an ever-growing change in dating and mating is the rise of interracial dating. Overall, interracial marriage is rare. In the United State, only 4 percent of marriages are between couples of different races (Fisman and Iyengar, 2008). While it is likely this points to a general tendency for people to seek mates within their own race, marriage is the result of a lengthy search, which may involve a number of interracial potential partners.

In many cultures, parents are concerned about the background of their children's partner and try to exert some influence over their choice. This parental tactic is sometimes successful. In general, groups that are especially concerned about ethnic community survival place a premium on dating others from within the same ethnic group. For example, this is the case among Jews in Canada (Weinfeld, 2001). Similar findings can be found across most ethnic groups.

However, not all children respond to their parents' wishes as expected, and intergenerational conflicts can occur. A comparison of women born and raised in India with women of Indian descent raised in the United States finds that some believe Indian women raised in the United States are "not Indian enough" on issues regarding marriage and dating, because

Figure 3.3 Generations divided on interracial dating

Percent who agree or disagree that "it's all right for blacks and whites to date each other" by year born.

Source: P. Taylor, C. Funk, and P. Craighill. 2006. Guess Who's Coming to Dinner: 22% of Americans Have a Relative in a Mixed-Race Marriage. *PewResearchCenter: A Social Trends Report*, p. 2.

of their assimilation of U.S. beliefs (Srinivasan, 2001). Similarly, among Asian American college students, intergenerational conflicts about dating and marriage are more common among immigrant families than U.S.–born families (Gim Chung, 2001). Growing up in a multicultural society widens the number of available cultures in which one can find dates, and interracial dating is on the rise in Canada and the United States. A 1995 study of black, Latino, and white individuals found interracial dating in more than 50 percent of each ethnic group (Tucker and Mitchell-Kernan, 1995). In the 2000s, it seems that younger, more educated, more popular individuals are engaging in interracial dating (Fleras and Elliott, 2003). A study of student dating at one U.S. university found that 66 percent of students interviewed had been involved in an intercouple (that is, interfaith, intercultural, or interracial) relationship at some time. This practice is increasing most in university towns and large cities where diverse populations come together. Interestingly, it is causing some schools to re-examine their policies. In 2005 Bob Jones University, a U.S. fundamentalist Christian University, dropped its ban against students dating interracially (Reiter, Krause, and Stirlen, 2005).

Same-Sex Dating

Much like interracial dating, same-sex dating is becoming more mainstream. As a result, many of the misconceptions surrounding gay and lesbian couples have lifted

(Oswald, 2002). One instance was even covered by the media extensively, leading to the production of a TV movie about the case: *Prom Queen: The Marc Hall Story*. Marc Hall, a student at Monsignor John Pereyma Catholic high school in Oshawa, Ontario, was prohibited from bringing his 21-year-old boyfriend to the prom. Officials from the Durham Catholic District School Board admitted that Hall had a right to be gay, but argued that allowing the date would send a message that the Church supported his "homosexual lifestyle." On May 10, 2002, Ontario Superior Court Justice Robert McKinnon ruled that a gay student had the right to take his boyfriend to the prom. Hall went to the dance (CBC News, 2005 June 29).

Where gays and lesbians meet and mate has changed over time. In 1990, gay bars were the most common first meeting place, regardless of whether individuals were looking for a short- or long-term relationship (Berger, 1990). Today, there are many other avenues open to gay and lesbian youth, including well-established subcultural institutions (bars and nightclubs, theatres, comedy clubs, gay travel tours, and so on), and internet dating.

However, so far, little research has been done comparing same-sex and opposite-sex dating practices.

MATE SELECTION

The term "mate selection" may seem odd, given all the constraints on our choices, both logistical and social. Our society is permissive; traditional societies have more many and specific rules about who can marry whom. Some societies practise **endogamy**, which is the requirement common in small, traditional societies that people marry within their own social group (such as their own class, caste, or ethnic group). Other societies practise **exogamy**, which means marrying outside one's social group. Exogamous societies are occasionally small and based on extended kinship, like the !Kung bushmen of the Kalahari Desert.

Marriage rules always aim to ensure a kin group's advantage. Wherever land or other immovable property might be lost through marriage, the pressure toward endogamy is strong. Endogamy is also likely when a group is suffering discrimination by outsiders and has to strengthen its social bonds by highlighting group boundaries in marriage. By contrast, exogamy gives the members of a small society more chances to survive by increasing the size of the group they can call on in the event of a famine, war, or other trouble. It is a good survival strategy where group resources are few and the group does not feel threatened by (all) outside groups, or where there are few if any family properties to be lost (or gained) through marriage.

Our own society has no clear rules of endogamy or exogamy, but it sometimes seems endogamous, since most people fall in love with and marry people who are like themselves in important ways.

Homogamy

The theory of **homogamy** proposes that people tend to fall in love within their own social group, as defined by class, educational level, religion, and race or ethnicity. This tendency of like marrying like—also referred to as *assortative mating*—is found for a wide variety of characteristics: age, geographic location, various physical traits and overall physical attractiveness, and mental traits, including attitudes, opinions, and personality (Buss, 1985).

There are good reasons people tend to be homogamous. First, **propinquity (closeness) theory** says that people are more likely to find a mate among those with whom they associate. Given the social circles within which we move, we are more likely to meet others who are (at least socially) like ourselves than to meet people unlike ourselves. Second, we like people who think the way we do and act the way we expect them to; we feel comfortable in their presence. Third, instrumental and expressive exchanges are easier to balance when like is marrying like. That's because people are bringing similar, therefore more equal, qualities and resources to the marriage.

Educational and Other Status Homogamy

Some characteristics of prospective mates are more important than others in determining mate selection. For example, in our society, education—an achieved status—is a more important criterion in the selection of marriage partners than social class origins,

There is an increasing prevalence of people who marry spouses of the same or similar educational attainment, most likely because of extended education and post-graduate programs.

which are ascribed (that is, inherited at birth). Educational homogamy has become the most relevant aspect of homogamy in Canada and the United States. Since 1960, educational homogamy has continued to increase. There is an especially strong decline in the odds that someone with low levels of education will "marry up" educationally—that is, marry someone with more education. Educational intermarriage continues to decline for those with "some college education" and those with more. Instead, college graduates are much more likely to marry each other, rather than others with less education (Schwartz and Mare, 2005). There may be several explanations for this, including the increased importance of educational attainment for upward mobility, and the increased numbers of young people who prolong their education through secondary school, college, or university, and even post-graduate programs. These young people who spend a longer period of time within these institutions are more likely to meet and date people in the same settings who often have similar interests.

Age Homogamy

One of the most consistent and persistent facts of marriage is the age gap of the partners involved. In the days when marriage meant financial security, women may have looked for a financially secure man who could provide for them. That often meant an older, established, and more mature man. Even today, the age difference persists. It could be argued that with the gender gap in earnings potential, marriage is still a matter of security for many women who cannot earn as much by their own labours in the market as they can by marrying someone with higher earning power. However, this is not likely the best explanation.

Age difference can reflect different power and experience, although this is not always true. It can mean that men exercise greater financial leverage in marriage. The younger partner may be in a weaker bargaining position. It is also possible, even probable, that if the man is a little older, his career is more established and that sets the course for the marriage in terms of who is likely to follow whom for a job, promotion, or transfer. However, this does not indicate that the greater the age difference, the more financial security the union brings. Research shows that, in fact, most Canadian age-discrepant couples have lower combined incomes than those with similar ages (Boyd and Li, 2003). Research also finds that when people remarry after divorce, there is less age homogamy in the remarried relationship. Findings showed that both men and women tended to remarry someone younger than themselves (Gelissen, 2004). Whatever reasons there may be for marrying someone older or someone of a similar age, Canadians are not in favour of one over the other.

The **marriage gradient**, a well-known sociological idea, takes unequal marriages one step further. First discovered by Jessie Bernard (1973), the marriage gradient reveals that we sort ourselves into couples not only by age but also by differential status. Men, on average, marry women with a little less education or a lower occupational status than their own.

There are two interesting consequences of this. First, when taken together, the unequal matches form an off-centre parallelogram of higher-status men linked with lower-status

- A little more than half of Canadian couples (58 percent) are three years apart or less in age; just over 40 percent are four or more years apart (Boyd and Li, 2003).

- In 2002, 23 percent of boys and 19 percent of girls aged 14 to 15 are estimated to have had sexual intercourse (although percentages differ depending on the survey population and honesty of respondents) (Boyce, Doherty, Fortin, and MacKinnon, 2003).

- Interracial marriage in Canada is on the rise. In 2006, there were 289 420 married and common-law mixed-race couples. This is one-third more than in 2001, the first time this data was collected. In the majority of these couples (85 percent), one partner is white and the other from a visible minority group. The remaining 15 percent are couples in which both partners are from different visible minority groups.

- In Canada, Japanese people are most likely to enter mixed-race unions (75 percent). Next are Latin Americans (47 percent) and blacks (41 percent). South Asian and Chinese people are least likely to form a union with a partner outside their ethnic group (Statistics Canada 2006a; CBC News, 2008).

women. Since the world comprises men and women of all statuses, there are bound to be some men and some women prevented from making marriage matches. But they are not the same kinds of people. Men who are left out of the marriage gradient are those at the bottom, for whom there is no one of lower status to marry. Women who are left out of the marriage gradient are those at the top, for whom there is no one of higher status to marry. Thus, one must be wary when comparing the married with the unmarried: unmarried men and women are likely to be markedly different.

When men and women pair off unequally by status and age, the impression is created that differences between men and women are larger than they are. It works like this: We see couples in which she is younger and lower in status than he is. Some people might conclude from this that there is a natural sex difference. In fact, social choices in marriage partners tend to exaggerate existing sex differences. By the marriage choices we make, we reproduce cultural prejudices about the natural abilities of women compared with men, in relation to education, wealth, and status.

Despite this marriage gradient, research shows great age and educational homogamy. Indeed, it points to increasing age homogamy among people in their first marriages, and a parallel, though smaller, increase in the same direction in later marriages. The increasing age homogamy suggests a decline in women's reliance on men as "breadwinners."

Ethnic Homogamy

At the turn of the century, endogamy was strong for all North American ethnic groups. Ethnic homogamy was strongest for the new immigrants from southern and eastern

Europe, with weaker endogamy in the second generation (Pagnini and Morgan, 1990). Today, ethnic intermarriage is more common for all groups. Second-generation European Canadians and Americans marry increasingly out of their national origin group. The ethnic boundaries that separate potential mates have weakened over time (Kalmijn, 1993). That's likely because people from different ethnic backgrounds are, during adolescence and early adulthood, attending educational institutions where they meet and mate with others of similar educational attainment.

Between 1970 and 2000, the number of interracial marriages rose tenfold, with many saying that this signifies increasing status equality between Caucasians and minorities (Fu, 2008). Data from the 2000 PUMS census, however, provide some interesting findings on the effect of interracial marriage on family socio-economic well-being. First, husbands and wives have similar education, job prestige, and income in both endogamous and exogamous marriages, supporting the idea there is an equal status exchange in intermarriages (Fu, 2008). Second, even though spouses may not always have equal status, especially in income, the net differences are similar in endogamous and exogamous marriages. This has an important impact on social inequalities, as those with high education and high social status tend to marry one another, leaving those with less to marry one another, aggravating social divides.

Usually only the "high achievers" from minority groups marry out, but the opposite is true for Caucasians. Between groups of equal status, individuals in interracial marriages tend to be from the higher strata of their group (Fu, 2008). This pattern of individual status matching results in the perpetuation of income and poverty inequality among ethnic groups. "Low-status minority families that carry on their racial and ethnic heritages through endogamy tend to have lower status within their group, while those with higher status tend to marry out and no longer carry the sole racial and ethnic heritage to the next generation. If this pattern persists, underprivileged minorities may suffer from low family resources across generations." (Fu, 2008: 152). In this way, intermarriage poses a social dilemma. On the one hand, it can foster greater acceptance between ethnic and racial groups, while, at the same time, preserving ethnically and racially defined social classes.

Religious Homogamy

The data also reveal weak and diminishing barriers to religious outmarriage. Even among the Jews, a group that is especially concerned about its group survival, the high degree of homogamy is achieved largely by selection but also by increasing acceptance of religious conversion (before or after marriage) (Weinfeld, 2001: 154–160).

Intermarriage between Protestants and Catholics has increased dramatically since the 1920s (Richard, 1991), indicating that the social boundaries separating educational groups are stronger than religious (or ethnic) boundaries. In addition, interfaith marriages have become increasingly homogamous with respect to education, showing that education has replaced religion as a key factor in spouse selection (Kalmijn, 1991).

However, the freedom to marry a partner of a different faith often depends on how conservative the religion is. Again, using the example of Protestants, there is a much stronger preference for religious homogamy among conservative Protestants in comparison to mainline Protestants (Logan, Hoff, and Newton, 2008). The same principle probably applies to Catholics, Jews, and Muslims, for example. Many conservative or pious members of a religion are more likely to prefer religious homogamy and push their children in that direction.

The research on the religious homogamy and its affect on marital satisfaction is mixed. However, in general, the link between religious homogamy and marital satisfaction seems to have weakened over the past 50 years. There has been an overall decline in perceptions of religious authority among younger generations, causing less importance to be placed upon religion and its traditions (Myers, 2006).

Similarity and Couple Happiness

The literature consistently argues that social similarity of partners promotes marital satisfaction. Homogamous couples are significantly more satisfied than dissimilar couples (Gaunt, 2006). This applies not only to age and religion but to attitudes. A study of long-term committed couple relationships finds that agreement on a wide variety of issues is one factor that contributes to the longevity of the marriage, marital satisfaction, and overall happiness (Lauer, Lauer, and Kerr, 1990). Men and women whose attitudes diverge from those of their spouses are less satisfied with their marriages (Lye and Biblarz, 1993).

Different aspects of couple similarity may become more important depending on time and place. For example, studies have found that congruent religious beliefs are no longer significant predictors of marital satisfaction (Myers, 2006). While this is a general finding, we must be cautious about its applicability. Again, more conservative members of religions would probably be more likely to emphasize the importance of religious beliefs.

The Ideals of Mate Selection

Some believe that mating and marriage are about the capture and possession of "erotic property" (Collins, 1975). This view is consistent with what we have said so far about the role of romance in the mating process and can account for the complicated and unreal beliefs people hold about mating and their mates.

Experts who provide premarital counselling note a variety of unrealistic beliefs that are common among people when they choose mates. They include the beliefs that

- people will find the perfect partner;
- there is only one good partner for each person;
- love is enough to smooth over the rough patches in a relationship;
- when all else fails, the mates will try harder and succeed; and
- opposites complement each other (that is, heterogamy is better than homogamy).

People tend to hold such beliefs because, for many, mate selection is the capture of erotic property, and people's ability to reason is often clouded by passion.

GENDER DIFFERENCES IN ATTRACTION

Although the gender difference is larger in self-report data than in observed social behaviour, men's preference for physical attractiveness, youth, and reproductive value in a mate is documented in many studies (Feingold, 1995). The results are similar no matter how we obtain the data: whether by survey, experiment, or otherwise, findings consistently indicate the emphasis men place on physical attractiveness. A study examining speed-date behaviour found that women put greater weight on intelligence and race of a partner, while men respond more to physical attractiveness. Further, they found that men do not value women's intelligence or ambition when it exceeds their own (Fisman and Iyengar, 2006).

Both men and women may value inexperienced marriage partners, regardless of their own experience level (Jacoby and Williams, 1985; Williams and Jacoby, 1989). However, Oliver and Sedikides (1992) find strong evidence of a double standard. Men prefer low levels of sexual permissiveness for committed partners, and they rate permissive potential mates lower on marriage desirability. For men, permissive partners may be attractive as dates but are less attractive as potential marriage partners.

For their part, women prefer low levels of sexual permissiveness for both low- and high-commitment partners, rating permissive potential mates lower than non-permissive ones on both dating and marriage desirability. In casual mating opportunities, and when considering how to choose a long-term partner, undergraduate women are more selective than men overall. Especially important are status-linked variables and the anticipated investment of a partner in a relationship.

In a study of strategies used to attract mates, women try to attract "investing" mates, who are willing to consider eventual parenthood, by acting chaste and stressing their fidelity. Men who show more interest in eventual parenthood than other men attract women by highlighting their own chastity, fidelity, and ability and willingness to invest (Cashdan, 1993). By contrast, non-investing men, and women who expect non-investing men as partners, flaunt their attractiveness and sexuality to draw in as many partners as possible.

Some of this gender difference may be a matter of mere self-presentation. An experiment by Hadjistavrolous and Genet (1994) finds that women intentionally under-report the impact of physical attractiveness on their preferences. Connected to a lie detector–like apparatus, women undergraduates admit being more strongly influenced by the physical attractiveness of potential male dating partners, and give lower desirability ratings to physically unattractive men. So, some of this gender difference is cultural, a result of what we are taught to say that we want, and not a biological difference between men and women.

Though one might expect that women's attainment of higher education—and more direct access to their own economic resources—would reduce such gender-based differences in mate choice, survey results indicate the opposite. Rather, consistent with what we've said about the strength of educational homogamy, higher education increases women's socio-economic standards for mates, thereby reducing their pool of acceptable partners (Townsend, 1990).

WHY PEOPLE DO NOT OPTIMIZE

Unlike the ideals many hold about marriage, people do not seek the ideal or **"optimal mate"** solution to their most important personal concerns. They do not try to optimize; rather, they "satisfice": they seek a "good enough" solution, within the constraints life has handed them (March and Simon, 1958). The difference between optimizing and "satisficing" is the difference between searching a haystack for the sharpest needle and merely searching for a needle that is sharp enough to sew with. For most purposes, whatever satisfies us is ideal.

Suppose that, as an idealistic teenager, you had listed 10 qualities you felt you absolutely must have in a mate. If we assume that one in five people has each of these qualities, and the qualities you are looking for in a mate are uncorrelated, only one person in five to the 10th power—one in 9.8 million—will meet all your requirements. That may be less than one adult person of the right sex, aged 20 to 60, in all of Canada. Equally, there is only one chance in 9.8 million your "perfect mate" will consider you the perfect mate. So, by this scenario, the chances of meeting and marrying the perfect mate are one in 9.8 million squared (or nearly zero).

Even more modest goals cannot be optimized. Suppose that, instead of needing your perfect mate to be among the top fifth in attractiveness, you need him or her to be only in the top half. You similarly lower your standards for your other requirements. This makes your mating problem more manageable: now, you only need to look for that one "perfect" person in a thousand (that is, two to the 10th power).

With this in mind, you may try to solve the shopping problem by reducing the number of qualities you look for in a mate. Suppose your potential mate has to excel in only one respect and satisfy you in four others. Now you and your perfect mate are each looking for someone who is in the top fifth in one quality and in the top half in just four other qualities. The likelihood of finding a person with the qualities you seek is one in 1250. The probability that you will satisfy his or her needs is also one in 1250. Even so, the chance of meeting and mating is still well below one in a million (that is, one in 1250 squared).

However you revise the shopping list and extend your range and number of contacts, the chance of finding the perfect mate this way is nearly zero. Most people cannot and do not find a mate in this way. Rather, people fall in love with those who are close at hand. As in so many areas of life, we come to value what we know best and have available: people like ourselves. We become satisfied with the possible, not the ideal; then we come to love the person who satisfies us.

Whether we choose homogamy or heterogamy (intermarriage) depends on what kinds of people are available nearby. That explains why our chances of mating with people of other religious, ethnic, and racial groups increase when we have more contact with them. People marry others who are socially and geographically near at hand, even if "better" mates can be found much farther away.

This process of "satisficing" may sound unromantic, but in practice the feelings of love are genuine. People in love believe that they have discovered the one perfect mate. In a sense, they have. But they have not (and could not have) done it by following a shopping list of the "right" characteristics. Instead, they have decided, after the fact, that their mate is perfect—and that is what's so amazing about falling in love.

DATING VIOLENCE

Unfortunately, every discussion of dating and mating must include a discussion of interpersonal violence. This is ironic because, as we said at the beginning of this chapter, dating in our society is charged with romantic illusion and emotional intensity. There is an element of choice that is lacking in many other cultures, and a sense that the choice—though reversible through separation or divorce—is nonetheless enormously consequential. We need to examine the possible relationship between our pattern of romantic mating, on the one hand, and the high rate of violence between dates, mates, and lovers, on the other hand.

Dating and Mating Trends

- University students are active internet users, often communicating with others through social networking sites to find dates and sexual partners (Boies, 2002).

- Women prefer more concrete consent before sexual involvement than men (Humphreys and Herold, 2007).

- Seventy-three percent of Canadian men in a random sample claim they have never been sexually coercive. Of those that state they have, childhood abuse, adolescent promiscuity, and restrained emotions were all factors that influenced aggressive sexual behaviour (Senn, Desmarias, Verber, and Wood, 2000).

- There is a difference between the attitudes of Easterners and Westerners regarding sexuality. Asian university students are significantly more conservative toward sexual behaviour than are Canadians. At the same time, Asians appear to be more tolerant of sexual harassment. Having lived longer in Canada predicts less tolerance of sexual harassment by Asian students (Kennedy and Gorzalka, 2002).

- Most people consider date rape as gender-neutral. However, among those who consider it gender-specific, there is a tendency to assume the perpetrator as male and the victim as female (Verberg, Wood, Desmarais, and Senn, 2000).

- Among those using on-line dating services who are seeking sexual opportunities, the majority are married or living common-law (Brym and Lenton, 2001).

- In couples with an age difference of 10 years or more, the older partner is most often 50 to 64 years old (Boyd and Li, 2003).

- As adolescents grow older, they are more likely to engage in sexual intercourse but also more likely to use a condom, a positive finding in the sexual health of Canadian youth (Saewyc, Taylor, Homma, and Ogilvie, 2008).

The U.S. National Violence Against Women Survey has been conducted several times in the past few decades. The survey asks 8000 female and 8000 male participants detailed questions about experiences of violence in intimate relationships (Tjaden and Thoenness, 2000). The most recent findings stem from the survey conducted in 2000. The findings indicated that partner violence is pervasive, especially for women: 25 percent of women and 7.5 percent of men reported being raped or physically assaulted by a partner. Estimates from the survey indicate nearly 1.5 million women in the United States are raped or physically assaulted annually. However, this is not consistent with findings from the National Family Violence Survey, which consistently reports that men and women are equally likely to be physically assaulted. Anyway, this shows the importance of recognizing that women also commit acts of physical violence, a fact often ignored by popular conceptions of abuse.

We will have more to say about domestic violence, in Canada and elsewhere, in a later chapter. As will then become apparent, research on this topic is significantly hindered by disputes about the definition and measurement of domestic violence

Unfortunately, physical violence is often accompanied by emotional abuse. The survey found that women whose partners were jealous, controlling, or verbally abusive were significantly more likely to be raped, physically assaulted, or stalked. These findings show that education and treatment should be targeting emotional abuse just as seriously as physical abuse.

The survey also examined violence among gay and lesbian dating partners, finding that lesbian couples were significantly less likely to experience violence, while the opposite was true for gay men. Men in homosexual couples experienced more partner violence than men in opposite-sex partnerships. This would support this survey's findings that dating violence is perpetrated primarily by men; however, more research is needed on same-sex relationships to better understand these findings.

Young people are beginning their sex lives at much earlier ages, which increases the general susceptibility to dating violence. People who are dating, not married, or in a committed relationship are also especially vulnerable to partner violence. Thus, "date rape" is a growing concern among sociologists. But in this area of research, getting good data is difficult; young men and women tend to disagree about what happens on dates. Nonetheless, there is strong and active interest in collecting better and better data. There is also a gap in the willingness of boys and girls, men and women, to report dating violence. Girls are much more likely to report physical violence and psychological abuse in dating relationships than boys (Swahn, Simon, Arias, and Bossarte, 2008). This is related to general social views about male and female roles and ideas surrounding violence. However, girls are often the perpetrators of violence in dating relationships, which must not be ignored in education on prevention and coping.

A survey by sociologists Walter DeKeseredy and Katharine Kelly (1995) conducted on 44 college and university campuses across Canada found four women in five saying they had been abused by a dating partner, with nearly as many men admitting having done so.

Where violent abuses are concerned, women are more than twice as likely as men to admit their occurrence. Where less violent abuses are concerned, men and women acknowledge them equally often. The 2004 General Social Survey (Statistics Canada, 2005c), the most comprehensive survey on family violence, found a clear inconsistency in the reports by women and men. This consistent discrepancy leads to one of three possible conclusions. Either (1) violent and abusive men date a lot more women than gentle, non-abusive men, (2) women tell a lot of lies about their dates, or (3) many men are ashamed to admit the things they have done to their dates and therefore lie. The third option seems the most probable based on what we know as sociologists.

These disturbing findings reveal that violent abuse on dates is not only physical but also sexual. Bear in mind that most instances of forced sexual activity occur between people who know each other. The result is, too often, that women blame themselves for the experience. Because they know the assailant, they react passively to the sexual assault. Because they react passively, they blame themselves for not reacting more forcefully. A few even continue the dating relationship. Many girls tolerate sexually coercive behaviour because non-physical coercive tactics are seen as socially acceptable. For example, many girls find it hard to deal with being verbally pressured into unwanted sex because verbal pressure is not identified as overt abuse. However, the results are real. Verbal sexual coercion is associated with relationship dissatisfaction and troubles with sexual functioning that each lead to further negative consequences (Katz and Myhr, 2008).

Date rape grows out of common practices of sexual harassment, which is especially prevalent in schools and workplaces (McDaniel and van Roosmalen, 1991). Sexual harassment in elementary and high schools is a widespread issue. A study of sexual harassment is several U.S. schools found that 81 percent of students reported they experienced some form of sexual harassment during their school years. About a quarter of those students reported that they were targeted often. Also, they found that sexual harassment increases with age, while at all ages, girls experienced more sexual harassment (Gruber and Fineran, 2007). Such early actions and attitudes toward women set the stage for later abuse in relationships and dating.

Part of the problem is found in gender differences in labelling behaviours. College-aged men are much less likely to label such behaviour as "harassment" than their female peers. But after exposure to the workforce, men's awareness grows and they, too, come to see certain behaviour as harassment. Overall, women label more behaviours as harassment than men do, but this gender difference decreases with men's experience in the workforce (McDaniel and van Roosmalen, 1991).

Besides gender differences in perception, recent research highlights the importance of interpersonal and contextual explanations of dating violence. Foshee and colleagues (2008), for example, find those adolescents from minority families, single-parent families, or whose parents have lower educational attainment report significantly more experiences of physical dating violence. Usually, this connotes an acceptance of dating abuse and gender stereotyping in the less educated, minority population (Foshee, Karriker-Jaffe, Luz McNaughton Reyes, Ennett, Suchindran, Bauman, and Benefield, 2008).

Research on the effect of low socio-economic status on the risk of dating violence is divided (see O'Keefe, 1998; Lavoie, Hebert, Tremblay, Vitaro, Vezina, and McDuff, 2002). There is some evidence to suggest that good parenting processes (satisfactory supervision, fostering a sense of closeness, and provision of support) can reduce the risk of dating violence by promoting self-esteem in the adolescent. These relationships, in turn, are conditioned by the parental socio-economic status (Pflieger and Vazsonyi, 2006). Low-income families have fewer resources and experience more life stressors, which lead the children to experience low levels of self-esteem and externalize their feeling by venting their frustrations outside the home. Adolescents with low self-esteem may interpret their dating partner's actions more negatively or as a personal rejection. Poor relationships with their parents, especially lack of closeness to their mothers, may also result in an inability to effectively deal with complex emerging emotions and conflicts. So, the likelihood of endorsing dating violence beliefs and acting upon them is greater among low-income families. This is because the build-up of stressors may predispose youths to aggression in a dating context or to becoming the victim of dating violence (Pflieger and Vazsonyi, 2006).

CONCLUDING REMARKS

Mating, and especially marriage or a long-term committed relationship, gives people the chance for both greater life satisfaction and deeper dissatisfaction than the single life normally does. If you marry, you will probably increase your standard of living and longevity, especially if you are a man. Marriage has riskier, less predictable outcomes for women, especially when there are children involved or when women lack skills that would allow them to earn a living. Men gain the most from a marriage that works, and women—especially mothers and poorer women—lose the most when a marriage fails.

Deciding whether to marry should mean assessing your relationship realistically. If you think that there is too much fighting and not enough hugging in your relationship, marriage will not solve the problem. As we will see, the "enchanted" newly-wed period is normally followed by many years of declining satisfaction, especially if children are present. The typical marriage may worsen before it starts to improve.

Most important, flee a relationship that is marked by physical or emotional violence. The violence is likely to recur. You are not to blame, and your partner is not likely to change. Message to men: Seek professional help if you tend to express your relationship frustrations in a physical or violent way. Doing so is not unavoidable, normal, or acceptable in modern close relations.

Do people get what they want from mating and marriage? On the one hand, the range of possible choices is wider than ever: people are increasingly free to marry or not to marry, to have the kinds of relationships they want to, and to choose their own mate. On the other hand, what we want is patterned by our social experience. People learn to want marriage as the preferred form of adult life. We mate with people who are nearby and socially like ourselves, not with "ideal" mates. However, we can grow to think our partner is, in fact, the "perfect" mate.

CHAPTER SUMMARY

This chapter discusses mate selection as an exchange process in which a fair or equal exchange is most likely to prevent disappointment or resentment of either partner. The way in which we choose a mate has changed from when romantic love emerged during the Middle Ages to present-day internet dating services. However, in the game of love some things have not changed: love is still a deeply important construct in our society; a loveless marriage is still considered a tragedy.

As we look at the origins of our dating and mating rituals in the courtly love tradition, we see the origins of the sexual scripts of men and women. These dating rituals contributed to a sexual double standard in which boys were the initiators and girls were the receivers. Although love is the ideal basis of a marriage in the Western tradition, in other traditions a material exchange is more important. The process involved in arranging a marriage is different from the marriage market of modern singles bars, although in both cases an exchange is the basis of interaction.

We compare our marketability on the basis of physical features, earning potential, and personality; we search for "the one" on campus, in workplaces, among friends, on the internet, or on holiday. As we select our mates it is clear that there are rules about whom we may date and whom we are most likely to date and mate with.

Like marrying like, or homogamy, is one way the exchange process of dating becomes apparent. Similarity seems to play a large role in whom we choose to date and mate with. Educational homogamy has increasingly become an important factor in dating. Couple happiness is deeply connected to the social similarity of the partners in the marriage.

Dating and mating sometimes ends in violence, the irony of a love-based exchange. Sociologists face many problems in getting reliable data about violence; men and women are unlikely to report it, whether as perpetrator or as victim. Sexual harassment is a too common experience for many Canadian women.

Key Terms

endogamy Marriage to a member of one's own tribe or social group.

exogamy Marriage outside of one's own tribe or social group.

expressive exchange An exchange of emotional and sexual benefits.

homogamy The selection of a mate with similar social attributes such as class, education level, religion, race, or ethnicity.

instrumental exchange An exchange of practical and useful benefits, such as unpaid work or financial support.

marriage gradient A systematic difference between mates, such that men are typically older and of higher social or economic status than their female partners.

monogamous Married to one person for life.

optimal mate One's theoretical ideal mate.

propinquity (or closeness) theory A theory of mate selection that people are more likely to find a mate among those who are geographically nearby.

romantic love An idea of love that is influenced by idealistic concepts of mating, like chivalry and a search for one's soulmate.

sexual double standard The application of different rules, or standards of sexual behaviour, to men and women.

sexual scripts Attitudes and activities that a culture links to each gender, or that are typically expected of members of a particular gender in regards to dating.

Critical Thinking Questions

1. Discuss the marriage gradient and its outcomes. How may the more harmful consequences be reduced?

2. What are the different types of homogamy? Specifically, discuss educational homogamy and the effect it may have on existing social divisions.

3. Describe some theories of mate selection. Using what you read in the chapter, which theory or theories do you think are most relevant today?

4. What is the problem with verbal sexual coercion in dating relationships? How may it be resolved at both a micro and macro level?

5. Discuss gender differences in personal ads. Explain why it may be that the values singles state they are looking for are not always values found within the people they date.

6. What is expressive exchange? How is it different from instrumental exchange?

7. What is a "flirting script," and how has it changed?

8. Using what you've read in this chapter, what are some problems with society's ideal of "romantic love"?

9. How do propinquity (closeness) theory and homogamy theory differ?

10. Explain which factor you think has the most influence on mate selection and why.

Weblinks

New Directions
www.newdirections.mb.ca
This non-profit agency funded by the United Way provides information on families and parenting.

Second Wives Club
www.secondwivesclub.com
This site provides an array of articles, information, and discussion for remarried women and stepmothers, as well as links to other family- and woman-oriented advice and information sites.

Match.com
www.match.com
This dating site caters to all types of singles in many areas, including lesbian and gay individuals.

Matchmaker.com
www.matchmaker.com
This fun, less traditional dating service allows you to participate in a trial match without spending money or giving away personal information. The site categorizes its participants by gender, sexual orientation, expected level of commitment, and ethnic and religious backgrounds. Ironically, it does not sort its participants by occupation or interests/hobbies.

DoSomething
www.dosomething.org
This site encourages teens to become empowered agents of change in their own communities, and includes a large section on dating violence aimed at adolescents. The Teen Dating Bill of Rights and Pledge encourages respect and responsibility in relationships.

Family Violence: A Fact Sheet from the Department of Justice Canada
http://canada.justice.gc.ca/eng/pi/fv-vf/facts-info/fv-vf/fv2-vf2.html
This site provides information on various topics in relation to family violence, including spousal abuse and dating violence. It also provides suggestions on preventing family violence and links to resources.

About: People and Relationships
http://about.com/people
This site provides a vast array of information, including data on dating and relationships, marriage, divorce, homosexual life, and senior life.

Chapter 4
Types of Intimate Couples
Marriage, Cohabitation, Same-Sex Relationships, and Other Forms

Chapter Outline

Intimacy is one of the fastest-growing areas of theory and research in sociology (see Giddens, 1992). In intimate couple relations, sociologists argue, the family is being redesigned. Intimacy involves a mix of emotion, caring, and often interdependency—none of which are well understood by sociology. We will have much more to say about this in the next chapter. This chapter is about the different forms this intimacy takes. We ask, Does form matter?

The importance of having a long-term intimate relationship may be both greater and lesser than it was historically. Personal need and social pressures continue to push us to find a close intimate partner with whom to share our lives. Most young people consider this a top- (or near-the-top-) priority life goal (Bibby, 2001; Vanier Institute of the Family, 1994), and 90 percent of today's Canadian teens plan to marry, have children, and stay with the same partner for the rest of their lives (Bibby and Wayne, 2004). People are very interested, as we have seen, in finding a long-term intimate relationship. Less emphasis, however, is placed on helping the partnerships work well once matches are made, as we saw in Chapter 3.

We live longer now, so a lifetime commitment involves a much longer period than it did for your grandparents. When marriage for life often meant 20 to 30 years, most of which were spent having and raising large families, couples had a different kind of intimate relationship. Now, couples may spend years childless, then have children, and find that they still have a lifetime together after the children leave home. Being a close couple for a lifetime is a different prospect now, and continues to change.

Today, more people live in families without an ongoing close personal relationship. Long life expectancy and family changes increase the likelihood of spending a significant portion of one's life, perhaps at different periods, outside a couple relationship.

Official definitions of family, as discussed in Chapter 1, rely on some concept of an ongoing intimate relationship. Despite the immense changes that have occurred, governments still define families in terms of legal or semi-legal relationships and shared residence, not in terms of what they share and what they do for each other.

Twenty years ago, the *Tax Guide for Canada* had no definition of "spouse"; none was needed to guide people in preparing their tax returns. By the end of the 1990s, however, a full page in the guide was devoted to defining a spouse.

The definition of spouse has expanded to incorporate the different types of unions in which the members are not traditionally classified as "partners." This reflects society's adaptability and malleability to recognize and catch up with the changing nature of intimate relationships.

INTIMATE RELATIONSHIPS: MORE DIVERSE AND MORE COMPLEX TOO

Rates of traditional marriage are declining. In 2006, the proportion of married-couple families accounted for 68.6 percent of all census families, down from 70.5 percent in 2001 (Statistics Canada, 2007a). That is not to say, however, that the proportion of people who are in intimate relationships is also declining. In fact, the number of common-law-couple families rose from 13.8 percent to 15.5 percent (Statistics Canada, 2007a). These are significant changes from the rates two decades ago, when common-law-couple families accounted for only 7.2 percent of all census families, while married-couple families represented 80.2 percent (Statistics Canada, 2007a). Deviance from tradition is further exemplified by the inclusion of same-sex married couples for the first time in the 2006 Census. Following the legalization of same-sex marriages for all of Canada in July 2005, 16.5 percent of same-sex couples were married couples (Statistics Canada, 2007a).

Further highlighting the diversity of close relations in Canada is the variation of marriage rates in various communities, For one, more than one-half of the total Aboriginal population has never married, while more than one-third is married (Frideres in Cheal, 2007). More interestingly, the rates of divorce and separation in this population are comparable to that of non-Aboriginal Canadians (Frideres in Cheal, 2007). These findings point to the role of cultural specificity of marital status among different populations in the emerging diversity of marriage in Canada.

Close relations are becoming more complex too. There are many more households in Canada than in the past, for example, but fewer are family households (Statistics Canada, 2007a). This means that more Canadians live alone or with others in what they, and the 2006 Census, see as non-family households. For instance, since 2001, there has been a large increase in one-person households, and in 2006, 26.8 percent of the total number of private households were one-person households, while only 8.7 percent were households of five or more persons (Statistics Canada, 2007a). Some of those living in non-family households preserve close intimate relationships with someone not in their household; they may have a commuter marriage/relationship or (especially for young adults or seniors) a significant other who does not share their home.

RELATIONSHIP TRENDS AND PATTERNS

Two seemingly contradictory trends characterize present-day marriage: growth in popularity of alternatives to marriage and the continuing popularity of marriage. Since the 1970s, there has been a decline in rates of legal marriage in Canada. This trend continues in

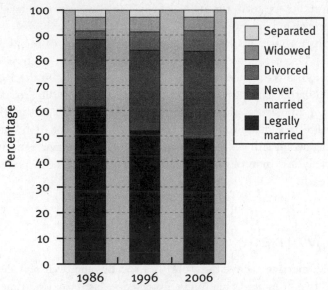

Figure 4.1 Unmarried people outnumber legally married people for the first time in 2006

Source: Statistics Canada website. 2006 Census: Families, marital status, households and dwelling characteristics. *The Daily.* Retrieved May 12, 2009, from www12.statcan.ca/census-recensement/2006/as-sa/97-553/figures/c7-eng.cfm.

the most recent data available (Statistics Canada, 1998b; 2007e), which show that a lesser proportion of all families are married families. The crude marriage rate was 4.7 for every 1000 population in 2003, compared to the most recent peak of 7.0 in both 1988 and 1989 (Statistics Canada, 2004c). Further, the 2006 Census found that for the first time ever unmarried people aged 15 and older outnumbered legally married people in Canada (see Figure 4.1). While these are large changes, the fact remains that most of both men and women, even in Quebec where cohabitation rates are very high, do marry at some point. And when asked, most Canadians value marriage and want to get married (Vanier Institute of the Family, 2004). "From a longer-term perspective, Canadians are still hooked on legal marriage" (Vanier Institute of the Family, 2004: 23). We need to consider, however, what else is happening with the formation of couple unions.

Age at Marriage

First, people marry later now than they did in the 1960s and 1970s. Even though the 1960s was supposedly a time of "free love," the age at marriage during that period was lower than it had been for a long time and lower than it has been since (about 22 years for women, 25 years for men) (Ram, 1990: 80). The long-term trend toward postponement of marriage continues; by 2003, the latest data available, women were aged 28.5 on average at first marriage and men were aged 30.4 (Statistics Canada, 2007e).

The reasons for later marriage are complex and related to social and economic opportunities and expectations. One factor is today's uncertain job prospects for young people. Compared to young people in the 1980s, young people in the 1990s seemed to have lower cumulative earnings (Statistics Canada, 2002c), leading to speculation that postponement of union formation may be, in part, economic. Another factor seems to be people's desire to pursue non-family interests such as education, travel, or work. Although young people still value marriage and family, as we have seen, they value marriage considerably less than older people. Younger people seem to prefer not to jump into marriage early.

Types of Marriage

Broadly defined, **marriage** across the world is a socially approved sexual and economic union between two or more people that is expected to last for a long time. People often enter this union with public formalities or a ceremony, such as a wedding.

In Canada, traditional forms of marriage and the family are experiencing dramatic change. Because the family is such a basic institution, and marriage is such an intimate relationship, change can seem threatening. Yet there is no single universal or necessary form of couple relationship. In order to understand the change in our own society, and what it may predict for the future, we will take a larger view of the institution of intimate couples and the many ways societies organize marriage-like arrangements.

In some societies, people wed more than one mate at a time. **Polygamy** is the generic name for this arrangement. Within this general category, **polyandry** is the marriage of one woman to more than one man, and **polygyny** is the marriage of one man to more than one woman. Polygamy was common in most pre-industrial societies and is still permitted in a few. But polygamy is banned in all industrial societies.

Polyandry, on the other hand, has always been a rare form of marriage. It occurs in societies like Nepal, where living conditions are harsh, and few men are able to support a wife and children on their own. A woman is therefore "shared" by a group of men—usually, brothers—and she is a wife to all of them. Female infanticide is practised, justified by the argument that the number of women "needed" in such a society is much less than the number of men. Anthropologist Marvin Harris (1997) suggests that societies with low population pressure (the relation between population density and arable land) favour polygyny; societies with high population pressure favour polyandry. Policies and laws on polygamy in Canada are being considered in light of the open practice in a small southern community in British Columbia and the possibility that refugees or immigrants to Canada may have foreign polygamous marriages (Beeby, 2006).

Monogamy—marriage between one woman and one man—is the form most familiar in Canada. However, variations on monogamy are also becoming more common, such as **cohabitation**, or non-marital couples, and same-sex couples. The 2006 Census of Canada found that 0.6 percent of all couples reported themselves as same sex (Statistics Canada, 2007a). Another form is what sociologists have called **serial (sequential) monogamy**. Serial monogamy is the marriage of a person over the life course to a series (or sequence) of partners, though only one at a time. In a society with high rates of divorce and remarriage such as ours, a growing number of people practise serial monogamy.

Is Marriage Still Valued?

Despite changes in timing and permanence, marriage continues to be central to interpersonal life in North America. See, for example, the popular book *The Case for Marriage: Why People Are Happier, Healthier, and Better Off Financially* by Linda J. Waite and Maggie Gallagher (2001). Cultural stereotypes and supports favouring traditional family life have not changed. Beaujot (2000) reports that Canadians typically see marriage as "natural" and believe it to be the foundation of family. Also, the vast majority (85 percent) feel that marriage provides more advantages than singlehood (Beaujot, 2000: 108–9).

Yet, in the early 1990s, David Popenoe (1993) wrote a famous article on the alleged "decline" of the family between 1960 and 1990. He attacks the devaluation of marriage and notes the increased acceptability and rates of divorce. He claims that the psychological character of marriage has changed over the years; whereas before it was understood as a social obligation for economic stability and procreation, it is now seen as a path to self-fulfillment where couples enjoy a true companionship (Popenoe, 1993: 533). Popenoe claims this has led to a deinstitutionalization of marriage and expresses his concern about the impact of the relative fickleness of marriage today and the breakdown of the nuclear family on children (1993).

Other sociologists, however, have argued that the shape of marriage is simply changing, not declining. Stephanie Coontz (2005) writes that today, we are pioneers "picking our way through uncharted and unstable territory" (282–283). Further, she writes that marriage or other intimate relationships today are carried out within an economy and culture that allows for more individualistic choices than in the past and, thus, must be based on respect and companionship (313).

Therefore, it may be the case that people today still value marriage enough to consciously make the choice to enter or stay in marriages even though divorce and cohabitation are socially accepted. This may lead us to asking whether currently couples actually value marriage *more* than couples did in the past, who stayed together out of social duty rather than true happiness, love, and respect for each other?

Zheng Wu's (2000) study of cohabitation and marriage in Canada reveals that "there is clear evidence that people now place less emphasis on marriage than they did a decade ago . . . The centrality of marriage seems to have weakened (71)." For example, the Statistics Canada 2001 General Social Survey finds about one-half of mature singles (single men between the ages 30 and 55 and single women between ages 28 and 55) in Canada did not expect to marry. Among these groups, either the option of marriage was not seen as real or love, marriage, and family did not have high priority (Statistics Canada, 2005d). Wu (2000) also notes that Canadians have become more accepting of non-marital sexual behaviour and non-marital cohabitation. As mentioned, common-law unions in the 2006 Census of Canada represented 16 percent of all couples, up from 6 percent in 1981 (Statistics Canada, 2002g, 2007a). In Quebec, the proportion was 35 percent of all couples.

People have individual reasons for choosing to live common-law rather than getting married, but the question remains whether the chosen difference ceases if law and policy make the two equivalent. A similar question occurs with respect to gay and lesbian unions. The differences between gay and straight relationships that may be valuable to some gay and lesbian partners could be seen as either diminished or enhanced now that the option of legal civil marriage exists (Canada, Department of Justice, 2005b). It is important to society to make gay and lesbian relationships equivalent to heterosexual relationships in terms of responsibilities and benefits. However, equivalence could lessen ways in which heterosexual relationships might benefit from being more like gay and lesbian couples, especially in partner equality. In this and subsequent chapters, we will consider gay and lesbian couples in various ways as vital family forms.

Changing Attitudes That Affect Marriage

In the 1960s, marriage was a social ritual by which young people were expected to declare their adulthood. Parents of baby boomers (children born between 1946 and 1964) epitomized this sentiment. These couples married in their early 20s and had lots of children—about twice as many as the generation before and the generation after!

The sexual revolution and the women's movement paved the way for changes in attitudes to sexuality, and to women's place in the family and the economy. This shift in attitudes is reflected in changes in the timing, structure, and permanence of marriage. Marriage rates began to decline in the 1960s, declined rapidly in the 1970s, and have continued to decline at a slower rate since 1980. A slight recent decrease is currently seen across Canadian provinces, though not in British Columbia, Ontario, or the Yukon, where marriage rates have gone up (see Table 4.1). The slight increase in marriage rates in British Columbia and Ontario may be explained by the fact that these are the two provinces in which same-sex couples have been allowed to marry since 2003. The proportion of adult years spent outside marriage has also changed, and it is higher than ever before. It began to rise as the average age at first marriage increased after 1960, a trend that continues today, as noted above.

Table 4.1 Marriage Rates by Province and Territory

	Marriages			
	2002	**2003**	**2002 to 2003**	**2003**
	Number		**% Change**	**Crude Marriage Rate per 1000 Population**
Canada	146 738	147 391	0.4	4.7
Newfoundland and Labrador	2959	2876	–2.8	5.5
Prince Edward Island	901	823	–8.7	6.0
Nova Scotia	4899	4742	–3.2	5.1
New Brunswick	3818	3724	–2.5	5.0
Quebec	21 987	21 138	–3.9	2.8
Ontario	61 615	63 485	3.0	5.2
Manitoba	5905	5659	–4.2	4.9
Saskatchewan	5067	4977	–1.8	5.0
Alberta	17 981	17 622	–2.0	5.6
British Columbia	21 247	21 981	3.5	5.3
Yukon	143	158	10.5	5.2
Northwest Territories	144	139	–3.5	3.3
Nunavut	72	67	–6.9	2.3

Source: Statistics Canada website. 2007. Marriages. *The Daily*. Retrieved May 12, 2009, from www.statcan.gc.ca/daily-quotidien/070117/dq070117a-eng.htm.

For most North Americans, the quality of a relationship appears to matter more than its structure (for example, married versus common law). The important question for most people is what makes the relationship satisfying. That said, a majority of people still like getting married, and marriage-related ceremonies are part of our culture's dream-life.

Many people still find the idea of legal marriage compelling, despite what they know about the realities of marriage and divorce. Enormous numbers of North Americans are neither rejecting the family or other long-lasting, close relationships nor accepting family in a traditional form. Most are hoping to revitalize and reinterpret family (Baker, 2001; Beaujot, 2000; Scanzoni, 2000, 2001), suiting their families to themselves and their needs.

Efforts to reinterpret the family are reflected in the recent legalization of same-sex marriage. Reactions to the legislation, which had been proposed for some time before passing, reflected the clash between traditional and non-traditional conceptions of marriage. Those who view marriage as a sacred arrangement whose main purpose is procreation were upset by the use of marriage vows to legitimate same-sex cohabitation. Those who view marriage as an enduring close bond whose goal is love, companionship, and sex were pleased to see the ceremonial forms made available to a wider range of people who care for each other deeply.

Living Solo

Most North Americans today postpone marriage or establishment of a long-term committed relationship until they have completed their education. For a small minority, this is high school. For most, it is something beyond high school, such as technical training, college, or university. This means that most people marry in their mid-20s or later. In both Canada and the United States, many young people come to marriage with much experience with dating and sexual experimentation; many have lived with someone, either the marriage partner or someone else.

Moreover, marriage is not for everyone. Over the last two decades, one-person households have increased substantially in Canada. More than one-quarter of all households in Canada consist of a person living alone (Statistics Canada, 2007a). Interestingly, it is older Canadians who most often live alone, while more and more young adults live at home with parents (Statistics Canada, 2004d). In part, the growth in living alone is because of an aging population containing more widowed people.

To live without a life partner is not new, nor is it more common now than it was in the early part of this century, though more concerns are expressed about it now. Alone, however, need not mean lonely. Many who live solo are not isolated from their communities or circles of friends. People who are devoted to their work may prefer not having a life partner; many great artists and writers have remained unmarried and unattached in any permanent way. And the need for marriage for security and acceptability for women has declined, even though it is not gone.

Commuter/LAT Relationships

However, many people still feel a strong urge to marry. Indeed, some people would prefer (or decide) to marry and live apart than postpone or avoid marriage. Consider so-called **commuter marriages**, or what is now called a **living apart together (LAT)** relationship. A LAT is a marriage or other intimate relationship between partners who live in two separate households (Borell and Karlsson, 2002). Of Canadians who have a partner, 1 in 12 lives separately from the partner (Statistics Canada, 2003b). Typically, couples take up separate residences after having shared a common one. More often now, couples live in two different homes from the beginning of their relationship, which is why some European sociologists call this arrangement "living together apart." Nault and Belanger (1996) also note committed long-term relationships in which both partners live with their parents. This is an aspect of the growing "cluttered nest" phenomenon that occurs when adult offspring return to the family home, or never leave it. And while LAT

Figure 4.2 Living apart together arrangements by age group, 2001

Source: Adapted from the Statistics Canada website. 2003. Couples living apart. *Canadian Social Trends.* Retrieved May 13, 2009, from www.statcan.gc.ca/pub/11-008-x/2003001/article/6552-eng.pdf.

arrangements are most common for the young, they are nonetheless a preferred arrangement for a portion of the older population (see Figure 4.2).

For some couples, a LAT marriage is only a short-term arrangement. For others, it becomes a long-term lifestyle. Though LAT relationships remain a minority, nothing illustrates so well people's continued commitment to close involvement with a partner despite enormous odds and the conflict between the cultural values of living together versus pursuing career success. LAT relationships force couples to create intimacy differently than couples who see each other every day. While couples living in LAT relationships tend to have an enhanced appreciation for their spouse or family, it remains a complicated way to live (Groves and Horm-Wingerd, 1991; Forsyth and Gramling, 1998; Borell and Karlsson, 2002).

Divorcees sometimes opt for this arrangement when entering a new relationship (Levin, 2004). After experiencing an unsuccessful marriage, these people tend to become more careful with later relationships. Choosing to live apart from their partners may be a strategy to avoid another painful separation. As well, some may fear that moving in together could change the current dynamics in the relationship or the sharing of assets. Others may simply not find jobs in the same area, so living apart is the only option.

Economic, cultural, or even policy pressures may explain why couples choose LAT relationships. The main reason behind LAT relationships is typically career advancement. Today, more women and men in committed relationships are in professional careers that make it hard for them to move when their spouses move. Laws and policies also make relocating to another country as a couple challenging. At the same time, tight job markets are forcing more people to relocate. In addition, people travelling because of work may meet a partner abroad. If relocation is not an alternative, they may form a long-distance relationship (Levin, 2004). In addition, technology makes staying in touch easier for couples living apart, making LAT relationships more workable.

The Falling Marriage Rate

Fewer people than ever are marrying, and those who do are spending a smaller proportion of their lives in spousal relations, and marriages last a shorter average time than in the past (Wilson in Baker, 2005). These trends inevitably lead to a decline in the numbers of those experiencing marriage. Let's examine two theories to explain this: an economic explanation and a demographic explanation.

A leading economic argument is that marriage rates have fallen in recent decades because marriage is less necessary for both men and women, and the alternatives to marriage are more attractive. For women, financial independence and reproductive control have begun to tip the balance to cohabitation or singlehood. Women have less to gain from marriage and more to gain from paid work than in the past. Combining marriage, parenthood, and labour force participation is hard work, especially for women.

Despite marriage rates being currently in decline, we cannot conclude that people are avoiding stable, emotionally committed relationships. In fact, when we look at the increased numbers of cohabiting couples, we realize that North Americans are still inclined to have intimate couple relationships and commitments, even if they are taking a slightly different form.

COHABITATION

One significant change in family life in the Western world has been a sharp increase in cohabitation—people living together without being legally married. In the past, cohabitation, also called **common-law union**, used to be more prevalent among working-class people. It also used to be seen as a lesser form of couple relationship than legal marriage. Now, however, cohabitation has become more common among all social classes and is much more accepted.

Cohabitation is, however, a less stable form of union than legal marriage. Some authors have attributed this fickleness of common-law unions to the fact that only a few people make a deliberate decision to begin cohabitation. Instead, a gradual movement into cohabitation occurs, without clear communication between partners about the meaning of the transition (Manning, Smock, and Majumdar 2005). Research shows that for many individuals, beginning to cohabit "just happened." With such a slide into cohabitation many couples are at risk for later distress due to a lack of a stable foundation of mutual commitment (see Stanley, Rhoades, and Markman, 2006).

Cohabitation has also been associated with fewer advantages than marriage. Cohabitating couples tend to have less involvement with extended families and less responsibility to the other partner during crisis; moreover, the union is rejected by some religious institutions (Waite, 1999, 2000). Domestic violence rates are also higher in cohabitating relationships, and levels of psychological well-being are lower. However, many cohabiting couples may disagree, as the numbers of long-lasting, happily cohabitating couples are growing rapidly. The 2006 Census finds a large growth in cohabitation among Canadians (Statistics Canada, 2007a).

Like all other relationship forms, cohabitation is not a homogeneous category. For instance, Canadian residents who are immigrants are less willing to cohabit than Canadian-born residents, the English-speaking less than the French, and women less than men (Milan and Peters, 2003). Further adding to the complexity and variable stability of cohabiting relationships are the multiple reasons for which a couple decides to cohabit (Heuveline and Timberlake, 2004). Recently, for a significant proportion of couples, cohabitation has replaced dating relationships, which do not necessarily involve any long-term commitment and least of all marriage (Rhoades, Stanley, and Markman, 2009).

The Prevalence of Cohabitation in Canada

- In 2006, married couples made up the largest portion of couples, at 68.6 percent. However, this number has been in steady decline over the last two decades. It is down 1.9 percent from 2001 (Statistics Canada, 2006a).

- As the percentage of married couples decreases, the percentage of couples cohabiting increases. The number of common-law-couple families increased a substantial 18.9 percent from 2001 to 2006. This number has risen five times faster than that of married-couple families and twice that of lone-parent families (Statistics Canada, 2006a).

- Starting conjugal life in a common-law relationship increases the probability of this first union ending in separation, regardless of whether the common-law partners eventually marry (Statistics Canada, 2004d).

- Average length of cohabiting relationships in Canada is about five years (Bibby, 2004a).

- Canadians who have experienced divorce tend to opt for cohabitation for their second union rather than remarrying (Wu and Schimmele, 2005a).

- In Quebec, where the proportion of cohabiting couples has been on the rise for half a century, the percentage is still growing. In 2006, one-third of couples (34.6 percent) lived in a common-law union. This level is more than double the level in the other provinces and territories (Statistics Canada, 2006a).

- The number of common-law-couple families in Quebec accounts for 44.4 percent of the national total. About one-quarter of all common-law-couple families in Canada live in Montreal and Quebec City (Statistics Canada, 2006a).

- Ontario has the lowest proportion of common-law-couple families (10.3 percent), as well as the highest proportion of married-couple families (73.9 percent) in Canada (Statistics Canada, 2006a).

Under these circumstances, one would expect very high rates of eventual dissolution, much like a short acquaintanceship leads to an increased likelihood of divorce among the married.

For many, living together is a practical way of splitting expenses. For couples who move in together for this reason, cohabitation is economically advantageous, simple, and generally not a long-term commitment. Divorced adults may also find economic advantages in cohabitation. For instance, splitting expenses with a partner may benefit many divorced men who have to support a child who lives elsewhere. Interestingly, despite the advantages that come with splitting expenses, overall cohabiters are far less likely than married couples to pool their finances (Heimdal and Houseknecht, 2003). In concert with the previous finding, cohabitation is more common among working women than among women who stay at home (Wu, 2000). This suggests that marriage sometimes is a less attractive option for women who are financially independent.

For others, cohabiting unions constitute a "prelude to marriage" or a "trial marriage"—that is, a period in which to test the solidity of the relationship without the legal commitment. For instance, Bianchi and Casper (2000) have found that nearly 50 percent of American couples who cohabit do so as a precursor to marriage. Such cohabiters are committed to each other and plan on getting married. Nevertheless, the Bianchi and Casper (2000) study illustrates that after five years, only 52 percent of these couples had married, 31 percent had separated, and 17 percent were still cohabiting.

Another group of cohabiters is older, previously married people. More than 40 percent of women cohabitants have previously been married (Statistics Canada, 2001a). These women have their own reasons for living together instead of marrying. Some are separated but not yet divorced from a partner, so they cannot legally remarry. Some often wish to avoid foregoing their newly acquired independence. Religious beliefs prevent others from divorcing and remarrying. Some widows do not want their pension benefits reduced by remarriage (Connidis, 2001). They may also be afraid that a marriage will force on them the role of a nurse for an ailing husband (Davidson, 2001).

For older adults who have already been married, cohabitation seems to carry far fewer risks than it does for younger adults. Thus, higher levels of happiness and stability have been found among older cohabiters when compared to their younger counterparts (King and Scott, 2005). This can be explained by the fact that for these people cohabitation becomes a substitute to marriage with a similar level of commitment, not just the road to an eventual marriage. Marriage as a goal loses its importance, as older individuals have already reached it once.

Increasing evidence suggests that for more and more people cohabitation is not a trial marriage but an alternative form of family union. While some people may prefer cohabitation precisely because it does not have the same expectation of permanence, others see cohabitation as permanent and make a deliberate choice not to marry.

In the last 20 years, cohabitation has become a long-term alternative to marriage. In this form, cohabitation is a marriage-like commitment without the wedding and with obligations to each other, often spelled out in law. Cohabitation gives people many of the

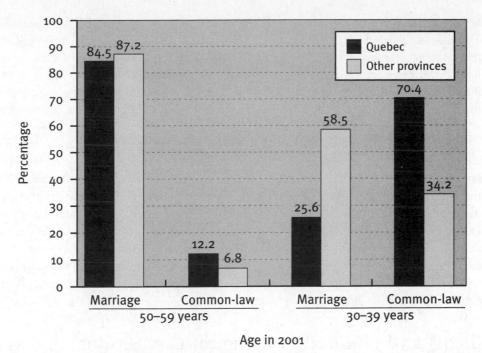

Figure 4.3 Probability for women of experiencing marriage or a common-law union as a first union, Quebec and other provinces, 2001

Source: Statistics Canada website. 2002. Changing conjugal life in Canada. *General Social Survey.* Retrieved May 13, 2009, from www.statcan.gc.ca/pub/89-576-x/89-576-x2001001-eng.pdf.

expected benefits of family life—emotional and sexual satisfaction, mutual dependency, and support, for example—while they retain (or at least perceive) a greater degree of choice. Cohabitation may be a personal "vote" against the restrictions, legal and often religious, of traditional marriage.

Despite Quebec's history of strict Catholicism, cohabitation is more common there than in any other Canadian province (see Figure 4.3). As of 2001, cohabitation in Quebec is as popular as it is in Sweden, where 30 percent of couples are cohabiting, and significantly greater than in France (17.5 percent) or the United States (8.2 percent) (Statistics Canada, 2002a). The percentage in Canada outside Quebec (12 percent) falls between these two countries. By age 35, 44 percent of Quebec men and 40 percent of Quebec women have cohabited, compared to only 28 percent for either sex in the rest of Canada.

Legal Implications

The major difference between marriage and cohabitation is that the former is an explicit legal commitment and the latter is not—or not in quite the same way. In some provinces, such as Ontario, cohabitation may mean differences in rights to spousal support or property acquired during the relationship. In other provinces, such as Alberta, the law regarding common-law relationships has been changed with the introduction of *adult interdependent relationships*. The Adult Interdependent Relationships Act, applied in Alberta since June 2003, provides some but not all the rights and benefits of marriage to "adult interdependent partners" (Renaud, 2004). The term includes same-sex couples and people sharing committed, responsible relationships, such as adult siblings who live together or an adult child sharing a home with an aging parent.

Even so, law and policy increasingly regard a long-term cohabiting relationship as a legally binding partnership. Most provinces in Canada treat common-law unions that last for some specific period, typically more than two years, the same as married unions; the obligations of the partners to their children are the same, and the split of property if the union ends may be the same as it would be for married couples, although this varies. Long-term cohabitants are legally expected, in most jurisdictions in Canada, to support each other during the relationship and after a breakup. The degree of this expectation, however, varies from province to province, and from state to state in the United States. One thing is clear, however: The difference between marriage and cohabitation is blurring.

Births and Children in Common-Law Unions

Increasingly, couples in cohabiting relationships are having children, another indicator of their degree of commitment and permanence. In 1993–94, 20.4 percent of all Canadian children were born to women living in common-law unions with the child's father. This is considerably different from the picture in 1963, when fewer than 5 percent of children were born to cohabiting parents (Marcil-Gratton, Le Bourdais, and Lapierre-Adamcyk, 2000; Vanier Institute of the Family, 1994). In Quebec, 44 percent of births were to common-law couples in 1997, more than twice the percentage in 1990 (Statistics Canada, 2004d). This trend can also be observed in the United States. As of 2001, 37 percent of all births in the United States occurred outside marriage; more than half those births (52%) were to cohabiting couples (Mincieli, Manlove, McGarrett, Moore, and Ryan, 2007). The old stigma of births "out of wedlock," once known as illegitimate births, is largely gone, especially when the parents are in a stable, caring relationship. This attitude change is captured in Figure 4.4, which shows an increasing number of children younger than age 15 that live with parents in a common-law relationship and in lone-parent families.

In the 2001 Census of Canada, about 13 percent of all children younger than age 14 lived with common-law parents. The rate in Quebec in 2001 is 29 percent (Statistics Canada, 2002g). This suggests clearly a change in the historical assumption that baby carriages follow marriage and not the other way around. As unions and marriages become less based on gender specialization and economic dependence of the woman on the man, choices emerge on how families can be created. The growth in child-bearing in cohabiting relationships may signal that change in both attitude and behaviour.

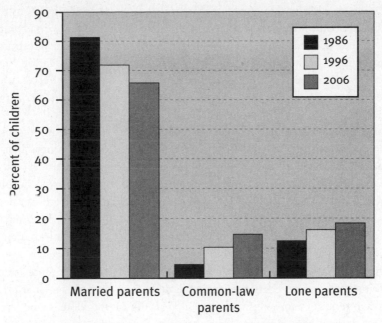

Figure 4.4 Percentage of children under age 15 living with parents

Source: Adapted from Census snapshot of Canada: Families on the Statistics Canada website, Censuses of Population, 1986, 1996 and 2006. Percent of children under age 15 living with parents (table). Accessed April 14, 2009, from www.statcan.gc.ca/pub/ 11-008-x/2007006/article/10380-eng.pdf.

Effects of Cohabitation on Marriage

Some common-law partnerships are a prelude to marriage, with just under one-half of the people ever in a common-law union ending up marrying their common-law partner.

One might expect that people who have cohabited would know when they were ready to commit themselves to marriage. But cohabitation is no better a "screening device" for mates, or preparation for marriage, than traditional courtship. Prior cohabitation is found to be positively related to marital disagreement (Wu, 2000). For instance, it has been shown that in the first two years of their marriage, couples who have cohabited have less positive problem-solving behaviours and are generally less supportive of each other than those who have not cohabited (Cohan and Kleinbaum, 2002). Surprisingly, the probability of divorce is greater, on average, for couples who marry after having lived together than for couples who marry without first living together (Statistics Canada, 2004d). Estimates suggest the chance of marital dissolution is two to three times higher among couples who lived together before marriage (Le Bourdais, Neil, and Turcotte, 2000; Marcil-Gratton et al., 2000; Wu, 2000).

Serial cohabitation has also been associated with higher likelihood of divorce. A study by Bumpass and Lu (2000) found that the percentage of cohabiting unions ending in marriage declined from 60 percent to 53 percent from the early 1980s to the 1990s. Furthermore, recently, marriage rates have been low, especially among disadvantaged and minority couples (Lichter, Qian, and Mellott, 2006), with less than one-third of poor cohabiting couples ending in marriage. The inclination of these relationships toward dissolution sets the stage for forming new cohabiting relationships. Serial cohabitation may therefore precede an increasing proportion of all first marriages and represent an overlooked but important risk factor for divorce.

So can we conclude that if a particular couple wants to ensure a long relationship they would do better to get married right away rather than to cohabit first? Not necessarily. The reasons for the increased level of divorce may be complex and even contradictory. It may be that it is not cohabitation per se that relates to the higher risks of splitting up, but the social risk factors that people bring into the relationship. First, people who cohabit may be already divorced once. If so, the difference in divorce rates may be not a result of cohabitation but a reflection of the characteristics of a self-selected group.

Moreover, the data hint that people who are willing to cohabit may also be more open to divorce. Along these lines, Canadian sociologist Zheng Wu states that "people who cohabitate tend to have less conventional views towards marriage or see themselves as poor risks in terms of a long-term relationship" (2000: 3). Individuals who live together before marriage may have different characteristics than those who do not, in terms of religion, family supports, and perhaps class or ethnic backgrounds, so they may not be directly comparable to those who marry.

People who cohabited prior to marriage are generally less religious and conventional; they are probably less hesitant to end marriages when they face marital problems than people who did not cohabit before marriage. Moreover, the experience of living together may itself be a factor. Living together without marriage can change a couple's views of marriage and divorce, and foster less conventional attitudes about marriage and family life. (Wu, 2000: 3)

Overall, the evidence shows a weaker commitment to the institution of marriage among those who cohabit and then marry (Bennett, Blanc, and Bloom, 1988). Yet, some research has found positive effects of cohabitation on marriage. Work by Manning et al. (2004) illustrates that marriage following a cohabiting birth is associated with greater union stability. Some studies find that cohabitation leads to a more egalitarian household division of labour and less traditional gender ideologies among married individuals who cohabit premaritally, as compared to those who do not (Le Bourdais, Lapierre-Adamcyk, and Pacaut, 2004).

Teachman and Polonko (1990) argue that the effect of cohabitation on marriage duration must be assessed more carefully. The durability of the relationship should be considered not in terms of the length of the marriage alone but in the total length of the relationship. When this is done, there is no difference in marital duration between those who cohabit and those who do not before marriage.

In short, we have no sociological evidence that cohabitation itself causes a decline in the quality of a later marriage; but neither is there any clear evidence that cohabitation improves mate selection or prepares people for marriage.

- Along with cohabiting-couple families, the percentage of lone-parent families is also increasing. From 1986 to 2001, the proportion surged by 58 percent, while that of two-parent families only increased by 10 percent. Most lone parents were either separated, divorced, or widowed. The number rose by another 7.8 percent from 2001 to 2006 (Statistics Canada, 2006a).

- Although lone-parent families are still usually headed by women (80 percent in 2006), the number of those headed by men increased 14.6 percent from 2001 to 2006, more than double the rate of those headed by women (6.3 percent) (Statistics Canada, 2006a).

- While the proportion of lone-parent families did not change significantly throughout the twentieth century, the reason people were parenting alone did. In the 1950s, single parents were usually widows or widowers. In the 2000s, most single parents are separated or divorced (Statistics Canada, 2006a).

- The percentage of children age 14 and younger living with married parents declined by 15.5 percent from 1986 to 2006. In 2001, the count was at 68 percent; in 2006, it was at 65.7 percent (Statistics Canada, 2006a).

Young People's Attitudes

Reginald Bibby's 2001 study of Canadian youths found that the vast majority—86 percent—approve of cohabitation. Further, about 63 percent of teenagers feel it is okay for a couple that is not legally married to have children together, and fully three-quarters think that homosexual couples should be entitled to the same legal and human rights as other Canadians.

Other studies also show an increased acceptance of cohabitation by young people. Dating and sexual experience, as well as parental influence, affect adolescents' attitudes toward union formation. Sexual activity is associated with positive views about cohabitation. Cunningham and Thornton (2004) find that 18-year-olds with more sexual partners are more positively inclined toward cohabitation. Virgins may be more conventional and more oriented toward the traditional marriage pathway that excludes cohabitation. Teens who experience parental divorce may be especially hesitant to marry and may view cohabitation as a way to avoid divorce and to test the relationship (Smock, Huang, Manning, and Bergstrom, 2006). Similarly, adolescents living with cohabiting parents may be more likely to cohabit as a result of modelling the behaviour to which they were exposed.

A study by Manning, Longmore, and Giordano (2007) finds that adolescents are less certain about their cohabitation than their marriage expectations. Furthermore, the authors find that not all adolescents consider cohabitation and marriage as mutually exclusive, with one-half of the respondents expecting both to cohabit and to marry sometime in the future. While the study illustrates a general support for cohabitation among the American teenagers interviewed, this support is not unequivocal, with 25 percent of teens ever expecting to cohabit.

Older Couples

As the majority of baby boomers will soon be older than age 65, some attention should be paid to older couples. Légaré, Martel, Stone, and Denis (2000) found that 40 percent of Québécois seniors are involved in mutually supportive relationships, most often with their partners.

Many older couples do not live alone—they live with extended families, especially children. This further contributes to the "cluttered nest" phenomenon. Older couples live with their children for many reasons: illness, limited income, loneliness, or unsuitable housing. Though many older people might prefer more independent living, shrinking social services make this independence difficult.

For instance, when examining whether Canada's public pensions—Old Age Security and Canada Pension Plan—provide enough income to seniors living in Nova Scotia in 2005 for a basic nutritious diet, Green, Williams, Johnson, and Blum (2008) found that single-member households could not meet basic food expenses. Moreover, although living with a partner protected against inadequate financial resources, the disposable income left over for that household after subtracting basic non-food and food expenses was negligible: roughly $300 (Green et al., 2008). Such shortcomings in Canada's retirement systems to ensure adequate financial resources for the basic needs of seniors contribute to the formation of multigenerational households.

Cluttered nests are more common among older immigrants than Canadian-born seniors. Some studies have attributed such discrepancies to differences in cultural values between immigrant and Canadian families. For instance, strong family values and norms of filial piety have been quoted as reasons for the choice of most older Chinese immigrants to live with their family members (Liu, Ng, Weatherall, and Loong, 2000). Recent studies have found, however, there is an increasing tendency for older couples to live alone. This phenomenon has been linked to acculturation—the process by which culturally diverse groups become more homogeneous through changes in identity, values, beliefs, even physical, political, and economic adjustments (Greenland and Brown, 2005). For instance, in a study examining the preferred living arrangements of Chinese Canadians age 55 and older, just over one-half of the older Chinese Canadians reported a preference for not living with children (Lai, 2005). This preference was influenced by a longer residence in Canada, older age, having received income from government programs, and having higher levels of social support (Lai and Leonenko, 2007).

Other studies, however, suggest that acculturation is not the reason for changing preferences in living arrangements. Research by Wilmoth, Dejong, and Himes (1997) points toward immigration policies—and not economic resources, functional limitations, or acculturation—as an influence on the decision of older couples to move in with their children.

A 1998 study showed that because older immigrants arriving in Canada are not eligible for government transfer payments or welfare benefits for up to 10 years, there is an 18 times greater chance that they will live with family than those seniors born in Canada (Basavarajappa, 1998). Moreover, in April 2005, Joe Volpe, then minister of citizenship and immigration, announced measures to speed up the processing of sponsorship applications for parents and grandparents coming to Canada as family-class immigrants. With these measures, the number of parents and grandparents immigrating to Canada is increasing (Government of Canada, 2005), contributing to more cluttered nests.

The 2001 Census of Canada reveals that more seniors now live with their spouse or partner than previously (Statistics Canada, 2002g). This is not surprising since there has been an extension in healthy life expectancy among Canadians, enabling them to live independently and in an intact couple for a longer period of their lives. More men than women now live with their spouses until late in life. This is because men die earlier, and also often marry younger women; thus, they more often leave widows. The 2001 Census also found a growing tendency for seniors, especially women, to live alone: 35 percent of women aged 65 and older lived alone in 2001, while 38 percent of women aged 85 and older lived alone in 2001 (Statistics Canada, 2002g).

Close Relations of Older Couples

- Although more seniors are living with their partners, men are far more likely than women to spend their senior years with a spouse or partner because of their lower life expectancy and tendency to marry younger women. Almost two-thirds (64 percent) of men aged 65 to 74 lived with a spouse or partner in 2001 compared to 48 percent of 65- to 74-year-old women (Statistics Canada, 2002g).

- Like among their younger counterparts, alternative relationships are popular among older adults. Eight percent of women from age 50 to 59 are in a common-law relationship as their first union. Eventually 20 percent of women age 50 to 59 will be involved in a common-law relationship (Statistics Canada, 2002h).

- While the majority of people in LAT relationships are young adults, in 2001, 44 percent of people in such unions were aged 30 and older. About 19 percent of those in LAT arrangements were in their 30s, 14 percent were in their 40s, and the remaining 11 percent were aged 50 and older (Statistics Canada, 2003b).

- Cohabitation among older adults has been associated with poorer health when compared with the married elderly. In the United States, older cohabiting men report more depressive symptoms than do married men (Brown, Bulanda, and Lee, 2005). Finnish cohabiters aged 65 and older also have poorer health outcomes, with an excess mortality of 35 percent to 40 percent compared with married couples (Koskinen, Joutsenniemi, Martelin, and Martikainen, 2007).

- Other studies have shown that for older adults who have already been married, however, cohabitation becomes a substitute to marriage, a relationship in its own right with a similar level of commitment. At least one study has found that older cohabiters experience higher levels of happiness and stability than younger ones (King and Scott, 2005).

Day-to-day caring for one's partner becomes an important factor in older couples, as they become more prone to illness. Caring for one's spouse in old age is a key issue for current debates about Canada's aging society. This task can put extra pressure on the relationship (Keating, Fast, Frederick, Cranswick, and Perrier, 1999). For instance, when deciding to place their partner in a chronic care hospital, 48 percent of spouses associate the institutionalization of their husband or wife with the ending of their marriage, due to a loss of companionship—sometimes preceded by non-responsiveness of the partner due to cognitive impairments (Gladstone, 1995).

Providing care can also undermine the caregiver's emotional and physical health through feelings of guilt, not enough personal time, increased stress, social isolation, and poor sleeping patterns. For example, Rosenthal and Dawson (1991) found that women who chose to institutionalize their spouse are ridden by feelings of ambivalence: relief, on the one hand, since they know their husband is receiving good care, and sadness and loneliness, on the other, since their husband no longer shares their home.

Women are usually more likely than men to experience these effects and suffer from "caregiver burnout" (Keating et al., 1999; McDaniel, 1999). Gendered roles and expectations may explain why older women find caring for ailing partners more distressing than do men, who report more positive experiences (Davidson et al., 2000; McDaniel, 1999). We will discuss gender roles and wellness further in the next chapter.

Same-Sex Couples

Recent media attention and increasing social acceptance of same-sex couples may lead some readers to believe that these arrangements are new ways to live in intimate relationships; it is not so. Gay and lesbians have formed and lived in couples since the beginning of families. It is, however, difficult to know how many gay and lesbian couples there are. Much is to be learned sociologically about couplehood by looking at gay and lesbian couples.

In looking clearly at how lesbians live in close relations, Dunne (1997a) says we can learn about the links of intimate relationships to economic and social systems. In a different study, Dunne (2001) suggests that the exploration of non-heterosexual experience also provides an opportunity to consider alternative ways of parenting, gender, and close relations. For instance, she argues that gay men who become fathers construct parenting identities and practices beyond the borders of heterosexuality. Dunne claims that by observing lesbian and gay people we notice the construction of more innovative and egalitarian approaches to work and family life and not a mirroring of the polarized division of tasks that characterizes heterosexual arrangements.

Coming out of the theoretical tradition known as queer theory, Michelle Owen (2001) argues that "families headed by same-sex couples signal both a 'normalization of the queer' and a 'queering of the normal'" (97). On one hand, many same-sex families want to be recognized as just like heterosexual families. On the other hand, the very situation of being a same-sex couple raising children resists the dominant model of family because the dominant model operates on the premise of gender difference.

Since conventional family norms do not apply in the same way, gay and lesbian couples must renegotiate and re-create for themselves how roles, responsibilities, and the balance of power will be distributed in their family. Thus, same-sex couples "normalize the queer" by forming families, raising children, and struggling to be recognized as being just like heterosexual families in their abilities to parent, provide stability, and be self-sufficient. At the same time, they "queer the normal" because their very existence signals that families are defined as being heterosexual.

The use of heterosexuality as a point of reference is also evident in research conducted on lesbian parenthood. Some authors have argued that research on lesbian mothering practices is conducted on the basis of comparisons between lesbian and heterosexual mothers to determine whether lesbian mothers' practices can be characterized as forms of assimilationism or resistance (Hequembourg, 2007). When trying to legitimize lesbian-headed families, many researchers and civil rights activists accentuate the similarities in

It was estimated that by the years 2005 and 2006, the number of older immigrants to Canada would increase substantially, creating cluttered nests and contributing to caregiving needs.

Same-Sex Couples in Canada

- The 2006 Canadian Census enumerated same-sex married couples for the first time since gay and lesbian marriage was legalized in July 2005 (Statistics Canada, 2006a).

- Same-sex couples represented 0.6 percent of all couples in Canada. One-half of the same-sex couples live in the three largest metropolitan areas of Toronto (21.2 percent), Montreal (18.4 percent), and Vancouver (10.3 percent). Ontario, Quebec, and British Columbia were the first provinces to legalize same-sex marriage (Statistics Canada, 2006a).

- Most of the same-sex married spouses are men (53.7 percent in 2006). This proportion is similar among same-sex cohabiting partners (Statistics Canada, 2006a).

- About 9 percent of same-sex couples had children (aged 24 and younger) living with them in 2006. This is more common among women (16.3 percent) than men (2.9 percent) (Statistics Canada, 2006a).

- The percentage of same-sex couples in Canada is similar to those in other Western countries, such as New Zealand and Australia (Statistics Canada, 2006a).

lesbian and heterosexual mothering practices, while undermining the role of sexuality plays in influencing mothering abilities. On the other hand, those who wish to discredit lesbian-headed families rely mainly on pointing out differences between lesbian-headed mothers and heterosexual mothers.

Such dichotomous analyses of the parenting skills and outcomes of children raised in lesbian- and gay-headed families are thought to lead to an inaccurate image of lesbigay couples. Judith Stacey and Timothy Biblarz (2001), for example, claim that a majority of family research emphasize lesbian mothers' similarities with other mothers while overlooking the small but interesting differences that arise in day-to-day parenting practices. In this way, even sympathizers of lesbigay couples risk to unintentionally construct an image of lesbigay families that does injustice to their essence. This suggests that, for practical and theoretical purposes, lesbigay relationships and families should be accepted as another alternative to the many existing family forms, and not considered an extension or opposition to heterosexual close relations. Therefore, same-sex families force us to examine in new ways how we think of family, what we do as families, and what we want the family to be. We discuss this further in Chapter 10.

POLICY CHALLENGES AND DEBATES

In July 2002, an Ontario court ruled to allow same-sex marriage, finding that prohibiting gay couples from marrying is unconstitutional and violates the Charter of Rights and Freedoms. In 2005, federal legislation made same-sex marriage legal across the country.

Both opposite-sex and same-sex partners can now choose to marry, and even if they do not, after a period of cohabitation they may still be granted spousal status.

Some argue that legalized same-sex unions are helpful to the institution of marriage, for they erase stereotypical gender roles that produce sexist legal treatments when dealing with heterosexual couples. As well, assumptions about the assumed complementary nature of female and male roles, and their importance in relation to the socialization of children, are eliminated. Fiona Nelson (1996), in her study on lesbian parenting in Canada, makes a similar point. She argues that because lesbian families need to redefine who a mother is and what she does, they throw into question the very idea of motherhood. Forcing us to rethink our understanding of motherhood and families in this way is, according to Nelson (1996: 137), a revolutionary turn that "has implications for family-focused policies and programs." From an economics standpoint, Christopher Portelli (2004) argues that same-sex marriage would strengthen the incentive to marry, increase the efficiency of marriage markets, provide for more children to be raised in two-parent environments, and benefit economies overall.

On the other hand, some argue that the terms on which recent same-sex legal struggles have advanced in Canada have led to the reinforcement of conservative and heteronormative discourses on marriage and family (Young and Boyd, 2006). In particular, the authors argue that the focus on feminist voices on various issues related to the family and economic security has diminished, leading to the survival of conservative discourses on marriage and family, despite the legal recognition of same-sex relationships (Young and Boyd, 2006).

Generally, the involvement of policy or the state (with all its agents and agencies) in marriage has been limited to laws about who cannot marry whom and what procedures must be followed to enter legal wedlock. There has been some resistance on the part of governments to involve themselves closely in the inner workings of marriage, which are largely seen as a private family matter.

Of course, the reality is that the state and state policies have actively shaped the ways in which we form and live in families, as well as our sense of family. Ideas about individual responsibility, the vulnerable dependent, sex and morality, and life chances and choices are all reaffirmed through our laws and policies. Therefore, it is not surprising that changes to these basic ideas cause concern and debate about family policies.

Two factors propelling the re-evaluation of policies on marriage and mating are recent concerns about family poverty, especially the poverty of children in mother-headed lone-parent families, and the rapid growth in women's labour force participation.

Are Policies Making Marriage Less Attractive?

It has been suggested that marriage laws may be a disincentive to marriage. Laws may discourage couples from marrying if aspects of legal marriage are seen as bringing major, and possibly unwanted, changes in a couple's relationship. On the other hand, if legal marriage is seen as changing nothing much, they may not find it attractive as an alternative to living common law.

At the same time, a strong argument is emerging from the family economy litera-ture that many tax policies are based on an outdated view of what families are. Given that, increasingly, Canadian family policy is delivered through the income tax system, it does make a difference what model of family is used. Men are defined much more often as the economically dominant partner in a marriage or common-law union, and women as the subordinate partner. All kinds of tax options encourage husbands to buy retirement plans in their wife's name, to assign income to the lesser paid partner. "Our tax system cannot achieve the modern social welfare and equity goals claimed for it so long as we continue to base policy decisions on an image of family that belongs to old reruns" (Phillips, 1995: 31).

Another policy debate involves the question of who should be entitled to the work-place benefits that marriage allows. Groups have lobbied for a broad definition of "spouse" in spousal rights. Access to such benefits, including health care, is especially important in the United States. In Canada, public health-care insurance makes the issue less pressing, but an incentive for being declared a spouse remains.

Alternative ways have emerged for gay, lesbian, and heterosexual couples to form in-timate couple bonds. One is the *pacte civil de solidarité (PACS)*, or civil solidarity pact, available only in France (Daley, 1999). The PACS began as an effort to legalize gay and lesbian unions and was instituted into law in early 2000 after intense debate and public protests. In the first four months, more than 14 000 couples had made PACS unions. Interestingly, many were heterosexual.

PACS is a kind of middle ground for couples, either gay or heterosexual, allowing for official recognition of non-married couples (Johnston, 2008). In a PACS, each partner is responsible financially for the other, in both support and debts. A PACS, however, is eas-ier to dissolve than a marriage and can be done without a lawyer, while divorce in France is a very long, involved process.

Perspectives of Low-Income Groups on Marriage and Cohabitation

Marriage among low-income groups has been declining since the mid-1900s. Whereas in the past, marriage rates were similar for the rich and the poor, today those living in poverty are only about half as likely to marry as those whose incomes are three or more times above the poverty level (Edin and Reed, 2005). These trends have raised concerns among policy makers about the well-being of children born out of wedlock and living in poor, single-parent households.

As we learned in Chapter 2, the 1990s was a decade of welfare reforms in both the United States (Kissane and Krebs, 2007) and Canada (Williamson and Salkie, 2005). In the United States, in particular, welfare reform was closely tied to promotion of traditional marriages as a way to relieve poverty among single mothers and their children.

The real impact of these reforms was to simply shift women and families from the rank of poor welfare recipients to that of the working poor. Women living in poverty are still more likely to get pregnant out of wedlock, remain unmarried, and thus work in low-paying jobs (Kissane and Krebs, 2007). While it is true that married women fare better economically, what the policies failed to take into account was that non-marital birth mothers are less likely than other women to marry "economically attractive" men after welfare reforms (Graefe, Roempke, and Lichter, 2007). Their husbands are more likely to have lower levels of education, more likely to be unemployed, and thus unable to earn a family wage. Therefore, for low-income women, marriage is not necessarily a route to up-ward social mobility. Rather, socio-economic differences and mate selection patterns maintain class boundaries and increase family income inequality.

Low-income men and women still value and aspire to marriage; however, "they believe they are currently unable to meet the high standards of relationship quality and financial stability they believe is necessary to sustain a marriage and avoid divorce" (Edin and Reed, 2005: 117). Therefore, instead of promoting marriage, governments should provide people with tools that would enable stable marriage formation. Increasing job stability, improving male earnings, and providing affordable housing and child care are among some possible initiatives. Another way to alleviate poverty among single mothers is to promote educa-tion. Research shows that post-secondary education "is the single most important factor with potential for breaking the cycle of poverty and is most promising in reducing poverty and reliance on public assistance" (Pandey and Kim, 2008). In addition, there is a positive relationship between education and marriage prospects. Women with post-secondary edu-cation are more likely to marry educated men (Graefe and Lichter, 2008), who, in turn, are more able to earn a family wage and support a middle-class lifestyle.

Cohabitation is another important family form to consider in the discussion of changing marriage patterns among low-income groups. In Quebec, where cohabitation is socially accepted and almost equivalent to marriage, cohabitation is not strongly related to socio-economic characteristics (Kerr, Moyser, and Beaujot, 2006). In fact, cohabiting men and women have similar and, in some cases, even slightly higher incomes than their married counterparts. In contrast, data from the rest of Canada resembles the broader North American pattern, "whereby persons with less education, lower incomes and more uncertain economic prospects are more likely to be in a cohabiting type of relationship and less likely to marry" (Kerry et al., 2006: 86). Therefore, cultural attitudes and norms play a role in controlling the extent to which family structure predicts the economic well-being of families. It appears that where co-habitation is widespread, the characteristics of cohabiters do not differ greatly from those of married individuals. Elsewhere, marriage seems to be, to an extent, selective of higher status.

Perspectives of Immigrants on Marriage and Cohabitation

In most immigrant cultures, marriage is regarded as the most desirable intimate union. In some others, marriage is the only union that is culturally acceptable. These views are based on traditional notions, most of which have their foundation in religious beliefs. Even after acculturation into the new country in terms of language and some social views, many immigrants (usually older people) hold on to traditional cultural values regarding marriage. In part, this is due to a social stigma attached to intimate unions outside of marriage.

Therefore, most immigrant parents prefer traditional union formations and often go out of their way to influence their children to adopt the same perspective. For instance, De Valk and Liefbroer (2007) studied to what extent immigrant parents of Turkish, Moroccan, and Dutch descent in the Netherlands influenced romantic partnerships of their youth. Those children with a Turkish or Moroccan background, especially those who identified most strongly with their cultural background, preferred marriage. On the other hand, cohabitation was most popular among Dutch adolescents. Further, there is evidence that a close family relationship between immigrant youth and their parents predicts the likelihood that children will share cultural values with their families. According to Hynie, Lalonde, and Lee (2006), who studied Chinese immigrants in North America, this occurs through a transmission of values.

Marriage Policy and Canadian Immigrants

There may be a difference emerging between recent immigrants and the Canadian-born in terms of marriage policy. Immigration policy in Canada has long highlighted, along with market forces, family reunification. The definition of family is, of course, critically important in carrying out family reunification.

Who exactly counts as family and is thus eligible for immigrant status in Canada has narrowed over recent years. The shrinking definition of family has excluded adult children of a couple, for example. A paradox emerges. Although in Canada, as we have seen, more couples are living common law, for purposes of immigration a person does not qualify as a spouse unless there has been a formal, binding, traditional marriage. Thus policy preserves a wide and widening gap between new and other Canadians.

With the increasing diversity of immigrants and refugees come other policy and legal challenges. One is polygamy, typically foreign marriages of one man to several wives. A 2006 study for the federal Justice Department (Beeby, 2006) argues that Canadian law does not well serve women immigrants in polygamous marriages. This will no doubt continue to be debated and discussed.

CONCLUDING REMARKS

There can be no doubt that people worldwide are redefining what it means to be an intimate couple. The family remains the arena in which personal, emotional, and psychological growth can take place. But more than ever, couple relationships have come to be voluntary acts—choices made freely by individuals. As well, there is a sense that what's done can be undone. Intimate partners are not as closely dependent on each other economically as they once were, and they can opt out of couple relationships that do not meet their personal expectations.

In Western countries, people are less inclined to marry legally than in the past; more people view singlehood positively. Cohabitation offers many of the benefits of marriage, without the same social and religious constraints.

Yet, where marriage and divorce are concerned, variations persist among industrialized countries. For example, in Sweden reforms have removed many of the traditional incentives to marry. Marital-type property rights of married couples were extended to cohabiting couples in 1987. So, legal marriage offers no direct economic policy benefits to Swedish women or men. Even spousal support after divorce is uncommon, having been abandoned as early as 1973 (Fawcett, 1990). It appears that all Western countries are moving in the same direction, toward diversity of ways to form intimate couple unions.

From the data we have examined in this chapter, we see a continued increase in the acceptance of varied intimate partner forms, without a decrease in the strength of commitment overall toward exclusive intimacy within a spousal relationship.

CHAPTER SUMMARY

Close relations in couples have become much more diverse and individualized, especially in the last few decades. At the same time, debate over who can be a couple and how couples should (or should not) be legitimized has intensified. In this chapter, we have looked at the variety and types of intimate couples. We have examined how couples are changing, and why; what the differences are, if any, in family experiences with different forms of couplehood. We have seen that, around the world, cohabitation is becoming much more common and couples are redefining what they mean by a "close relationship."

Now, more than ever before, the decision to be a couple and the decisions of what kind of couple to be are left to the individuals. Also, there is an increasing sense that one can separate from one's partner and start again. Legal marriage is less popular, and singlehood is seen as more respectable and positive. When we look at marriage as an exclusive contract of intimacy

between two people, we see that marriage in all its forms is still a popular arrangement.

Living together or cohabiting has gone mainstream; it is more popular and much more often leads to a lifelong union. Ironically, the chance of divorce is greater for couples who lived common law before legally marrying.

We discovered that first marriages are taking place later in Canada, and that many people wait to begin a committed relationship until after they finish their education. Most Canadians marry in their mid-20s or later. Homogamy, or like marrying like, is visible in marriages as well as in dating. However, men still tend to marry younger women and women with less education and slightly lower occupational status than their own.

Many Canadians live alone, some as widowers or widows, some as divorcees, some as single persons by choice. The reasons for this vary; interestingly, one way some women solve their conflict between career and family is to choose career and independence by living alone. A commuter marriage, when partners live in separate homes, often for career-oriented reasons, comes about for similar reasons. Commuter marriages/relationships are not common but may increase for practical reasons, such as the scarcity of good jobs.

Common-law relationships affect our ideas about families. For example, births in common-law arrangements are increasing, and the stigma attached to children of such unions has almost disappeared. Despite its increased social acceptability, in places where cohabitation is rare, it is more likely associated with lower socio-economic groups.

Another change that is occurring is greater societal acceptance of same-sex couples. Increasingly, same-sex couples are being granted rights and duties similar to heterosexual couples, including the right to marry legally.

Key Terms

acculturation A process in which culturally diverse groups become more homogeneous through changes in identity, values, beliefs, even physical, political, and economic adjustments.

cohabitation A sexual relationship in which two people live together without being legally married.

common-law marriage A valid and legally binding marriage entered into without civil or religious ceremony, resulting from a cohabiting relationship that lasts for more than three years.

commuter marriage (also called living apart together, or LAT) A marriage between partners who live in two separate households for any of a variety of reasons.

living apart together (LAT) relationship An intimate relationship between partners who live in two separate households for any of a variety of reasons.

marriage A socially approved sexual and economic union between two or more people that is expected to last a long time.

monogamy A form of marriage in which one is allowed only one partner.

***pacte civil de solidarité* (PACS, civil solidarity pact)** An alternative form of couplehood in which a partnership is legally recognized and each member is financially responsible for the other, but that is easier to dissolve than a marriage.

polyandry The marriage of one woman to more than one man.

polygamy The marriage of one person to two or more partners at the same time.

polygyny The marriage of more than one woman to one man.

serial (sequential) monogamy The marriage of one person to two or more partners in a lifetime, though only one at a time.

Critical Thinking Questions

1. We saw that some sociologists have described marriage as having become a private relationship based on personal satisfaction rather than a covenant based on mutual fulfillment and responsibilities. Do you think this translates into a decline of the power of marriage as a social institution?

2. Do you think it is possible for "polyandry" and/or "polygyny" to replace "serial monogamy" in Canadian society? Why or why not?

3. In the past, couples who moved in together often had been in a long-term relationship and were planning on getting married.

Cohabitation in the form of trial marriages, consisting of living together to eventually graduate to a more permanent relationship, was prevalent 20 years ago. How have the nature and goals of cohabitation changed?

4. Marriage as an institution has been deemed as an agency of social control through its contribution to the emotional stability and overall well-being of adults and children. To what extent can alternatives to marriage serve the same purpose?

5. In most provinces in Canada, cohabiting couples are given rights similar or equal to married couples and the same responsibilities in the case of separation. In view of such similarities, does cohabitation still constitute an alternative to marriage?

6. In the past, lesbigays rejected motherhood as well as traditional family values. Yet the movement toward integration within the mainstream family culture and a focus on stable couple formation and family life emerged when marriage was considered a traditional heterosexual institution, How can we explain this apparent contradiction—a desire for mainstream integration and a rejection of heterosexual norms?

7. With increased life expectancy, older couples live together for longer. However, they are more prone to illness, which leads to seniors becoming caregivers for their partners. What is the role of formal and informal supports for these caregivers?

8. What is the effect of the inability of immigration policies for family reunification to keep up with our changing perceptions of what constitutes partners/family?

Weblinks

Citizenship and Immigration Canada
www.cic.gc.ca/English/immigrate/sponsor/spouse-apply-who.asp
This site provides information about sponsorship programs and eligibility of spouses, common-law or conjugal partners, or dependent children who may immigrate to Canada as permanent residents.

Equal Marriage for Same-Sex Couples
www.samesexmarriage.ca
This site documents the journey toward the legal recognition of gay marriage rights in Canada and around the world. The site providing links to articles in the media that document the efforts, stories, as well successes of activists in their feat to legalize gay marriages

Loving More
www.lovemore.com
The Loving More site provides information for people of all orientations who are interested in exploring relationship options including group marriage, open couples, intimate networks, and expanded families. It provides information about annual conferences, retreats, and seminars aimed at familiarizing people with polyamory.

The Vanier Institute of the Family—Fascinating Families
www.vifamily.ca/families/families.html
Fascinating Families is a web feature of the Vanier Institute of the Family that highlights current family-related facts. The information helps to understand the strengths of Canadian families and the challenges they face by discussing the implications of recent trends for families in Canada through a "family lens."

Seniors Canada
www.seniors.gc.ca
This site provides general information about different areas of Canadian seniors' lives, such as marriage, divorce, family violence, health and wellness, and care facilities.

Chapter 5
Happy and Healthy Relationships

Chapter Outline

The world can be a cold, lonely place for people who are on their own, without a close intimate relationship. Perhaps that is why, over the course of their lives, most people enter one or more intimate relationships. Two things can be said with certainty about any relationship: None is perfect, and no long-term relationship is easy to preserve. Close relations can be frustrating, boring, irritating, exhausting, and disappointing. People in close relations can be just as lonely as single people. Yet, most people continue to enter and remain in these relationships and, if they end, seek new relationships.

This chapter is about why people enter and stay in close intimate relations—what benefits they receive by doing so—and how some manage to "succeed" better than others do. We will consider the reasons some people have happier, closer, more fulfilling relationships than others. We will also study the reasons people in committed long-term relationships are, on average, happier and healthier than unattached people—despite the many difficulties associated with setting up and preserving intimate relations.

For simplicity in the discussion that follows, we will call long-term, intimate relationships "marriages." However, while doing that, we will remember that "legal marriage"—marriage with the conventional paperwork—is no guarantee of happiness, permanence, or even intimacy. Besides, as we see repeatedly throughout this book, people can enjoy long-term intimate relations in cohabiting relationships that are not considered "legal marriages." Making this terminological change, however, will erase the need to keep speaking of "close relationships" and "intimate relationships" as though we might possibly mean non-intimate friendships, long-term work relations, or close but not intimate kinship connections. For indeed, this book titled *Close Relations* is not about those kinds of relations—it is mainly about marriage and marriage-like relations.

SOCIOLOGICAL FINDINGS ON MARITAL QUALITY

Sociologists have measured the link between marriage and well-being for more than a century. In fact, they have gone about this in at least three different ways: (1) by examining the suicide rates of attached and unattached people, (2) by asking people to report their feelings of happiness or satisfaction with life, and (3) by looking for signs of poor mental or physical health, or changes from previous healthfulness, among people with different relations. Interestingly, these different methods have yielded similar results.

One of the earliest sociological studies, Émile Durkheim's classic work *Suicide*, discovered something that today we think of as almost common sense. In looking at the patterns of French suicide rates in the late nineteenth century, Durkheim found that socially integrated—that is, socially attached—people are less likely to kill themselves. The more attached they are—as spouses or parents, for example—the less likely people are to commit suicide.

People who are isolated and unregulated often suffer from rootlessness and aimlessness that Durkheim called **anomie**, a condition that increases the risk of suicide. Close relations reduce the risk by providing attachment and care. Close relations also provide order. They set healthy limits on people's hopes and ambitions. Emotional ties connect married people to those they live with. Duties to protect and support these people regulate their lives. Intimate partners typically agree to control their sexual wishes, for example.

On the other hand, unattached people—especially people with no partner, children, or other close family (for example, dependent parents, brothers, or sisters) to care for—are free to go where they want, when they want, with whom they want. Paradoxically, with less integration and order, these people are more likely to commit suicide than attached people. Thus, freedom carries risks as well as benefits.

Today's statistics support Durkheim's theory. Suicide rates remain higher among unmarried than among married people, just as they were a century ago. In Durkheim's frame of analysis, there will always be limited fulfillment and satisfaction unless we involve ourselves with others, in close relations.

However, researchers rarely rely on suicide statistics to measure people's well-being. Although suicide may be a sign of unhappiness, few people who are unhappy commit suicide. Besides, divorce and singlehood are not the only causes of suicide. Therefore, sociologists have developed various ways to measure health, happiness, and satisfaction. The reasoning runs, good marriages should provide more benefits than bad close relations or good distant relations. This reasoning can be subjected to empirical analysis.

Close Relations, Good Health

Research consistently shows that marriages—despite the effort they take and the conflict they often breed—*are* good for people. Committed marriages can do people a lot of mental and physical good, though bad ones can do them much harm. Best of all, people can *choose* to form close relations, and they can act to improve their relations. So, in the end, the benefits of a marriage are available to everyone.

Research also shows that the closer the marriage, the better: marriage is better than a dating relation is, and dating is better than nothing (Laumann, Gagnon, Michael, and Michaels, 1994). Other things being equal, married people are healthier and happier than unmarried people are. Compared with married people, separated, divorced, and unattached people are, on average, less happy, less healthy, more disturbed, and run a higher risk of early death (Keyfitz, 1988). Cohabiting people are typically less stable and satisfied than married people. However, other things being equal, people in long-term committed cohabiting relations are happier and better off than unattached people.

Even though high divorce rates in North America may cause people to have more skeptical ideas surrounding marriage, most people still marry, and it continues to have strong benefits for those people. Research has found the benefits of marriage for some groups have increased over the past several decades. During the past few decades, there has been a dramatic rise in inequalities in health among men, such that unmarried middle-aged men are about one-third more likely than married men to die in any given year. This study included causes ranging from cancer to respiratory disease to suicide (Jaffe, Dena, Manor, Eisenbach, and Neumark, 2007). Findings such as these show the strong associations that consistently link marriage and health.

Among attached people, happiness and health depends a lot on the quality of a marriage—on how a couple gets along. In some marriages, the two partners are simply not compatible. In others, they do not know how to solve their problems. This chapter will explore these issues and discuss the ways that couples improve troubled relations.

Because a good marriage produces happiness and health, we can gauge the quality of a marriage from the partners' mental and physical health. In fact, we may be able to make a better guess about the quality of a marriage by looking at the health of the people in it than by listening to what the same people tell us about the marriage. To take an extreme example, a battered wife may give all the "right" answers on a survey about marital happiness. Yet, signs of poor health such as depression, lack of sleep, and poor eating—not to mention, signs of physical violence—will reveal that the marriage is in trouble.

Marital problems can infect every part of a person's life. Often, marital dissatisfaction and unhappiness take physical forms. Symptoms of stress from marital dissatisfaction occur in an ever-widening range of illnesses. For example, people with cancer vary in their adjustment to the illness. Cancer patients in bad marriages report more depression and anxiety, less commitment to good health, and more illness-related family problems than patients in good marriages (Rodrigues and Park, 1996). Marital functioning can indirectly influence health by moderating daily life habits and mood swings.

Marital stressors are found to be related to various health problems, both mental and physiological (Kiecolt-Glaser and Newton, 2001). As shown in Figure 5.1, the cause-and-effect relationship goes both ways: for example, psychiatric symptoms can lead to marital difficulties, or marital difficulties can exacerbate psychiatric symptoms. People in unhappy marriages often show signs of psychological difficulty. The symptoms include a weaker will to live, less life satisfaction, and reported poorer health, compared with people in happy marriages (Shek, 1995). A bad marriage may even lead to work loss, especially for men in the first decade of an unhappy marriage (Forthofer, Markman, and Cox, 1996). A bad marriage is far worse, especially for women, than singlehood or divorce. This explains why many people divorce or avoid marrying altogether.

Conversely, a happy marriage can improve every part of a person's life, including health and parenting skills, especially if the mother is satisfied with the marriage (Feldman, Fisher, and Seitel, 1997).

Figure 5.1 Percentage of adults who were in fair or poor health, by age and marital status: United States, 1999–2002

NOTE: Fair or poor health status is based on the question "Would you say [person's] health is excellent, very good, good, fair or poor"; results based on interviews with 127 545 adults.

Source: U.S. Centers for Disease Control and Prevention/National Center for Health Statistics. *National Health Interview Surveys 1999–2002.* www.cdc.gov/nchs/data/ad/ad351.pdf.

Marriage quality affects the mental health of wives more than it affects husbands (Horowitz, McLaughlin, and White, 1998). Women tend to respond in a more directly emotional manner to adverse experiences. Under conditions of stress, men tend to act out—to drink or act violently, for example; while under the same conditions, women are more likely to suffer depression.

What Makes Marriage Work

■ Men report higher marital satisfaction and benefit more from marriage than women do. Marital satisfaction predicts life satisfaction, but more so for women than men (Ng, Teik-cheok, Gudmunson, and Cheong, 2009).

■ Sharing—ideas, thoughts, worries, and dreams—with one's partner leads to greater marital satisfaction and intimacy (Duffey, Wooten, and Lumadue, 2004). Partners who share on a regular basis are usually more able to resolve conflicts effectively (Knee, Lonsbary, Canevello, and Patrick, 2005).

■ Sexual problems in couples often have an underlying cause that has to do with marital dissatisfaction, especially conflict resolution issues (Metz and Epstein, 2002).

■ Couples who regularly take part in religious events or carry out religious duties are more satisfied maritally and are better able take care of children than couples who do otherwise (Ahmadi and Hossein-abadi, 2009).

■ More than 80 percent of women agree it is more important to have a husband that can communicate about his deep feelings than one that makes a good living (Whitehead and Popenoe, 2001).

■ Around 70 percent of divorces result from low-conflict marriages and 30 percent from high-conflict marriages (Naiman, 2005).

Happiness and satisfaction change over time. As partners come closer to fulfilling their ideals for good marriage, they experience increases in well-being and satisfaction with the marriage. They report more enjoyable sex, less anxiety, and more overall happiness with life (Freiband, 1996).

A good marriage is especially important to people who are sick, weak, or vulnerable in other ways. For example, pregnant women benefit from being in a good marriage with a kind and understanding partner. The quality of the attachment between a pregnant woman and her partner increases the woman's sense of well-being (Zachariah, 1996). Intimacy gives both partners health protection within a stable and caring family environment. Intimacy may also promote coping strategies in dealing with stressful life events (Ren, 1997). Recent studies have shown that the positive effects of marriage are not only found among married heterosexual couples, but also among gay and lesbian married couples (Wienke and Hill, 2009). Many people cannot handle stress all by themselves. A partner or family can provide support during these difficult times.

Why does a good marriage increase life satisfaction, health, and longevity to such a degree? We must consider the idea that the correlation may go in the opposite direction. Perhaps it is not always that marriage makes people happier, but that happier people get married. Studies have found that this is partially the case. Happier singles do opt more for marriage (Stutzer and Frey, 2006).

The likeliest explanation for the often-found link between marriage and health is that a good marriage provides economic and emotional support. Emotional stability in turn strengthens the immune system, making partners more able to avoid or recover from illness. It also increases the will to live and promotes prudence and self-care. As well, marriage provides economic support. Married people who live together are able to pool their funds to avoid economic hardship. This increases their access to health care and also permits them to focus on healthy lifestyles. These two factors are likely the best explanation for the good health of people in good marriages.

However, this may not explain the entire effect, so other theories are needed. Perhaps some of the correlation between marital closeness and happiness may be a mere result of social construction. We have structured society to enforce the idea that marriage is good and there is something wrong with people who do not form permanent or long-term relations. As a result, single people (also, separated and divorced people) may suffer from cultural biases and social prejudices against them. This prejudice may lead to some or all of their unhappiness.

A strong argument against this prejudice for marriage under all conditions is provided by sociologists Huston and Melz (2006). They challenge the view that marriage is universally worthwhile and therefore should be widely promoted, arguing that, under specifiable conditions, people inclined to marry are wise to hold back if they see warning signs of future problems. Marriages, they argue, are fashioned in the images of the partners; therefore, people are well advised to be wary of potential mates with "difficult personalities." They write, "Rocky courtships give birth to marriages that are marriages that are conflict-prone, unhappy and fragile . . . We have found that the difficult personality that lay beneath rocky courtships . . . reduces to three qualities: lack of conscientiousness, independent-mindedness, and anxiety" (Huston and Melz, 2006: 950).

This, as will be obvious, argues against the ideas promoted in this chapter and elsewhere in the book that marital success is not about successful mate selection but about cultivating skills of intimacy, communication, and conflict resolution. We will lay out our evidence shortly. However, Huston and Melz (2006) also recognize that poverty increases the strain on marriage, increasing the risks of conflict and divorce. Therefore, they argue, there is little point in arguing in favour of universal marriage unless we are willing to do something about poverty. As they say, "The promotion of family health and stability will require an approach that attends to couples' psychological, social, and economic needs" (Huston and Melz, 2006: 943).

A Continuum of Closeness

Consider these points in the context of an important finding about marriages by Laumann, Gagnon, Michael, and Michaels (1994). Imagine, first, that there are four (and only four) kinds of current relationship statuses: single, dating, cohabiting, and married. Let us take "dating" to mean being involved in an intimate sexual relationship with someone who lives in another household, while "cohabitation" means being involved in an intimate sexual relationship with someone who lives in the same household. Together, these create a continuum of closeness, where legal marriage is at one end and single or non-dating status is at the other.

How does being in one of these statuses compare, in health terms, with being in another of these statuses? In addition, does it matter how a person got into one of these statuses? These are questions that sociologist Edward Laumann and his team at the University of Chicago addressed (1994) to data collected from adults aged 18 to 59 who were part of the National Household Survey of Life Styles (NHSLS). The team cross-tabulated answers to questions about health, happiness, and physical and emotional satisfaction with the respondent's most recent partner against information about the respondent's relationship history and status (see Table 5.1).

The findings for women are clear-cut and convincing. On every dimension, women currently in their first marriage are better off—healthier, happier, more physically satisfied, and more emotionally satisfied with their partner—than any other women. After women who are in their first marriage, women who have never married or are cohabiting are the next healthiest, happiest, and most satisfied women.

On almost every dimension, the opposite is true for women who, after divorce, separation, or widowhood, are single. They are least likely to report they are happy and physically or emotionally satisfied with their most recent partner. The only women in poorer health than these single women are cohabiting women who have previously divorced, separated, or been widowed. In short, close intimate relations—marriages, as we are calling them—are good for women's health and happiness.

Table 5.1 Percentage Distribution of Quality of Life Outcomes by Marital, Cohabiting, Dating, and Single Status: American Adults 18–59, NHSLS

Men	Excellent or very good health	Very or extremely happy	Very or extremely physically satisfied with partner	Very or extremely emotionally satisfied with partner
Never married, single	90.6	44.8	71.7	46.2
Never married, dating	95.3	60.7	81.7	72.6
Never married, cohabiting	88.3	55.0	82.8	84.5
Currently in first marriage	91.5	70.4	89.1	88.4
Divorced/separated/ widowed, single	87.5	31.4	67.5	47.5
Divorced/separated/ widowed, dating	85.9	42.7	84.3	69.5
Divorced/separated/ widowed, cohabiting	79.0	63.2	97.4	92.1
Currently remarried	87.1	68.3	89.2	84.9

Percentages

Women	Excellent or very good health	Very or extremely happy	Very or extremely physically satisfied with partner	Very or extremely emotionally satisfied with partner
Never married, single	88.5	54.2	65.3	56.0
Never married, dating	87.8	51.3	83.9	74.2
Never married, cohabiting	90.4	61.1	84.5	73.2
Currently in first marriage	90.9	68.8	86.2	83.6
Divorced/separated/ widowed, single	86.8	36.7	50.0	38.2
Divorced/separated/ widowed, dating	83.5	41.1	84.1	67.5
Divorced/separated/ widowed, cohabiting	76.8	50.9	85.5	74.6
Currently remarried	80.3	66.2	85.2	80.1

Source: Edward O. Laumann, Jenna Mahay, and Yoosik Youm. "Sex, Intimacy and Family Life in the United States," Presented at the ISA Conference, Brisbane, Australia, XV World Congress of Sociology, July 8–13, 2002, Plenary Session, Symposium III, Table 4. Reprinted with permission.

The patterns for men are far less clear. The healthiest men in this sample have never married and are dating. The happiest men are currently in their first marriage. The most sexually and emotionally satisfied men have been divorced, separated, or widowed, and are currently cohabiting.

However, men who are in their first marriage are consistently closer to the top scores in health, happiness, and satisfaction than any other group of men. Men who have been divorced, separated, or widowed, and are single are consistently closer to the bottom scores in health, happiness, and satisfaction than any other group of men. So, in the end, the patterns for men and women are not unrelated.

These survey data argue that relationships stretch along a continuum of closeness. This has been well supported by other research. Dush and Amato (2005) also examined this continuum of closeness. They included additional types of relationship, including married and cohabiting, as well as steady dating, dating multiple people, and, finally, not dating.

Consistent with Laumann's research (1994), well-being was highest among married, followed by cohabiting, followed by steady dating and lowest for non-daters. Well-being decreases from first marriage, down through cohabitation, dating, to singlehood. First marriages are more valuable and satisfying than later marriages; and people who have ever gone through a marriage breakup are less happy and healthy than people who have not.

Bear in mind, these are only correlations, not proofs of a causal link between good relations and good health. Therefore, we cannot be certain from the data that good marriages confer good health and happiness. It is also possible that good health and happiness produce good marriages. Another possible interpretation is that the psychic injuries associated with marriage breakdown (that is, divorce or separation) or widowhood make it difficult for people to experience the same high levels of satisfaction in second or later marriages. That said, this study by Laumann and his colleagues (1994) supports the findings of dozens of other researchers.

TYPES OF UNION AND MARRIAGE QUALITY

There are several explanations for the trends discussed in relation to relationship quality. Defining a "good" marriage is not as difficult as it might seem. People in good marriages manage to achieve a good fit between the partners' individual needs, wishes, and expectations, a fit they regard as unique and irreplaceable (Wallerstein, 1996).

As we have seen, reported well-being varies from one relationship to another—for example, from marriage to cohabitation to dating. Likely, people in different kinds of relations bring different standards to bear when evaluating their relationship and their lives within them.

For example, cohabiting marriages typically last a shorter time and yield less satisfaction than legal marriages. Studies comparing marital quality between three types of marriage—long-term cohabiting, married, and remarried—reveal that cohabiting couples have the least happiness (Skinner, Bahr, Crane, and Call Vaughn, 2002). This may be because of the lack of acceptance of cohabitation by the public, leading to a decrease in social support. Couples that cohabited before marriage were less happy than those who had not. In addition, long-term cohabiters were reportedly more violent (Stafford, Kline, and Rankin, 2004).

People in different kinds of marriages may also draw satisfaction from different things. Cohabiting couples place more emphasis on spending time together and enjoying physical intimacy, while married couples place more emphasis on emotional stability (Cannon, 1999). For the (on average) longer-lived marriages, physical intimacy has become less significant.

Cohabiters reported less commitment than married individuals as well as a greater conflict frequency (Stafford et al., 2004). The greater stability of married couples is particularly important for their well-being. As a result, less instability and more happiness are found among cohabiters who marry than among those who continue to cohabit (Brown, 2004). Brown also noted that cohabiters expressing plans to marry enjoy levels of relationship quality similar to those who did marry.

There is a common belief (highlighted by those who reject same-sex marriages) that homosexual marriages are markedly different from their heterosexual counterparts. However, evidence suggests that the same kinds of marriage dynamics are found in all couples. Gays and lesbians show selection patterns similar to heterosexuals—they also tend to find partners who match them in age, race, education, and income (Jepson and Jepson, 2002).

"Coming out" is relevant to the marital quality of same-sex couples. Evidence shows that it is essential for the health of the marriage that the partners reveal their sexual orientation to their families. Gay men who come out to friends and family are more likely to engage in a long-term marriage than men who do not (Eaton, 2000). Similarly, lesbians who come out to a wide group of people report more satisfaction in their marriage than those who do not (Jordan and Deluty, 2000).

If one partner is openly gay to friends and family but the other is still hiding his or her sexuality, conflict can result and marital quality can decrease (Haas and Stafford, 1998). One partner may not feel he or she is getting the needed social support, or may feel insulted the other partner refuses to admit openly the marriage is a legitimate one.

This has a counterpart in heterosexual marriages: for any partners, declaring the importance of the marriage to friends and family marks a turning point in the relationship. It signals a commitment and invites support. Both commitment and support strengthen couple closeness and satisfaction with the marriage.

HOMOGAMY

Some researchers have argued that marital closeness and satisfaction depends on how similar the partners are, especially in terms of certain characteristics, as we said in Chapter 2. This has not been a universal assumption. In fact, sociologist Robert Winch theorized, "Opposites attract." Couples who are unlike, he argued, should be more satisfied with their marriages because their differences (in personality or skills) are complementary. Marriage is a series of exchanges, Winch reasoned. Therefore, couples ought to be more satisfied if each partner brings something the other cannot provide for him or herself. A marriage between partners with different skills and aptitudes would be more "efficient."

Winch's (1962) first qualitative study of couples supported his theory. On balance, however, research data have not supported his theory. Heterogamy is everywhere on the increase with the growth of career opportunities for women. For example, Asian Canadian women who are more educated and participate more in the labour force are more likely to have an interracial marriage (Tzeng, 2000). These women avoid within-group marriages because of a wish to avoid traditional constraints on Asian wives (Tzeng, 2000). However, the increase of heterogamy is also associated with decreased marital happiness and interaction between spouses (Amato, Johnson, Booth, and Rogers, 2003).

Contrary to Winch's theory, most research findings show there is a strong connection between spousal similarity and marital satisfaction. Gaunt (2006), for example, found that for both men and women similar personality traits and values were strongly and consistently associated with happiness and marital satisfaction.

However, as discussed in Chapter 3, similarity in religiosity had a weaker association. This is as expected, due to less emphasis on religion and weakening beliefs in its authority. Gaunt found that similarity in self-direction, conformity, and achievement values were most important for wives' satisfaction and affect. Similarity on values around good will and charity were important for men's satisfaction and affect. In general, according to Gaunt's findings and consistent with other research, marital satisfaction showed the strongest and most consistent associations with couple similarity in almost all domains.

Homogamy increases marital satisfaction by reducing the number of issues on which the couple may disagree. As a result, other things being equal, partners who think they are a lot alike voice more satisfaction with their marriage. In fact, sometimes it is merely a belief in similarity that provides satisfaction. Research has found that an *assumed* similarity between partners may sometimes be just as important for marital satisfaction as *real* similarity (Blackmon, 2000; Hassebrauck, 1996; Yaffee, 2003).

Marital Satisfaction among Immigrant Couples

The experience of immigration is a stressful one, and stressful situations strain close relations. Current sociological research readily addresses the impact of migration on an individuals' well-being but scarcely examines how immigrant couples adapt to the environment in their new country. This is a significant research limitation, since couples and families—not individuals—usually migrate (Ataca and Berry, 2002).

According to Hyman, Guruge, and Mason (2008), there are many negative effects of immigration on marital satisfaction. Most significant of these is conflict related to gender roles and responsibilities. As we will see in a later chapter, this is an important point given the high rates of spousal violence in immigrant marriages. At the same time, immigration is a mutual challenge that can instead strengthen the bonds of marriage by increasing interdependence, improve communication and intimacy, and simplify joint decision-making (Hyman et al., 2008).

So, what is needed in a marriage to survive immigration? Most essential are communication and trust, as in all marriages. Moreover, satisfaction depends on the couple's adjustment to changing gender roles and responsibilities in the new society, increased intimacy and sexuality, and conflict management (Hyman et al., 2008; Cheung, 2008; and Huang and Akhtar, 2005). Some external factors are also significant, including a good balance between old and new cultures and the availability of support networks, whether formal or otherwise (Cheung, 2008).

THE LIFE CYCLE OF A MARRIAGE

In many marriages, the expected sequence of events is dating, cohabiting or legal marriage, children, and then possibly grandchildren. This "typical" sequence of events characterizes long-term stable marriages (Ravanera and Rajulton, 1996). Many couples also expect that their marriage will become even more satisfying as they enter each stage of life. However, here people's expectations may be unrealistic. In fact, marital satisfaction does not increase, or decrease, linearly over time. Marriages have some predictable difficulties.

Beginning Marriages

In the beginning, sex is especially important for close relations. The quality and frequency of sexual intercourse becomes an important indicator of couple satisfaction and relationship quality, but overall it tends to decline through the marriage. Experience affects marriages too. The choices couples make about their sexual behaviours are as much a result of earlier sexual experiences as they are of later ones. Preconceived notions about sex and proper sexual behaviour can enable or constrain sexual activity. As discussed in Chapter 3, in many cultures—including our own—the sexual double standard heavily influences many sexual relations. Participants may not always recognize the double standard is affecting their marriage (Greaves, 2001). Often, women in new relationships will be sexually compliant, consenting to sexual activity with a partner without experiencing a desire for that sexual activity (Katz and Tirone, 2009).

In a sense, they fake the desire. Researchers found that women who did so claimed they did so to promote partner satisfaction and avoid tension and emotional discomfort. This is not to say that all women in new relationships engage in sexual activity out of a sense of obligation. Nonetheless, gendered sexual expectations—and a double standard—persist. Women in this study were asked about their investments in "ideal womanhood" and how important they thought it was for a woman to meet society's ideals. Those reporting a strong investment in ideal womanhood were the women most likely to report sexual compliance. Still, both men and women in this situation tend to report satisfaction. That is because sex is important for both men and women in new relationships.

Sex becomes less important with the passage of time. For gay and lesbian couples, as well as for heterosexual couples, the frequency of sexual intercourse declines with passage of time in a relationship. Around this central fact, different kinds of couples have different sexual expectations. Studies find that in the beginning gay male couples have more sex than other couples do, while lesbian couples have less (Peplau and Fingerhut, 2007). This may be due to learned attitudes toward sexuality and openness.

Far more important is that sexual activity for all couples declines over time, especially with the arrival of children.

Children

In general, the transition to parenthood is associated with less sex and steeper declines in marital satisfaction, compared to couples who remain childless (Lawrence, Rothman, Cobb, Rothman, and Bradbury, 2008).

That said, a lot of the effect of children on marital satisfaction depends on timing and planning. Not surprisingly, husbands and wives who plan the pregnancy experience less decline in marital satisfaction than those whose pregnancy is unplanned and unexpected (and possibly unwanted).

The same trend is found in lesbian couples. Shortly after the birth of a child, lesbian couples report less love and more conflict in their marriage (Peplau and Fingerhut, 2007). Therefore, despite the more egalitarian division of labour in lesbian homes, children are nonetheless stressful.

There are many explanations for this near-universal decline in marital satisfaction following childbirth. Four models have been proposed in explaining the decrease of marital satisfaction with the arrival of children (Twenge, Campbell, and Foster, 2003):

Role conflict model: The arrival of children often leads to changes in social roles, bringing them closer to the traditional ones—wives providing childcare and husbands being the breadwinner.

Restriction of freedom model: Children drastically reduce the time wives have for their husbands or themselves. The presence of a pre-school-aged child reduces significantly the activities wives do alone, or parents do as a couple or with non-family members. This radical shift from spousal (adult-centred) activities to parenting (child-centred) activities creates an emotional distance the partners find hard to bridge.

Sexual dissatisfaction model: With the presence of children, sleepless nights increase. Privacy, and often romance, disappears. It is more difficult to have sexual relations.

Financial cost model: Children are expensive.

Mothers, usually the main providers of child care, have to change their time use much more than fathers after the birth of a baby. According to the role conflict model, mothers may have to give up previous jobs to provide caregiving. Their happiness decreases if they resent the fact that they had to give up their careers. Fathers, on the other hand, may be spending more time at work to meet increased financial needs. Many studies point to the importance of men sharing child-care and household responsibilities as one of the most important factors in determining the effect children will have on a marriage. As well, access to and ability to afford daycare is important. More recently, women are increasingly not stay-at-home mothers and must work. If women perceive their work role as independent from their mother and wife role, they are likely to feel guilty. Men tend to feel less guilt and anxiety about working and being fathers because traditionally those roles have been viewed as interdependent; they must work as part of their role as a husband and father.

However, Bonnie Fox (2001) points out that the transition to parenthood often increases gender inequality in the marriage. With parenthood, the marriage changes. Wives, as mothers, devote more time to their infants and less time to their husbands. Husbands often resent this change, and to reduce resentment and conflict, wives may become more subservient, or cater to their partners' needs more than they otherwise would have.

> In short, how a woman defines mothering is partly a product of negotiation with her partner. Because intensive mothering requires considerable support, it is contingent upon the consent and active cooperation of the partner, which makes for all sorts of subtle inequalities in the relationship ... [a] strong relationship between the father and his child ... is partly contingent upon the woman's active creation of it. (Fox 2001, 11–12).

After the birth of a first child, marital quality and quantity of free time declines immediately (restriction of freedom model). The partners are often too busy to spend even limited "quality time" with each other. Parenting affects sexuality (sexual dissatisfaction model).

Sexual activity falls off dramatically and may never return to its original level. Researchers report that with preschoolers present in a household, sexual inactivity is likely and prolonged. It is amazing that couples with preschoolers have more children! Both husbands and wives become concerned about financial matters, leisure, and relations with family and friends. New sources of conflict emerge for the couple (Wadsby and Sydsjoe, 2001).

Having children also affects the mental and physical health of a couple; however, the findings on the effects are mixed. Children younger than age 18 take time and work, create feelings of overload, and lower marital quality—all of which can cause depression (Bird and Rogers, 1998). However, Helbig, Lampert, Close, and Jacobi (2006) found that parenting decreased the likelihood of depressive disorders and substance abuse for both men and women. As well, an absence of partnership was associated with increased rates of all common mental disorders (Helbig et al., 2006).

A good marriage can decrease postnatal depression in first-time parents and can decrease couple morbidity. Many couples also come to rely on their parents—especially their mothers—for practical help and emotional support (Matthey, Barnett, Ungerer, and Waters, 2000).

As mentioned, a husband's participation in pregnancy and parenthood is essential in helping keep the marriage healthy. Wives in strong, supportive marriages are more likely to view the fetus in a loving, warm, and joyful way, for example. These mothers are also more likely to report better marital adaptation and less likely to feel abandoned by their husbands in pregnancy (Sitrin, 2001). Once the children are born, women often have a harder time than men adjusting to the change in their marriage. Given the extra pressure, mothers often experience stress first (Graham, Fischer, Crawford, Ftizpatrick, and Bina, 2000). Thus, it is important that women receive social support from their family to help with marital adjustment.

Infertility

While having young children has been shown to increase stress and marital problems, a lot of other research has focused on the inability to have children, often involuntarily. More recently, this has become a more prevalent issue. Women are waiting longer to have children as they complete their education and work toward establishing careers. Because of this, women and men often find themselves in situations in which it is difficult to have children due to age and infertility. This has been associated with stress, anxiety, and sexual problems in both men and women. Women often experience high levels of depression because of this inability. In recent times, there is a built-in biological life course discord. While biologically, women and men are in their prime child-bearing stages in young adulthood, culturally, they are now expected to wait longer in order to ensure they are "ready." As a result, infertility is an increasingly important marital strain. This fact becomes clear when we consider that the infertility treatment market was worth more than $1 billion in 2006 (BioPortfolio, 2006).

In these circumstances, couples that turn to these expensive solutions are likely to increase the effects of financial strain already brought on by children. As with other strains, there are many ways couples may cope with the stress brought about by infertility, some more effective than others. *Active confronting coping* means asking for advice, trying to solve the problem, and discussing feelings about infertility. *Meaning-based coping* involves attempting to grow as a person in other ways and redirecting life goals. These both have been linked to short- and long-term adaptation to infertility (Peterson, Pirritano, Christensen, and Schmidt, 2008). Facing infertility is a unique experience and can cause intense feelings of powerlessness; however, as with all other marital stressors, coping abilities are key.

The Midlife Marriage

Midlife couples face unique difficulties in their lives often due to the many transitions that they are likely to face at this stage. For one, couples may be dealing with parenting their children and also taking care of their elderly parents, although it is debatable if this has a negative impact on couple health (Henry and Miller, 2004: 407). Moreover, menopause and parental death may also put strain on the marriage (408). In general, midlife married couples were more like to report problems with financial matters, sexual issues, and ways of dealing with children (413). Problems were least reported in areas of values, commitment, spiritual matters, and violence (405). Thus, the midlife couple faces unique challenges that are different from couples of a newborn baby and, as we will see, couples in later life as well.

Later in the Marriage

Marital satisfaction, which decreases with the arrival of children, typically reaches an all-time low when the children are teenagers. Then, as children approach late adolescence and start to leave home, marital satisfaction may start to increase.

Once the children leave home, creating what we often call an "empty nest," many marriages improve nearly to newlywed levels of satisfaction. Parental and work responsibilities decline around that time, partly explaining this return of marital satisfaction in later life (Orbuch, House, Mero, and Webster, 1996).

Many couples rediscover each other now because they have more leisure time to get reacquainted. So, compared with younger married couples, older couples report much less distress, less desire for change in their marriage, and a more accurate understanding of the needs of their partners (Rabin and Rahav, 1995).

The need for companionship in later life is strong for both men and women. As we have already seen, today Canadians are living longer than at any other time in the past. With extended lifespan, however, comes singlehood during the senior years. Moreover, much like their younger counterparts, seniors who find themselves on their own look for a marriage and the benefits it brings. Many are eager to couple again if they find a suitable partner. For instance, in a qualitative, exploratory study of a sample of middle-class, Jewish seniors who entered a new union after the age of 65, Schlesinger and Schlesinger (2009) found that the main reason for entering a union after the death of a spouse for senior men is to alleviate loneliness. Women, on the other hand, enter into a new marriage for more reasons than companionship, such as sexuality, friendship, intellectual interests, and support for children and grandchildren. Regardless of the reasons behind them, the new unions are positive in a variety of ways for both senior men and women. So, in the third age, couplehood is an experience of wellness, rather than the dysfunctional marriages potentially experienced in the earlier unions (Schlesinger and Schlesinger, 2009).

WHAT MAKES A MARRIAGE SATISFYING?

Other marital problems can also be predicted and avoided. We will now discuss separately, and in turn, several factors that affect marital satisfaction.

Love

Many people consider love more important than anything else in keeping alive a marriage. For people in cultures that define marriage in romantic terms, this will necessarily be true.

What, then, of marriages that are not based on romantic love in the beginning? In many societies, so-called "arranged" marriages are the norm. Arranged marriages in

China, the Indian subcontinent, and the Arab world are often built on parents' views that the future partners share important qualities. In arranging the marriage, parents usually choose carefully—and homogamously—for their children. Arranged marriages tend, as a result, to be stable and sometimes very happy. But are they happier than love marriages?

Westerners tend to assume that they cannot be. Folk mythology in cultures that support arranged marriages says that arranged marriages become, over time, even more satisfying than love marriages. Allegedly, arranged marriages "heat up" with time, while love marriages "cool down." Research on this question is mixed. In China, where the arranged marriage has a long history, a survey by Xiaohe and Whyte (1990) found that love marriages are more satisfying at every stage or duration. In countries where arranged marriages were once the norm, love marriages are coming to replace them, especially among more educated and economically independent young people. However, overall, there is little evidence that in the end, one system works better than the other does.

In Canadian society, as we have said, most people marry for love. They see love as the basis of their union, without which the marriage would not satisfy either partner. However, this is not to say that people ignore practical considerations, like the earning power or social status of a potential mate. According to our ideology about marriage, people are not supposed to think about those things. However, people who must live hand-to-mouth cannot afford to think as much about love; often, they have to be more practical. The more financially secure people feel, the more willing they are to indulge romantic impulses: they can afford to indulge their emotions.

Typically, people who assign the most importance to love as a basis for happiness have the highest divorce rates (Levine, Sato, Hashimoti, and Verma, 1995). They are likely to look for and find flaws in their love marriage. As well, a marriage based on romantic ideals may not be able to weather the often-harsh realities of the situations couples must face together throughout their marriages.

In close relations, feelings of passion and companionship usually continue throughout life, yet some types of love are more common than others at particular stages of a marriage (Noller, 1996). What some consider **immature love**—exemplified by **limerence**, love addiction, and infatuation—is characteristic of the first year or two of a marriage. As anyone who follows Hollywood marriages will know, this love is not always the best base for a lasting marriage and family. Another kind of love, less euphoric and less chaotic, supports marriage and family life, and it can continue throughout life. It creates an environment in which both the lovers and those who depend on them can grow and develop. **Mature love** is more common later in a romantic marriage. It is, without a doubt, central to the marital satisfaction, and life satisfaction, of present-day Western people—enacting current notions of intimacy.

Sexual Satisfaction

Sex may be most important in the early years of marriage; however, it is still important in middle age. Longitudinal research finds that in middle-aged couples sexual satisfaction serves as rewards and positive interactive experiences and makes important contributions to couples' positive evaluations on marriage. This research is helpful, as it found that there was little evidence to suggest that marital quality affected sexual satisfaction. This suggests that the affects of sex on marriage are important for men and women, while also establishing a causal sequence (Elder, Kirkpatrick Johnson, and Crosnoe, 2004). With respect to age, the frequency of sexual behaviour in men and women was believed to decline into older age, often accompanied by a decrease in sexual desire. Some researchers have attributed these declines to increasing incidence of illness and/or medication use. However, in their study of sexual desire in a sample of people age 45 and older, DeLamater and Sill (2005) found that, even when controlling for illness and medication use, a significant negative effect of age on sexual desire in both men and women was observed. However, such studies that suggest an association between older age and decreased sexual interest have recently been criticized because of their reliance on cross-sectional data and unrepresentative samples consisting only of heterosexual, Caucasian, and well-educated adults (Skultety, 2007). More and more studies point toward the importance of sex behaviour and sexual satisfaction in middle and older age. With increased life expectancy, couples now live together longer and remain sexually active longer. A recent international study of men and women aged 40 to 80 found that sexual well-being is strongly related to overall happiness. The study, by Laumann, Mahay, and Youm (2002), surveyed 27 500 people on their health, happiness, relationships, and attitudes to sex. Most middle-aged and older respondents with partners remained sexually active. The study found that people in countries with greater gender equality are most likely to report being sexually satisfied. Of the 29 countries surveyed, Canada ranked third, behind only Spain and Austria (see Table 5.2). The lowest rankings were for Japan

Table 5.2 Percentage of Respondents Who Report Sexual Satisfaction

The Top Ten		The Bottom Five	
Austria	71.4	Thailand	35.9
Spain	69.0	China	34.9
Canada	66.1	Indonesia	34.0
Belgium	64.6	Taiwan	28.7
United States	64.2	Japan	25.8
Australia	63.6		
Mexico	63.2		
Germany	62.0		
Sweden	60.5		
United Kingdom	59.8		

Source: Edward O. Laumann, with permission.

and Taiwan, possibly because in male-centred cultures where reproduction is seen as the main purpose of sex, there is less emphasis on pleasure, especially for the woman.

Intimacy

Most people would agree that feelings of intimacy are also important in making people satisfied with their marriage. "Intimacy" comes from the Latin word meaning "inward" or "inmost." To become intimate with someone else means admitting them to our (largely) private, unique world and trusting them with our most valued possessions. Building this intimacy with a partner is the key to a mature, surviving marriage.

Intimacy is *not* mainly about sex. Many sexually active couples are not truly intimate with each other, and many who are intimate have no sexual relations. Consider the odd status of friendship—especially same-sex friendship—in our culture: often, our friendships are far more intimate (in the original sense of the word) than our marriages.

However, another form of intimacy can exist between partners as well. Anthony Giddens claims that a particular form of intimacy called "the pure relationship" is increasingly being sought in personal life (Jamieson, 1999). The type of intimacy that Giddens is describing in the "pure relationship" encourages "confluent love," which is based on the equality of emotional exchange and partners being open and vulnerable with each other (Ariss in Cheal, 2007). Giddens also claims that with confluent love, intimacy and sexuality are explicitly connected (Jamieson, 1999). Moreover, this form of intimacy is said to be free from gender-based marriage aspects often found in modern notions of romantic love (Ariss in Cheal, 2007). However, Giddens's ideas have been criticized for downplaying the notions of private and public roles in intimacy and also how the responsibilities of children can negatively affect a couple's marriage (Ariss in Cheal, 2007).

Typically, men consider cheating by their partner to mean sexual interaction with another man. Women may also consider cheating by their partner to mean *emotional* intimacy with another woman, whether sexual relations occurred or not. In good marriages, we find intimacy of both kinds, sexual and emotional. Satisfied partners are more sexually intimate with each other, as measured by how often they display affection physically, touch each other, kiss each other, cuddle, and have sex. These loving behaviours are mutual. Shows of affection by one partner in a good marriage usually prompt loving behaviour by the other partner. Intimacy grows naturally in a sympathetic marriage.

A recent obstacle to intimate fidelity has come about with internet chat rooms. It has become easier than ever to enjoy the stability of marriage and the thrills of the dating scene at the same time (Mileham, 2007). Often this infidelity will come in the form of anonymous online interactions of a sexual nature. The anonymity makes the internet a safe place for infidelity for married individuals. Research finds that married people involved in this tend to rationalize it as innocent and harmless. Even people who report happy marriages have joined chat rooms for these purposes, researchers find.

There are many reasons why a loving, committed couple can have problems with emotional intimacy. It can be problematic if one or both partners never learned how to express feelings and respond to others' expressions. Couples can also have problems with sexual intimacy when they have different levels of desire. Usually, but not always, the partner with less sexual desire is the wife (Trudel, Landry, and Larose, 1997). This can be a problem since Anglo American (and Canadian) culture places a high premium on sex, both as a source of pleasure and as an indicator of intimacy and marital happiness. Besides, sexual satisfaction contributes significantly to marital satisfaction (Kumar and Dhyani, 1996). Couples in which sexual activity is rare and one or both partners show little sexual desire may have problems getting along together. Little is known about couples that are not sexually intimate but still have strong and loving marriages.

Men and women experience sexual intimacy differently. They want, need, and expect different things. So, opposite-sex coupling is a big experiment in heterogamy, where opposites attract but all the problems of difference are on display. Men and women are usually raised in such a way that they are praised for gender-conforming feelings and behaviours, while at the same time expected to marry opposite sex partners. While this norm is becoming less concrete with the acceptance of same-sex marriages, it is no wonder that opposite-sex marriages have problems to solve.

This gender difference has consequences in every aspect of a marriage, including sex. For example, wives report less sexual satisfaction than husbands do. As well, the predictors of sexual satisfaction differ for husbands and wives (Song, Bergen, and Schumm, 1995). For women, sex occurs within a gendered or gender-unequal society. Many women have to find sexual pleasure within a marriage that also provokes feelings of powerlessness, anxieties about contraception, and exhaustion from child care and outside employment.

For many reasons, including these power issues between men and women, sexual incidence and frequency decline with time. Age, duration of marriage, and the presence of children all affect the frequency of sex. Yet, given all these variables, happily married people still have sex more often than less happily married people do. While the cause-effect relationship is not determinative, as mentioned, some research shows that it is sex that affects marital satisfaction and not vice versa. However, it is probable that marital satisfaction also has some effect on frequency and satisfaction of sex.

Coping and Conflict Management

How well a couple manages the conflicts that arise in their marriage shapes their marital satisfaction, and these conflicts and stresses come in many forms.

Less satisfied couples are more likely to avoid discussing important aspects of their marriage, such as their financial situation and their children, and they are more likely just to make small talk (Nielsen, 2002). When talking about important issues, they also talk more negatively than couples with high marital satisfaction (Nielsen, 2002).

Health-induced strains also reduce marital satisfaction. Taking care of a severely ill partner puts an enormous chronic strain on a marriage. This leads to dissatisfaction, especially for the caregiving partner. Dissatisfaction is especially likely if a caregiver feels the ill partner brought on his or her own health problems, or has other reasons for feeling cheated in the marriage (Thompson, Medvene, and Freedman, 1995).

Traumatic events in the course of a marriage lead to distress, which has effects on marriage. For example, the death of a child reduces marital satisfaction by straining emotional and sexual intimacy for years afterward. Often, marriages fall apart after a child's death. Partners have a hard time thinking and talking about their suddenly changed lives, with their child missing. The grieving parents often need help reorganizing the ways they think and talk about themselves and their family (Riches and Dawson, 1996).

Lesbian and gay couples report a similar frequency of arguments and tend to disagree about similar topics, with finances and household tasks at the top of the list. Research has also found that same-sex couples tend to employ similar methods of coping. For example, same-sex couples tend to positively problem solve through communication, negotiation, and compromise. While they also employ less positive forms of problem solving, they do so at similar rates as heterosexuals (Peplau and Fingerhut, 2007).

Whether strains are chronic or traumatic, they are distressing and increase the likelihood of marital conflict. It is clear that married people cannot avoid conflicts, whatever their cause, and trying to avoid disagreements altogether is usually unwise. Research has shown that marital adjustment is affected less by the presence or absence of hardship than by marital skills and beliefs—coping abilities. With the passage of time, many couples figure out how to defuse and laugh at their disagreements. In older couples, conflict resolution is usually less hostile and more loving than in middle-aged couples. However, styles of conflict resolution vary by gender, and this difference causes more conflict. Wives tend to be more emotional than husbands are; husbands tend to be more defensive and less expressive (Carstensen, Gottman, and Levenson, 1995).

Which is better—making a fuss or refusing to say anything at all? Research suggests that becoming quiet and withdrawn does the most to keep the peace and preserve marital happiness, providing this is not simply a means of avoiding the discussion of problems. Many new parents cope (effectively) with the increased stress that accompanies childbirth by adopting this strategy of quiescence (Crohan, 1996). However, this is only a short-term strategy while the couple decides how to address their problem in a more useful way.

On the other hand, hostile argument is unhelpful. It neither makes the disagreement disappear nor improves the marriage. Partners who lack the skill to argue usefully (see "Rules for Successful Communication" later in the chapter) may fall into a pattern in which both partners assert but neither accepts the other's effort at control (Sabourin, 1995). Each responds to the other's comments with one-upmanship, and the argument escalates, sometimes resulting in violence. Violence, as we discuss further in Chapter 8, is *never* a satisfactory way to deal with marital conflict.

Love/choice marriages lead to happier marriages than arranged marriages.

- Evidence is mixed on this. Some studies have shown no difference in marital satisfaction between love/choice and arranged marriages (Myers, Madathil, and Tingle, 2005). In one study, Asian Indians in an arranged marriage who lived in North America were more maritally satisfied than their North American counterparts (Madathil and Benshoff, 2008).

Couples of different religions have less happy marriages.

- Evidence here is mixed. Some find that religious heterogamy has no significant effects on frequency of arguments (Curtis and Ellison, 2002) or on marital satisfaction (Vaijayanthimala, Kumari, and Panda, 2004).

Financial situation has no effect on marital satisfaction. If you love each other enough, you can get through any of life's challenges.

- Research shows that people of a lower socioeconomic status (SES) have a more difficult time handling marital conflicts because of being stressed about other life problems caused by lack of sufficient income. Negative emotional states are prevalent, as are considerations of divorce (Grable, Britt, and Cantrell, 2007). These findings indicate that couples who are not financially satisfied are more likely to have marital problems.

In short, some mixture of emotional expression and emotional restraint is called for under conditions of stress. In the end, everything has to be discussed in a calm, friendly way. Most important, the partners should understand that each has his or her own way of dealing with the stress, and they need to show patience and sympathy for each other.

Gender Role Attitudes and Equity

People are more satisfied with a marriage that meets their expectations of what a marriage should be, and how a partner should treat them. Increasingly, this means that, in our society, people, especially women, are much more satisfied when their partner treats them as an equal in the marriage.

The most dissatisfied wives today are younger mothers who are doing most of the household work—often, far more than their husbands are doing—as well as working outside the home (Stohs, 1995). (We return to the division of household labour in more detail in Chapter 7.) It is not just the objective reality of wives doing more housework, but the subjective perception that the wife feels she is under-rewarded and undervalued (DeMaris, 2007). This gender inequality, objective and subjective, increasingly leads to marital conflict.

Couples today argue more about household work than about paid work or anything else. Conflicts about paid work usually revolve around the husbands' working hours, with most wives preferring their husbands to spend less time at work (Kluwer, Heesink, and van de Vliert, 1996). Child care is an area of particular conflict when household work is discussed. Whisman and Jacobson (1989) report an inverse relationship between marital satisfaction and power inequality. That is, happy couples more often share the power. Equality also brings couples closer together, so partners are better able to see accurately the other's wishes and emotional state (Kirchler, 1989; DeLongis and Lehman, 1989).

Mates who see themselves as equal partners are more satisfied with their marriage, and better adjusted, than are traditional partners, and report using fewer power strategies in trying to get their way (Aida and Falbo, 1991; Diez-Bolanos and Rodrigues, 1989). Non-traditional gender attitudes, and husbands' approval of their wives' careers, promote higher marital satisfaction (Ray, 1990).

While the gendered division of labour persists in heterosexual marriages, many people are not knowledgeable about how labour divisions function in same-sex marriages. Firstly, most gay men and lesbian women are in dual-earner marriages. Research finds that in same-sex marriages the tasks are divided more fairly and equally. Lesbian partners tended to share tasks, while gay men tended to specialize in different tasks. Most same-sex couples tend to highly rate power equality in terms of what they value in a marriage (Peplau and Fingerhut, 2007).

Are marriages better for men or for women? Given what we have said about the importance of equality for marital satisfaction, the answer should be that close relations are equally important for both. However, in our society close relations are still better for men than for women (Keyfitz, 1988)—despite findings cited earlier that women are more likely to acknowledge the benefits of marriage. Indeed, men and women often have different experiences of marriage. Two intimate partners can have different, and even opposing, views about the quality and value of their marriage.

Conflicts in close relations can have a greater toll on women, especially when coupled with conflicts at work. This may be because women are more likely to blame themselves for marital conflict. Husbands are also more likely to blame wives for marital conflict (Simon, 1995).

In addition, the greater loads of child care and domestic labour are stressful for women. In addition, stronger pressures to marry—from society, family, and personal expectation—increase the likelihood that women may form an unsatisfactory marriage.

We noted earlier that married people are healthier than unmarried people are. Significantly, this is truer for men than it is for women. As a result, Canadian married men have a life expectancy five years longer than single men do, while married women live only one and a half years longer than unmarried women (Keyfitz, 1988). Men also gain more satisfaction from a marriage because men and women hold different positions in society.

Women, as a group, have less power. Even if close relations yielded women as much mental, emotional, and financial benefit, they would profit less than men because they had invested more. This is especially true where the partners have children to care for. As we will see in Chapter 7, women still do most of the housework, whether or not they also work outside the home. When the household division of labour is unequal (favouring

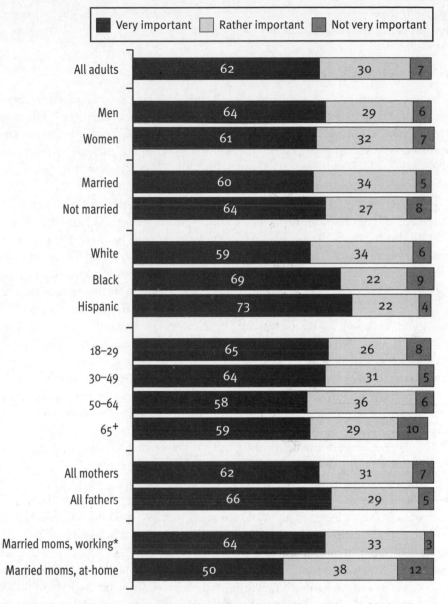

Legend: ■ Very important ☐ Rather important ▪ Not very important

	Very important	Rather important	Not very important
All adults	62	30	7
Men	64	29	6
Women	61	32	7
Married	60	34	5
Not married	64	27	8
White	59	34	6
Black	69	22	9
Hispanic	73	22	4
18–29	65	26	8
30–49	64	31	5
50–64	58	36	6
65+	59	29	10
All mothers	62	31	7
All fathers	66	29	5
Married moms, working*	64	33	3
Married moms, at-home	50	38	12

NOTES: Whites include only non-Hispanic whites. Blacks include only non-Hispanic blacks. Hispanics are of any race. The terms "mothers" and "fathers" refer to those with children younger than age 18. *Consists of married mothers employed full- or part-time. "Don't know" responses are not shown.

Figure 5.2 The importance of sharing household chores for a successful marriage

Source: "Modern Marriage." July 18, 2007. PewResearchCenter: Social and Demographic Trends. http://pewresearch.org/pubs/542/modern-marriage.

husbands), wives—especially employed wives—are more likely to become unhappy and depressed (Pina and Bengston, 1995).

Work, Money, and Marital Quality

With more women entering the workforce and the subsequent rise of dual-earner families, the influence of work and money on marital quality deserves a more detailed discussion. As researchers Dakin and Wampler (2008) point out, "because money is woven into many parts of the family and marital fabric, it is essential to better understand this family financial phenomenon" (Dakin and Wampler, 2008: 300). They point out that disagreements over finances are among some of the top reasons for divorce.

Financial stress can include cognitive, emotional, and behavioural responses that can lead to spousal hostility and a decrease in spousal warmth (Dakin and Wampler, 2008). It also increases the likelihood of depression in both partners. Depression leads partners to withdraw their social support and undermine each other. These behaviours, in turn, reduce marital satisfaction and intensify the depression (Vinokur, Price, and Caplan, 1996). For families living in poverty, financial problems constitute one of the most significant stressors, as they find it difficult to meet their basic economic needs (Dakin and Wampler, 2008). Researchers studying marital quality among low-income married couples in America find that religiosity can buffer some of the negative effects of economic stress on married couples, if they share similar beliefs, pray together, or attend religious services together (Lichter and Carmalt, 2009). These results indicate that social institutions, shared beliefs, and engagement in common activities may have the capacity to enhance and strengthen marital bonds independent of financial circumstances.

The stresses of work can also reduce marital satisfaction. Often, conflicts resulting from a partner's employment cause distress and, in turn, produce hostility and reduce warmth and encouragement between partners (Matthews, Conger, and Wickrama, 1996). Unemployment because of job loss also causes marital conflict, either from the loss of ordinary ways of family living or an unwanted role reversal (especially for males). A good illustration of this comes from studying couples where a husband is diagnosed with multiple sclerosis (MS), a debilitating neurodegenerative disease. Job loss because of MS is nearly inevitable and, out of necessity, results in wives becoming the main breadwinners, which many couple cite as the hardest thing to adjust to (Courts, Newton, and McNeal, 2005). The wives often find themselves with greater caring and financial responsibilities, whereas husbands diagnosed with MS feel that they have become a burden to their wives and lost their independence and manhood in the face of the disease and unemployment (Edmonds, Vivat, Rubman, Silber, and Higginson, 2007; McCabe, 2006). This puts considerable strain on the marriage, as new ways of dividing responsibility within the household must be negotiated. The couples who successfully adjust to role reversal and experience a strengthening of their marriage cite open and honest communication as the key coping strategy (Courts et al., 2005).

Retirement from work can either increase or decrease marital satisfaction. Leaving a high-stress job normally increases satisfaction. However, poor health and other changes that often cause or go with retirement reduce satisfaction (Myers and Booth, 1996). Retirement, like unemployment, may also reverse gender roles or reduce social support. In general, people need to prepare for retirement and, often, adjust their marriages to handle their new situation.

Leisure

Marriage, and especially children, reduces the free time of both partners, but especially that of women and mothers in marriages. On average, marriage increases a woman's total work time by more than seven hours per week. By contrast, the work time of husbands only increased by an average of 3.5 hours per week (Zick and McCullough, 1991). This sharp, unequal increase of work for women can put strain on a couple and reduce their satisfaction with the union. If nothing else, it means there is less time for the couple to spend with each other.

The more unequal the incomes of the partners in the marriage, the more unequal will be the split of leisure time. When men's income is more similar to their partners', or their partners' income exceeds theirs, they are more likely to contribute more to housework and child care. Since men typically earn more than their female partners do, they typically have more leisure time.

COMMUNICATION

We have saved for last the most important reason for marital satisfaction: good communication. Some of the problems we have discussed so far can be solved only by choosing a mate wisely, developing better coping skills, or reorganizing the household division of labour and increasing equity. However, most problems can be improved by working on spousal communication issues. Both quantity and quality of communication are important in a marriage.

The quality of spousal communication includes (1) how open partners are, (2) how well they listen, (3) how attentive and responsive they are, and (4) whether and (5) to what extent they confide in each other. These are all important to establishing a good, satisfying marriage.

"Quantity" means how often partners talk with each other. Successful couples talk a lot, even if they have tight schedules and little time to spend together, even if the topics of conversation are trivial. Satisfied couples engage in much more communication than dissatisfied couples, who engage in little communication on most of the topics commonly discussed by satisfied couples (Richmond, 1995). This is true of same-sex couples too: lack of communication proves to be the most significant factor breaking up gay men in long-term marriages (Alexander, 1997).

Satisfied couples chitchat: they make small talk, banter, and joke around. Dissatisfied couples talk less, or mainly talk about weighty matters when they talk at all. Couples do not all have to communicate at the same rate to be successful; however; it is the couples' *sensed* quality of communication that contributes most to marital satisfaction. The perceived accuracy, appropriateness, and effectiveness of communication contribute more to satisfaction than how much a couple may talk to each other (Glick, 1997).

Communication and Gender

Communication is a gendered marital challenge, in that women sense more communication problems than men do and are more likely to see men as the source of these problems. Men, on the other hand, view the communication problem, if it is a problem at all, as shared (Eells and O'Flaherty, 1996). Some supposed gender differences in language are stereotypical and have not been empirically confirmed. However, researchers *have* found gender differences in such dimensions as how much women and men talk, length of utterance, use of qualifying phrases, swearing, breaking of silences, and compliment styles (O'Donohue and Crouch, 1996; Tannen, 1993). There are also differences in the emotional content of the talk, with women typically expressing more emotions than men do.

Therefore, men and women speak differently, and this difference can become a problem. Consider an important form of marital communication called *debriefing*—conversation about what happened during the day. Men view their debriefing talk as having an informative report role, that is, to bring their partner up to speed on current events. In women's view, the talk may be about current events at home or at work, but the real purpose is downloading grievances, receiving and providing support, and renewing contact with the mate.

Communication is not just verbal and is not always straightforward, but may often be more subtle. A word, phrase, or even type of body language can have intensely different meanings for different people. It is partly to avoid these problems, and partly to separate themselves from others, that many couples develop their own private **idioms**. These idioms take a variety of forms: special pet names for each other, inside jokes, and words or phrases for intimate activities, special activities, or places. Couples in the earliest stages of marriage report using the most idioms, and those in later stages use the fewest, for various reasons. One is the arrival of children. When teaching children to speak, you want to teach them words that will help them in the outside world. Family idioms will not do that.

At the beginning, however, the use of idioms improves communication because the couple has defined their meanings together. As a result, satisfied couples use more idioms than couples that report lower levels of marital satisfaction. For interracial couples who may have grown up in different cultures, the use of idioms can reduce conflict and increase openness by creating a language that both parties are now familiar with (Shi, 2000).

Communication Differences between Genders in Marriages

Studies indicate that women, more than men, are sensitive to the interpersonal meanings that lie "between the lines" in the messages they exchange with their mates. That is, societal expectations often make women responsible for regulating intimacy, or how close they allow others to come. For that reason, women pay more attention than men do to the underlying meanings about intimacy that messages imply. Men, on the other hand, are more sensitive than women are to "between the lines meanings" about status. For men, societal expectations are that they must negotiate hierarchy, or who's the captain and who's the crew (Tannen, 1993).

Women tend to be the marriage specialists and men tend to be task specialists. Women are typically the experts in "rapport talk," which refers to the types of communication that build, maintain, and strengthen marriages. Rapport talk reflects skills of talking, nurturing, emotional expression, empathy, and support. Men are typically the experts in task accomplishment and addressing questions about facts. They are experts in "report talk," which refers to the types of communication that analyzes issues and solves problems. Report talk reflects skills of being competitive, lacking sentimentality, analyzing, and focusing aggressively on task accomplishment.

These differences can create specific, and commonly experienced, misunderstandings. Here are two examples.

MISUNDERSTANDING #1

He: I'm really tired. I have so much work to do—I don't know how I'm going to get it done!

She: Me, too. There just aren't enough hours in the day!

He: There you go again! You never think my contributions to this marriage are good enough!

In this conversation, she is trying to communicate something like "We're partners and share similar experiences." Her intended "between the lines" message is: "I understand what you're going through; you're not alone." The "between the lines" message he hears emphasizes competition for status: "What are you complaining about? You aren't any better than I am!" or "Your contributions to our marriage aren't any more significant than mine!"

MISUNDERSTANDING #2

She: I'm really tired. I have so much work to do—I don't know how I'm going to get it done!

He: Why don't you take a day off and rest, if you're so tired?

She: (sarcastically) Thanks a lot! You think my contribution to this household is so trivial that I can do nothing and the difference won't even be noticed?

Here, he is trying to communicate something like "Oh, you need advice and analysis? I'll focus on the details and facts, and offer a solution." His intended "between the lines" message is: "I will help you solve your problem because I think I know something that might help." The "between the lines" message she hears him saying: "I don't want to understand your feelings; I'm different from you and I know what you should do."

WHAT DOES ALL THIS MEAN TO US?

Understanding differences is the key to working them out. When we misunderstand one another, we often think that the other's motives are not reasonable, are mean-spirited, or worse! But by knowing that women and men sometimes see—and hear!—things through different filters, we can begin to share with one another the distortions we experience, and thereby find our way to clarity.

Source: Cynthia Burggraf Torppa. 2002. Gender Issues: Communication Differences in Interpersonal Relationships fact sheet. Ohio State University Extension. Retrieved from http://ohioline.osu.edu/flm02/FS04.html. Reprinted with permission.

Non-verbal Communication

Another important part of successful communication is the encoding and decoding of non-verbal information. Non-verbal communication includes posture, the direction of the gaze, and hand position. Researchers find that dissatisfied couples are especially prone to misunderstanding each other's non-verbal cues. This lack of understanding can cause problems, especially when a person's non-verbal cues contradict the speaker's verbal cues.

For example, if one partner is apologizing sincerely, and the other partner misreads the non-verbal signals as insincerity, a simple miscue can turn into a full-blown argument. Long-term couples may also ignore each other's verbal cues and rely mostly on non-verbal ones, causing more misunderstanding. Older long-married couples display lower frequencies of responsive listening than younger couples, which can increase conflict in a situation where a partner uses verbal cues (Pasupathi, Carstensen, Levenson, and Gottman, 1999). Non-verbal accuracy increases over time in marriages, but it increases more for people who are satisfied with their marriages.

Styles of Communication

A common style of communication that increases marital conflict is the so-called "demand/withdrawal pattern." In this pattern, one party—the demander—tries to engage in communication but nags, bullies, or criticizes the other partner. Partners with more power in the marriage are more likely to be "the demander." The withdrawer, on the other hand, tries to avoid such discussions through silence, defensiveness, or withdrawal (Walczynski, 1998).

Like any behaviour that can reduce marital satisfaction, the demand/withdraw pattern of communication has health outcomes. Among married couples aged 23 to 71 years

The Importance of Intimacy

- Men and women are more similar than they are different when it comes to communication in good marriages. Usually, differences arise in the context of conflicts (Emmers-Sommer, 2003).

- Over the years, divorce rates have remained positively correlated with suicide rates, so that whenever the divorce rate is higher, the suicide rate is higher too. This seems to bear out Durkheim's theory that the lack of social integration plays a role in suicide (Lester, 2003).

- People tend to marry partners with similar attitudes and values, but not necessarily similar personalities. However, similar personality traits such as attachment, extroversion, or conscientiousness increase marital happiness (Luo and Klohnen, 2005).

- Emotional intimacy is strongly associated with social intimacy ("We enjoy spending time with other couples"), intellectual intimacy ("My partner helps me clarify my thoughts"), and recreational intimacy, as well as conventionality ("My partner has all the qualities that I want in a mate") (McCabe, 1999).

old, withdrawers—nagged spouses—had higher blood pressure and heart rate reactivity than the other groups. Husbands of withdrawer wives had even higher blood pressure than the husbands of demander wives. Demander (that is, nagging) husbands with withdrawer wives experienced the highest blood pressure of all the groups (Denton, Burleson, Hobbs, Von Stein, and Rodriguez, 2001).

This suggests that neither nagging nor being nagged is a recipe for good communication. It alienates your partner and makes him or her sick. It may even make you sick. So, demanding and withdrawing is not a good communication pattern; nor is mutual nagging or mutual withdrawing. Partner communication patterns must be effective and similar enough to uphold marital quality and couple happiness. If partners discuss this problem, and what both parties want, their commitment to their marriage will increase.

Rules for Successful Communication

Talking openly is easier when you and your partner are already satisfied with your marriage. Even so, good communication is hardly ever the automatic result of a good marriage. Couples who love each other intensely and are committed to each other may still have trouble learning to talk effectively. Like all our other social skills, communication is something we learn, and continue to learn, throughout our lives.

What counts as good, effective communication varies over time and across cultures. In our own society, however, most people agree that certain forms of communication harm the marriage because they undermine the listener's self-esteem. For example, personal insults, ridicule, questioning a person's authority or competence, or dismissing or belittling the person's achievements are negative, hurtful, even emotionally abusive, forms of communication. Giving a partner the cold shoulder can sometimes hurt even more than a personal insult.

Some rules of successful communication emerge from sociological research on families. One purpose of communication is to send information, of either a factual or an emotional nature. The first rule then is that communication must be clear if it is to be effective. Both partners should say what they mean and mean what they say. Many learned at an early age that communication is not only a tool for making our thoughts and feelings known but also a powerful tool for hurting and controlling people.

The second rule of communication is: Be willing to hear and to respond to your partner's comments, complaints, and criticisms. This involves the difficult task of being an effective listener. A key to beginning and continuing good communication in a marriage is recognizing our own defects and trying sincerely to work on correcting them. Communication is important at all stages of a marriage, but it can be especially important in the beginning. This is because during the so-called honeymoon period there is an increased sensitivity to the communication of a partner, as well as a strong wish to please and understand the other person. It is during this period that couples set up the basic interactional patterns of the marriage. Indications of marital quality, such as the methods a couple uses in solving its problems, are often first evident at this time.

The third rule of communication is: Let your behaviour speak for you (and be sure to "listen to" your partner's behaviour too). Often, we have trouble putting our thoughts and feelings into words. That is why actions can be meaningful in communicating feelings and desires. Establishing family rituals can help a couple build and express stability. Among couples with small children, marriage satisfaction is highest for people who have created family rituals and believe that these rituals are important.

In lesbian marriages, family routines are of utmost importance for increasing and expressing couple happiness. Caron and Ulin (1997) found that openness with a partner's family and friends is associated with the quality of the couple's marriage. For example, the couple's presence at family events and participation in the family ritual strengthens the marriage. Family involvement also increases marital quality for gay men (Smith and Brown, 1997), but only if the family confirms the partners as a couple. Otherwise, extra stress is introduced into the marriage.

WAYS TO INCREASE MARITAL WELL-BEING

Close relations are emotionally satisfying only if they are "good," which is to say the partners *feel* the marriage is giving them something they value. Throughout the chapter, we have discussed the many benefits of being involved in close relations; however, these are dependent on the quality of those close relations. A marriage must increase and preserve both partners' sense of well-being if it is to survive. Social science evidence shows that marriages that fail to satisfy—whether because of differences between the partners, absence of love, too little intimacy, too much conflict (or abuse or violence), or poor communication—are less likely to survive.

An important concept affecting marital well-being is forgiveness. Forgiveness is strongly related to conflict resolution in marriages. Studies have found that retaliation and avoidance are linked to ineffective conflict resolution. Consistent with what we have said about the importance of effective communication, unresolved conflicts due to ineffective communication spill over into future conflicts and create a negative cycle (Fincham, Beach, Vangelisti, and Perlman, 2006). In looking to ensure marital well-being, it is important to remember that as tempting as it is to walk away from issues and troubles, this is not a good reaction in the end.

Finally, marital quality depends on a couple's ability to adapt effectively in the face of stressful events, given their own enduring vulnerabilities (Karney and Bradbury, 1995). Every person, and every couple, has vulnerabilities. Every person and couple faces stressful events and must find ways of adapting or coping. From this perspective, there are three ways to increase marital well-being: (1) by better adapting to stressful events, (2) by better avoiding stressful events, and (3) by reducing the couple's stock of vulnerabilities.

Many couples try to improve their marriage on their own and do so successfully. Others seek help from family and friends, discreet and sympathetic (but unspecialized) advisers such as priests/ministers/rabbis/mullahs, family doctors or lawyers, or teachers. Sometimes (perhaps a lot more often than we would suppose), people talk with wise amateurs: bartenders, cabbies, dental assistants, and hairdressers. Others, or sometimes

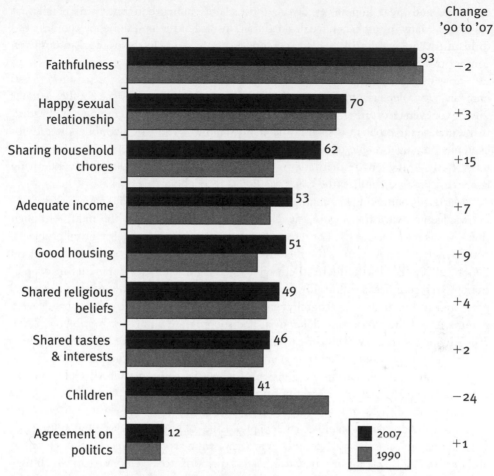

Figure 5.3 What makes a marriage work?

Source: "Modern Marriage." July 18, 2007. PewResearchCenter: Social and Demographic Trends. http://pewresearch.org/pubs/542/modern-marriage.

the same people, consult specialized advisers, including psychologists, psychiatrists, and marital and family therapists.

Speaking to an outsider gives a person a chance to air his or her views to an objective listener in an unemotional setting. Sometimes, just doing this is enough to help a person see the source of problems, and the possible solutions. Other times, something more is needed. Then, a professional therapist with many hundreds of past clients and many thousands of hours of listening may be better able to help.

Marital Therapy

Many couples do not know how to handle the unexpected bad feelings they sometimes experience in their marriages. After all, the overwhelming majority of couples begin with true love and great hopes, yet divorce still claims more than one-third of all first marriages. Many researchers have decided that, instead of therapy, unhappy couples need to learn psychological skills, called "psychoeducation," to help them avoid intensifying conflict (Marano, 1997).

However, no marriage can avoid conflict altogether. Sometimes for reasons of cost, immediacy, or tolerance of partner(s), the goal treatment may be to reduce conflict without solving (or even recognizing) the problem that is causing the conflict. This is wrong-headed. If the underlying problem is spousal inequality, family poverty, or alcohol addiction, for example, helping a couple to avoid escalating its conflicts may merely mask the problem temporarily. In the long term, therapy—if it is to succeed—has to address the underlying issues that produce conflict: the issues we discuss throughout this book.

Marriage counselling has changed over the years, both with an increase in therapist's knowledge and with the ongoing development of new theories in the field. Although therapy was once seen as the last resort for couples wishing to fix their marital problems, couple therapy is now seen as the preferred mode of treatment for couples (Johnson and Lebow, 2000: 23). Furthermore, there have been significant developments in couples therapy in recent decades. Initially, feminist writers in the 1990s claimed that therapists promoted and maintained patriarchy within the marriage, in which the husbands were dominant and the wives were deferential and subordinate (Johnson and Lebow, 2000: 30). Therapists are now beginning to understand the importance of rebalancing power within the marriage and attempting to understand the gender meanings assigned to controlling money and allocating the division of labour with the household (Johnson and Lebow, 2000: 30).

Moreover, in light of same-sex marriage, therapists have begun to understand and appreciate the diversity of families and couples. Issues of ethnicity, class, and culture can have implications for the ways couples view their own marriage and each other (Johnson and Lebow, 2000: 32). For instance, this has led therapists to develop ways in which they can better understand the differing gender roles between African American partners (Johnson and Lebow, 2000: 32).

Whether a marital and family therapy (MFT) program is "effective" depends on the treatment goal. Is the goal to reduce conflict, to increase understanding, to avoid divorce, or to help a couple to break up in a friendly, peaceful way? Is the goal to improve the well-being of the marriage as a whole, or of a particular partner? Increasingly, marriage therapists are seeing just one partner (Bennun, 1997). It is not clear that helping one partner helps the marriage nor that helping the marriage helps either or both partners.

Thus, often, therapists must decide whether to apply psychological theories to help individual clients in a troubled marriage, or to apply sociological theories to help improve the marriage itself. Some partner-aided therapy with depressed patients leads to reduced depression and thinking that is more productive. However, there is no evidence that this treatment affects marital satisfaction or communication and expressed emotion between the partners (Emanuels-Zuurveen, and Emmelkamp, 1997). For some, couples therapy

Couples who see themselves as equal partners use fewer power strategies and report more satisfaction with their marriage than traditional couples do.

improves both individual psychological functioning and marital satisfaction. This shows that couples therapy can accomplish both goals simultaneously, while individual therapy cannot (Hannah, Luquet, and McCormick, 1997). One study (Vansteenwegen, 1996a) finds that seven or more years after completing couples therapy, the individual changes were longer lasting than changes in the marriage itself.

Couples that seek MFT want to be helped, which increases the odds the process will help them. However, some respond to therapy better than others do. Gray-Little, Baucom, and Hamby (1996) find that what they call wife-dominant couples improve more than any others from therapy. Egalitarian couples continue to work well before and after therapy, while anarchic (and to a lesser degree, husband-dominant) couples change little and continue to work poorly. Younger couples and those who initially believe therapy can help them are also more successful couples after treatment (Vantsteenwegen, 1996b).

A couple's expectation of their therapist can affect success rates as well. Couples expect marriage therapists to be active, directive, and focused. Couples identify poor therapists as those who waste time or are unclear in therapy. Both successful and unsuccessful couples think that therapy needs a safe environment and proper structure (Estrada and Holmes, 1999).

Many of the "successes" of marriage counselling are partial successes in the sense that some goals are accomplished while others are not. Ideally, both partners will be satisfied with the outcome of therapy. However, in two-fifths of the couples that receive therapy, one partner is more satisfied than the other. In only one-third of cases are both partners satisfied (Follette, Jacobson, Revenstorf, Baucom, Hahlweg, and Margolin, 2000).

Moreover, helpful therapy does not always ensure the survival of the marriage. Sometimes, open discussion reveals that a marriage is deeply and irrevocably flawed. In some cases, therapy reveals that two people are unsuited to each other. They may be wisest to break up. In a comparison of couples who divorced and those who stayed together after therapy, the divorced couples reported finding therapy just as useful as those who stayed together. In fact, these couples viewed the divorce as a positive result of therapy (Vansteenwegen, 1998).

The findings on the effectiveness of MFT vary widely. In a survey by the Ontario Association for Marriage and Family Therapy, 83 percent of clients reported that they had achieved their goals completely (Ontario Association for Marriage and Family Therapy, 1996). Another survey finds moderate but significant effects (Shadish, Ragsdale, and Glaser, 1995). Recent studies have found that slightly more than half of couples claim to have benefited from marriage counselling and about 60 percent of those couples stayed in treatment during the follow-up period (Follette et al., 2000). While these numbers may seem disappointing, relapse into old behaviour is low and couples are usually satisfied with the treatment.

In short, therapy does help couples. Counselling can provide important insights that can be used to learn about each other and aid in effective communication.

CONCLUDING REMARKS

There are no guarantees in life and no fixed rules we can follow to ensure a satisfying marriage. Yet, one reason we place so much importance on our marriages and family lives is that these are areas over which we can have a good deal of control. We may divorce if we no longer want to be married to our partner, remarry, perhaps encourage adult children to leave the house, adopt children, and so on. We assume that satisfaction will result if only we make the right decisions.

However, conflict is bound to arise, and a successful marriage is one in which conflict is managed well. Long before forming a marriage, couples should start to discuss what they expect from it, what they want from life, what they are willing to give up, and what they are not. A marriage is, in the end, a plan to try to solve problems together. People who can't solve problems together won't be married for long or, if married, they will be miserably unhappy.

CHAPTER SUMMARY

People cannot achieve a satisfying marriage by following a set of strict rules. However, this chapter has shown that there are better and worse ways of preserving a marriage. Couples should remember that conflict is inescapable. By relying on good communication, many couples pull through. As couples age they often learn to defuse conflicts quickly. By joking about the conflict, they address it directly and keep it under control, and are likely to establish forgiveness. Conflicts about time are common; women who do most of the child care and have paid jobs too are the most dissatisfied of all married women.

As well, life means dealing with the unexpected. Negotiation is key to working out problems in marriages. Interestingly, the fairer the distribution of power seems to the partners, the more satisfied they will be.

As we have seen, married people—and others in enduring close relations—tend to live longer, happier lives. Satisfaction in a marriage means different things to men and women. Men value emotional independence in their wives, while wives feel happiest when their husbands are "there for them," or emotionally available.

The life cycle of a family is full of difficulties; for example, planning to have a child and then setting out to produce one increases marital happiness. Yet marital happiness usually decreases once the child arrives or if that goal is unable to be met, as in the case of infertility.

Intimacy is an important part of a good marriage. Sexual intimacy is a reliable sign of happiness throughout a marriage, although after children appear, sexual activity typically decreases, often for extended periods of time.

One cause of increased marital satisfaction is homogamy—similarity in attitudes, interests, and behaviours. Not only do people tend to date people like themselves, they usually do better to marry people like themselves. If partners disagree on a woman's role, the marriage is often less happy.

Communication is the key to a successful marriage but, like many skills, it is easier to applaud than to acquire. Good communication may seem irrelevant to couples that choose to divorce and start afresh. Others face their problems squarely, with the help of counsellors who may help them communicate and solve their troubles.

Key Terms

anomie According to Durkheim, a lack of control, or a lack of norms.

idioms Various verbal forms, including pet names and inside jokes, that couples use to separate their relationship and define themselves as a couple.

immature love A type of love typified by limerence, love addictions, and infatuation; characteristic of the first year or two of an intimate relationship.

limerence Infatuation or preoccupation with a relationship partner that is characteristic of the early stages of intimacy.

mature love Love that allows the lovers and those who depend on them to grow and develop—provides constraint, stability, and certainly.

Critical Thinking Questions

1. What is meant by *relationship quality*? Contrast men's and women's views of relationship (or marital) quality.

2. How do children and childlessness effect close relations? How might the birth of a child versus childlessness have different effects on marriage?

3. What role does homogamy play in marital satisfaction and how might this change in the future?

4. What is the meaning of *intimacy*? What are the differences between sexual and psychological intimacy and how do you think barriers to these will affect men and women in the future?

5. What are some of the stresses that an intimate relationship may experience? Using what you have read, what do you think are the most detrimental to close relations?

6. What are the ways married people can cope with and resolve conflicts?

7. How important is communication between partners and how can it be improved?

8. Using what you have learned in the chapter, what do you think are the most important keys to marital well-being?

9. Discuss stressors that effect different stages of relationships from beginning to later stages of close relations. Which stage do you feel is most stressful and what are some ways to cope with those stressors?

Weblinks

Relationship Information Online
www.relationshiproadblocks.com
This site provides advice and information about relationships in a variety of forms, including polls, articles, and blogs.

The American Communication Association (ACA)
www.americancomm.org
The ACA was created to promote academic and professional research, criticism, teaching, practical use, and exchange of principles and theories of human communication. This is a resourceful educational site offering up-to-date information on communication.

Professor's House
www.professorshouse.com
From advice on the home, children, and pets, with a large information base on communication, this site provides advice on dealing with just about any issue that arises in dating and marriage.

Ask the Internet Therapist
www.asktheinternettherapist.com
This resource provides a new and original form of marriage counselling. For those with time constraints or who do not wish to travel to visit a therapist, a new option is online counselling. For a fee, the site offers on-the-spot counselling from an array of medical professionals. They also offer phone and video counselling.

Chapter 6
Parenting
Child-bearing, Socialization, and Parenting Challenges

Chapter Outline

In the days of your great-grandparents and before, it was assumed that people would marry and—as soon as it was sensible—start producing children. Marriages without children were considered to be scarcely marriages at all. Today, we think differently about these matters. We do not assume that everyone will want to have children or will start to have children soon after marrying; and we do not assume that, in important ways, a family without children is no family at all.

As we shall see, there are many reasons for this dramatic change—a change that has accompanied dramatic changes in family life and, especially, dramatic changes in women's social roles. Today, with the availability of good contraception, people are better able to decide whether and when to have children, and the reasons they should or should not do so.

ENTERING PARENTHOOD

Decisions about Entering Parenthood

Researchers have proposed several theories about the ways in which people decide to enter parenthood. One theory proposes that child-bearing reflects deep and lasting beliefs. Habitual, sometimes unexamined family and religious values underlie a couple's decisions about parenthood in this scenario. An opposing theory supposes the couple does a complicated cost/benefit analysis of child-bearing. Into the equation go things such as the costs of having children, lost income opportunities for whoever will take on the largest part of child care, and other goods (new house, car, travel, and so on) the couple may have to forgo.

Likely, deciding to enter parenthood combines rational choices and emotional longings—life hopes for parenthood, self-realization, social and cultural influences, and estimated costs and benefits (McDaniel, 1996b).

Entering Parenthood in the Past

Child-bearing today is much less common than it was in the past, the result of a slow and (almost) consistent decline that took more than a century. Historical records show a marked decline in the Canadian **birth rate** from the mid-nineteenth to the mid-twentieth century, in average numbers of children borne (Gee, 1986: 269). Women born in Canada between 1817 and 1831, for example, had about 6.6 children, compared with 1.7 children for women born between 1947 and 1961. Since 1961, the numbers of births has continued to fall, especially among native-born, highly educated women.

The improvement of birth control played a role in this fertility decline but not as large a role as is often thought, compared with significantly changed views about the value of children. The decline in numbers of children born into families was largely because of the changing social and economic circumstances in which families lived. As Canadian society industrialized, fewer people needed children to work on the farms. Children cost more to raise in towns and cities than they did on farms. Children in cities, thus, changed from an economic benefit to an economic liability.

So, a century-long downward trend in child-bearing continued with only a brief interruption—the so-called "baby boom" between 1947 and 1967 (Statistics Canada, 2008a). Today, the average number of births per woman is roughly 1.5, an all-time low. Most Canadians continue to enter parenthood in their mid- to late 20s. However, "nearly one half of the women who gave birth in Canada were age 30 and older. In fact, in Ontario and British Columbia, mothers age 30 and older were already in the majority. This reinforces the long-term trend among Canadian women: they have been waiting longer and longer to start families" (Statistics Canada, 2005a).

These changes in numbers and timing, along with other social and economic changes, open the door for women to combine paid work with families—a topic we will discuss at great length in another chapter. The result is a variety of family types and forms.

Entering Parenthood Today: Family Planning

Most people who are sexually active in the 2000s know something about contraception. Why contraceptive practice varies remains to be fully understood, but family research provides some answers.

In Canada, knowledge about contraception is widespread (Balakrishnan, Lapierre-Adamcyk, and Krotki, 1993: 197). Prevalent use of contraception has been a factor in the decline in the Canadian birth rate and in family size—but it is not the cause of this decline, only the means. People use contraception only if they want to limit their fertility, to have smaller families. Then, the widespread availability of effective contraception allows a separation of sexual intercourse from pregnancy, which changes both the practice of sex and the opinion of parenthood. As a result, many people now see the entry into parenthood as a distinct choice, for good or bad.

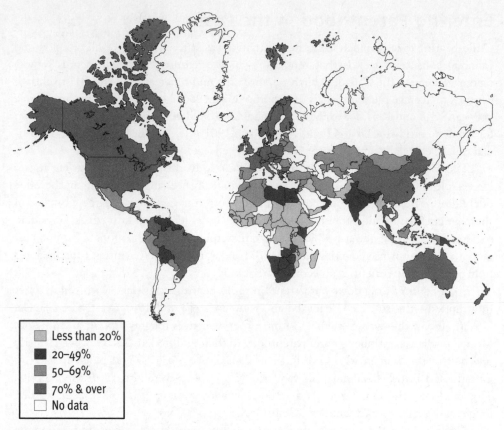

Figure 6.1 Contraceptive use

Source: Millennium Development Goals Report 2008 © United Nations, 2009. Reproduced with permission.

Contraceptive use varies throughout the world, as it does in Canada. Typically, contraception rates are higher where literacy is higher and women receive more education, social and economic opportunity, and general empowerment. The highest rates of contraceptive use are found in the People's Republic of China, with 83 percent of women of reproductive age using modern contraception, compared to Canada and the United States, where the percentages are 73 percent and 70.5 percent respectively. In Northern Europe, three-quarters of women of reproductive age are using it. By contrast, only one woman in five of reproductive age is using modern contraception in Africa, and just one in four is doing so in Western Asia (including the Middle Eastern countries) (United Nations, 2004).

Contraception is taking hold even in traditionally religious high-fertility areas of the world. Within rural areas, accessing health care and contraceptive advice poses challenges. Sutherns and Bourgeault (2008) set out to study conditions of maternity care in rural areas. A comparative, qualitative study examined women's experiences with maternity care in two provinces, Ontario and Alberta. They concluded that finding out about birth options in rural Canada is harder than in urban areas. Care close to the patient gives better health-care outcomes than more sophisticated but less accessible secondary care. If so, one wonders why there has not been more investment in better care for individuals living in rural areas of Canada. A failure to provide this may result in a shift from rural neighbourhoods to areas where access to medical care is more widely available, as well as more troubled pregnancies and sickly infants.

Entering Parenthood Young

Increasingly, public concern has focused on "children having children." Yet the rate of pregnancies among Canadian teenagers has dropped dramatically by one-third since 1974. Also, the proportion of Canadian pregnancies accounted for by teenage girls dropped from 14 percent in 1974 to 8 percent in 2001 (Statistics Canada, 2005a).

Teen pregnancy rates vary enormously across the industrialized West. In Sweden, child-bearing among women younger than age 18 has almost disappeared (Hoem and Hoem, 1988: 22). By contrast, the United States has the highest rate of unmarried teen pregnancy in the world—about three times Canada's rate (Statistics Canada, 2008c).

Given their easy access to reproductive control, why would young men and women in North America "choose" to reproduce? One theory is that teens are confused by mixed messages. Another is that religious groups may discourage access to contraception and birth control.

A study that interviewed pregnant or parenting adolescents found four other factors which predict risky sexual behaviour that could lead to teenage pregnancy: presence of a family member with a drinking problem, physical assault by a family member, (early) age of first drunkenness, and (early) age of first wanted sexual experience (Kellogg, Hoffman, and Taylor, 1999). Comparative research (Jones, Darroch Forrest, Goldman, Henshaw, Lincoln, Rosoff, Westoff, and Wulf, 1993) suggests that another source of the problem may be cultural: excessive sexualization of the mass media combined with a relative absence of sexual education in the schools and access to contraception in the community.

Adolescent parenting is associated with socio-economic disadvantages for the mother and poor outcomes for the child. Younger mothers have higher than average rates of low birth-weight babies, which is a serious public health concern due to the link between low birth weight and "poor infant health and mortality" (Statistics Canada, 2005a). Canadian research using data from the National Longitudinal Survey of Children and Youth finds that the children of young mothers are especially likely to have problems. Children born to teen mothers are more likely to have a behavioural disorder, especially during preschool years, and to have poor listening vocabulary on entering school (Dahinten and Willms, 2002). A follow-up study found that as these children grow older (10–15 years old), they have significantly lower math scores and commit more property offences than children born to older mothers (25 29 years of age) (Dahinten, Shapka, and Willms, 2007).

Teen mothers themselves do not fare well. They report lower levels of family func-tioning than older mothers. One in four teen mothers reports being depressed—twice the prevalence of mothers who had their first child in their late 20s. Teen mothers are much more likely to be single parents and not work outside the home, which puts them into a disadvantaged financial situation. For example, the average family income of mothers who had a first child as a teen was $25 000—half the national average (Dahinten and Willms, 2002). Their education was lower than that of older mothers.

People who enter parenthood unexpectedly often find the parenting role stressful and their children difficult. Beyond this, adolescent women often have little understanding of the developmental milestones in their infants' behaviour. These mothers, themselves young, are still forming their own identities, which can further aggravate the stress of parenting. Outside support often helps an adolescent mother to handle the demands her child poses. Researchers (Luster, Perlstadt, and McKinney, 1996) report that an intensive family support program improves adolescent mothers' care of their infants.

We know far less about the fathers of babies born to teen mothers. Using birth records, Millar and Wadhera (1997) found that more than three-quarters of births to teen mothers involved men who were older by an average of 4.1 years. Twenty-four percent of fathers were six or more years older than the teenage women they impregnated. These findings raise many questions about responsibility for pregnancy and contraception.

Likely, employment opportunities influence fathers to stay or leave: they are more likely to stay if they can find a job to support the mother and child. At the macro- or societal level, teen pregnancy results from inadequate educational opportunities, job opportunities, career goals, and access to birth control and abortion services. At the micro-level, the problem of teen pregnancy results from poor parenting, including poor parental communication, the setting of a poor example, and poor guidance and help.

Child Rearing Alone

According to the 2006 Census, lone parents make up 15.7 percent of families in Canada. This is an increase from 14.5 percent in the 1996 Census (Statistics Canada, 2007a). Most (81 percent) of these families are headed by a woman (Vanier Institute of the Family, 2000). A small fraction of these lone-parent families results from a teen pregnancy or unwed (often unplanned) pregnancy. Most result from the dissolution of a relationship.

Single mothers face a higher-than-average risk of physical and mental health problems. Their children also have an increased risk of social, academic, emotional, and behavioural difficulties. We will talk about this issue more later in the chapter.

The Decision Not to Have Children

Canadian couples who had no children living at home accounted for 38.4 percent of all families in 2006, up from 38 percent in 1991 and 34 percent in 1981 (Statistics Canada 2007a). Some of these couples have adult children who have moved out. Some couples may simply be postponing their entry into parenthood and eventually will become parents.

While many would assume that people who decide not to have children feel less fulfilled than parents, this is not necessarily the case. Childless people typically have no fewer friends than parents do, though they may have fewer close relatives. In addition, childless people also experience less stress than individuals with children (McMullin and Marshall, 1996), as we noted in the previous chapter, and their marital satisfaction is higher at all stages of the relationship.

Adoption

By considering parenthood and family in terms other than biological reproduction, we pose an important question about what "families" really are nowadays. The way a modern society answers this question lies at the root of today's adoption policies and practices.

Not long ago in North America, officials handled adoption in secrecy and closed their records on the child's adoption to the child and to the adoptive and the biological parent(s). However, perpetuating such a fiction often led to problems for children who discovered the truth. Most family researchers today agree that it is better to tell children that they have been adopted when they are old enough to understand what that means. By openly talking to the child about his or her adoption, parents make it a positive fact of the child's life.

Dramatic changes in the popular view of adoption, and in people's behaviour toward it, are also a natural result of changes in the modern family—for example, in the growth of heterogamy. Today, adoptive parents, especially in Canada and the United States, may

Especially in Canada and the United States, adoptive parents may belong to a different ethnic or racial group from their adoptive child. This results in a blend of identities for the child.

belong to a racial or ethnic group different from that of their adoptive child. The increasing awareness of the value of the child's original ethnic or racial identity encourages adoptive parents to go beyond their own community in search of their child's original community. Such parents generate a blend of identities for their children, often involving representatives of the child's original community.

Some people believe that openness about adoption reassures the birth parents about their child's well-being, helps children form an identity, and gives them a greater sense of security. Others believe that contacts with birth parents interrupt and destabilize the adopted family and confuse the child's sense of identity. More research is needed before we can say much about the conditions under which adopted children benefit from linking with their natural parents (Miall and March, 2005a).

Assisted Fertility

In a *pronatalist* society, people expect all women to bear children and stigmatize women who fail to produce children. In high fertility cultures, most women fully internalize and support the pronatalist discourse (Remennick, 2000). Women facing stigma because of infertility develop various coping strategies that include selective disclosure or guarding their "hidden disability."

Infertility is associated with lower levels of satisfaction with an intimate partner. Infertile women older than age 30 have an even more negative vision of the future than infertile women younger than age 30 (DeBoer, 2002). Many Canadian women regret their inability to become pregnant and seek medical help—often in the form of long-term and burdensome infertility treatments at high personal and financial costs.

Medically assisted procreation (MAP) is an aid to couples facing infertility or sterility. The chance of success with many procedures is not high at all, however. In vitro fertilization, for example, succeeds in a healthy baby in only a small percentage of cases treated (McDaniel, 1988). Artificial insemination has a slightly higher rate of success. For some women, the new technology succeeds too well. They bear far more children than they had bargained for. The year 1998 marked the first time a set of octuplets all survived birth. And, of course, a famous set of octuplets were born in 2009 by artificial reproduction to a California women who already had six children. However, we are only at the beginning of this new process and have much more to learn about the conditions under which assisted fertility succeeds socially as well as technologically.

According to information from the Canadian Fertility and Andrology Society (CFAS), rates of assisted reproduction in Canada were high and rising rapidly. However, a successful outcome is not the only factor affecting women's reaction to their experiences with assisted fertility. Some women, for example, resent the experience of male domination in fertility clinics (Birenbaum-Carmeli, 1998) or find the clinics objectifying.

Having sympathetic friends also improves women's experiences with assisted fertility. Overall, disclosing their infertile status increases women's perceived levels of social support and their satisfaction with assisted fertility treatment.

Sociologists have not yet thought through all the ethical issues presented by NRTs. They need to be involved in the critical assessment process. Eichler recommends research on the long-term outcomes of intensive unsuccessful treatment for infertility, the type of information given to clients, and effects of the anonymity of genetic parentage on offspring and others.

New reproductive technologies have allowed some people who might otherwise have remained childless to bear children. However, many couples experience an emotional roller coaster: their hopes and expectations are raised and then dashed. We are only at the beginning of many changes in this area of human experience

HOW PARENTHOOD AFFECTS RELATIONSHIPS

Parenting, the research suggests, has a generally negative effect on marital relationships. A meta-analysis of the literature on this topic by Twenge, Campbell, and Foster (2003) finds that parents typically report lower marital satisfaction than childless couples. The researchers also find decreases in marital satisfaction with increases in the number of children; children may be cheaper by the dozen but clearly not better.

However, though these observed differences are statistically significant—that is, not due to chance—they are often small, and other factors affect marital satisfaction as much or more. Moreover, marital satisfaction also means different things to parents and nonparents. First-time parents and childless couples attach different weights to various ingredients of marital satisfaction: for example, to the importance of sexual intimacy versus building a future together. If we consider these differences in definition, some of the reported differences in marital satisfaction lessen.

As well, many factors influence how parenthood affects a marital relationship and how parents evaluate parenting. And, although marital quality tends to decline over time, some couples begin with much higher levels of marital quality than others. Some contextual factors—ethnic and religious beliefs, financial distress, chronic illness or disability, or social support, for example—affect the rate of decline induced by parenthood. In general, people who hold positive attitudes toward traditional family and gender issues experience a smaller-than-average decline in marital satisfaction due to parenthood.

Does parenthood, then, reduce marital satisfaction? When answering that question, it matters whether the couple in question is married or cohabiting (Manning, 2004), resilient or fragile, and what expectations the partners have brought to the relationship and to parenting. It matters whether the birth was planned or unplanned, desired or dreaded, on time or "too early." Sometimes, child-bearing even leads to union dissolution—especially where there are children from previous relationships, marital conflict, a lack of trust, and a lack of shared activities (Waller and McLanahan, 2005). A sense of secure attachment makes it much easier for a couple to endure the strains and disruptions associated with new parenthood (Simpson, Rholes, Campbell, Tran, and Wilson, 2002), as does strong support from family and friends (Schulz, Cowan, and Cowan, 2006).

New parents and couples with young children face a variety of new concerns: inappropriate expectations, problems with returning to work, changes in sexual intimacy, new intrusions by (and reliance on) in-laws, an absence of sleep and leisure time, and new problems communicating all these concerns. Preserving closeness is critical to keeping marital satisfaction alive during the transition to parenthood. Couples have trouble doing this, especially if they start out with low levels of attachment or have childhood memories of their parents lacking attachment (Curran, Hazen, Jacobvitz, and Feldman, 2005).

As the children get older, parent–child conflicts can introduce or intensify parent–parent conflict, again reducing marital satisfaction (Hiotakis, 2005). Women with children younger than age 18 who are unsatisfied with housework, parenting, or marriage often prefer to stay at work for longer hours rather than come home (Hochschild, 1997). In short, the entry into parenthood has major effects on relationships, at least in North America. It can affect the career patterns of both parents, but especially the mother. It also affects patterns of household work, the distribution of power, marital satisfaction, and economic well-being within the household.

McMahon (1995) shows that parenthood can also be transforming and increase the woman's sense of social power. Contrary to popular images of self-sacrificing mothers, the mothers McMahon interviewed do not see themselves as denying their own identities. However, the presence of children in the family often decreases adults' mental well-being.

According to McLanahan and Adams (1987, 1989), this effect is due to the strain parenting puts on a couple's time and money, especially poor and working-class people with little flexibility in their work patterns.

Life Course Concerns

Faced with the practical problems of parenting—a shortage of time and money—women adopt strategies to time their education, career, marriage, and childbirth. Having a child later in life may be physically more risky for the mother and child, but it allows the mother to complete her education and prove herself occupationally. Having a child earlier in life lessens the likelihood a woman will complete her education and leaves her more vulnerable to reduced wages (Taniguchi, 1999). A cross-cultural study by Sayer, Gauthier, and Furstenberg (2004) found that more educated mothers spend significantly more time with their children. For various reasons, professional working mothers are better able to prioritize their life events so more time can be spent with their children.

Parenting carries significant costs in time and money nonetheless. As we saw in the previous chapter, new parents undergo a significant drop in the time they spend together as a couple. As for money, researchers have estimated the direct costs of raising one child are close to $150 000 (Scott, 1996: 18). The emotional costs of parenting become especially burdensome and the potential costs to marriages especially great if people see children as easily damaged by stress or poor parenting (as Freud argues), or as infinitely malleable by their environments (as behaviourism suggests).

However, not all the outcomes of entering parenthood are bad for close relationships. Entering parenthood often gives the new parents a sense of meaning and direction. Becoming parents can also improve their status in the eyes of their families and society, and represent entry into adult responsibilities.

In sum, the effects of children on marital happiness result from an interplay between many factors such as sex role traditionalism and income earning status, among others (Tsang, Harvey, Duncan, and Sommer, 2003). If this were an advice book, rather than a sociology textbook, it might say the following: Do not enter parenthood before you are emotionally, socially, and financially prepared. Have a child who both parents want and for whom both are willing to sacrifice. Most important, realize that babies take up much time and family resources.

Family and Household Size

As discussed in Chapter 2, declining fertility has led to smaller households and more people living alone. For individuals, this change has meant that we have fewer siblings, uncles and aunts, nephews and nieces, and cousins than our parents did. We have become far more reliant on our partner and one or two children and, most important, on our friends.

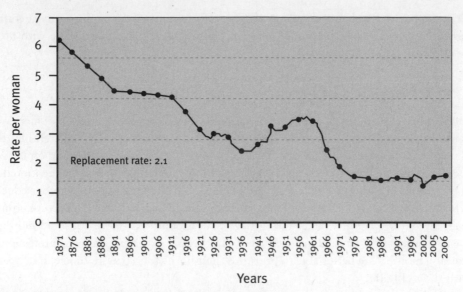

Figure 6.2 Total fertility rate, Canada, 1871–2006

Source: Statistics Canada website. 2008. Births. *The Daily,* September 26, from www.hc-sc.gc.ca/sr-sr/pubs/hpr-rpms/bull/2005-10-chang-fertilit/intro-eng.php.

Compared with the past, a far higher proportion of the children in our society are first-borns or only children—often pampered and prematurely ushered into adult-like competition for achievements and awards. Our families, much smaller than in the past, are infinitely more mobile, so more of us move from one community to another, becoming more isolated and self-sufficient as we go.

Socialization

Children do not arrive "ready to go" but must be carefully taught how to take part in families and in society. Sociologists define **socialization** as the social learning a person goes through to become a capable, functioning member of society. The **primary socialization** of children is usually the responsibility of the child's family. It has a deep impact on the individual's life by helping to set the child's future values, goals, and, to a certain extent, personality. It is in the family that a child first learns how to gain rewards by doing set tasks and how to negotiate to achieve a consensus on rules.

Often parents decide how to socialize their children based on particular cultural or traditional values. Parents choose what skills and behaviours to teach their children based on what they feel will help them become healthy and successful members of society. Aboriginal families, for instance, are more likely to promote more education and achievement-oriented behaviours in their own children than European Canadian mothers (Cheah and Chirkov, 2008: 415). This could be in part because of the strong

Aboriginal belief that education is a means of improving one's social position and promoting success in society. Moreover, Aboriginal mothers felt it was more important that their child maintain a sense of cultural traditions and spirituality than European Canadian mothers (Cheah and Chirkov, 2008: 415). Aboriginal mothers may have felt this was particularly important because of the historical attempts to assimilate the Aboriginal population into Canadian society. Thus, the socialization of children is a complex process that involves the transmission of cultural and traditional beliefs promoted by parents.

Most important, children in well-functioning families learn that they are valued human beings. Most children follow a set pattern of growth, physically, emotionally, and morally, within a range. The family environment affects these patterns by encouraging each step and modelling how to communicate. Like the spousal relationship, the parental relationship relies on good communication. Talking to children helps them learn to speak and understand language. More than that, it helps them become social beings.

Myths and Facts about Parenting

- Children and parents learn together. And parenting changes with the changing needs of children. You don't have to know everything. No parent has all the answers. There is no such thing as one "right way" or "one-style-fits-all" parenting. Parents need to understand and be able to respond to the unique personalities, strengths, and vulnerabilities of each child. Have reasonable expectations of yourself. Have confidence in what you do know. It's okay to say I don't know. Find out more about the things you feel less confident in.

- Children and parents learn from each other. As a parent, you constantly learn more about your children as they grow and change. Every parent has to work it out as they go along. Every parent makes mistakes and learns through experience. Mistakes only count if you keep repeating them.

- There is no such thing as a perfect parent. Accept that there may be things you could do differently or better next time (although you usually only know this by looking back after-

ward). Do not be too hard on yourself. Appreciate that parenting has its ups and downs and accept that this is normal. And there is no such thing as a perfect child.

- There are many ways to parent. There is no one right way to do it. Historically, extended families and neighbourhoods shared the responsibility of caring for children. Today, more than ever before, parents are viewed as solely responsible for raising their children.

- Many other parents feel the same way you do—confused! Asking for support is a positive thing to do for you and your child. Seek support from family, friends, and community and family support services. Parenting is a community activity—many people play a significant role in children's lives. Grandparents, uncles, aunts, friends, teachers, and neighbours all contribute to and support family life.

Source: Adapted from Australian Childhood Foundation at http://raisingchildren.net.au/articles/parenting_-_myths_and_facts.html/context/302.

Gender Socialization

Most children grow up securely attached to their family or other caregivers and able to take their place in society. It is in this secure family context that they begin to learn social roles, including one of the earliest and most consequential—their gender. People learn their gender-based habits of behaviour through **gender socialization**. The major agents of socialization—family, peer groups, schools, and the mass media—all serve to reinforce cultural and conventional definitions of masculinity and femininity. Gender socialization starts at birth and continues throughout life. Young children learn gender identities by watching others at nursery school or daycare, role-playing games, experimenting with hair and clothing styles, and body decoration.

Parents routinely assign more household tasks to daughters than to sons. The tasks people assign to their sons are usually more fixer-upper tasks, and less often cleaning, child care, or meal preparation. Daughters get to do the latter. Not surprisingly, children often form traditional, gender-based attitudes toward housework before the end of high school. Men, older people, and poor people are especially likely to hold and teach traditional, gendered attitudes. As a result, fathers demand more help from teenage daughters than from teenage sons.

Gender socialization affects the career paths children take in later life. Children are likely to follow in their parents' footsteps occupationally. Learned gender differences also show up in our intimate relations—for example, in our communication—as we noted in an earlier chapter. For example, we teach women to behave in a demure, innocent, and disinterested fashion when sex is the topic of discussion with men. (Women are more forthcoming in discussions with other women.) Learned patterns of communication create and preserve distinctions between women and men, and reinforce social expectations between the sexes. Often, they complicate our understanding of what is going on between men and women.

Ethnic Socialization

Many parents, especially those who raise their children outside their country of origin, want to ensure that later generations are aware of their culture and history. **Parental involvement** affects the identities children take on in later life. For example, among Australians of mixed Aboriginal and European heritage, children are more likely to call themselves Aboriginal if parents provide an upbringing rich in Aboriginal life experience (Ramsay, 2000).

Though other cultures are likely to figure in a child's final conception of himself or herself, how strongly children hold on to their parents' cultural heritage depends on the efforts of their parents. Family rituals and routines play an important part in upholding a family's ethnic heritage. McCarroll (2000) finds they have a great impact on children's developing racial attitudes, for example. However, despite parents' best efforts, children still may choose to ignore ethnic traditions or identify with different groups. The child is not merely an empty vessel waiting to be filled with cultural information but an active participant in development. The desire to stray from parents' cultural expectations may lead to conflict in families.

PARENTING PROCESSES

Family researchers have found what most of us would judge to be better and worse ways of preparing children to take part in society. Some parents put a high value on obedience, for example. Other parents value independence. Some parents want their children to be co-operative and adaptable; others, to be competitive and ambitious. However, "good parenting"—whatever its intended goals—is most likely to produce children who are healthy, law-abiding, and successful at school. Poor parenting is most likely to produce opposite results.

When a child is failing, delinquent, or disturbed, this is not always the result of poor parenting. Genetic factors can also increase the risks of childhood failure, delinquency, and depression.

That said, parents still play the primary role in preparing a child for the life he or she will face outside the family home. "Parenting" involves much more than taking care of a child's basic needs for food and shelter. It means helping to mould that child into a functioning member of society. This, in turn, requires that parents create the right conditions for the emotional and cognitive development of their children. These "right" parenting conditions include providing love and attachment, emotional stability, protection and control, and fair and moderate discipline.

Love and Attachment

Most parents probably love their children, just as one would hope. Problems can occur, however, when parents do not know how to express this love to their children; children who feel unloved by their parents suffer emotional damage. Sometimes, too, children have difficulty receiving expressions of love. For example, autistic children may not find a gentle, loving touch pleasant. Depressed children may discount expressions of affection. Less severely, children with temperaments different from those of their parents may get the wrong message. In addition, some parents and children might have higher relationship expectations than either party can meet. Relations between children and their fathers are especially problematic. Children usually remain closer to their mothers than to their fathers. Thus, more children may feel ignored by their fathers than by their mothers.

These patterns, as well as the relations between siblings, are subject to change as children and their parents age (Burholt and Wenger, 1998). Yet, feelings of neglect or dislike are surprisingly resistant to change. For example, delinquent girls are more likely than other girls to say their mothers and fathers spend too little time with them. Often, they feel that neither parent gives them enough love.

Why are children who feel unloved more likely to break society's rules? Explanations vary. Perhaps only delinquent peers are available to the unloved children, and they learn delinquent ways from these peers. Or perhaps they are angry with their parents for (seemingly) not loving them, so they deliberately choose friends of whom their parents will disapprove.

John Bowlby, a British psychoanalyst, was the first to state a formal theory of attachment (1969). While trying to understand the distress that infants suffered after a separation from their parents, Bowlby noted that infants would make great efforts to prevent separation from their parents or to re-establish closeness after a separation. Research showed that, far from being unusual, such behaviours were common to various mammals. In fact, they may be adaptive responses to separation from a primary attachment figure—someone who provides the support, protection, and care on which an infant depends. That is, they may have significance for the evolution of human beings.

According to Bowlby, infants often want to know whether the attachment figure is nearby, on hand, and attentive. If the answer is "yes," the child feels loved, secure, and confident, and is likely to explore the environment, play with others, and be sociable. Otherwise, the child suffers anxiety and is likely to search visually, follow actively, or signal vocally. These behaviours continue until the child is near to the attachment figure again, or until the child "wears down." In the latter case, the child is likely to experience despair and depression.

In short, parental support and encouragement are important in creating a sense of attachment. Remember that children—indeed, people of all ages—form judgments about themselves by responding to how others treat them. People learn how to conform to rules, and how to obey authority, by generalizing from particular situations. Children with kind, encouraging parents usually get higher grades at school, have more social competence, and get into less trouble with teachers. They have learned that people in authority—first their parents, then their teachers—are there to help them, not hold them back.

Feeling valued inside the home, children feel valued outside the home and conform more enthusiastically to the rules of social institutions like the school. Research shows that more involved parenting reduces delinquency among inner-city boys, for example. Warm, sympathetic parenting leads to good social, psychological, and school adjustment. Even in adolescence, often a time of big changes and doubts, children whose parents are encouraging do better. Adolescents with unsupportive parents are more likely than other adolescents to start smoking cigarettes and engage in other risky behaviours.

Emotional Stability and Family Cohesion

Emotional stability ranks close behind love as a contributor to the healthy development of children. Anything that reduces the parents' capacity to provide stable, consistent support runs the risk of producing school problems, delinquency, or depression in the child. These destabilizing factors can include spousal conflict, addiction, depression, or physical illness. Children whose parents are emotionally unstable are more anxious, less secure, and more likely to act out than children whose parents are emotionally stable.

Similarly, instability often produces conflict, and children whose parents argue and fight a lot have lower self-esteem than those whose parents get along. Once again, family rituals are important for family stability and family cohesion. **Family cohesion** is a sense of attachment and relatedness among members of a family, both preserved and represented by shared activities, self-identification as a family member, and signs of familiarity and liking. Researchers report that children who live in families that have sit-down meals together at least three times a week are much less likely to become delinquents in their adolescence, or to turn to crime in adulthood. Family dinners are a sign of family cohesion and stability that contribute to the healthy emotional development of children. Also, families that enjoy recreational activities together are much less likely to produce delinquent children.

Protectiveness and Control

No less important than love and stability is parental **control and supervision**—how firmly, consistently, and fairly parents make and enforce rules for the child. Good rules guide and protect the child. They show the parents' concern and attachment. Children are less likely to become delinquents if their parents keep an eye on what they are doing, offer them support, and give them a chance to discuss whatever it is that is bothering them. This is true of children in two-parent families, mother-only families, and mother-stepfather families. The quality of family relationships counts more than the number of parents in forming and socializing children.

Youths who are supported at home develop identities conducive to success, while youths deprived of support at home, school, and community form identities that make school success much less likely. Unhappy marriages often produce more troubled and troublesome children, for two reasons. First, an unhappy marriage can cause children to feel unloved. Unhappily married people often spend too little time with their children. The parents are depressed, stressed out, and self-absorbed. Second, marital conflict disrupts the normal practices of discipline, especially by mothers, who are typically the family disciplinarians in Canadian society. This, in turn, reduces the attachment between parent and child.

The **authoritative parenting** style (high acceptance, high control) turns out children who achieve the highest levels of academic performance and mental well-being. Other forms of parenting produce less desirable outcomes. For example, **authoritarian parenting** (low acceptance, high control) keeps the child from developing expressiveness and independence. This parenting style also increases the risk of adolescent drug use. Children whose parents are controlling but not as caring are more likely to become delinquents (Man, 1996), to become depressed, and to fail in school (Radziszewska, Richardson, Dent, and Flay, 1996).

This does not argue for lax parental control, however. **Unengaged parenting** (low acceptance/low control) can also be harmful. **Permissive parenting** may produce poor results too. A study of high school students in the San Francisco Bay area found that permissive (high acceptance, low control) parenting produces poor grades (Vergun, Dornbusch, and Steinberg, 1996). Low-achieving students are more likely to come from families with permissive parenting styles (Bronstein, Duncan, and D'Ari, 1996; Radziszewska, 1996). What is more, differences in adjustment add up over time, and the harmful effects of careless parenting continue to take their toll as behaviour problems, internal distress, and poor school performance (Steinberg, Lamborn, Darling, Mounts, and Dornbusch, 1994).

Naturally, many parents combine elements of the different styles, being more permissive of certain behaviours than others, and more engaged in some circumstances than others. Children, too, are born with different temperaments, and two children may respond quite differently to the same parenting actions. However, parenting styles yield different results depending on the neighbourhood the families live in, their ethnic group, and the child's developmental stage, among other things. Studies have found that restrictive parents may provide an element of protection in unsafe neighbourhoods, for example, but the same amount of control may hinder the child in a safe neighbourhood (Dearing, 2004). Also, the age of the child can turn this relationship around: a high degree of protectiveness can hinder the development of older children but benefit younger children.

Younger children require more supervision, for example, especially given the environment. As well, location matters. Rural dwellings often pose a threat to children because of the dual nature of the land serving as place of occupation and residence.

Far more important but less understood is the cross-cultural variation in parenting styles and their effects on children. Some believe that authoritarian parenting, which is very common in many "traditional" parts of the world, carries less stigma and causes less harm than it does in Canada, where such parenting may be considered abusive.

Cultural variations in parenting are also clear in a study done by Dwairy and Menshar (2006) on the parenting styles used for Egyptian adolescents. The authors found that, among Arabs, the common types of parenting styles differ in rural and urban populations, and are also gender-specific. In rural communities, the authoritarian style is more prominent, especially for the parenting of male adolescents; parents here tend to use an authoritative style with girls (Dwairy and Menshar, 2006). On the other hand, an authoritarian parenting style is used with girls in urban communities, and not with males (Dwairy and Menshar, 2006). Thus, parenting styles are adjusted to environment—whether rural or urban—and also to the varying need for control and obedience among sons and daughters in these contexts.

In this research, and other research in Israel and Egypt, the same authors report that consistent discipline is better than inconsistent discipline, and consistency is more important than style of parenting. They report, for example, that they can find no definitive proof that authoritarian parenting is harmful to Arab and Bedouin children, who are accustomed to this treatment. This raises the always important question of whether parenting behaviours are important in themselves or important only to the extent they are perceived as unusual, abusive, or malevolent.

So, one cannot ignore the influences of factors such as culture, religion, neighbourhood, or (of course) age. One parenting style does not work well under all circumstances. However, in North American, researchers generally find that children whose parents are authoritarian, unengaged, or permissive are most likely to show problems of adjustment, poor academic achievement, or substance abuse. The authoritative parenting style offers the best mixture of love and control—not too much or too little of either.

Fair and Moderate Discipline

The issue of discipline is related to control. Overzealous discipline may wipe out the benefits of control, as may inattentive discipline. The trick is to provide the right amount of discipline, and provide it in the right way—that is, using the right technique.

Hoffman (1979) distinguishes between three basic types of disciplining techniques: power assertion, love withdrawal, and induction. In using **power assertion,** a parent or other caregiver threatens a child with punishment for non-compliance. The child changes his or her behaviour to avoid punishment. The child's seemingly moral behaviour is externally, not internally, driven. Similarly, in **love withdrawal**, a parent threatens a child. Instead of the punishment taking a physical form, it takes an emotional form—producing in the child anxiety over the loss of love. As with power assertion, the child complies with parental demands to avoid punishment.

Induction, on the other hand, stresses the possible benefits of the child's behaviour for others. Inductive discipline—teaching good behaviour by setting a good example, then rewarding imitation—is better for the child than power assertion. When children raised inductively break the rules, they are aware of contributing to another's distress and feel guilty. Feelings of guilt, unlike feelings of fear or anxiety, exercise an **internal moral control** over their behaviour. Parental affection and inductive discipline foster moral internalization, while power assertion reduces moral learning (Hoffman, 1979).

Inductive techniques offer many benefits by, for example, forcing parents to explain and show good behaviour. Yet, many parents continue to use some degree of physical punishment—a form of power assertion—as a disciplinary tool. Physical punishment and power assertion appeal to parents who do not have the time, patience, or inclination to teach rules inductively.

Spanking and other forms of corporal punishment continue to be prevalent in Canada, as revealed in a review of the literature by the Global Initiative to End All Corporal Punishment (www.endcorporalpunishment.org): for example, a survey of 1000 people in an SES/Sun Media poll found that 64 percent support the use of force such as spanking by parents to discipline a child, though a wide majority oppose physical force being used by others. Support for spanking as a reasonable measure was highest in the West at 71 percent and Ontario at 62 percent (Spanking poll backs ruling, 2004).

Davis (1996) notes that when parents threaten physical punishment as a form of discipline, usually they want compliance with some simple demand. For example, the parent wants the child to sit still, be quiet, come with the parent, or stop touching things. Children typically respond by ignoring the parent. About half the adults making these threats also hit the children. What we learn from this scenario is that parents use physical punishment routinely, and it is routinely ineffective! At its extreme, harsh childhood discipline produces delinquency and low self-esteem (Peiser and Heaven, 1996). A broad range of studies has also found harmful outcomes in adulthood, including depression, alcoholism, aggressive behaviour, suicide, and a tendency to physically abuse wives and children.

Parents use physical punishment for various reasons. Probably, inexperience is chief among them. For example, teenage mothers are more likely than other mothers to punish their children physically, and the youngest adolescent mothers favour the use of physical punishment most strongly. They also report less personal happiness than other adolescent mothers. Nonetheless, the single most important factor predicting physical punishment by an adult is violence that adults have experienced during their own childhood. People whom parents often yelled at and spanked are more likely to yell at and spank their own children (Barnett, Quackenbush, and Sinisi, 1996).

Runaways

How can we tell if parenting is "good" or "bad" without simply applying a personal moral judgment? There are at least two ways to do this. First, let's agree that good parenting ought to promote in children good mental and physical health, school readiness, an ability to get along with other children, and a willingness to follow social rules and obey the law. If so, we can examine research that shows the kinds of parenting practices that are most commonly associated with these outcomes. Good parenting will increase the likelihood of these desirable outcomes; bad parenting will increase the likelihood of the opposite.

Second, if we can all agree that children who receive good parenting are likely to want to remain at home with their families until they go away to school or (at least) are able to support themselves, then we can examine research that shows the kinds of parenting practices that are most commonly associated with these outcomes. Good parenting will produce this desirable outcome; bad parenting will produce the opposite: children who run away from home.

The research on street youth shows clearly that children who receive bad parenting are more likely than other children to run away from home. The decision to run away from home typically involves various interpersonal and family relationship problems. These include difficulties at school and problems with siblings (Spillane-Grieco, 1984). Most street youth have run away from families that suffer serious emotional, mental, or substance abuse problems. In short, most runaways are young people fleeing dysfunctional families.

Many of these runaway children have been abused. Abuse aside, the children often come from "chaotic/aggressive families" and reveal a pattern of youth aggression and deficient parental skill (Teare, Authier, and Peterson, 1994). Abused runaways are even more likely than those who were not abused to describe their parents in ways that suggest serious anti-social personality and drug problems (Stiffman, 1989a). Besides physical and psychological abuse, sexual abuse may be present too; it is more common in broken families, reconstituted families (those comprising formerly married partners and their children), and financially unstable families (McCormack, Burgess, and Gaccione, 1986).

The classic work in this area is *Mean Street: Youth, Crimes and Homelessness* by Canadian sociologists John Hagan and Bill McCarthy (1998). These authors collected survey and interview data from more than 800 homeless adolescents in Toronto and Vancouver, as well as 400 high school youth living at home.

Hagan and McCarthy (1989) found that most homeless youth come from dysfunctional families. These include families who are experiencing economic strain where that strain is translated into abusive or careless parenting styles. A disproportionate number of street youth come from homes where there is family violence and sexual abuse.

Once they arrive on the street, runaway youth become increasingly immersed in networks of other street youth and street adults, many of whom are heavily involved in crime. Crime is a practical response to need. Employment is a turning point in the lives of street youth. It has an important effect on street youths' involvement in crime and other dangerous activities characteristic of street life. Street youth who find stable, long-term employment are less involved in several types of crime and spend less time hanging out on the street. Most of them are in and out of employment, not continuously unemployed.

Elgar, Arlett, and Groves (2003) study the differences in self-reported attachment characteristics, substance use, and behavioural problems in juvenile delinquents from rural and urban areas. As noted in previous studies, insecure attachment characteristics correlated with behavioural problems, substance abuse, and poor family functioning. In comparison to rural delinquents, those from urban areas reported more substance use problems, problems with peers and family members, and externalizing behaviour such as hyperactivity, aggression, and inattention (Elgar et al., 2003). Such results may be caused by opportunities for those living in urban areas to associate with certain peer groups. This is a key finding for professionals, which can lead to improvements in administration and delivery of psychological treatments in youth correctional settings (Elgar et al., 2003).

In short, happy, healthy parents who treat their children authoritatively are more likely to produce happy, healthy children. Parents who are unhappy, unhealthy, abusive, or unaware of good parenting practices produce children who are more likely to run away from home.

Famous Quotations about Children

Of all the animals, the boy is the most unmanageable.

—Plato

A child thinks twenty shillings and twenty years can scarce ever be spent.

—Benjamin Franklin

If children grew up according to early indications, we should have nothing but geniuses.

—Goethe

Nothing has a stronger influence psychologically on their environment, and especially on their children, than the unlived lives of the parents.

—Carl Jung

Healthy children will not fear life if their elders have integrity enough not to fear death.

—Erik Erikson

What's done to children, they will do to society.

—Karl Menninger

Juvenile appraisals of other juveniles make up in clarity what they lack in charity.

—Edgar Z. Friedenberg

Children are remarkable for their intelligence and ardour, for their curiosity, their intolerance of shams, the clarity and ruthlessness of their vision.

—Aldous Huxley

Children have never been very good at listening to their elders, but they have never failed to imitate them.

—James Baldwin

Children have no use for psychology. They detest sociology. They still believe in God, the family, angels, devils, witches, goblins, logic, clarity, punctuation, and other such obsolete stuff.

—Isaac Bashevis Singer

Childhood—a period of waiting for the moment when I could send everyone and everything connected with it to hell.

—Igor Stravinsky

If a child is to keep alive his inborn sense of wonder without any such gift from the fairies, he needs the companionship of at least one adult who can share it, rediscovering with him the joy, excitement and mystery of the world we live in.

—Rachel Carson

Source: www.famousquotesandauthors.com/topics/children_and_childhood_quotes.html.

Stresses Associated with Parenting

As we have already seen, parenthood itself causes stress. The most important predictors of parental (especially maternal) stress are the age and sex of the child. The stresses are especially great for young women who have experienced an unwanted pregnancy or physical abuse.

Caring for Sick Children

Researchers have given much attention to the stress caused by a severely ill child. Not surprisingly, the illness is stressful for the sick child: many children who become chronically ill by age 15 also suffer from serious psychological and behavioural problems as a result. The parent who undertakes the most care often suffers a decline in health as well. Other family members also suffer from emotional and psychic depletion.

Just as fathers are often estranged in the mother-child relationship, siblings are often left out of the intense relationship between the parents and their sick child (Lademann, 1980; Larcombe, 1978). Lacking the communication skills of adults, siblings have a hard time giving voice to their feelings and wishes; serious behavioural problems at school and at home may result. Adults and children in daily contact with these siblings often remain ignorant of the source of these behavioural problems.

The effects of severe illness vary from one family to another, partly because of variations in the illness itself, but the well-being of the whole family often declines. The more severe the decline of the caretaker parent and the longer the illness goes on, the more strain the entire family experiences, and the more difficult it is to cope.

The problems that families face in trying to cope with a severely ill child are often closely tied to problems that existed before the onset of illness (Ilze, Kalnins, Churchill, and Terry, 1980). In short, a family's capacity to cope under conditions of great stress is correlated with its previous level of functioning (Steinhauer, Santa-Barbara, and Skinner, 1984).

While most of the literature reflects a high rate of dysfunctional response to child illness, it sometimes strengthens family ties (Motohashi, 1978). For instance, researchers have begun to recognize that having a child with a disability or an illness in the family does not lead inevitably to negative outcomes in familial health as once believed. In fact, a study by Van Riper (2007) on families with a child affected by Down syndrome found that through enacting family resources, successful problem solving, and coping, families were able to survive and thrive after the birth of their child with Down syndrome. More importantly, researchers have noted that although parents may face initial negative outcomes after the birth of their child with a disability, over time parents can come to experience positive outcomes such as psychological well-being, personal growth, and increased satisfaction with parenting (Van Riper, 2007). In some families, members talk meaningfully for the first time (Valens, 1975) and become pillars of support for one another. People occasionally discover unknown and creative personal resources (Anthony, 1970). Though a child's illness poses huge obstacles, these family breakthroughs prove that successful coping is possible.

VARIATIONS ON A THEME

Diversity is normal and natural in family relations. Different kinds of parents can do an equally good job of raising their children if they provide the basics of good parenting that we have already considered. The form or composition of a family may not have any effect on the quality of parenting provided.

Single Parents

There is something to be said for single-parent families. Where they have resulted from a divorce or separation, typically single-parent families provide children with a significant decrease in conflict, anxiety, and depression. This, in turn, may lead to better, more consistent parenting and a closer bond between the child(ren) and the custodial parent. As well, the single-parent family provides "opportunities for change and growth, and for freedom from limits of the heterosexual nuclear family based on marriage . . . Despite their problems, these families can be viewed as representing a stage of one's life or a preference to marriage, rather than as a failure or a disaster . . . [and] a viable alternative to other ways of carving out a life for oneself and one's children" (Lynn, 2003).

However, other things being equal, single-parent families have a harder time than two-parent families preserving a high quality of life for themselves and their children. In large part, the problems of single parenting result from a single parent having to do the parenting work of two people—a nearly impossible job. If this problem is overcome, good parenting can result.

Difficulties associated with single parenting are usually the result of lack of partner support, life distress, social isolation, and a shortage of money (Stern and Smith, 1995). According to Kesner and McKenry (2001), the increasing number of children who live in single-parent households can be linked to other serious social problems, including delinquency and welfare dependency.

Low income for many of these single mothers is a direct outcome of divorce (Duffy and Mandell, 2001). In turn, low income is likely to hinder the school performance of children in single-parent families. However, research using data from the National Longitudinal Survey of Children and Youth (Lipman, Offord, Dooley, and Boyle, 2002) shows that disparities in school readiness between children in single-parent families and those in two-parent families are only partly attributable to differences in family income. Children in low-income *single-parent* families are much more likely than children in low-income *two-parent* families to present various emotional, behavioural, and academic problems. Gender of the child also plays a part, with boys being more prone to behaviour problems.

Parenting in the Context of Poverty

Families living in poverty face many challenges in raising children because of limited financial and social resources, stress, and neighbourhood disadvantage.

McLanahan (2009) undertook a longitudinal survey of about 5000 parents to elucidate the relationship between poverty, extramarital child-bearing, and their outcomes for both parents and children. She found that unmarried mothers have the lowest income and educational attainment before the birth of the first child. Except for divorced mothers, single mothers also experience the smallest income growth in the five years following childbirth. Economic disparity predicts greater mental health problems and maternal stress. This negatively affects the quality of parenting and works with limited parental resources to decrease children's life chances and thus perpetuates poverty.

In a Canadian study of parents considered high risk by child protection agencies, the researchers identified poverty as a key obstacle to parenting capacity. Parents unable to supply the basic needs for their family experience despair, depression, and social isolation, and feel they are inadequate caregivers. They describe their financial situation "as a struggle, a fight, a daily preoccupation that consumed parental time, strength and patience" (Russell, Harris, and Gockel, 2008: 93). In such desperate circumstances, some families solve the problem by placing their children with other family members or even turning to temporary foster care until they can stabilize their financial situation.

The effects of socio-economic disadvantage extend beyond the immediate family members to later generations (Scaramella, Neppl, Ontai, and Conger, 2008). Parents who experience adolescent poverty are more likely to have children who reach parenthood at an earlier age. Younger parents, in turn, employ harsher parenting practices that increase the number of externalizing problems experienced by the third generation of children. Thus poverty can have long-term and cross-generational effects on family outcomes.

Children growing up in low-income families experience greater behavioural and cognitive problems as early as preschool (Noel, Peterson, and Jesso, 2008). Financial stability allows parents access to educational resources and activities, as well as the ability to devote more time to pursue these activities with their children (Ermisch, 2008). However, other studies find that the effect of economic disadvantage on preschool child cognitive performance can be mediated by parenting quality (Lugo-Gil and Tamis-LeMonda, 2008).

Parental income and educational level also positively affect adolescent educational attainment. Sympathetic parenting, sibling relations, and academic engagement are important mediators of this relationship (Melby, Fang, Wickrama, Conger, and Conger, 2008). Therefore, besides providing financial support for low-income families, parenting quality should be strengthened by introducing high-quality child care and community services that improve family literacy, education, and reduce parental stress.

Social support is a resource that mitigates the negative effects of poverty by providing financial, child-care, or housing support (McLanahan, 2009), which, in turn, reduces parental stress and improves the home environment for the child. In a literature review, Attree (2005) found that low-income single mothers have smaller informal and formal support networks than two-parent families. Further, the most socially isolated women are least likely to seek professional help for coping with parenting in poverty because they feel the services do not cater to their specific needs and because they fear being labelled as "inadequate" parents. Thus it is important to incorporate parental feedback in the design and

Myths and Facts about Single Parenting

Since culturally, traditional nuclear families are the norm and predominant, single parenting is an aberration and single parents are often left lonely and isolated.

■ Recently, single-parent families have shown a sharp rise. In the United States, about 59 percent of American children have lived in a single-parent home at least once during their minor years and more than 16 million children currently live in single-parent homes. They are often "bi-nuclear" families, where despite divorces and remarriages, both the parents are actively involved in parenting and offer their children two separate homes.

Children from single-parent families have emotional and behaviour problems and do poorly in school.

■ The outcomes of the oft-quoted 10-year study of Judith S. Wallerstein and Julia M. Lewis (2004) cannot be [fully] trusted as it started with subjects with problems, for example, children with psychological disorders or juvenile delinquents. Children of single parents can be as healthy and emotionally secure as those from traditional families.

Single-parent families mean "broken homes."

■ Parents who choose divorce or not marrying as a way of life aren't necessarily trying to make a broken home work. Many times, it turns out to be the healthiest choice to give children a peaceful and stable home environment. The outcome of single-parent families actually depends on the social network and support to the family and good communication within the family.

Being brought up in single-parent families is detrimental to children's self-esteem.

■ Children's self-esteem is often linked to the income level of the family. Parents can teach resilience and self-esteem skills to their children by being a model to them, boosting their self-respect and self-nurturance and making them realize that their possessions do not determine who they are.

Families need to be self-sufficient, while single-parent families aren't.

■ The emphasis on self-sufficiency often produces unnecessary shame and guilt in parents who are emotionally and financially challenged, including single parents. One has to learn to be interdependent, give and receive; taking our own responsibilities and asking for support and engaging even professional help when needed.

Source: Adapted from www.iloveindia.com/parenting/single-parenting/index.html.

delivery of social care services. A potential strategy is to increase peer-led interventions, which act to support existing informal networks.

The *duration* of poverty also plays a part. Long-term low income has especially harmful outcomes for children (Jones, Clark, Grusec, Hart, Plickert, and Tepperman, 2002). Persistent poverty, as well as workplace stress, increases parental stress and family conflict. It increases the likelihood of parental depression and hostile and ineffective parenting patterns—yelling, smacking, and providing no quality time or even time to help a child with homework. Poor parenting behaviours, in turn, produce undesirable child outcomes: reduced mental health (for example, more depression), worse physical health (for example, more physical injuries), and poorer school performance (for example, more school absences).

Finally, broader contextual factors influence the relationship between family processes and child outcomes. In neighbourhoods characterized by high levels of violence, social disorder, and fear, children experience greater internalizing problems, such as anxiety and depression (Caughy, Nettles, and O'Campo, 2008). Low-income families increasingly find themselves in these economically impoverished communities with a "negative social climate." Although a high degree of positive parental involvement can mitigate the neighbourhood effects on behaviour problems, it takes an enormous amount of effort and motivation to get access to appropriate resources for their children.

Gay and Lesbian Families

Until recently, most family studies ignored same-sex couple families and their parenting practices. Doing so resulted in an incomplete picture of what families are and do. As more countries accept or legalize gay and lesbian unions, the number of couples with two same-sex parents wishing to adopt or raise a child will naturally increase. Though a larger fraction of the public is coming to accept homosexuals, attitudes toward gay parents remain conservative, especially among older and rural people. Only around 20 percent of Canadians surveyed in Miall and March's (2005b) study, for example, were in favour of homosexuals adopting children, compared with the 92 percent who supported adoption by traditional married couples. Research finds stereotypical views about homosexuality even among young, highly educated people. These views include the beliefs that homosexual parents create a dangerous environment for the child, provide a less secure home, and offer less emotional stability. As far as we know and contrary to popular belief, gay and lesbian parents raise fine, healthy families as often as heterosexual families do (Wainwright, Russell, and Patterson, 2004).

Data are still rare on how many gay and lesbian couples are parenting children. Official definitions of family still often exclude gay and lesbian families. Besides, some gay and lesbian couples are not "out," preferring to keep their sexual preferences secret. During the 1980s, lesbian access to clinic-based donor insemination was limited because such access was thought to threaten both the traditional family and the medical definition of infertility. As a result, many people made insemination arrangements privately (Haimes and Weiner, 2000).

Lesbian couples would seem to be especially advantaged as parents. Apart from considerations of age, education, and health, lesbian couples have the luxury, for example, of deciding which partner will carry the child and how to create gender-unrelated parenting roles (Reimann, 1999). Also, as women, they would be more likely than men to have learned gender-related roles of nurturance.

However, gay/lesbian families face great challenges in being accepted by law and society. One well-publicized case—Ms. T. in Alberta in 1997—brought out previously unspoken but strongly held attitudes toward raising children in same-sex-couple families

(Abu-Laban, McIrvin, and McDaniel, 1998: 82). The Province of Alberta judged Ms. T., a woman who had successfully raised 17 foster children over many years, an unfit foster mother when authorities discovered that she had moved from a heterosexual to a lesbian relationship. They did not raise such questions about her capacity to parent when they saw her as heterosexual.

Many studies support the finding that gay and lesbian parents are just as capable in child rearing as heterosexual parents. Children raised by homosexual parents do not have different behavioural and educational outcomes than children of heterosexual unions, nor do they feel any less loved or accepted by their parents (Mattingly and Bozick, 2001). Rather, the quality of family relationships affects the child's well-being. Also, adolescent children of same-sex parents do as well as children of opposite-sex parents. The self-esteem levels, functioning in home and at school, and the romantic lives of these adolescents are the same despite family type (Wainwright, Russell, and Patterson, 2004). Further, there is no more chance of children growing up gay or lesbian in a same-sex family than in a heterosexual family (Mooney-Somers and Golombok, 2000; Fitzgerald, 1999).

Aboriginal Families

Understanding the parenting of Aboriginal families entails taking into consideration the large-scale disruption to their familial and cultural lives by the dominant Western society over the centuries. Frideres (in Cheal, 2007) has claimed that the familial organization of Aboriginal families and parenting has been profoundly altered on two separate occasions during the twentieth century. Firstly, Aboriginal children were forcibly removed from their families and moved to residential boarding schools under a government policy of assimilation, where Aboriginal children were no longer allowed to speak their own language or practise their spiritual values (Frideres in Cheal, 2007). The teachers, often members of religious groups or orders, served as "parents" to the children, who often did not see their own parents for up to 10 months a year. Some children never saw their parents. The residential school "parents," however, were strict disciplinarians. Children were forbidden to speak their own languages, wear their own clothes, or maintain cultural traditions or religions. Harsh punishment was meted out to children reluctant to obey their school masters (Bradbury, 2001).

Frideres (in Cheal, 2007) has stated that this has led to an underdevelopment of parenting skills by several generations of Canadian Aboriginals. More importantly, the government policy of assimilation has led to nearly three generations of Aboriginal families being destroyed by forced separations and caused many children to be alienated and removed from their parents' care. Furthermore, an important component of the assimilation of Aboriginal children was imposing upon them European ideals of marriage, sexuality, and patriarchy (Bradbury, 2001: 71). The priests/teachers/school authorities sometimes worked out arranged marriages for the children when they grew old enough (Fiske and Johnny, 1996). Essentially, these children were being resocialized for assimilation into mainstream society. This "experiment" in cultural domination has long since been declared a disaster—not only for Aboriginal families, who lost cultural traditions and often did not have or could not learn the skills needed to parent their own children, but for the entirety of Canadian society (Bradbury, 2001; Dickason, 2002). Claims for abuse and compensation are being made by the now adult children in Canada (see the Assembly of First Nations' Web site at www.afn.ca for details on these claims).

Secondly, during the 1960s and 1970s, another series of social service initiatives by provincial governments led to the removal of Aboriginal children from their homes to live with non-Aboriginal families (Frideres in Cheal, 2007). This in turn has had a large detrimental effect on Aboriginal families and parenting practices. As Cheah and Chirkov (2008: 407) have noted, the separation of Aboriginal children from their families has led to the breakdown of traditional Aboriginal child-rearing patterns and also the spread of cultural and parental knowledge throughout generations. This has led to many negative consequences, such as an increase in drug and alcohol dependency along with suicide among the Aboriginal population (Cheah and Chirkov, 2008: 407). Therefore, the breakup of Aboriginal families by government policy is also an example of how larger societal and political changes can impact familial functioning at the most basic level.

Custodial Grandparents

Grandparents can be valuable family members. Many two-parent families (with both parents working) depend on retired grandparents for child care. In this capacity, grandparents help to reduce stress for the parents, and especially for the mothers. For example, the stress of day-care dropoff and pickup is reduced if children are left with the grandparents. Many grandparents stock their home with toys, equipment, and goodies that their grandchildren enjoy.

Many of the cultures immigrating to Canada and the United States also place a high value on custodial grandparenting and—where available—parenting shared by extended families. Caring for children again comes with a unique set of opportunities. Older grandmothers believe they have more information about grandchildren than younger grandmothers, and women who become grandmothers later in life believe themselves to be stronger in teaching grandchildren (Watson, 1997). Research by Harrison, Richman, and Vittimberga (2000) finds that grandparents report lower levels of parental stress than parents from both single- and two-parent families.

Grandparents are especially effective because they give their children an opportunity to learn from skilled caregivers. Young mothers who live in three-generation households with their own mothers are also found to give their children better quality care than other young mothers (Cox, 2000).

Cultural Variation

Because of the recent immigration of many different cultures into countries such as Canada, much of the younger population today is made up of young immigrants who come from societies with high fertility rates. Many young people immigrate to start a family and a new life in their host country.

For people who are already parents before deciding to move, immigration poses many difficulties for parenting attitudes and practices. For instance, one study describes the stressful process of immigration to the United States for Mexican fathers (Behnke, Taylor, and Parra-Cardona, 2008). Most of these fathers face cultural and economic difficulties and experience the effects of these challenges on fathering, such as restructuring of parental roles and family dynamics.

These problems are of importance, since research has showed that father involvement is significant for positive development in all adolescents, whether from native-born or immigrant families (Bronte-Tinkew, Moore, Capps, and Zaff, 2006). For youth from immigrant families, father involvement and being a first-generation immigrant is associated with reduced risky behaviour such as substance abuse (Bronte-Tinkew et al., 2006). This may be because the fathers of these children hold strong cultural beliefs about use of alcohol or drugs, whereas youth that have integrated into the new culture may not hold such beliefs as dear.

Another example of the challenges of parenting in a new context is the cultural differences between the parents and their usually more acculturated child. Chinese mothers in a study by Buki, Ma, Strom, and Strom (2003) stated that the biggest challenge is the difference in adjustment to the new culture between them and their children.

Also, many children of immigrants face the challenge of balancing two cultures. Parental understanding about this conflict can greatly ease tension. According to Abad and Sheldon (2008), if fathers, typically the "instrumental caregivers" (meaning they are responsible for helping and encouraging the child to develop independence and generally become a functioning adult), support children in their wants and endeavours, children are much more likely to report greater well-being.

As well, some styles of parenting are significant for the well-being of both immigrant parents and children. As mentioned earlier, parenting styles are often different between Western and other cultures. Generally, Hispanic and Asian families have been shown to use authoritarian practices much more readily than North Americans of European descent (Varela, Sanchez-Sosa, Riveros, Vernberg, Mitchell, and Mashunkashey, 2004; Pong, Hao, and Gardner, 2005). For example, Chinese adolescents may report that their parents are warm but too controlling. In Shucksmith, Henry, and Glendinning's (1995) terms, we would characterize these Chinese parents as falling somewhere between authoritative and authoritarian. Further, European parents do not usually use physical punishment to discipline their children and are generally more accepting and supportive of their children's wishes about life choices (Jambunathan, Burts, and Pierce, 2000).

When some immigrant parents come to Canada, they often have trouble learning to loosen the child-parent tie—to accept more permissive standards of parenting, which children raised in North America come to expect. Because of an authoritarian parenting style, some children of immigrants report aggression in the parent-child relationship (Lau, Takeuchi, and Alegria, 2006).

In many cultures, parents exert a high degree of close control for extended periods. We often stereotype Jewish mothers for this quality. Research confirms that some

Famous Quotes about Parenthood

Every beetle is a gazelle in the eyes of its mother.
—Moorish proverb

God could not be everywhere and therefore he made mothers.
—Jewish proverb

An ounce of mother is worth a pound of clergy.
—Spanish proverb

A father is a banker provided by nature.
—French proverb

Parentage is a very important profession, but no test of fitness, for it is ever imposed in the interests of the Children.
—George Bernard Shaw

Parents are sometimes a bit of a disappointment to their children. They don't fulfill the promise of their early years.
—Anthony Powell

When one has not had a good father, one must create one.
—Friedrich Nietzsche

Who doesn't desire his father's death?
—Fyodor Dostoyevsky

The fundamental defect with fathers is that they want their children to be a credit to them.
—Bertrand Russell

Perhaps host and guest is really the happiest relation for father and son.
—Evelyn Waugh

The first half of our lives is ruined by our parents and the second half by our children.
—Clarence S. Darrow

I must study politics and war, that my sons may have the liberty to study mathematics and philosophy, geography, natural history, and naval architecture, navigation, commerce, and agriculture, in order to give their children a right to study painting, poetry, music, architecture, statuary, tapestry and porcelain.
—John Adams

Parents are the bones on which children cut their teeth.
—Peter Ustinov

Parents accept their obsolescence with the best grace they can muster . . . they do all they can to make it easy for the younger generation to surpass the older, while secretly dreading the rejection that follows.
—Christopher Lasch

Source: www.famousquotesandauthors.com/topics/parenthood_quotes.html.

groups—for example, Greek and Lebanese mothers—use this approach more often than other groups—for example, Vietnamese mothers. To describe the complete variety of cultural approaches to parenting, and its associated outcomes, would take a book in its own right. However, amid this panoply of approaches, the basic principles about good parenting stated earlier continue to apply, at least in the Canadian context.

CONCLUDING REMARKS

We have seen in this chapter that parenting has changed and continues to change. The ways in which people become parents, the processes by which they begin parenting, and the kinds of families into which children are born and live have all changed and diversified in recent years. The need for good parenting, however, remains.

Families are complex and important. How well families raise their children affects the kind of adults those children will become and the world we will live in. How well parents have managed to balance discipline and freedom will affect how the children act and feel when they become teenagers. In Canada, teenagers who see their parents as accepting and warm, and as less controlling, have higher self-esteem than other children. They are healthier and perform better in school. In turn, parents with higher self-esteem are more likely to give their children freedom and acceptance, and to have better communication with the children as a result.

Childhood experiences resonate through adult life. For example, children punished physically by their parents are more likely to grow up to be aggressive toward other family members. Treating children this way dramatically increases their potential for violence as teenagers. Nevertheless, not all family difficulties (or lucky breaks, for that matter) are the result of parental influences and choices. Many important forces are not under parental control. Sometimes factors beyond the parents' control, such as the sickness of a family member or a sudden change in socio-economic circumstances, interrupt the socialization.

Also, bear in mind that not only do parents socialize their children, but children socialize their parents too. Children's influence over their parents is more powerful under some conditions than others. For example, a parent who feels guilty about neglecting the child or about divorcing a spouse, or who feels unloved or emotionally insecure and therefore depends on the child for important gifts of affection and attention, may change parenting styles to get the wanted effect. Children's socialization of parents may also be healthy, with sensitive parents adapting their style to fit the child's personality.

As we have seen in this chapter, parenting makes a difference to the ways that children grow up. In the next chapter, we further explore a topic with much significance for both parent-child relations and the family as a whole: the domestic division of labour.

CHAPTER SUMMARY

In this chapter we have examined parenthood from the perspective of societies, parents, and children. Today most people have fewer children, reproduce at a later age, and compress their parenting into a smaller time frame than in the past, allowing more time for careers and family. We can plan our families in this way because of reliable contraceptive devices.

The teen pregnancy rate is low in Canada, compared with the United States. Teen preg-

nancy can lead to many difficulties later. For example, many teenage mothers never make up their lost opportunities. They may also be unable to provide good parenting.

Once you have a child you must be a parent, and as a parent, you are responsible for primary socialization during your child's first years. Gender socialization begins as soon as the parent knows the sex of the child, perhaps in utero. One of the jobs of the parent is to ready the child for entry into society, and some parents do it badly. Runaways are children who have judged their parents' parenting styles as so inadequate that they prefer life on the streets to life in the home of the parents.

Though class and cultural variation in styles of parenting remain, they are narrowing in many ways. The same principles of good parenting apply whatever the cultural group or class.

Key Terms

authoritarian parenting Parenting characterized by low acceptance and high control, which can hinder the development of expressiveness and independence in children.

authoritative parenting Parenting characterized by high acceptance and high control, which produces the best outcomes in children.

birth rate Number of births per 100 000 people in a given year.

control and supervision The extent to which parents oversee and censure their children's behaviour.

family cohesion A sense of attachment and relatedness among members of a family, both maintained and signified by shared activities, self-identification as a family member, and signs of familiarity and liking.

gender socialization The social learning process a person goes through to acquire gender roles and gender-based habits. This is usually done through family, peer groups, schools, and the mass media.

induction A form of discipline focused on using reason to encourage children to behave in certain ways in order to benefit themselves or others. For

example, a child will be told to put away her toys so that others will not trip over them.

internal moral control An emotional feeling, such as guilt, that inhibits non-compliance.

love withdrawal A form of punishment to a child for non-compliance, where a child is denied the expression of love.

parental involvement Spending time with children, talking about them, and thinking about them.

permissive parenting A type of parenting with high acceptance and low control.

power assertion Threatening a child with punishment, usually in physical form, for non-compliance.

primary socialization Learning that takes place during childhood.

socialization The social learning process a person goes through to become a capable, functioning member of society; to prepare for life in society.

unengaged parenting A type of parenting with low acceptance and low control.

Critical Thinking Questions

1. Why and how might the ways a society defines "family" affect people's attitudes toward child-bearing, contraception, adoption, and abortion?

2. How and why might literacy and education affect contraception, child-bearing, and parenting even in a society as developed as Canada?

3. What are the social pros and cons around medically assisted procreation? What ethical issues are likely to enter into "engineered" pregnancies?

4. How and why do parents socialize their children? How and why do children socialize their parents?

5. Are there conditions under which attachment to one's parents is likely to be a bad thing? Explain.

6. How should our society draw the line between fair and justified discipline, on the one hand, and child abuse, on the other?

7. How does homecare for a chronically sick child affect the family as a whole, and each

member of the family separately: the father, the mother, the sick child, his or her siblings?

8. Can different "kinds" of families—for example, two-parent versus one-parent families, cohabiting versus married parent families, heterosexual versus homosexual families, native-born versus immigrant families—parent their children equally well? Explain your answer.

Weblinks

Planned Parenthood
www.plannedparenthood.com
For more than 90 years, Planned Parenthood has promoted a common-sense approach to women's health and well-being, based on respect for each individual's right to make informed, independent decisions about sex, health, and family planning.

The Heritage Foundation
www.familyfacts.org
A religious-oriented site promoting positive values around a variety of family issues, including parenthood, marriage, and other related topics. It provides a continuous update of new research findings that support its message.

Parenthood.org
http://parenthood.org
Providing support for families and parents, this site is allegedly run by parents for parents and offers access to new text-audio-video-live cam chat and information boards on a variety of topics.

About: Toddlers
http://babyparenting.about.com/od/blogs/Blogs.htm
Here you will find blogs written by parents about the puzzling problems they face and solve daily.

Daily Strength
http://dailystrength.org/support-groups/Childrens-Health-Parenting
This site offers parents free, anonymous online parenting advice from "people just like you," on topics that include children's mental and physical health and developmental and learning disorders.

Dads of Michigan
www.dadsofmichigan.org/parenting.html
Dads of Michigan is dedicated to promoting the idea that "Fathers are parents too." It organizes local events, maintains a message board, and takes other practical steps to keep men active in their children's lives.

Parenthoodkids.com
www.parenthoodkids.com
This site is "designed for kids of *any age*, and even for the young at heart! You will find resourceful information about homeschooling, recipes for fun foods that kids love to make and eat, games to play online, and birthday party game suggestions as well as games for everyday fun."

Open Directory Project: Parenting
www.dmoz.org/Recreation/Humor/Parenting
This site is devoted to showing the humorous side of parenting, collecting together a variety of blogs, columns, and memorable quotes.

Chapter 7
Work and Family Life

Chapter Outline

This chapter will focus mainly on the family work done by intimate partners, for example, husbands and wives. We shall not consider the work of children or other family members— not because their contributions are unimportant but because of space considerations and limited data. Second, in this chapter we will return time and again to the stress caused by the conflicting demands of paid work, domestic work, and child care.

Housework and child rearing have not always been solely women's responsibility. In some past societies, men took a central role in caring for and raising children. The older idea of child rearing was that we should toughen children up for the real world, to earn a living to help the family, a task to which parents often put them at early ages. Besides, in the pre-industrial family, women were essential to market production. Women also worked on farms and provided a wide range of care, delivering babies, helping tend to the sick, and looking after people with disabilities or the severely ill. Women, then, were an important part of economic production in pre-industrial and early industrial societies, especially in the primary production sector of society.

The term "housework" came into being only with the rise of industrial capitalism, when unpaid domestic labour became distinguished from paid labour. While women could work for pay outside the home, in the nineteenth century skilled working-class men sought to bar women from trade unions. Housework as we define it is, thus, not a carry-over from precapitalist life or a creation of capitalism. It is the result of an interaction between capitalism and patriarchy that allowed men to defend their privileges under new economic and social conditions (Jackson, 1992).

From the beginning, housework has been hard work for women. As historian Susan Strasser, author of the classic *Never Done: A History of American Housework*, has noted about colonial America,

> Women spun wool and flax, wove cloth, sewed it into clothing, grew food and pre-pared it for eating or storage, and made soap and candles. Other family members shared those tasks and (according to a gendered division of labor) worked in adjoining fields and small crafts shops. The colonial household, then, served as the central institution of economic production (Strasser, 2006).

Women's work played an important part in Alberta's settlement history. Within the agricultural communities, gender roles were restricted, with the expectation that women should be "caring, nurturing, and domestically proficient" whereas "the good male farmer is tough, hard-working, and in control of his environment." (Heather, Skillen, Young, and Vladicka, 2005: 89). Thus, in the late nineteenth and early twentieth centuries, while males went out seeking work, women stayed home, acting as "community builders" and ensuring the survival of the family's farm.

Nineteenth-century farm families spent much of their time repairing household supplies and equipment. Upper- and middle-class families, who could afford it, hired domestic help, especially for tasks like laundry and work involving special skills (Strasser, 2006). However, in other homes these household tasks were performed by the homemaker and her daughters. Even non-farm women performed a significant economic role in household food production. Although the husband earned the wages, female home support always made an important contribution to family finances (Armitage, 1979). And not only was the domestic work heavy in these households, it was never-ending. Nearly every chore meant building a fire and hauling water, for example.

Interestingly, although these farm women were often involved in activities that resisted the traditional roles expected of them, they tended to reject a feminist label. Taking on a feminist identity would have resulted in tension and social rejection (Heather et al., 2005). Instead, these women continued their proactive role within the community, revolutionizing and improving the lives of agriculturalists.

Yet women had mixed feelings about their gruelling role as domestic labourers. Consider the author and editor L. M. Child (1802–1880). Although she criticized the drudgery of domestic work, she also idealized it. Like her contemporaries, Child saw women as upholders of society's moral standards. By ensuring domestic and social tranquillity, women preserved the family unit. As Child's letters reveal, women did not necessarily feel oppressed by this responsibility (Jeffrey, 1975).

In modern rural households, housework is still divided, but the family is involved in nearly all its aspects. Valdivia and Gilles (2001) found that rural families constantly negotiate access to natural resources, labour, capital, knowledge, and markets. Unsuccessful negotiation threatens family survival and reduces biodiversity, as seen in studies from Latin America, Asia, Africa, and North America. Women there are major sources of family well-being, but they are also stewards of natural and productive resources, highlighting the influence rural women have on the environment and society (Valdivia and Gilles, 2001).

The twentieth century saw a surge toward the industrialization of farming, especially the incorporation of technology, science, and global markets into agriculture (Heather et al., 2005). And shifts toward enlarging and intensifying agriculture continue to alter the relationship between rural communities and farming (Smithers and Johnson, 2004). New farming methods have replaced traditional ones by increasing capital and technology; and much change has also resulted from new policies and rules around environmental sustainability and food quality (Smithers and Johnson, 2004).

Yet, as globalization has progressed, federal government support for agriculture in Canada has been reduced. Without new economic regulations, farming families now find it more difficult to succeed financially in a competitive economy (Smithers and Johnson, 2004). For example, in a survey conducted by Smithers, Johnson, and Joseph (2004), most farmers noted the cost of farmland was increasing due to the reduced scale of operations and more competition between neighbouring farms.

As described in Chapter 2, not only did industrialization change the lives of rural families, but it also brought an influx of people into urban areas. However, it was only with the arrival of the urban bourgeois family that the idea of home as a retreat emerged. This change came about through separation of the workplace from the home, new definitions of women as homemakers and full-time mothers, and a growing industry that catered to home efficiency. By contrast, working-class families remained less insulated from the workplace. Rather than serving as a refuge, working-class homes served mainly to reproduce the capitalist workforce, thus linking domestic and work life (Hareven, 1991). In the working-class family, households and the economy interpenetrated each other, linking the personal and the political (Armstrong and Armstrong, 1985).

Much of the change in family roles that we associate with modern life can be traced to the rise of urban, industrial society. New "labour-saving" appliances—the electric iron and the vacuum cleaner, for example—eased women's entry into paid work. By the 1920s, the urban middle-class had available many of our familiar household conveniences, including hot and cold running water, gas stoves, washing machines, refrigerators, and vacuum cleaners (Mintz, 2006). As mass-produced clothing became available and desirable and more women worked outside the home, fewer women sewed out of necessity. Home sewing moved beyond its purely functional role to become a way of expressing personal tastes (Gordon, 2004).

Ironically, with the spread of new household technology, the time spent on housework did not lessen. Time saved on cooking and cleaning was used instead for shopping, household management, and child care. The responsibility for these tasks still fell on individual households, and became an even greater concern as increased numbers of married women took paid work outside the home (Strasser, 2006). Oddly, the resulting stresses became personal problems and did not yield collective solutions. Housework remains one of the few technological realms in which decentralization continues—because women are the principal workers in households (Cowan, 1979).

Meanwhile, standards of housework rose. The evolution of laundering practices in both urban and rural areas in the nineteenth century, for example, reflects the evolution of the bourgeois cult of cleanliness as a condition for all public appearances. New cleanliness norms served as instruments for social control and normalization. The "hygiene revolution" of the late nineteenth and early twentieth centuries led to a wider acceptance of the ideal of cleanliness, and put pressure on women to keep their families clean and well groomed (Laermans and Meulders, 1998).

Increasingly, with the spread of new technology, women were called on to learn and practise home economics—a form of education that many viewed as preparation for social reform (Apple and Coleman, 2003). Women's institutes tried to redefine domestic labour as skilled, giving women status (Morgan, 1996). The professionalization of traditional domestic skills served as a means of raising women's social standing, largely through the application of something like Frederick Taylor's scientific management methods to housework (Turnbull, 1994; Strasser, 1978).

So, industrialization simplified many household tasks, allowing women to do more in less time. However, rather than enjoying spare time as a result, time use studies show that women devoted the same amount of time as ever to their housework. People now expect women to make their homes attractive out of love rather than any interest in market rewards. The fusing of love with domestic consumerism and household duties for women changed forever the relations between the sexes on the domestic front. Campaigns to promote the new household technologies highlighted the love ingredient of housework, lest women abandon their domestic work with the "mechanization" of housework (Fox, 1993: 151).

As mentioned earlier, home economists worked to raise the esteem of homemakers by promoting the idea that new home technologies needed skilled operators. High standards of cleanliness were associated with health and children's well-being. Concerns about the home being too dirty for curious young children led mothers to assume responsibility for cleaning as part of their identity as women (Fox, 2001). Society charged homemakers with the duty of health promotion, a noble cause but unpaid and hugely undervalued. With this "scientization" of housework, women were assigned the role of preserving the home as their central lifework, with limited access through their homemaking skills to the markets they had enjoyed before industrialization. This was evident, for example, in the influential writings of Charlotte Perkins Gilman, who around the end of the nineteenth century was imagining—or we should say, re-imagining—the future organization of work in households. Among other things, she imagined a much more communal connection among families and households.

But her imaginings did not come to fruition. To go with a growing drive to consume, women began to take paid jobs outside the home to increase the family income. This need for outside work coincided with a growing demand for women workers in factories, especially during the Second World War, and for even more in offices from the 1920s onward. The development of new office technology lessened the need for strength (and often skill) that had characterized earlier forms of work, making possible the vast movement of new female workers into the public, paid workforce.

THE WORTH OF HOUSEWORK

For various reasons, as the twentieth century progressed, people began to ask questions about the value of the domestic work they had been doing. Some thought that mechanized homemaking could be valued like work outside the home and factored into calculations of the gross national product. Others argued, in contrast, that we could measure housework but still should not include it as a market exchange, since the work done by women at home ought to be freely provided. Yet the amounts in question are enormous.

In 1995, for example, the United Nations estimated that unpaid work carried out by women around the world would translate to $11 trillion at fair market value (Nova Scotia Advisory Council on the Status of Women, 2000).

For the first time in any country in 1996, a government recognized unpaid work by including questions on it in the Census. In the Census of Canada sample of one in five households, all respondents aged 15 and older, excluding full-time residents of institutions, were asked to report the number of hours spent in the previous week doing (1) unpaid housework, (2) unpaid child care, and (3) unpaid care or help to seniors. They were also invited to identify "periods when [they] were carrying out two or three of these activities at the same time." It remains to be seen whether this practice of "counting housework" will catch on widely.

Another important step in recognizing unpaid work was the payment of family allowances discussed in Chapter 2. Although family allowances (begun in Canada after World War II) were meant to buy needed items for children, they were also a small way to give women payment and recognition for child-rearing. These monthly payments, based on the number of children at home, went to all women with children—but only to women, never to men. For many women who worked solely at home, this was their only independent income. These payments may also have served to perpetuate the gendered division of labour. Quebec alone now continues with some form of family allowances (Le Bourdais and Marcil-Gratton, 1994).

However, the federal government stopped its program of family allowances in 1992, replacing it with the Child Tax Credit program, which targets low- and middle-income families. Quebec intended its own program of baby bonuses both to increase the numbers of births and to provide support for women raising children. One must keep in mind that the amounts paid in no way compensate for the costs involved in raising a child. However, they gave important recognition to the important, mainly unpaid work that Canadian women contribute to the economy.

The More Things Change

Women still do most of the housework. Wives, whatever their employment status, consistently do about twice as much housework as husbands do (Davies and Carrier, 1998). Husbands with children whose spouses work full-time engage in more unpaid work than husbands with children whose wives are not working full-time (Hook, 2006). Yet even so, the distribution of domestic labour is far from equal; the greatest share of unpaid work by married men did not exceed 37 percent in any of the 20 countries Hook surveyed. Nakhaie (1995) finds that when husbands' work hours increase beyond 30 hours a week, their contribution to housework decreases; but when women's work hours increase beyond 30 hours a week, their proportionate contribution to housework *increases*. Though husbands with fewer paid hours have more time to do the tasks, instead of doing more housework, they wait for their spouses to complete those tasks—even if those spouses work longer hours!

Because women have the primary responsibility for domestic work, they are undertaking a "double day" (Armstrong and Armstrong, 1994) when they enter the labour force—especially if they are mothers. (Most mothers of young children are in the paid labour force.) As a result, many women have little leisure time and have difficulty separating it from work time. "The ensuing exhaustion of women encourages dissatisfaction, especially when their partners do not share the responsibility of work in the home" (Armstrong and Armstrong, 1994: 227).

On farms, women often work a "triple day," since they have to care for the household, the farm, and possibly hold a job outside the home as well (Martz, 2007). As Irish sociologist Patricia O'Hara (1998: 37) notes, it is no wonder farm women have been advising their daughters to leave the rural areas, and especially agriculture.

An unequal domestic division of labour is also evident among Aboriginal peoples in Canada. For many Aboriginal communities, including the Inuit living in eastern Arctic settlements, modernization has led some to speculate that traditional gender roles—especially the division of labour within the household—may change drastically. For men in these communities, modernization has meant the transition from hunting to a wage economy (McElroy, 1975).

However, Inuit women were slow to alter their traditional domestic roles within the household, even though some had also taken on paid work. Sociologists have noted this relative stability of women's roles within the household, despite cultural change. Some studies suggested that Inuit women may feel isolated and alienated by the changes around them. However, in McElroy's (1975: 682) study, young Inuit women began to move toward a stronger acceptance of Euro Canadian values, with many seeking more wage employment, higher levels of education, and later marriage than before. Since then, the domestic division of labor has continued to change in Inuit communities, as elsewhere.

Men contribute to domestic work too, but their contribution is most notably on household maintenance and repairs. Often, less time overall is spent on these kinds of tasks than women spend on day-to-day housework and child care. Two more factors matter in how men's contributions to the home play out in society. First, men can often postpone these sorts of household tasks until time allows. This means that men's work at home is less constraining than women's. Second, and importantly, no one sees men's work at home as defining them in the way that women's does. Men who fix up and care for their homes are less often defined by that work, whereas some people still define women as wives and mothers first and workers second.

Domestic work is a mirror of what society expects of men and of women (Oakley, [1974] 1985). Getting beyond the power of gendering is not easy for couples, even for New Age postmodern couples. Besides, gendering in the paid workforce often promotes gendered work at home.

However, inequality in domestic work is not merely a result of patriarchal culture, as shown by the similarity of arrangements in gay and lesbian couples. Unlike heterosexual couples, factors such as income, education, and time availability have little bearing on the distribution of tasks among homosexual couples (Illig, 1999). Division of labour practices among gay and lesbian families are not based on gender; yet the division of household work is not egalitarian (Oerton, 1998): often a pattern of primary breadwinner/primary caregiver emerges. This suggests the inequitable division of household labour in opposite-sex families is a result not of patriarchal values and traditions alone, but of the demands of child rearing and an unequal contribution of time to the paid labour force.

Figure 7.1 provides data from a recent Canadian report on the changing nature of the family workweek (Marshall, 2009). Several important trends in the past 30 years can be noted here. First, note the change in hours worked. In 1976, couples spent a total of 57.6 hours in paid work per week; by 2008, this number had increased by 13 percent to 64.8 hours (Figure 7.1a). Household heads were not necessarily working longer; rather, there were more income contributors within the average family—usually, two adults.

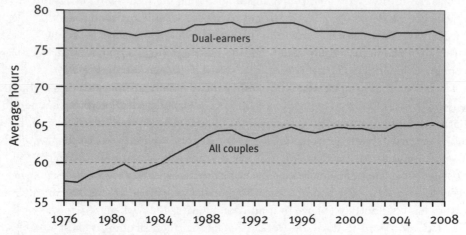

(a) The increase in total family work hours is due to more dual-earners, but the dual-earners' hours are stable.

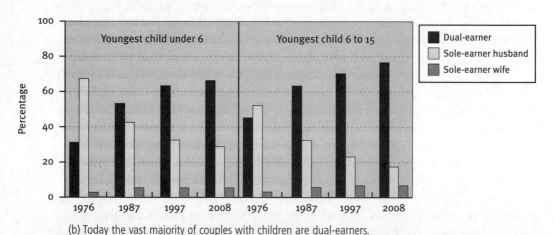

(b) Today the vast majority of couples with children are dual-earners.

Figure 7.1 The changing nature of the family workweek in Canada

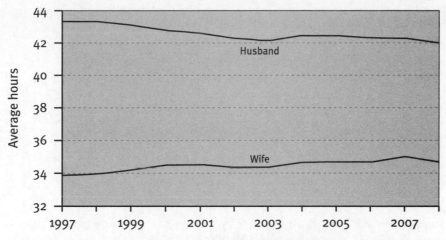

(c) Slight but steady narrowing of dual-earner hours since the late 1990s.

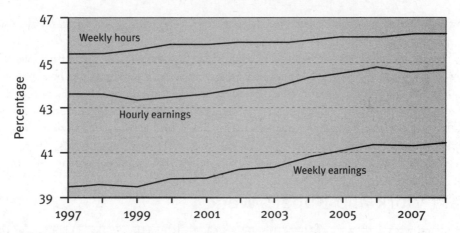

(d) Dual-earner wives' contribution to family hours and earnings increasing.

Figure 7.1 (*Continued*)

Source: Katherine Marshall. 2009. The family work week. *Statistics Canada Perspectives*, Catalogue no. 75-001-X. Retrieved from www.statcan.gc.ca/pub/75-001-x/2009104/pdf/10837-eng.pdf.

Accordingly, the data in Table 7.1 show a large increase in the number of dual-earner families in the last three decades—a jump from just over one-third to three-quarters of all couples in 2008. **Dual-earner couples** work an average of 77 hours per week—nearly twice the number of hours of a **single-earner couple**. This suggests that, in most dual-earner couples, both spouses are working close to full-time.

What's more, most of the families with children are dual-earners, a statistic that has been on a steady rise since the mid-1970s (Figure 7.1b). This means that most families now have less time available to engage in unpaid work and leisure activities—for example, in housework, cooking, or child-care. Parents are under more pressure to negotiate

Table 7.1 The Degree of Labour Participation Varies by Age and Family Status

	Total 15+	Age groups			
		15–24	25–54	55–64	65+
All members of economic families	69%	65%	86%	59%	9%
Family head	71	76	86	59	10
Spouse of head	71	81	88	61	11
Child of head	66	62	82	56	*
Other relative of head	53	65	80	52	4
Unattached individuals	60	77	86	56	6

Source: Roger Sauvé. 2009. *Family life and work life: An uneasy balance.* Ottawa: Vanier Institute of the Family. Retrieved from www.vifamily.ca/library/work/sauve/worklife.pdf.

how they divide their time at home, especially their caregiving, and this pressure can be a source of stress and conflict, as we will see later in the chapter.

Finally, on a more positive note, it seems that the number of hours partners work is now converging (Figure 7.1c). There may be several reasons for this, including "changes in the industrial and occupational structure, educational attainment and labour market opportunities, and individual and family preference and choice . . . These trends are more likely to affect men's average hours since they have traditionally been more likely to work long hours." (Marshall, 2009: 8). However, wives' earnings are also increasing (Figure 7.1d), signalling the beginning of a change in breadwinning roles (Marshall, 2009).

Paid Work and Unpaid Work

Gendered work is slow to change. Despite a steady advance in gender equality over the past several decades, discrimination against women remains an important problem. Gender stereotyping and inequality continue in the workplace. A *glass ceiling* results in earning differences between women and men. Because of stereotypes of women as largely nurturing and emotional, and of men as more dominant and rational, some women have been excluded from jobs that call for a broad education and skill development. For these reasons, even today, women are still under-represented in leadership positions.

"Women's work"—clerical jobs, sales, light manufacturing, and the catchall category of "service work," which includes nurses' aides and grade-school teachers, waitresses, and welfare caseworkers—pays poorly. In general, women's work not only pays less than men's but also is less inflation-proof. The occupational segregation of women in our society makes for an important difference between women's poverty and men's. For men, poverty is often a result of unemployment, and is curable by getting a job. But for women, concentrated in the low-wage stratum of the workforce, a job may not erase poverty, only reduce it. The low wages and job instability of the secondary work sector often mean that even full-time workers live in poverty.

Women's financial contribution to the economic well-being of families cannot be overstated. Many families need women's wages to keep the family from poverty. Without the contribution of women's wages, the number of families with low income in 1994 would have more than doubled to 400 000 from 184 000 (Statistics Canada, 1996b). However, many continue to ignore the significance of this contribution. Armstrong and Armstrong (1994: 225) argue compellingly that the nature of women's work in the home and in the labour force reinforces and perpetuates the division of labour by gender.

Yet, some studies have shown that participation in the labour force can have benefits for women, such as improved self-esteem, mental and physical health, and status and resources (Tingey, Kiger, and Riley, 1996). Besides, as women do better economically, their families do too. Cohen (1998) found that in families where women have higher incomes and occupational status, the families spend more money on housekeeping services and dining out. Though this choice is more popular among wealthier and white families, it is still one way that women can reduce the stress of the double day.

Finally participation in the labour force is not uniform across the lifespan. Figure 7.1 shows that participation is highest among family heads and their partners (71 percent), followed by their children (66 percent). Further, participation is at its peak for people aged 25 to 55, when 86 percent of adult family members are working for pay. Participation drops to 59 percent for people aged 55 to 64 and then down to less than 10 percent for people more than 65 years old (Sauvé, 2009).

Canadian Workforce Trends

- Women are still more likely than men to work part-time, drop out of the paid workforce, or hold two paid jobs to support the family. In 2006, 32 percent of female Canadians said they were working part-time to care for children or meet other personal or family responsibilities, while only 6 percent of males cited these reasons (Sauvé, 2009).

- Dual-earner couples are now the dominant family form, comprising 7 out of 10 couples in 2008. With more contributors to the family income, the overall family work hours have increased and the disposable family time has thus been reduced (Marshall, 2009).

- Increased work time means less family time. The average time spent with family members on a typical workday has shrunk from 250 minutes per day in 1986 to 206 minutes in 2005—a drop of 18 percent (Sauvé, 2009).

- Seventy percent of mothers with children younger than the age of six are taking part in the labour force, an increase from 25 percent in 1965 (Human Resources and Skills Development Canada, 2005a).

- One-quarter of dual-earner men and one-third of dual-earner women report feeling severely time stressed, but given the choice of fewer hours, most say that they prefer their current number or even more hours (Marshall, 2009).

- The peak participation in the labour force is seen among people aged 25 to 54. This "core age" group, which makes a critical contribution to the economy, will grow by less than 10 percent in the next 20 years, resulting in a likely labour shortage (Sauvé, 2009).

DOMESTIC WORK: CARING FOR FAMILY MEMBERS AND HOME

Child Care

As the work lives of women and men become more similar (although, as we have seen, not yet identical), child care becomes the great divide on the domestic scene. Baker and Lero (1996: 103) argue that "the gender-structured nature of the labour market, differential use of parental and child-rearing leave by men and women, and different gender expectations by families and communities preserve the unequal sharing of economic and social parenting."

Not only does the presence of a child or children add to domestic demands; with the arrival of children, parents often take on particular gendered roles. We tend to see practical day-to-day parenting as women's work, and specialized economic responsibilities as men's work—in part because women are typically the lower earners. Thus, one study finds that parenthood had no effect on husbands' employment or housework hours; in contrast, motherhood increases wives' housework hours and reduces employment hours (Sanchez and Thomson, 1997).

Parents seldom share child care equally (Wilson, 1996). Statistics Canada data (cited in Armstrong and Armstrong, 1994: 10) reveal that women are almost three times as likely as men to give physical care to children younger than the age of 5 and two-and-a-half times as likely to provide care for children between ages 5 and 18. The 2001 National Work-Life Conflict Study funded by Health Canada reported that 63 percent of female respondents had primary responsibility for child care, compared to 6 percent of male respondents (Higgins and Duxbury, 2002). These numbers have not changed much from their 1991 study.

This is not to say that men contribute nothing to child care. On the contrary, in the past decade, more and more men have spent unpaid time caring for children younger than age 15, with 79.5 percent currently doing so—nearly comparable to the 86 percent of women who do so (Statistics Canada, 2006i: 31). Yet, women remain much more likely to spend *longer hours* in unpaid child care. For example, in 2006, nearly half of the women (47.3 percent) with a child younger than age 15 spent 30 or more hours a week caring for children, compared with just over one-fifth (21.8 percent) of men who did the same (Statistics Canada, 2006i: 31).

Working in the paid labour force is difficult for women if they are also minding young children. Even if they make satisfactory child-care arrangements, the plans often fall apart if the child gets sick, as most children do at some point. Such times reveal who is finally responsible for child care, as many—especially men—still consider care of a sick child to be women's work (Wylie, 200). Many still expect women to take the time from work to do the caring, though few people expect the same of men.

Women often must fulfil the family's nurturing, caring roles, especially toward family members who are ill or have disabilities. This is especially true in rural areas, where people have shorter life expectancies and higher rates of disability, and experience more accidents, poisonings, and incidents of violence than their urban counterparts (Edelman and Menz, 1996; Sutherns, McPhedran, and Haworth-Brockman, 2004).

Wathen and Harris (2007) examine the issue of women's health within a rural setting in their paper "I Try to Take Care of It Myself." They find that, either from a sense of self-reliance or feelings of helplessness, women use both formal and informal sources of information to deal with health problems. The authors debate the notion of patient empowerment, questioning whether the idea of collaboration between patients and doctors is realistic, due to the time constraints of professionals. They conclude that, to serve rural residents adequately, reliable on-line information, featuring the participation of health and information professionals, is needed (Wathen and Harris, 2007).

Because of women's family care responsibilities, some employers are reluctant to hire women with young children, especially single mothers. The National Childcare Study in Canada (cited by Armstrong and Armstrong, 1994: 106) found that each added child lowers the chance that a single parent will be employed.

With most mothers of young children in the paid labour force, young children need care while parents work. The National Childcare Study (Baker and Lero, 1996: 89) reports that care is needed for 64 percent of families with one child younger than age 13, 59.3 percent of families with two children younger than age 13, and 48.3 percent of families with three or more children younger than age 13. The gap between demand (estimated to be 2.2 million) and supply of licensed child-care spaces (333 000) is huge. Only 15 percent of the children who need care have access to it (Baker and Lero, 1996: 91).

A lack of access to quality, low-cost child care creates stress for all parents. However, low-income single mothers are especially vulnerable because "without subsidies to help cover the costs of child care, paid work may not be financially feasible for lone mothers earning minimum wage" (Mason, 2003: 49). The lone mothers who enter and remain in the labour market either receive assistance from mothers, sisters, or friends or they work in family-friendly environments (Mason, 2003).

An alternative to low-cost child care is grandparental care of their grandchildren. However, whether the participation of the older generation reduces the stress associated with child rearing and employment demands for mothers is unclear. The effects of grandparents in the household are illustrated in a study of Taiwanese immigrants conducted in Vancouver. Sun (2008) finds that grandparental child-care assistance is appreciated differently by mothers and fathers, with mothers preferring help from their own mothers and not their mothers-in-law. Fathers, on the other hand, are just as happy to receive help from their own parents and their parents-in-law. Sun (2008) also suggests that mothers may feel ambivalent about receiving the older generation's assistance. However, this is hard to assess since mothers-in-law hold authority over daughters-in-law, preventing any direct communication of the daughters-in-laws' views and grievances.

On balance, however, child care by parents improves with help from the older generation. In most families, fathers continue to serve mainly as economic providers, seemingly disconnected from issues of child care when the older generation is available. Overall, this study shows that help from paternal grandparents encourages mothers to play more active roles outside the home, while providing a nurturing environment for the children of employed mothers. However, this also reinforces the traditional gendered division of child-care labour in the family.

Elder Work and Care: Emerging Challenges at Home

Despite increased life expectancies for older people, widowhood is still a prevalent reality for older women. Widowhood has been deemed one of life's most stressful events, requiring more adaptation than any other life transition (Thompson, Breckenridge, Gallagher, and Peterson, 1984). With the death of a spouse, the partner left behind has to not only deal with the pain and grief caused by the loss of their significant other, but must also reconstruct their identity as a newly single person. This will, among other things, entail alterations in the daily tasks and routine responsibilities that were once shared by the couple.

Research on the daily routines of older (age 65 and older) bereaved persons (Utz et al., 2004) examined the effect of gender on housework changes after the loss of a spouse. The authors find that, compared to married men, widowers perform significantly more housework, while widows perform significantly less housework than married women. Specifically, bereaved husbands do nearly 7 more hours of housework than married men, in contrast to bereaved wives, who do 3.5 hours less than married women. Further, the study finds that although changes in the health status of a spouse lead to increased participation by husbands in housework, they do not significantly reduce women's performance of housework. No matter what happens (short of death), women are still expected to keep up the household. These findings show that throughout the life course, traditional domestic roles resist change.

Care of older members has become a major source of stress in Canadian families. Increased life expectancies among the old-old (those older than age 85) have meant the demand for care has increased. However, the inability of public funds for health and social services to keep up with this demand has limited the choices available for care (Fast, Keating, Oakes, and Williamson, 1997). Thus, many families view elder care as a private responsibility that they must fulfil. Increasingly, the burden for elder care has fallen on the shoulders of middle-aged women, most of whom are in the paid workforce. If even some of these caregivers give up paying jobs to provide informal care, the long-term societal effects may be serious, with older women having fewer pension rights and possibly a greater risk of poverty. In short, since poverty is a greater risk for women than for men, especially for single mothers, enormous problems over the life course may burden women we ask to take on more caregiving for older family members.

Another factor contributing to the stress caused by elder care is inadequate communication. Few children want to talk to their parents about death, inheritance plans, or funeral plans. One study found that almost 80 percent of elderly mothers had not discussed future caregiving preferences with their adult daughters and did not feel they needed to. They felt their daughters had already learned their preferences through long-term interaction with the mother or by watching them provide care to an earlier generation

(Pecchioni, 2001). This lack of communication can lead to strain and unhappiness later, especially if the mothers and children have different ideas about what the mother prefers.

Also, family sizes have shrunk over the last few decades. This is pressing in Asian countries (for example, Japan, Korea) that follow the Confucian tradition of filial piety, and among immigrants to Canada from these countries. The capacity and willingness of children to honour traditional elder-care duties is compromised both by the demands of the modern workplace and by a growing shortage of siblings.

Nowhere is this care shortage more marked than in China, owing in part to the Chinese one-child policy. Not only are Chinese children less willing today to care for their aging parents, but they are also less willing to honour any of the traditional practices of an extended family. For example, they are less willing to live with grandparents and less willing to share the same household with their parents when they become older and more dependent (Zhan, 1998). Many of these children also fear that, on marrying, they may become long-term caregivers for as many as four older parents.

Similar problems arise in Canada for adult children whose parents have divorced and remarried. Their duty to care for older parents and step-parents (also grandparents and step-grandparents) is problem enough (Ganong-Coleman, 1998). Extra divorces add further strain, especially when these children are trying to build their careers, protect their own marriages, and raise their own children.

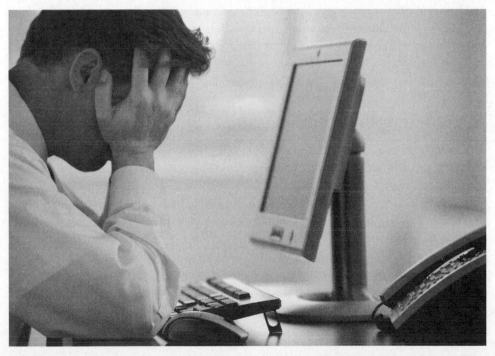

High levels of stress, whether work-related or due to marital hostility, decrease both work productivity as well as family functioning.

With the large baby boom generation getting older, many families find themselves part of what we call the "sandwich generation"—they are caring for both dependent children and older parents. Thirteen percent of respondents in the 2001 National Work-Life Conflict Study were part of this group (Higgins and Duxbury, 2002). The number is likely to grow as the population continues to age and as young adults stay at home for longer periods of time (Statistics Canada, 2002i). Most dual-earner couples, facing increased role demands, reduce their engagement in other roles so as to meet increased demands on their time and energy (Cullen, Hammer, Neal, and Sinclair, 2009).

At the same time, today many older people are also responsible for caring for their grandchildren. In fact, in the United States, more grandparents than ever before are raising their grandchildren in the absence of their biological parents (Mills, Gomez-Smith, and De Leon, 2005). Often, caring for grandchildren causes psychological distress, especially for grandmothers. This distress is amplified by having a family income below the poverty level, not receiving welfare payments for child-care, and not having a usual place to receive health care (Mills et al., 2005).

This family situation is paralleled in Canada. Between 1991 and 2001, there was a 20 percent increase in the number of Canadian children younger than age 18 living solely with their grandparents. Further, this arrangement is especially common in families of First Nations origin, including North American Indians, Métis, and Inuit, with one-third of First Nations Canadian grandparents raising two or more grandchildren. In comparison to other grandparent caregivers, First Nations custodial caregivers are also more likely to be simultaneously caring for a senior, and spending more than 30 hours each week on child-care and housework responsibilities (Fuller-Thomson, 2005).

Overall, caring for another family member, whether it be an older parent, a child, or a grandchild, is a major stress factor for Canadian families in the realm of domestic work.

Economic Independence and Domestic Work

The movement toward greater household equality is a slow, complex process, as is any change of practices within a family. In part, this is because husbands translate their income advantage into a sharp division of labour at home. So, women's growing economic independence does not translate readily into independence from domestic work. Some wives have discovered that earning an income—even a good income—is not enough in itself to change the housework a spouse does.

Sociologists have found that increases in women's paid work alter authority relations between husbands and wives. Wives who work for pay see themselves as having (and do have) more bargaining power in the relationship. For example, employed spouses are more likely to have an equal voice in decisions about major purchases (Baker and Lero, 1996: 97–98).

Researchers, responding to public concern, have thoroughly studied the results of mothers' paid work. Few question the effects on children of *men's* paid employment. But many believe that women who work must necessarily be neglecting their families.

Does maternal employment affect the emotional and psychological development of children? On the positive side, some research finds that school-aged children and adolescents with working mothers hold fewer stereotyped ideas about male and female roles, and daughters of these mothers are more achievement-oriented. On the negative side, some research finds that children whose mothers work for pay are more likely than other children to experience "insecure attachment" to their mothers.

Likely, a child's insecurity is correlated with the quality time he or she spends with parents, starting at an early age. Bonding develops over time and is based on long-term expressions of love, caring, communication, and active listening. All children need this love, supervision, and discipline. Whenever parents fail adequately to provide for these needs, their children will suffer. Setting aside time for quality interactions with children is important, especially for working parents. When parents are unable or unwilling to do this, it becomes a family problem—no less a father's problem than a mother's problem.

Children's overall adjustment, however, depends not on the mother's employment alone, but also on both parents' attitudes toward the mother working. Enjoyable features of work— such as the complexity of work with people, the challenge, and the stimulation—all contribute to good parenting (for example, gentler discipline, more warmth, and responsiveness).

Research shows that women with especially challenging, interesting, and complex jobs have less troubled or delinquent children—because the moms are happier with their lives and work. The economic benefits of employment, and opportunities for workplace autonomy that improve parenting skills, overshadow the disadvantages that stem from decreased time working mothers spend with their children (Cooksey, Menaghan, and Jekielelek, 1997: 658). And although we have described the stress working women face, filling multiple roles does not *necessarily* cause stress. What determines whether a working mother feels stressed and whether this stress harms the family is whether the working mother feels she has control over her life (Tingey, Kiger, and Riley, 1996). Anything that makes good parents healthier and happier in the long run makes the children healthier and happier.

The Effects of Domestic Work on Paid Work

Many Canadians assume that women are mainly responsible for work at home. As a result, they imagine that women will have weak connections with, and weak commitment to, the paid labour market. And some evidence supports this supposition. Mothers, for example, take greater advantage of parental and family leaves, **flextime**, and "family-friendly" workplace policies than do fathers, largely to care for dependent children. Women also more often turn down work that requires travel, or decline transfers or promotions that mean a geographical move, because of their responsibilities for children and families. Of course, if men were primary caregivers, they would act the same as women do in the workplace. And if raising children were equally shared and socially promoted, women might take less time off and men take more, to balance each other out.

Fathers currently tend to contribute to family welfare by increasing their paid work rather than by increasing their contributions to domestic work. Though they are more likely than mothers to move from one job to another or one employer to another, they are less likely than mothers to leave a job (or employer) or change to part-time work because of increased family responsibilities. Men still earn more, so it seems to make sense for women, who are typically paid less, to cut back hours.

One result of their primary responsibility for domestic work means that women who spend their adult lives caring for families and homes are unlikely to build up their own economic resources through savings, pensions, contacts, or job status. For this reason, divorce and widowhood are harder on women. Widows who spend their adult lives in **family work**—including, increasingly, caring for a severely ill or dying spouse—typically find themselves without any pension. After years of working as homemakers, women whose marriages end in divorce all too often fall quickly into poverty. Economic dependence also makes it difficult for women to leave an unhappy marriage or abusive relationship.

The gendering of domestic work also affects custody arrangements after divorce. One study found that working mothers (whether full-time or part-time) are more likely to share their children's care with a former spouse (Juby, Le Bourdais, and Marcil-Gratton, 2005). Fathers are also more likely to gain full custody when their former wife is successfully integrated into the workforce, especially if these men were involved in the home during marriage. Thus, a more equal division of household labour and workforce participation can improve the economic condition of divorced mothers by raising their income and sharing the costs of raising children through shared custody.

In 1983, it became possible for women leaving the workforce to care for small children (younger than age seven) to receive continuous pension coverage. However, the challenge is to find an equitable way to provide pensions to women who have spent their *entire* lives doing family work. Given that many women, and some men, may spend portions of their working lives as homemakers or informal caregivers, the question is whether pensions should credit this work.

WORK AND FAMILY LIFE

The Problem: Balancing Work and Family Life

Both paid work and family life make enormous demands on our time, energy, and emotions. Life often calls on us to make choices between work and family. People in widely varying societies, doing different kinds of work, have tried to solve this problem in different ways. Today, for many Canadians the work–family problem has worsened, as many people have taken to working longer hours to make ends meet. (Figure 7.2 illustrates some of the contemporary factors that contribute to work–life conflict. Figure 7.3 presents a theoretical framework of work–life balance.)

Of course, by historical and comparative standards, most Canadians are not working more. Due to extended full-time education, paid work today tends to start later in life and end earlier in life (through retirement) than it did a century ago. Likewise, workweeks have shrunk from 50 hours to an average of 42.2 hours (Higgins and Duxbury, 2002).

Figure 7.2 Why is work–life balance so important in today's world?

Source: Addressing Work–Life Balance in Canada, www.hrsdc.gc.ca/eng/lp/spila/wlb/awlbc/01table_of_contents.shtml, Human Resources and Skills Development Canada, 2005. Reproduced with the permission of the Minister of Public Works and Government Services Canada, 2010.

Figure 7.3 Theoretical framework of work–life balance

Source: The 2001 National Work–Life Conflict Study: Report One, Public Health Agency of Canada, 2002 © Adapted and Reproduced with the permission of the Minister of Public Works and Government Services Canada, 2009.

However, overtime work is on the rise. The number of respondents who work more than 50 hours has more than doubled over the past 10 years (Higgins and Duxbury, 2002).

Time Crunch

Why do people work longer hours if it means shortening the time they can spend with their families? Sociologists disagree about the answer to this question.

In her book *The Time Bind*, sociologist Arlie Hochschild (1997) suggests that today, paid work gives women with more rewards and less stress than does family life. Increasingly, workplaces are turning into home-like environments. And increasingly, the demands of family life are, for mothers, becoming less manageable and less egalitarian than the demands of paid work life. This, says Hochschild, accounts for some women spending so much time at work. (Also, full-time work receives more pay and more benefits than part-time work; and job-sharing arrangements are not widely available.) By contrast, more time off paid work means spending more time at home, doing more unpaid domestic work.

Juliet Schor, in her book *The Overworked American* (1992), offers the alternative theory that many people work harder today to pay for their consumer purchases. In a culture like ours driven by consumerism, more and more people are willing to trade away their free time for more goods. Rising costs of housing and higher education may also be factors. Yearly vacations, however attractive, may not be achievable goals without a time crunch to pay for them.

Besides this, employers demand more of our time. During the economic downturn of the 1980s and 1990s, to prove their worth to an employer, more people began to work overtime. Rather than hiring (or keeping on) more workers, employers preferred to pay their remaining full-time workers overtime wages or to push their employees to provide more work for the same pay. These expectations applied to women as well as men. Even today, many women are working longer hours because, like men, they are in jobs and careers where employers expect it. Many women value their careers and want to develop them, even though this usually means working longer hours. Besides, many women understand that earning an independent income raises the likelihood of equal treatment in society and within the household.

It is unfortunate that the organizational practices in many workplaces are based on the "assumption that dedicated workers can free themselves from private duties, so nothing needs to interfere with the demands of their jobs" (Echtelt, Glebbeek, Lewis, Lindenberg, 2009: 190). Feminist sociologist Joan Acker argues that in Western market economies, jobs already contain a gendered division of labour, despite what appear (on paper) to be "gender neutral" policies. The separation between the public and private spheres of life, and the corporate lack of responsibility for society's reproductive interests, "effectively denies women the opportunity to combine work and family life in a natural and optimal way" (Echtelt et al., 2009: 190).

Compare this with the situation of workers in Holland, in workplaces characterized by greater flexibility and autonomy. Employees there can decide when and where to work and thus effectively combine work and family life. However, a worker's success in this "post-Fordist" workplace depends more heavily on high performance, which leads to time competition among workers, intensified work, longer hours, and more pressures to outperform oneself (Echtelt et al., 2009). Thus, the modern gender-neutral workplace, with more flexibility and more overtime than the traditional workplace, may end up reproducing the traditional male model of work and worsening work–life conflict.

Finally, to some extent, we are all victims of the technology we have produced to simplify work. The computer—at home and at the office—has revolutionized the pace of work by speeding up research (through the internet), communication (through e-mail), and text production (through word processing.) The cell phone has made everyone available for work everywhere, always. By combining computer and cell phone—as with the BlackBerry—we have voluntarily made ourselves on call 24 hours a day. Because of these technological changes, we have come to expect near-instant responsiveness from the people we work with, and they expect it of us.

Descriptions of the resulting problem fall into several categories—overload, culturally induced stress, and spillover. By **overload**, we mean the excessive amount of work many people—especially mothers—have to do. By **culturally induced stress**, we mean the load of stress and guilt that people in our culture feel when they fail to get all the work done. Finally, by **spillover**, we mean the strains and demands that workers bring home from the workplace and that the family struggles, often unsuccessfully, to meet.

Overload

As we have seen, the unequal division of domestic labour dumps much work on the shoulders of women—especially mothers—who also work for pay. Results include stress, resentment, lack of self-esteem, and poor health. As well, most women have to work longer hours to earn the same amount as men, due to their lower overall earning power (the **wage gap**).

Because women spend more combined time on paid work and domestic work than men, they experience more overload, especially during early parenthood. However, the extent of the overload varies over the family's life cycle. Especially when their children are young, women in dual-earner families report more overload and more symptoms of distress than men. Among dual-earner couples with children in the home, both wives and husbands experience stress due to paid work. However, only wives experience significant stress due to family life (Rwampororo, 2001).

The problem of overload may lessen in time, as more people become adept at juggling their duties (Tingey, Kiger, and Riley, 1996). However, time management behaviour does not currently reduce the effects of strain on feelings of *stress*.

Control is an important factor in the perception of overload, for both men and women. Without a sense of control either at work or at home, both women and men are at risk of developing depression and anxiety. However, other things being equal, paid work stresses women more and causes women more absenteeism from work than it does men (Jacobson, Aldana et al., 1996). Largely, this is because of the jobs that women hold. Women are more likely than men to hold paid jobs that are intrinsically stressful. Many women's jobs combine heavy, continuing demands with a lack of decision-making authority (Karasek and Theorell, 1990). Women doctors, with more job autonomy, experience fewer harmful effects of work overload than women secretaries, for example.

Although many believe that reduced hours of work decrease distress, empirical findings on this point are inconsistent. Giving up some aspects of work for more time off may be more stressful for some employees than for others.

Distress may be caused by parents' concerns that they are not spending enough time with their children. Although mothers and fathers who work more hours often spend the same amount of time or more with their children (Zuzanek, 2002), they still experience higher levels of stress, time pressure, and less satisfaction with the work–family life balance. Thus, perception plays a larger role than hours per se.

There are growing concerns about the dissatisfaction workers feel about their present work–life balance. Many factors can tip the balance. Employers and employees are now realizing that this dissatisfaction affects not only the health of employees but their rates of absenteeism and the productivity of the company as a whole (Human Resources and Skills Development Canada, 2005a). As more attention is drawn to this problem, stronger measures will be taken to improve the situation.

Cultural Sources of Distress

Different cultures produce different patterns of work and stress. So, we cannot ignore the cultural context when discussing the family division of labour and its effects. In some cultures, where traditional conceptions of male and female are unyielding, working mothers who fail to live up to traditional standards may feel especially guilty or ashamed.

For example, female Bulgarian and Israeli schoolteachers, who favour a traditional division of household labour, report higher levels of home–work conflict than American, Australian, and Dutch schoolteachers, who favour an egalitarian division of household labour (Moore, 1995). Both have similar amounts of work to do. However, the women who, for cultural reasons, continue to strive for high levels of homemaking experience the most conflict.

Sometimes, the problem is normative unclarity about how people are supposed to behave. For example, Argentinean professional women ages 20 to 45 feel they lack a clear definition of their roles as workers and mothers, and suffer especially high levels of stress and conflict as a result. The recent, rapid changeover from a male-dominated macho society to one in which working women play an important economic and social role has taken many couples by surprise.

Men in Latin American countries have a reciprocal problem. To some degree the family in Costa Rica, for example, has always been an unstable entity and a source of stress for women and children because of this gendered power imbalance. Today, this is becoming a problem for men as well. They feel their traditional bases of power and identity are being undermined by changes in the labour market and by legislative and policy initiatives supporting women. They, too, need a clearer idea of what it means to be a man in the modern home and the modern workplace (Chant, 2000).

International Differences in Work–Life Balance

- Taiwan—Taiwan has recently gone through a rapid modernization of work and lifestyles, so that more employees are now exposed to stressful Western and industrialized work situations. The rising female participation in paid work makes it even harder for families to maintain a work–life balance. In traditionally collective societies like Taiwan, Western-style flexible work options are not as effective as reductions in maximum work hours, monetary compensation for overtime, or training of managers to act as first-line counsellors for employees (Lu, Kao, Cooper, Allen, Lapierre, O'Driscoll, Poelmans, Sanchez, and Spector, 2009).

- Japan—The participation of the Komeito Party in Japan's coalition government influenced the introduction of three family-friendly policies—a child allowance, child-care services, and facilitation of the work–life balance—as means of lowering the fertility rate. However, a continued commitment to traditional gender roles and a lack of enforcement of family-related policies have undermined the effectiveness of these interventions (Roberts, 2005; Suzuki, 2008).

- France—Extensive state-sponsored child care means that nearly all children between the ages of three and six, and a minority of two-year-olds, attend state nursery schools. Even though French family policy favours higher rates of fertility, rather than increases in women's equality, the child-care policy has meant that more than 56 percent of women are employed and a majority of these are working full-time (Crompton and Lyonette, 2006).

- Russia—Although traditional gender role attitudes about housework still persist, the Russian government has, for a long time, supported Russian women in their pursuit of full-time employment. Pregnant women are entitled to fully paid leave 10 weeks prior and 8 weeks after giving birth, followed by up to 70 weeks of partially paid leave. As a result, Russia even surpasses Sweden in the proportion of dual-earner and female-led families (Motiejunaite-Akvile and Kravchenko, 2008).

- Sweden—State policies recognize the importance of sharing care responsibilities and encouraging father involvement in the child-care process. Parental leave of 68 weeks is divided between both parents, with 8 weeks reserved for each of them individually. This arrangement, together with widely available, affordable, and high-quality child care, promotes dual-caring and flexible work arrangements for women (Motiejunaite-Akvile and Kravchenko, 2008).

- Britain—British women have the second-highest part-time employment (44 percent in 2001) in Europe, after the Netherlands, but the state provision for working mothers and carers has seen little growth. Working parents there are expected to make their own child-care arrangements, and the increase in child-care places has been largely a result of the involvement of the corporate, private sector (Crompton and Lyonette, 2006).

Workload problems affect people differently, depending on their cultural or social group. In Canada, mothers from higher socio-economic backgrounds have a better chance to enter and stay in paid employment even if they have responsibility for children. In short, high-income women are better able to deal with the dual burden of work and marriage than poorer women. This means the problem of work–family overload is greatest for women who are already the most socially vulnerable.

Gender Relations, Housework, and Paid Work in Immigrant Families

Gender relations in Western societies are more egalitarian than elsewhere, with both men and women increasingly obtaining the same education and pursuing careers with similar prospects. With immigration, many women from strictly patriarchical societies with traditional gender roles still largely in place are experiencing this different outlook on society more readily (Darvishpour, 2002).

Many women who immigrate to Canada have never done paid work before because of household responsibilities and strict gender roles that have limited these opportunities. However, after moving to Canada, some have no choice but to pursue employment to support their family (Remennick, 2007). Given the opportunity, some women are even tempted to seek economic independence, having only stayed with their husbands because of cultural ties and economic dependency (see Nissimi, 2007, for a description of this in the Mashhad immigrant community).

Some researchers argue that this can lead to a decrease in the prevalence of patriarchy, or at least a reconfiguration (Hyman, Guruge, and Mason, 2008). On the one hand, this may be beneficial, with women from traditionally patriarchical societies gaining autonomy. At the same time, this loss of power can cause insecurity in males who are used to domination. This can lead to domestic conflict (Hyman, Guruge, and Mason, 2008; Tang and Oatley, 2002; and Darvishpour, 2002).

According to Read (2004), the employment of immigrant Arab women remains rare, while the employment of native-born women of Aran ancestry is comparable to that of other native-born women. Immigrant women tend to follow the traditional gender norms of their culture, which emphasize their responsibility primarily as mothers (Read, 2004; Williams and Vashi, 2007). Acting against these traditional expectations often causes serious tensions within the family and may even escalate to family violence, which we will discuss in a later chapter (Smith, 2008).

On the other hand, if a husband is supportive of more egalitarian gender roles and sharing of tasks, the marital satisfaction and well-being of the wife is greatly increased (van de Vijver, 2007). However, although some men from patriarchical societies are willing to support their wives in finding a fulfilling job or even career, many are still reluctant to take on roles traditionally associated with the female gender—the majority of childcare obligations and especially housework. The good news is that as the generations in the host-country progress, more egalitarian views increasingly emerge. Many immigrants find a sense of balance between the values of their old culture and the new values they have adopted from their new one.

Spillover

Work-to-family spillover is the tendency for stressful or difficult jobs to have a negative impact on workers' family lives. The factors that cause work tensions to spill over into family life are the same as those that undermine workers' health: they include inflexible work schedules and high levels of job responsibility with low control over how work is conducted.

Generally, the solution to problems of spillover is to provide more flexibility, both at home and at work. More job flexibility improves the work–family balance and benefits both individuals and businesses. Given the same workload, individuals with perceived job flexibility have a more favourable work–family balance and can work longer hours before experiencing imbalance (Hill, Hawkins, Ferris, and Weitzman, 2001).

A study of female hospital workers and their families finds both spillover from paid work to the home and, to a lesser extent, from the home to work (Wharton and Erickson, 1995). Simple exhaustion is one of the most important effects of work on family life. Work-induced emotional exhaustion—along with time pressure and mood shifts— profoundly affects a person's state of mind. Emotional exhaustion, like family conflict, increases the likelihood that work will interfere with family life by disrupting spousal and parenting relationships (Leiter and Durup, 1996).

Work-related emotional exhaustion can harm a relationship almost immediately (Leiter and Durup, 1996). Strain and exhaustion because of job stress often make parents more hostile and less responsive, for example (Kinnunen, Gerris, and Vermulst, 1996). Ironically, the major stressors affecting mothers of preschool children are lack of time, child-related anxieties (for example, about how the child is developing), and guilt (Rankin, 1993).

Paid work may also affect family life by dominating the thoughts and interactions of the spouses. Some workers without a long-term emotional relationship feel their work keeps them from becoming intimately involved with another person. Conversely, people in close relationships report spending a lot of time discussing their work with their partner. In nearly half of couples (Miller and Gillies, 1996), work-related subjects lead to conflict, however. Four respondents in ten say that their partner complains regularly that they (that is, the respondents) are too absorbed in their work (Miller and Gillies, 1996).

The spillover of stress from work to family occurs in different ways for men and women. Mothers who have been stressed by their work are more likely to ignore their children. Fathers who have been stressed by their work are more likely to pick a fight with their children. Both child neglect and conflict increase the likelihood of adolescent problem behaviour. Parent-adolescent conflict is highest when work stresses *both* parents.

Parents often withdraw from family activities after a difficult workday. As a result, parents (especially fathers) with high work-to-family spillover are less knowledgeable about their children's daily lives (Bumpus, 2001). Work-stressed fathers are especially uninformed about their children—and especially their younger sons—when relations are strained between them and their spouse (Bumpus, Crouter, and McHale, 1999).

Spillover also affects children's views of work. Adolescents who witness their father's bad moods and hear about his work experiences are likely to be influenced in their own work values (for example, in the value they attach to human-centred work). Views of mother's work are less likely to influence adolescent work values (Galambos and Sears, 1998).

Spillover does not always harm people, however, nor does the perception of spillover depend only on the hours worked. A Canadian study found that many lawyers who worked 50 or more hours a week did not feel their work intruded on other areas of their lives (Wallace, 1997). Often, the harmful effects of their long hours were offset by their interest in the work itself and the career rewards associated with success.

Spillovers in the other direction, from family to work, are also common and consequential. Among transit workers, for example, family-to-work spillover results from lack of backup child care and inadequate social support systems (Reisner, 2000). One in ten Canadians reported family-to-work interference in 2001, an increase from the 5 percent reported in 1991 (Higgins and Duxbury, 2003). Mothers are far more likely than fathers to report family-to-work spillovers. Their most commonly cited reason for missing work, coming in late, or leaving early is caring for a sick child. In one study, 16 percent of respondents missed one or two days of work during a period of six months because of childcare duties (Higgins and Duxbury, 2003).

Work-Related Stress

As we have noted, paid work produces stress—sometimes too much stress. In recent Statistics Canada data, more than one-third (34 percent) of respondents mentioned "too many demands and too many hours" as the main source of stress in the workplace. This was followed by poor interpersonal relations (15 percent), the threat of layoff/job loss (13 percent), risk of injury/accident (13 percent), and learning new computer skills (11 percent) (Sauvé, 2009). Stress of this kind harms both their family life and their functioning in the workplace. Certainly, a high level of work–life conflict is associated with lowered levels of family and parental satisfaction and impaired family functioning. Employers, in turn, report a higher turnover of employees, and high costs related to absenteeism and decreased worker motivation under these conditions (Sauvé, 2009).

Supportive work environments are important because they not only affect mothers' parenting but also influence the extent to which fathers can contribute to child rearing. In low-income families, workplace stress decreases the quality of father–infant interactions and father parenting in general (Benjamin, Crouter, Lanza, and Cox, 2008). Further, single mothers who work in low-paying or part-time jobs, or work non-standard hours, experience poorer home environments that tend to reduce the well-being of children and youth (Lleras, 2008).

For both genders, job functioning is reduced by high levels of work-related stress, health-related stress, and depressive symptoms. When work increases the stress workers feel, it increases the likelihood of hostile marital interaction. In that way, stress reduces the quality of both marital and family functioning (Larson, Wilson, and Beley, 1994). And as work increasingly interferes with family life, both emotional and practical supports within the family weaken.

That said, as bad as it may be to have a job, not having a job is worse because it means not having an income or social standing. Under conditions of unemployment, underemployment, and job insecurity, especially for male family members, family conflict intensifies, as does the risk of domestic violence. Unemployment harms the emotional health of the spouses, the quality of the marital relationship, the parent-child relationship, and family cohesion. Over time, job insecurity has a cumulative negative effect. For women, for example, job insecurity in one year increases job exhaustion and negative work spillover into parenting practices a year later (Mauno and Kinnunen, 1999).

The effects of unemployment on family life may vary from one culture to another. For example, in Israel, unemployed women report stress reactions and a decline in health because of their unemployment. Though married respondents of both sexes are likely to reject job offers that conflict with family responsibilities or provide unsuitable working conditions, they feel the lack of a job especially keenly, because it means a failure to meet family and social responsibilities.

A mother's paid work does the family a lot of good when it makes up for a father's difficulties with work, such as an inadequate or insecure income (Grimm-Thomas and Perry-Jenkins, 1994). Secure employment benefits the family even if it increases people's overall workload.

Six Key Findings about Work and Family Life

- Our lives are far from leisurely—contrary to what some theorists expected a century ago. On the contrary, the average number of hours in the workweek for full-time employees has risen between 1995 and 2005 (Statistics Canada, 2007d).

- A single mother's ability to remain in the workforce largely depends on the presence of relatives or friends who are willing to provide emergency child care and family-friendly work environments that allow for flexible schedules and numerous sick days. Because children have not built up their immune system to common illness, they often get sick when they first enter large social settings such as child care (Mason, 2003).

- In the past decade, there has been a significant increase in the number of grandparents looking after their grandchildren in the absence of parents, especially in Aboriginal communities (Fuller-Thomson, 2005).

- A cross-national comparative study finds that men do more hours of unpaid work in countries where "married, employed women work full-time hours, and when parental leave is short and available to men" (Hook, 2006: 653). However, when "married, employed women work few hours and men are ineligible to take parental leave, men's contribution to domestic work does not increase when children are born" (Hook, 2006: 653).

- Recent findings show the proportion of senior Canadians living alone increases with age (Statistics Canada, 2004e). Seniors aged 85 and older are most likely to live in health-care institutions. Yet, their number is decreasing.

- Less supportive work environments, characterized by high levels of workplace stress and low levels of worker autonomy, result in lower levels of high-quality parenting by fathers in low-income families (Benjamin et al., 2008).

EFFORTS TO SOLVE PROBLEMS OF WORK–FAMILY BALANCE

Individual and Family Efforts

People have used various strategies to deal with the conflicting demands of paid work and housework (Paden and Buehler, 1995; Wiersma, 1994). A common strategy has been for one parent, usually the mother, to stay at home looking after the young children. It is for this reason that women between the ages of 15 and 44 who have children at home are less likely than other women to work for pay.

Other strategies include one or both spouses working part-time, having fewer children, relying on extended family for support, and doing less housework. Some people redefine how much care their children need. Many families buy more services: for example, paying someone to clean the house, buying prepackaged dinners, or hiring sitters to look after the children.

Another way of dealing with the problem is by redefining the domestic division of labour—specifically, by assigning more of the basic domestic tasks to male family members and more of the discretionary tasks to female members. This is the most difficult approach because it means the couple must "invent" a new organization of family life, often without the co-operation of employers, schools, neighbours, or kin. It also means unlearning much of what they learned about family life while growing up and ignoring much of what the mass media have to tell us about "good families."

However, redefining the domestic division of labour to be more equal among family members may not be the way to relieve women's distress within the household—if the problem lies elsewhere. For instance, Rivières-Pigeon, Saurel-Cubizolles, and Romito (2002) examined the domestic division of labour in France, Quebec, and Italy among new mothers. They found that women's psychological distress was not associated with the unequal domestic division of labour with the household. Instead, women suffered more distress about the unequal division of child care.

Interestingly, many women have found housework to be gratifying and have enjoyed a high level of autonomy in doing household tasks. On the other hand, while many women have found child care to be gratifying, caring for a young child was still exhausting; and many women report feeling unhappy when they did not receive significant help from their spouses. New mothers felt especially upset about the unequal division of child care if they considered their spouse's involvement in child care to be a form of support for their relationship and an important part of being a father (Rivières-Pigeon et al., 2002). In short, redefining the domestic division of labour does not remove all conflict and distress from women's lives within the household. However it highlights the importance of reorganizing the division of child care responsibilities within the family, and reminds us that what is important is the ways people interpret their situation.

Self-employment is an increasingly attractive form of work that offers schedule flexibility, especially important for women (Carr, 1996). Education, age, and past work experience all influence parents' willingness and capacity to become self-employed. The growth of self-employment makes it possible for some women with few marketable skills, for example, immigrant women with an inadequate knowledge of English, to work at home making clothes for big manufacturers. Though paid low wages, these women can, in some respects, organize their paid labour around the needs of their families (Gringeri, 1995). However, having the work at home also creates more stress and time management problems. It may mean doing the work after-hours and on weekends, leaving no leisure time. Faced with these problems, the women may take it out on their partner and children, leading to an unhappy home life.

Unlike paid work outside the home, paid work done inside the home often does not significantly reduce the number of hours a person spends on domestic chores (Silver and Goldscheider, 1994). The result, argue some analysts, is that home-based manufacturing reinforces women's lesser status both at work and at home.

Another adaptation is the home office. New technologies, such as computers, fax machines, and e-mail, have led to changes in thinking about work and home. Many duties can be done just as efficiently in either a public workplace or a private one. As well, working from home removes the need for an employer to pay overhead to supply its employees with a workplace.

Yet, despite hopes to the contrary, **supplemental work at home (SWAH)** does not solve the problem of work/family spillover. (We discuss this later in the chapter.)

The Daycare Debate

For obvious reasons, families today increasingly use daycare. Among those who most need good quality daycare are the children of single parents. More than half of families with incomes below the poverty line are single-parent families headed by women (Statistics Canada, 2006a), and most do not receive enough financial support from the child's father. The increase in single-parent families has led to an increase in demand for child care and especially less expensive child care, so single mothers can support themselves and their children.

Today, more than half of Canadian children aged four to five spend part of their week in some care arrangement, while their parents study or work outside the home (Statistics Canada, 2005e). Unregulated care outside the home, often by relatives or neighbours, is the most prevalent form of care arrangement. Yet even unregulated child care can do children much good. Children from low-income families who are cared for in facilities outside the home, either regulated or unregulated, have superior vocabulary skills to those who do not take part in care arrangements.

As a result, investments in daycare for vulnerable children have large returns over time because they can reduce unemployment, dependency on social welfare, and increase tax revenue. Without such high-quality universal daycare, the care that working parents can provide to their children depends on their financial, cultural, and educational background. Parents with the necessary resources—the wealthiest 5 percent—may hire nannies to provide at-home child care. One parent in six leaves their preschool children with a non-parental relative (for example, a grandmother) (Statistics Canada, 2005e).

In corporate settings, on-site daycare is typically of high quality but it is still rare, and few children—especially children from poor families—have access to it. Daycare centres provide the most common form of child care. Some, however, are more like large babysitting services where the children do little more than play and rest. Poor-quality daycare results in, among other things, children becoming ill often (see, for example, Pruissen, 2006). This adds to lost paid time and adds stress to parents' lives.

Most research supports the benefits for children of good-quality non-parental daycare. Typically, children who attend such daycare facilities suffer no attachment anxiety. They develop more rapidly, with better social skills, than their home-raised peers because of a more varied social world (Broude, 1996).

Recent research based on the National Longitudinal Survey of Children and Youth (Kohen, Hertzman, and Willms, 2002) has identified three factors that make daycare beneficial to children: low child-to-adult ratios, educated staff with specialized training, and resources to provide stimulating activities. High-quality daycare centres increase children's linguistic, cognitive, and social competencies, and this has long-lasting benefits for children, especially those from low-income families.

Dutch research finds little evidence to support the theory that children in group daycare are more aggressive or less socially competent than their stay-at-home peers (Goossens, Ottenhoff, and Koops, 1991). Also, Swedish research finds both girls and boys benefit from early daycare, especially boys who experience daycare early, at ages six months to twelve months. Boys displaying learning or behaviour problems have been reared at home with no exposure to daycare or preschool (Andersson, 1996). A different study, however, finds that children who receive 20 or more hours a week of non-maternal care during their first year of life run a much higher risk of disciplinary problems. Of all the parent groups studied, heavy daycare users report the most frequent defiance by their children. Resistance often explodes, with the child moving from passive aggression to active rebellion when parents try to control the child (Belsky, Woodworth, and Crnic, 1996). In short, the evidence on this is still mixed. The quality of daycare is everything!

Children's adjustment to daycare, and their ability to benefit from it, depends on a co-operative relationship between parents and centre staff. This relationship affects both family life and the children's self-development (Sommer, 1992).

Maternal employment may also produce acute problems when the mother experiences a great deal of stress at work and receives little social support. Videotaped interactions show that when highly stressed mothers reunite with their energetic preschoolers at the end of the workday, the mothers often withdraw emotionally and behaviourally. They speak less and offer the child fewer signs of affection than less stressed mothers.

Largely, however, the research so far seems to say, "No, children do not receive worse parenting when both parents are working for pay" (see, for example, Paulson, 1996; Beyer, 1995). True, parenting styles may change when women start to work for pay, but it is still the **parenting style**, not maternal employment, that causes a problem.

Child care becomes easier for working parents when their children start school.

- This is not always the case for three reasons: work hours are rarely the same as those of school; it is hard to predict work schedules; and cuts in school funding make parents do more education work. In order to care for children and elders, Canadian adults can always choose to stay home.

Most Canadian households need two incomes to survive. Unequal division of housework is no longer an issue as men are taking more responsibility.

- This is partly true. Men are doing more than before, but women still carry most of the responsibilities.

Children leave home when they turn 18 and parents have one less burden.

- Children are certainly living at home longer. Because the years of education are longer, and work is harder to find, it takes young people an average of eight years to find a job that can support them fully.

It is now possible to look after children or older family members while holding a paid job, through flextime and working at home.

- Paid work and care for others are rarely successfully done simultaneously.

Care should be less problematic as Canadian employees have more flexible work schedules.

- More people are in contract or temporary jobs; however, work hours are longer, with more responsibilities and less security.

Source: Alice De Wolff. 2003. Working and having a life in Canada, a ten-year review. In *Bargaining for work and life.* Retrieved May 27, 2005, from http://ofl.ca/index.php/library/index_in/C41/.

The research suggests that all children need rich and stimulating experiences to support healthy development.

Today, there are not enough spaces at high-quality daycares to care for every child who needs care, and waiting lists are common. Various advocacy groups are pressing for better child care and fairer policies that will benefit all types of families. Quality care arrangements need to be made available and affordable for all children, regardless of background, developmental level, or ability to pay. Canada needs a national standard of quality and universal access to child care for those Canadian families who choose to use them; and it needs to coordinate the development and implementation of child services across the provinces. So far, however, the current federal government has backed away from this universalistic approach.

Corporate Responses

Large corporations have, over the last 20 or so years, become more sensitive to the needs of families. As a result, many have changed their policies, provided new employee benefits and services, and even reformed their organizational cultures—the way they think and talk about work issues. The changes have paid off. The more the organizations support employees with family responsibilities, the less strain employees experience between paid work and family roles. Supervisor flexibility and family-oriented benefits also reduce the work–family strain (Warren and Johnson, 1995; Thomas and Ganster, 1995) and increase work satisfaction, which, in turn, increases life satisfaction (Ezra and Deckman, 1996).

Employers are more likely to provide these benefits to reduce per-employee start-up costs such as training or to improve productivity. A survey of 4400 families with children younger than age 13 finds that employer policies affect how quickly working mothers re-enter the workforce after childbirth (Hofferth, 1996). A combination of parental-leave laws, organizational policies, and the cost and quality of child care jointly decides how soon a mother will begin (or return to) working outside the home after childbirth. Mothers' family circumstances and their family's attitudes also matter.

Family-friendly workplace policies are available to only a minority of families, however. The 1999 Workplace and Employee Survey (WES) suggested that most companies' practices do not promote the integration of work and family. While roughly one-third of Canadian employees have flextime, access to other family-friendly work arrangements is very rare.

Access to family-friendly practices is influenced by the company's size, industry, and by the type of work performed, with greatest access among well-educated managers and professionals. It is almost unrelated to the personal needs or family characteristics of its employees. Flextime and telework are most available in workplaces with fewer than 10 employees (Statistics Canada, 2003a).

Recent work suggests that an employee's relationship with his or her direct boss may be key to renegotiating the border between work and family. Surprisingly, employees report that supervisors with similar family responsibilities are *less* likely to help them cross the border between work and family (Winfield and Rushing, 2005). This finding suggests we will have continuing problems creating family-friendly workplaces.

Unions have played a large part in pressing for more workplace benefits and gender equality. Overall, firm size and unionization are the most powerful determinants of family-friendly policies in North American, especially American, companies (Glass and Fujimoto, 1995). Corporate cutbacks and falling union membership in Canada do not bode well for family-friendly policies.

Since most people do not want the problems associated with home offices or self-employment, they increasingly value flextime. Flextime involves working the same number of hours but having some freedom to decide when to work these hours. Flextime is popular among parents, especially women, since it does not lead to pay cuts or reduce chances for a promotion. Swapping shifts is another way of to create flextime, yet shift work carries costs. Part-time work is a widely used policy, for many reasons. In the Netherlands, some employers allow employees to save up overtime hours toward a longer leave (Todd, 2004).

Organizations like to put people on part-time work because they do not have to pay full benefits and can fire the employee at will. Part-time status puts women who choose this for domestic reasons on a "**mommy track**." Employers see the women on this track as less committed to their work and to their career and thus less promotable. One popular family-friendly workplace initiative is on-site daycare for young children. This program does not change how parents have to work, but it relieves some anxieties. Collectively, services sponsored by employers, groups of employees, or unions are called *work-related child-care centres*. Daycares do not necessarily have to be on-site; any support to child care, whether community based or in the form of off-site, consortium centres, is helpful to working parents (see Barbeau, 2001).

Computerized Work and the Family

Changes in work life because of computerization and other information technology may have a large influence on family life. The computerization of work and its transfer to a home setting—what is variously called telework, telecommuting, or computer-supported work at home (SWAH)—is still at an early stage, and research on this topic is still developing, but this much is known so far. First, telework blurs the boundaries between work and leisure, which complicates both work and leisure. Second, telework does not reduce the work done or the spillover from work life to family life. Third, telework does not appear to significantly change the gendering of domestic labour. Fourth, though telework may increase the time a parent spends near his or her spouse or child, there is no evidence that it improves (or increases) interactions between them.

A recent study by Scott Schieman and Paul Glavin (using 2002 data from an American national study) shows that greater schedule control—that is, having greater control over the start and finish times of work—is associated with more frequent work–family role blurring, especially for men. And, for both women and men, more job autonomy is associated with more frequent work–family role blurring among both women and men. Such autonomy and control typically increases the amount of work-related contact outside of normal work hours; and for both genders, receiving work-related contact (for example, telephone calls) outside of normal work hours increases work-to-family conflict. Thus, one disadvantage of the greater schedule control and autonomy associated with in-home work and computerization is blurred boundaries and increased conflict between work and family. And, as we have seen, more conflict between work and family predicts worse personal, health, social, and organizational outcomes.

The effects on individual workers are mixed. Telework reduces travel. Teleworking gives professional workers greater freedom and control because they are less closely supervised, although routine clerical work can be closely controlled through central keystroke checking. Employed parents who do SWAH report more task variety and job involvement than other parents. On the other hand, teleworking passes the costs of workspace on to workers, and gives workers more role overload, interference, and stress (Duxbury, Higgins, and Thomas, 1996).

Family Policies: A Cross-National Outlook

Balancing work and family life is a huge problem worldwide. As women enter the labour force, whether by choice or need, the work traditionally assigned to women—providing care to children, the infirm, and the elderly—must be done in other ways.

Cross-national research on 15 industrial societies (Shaver and Bradshaw, 1995) finds that people commonly apply three models to the relation between family and work. In the *traditional* model, the wife is economically dependent on her husband. In the *modern* model, the wife remains outside the labour market, but only while she has young children. In the *dual-breadwinner* model, the mother of young children is in full- or part-time employment. Welfare states typically embrace the dual-breadwinner model. They provide support to women, whether or not they have young children and work for pay, though the levels of support vary among welfare states.

Another way to conceptualize the issue of poverty is by focusing on the broader factors, such as political influences on the division of labour in families. Recall that single-women households, especially those with young children, experience the highest levels of poverty. The question that arises then is what kinds of government policies are most effective in alleviating poverty among single mothers. Using Nancy Fraser's classification, Misra, Moller, and Budig (2007) identify four types of welfare state strategies that carry specific assumptions about the role of women and men in the household:

- *The carer strategy:* This is closest to the traditional model of family and work, where the husband is seen as the breadwinner and the wife as the caregiver. Policies of these welfare states encourage and reward women for providing care and reinforce traditional gender divisions. Caregiver allowances, parental leaves, and flextime may be provided, but part-time employment is considered the best way for women to combine employment and care. Here, women's caregiving is the primary source of provision of care. Countries in this category include the Netherlands, Germany, and Luxembourg.

- *The earner strategy:* This strategy is based upon the dual-breadwinner model, where men and women are equally encouraged to participate in the labour market, through policies against gender discrimination in employment and so on. However, little or no effort is made by the government to directly address the work–family tension described earlier in the chapter, which questions the overall effectiveness of creating actual gender equality. In the United States, for example, women must rely on corporate and domestic support. The latter is often either too expensive or difficult to attain for single low-income mothers. The United States is unique among industrialized countries in its lack of public help for child-rearing mothers—for example, its lack of state-guaranteed minimum payments or employment policies that would help mothers increase their earnings. Other countries that can be broadly classified in this category include Canada and the United Kingdom.

- *The choice strategy:* As the name suggests, these societies use a progressive strategy to provide women with more opportunity to exercise a choice to either provide care or engage in full-time employment. In France, for example, the state provides child care, generous parental leave, and home-care allowances that support parental care for two or more young children. France and Belgium exercise this strategy; however, there is little push here to equalize men's contribution to child care and housework.

- *The earner-carer strategy:* Welfare states employing this strategy envision a society where informal carework and employment is equally shared between men and women. Both are encouraged to take parental leave, and men's involvement in the household is promoted through paternity leaves that only men can take. Yet, the state also provides high-quality child care outside of the home to facilitate women's maintenance of full-time employment. Sweden, Norway, and Finland employ this paradigm.

CONCLUDING REMARKS

As we have seen, the increase in time spent at work has created much stress within the family. Financial insecurity also increases stress within the family, and the past 20 years have provided many opportunities for families to experience financial stress. For many individuals, the costs of family life are starting to outweigh the benefits. The results of family stress, bad parenting, and work disruption because of family concerns are significant public issues. To meet the demands that work is putting on parents, family time has become increasingly regimented, with "quality time" scheduled among members.

Increasingly, dual-earner couples develop behavioural strategies to solve work–home conflicts. These coping behaviours are co-operative or social, in the sense that they transform the way the family system works to reduce pressures on one or more of the family's members, but neither strategy involves state expense. The organizational and institutional standards in any society decide the context within which men and women make education, labour market, and reproductive choices. Currently in North America, irregular school schedules and lack of child-care services reflect a social and political belief in the full-time homemaker. Women are forced to make a choice between family and work.

For most of this chapter, we have concentrated on the negative aspect of work—especially the stress it causes families. We should not leave the topic without recognizing that work can also be a deeply rewarding experience, with benefits for the family. For example, many studies of single mothers show that if the mother is in a job that she enjoys, the child often grows up unaffected by the absence of a father. Other studies show that professionals can sometimes apply to their family the problem-solving skills learned at work. This is an interesting aspect of the relationship between work and home that researchers should explore further.

Women and men also need to set up a new domestic economy. Too many men still believe they are entitled to full domestic service from their wives. The whole question of what is fair in marriage—especially when both mates are working for pay and workers have children to care for—needs to be discussed. Couples forming relationships need to talk openly about their wishes and hopes with respect to housework, child care, and elder care.

CHAPTER SUMMARY

This chapter looked at the intersection of what are arguably the two main aspects of an adult individual's life: family and work.

We showed family work to be just as important and valid as paid work, a major contributor to the socio-economic fabric of Canada. We examined child care, a major ingredient of domestic labour. Again, we found that mothers rather than fathers more often do this work. Satisfactory child care for working parents in Canada is lacking, with only 15 percent of children who need care having access to it. We also examined the growth in unpaid elder care, in which family members care for their older and frail relatives.

The basic problem facing working parents is that both work and family life take up enormous amounts of their time, energy, and emotions, and that it is difficult—but necessary—for adults to balance these often-conflicting demands. Imbalance leads to stress and marital conflict.

Work–family problems fall into one of three categories: overload, culturally induced stress, and spillover. Work-related stress is a major cause of marital problems in many families because it creates other problems, such as preoccupying the thoughts and interactions of the spouses or intensifying arguments over domestic responsibilities.

Both micro and macro solutions are needed. By *micro*, we mean personal and family solutions, such as postponing work to become a homemaker, restructuring work arrangements and schedules, or opting for daycare. By *macro*, we mean corporate responses, such as setting up flextime policies and on-site daycare services for the children of employees, and state responses, such as expanding parental leave policies and offering economic and social support for single parents.

Key Terms

mommy track A term used to describe women who are seen as less committed to their work and to their career and thus less promotable.

culturally induced stress The stress and guilt people in our culture feel when they try to cope with the workload and their inability to get it all done.

dual-earner couples Both spouses or cohabitants are employed in full-time or part-time work.

family work Tasks involved in preserving a family, such as coordinating family activities with paid work and housework.

flextime Working the same number of hours but having some freedom to decide when to work these hours.

housework Tasks involved in maintaining a home, such as cleaning and cooking.

overload The excessive amount of work many people, especially mothers, have to do.

parenting style The way in which a parent acts and communicates with children.

single-earner couples A union where only one spouse or cohabitant is employed, while the other is unemployed or not in the labour force.

spillover The situation in which concerns related to one part of one's life intrude on another part.

supplemental work at home (SWAH) Work in the home office that is aided by technological advances such as computers.

wage gap The differences between the sexes in number of hours spent working and average dollar earned per hour. Most women work longer hours to earn the same amount as men, due to women's lower overall earning power.

Critical Thinking Questions

1. Based on what you have learned in this and previous chapters, do you think that families are becoming more or less egalitarian in terms of paid and unpaid work?

2. Chapter 2 described welfare reforms in the 1990s. Building on what you learned in this chapter, how do you think welfare reforms have affected family life for low-income families?

3. Discuss possible problems in making cross-national comparisons of work and family life. Can you think of ways to conduct research to get more accurate comparative data?

4. This chapter has outlined several ways that technology has influenced the evolution of housework and paid work. Can you think of other modern-day technologies (BlackBerries,

the internet, and so on) that are changing the dynamics between work and family life or may do so in the future?

5. What are some of the most pressing challenges families will have to face in the future with respect to managing family life and work?

6. Discuss possible strategies that employers could undertake to alleviate work-related stress.

7. How can families effectively reorganize themselves to cope with various caregiving demands?

8. To what extent do the state and private corporations have a responsibility to or a right to influence the division of labour within a household?

Weblinks

ElderCare Canada
www.eldercarecanada.ca
This site is an advice and action consulting service aimed at "adult children" seeking advice and hands-on help for all aspects of care for aging parents. Toronto-based, its services are available to clients across Canada, as well as internationally.

Centre for Families, Work and Well-Being
www.worklifecanada.ca
This educational site gathers interdisciplinary research, responding to dramatic changes in family patterns, paid work, and broader economic and political structures.

National Study on Balancing Work, Family and Lifestyle
www.phac-aspc.gc.ca/publicat/work-travail/index-eng.php
This is a Public Health Agency of Canada site that contains ongoing reports on effective ways of managing work–life conflict.

Aboriginal and Indigenous Social Work
www.aboriginalsocialwork.ca
This site contains an overview of social work conducted with First Nations, native, Aboriginal, and indigenous communities. It is a good source for general links, general social

work links, and a range of valuable and useful information especially if you are a social work educator, practitioner, researcher, or student.

Canada Immigration
www.canadaimmigrants.com
This site provides interdisciplinary information about discrimination against highly skilled immigrants in the Canadian job market and discourse on solutions to eliminate systemic racism.

Organisation for Economic Co-operation and Development (OECD)
www.oecd.org
OECD has been one of the world's largest and most reliable sources of comparable statistics and economic and social data. As well as collecting data, OECD monitors trends, analyzes and forecasts economic developments, and researches social changes or evolving patterns in trade, environment, agriculture, technology, taxation, and more.

SingleMom.com
www.singlemom.com
This site provides resources aimed to help single mothers pursue their education, apply for financial assistance, and receive parenting and other advice.

Chapter 8
Stress and Violence
Realities of Family Life

Chapter Outline

- Stress
  - Types of Stressors
  - Caregiving as a Source of Family Stress
  - The Effects of Family Illness
  - Coping with Caregiver Stress
  - Health Stressors and Supports

- Support and Coping: A Systems View
  - Families Change in Patterned Ways
  - Each Family Has Its Own Characteristics
  - All Families Solve Problems
  - Some Families Need Help Solving Their Problems

Researcher and family therapist John Gottman (1995, 1999) has found that when long-time couples argue, they argue about many of the same things they did in years past. Some important disagreements never go away; they simply cannot be resolved. This finding supports Gottman's view that we cannot hope to eliminate the conflict in close relations, no matter how dedicated and skilled we may be as partners and communicators. Since conflict will never go away entirely, couples need to learn how to disagree in a friendly and respectful manner. Couples should realize the relationship will always retain some grit—something that will irritate, frustrate, and disappoint them. This will be a source of stress, but it will not be the only source.

In earlier chapters we have noted that close relations are hard work. Solving conflicts and communication problems, raising children effectively, earning necessary income, and getting all the household work done—these tasks are hard to do. They can be frustrating, draining, and upsetting. No wonder real people in real relationships can get exhausted, even depressed and ill. Family life gives people a lot but it also takes a lot, and we need to remember this while reading this chapter.

In the mass media, families are often portrayed as havens in a heartless world, but in reality, families can be danger zones. Family life is the site of our closest, most intimate relations. However, in the intimate family setting, people reveal themselves, invest themselves, and leave themselves open to emotional, financial, and physical harm. As we shall see, violence occurs too often in this vulnerable setting. The research on family life is full of attempts to explain why **domestic violence** is much more common than we would expect or hope. In this chapter we examine various forms of family stress and violence. We consider what it is about family life that often leads to stress, and the ways that stresses affect family relationships. Finally, we examine the common forms of intimate or family violence, especially child abuse and wife battering.

By discussing stress and violence in the same chapter, we are *not* claiming that stress is the only or even the main cause of domestic violence. Stress does *not always* lead to violence, nor does violence *always* result from stress. In fact, stress is often an effect as well as a cause of family violence. However, what ties these two topics together is the simple fact that both stress and violence show the striking gap between an idealized, sentimental fantasy about families and the way that flesh-and-blood families actually work. Few people, when they form a family, imagine just how stressful family life is going to be at times; and for some families, a high degree of stress is recurrent or continuous. And few people, when they form a family, imagine there is a risk of violence taking place. Family violence tends to be hidden, so we rarely know when it is going on in other people's lives, and we try to keep other people from knowing it is going on in our own lives.

Neither violence nor stress is part of the romantic ideal of family life that most of us have learned to imagine and embrace. So, for some readers, this chapter will be a shocking wake-up call. For others, it may simply confirm what they already know from their own first-hand experience. But it is important to remember—this can't be emphasized too often—that violence is not a normal, everyday result of stress. Stress is normal and common, and can be coped with. Violence is abnormal and mercifully still uncommon, and should not be coped with, but rather shunned and escaped.

STRESS

Family stress is "a state that arises from an actual or perceived imbalance between a **stressor** (that is, challenge, threat) and capability (that is, resources, coping) in the family's functioning" (Huang, 1991: 289). To explain the effect of stressor events on families, most current researchers employ a version of the **ABCX family crisis model** first elaborated by Hill (1949). In this model, A, which represents the stressor event, interacts with B, the family's crisis-meeting resources, and with C, the interpretation a family makes of the event, to produce X, the crisis.

This ABCX model focuses mainly on pre-crisis variables that make some families more or less able to cope with the impact of a stressor event. Researchers originally developed the model to study family adjustment to the crises of wartime separation and reunion (Hill, 1949). Sociologists have since used the model to examine differences in the ways families cope with a wide variety of difficult problems.

One factor that always influences stress is the nature of the stressor event itself, as measured by its severity, intensity, duration, and timing. We can evaluate stressor events as both *objective* and *subjective*. An outsider, such as a researcher, using agreed-upon standards of measurements, can provide an objective evaluation of the stressor, which corresponds to A in the model. To do so, a researcher would measure how long the stressed period lasted and the frequency with which it recurred. Typically, the longer a stressor event lasts, the more severe its effects. The more often it occurs, the more it strains a family's resources. So, the harder it is for the family to cope successfully.

Family members themselves also make a subjective evaluation of the stressor, which corresponds to C in Hill's model. How family members view and define that event controls the way they react to it. Their subjective evaluation of an event may not match the researcher's objective evaluation. However, what people believe about the event may even affect its outcome. Like any self-fulfilling prophecy, the family's belief in their ability to cope increases their actual ability to cope.

Since sociology is the study of social relationships and social institutions, sociologists are interested in learning how stress changes the roles and relationships that make up a family. For example, they study how stress changes the ways that spouses relate to each other, parents relate to children, children relate to parents, and siblings relate to one another. They study the ways stress affects patterns of communication and interaction, marital satisfaction, or parental competence within the family. How, they ask, does stress change the way that family members relate to extended kin, neighbours, community members, teachers, and employers? Finally, they find out how stress changes a family's ability to socialize children, or to provide a stable and healthy workforce.

Often, extreme stress reduces a family's ability to act well in these respects. For that reason, sociologists are interested in how family members cope and adjust to a long-term stressor. Finally, a family's success in coping with a stressor event will depend on the strength or quality of its crisis-meeting resources. As we will see, families that cope well with stresses are families that already had important resources—especially cohesion and flexibility—before the stresses began. We will find systemic differences between the families that pull together and the families that fall apart under the strains of stressor events.

Types of Stressors

Common causes of family stress fall into at least four categories:

- *major upheavals*, such as war and natural disasters that affect many people simultaneously.

- *major life transitions*—acute disruptions because of events that may affect some family members simultaneously but not others—such as the birth of a child, the death of a parent, divorce, and retirement.

- *chronic stressors*, such as disability, severe physical or mental illness, drug and alcohol abuse, occupational problems, unemployment, or imprisonment of a family member.

- *occasional stresses*, which may be severe but go away without permanent change. Examples include a car accident, a burglary, a sudden illness or death of a family member, or even seemingly pleasant but stressful stimuli like a holiday trip. We will not discuss these common stresses in this chapter.

Major Upheavals For North American families, the Great Depression of the 1930s was a near-universal stressor causing widespread unemployment and poverty. A classic study of family life during the Depression (Cavan and Ranck, 1938) found that coping ability rests largely on a family's previous organization. Families reacted to the Depression in the same way as they had reacted to earlier problems. Thus, families who had been well organized before more readily recovered from the emotional strain caused early in the Depression. All families showed increasing strain as the Depression continued. However, families differed in the degree to which they felt this strain and the ways they dealt with it.

For many, the Second World War *reduced* family stress by providing jobs for people who had been unable to find work during the recent Depression. However, the dramatically increased wages that many teenagers brought home weakened parental control and increased delinquent behaviour. Also, the loss of a father to military service, or a mother's change of roles from homemaker to working woman, forced all members of the family to adjust (Levy, 1945). War, like unemployment, brought families closer together if they were already cohesive. They drove families apart if members were already enmeshed in conflict.

Research today continues to examine the effects of war on family functioning, and continues to find that families living under long-term war conditions suffer great stress. Consider the families in West Beirut, Lebanon. After 12 years of war, they showed various stress-related problems: depression, interpersonal and marital conflict, and psychosomatic symptoms (Farhood, Zurayk, Chaya, Saadeh, Meshefedjian, and Sidani, 1993). In many war-torn countries, an atmosphere of fear and isolation prolongs stress-related disorders long after the deaths, imprisonments, and migrations of family members themselves (Quirk and Casco, 1994).

Family Life Transitions Typically, we think of family life transitions as including only those events that are predicted and expected in average families: birth, death, marriage, perhaps divorce, retirement, the empty nest, and so on. They all have disruptive, stressful effects, even though they are common and foreseeable. It seems fitting now, in Canada and other societies with large immigrant populations, to include migration as a typical family transition—one that is common if not always foreseeable, and often likely to produce disruption and stress.

Like war and economic difficulty, migration has been a continuing source of family stress in Canada over the past 100 years. Immigrant families typically face **acculturative stress** because of the strains of adapting to a new society. These include a lack of local language skills, low employment and economic status, limited educational background, and broken social networks (Thomas, 1995). Prolonged stress of this kind can harm a family. Therefore, time spent in a new homeland may increase the anxiety and depression of both parents and children (Liebkind, 1993). Often, women are especially stressed because they are often more marginalized by migration than men.

Typically, the children of immigrants assimilate more rapidly than their parents to local standards of behaviour. This often produces conflict between parents and their children. For example, Southeast Asian adolescents in North America report experiencing much parent-induced stress about academic performance (that is, studying for a test, pressure to get good grades) and parental expectations (that is, high expectations to do well). They fear failing to meet family expectations. This extends to interpersonal relations as well, especially for adolescent women (Duong Tran, Lee, and Khoi, 1996). Often, there is a mismatch between parents' more traditional beliefs about how a young woman should act, especially toward dating, and views that daughters adopt from the new culture (Zhou and Bankston, 2001).

Chronic Stressors Chronic stressors confronting families may include poverty, inequality, and unemployment. They all increase stress, reduce resilience, and hinder every part of a family's well-being, including its health. Taken as a package, economic stress—resulting from a lack of enough money, a fear of economic problems, job instability, and job insecurity—strongly influences family well-being.

Table 8.1 Some Common Misconceptions about Stress

The illusion of constant stress	This is the illusion that one is under constant stress without any sense of relief or any improvement in circumstances. However, research shows that people are not always under constant stress and, in fact, periods of greater stress can only have an impact if they have been felt in contrast to periods of lesser stress.
The illusion of ubiquitous stress	This is the idea that stress is everywhere and is an indisputable part of everyday life. The notion that stress is inherent in many life situations takes away from the fact that people suffer from a variety of stressors and to varying degrees.
The illusion of simple solutions	People are constantly searching for a "quick fix" to their stressful lives. There are many problems with searching for, and believing in, "simple solutions" to life stress. For one, simple solutions do not prevent the problem from reoccurring, do not fix the overall structuring of life that can regenerate the stressor, and, lastly, ignore the fact that most stressors are too complex to be fixed with a one-time solution.
The illusion that people cause their own stress	This is the illusion that people cause their own stress because they bring it on themselves by, say, engaging in a particular lifestyle. However, research shows that many stressors are randomly patterned, and even when social status and location are taken into account, there is still a large undetermined component to their occurrence.

Source: Blair Wheaton. 1999. The nature of stressors. In Allan V. Horwitz and Teresa L. Scheid (Eds.) *A Handbook for the Study of Mental Health.* New York: Cambridge University Press. Reprinted with the permission of Cambridge University Press.

Current research continues to examine the linkage between economic stress, poverty, and family dysfunction. Sociologists continue to find that economic pressure on a family increases parental unhappiness and marital conflict. In a study by Fox and Chancey (1998), for example, both women and men sensed economic well-being was the strongest predictor of measures of individual and family well-being. Also for both, a spouse's or partner's job variables were important predictors of measures of family well-being. The respondent's own job instability and insecurity created stress and appeared more important to women than men, and more so for family than individual well-being outcomes.

Single mothers are especially vulnerable to economic and social stress. A longitudinal study of mothers from London, Ontario, by Avison, Ali, and Walters (2007) found that single mothers experience significantly higher levels of psychological distress than their married counterparts. The reasons for this are rooted in a structural disadvantage of being the sole breadwinner and caregiver, having to balance work and parenting strain. So, even though both married and lone mothers do not differ in their ability to *react to* and *cope with* stress, single parents are consistently *more exposed to* stressful life events.

Lone mothers often pass their heightened stress, anxiety, and anger on to their adolescent children, especially when they spend a lot of time with their children (Larson and Gillman, 1999). Mothers who form strong bonds with their children and control them through manipulating guilt, shame, or fear pass their own anxieties on to their children when stressed. The psychological distress they induce weakens a child's ability to form and preserve a satisfying marital relationship, and thus leads to higher risks of separation and divorce in adulthood (Clifford, 1998). Children and teenagers living with lone mothers are also more likely to experience times of temporary or persistent poverty, which can be harmful in itself. For instance, children who live in persistent poverty experience significantly higher levels of depressive symptoms when they enter adulthood (Mossakowki, 2008). The duration of poverty is important; the more extended the period of poverty, the stronger the relationship to mental health. Also, the effect of past poverty duration remains significant when present socio-economic status and family background is controlled (Mossakowki, 2008).

At the same time, closer and more frequent contact between a lone mother and her adolescent child is likely to reduce stress from other sources. During early adolescence, closer watching by single mothers may increase their awareness of adolescent stress and in turn may buffer the negative effects of stress on adolescent adjustment (Hartos and Power, 2000).

Racism is another chronic source of stress for visible minorities—even for those who are economically successful. For those minorities who are less well off, like Aboriginal peoples, racism is the final insult. For such groups, community institutions such as churches, schools, newspapers, and voluntary associations help group members cope effectively with these and related problems.

Major stresses for Aboriginals, such as alcohol use, family breakdown, inadequate tribal leadership, unemployment, and issues surrounding children's education, place great demands on coping. Major family and tribal strengths include extended family support, spiritual values and religious practices, community generosity and support, tribal culture and traditions, and the determination of many tribal members to recognize and overcome their problems (Abbott and Slater, 2000).

Other visible minorities in Canada also rely on social supports to help them with problems of racism, isolation, and poverty. For example, among Somali immigrants, religious and cultural traditions help to promote family strength. Loyalty, respect, and stable hierarchical roles support spiritual unity. Beliefs in the sanctity of the family promote interdependence and sharing of resources for family survival. Community solidarity provides a context for values of peace and harmony that support psychological unity (Heitritter, 1999).

Caregiving as a Source of Family Stress

An aging, longer-living adult population leads to increased demands for care by families, and to increased family stress. More than 20 percent of Canadian seniors receive the help of family members because of long-term health problems (Keating, Fast, Frederick, Cranswick, and Perrier, 1999: 99). One result, as discussed in Chapter 7, is the so-called "sandwich generation": 42 percent of Canadian women ages 40 to 44 balance parental care, child care, and work outside the home. Broader changes also include a shift from institutional to community-based care, a growing ideological commitment (at least on paper) to elder care by the state, and funding cuts by the federal government for such services (Canadian Centre for Policy Alternatives, 2004).

Long-term care for the older family members, people with disabilities, or the severely ill can put great strains on a family's functioning. As a result, caregivers often have to change their social activities or their sleep patterns, or give up holiday plans (Keating et al., 1999). The "caregiving family" in our North American culture contains both people who provide assistance and people we see as having some duty to provide help but who do not. An idealized view of family caregiving may be used to put pressure on families to provide more care, but it does not always work well (Keating et al., 1994).

For one, caregiving can be particularly stressful for certain populations. Romanow suggests that rural communities are home to residents who have poorer health and more profound needs for primary health care, yet urban centres promote better access and quality of service (Ryan-Nicholls and Haggarty, 2007). Ryan-Nicholls and Haggarty (2007) also stress that recruitment and retention of health-care providers has contributed to this problem. Problems with access to health care in rural areas are evident when examining the many difficulties parents face in raising children with special needs. Roberts, O'Sullivan, and Howard (2005) examine the technologies available for serving people with special needs in rural and northern communities. Open and distance learning (ODL) has bridged the gap for those who lack access to education, and information and communications technologies (ICT) play a critical role in offering services and education for children with special needs, their families, health-care providers, and teachers, particularly in geographically isolated areas (Roberts et al., 2005).

Often most of the care responsibilities and the attendant strains fall on one family member, typically a woman (Keating et al., 1999). As discussed in Chapter 7, women are almost twice as likely as men to give personal care and, as a result, experience caregiving strain, work interference, income loss, and role strain (Fredriksen, 1996). Women forced to alter their work schedule are particularly stressed (Orodenker, 1990). Further, caring for others increases the probability of developing physical health problems and emotional and mental distress (Vitaliano, Scanlan, Zhang, Savage, Hirsch, and Siegler, 2002), thus exposing women to more disturbances. For instance, the risk of social or physical harm is particularly associated with caring for someone with dementia (Gilliam and Steffen, 2006).

Elder care affects many aspects of family life. For example, sharing a household with elderly parents limits activities (Deimling, Nolker, and Townsend, 1989). Men sharing households with their mothers-in-law are more likely to report interference in their social lives, family vacation plans, time with wives and children, and relationships with other relatives (Kleban, Brody, Schoonover, and Hoffman, 1989). Balancing caregiving and other responsibilities sometimes result in moments of "crisis." **Crisis episodes** in caregiving have been defined as significant events that are likely to lead to seeking help from professionals (Betts Adams, 2006), changing caregiving conditions (Usita, Hall, and Davis, 2004), or precipitating decision making (Taylor and Donnelly, 2006). Sims-Gould, Martin-Matthews, Gignac, and Monique (2008) analyze the nature of crisis episodes in employed caregivers' lives in a study of 5496 Canadian caregivers. They found that crisis episodes occur in two dimensions. First, crises can be enduring (chronic) or temporally bounded (acute), and second, they can be predictable or unpredictable (Sims-Gould et al., 2008). For instance, they classify a knee surgery required by the person cared for as temporally bounded and predictable, where a depression diagnosis as enduring and unpredictable. Similarly, events taking place in the caregiver's life can lead to crises. For instance, selling a family home is a crisis that is temporally bounded and predictable, and a divorce is enduring and unpredictable. The perception of the crisis is important in determining how the caregivers will approach the changing circumstances. If crises are perceived as temporary, caregivers may hesitate to make permanent changes in their work arrangements. That is, instead of missing work, caregivers reporting crises would use vacation time or make changes to their leisure, sleep, and social lives to deal with crisis episodes (Sims-Gould et al., 2008).

The Effects of Family Illness

Severe illness is another source of stress because of prolonged caregiving. The extent, duration, and results of these family strains vary with the nature, severity, and duration of the illness. For example, informal caregivers for non-institutionalized parents with dementia report heightened feelings of burden and depression because of the care recipient's aimlessness, aggressive behaviours, forgetfulness, and restlessness (Chappell and Penning, 1996). Strains also vary with the coping abilities and resources of the family and with the disease sufferer, whether a parent or child, old or young, male or female.

Many wives experience reduced anxiety when their mate is admitted to hospital for treatment. Many others suffer ambivalence: on the one hand, they feel relieved that they need no longer provide difficult home-based care and the husband is receiving excellent care; on the other hand, they feel guilty that they are failing to provide care themselves. As a result, in the first weeks after admission, wives display poor physical health, low morale, and high levels of depression.

Longer stays often undermine patient self-care and increase depression among caregivers (Sulman, Rosenthal, Marshall, and Daciuk, 1996). Overall, wives with better social support and better psychosocial health are more satisfied with the care their spouse is receiving (Rosenthal and Dawson, 1991).

Coping with Caregiver Stress

As we have seen, family life is full of stresses. However, many families deal with them successfully: family functioning soon returns to normal, though the stressor may still be present. Families learn to cope by organizing their lives around handling their problems. Support from family, friends, and community agencies buffers the impact of caregiving, work, and family role strain. Overall, caregivers with larger support networks—especially of women and kin—report lower levels of stress. Close relationships with people who are both personal supporters and caregivers lighten the load (Wright, 1994).

In this section, we will use caring for ill family members as an example of a family stressor. Like any stressor, it drains the resources of the family. Two broad categories of resources—material and emotional/psychological—are key in deciding which families can withstand crises successfully. Stressor events generally use up large amounts of all these resources. When a family member develops a severe illness, families may have to pay for costly medication and take time off from work to look after the ill person. Time and money ease these strains, but neither resource is equally available to all Canadians.

Everyone knows the meaning of *natural resources* like water, oil, natural gas, and so on. Most people could intuit the meaning of *financial resources* to mean cash on hand plus the credit available to borrow money as it is needed. *Psychological or emotional resources* are harder to define. These are the internal abilities to withstand misfortune. They may include coping skills that have been specifically learned and developed; they may also include aspects of personality such as self-confidence, calm, and bravery. Psychological/emotional resources also include feelings of trust and affection for other family members, an ability to communicate openly, and a willingness to risk change for the collective good. Family members contribute to the emotional resources of others by listening well and offering encouragement. This role is especially important in the spousal relationship. Families with a good stock of psychological/emotional resources are best able to withstand stresses.

Health Stressors and Supports

Like other good things, good health is in part a product of social relationships. Social support is important in achieving and keeping good health. Social support includes information that diffuses through social channels, but it is more than that. To be useful, social support must give caregivers the right information and encouragement at the right time. It is social interaction, and positioning in a network of relationships, that grants meaning and value to health information. That is, the information is confirmed by people in a social network whom the listener trusts and respects.

Illness is partly a biological event and partly a socially performed drama. In return for being allowed to deviate from their everyday activities and neglect their social duties, sick people have to appear ill, consult a doctor, and follow the doctor's advice.

Family and friends play an important part in this culturally scripted drama. It is through interaction in social networks that people recognize (or admit) health problems, contact health facilities, and comply with medical advice. A key player in this drama is the sick person's primary caregiver—usually, the sick person's wife, mother, or daughter. The caregiver may have a full-time or part-time paid job, besides domestic responsibilities. Whatever her other duties, the addition of primary caregiving drains a caregiver's time and energy. Often, however, the caregiver finds herself needing support.

Sometimes people can get this support from their doctor, but a doctor's time is limited. For example, wanting more information and more reassurance than their doctor has the time to provide, many patients and their caregivers look for help from *support groups*. These groups vary widely in size, composition, and activity. Medical professionals lead some, others are led by social service professionals, and others still by peers. They all share a wish to help patients and caregivers help themselves and one another. Recently, the internet has become a support medium in health care, complete with on-line research libraries, discussion groups, chat rooms, and expert advice available by e-mail.

However, doctors remain primary advisers to resolve confusion over conflicting information, despite being sometimes averse to information from outside sources. Interpersonal trust depends on the degree to which patients see their doctors as competent, responsible, and caring. Continuities of care, and meeting time that allows opportunities for response, patient instruction, and patient participation in the decision making, all encourage trust.

However, people get far more of the information and encouragement they need from their personal networks than from special-purpose support groups. Hundreds of empirical studies show that support from one's social network is a key factor in explaining resilience in dealing with life stresses and misfortune (Ganster and Victor, 1988).

Social relationships give people a *sense* that they are receiving social support, and this *sensed* social support is important to their well-being (Gottlieb, 1981, 1985). Strong social networks get people to address their medical needs and use health care regularly (Freidenberg and Hammer, 1998). It is through personal and interorganizational networks that individuals seek help with health problems (Pescosolido, 1996). Therefore, network characteristics make a difference to the care a sick person receives.

Large, cohesive networks typically promote higher levels of social participation, leading to higher levels of well-being and life satisfaction. So, membership in a large, cohesive social network is good for a person's health (Tennstedt and McKinlay, 1987; Wilson, Moore, Rubin, and Bartels, 1990).

Some health programs encourage forming new self-sustaining friendship networks. Women who take part in these programs improve their social networks and increase their quality of life and self-esteem (Anstorp and Benum, 1988). In Quebec, two of every three older adult (ages 65 and older) provide support to others, making them important actors in their own informal support networks. Old people living alone or having small kinship networks receive less support than others (Martel and Légaré, 2001).

A key part of all case management is reconstructing social support networks damaged by illness or an inability to cope with severe illness (Pescosolido, Wright, and Sullivan, 1995). Though high levels of social support often reduce a primary caregiver's sense of a burden, interaction with family and friends often declines after people become caregivers.

Take rest; a field that has rested gives a bountiful crop.

—Ovid

A crust eaten in peace is better than a banquet partaken in anxiety.

—Aesop, *Fables*

How beautiful it is to do nothing, and then to rest afterward.

—Spanish proverb

We live longer than our forefathers; but we suffer more from a thousand artificial anxieties and cares. They fatigued only the muscles; we exhaust the finer strength of the nerves.

—Edward George Bulwer-Lytton

One of the symptoms of an approaching nervous breakdown is the belief that one's work is terribly important.

—Bertrand Russell

There is more to life than increasing its speed.

—Mohandas K. Gandhi

It is impossible to enjoy idling thoroughly unless one has plenty of work to do.

—Jerome K. Jerome,
The Idle Thoughts of an Idle Fellow

Source: www.quotegarden.com/stress.html.

Little study has been directed toward understanding how and why networks change when people become caregivers to AIDS victims, for example (Suitor and Pillemer, 1988).

SUPPORT AND COPING: A SYSTEMS VIEW

What makes social life regular and predictable, despite change and occasional turmoil, is that every family is largely self-anchoring. Like any organization, group, or society, a family is locked into certain ways of thinking and behaving. There are various reasons for this: among others, the strength of family culture, the dominance and interest of certain individuals (for example, parent over child, husband over wife), and the use of routines to meet family duties (for example, to work every day to pay the mortgage). Change can help or hinder a family, often unexpectedly. In predicting how a family will respond to the problems associated with childbirth, for example, a lot depends on the family, its organization, and its history. Different couples face the problems in different ways. Though relationship satisfaction changes in complicated ways with the birth of a first child, for example, the types of changes that occur depend on whether the couple planned the pregnancy, the gender of the unplanned child, and the couple's problem-solving abilities.

Families Change in Patterned Ways

As we have seen in this book, families follow a life cycle. Change is often difficult.

Not only do families change organizationally over time, but individual family members change too. They grow, mature, and decline in various ways, socially, psychologically, physiologically, and otherwise, and these changes usually affect interactions with other family members. Family rituals—complex, meaningful patterns of interaction—are often used to mark these changes in the lives of family members. Rituals and traditions are important to families as sources of strength, to uphold a family's system of shared behaviours and beliefs, and to communicate its identity. Rituals also strengthen families by linking practices, beliefs, and values across generations (Newell, 1999). So, the collapse of family ritual is itself a problem that needs solving.

Some members of a family change more rapidly or radically than others. Such out-of-phase changes can cause conflict. This may be the case with adolescents and young adult children. While often their departure improves relations between the parents, in some families it loosens the glue that has held a couple together for many years, and the parents separate. Some families are better able than others to adapt to such changes over the life cycle. During middle and later life, many emerging mental problems—sexual problems, substance abuse, psychosomatic problems, issues related to retirement or menopause—are a result of increased stress that is unmediated by social support or effective coping strategies (Kahana, Kahana, and Kinney, 1982).

Older adults experience many interpersonal losses—partner, siblings, and peers—and these losses have a direct impact on all the generations of the family. They call everyone's attention to mortality and the generational shifts occurring in the family. Some move away from their families to start new lives.

Each Family Has Its Own Characteristics

All families are alike in facing certain problems. At the same time, every family is unique. Families, being little societies, all have their own history, culture, language, myths, pet peeves, irrational fears, and blind enthusiasms. Also, every family has a view (or multiple views) about different lifestyles. If, for example, a family has a negative view of homosexuality—its meaning, origins, effects—and one family member has just "come out," the family faces a problem compounded of the characteristics of one of its members and the views of others. The family must confront this problem in its own unique way, at its own pace, and find its own way through the distress and communication barriers that will likely affect all members.

All Families Solve Problems

Families, like other human groups, often become very good at solving problems and resolving their conflicts. For parents in particular, good problem-solving skills are important. Better problem-solving skills result in more marital satisfaction before the birth of a child and less decline afterward.

Families can change themselves in response to changes in their environment and are capable of learning from their mistakes and changing by design because they comprise human actors. Methods of changing family dynamics include changing beliefs, changing positions and roles in the family, building a sense of optimism, and developing social interest (Dinkmeyer and Sherman, 1989).

Many families also show an astonishing ability to bounce back from misfortune. Solving problems is easiest if the parties to a dispute are like-minded. Similarity in perceptions between partners is an important dimension of the family system; it makes family life simpler. The members of better-functioning couples have more similar perceptions of their marriage and their family. This likeness between partners, which tends to be stable over time, supports family cohesion and is supported by it (Deal, Wampler, and Halverson Jr., 1992).

Well-functioning families set goals, plan for them, and carry them out. In well-functioning families, problem solving is an education of self-discovery. Families learn different ways to resolve conflict and change disabling ways of dealing with one another (Cox and Brooks-Gunn, 1999).

Some Families Need Help Solving Their Problems

People do not typically grow up knowing how to conduct their personal affairs, or family lives, in the best possible way. No wonder we have problems co-operating to change effectively. Yet, though all families change and solve problems, some families do so better, more easily, and more quickly than others. There are reasons families vary in this way.

Some people have grown up with the benefit of experience in well-functioning families in which people co-operate to solve their problems. There are also *systemic* reasons why some families solve their problems more easily. To set goals, make plans, and carry them out, families need leadership. Stronger families contain individuals who are willing to take responsibility for the family interest and try to mobilize support for a plan of action. Improvements in family relationships are more likely in homes where the parents can describe strategies for fostering family ties, showing that they have spent time thinking about the problem.

Families with stronger traditions of leadership, co-operation, and communication are more readily able to talk about their problems and their plans. For example, among the families of patients surviving bone marrow transplants and maintenance chemotherapy, strong family relationships are associated with better adjustment in every respect: physical, emotional, and social (Molassiotis, Van den Akker, and Broughton, 1997). Besides benefiting from inner strengths, some families rely on the support of extended, even multigenerational kin. Grandparents, for example, can be important sources of wisdom and relative disengagement from many family conflicts.

Families that need outside help solving their problems, however, can often get the support they need. Some seek family therapy, counselling, or family mediation, which help different kinds of families to different degrees; it is often impossible to know in advance what option will work best. Some people find discussing their problems in a group setting to be beneficial. Family therapy and participation in a common support group can balance one another, giving relief from feelings of isolation and treating complex issues of family dynamics (Goldstein, 1990).

Older adults also turn to outside help in order to cope with the stress associated with problems that they face, such as the death of their partner. Bereaved persons rely on a network of friends to help them cope. In both cases, a gendered pattern emerges—women tend to receive more emotional support from their children after the loss of their partner (Carr, 2004). Furthermore, men have few confidantes to turn to, while women are usually part of larger and more emotionally connected friendship networks (Antonucci and Akiyama, 1995). Since psychological and physical well-being is determined by the level of support received, bereaved people will search for companionship. Carr (2004) finds that men's interest in dating and remarriage depends on the amount of social support received from friends. Carr (2004) shows that 6 and 18 months after spousal loss, men with low or average levels of social support from friends are more likely than women to report interest in remarrying someday. Her findings reveal that in the absence of support from friends, widowers seek emotional support elsewhere, suggesting that late-life romantic relationships may be a source of companionship much needed by older adults.

Therefore, to reiterate, every family, like every group, organization, or society, has resources that help it address its system problems and system changes. The members of a family vary in their *coping skills*. Second, and more important, an effective family has good *systemic properties*. Specifically, they have a high degree of *cohesion* and a high degree of *flexibility*. That means the family roles and relationships can change when necessary, yet they are strong enough to stay put when no one needs or wants change. This is different from personal coping: Families with strong systemic properties can even endure the weaknesses and poor coping skills of their individual members. As a result, family membership makes its individual members better able to deal with the misfortunes of life.

At the same time, too much of either cohesion or flexibility is to be avoided. An excess of cohesion is repressive. It stifles individual development and may produce family members who are less competent and flexible than they need to be as individuals. An excess of flexibility is also undesirable, since it points to a lack of enough normative support in the family. No wonder, then, that Durkheim found that, just as too little attachment (that is, egoism) and too little normative control (that is, *anomie*) predict suicide, so do too *much* attachment and too *much* normative control.

Some families, unable to deal effectively with their problems—whether alcoholism, homosexuality, or infants who are critically ill or have disabilities—cope through a harmful form of religious denial, such as the everlasting belief in a miracle (York, 1987). Since miracles are rare, the problems remain. Weak families indulge in unrealistic thinking, self-blame, distancing, and denial (Judge, 1998). Strong families use their social supports and other types of resources they may have at their disposal.

VIOLENCE

There is rich feminist and anti-racism literature on the topic of family violence, as well as research developing in disability, queer, and anti-oppression perspectives.

Particularly important is a structural feminist analysis, rooted in gendered inequalities. We will comment on this issue throughout the chapter. Due to space limitations, we have only the slightest opportunity to touch on these perspectives in this chapter, and thereby risk omitting many significant recent findings.

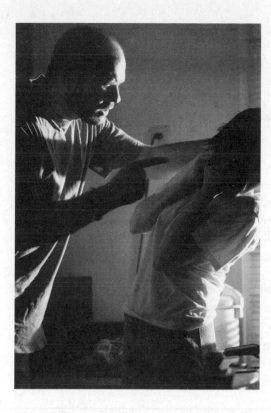

Men and women are equally as likely to commit small acts of violence; the greatest predictor is previous experience of violence at the hands of a mate or spouse, a parent, or witnessing it.

That said, the theme that runs throughout this literature is that the victims and survivors of violence are not to blame, nor is violence a result of family stress. All families experience stress at one time or another, but not all families experience violence. So stress is not integrally related to violence and abuse. This fact becomes plainly apparent in current research, which explores the relevance of broader social and structural factors that are commonly believed to be much more significant to the analysis of interpersonal violence. There cannot be a useful discussion of family violence without understanding the effects of poverty, immigration status, racism, and other forms of oppression that may affect an individual's perceived ability to leave a violent relationship. Much more than "learned helplessness" operates here to keep women, children, and older adults in abusive relations.

That said, a second theme also needs mentioning. In light of new research, victims of violence are more likely to be seen as survivors of violence. There is a growing literature on the ways abused and oppressed family members resist and fight back against abuse even while they remain locked in cycles of domestic violence they cannot escape and can scarcely avoid. So we must avoid objectifying the victims of violence and begin to recognize that the fight against abuse happens within family homes, as well as through legislation and other formal mechanisms.

So, how big a problem is family violence in our society? Discovering the exact statistics is difficult, partly for methodological reasons. To begin with, we have the problem of defining violence. What counts as violence varies from one culture to another and often from one family to another. Is female circumcision family violence? If it is, what about infant male circumcision? Also lacking is a widely accepted definition of what is a family (Gelles, 1994). Students of family violence come at the issue from a host of disciplines that include anthropology, sociology, psychology, social work, medicine, and criminology. Within each discipline, there are competing definitions of what counts as family violence, and various ways of measuring its extent. The term "family violence" did not even exist before 1930 (Busby, 1991: 336).

"Family violence" is an umbrella term covering different kinds of violence among different sets of family members. The oldest recognized form of violence is physical: the intentional use of physical force that one family member aims at hurting or injuring another family member (Busby, 1991: 335). It is estimated that family members, most commonly parents, carry out at least 20 percent of all physical assaults. Because of sexual violence's qualitatively different nature, researchers classify it separately from non-sexual physical violence and study it in its own right. Macmillan and Gartner (1999) note a variety of types of violence in the literature: "(1) *interpersonal conflict* violence, which almost exclusively involves pushing, shoving, grabbing, and slapping; (2) *non-systematic abuse*, which involves a greater variety of violent acts, including threats, the throwing of objects, kicking and hitting; and (3) *systematic abuse*, which involves a relatively high risk of all types of violent acts, including life-threatening violence such as beating, choking, and attacks with knives or guns" (p. 949). It is systematic abuse that most concerns researchers and policy makers.

Researchers also study emotional and psychological abuse. There are two reasons for including non-physical forms of abuse in studies of family violence: First, emotional abuse often accompanies violent acts. Second, emotional abuse is often as painful or destructive of the self-esteem and healthy emotional development of its victims as physical violence. Figure 8.1 covers some of the common forms of physical, sexual, and emotional abuse used against partners. Sexual abuse, neglect, and physical violence often stem from different causes. In the discussion that follows, we will focus on physical violence.

Data collection is a problem when trying to estimate the prevalence of family abuse in Canada, although family violence has to some degree been dragged out of the closet. We usually lack access to hospital records and case files gathered by social workers. Violence typically takes place in private, as part of a continuing intimate relationship. Despite these difficulties, sociologists have developed better techniques for estimating its prevalence. "Spousal Violence in Canada" shows recent statistics on the prevalence of spousal violence in Canada.

The first reliable and valid scale for measuring family violence, the **Conflict Tactics Scale**, measures verbal aggression and physical violence on a continuum. It looks at two dimensions. One is whether there have been three or more instances of violence in the previous year. The other is the severity of the act or acts. Factors included in the scale include the use of a weapon; injuries needing medical treatment; the involvement of a child, an animal, or a non-family member; drug or alcohol involvement; extreme dominance,

Figure 8.1 Power and Control Wheel

Source: Women's Safe Inc. Retrieved February 23, 2006, from www.theduluthmodel.org/pdf/PhyVio.pdf. The Power and Control Wheel was developed by the Domestic Abuse Intervention Project (DAIP), 202 E. Superior St., Duluth, Minnesota 55802. Reprinted with permission.

violence, or surveillance; forced sex; extensive or repeated property damage; and police involvement (Straus, 1996).

How common is **intimate partner violence**? We use this term, rather than *marital* or *spousal* violence, since both married and unmarried couples inflict violence on each other. In fact, one study found consistently higher rates of violence among cohabiting couples (Brownridge and Halli, 2002). Findings from five studies suggest that husband violence has occurred in up to *one-third* of couples who do not even report distress with their marriage and *one-half* of maritally distressed couples (Holtzworth-Munroe, Waltz, Jacobson, Monaco, Fehrenbach, and Gottman, 1992). On the other hand, some researchers have a tendency to inflate the number of events by using very broad definitions (see Chapter 3).

Who commits intimate partner violence? Men and women are almost equally likely to commit small acts of verbal, psychological, and physical violence in intimate relationships. Statistics Canada reports that women kick, slap, or throw things, whereas men are more likely to punch, choke their partners, or use a weapon (Serran and Firestone, 2004). Men are much more likely than women to commit the most physically and mentally harmful acts—for example, killing. Men are also more likely to engage in more prolonged violence than needed to actually kill their partners, often referred to as "over-kill," while the killing is also more likely to be sexualized than when women kill their partners (Gartner, Dawson, and Crawford, [2001] 1998). Women who do kill a partner do so for different reasons than men. Men kill partners who have just left them or are planning to leave them. (Also, men are likely to kill themselves after killing their "property.") Women are most likely to kill their partner if they have been suffering continued abuse and are prevented from leaving the relationship. They are unlikely to kill themselves or their children.

Moreover, records from women's shelters show five main types of battered women, determined by types of violence used and experienced: (1) women in stable, low-violence relationships who are likely to be violence instigators; (2) women in unstable relationships who suffer severe and often sexual violence; (3) severe and chronically abused women who have also seen their children abused; (4) women who were not abused but whose children were; and (5) chronically abused women who have grown to accept it.

One survey of self-reported domestic violence in Canada shows that (1) younger people are more violent to their spouses than older people; (2) unemployed people are more violent than employed people; but (3) lower-income and less educated people are no more violent than higher-income, highly educated people (Statistics Canada, 2005c).

These particular risk factors, and others, become increasingly obvious when examining intimate partner abuse among Aboriginals in Canada. Using survey data from 1999 and 2004, Brownridge (2008) has found that Aboriginal women are four times more likely

Spousal Violence in Canada

- Spousal violence reported to the police was more prevalent in Nunavut and Quebec (20 percent each) and lowest in British Columbia, Nova Scotia, and New Brunswick (8 percent each) (Statistics Canada, 2006e).

- Incidents of spousal violence were more common between current partners than former spouses (69 percent versus 31 percent) (Statistics Canada, 2006e).

- Common assault (61 percent) was the most frequently reported violent offence committed by a current or ex-spouse, followed by major assault (14 percent) and uttering threats (11 percent) (Statistics Canada, 2006e).

- Male victims of spousal abuse were twice as likely as female victims to report incidents of major assault (23 percent of male victims versus 13 percent of female victims). This may be because male abusers are more likely to use physical force, while female abusers rely on weapons (Statistics Canada, 2006e).

- Over the past decade (1997 to 2006), the largest proportion of spousal homicides has involved victims living in common-law relationships (39 percent), while another one-third (36 percent) of spousal homicides occurred between married persons (Statistics Canada, 2006e).

to experience intimate partner violence compared to non-Aboriginal women. More importantly, the high rate of violence against Aboriginal women has been linked to mental health problems, substance abuse, and an increase in HIV behaviour (Brownridge, 2008). Therefore, it seems that the Aboriginal community faces particular social and situational factors that increase the likelihood of violence in intimate relationships. For one, the Aboriginal community tends to be younger compared to the rest of the general Canadian population, have lower educational attainment, and have higher rates of cohabitation, factors that have been associated with partner violence (Brownridge, 2008). Furthermore, Aboriginals have higher rates of unemployment, are more likely to live in rural areas, abuse alcohol, and have higher fertility rates than non-Aboriginal Canadians, also putting them at an increased risk for partner violence (Brownridge, 2008). However, much of the elevated risk of partner violence for Aboriginal women has been linked to the colonization of Aboriginal peoples, which has negatively affected the community and its members' health (Brownridge, 2008), which will be discussed later in this chapter.

Causes of Violence

Violence between intimate partners raises many questions. Why would people abuse someone they have chosen to share their life with?

International Differences in Attitudes toward Partner Violence

- In East Asian cultures, outside intervention in family disputes brings dishonour and shame. This attitude makes it difficult for women to seek help and for professionals to treat them (Weil and Lee, 2004).

- Battered women in many countries in Latin America and the Caribbean are required to undergo medical examinations and receive certificates before they can file an official domestic violence complaint with the police. Often, medical examiners under-report the injuries suffered or see them as being less serious (Creel, 2005).

- In Sub-Saharan Africa, women's refusal of sex is often cited as the cause of family violence. Fear of violence prevents many women from insisting on condoms for birth control or disease prevention (Watts and Mayhew, 2004).

- Many women in Russia are killed by their partners or relatives; however, the country has no law specifically addressing domestic violence (Amnesty International UK, n.d.). In many countries in the region, laws or enforcement patterns do not treat family violence as seriously as other forms of assault (Stop Violence Against Women, 2003).

- In Turkey, men have the choice of marrying the victims (through forced marriages) that they sexually assaulted, raped, or abducted to reduce their punishment for these crimes (Amnesty International, 2004).

- In India, there is a high frequency of husbands physically abusing their pregnant wives. In a study done, almost half of the sample experienced being kicked while pregnant (Jain, Sanon, Sadowski, and Hunter, 2004).

Researchers continue to debate the causes of family violence (for a text that reviews many controversies in the literature, see Gelles and Loseke, 1993). Possible contributors range from personal factors, such as stress level or a history of abuse, to cultural ideologies of families and "discipline." We will examine a few of the more obvious and influential variables.

Previous Experience of Violence Violence tends to produce more violence. The single best predictor of violent behaviour toward a partner is the experience of violence at the hands of a partner, or at the hands of a parent, or having witnessed partner violence as a child. Abused people often abuse others even more vulnerable than themselves. Thus, husbands may abuse wives, and wives abuse children or older parents.

People who abuse their spouses often abuse their children as well; and the more often a person uses violence against a spouse, the more likely that person is to also use violence against a child. This relationship is especially strong for men. The likelihood of child abuse by a violent husband increases from 5 percent with one act of marital violence to near certainty with 50 or more such acts (Ross, 1996). Thus, children in abusive households are likely to both witness and experience domestic violence first-hand.

Children learn, by observation, to use violence to resolve disputes and vent frustration. Childhood experience doesn't explain all incidents of abusive behaviour, but it does account for many. According to Murray Straus (1992: 685), the more physical punishment a man experiences as a child, the higher is his likelihood of hitting a spouse. For it is in the family that children learn the normative legitimacy of family violence.

However, many children who suffer or witness abuse never become abusive adults. Boys are more likely to respond with violence, whereas girls more often internalize their problems, resulting in depression and anxiety.

Patriarchal Attitudes Some view domestic violence as a defence of patriarchy by men who fear that women's increasing economic and social independence is eroding their dominance. So, for example, an income disparity between husband and wife predicts the occurrence of wife abuse (McCloskey, 1996), particularly when it is the woman who has the higher income. Since employment is a symbolic resource in relationships—a source of status, power, and economic resources—spousal violence against women is most common when the wife has a job and the husband does not. Risks are low when neither partner is employed, or only the husband has a job (Macmillan and Gartner, 1999).

Interactional Styles On occasion, both husbands and wives are violent. Some researchers argue that, in these cases, violence is an *interactional problem*—a result of marital dysfunction. For example, Brinkerhoff and Lupri (1988) state, on the basis of a survey conducted in Calgary, that husband-to-wife, wife-to-husband, and mutual violence occur in families at every socio-economic, educational, and income level. The strongest predictors of violence are interactional—meaning that they arise from relationship processes such as marital conflict, usual modes of expressing aggression, and stresses induced by work.

So, Lupri (1993) used data from a representative national sample of Canadians to argue that male violence in the home is a widespread and, in that sense, "normal" element of marital interaction. Over the life course, partners negotiate and renegotiate their ways of interacting and dealing with conflicts, so patterns of violence change with age. According to this research, and contrary to common belief, wife-to-husband violence is frequent, and Canadian couples are reportedly more likely to engage in domestic violence, both severe and minor, than are American couples. The reason for this difference is unclear.

Psychologically abusive women show the same personality profiles as abusive men, characterized by jealousy, suspicion, immaturity, and insecurity. As to physical abuse, researchers report that more than 70 percent of these women have been physical to the point of shoving their husband or boyfriend or destroying their partner's possessions in anger (Stacey, Hazlewood, and Shupe, 1994: 124). Their spouses' superior strength kept them from more direct forms of assault, but many women nonetheless punched, slapped, kicked, or used a weapon against their partner. In such relationships violence is two-sided.

As Macmillan and Gartner (1999) have noted, "interpersonal conflict violence" is common and symmetrical, with equal numbers of male and female perpetrators. Battered women use more violence than women who are not battered, receive lower levels of social support, and experience higher levels of self-blame. Battered women, therefore, are more likely to use violence on their spouse when they feel they are receiving little social support, and even if they feel they are to blame for the conflict (Barnett, Martinez, and Keyson, 1996).

Most battered women in jail for killing their partner share a few distinctive characteristics. Typically, they were sexually assaulted during childhood, dropped out of high school, have an erratic work history of unskilled jobs, cohabited with their partner, experienced a drug problem, tried suicide by drug overdosing, and/or had access to the batterer's guns. These findings, based on interviews, help to explain why battered women kill their mates. After brutal, repeated assaults and death threats, and after failing in their attempts to escape through alcohol or drug abuse—even through attempted suicide—they see killing their abuser as the only way out (Roberts, 1996).

Women jailed for killing or assaulting their abusers are usually older, in the relationship longer, and have experienced a longer duration of violence in the relationship. They have also experienced more frequent and severe battering (including sex assaults) and suffered more injuries than a comparison group of battered women imprisoned for other offences. Further, battered women who killed or seriously assaulted their partners were more likely to believe that their lives were in danger. Often these women had no prior criminal record and had no history of violence before the killing (O'Keefe, 1997).

Status Inconsistency Status inconsistency—a state in which one does not quite fit into any social class—is another factor associated with increased risk of psychological and physical abuse, and an even greater risk of life-threatening violence. Violent men typically have lower levels of self-esteem than non-violent men from either stressed or happy marriages (Murphy, Meyer, O'Leary, and Daniel, 1994). These men tend to be more jealous and possessive (Shackelford and Mouzos, 2005) and to consider their wives' behaviour toward them to be more damaging to their self-esteem.

Alcoholism and Drug Abuse Excessive use of alcohol is a significant, though modest, predictor of both intimate-partner violence and child abuse (Merrill, Hervig, and Milner, 1996). Researchers have identified further variables that help explain the effects of alcohol on violence. Many drugs (including alcohol) are disinhibitors, causing people to relax their inhibitions, including inhibitions against violent behaviour. Other drugs increase adrenaline levels and, in this way, may cause anger or frustration levels to get out of control. Alcohol consumption is one of several high-risk behaviours that interact with poverty and stress to produce violence (Walters and Simoni, 1999).

In some couples, one or both partners excuse violence because of drinking or another extenuating circumstance. As a result, the violence has less impact on relationship satisfaction and thoughts of divorce (Katz, Arias, Beach, Brody, and Roman, 1995).

Lack of Coping Resources A lack of enough *coping resources* also increases the likelihood of violence in a family relationship. In one study, 90 percent of the violent families examined had serious problems such as financial difficulties and poor family cohesion. These families were also poorly integrated into society, with a resulting lack of social support (Bryant, Billingsley, and Kerry, 1963).

Social Isolation Lack of social support is a common predictor of physical child abuse. Mothers at the greatest risk of physically abusing their children are, typically, more socially isolated than others. Both practical support from work or school associates and emotional support from nurturing people help to decrease the potential for physical child abuse (Moncher, 1995).

Cultural Attitudes Attitudes that support violence as a whole, or violence against women and children in particular, also contribute to domestic violence. A society that overlooks violent behaviours may end up encouraging them.

Aboriginal communities, for example, are diverse and varied. In some Aboriginal communities, male authority and socio-economic stress are associated with restriction of women's activities and violence against women, but the levels of these factors vary widely across Aboriginal groups. Some Aboriginal groups practise matrilineal descent, while others are patrilineal, and this diversity has far-reaching implications for the community context in which domestic violence occurs. An approach that integrates both feminist and community approaches seems best suited to address the problem of domestic violence in Aboriginal North America.

Before the Aboriginal peoples were colonized, many communities were egalitarian and, as far as we can tell from records and reports, levels of intimate partner violence were low as a result. Violence in the home reportedly started when colonizers created hierarchies between men and women and used husbands to control women's sexuality. Violence by the state also helped create violence in the home. So, it should not be assumed that Aboriginal North Americans are just prone to violence, nor that their culture promotes violence; this habit is something that was introduced or at least reinforced by colonizers.

Acculturation may also contribute to violence by increasing the stress level. Findings by Firestone, Lambert, and Vega (1999) show that higher acculturation increases intimate abuse among immigrants. Abuse rates, for example, are higher among U.S.–born Mexican Americans than among immigrants. Results highlight the need for an improved understanding of acculturation stress.

Community violence—whether a result of patriarchal culture, substance abuse, warfare, poverty, or a combination of these—increases the likelihood of domestic violence. In Israel, Al-Krenawi, Slonim-Nevo, Maymon, and Al-Krenawi (2001) find levels of distress and symptomatic behaviour higher than Israeli norms among Arab adolescents who live under the threat of continuing blood vengeance. However, family functioning mediated these effects and emerged as the major predictor associated with mental health.

Likewise, Overstreet and Braun (2000) report that among African American children ages 10 to 15 living in or close to an inner-city public housing development, exposure to community violence produces perceptions of decreased neighbourhood safety and increased family conflict, which, in turn, leads to symptoms of post-traumatic stress disorder in the children.

It is unclear whether societies that overlook family violence have higher rates of violence than those that do not. However, societies that overlook violence offer less support to abuse victims. In the past, cultural myths prevented Canadian society from accepting domestic violence as a serious problem, and therefore recognizing the need for laws and institutions to protect victims. These myths included the belief that women typically provoke violence, and that family violence is a "private affair" and therefore police should stay out of it. To recognize a "battered-wife syndrome" was a big step toward condemning domestic violence (Fineman and Mykitiuk, 1994).

To understand the prevalence of domestic violence in our society, we must understand ordinary people's attitudes toward intimacy, gender, and violence. Even those who are innocent of violent behaviour may unwittingly support violence by their ways of thinking.

Traditional Family Values Values of male dominance, gender-based division of labour, and parental discipline of children are associated with high levels of family violence, including child sexual abuse (Higgins and McCabe, 1994). A review of previous studies finds that assaultive husbands are likely to support a patriarchal ideology, including approval of marital violence and disapproval of gender equality. Usually, people in our society who hold egalitarian sex-role beliefs are more sympathetic to battered women than are traditionalists (Coleman and Stith, 1997).

As a result, the remnants of antiquated notions of chivalry are sometimes used to justify gender inequality and therefore domestic violence against women. Also, because of cultural conceptions of masculinity, men are more tolerant of domestic violence than women.

A belief in patriarchy is more common among lower-status, less educated men. One would expect, therefore, violence would be particularly common among relatively uneducated people. However, this does not appear to be so (Statistics Canada, 2005c).

In their analysis of data from the Canadian Violence Against Women Survey (Statistics Canada, 1993), Macmillan and Gartner (1996) examine the effects of proprietary or "coercively controlling" attitudes on domestic violence. The jealous husband does not want his wife to talk to other men. He tries to limit her contact with family or friends, insists on knowing whom she is with and where she is at all times, and prevents her from knowing about or having access to the family income, even if she asks.

Often, psychologically and physically abusive men fear the loss of their partner, whom they consider sexual and emotional property. These abusive men show a high degree of jealousy and always try to oversee their spouse or girlfriend. High levels of reported coercive control predict domestic violence and especially the most serious, systematic abuse (Macmillan and Gartner, 1996). Violence is used to gain power in the relationship (Schwartz, Waldo, and Daniel, 2005).

The effects of traditionalism on beliefs about domestic violence are even more obvious in recently industrializing countries. For example, residents of Singapore disapprove of wife beatings, even when extramarital affairs or child abuses by women are involved. However, beatings are more acceptable if people see the wife as violating her

Table 8.2 What Is a Healthy Relationship?

Negotiation and fairness	Seeking mutually satisfying resolutions to problems and being able to compromise.
Non-threatening behaviour	Talking and acting so both partners feel safe and comfortable expressing their feelings.
Respect	Listening in a non-judgmental way and valuing each other's opinions.
Trust and support	Supporting each other's life goals and rights to personal goals, friends, activities, and opinions.
Honesty and accountability	Accepting responsibility for self and communicating openly and truthfully.
Responsible parenting	Sharing parental responsibilities and being a positive, non-violent role model for children.
Shared responsibility	Mutually agreeing on a fair distribution of work and making family decisions together.
Economic partnership	Making money decisions together and making sure both partners benefit from financial agreements.

Source: Adapted with permission from the Equality Wheel developed by Domestic Abuse Intervention Project (DAIP), 202 E. Superior St., Duluth, Minnesota 55802. Retrieved May 12, 2009, from www.theduluthmodel.org/pdf/NonVio.pdf.

prescribed sex role, especially in failing to be the "good mother" and the "loyal wife" (Choi and Edleson, 1996). In traditional or recently industrialized societies, women themselves have a hard time escaping from these traditional notions. Recent immigrants may hold on to such notions. For example, many Indian immigrant women in North America show the effects of patriarchal thinking in their acceptance of domestic violence.

Causes and Effects of Stress and Violence in Immigrant Families

Immigration is a major life transition. Therefore, it is the cause of stress for the families undergoing this significant change. More importantly, the stress of immigration may never completely diminish even after many years of being in the new country. A study done by Mirdal (2006) indicates that although the financial situation of immigrant women and their families had significantly improved in the years after immigration, the women still experienced a high level of stress regarding their immigrant status and the challenges of living in a county they still had some difficulty accustoming to.

So, how do immigrants deal with this stress? For one, many choose to live in areas that will be more familiar, both in language and culture, to their old communities. The cultural enclaves of the Greater Toronto Area are examples of such areas. Here, immigrants find social support from other immigrants and are less distressed with acculturation and the challenges this poses. Immigrant parents, for instance, are then less pressured to fit in quickly, and can in turn provide social support for their assimilating children (Thomas and Choi, 2006). As a result, the children can go on to integrate smoothly with peers in school and pursue higher education and employment in the new country. Research has shown that good familial relationships are fundamentally important in the acculturation of immigrant children (see Birman and Taylor-Ritzler, 2007, on information about acculturation of adolescents from the former Soviet Union).

On the other hand, studies have also found that less acculturated children experience less discrimination and psychological distress (Buddington, 2002). This may be because they retain their cultural identity by befriending peers of the same cultural background or find other ways of being connected to their indigenous culture.

Although not all stress escalates into familial conflicts resulting in domestic violence, there is some evidence that stress related to immigration can do this quite readily, especially among families from traditionally patriarchical societies. For instance, a study by Kim-Goh and Baello (2008) found that immigrant men with low education attainment levels are most likely to approve of violence, especially toward non-compliant wives. Therefore, it seems that the risk factors for abusive relationships in immigrant families include patriarchical authority, strict gender roles, lack of education, and women's financial dependence on partners especially related to immigration status (Morash, Bui, Zhang, and Holtfreter, 2007; Ammar, 2007; Hadas, Markovitzky, and Sarid, 2008). So, how are wives of such husbands to deal with this abuse, especially those who are economically and perhaps emotionally dependent?

Bui and Morash (2007) claim that social networks within immigrant communities are most helpful for these women. The support of family and friends is especially alleviating for distress associated with abuse. However, family and friends often discourage women from utilizing legal services to deal with abuse for various reasons, many of which relate to traditional gender roles and responsibilities. Also, closed networks limit opportunities for other sources of help available.

Types of Abusive Relationships

Child Abuse In 1946, the investigation of a child with an unexplained head injury led to the phrase **battered-child syndrome**. Before that, people often merely labelled beating a child "strict discipline." Systematic observation led researchers to find more cases. In 1962, Kempe, Silverman, Steel, Droegmueller, and Silver watched hospitals and found 302 (known) cases of child abuse in one year. Of these children, 33 died and 85 suffered permanent brain injury. The syndrome could affect children at any age but mainly affected children younger than the age of three. This study led to the first legislation that required professionals working with children to report suspected cases of abuse.

As we mentioned earlier, abused children often grow up to be abusive adults. Also, child abuse contributes to the risk of delinquent behaviour. Most young delinquents have suffered childhood abuse of some kind, and among those young offenders classified as psychopathic (meaning that they are unable to internalize moral standards or form deep attachments) the level of childhood abuse is even higher.

It may not be possible to provide a valid estimate of the population affected by parent–child violence, but the true number is likely high. Child homicide by parents offers an extreme but well-documented version of child abuse. In the first few weeks of a child's life, the risk of being killed by a parent is about equal for males and females. From one week to 15 years, males are the victims in about 55 percent of all parent–child homicides. In the 16- to 18-year age groups, this proportion increases to 77 percent (Kunz and Bahr, 1996). For a closer look at child and youth abuse in Canada, see "Six Key Findings on Child and Youth Abuse."

Both child abuse and elder abuse arise from attempts by the caregiver to control behaviour they find problematic. Male abusers typically use physical violence, whereas female abusers tend toward neglect or emotional manipulation (Penhale, 1993). Sometimes, adult children abuse the parents who abused them in childhood.

Note, finally, that lone mothers, although they are considerably more disadvantaged than partnered mothers, do *not* punish their children more frequently or more severely (Nobes and Smith, 2002). When fathers' actions are included, children from two-parent families are found to have been physically punished more frequently and severely (Nobes and Smith, 2002). This would argue against the notion that two-parent families are invariably better for children than single-parent families.

Six Key Findings on Child and Youth Abuse

- In 2006, children and youth younger than age 18 were most likely to be physically or sexually assaulted by someone they know (Statistics Canada, 2006e).

- The rate of sexual assault committed by family members was four times higher for girls compared to boys (Statistics Canada, 2006e).

- Boys were more likely to sustain physical injuries resulting from family violence (Statistics Canada, 2006e).

- The rate of physical assault by a parent was more than three times higher than the rate of sexual assault (Statistics Canada, 2006e).

- Six in ten homicides against children and youth were committed by family members in 2006 (Statistics Canada, 2006e).

- Infants (younger than one year of age) experienced higher rates of family-related homicide compared to older children, with baby boys being at a somewhat greater risk than baby girls (Statistics Canada, 2006e).

Elder Abuse Elder abuse receives less attention in our society than child abuse and spousal violence, partly because it is less common and perhaps also because we have less interest in older parents than in wives and children. Most would admit that children are our future; however, many see older adults as burdens we must put up with until they pass on (Biggs, Phillipson, and Kingston, 1995). Another reason may be the economic prosperity of the past few decades, which allowed many seniors to provide for their own needs instead of being dependent on their children. However, with the aging of the baby boom population and the decrease of available pension funds, we may see an increased interest in the well-being of older adults.

Abuse of older adults is sometimes described as a misuse of power and a violation of trust. Abusers may use many different tactics to exert power and control over their victims. Abuse may happen once or it may occur in a repeated and intensifying pattern over months or years. The abuse may take many different forms, which may change over time. There are various types of abuse:

- **Psychological abuse** includes efforts to dehumanize or intimidate older adults. Any act that reduces their sense of self-worth or dignity and threatens their psychological and emotional integrity is abuse. This abuse may include, for example, threatening to use violence, threatening to abandon them, and intentionally frightening them.

- **Financial abuse** encompasses financial manipulation or exploitation including theft, fraud, forgery, or extortion. Anytime someone acts without consent in a way that financially or personally benefits one person at the expense of another it is abuse. Such acts may include stealing their money, pension cheques, or other possessions, selling their homes or other property without their permission, failing to use their assets for their benefit, and wrongfully using a power of attorney.

- **Physical abuse** includes any act of violence, whether or not it results in physical injury. Physical abuse may include, for example, beating, burning, or scalding, and pushing or shoving. Other forms of physical abuse may include tying older adults to furniture, using or misusing physical restraints, and excessively restraining them with alcohol, tranquilizers, or other medication.

- **Neglect** involves failing to care for older adults who are dependent and cannot meet their own needs. This type of abuse may include, for example, failing to provide enough nutrition, clothing, and other needs, satisfactory personal care, safe and comfortable conditions, and access to medical or health services, aids, or assistive devices, or treatment for substance abuse.

- **Sexual abuse** includes behaving in a sexual way toward older adults without their full knowledge and consent. It includes all forms of sexual assault, sexual harassment, or sexual exploitation. (Adapted from Canada, Department of Justice, 2003).

Approximately 7 percent of the sample of more than 4000 adults 65 years of age and older who responded to the 1999 General Social Survey on Victimization (GSS) reported that they had experienced some form of emotional or financial abuse by an adult child, spouse, or caregiver in the five years prior to the survey, with the vast majority committed by spouses. (Other sources show more abuse by adult children.) Emotional abuse was more frequently reported (7 percent) than financial abuse (1 percent). The two most common forms of emotional abuse reported were being put down or called names, or having contact with family and friends limited. Only a small proportion of older adults (1 percent) reported experiencing physical or sexual abuse. Almost 2 percent of older Canadians indicated that they had experienced more than one type of abuse.

According to the incidence-based Uniform Crime Reporting (UCR2) Survey, in 2000 the largest category of police-reported violent crime committed against older adults by family members was assault—usually common assault, such as pushing, slapping, punching, and threats to apply force.

Older adults' experiences of abuse may be related to their living arrangement (living alone, with family members or others, or in an institution) and to their reliance on others for help and support in daily living (Canada, Department of Justice, 2003). For example, abuse in private homes may grow out of the older adult's financial or emotional dependence on family members or others, or vice versa. In long-term care facilities, abuse may relate to the often-intimate processes in which staff and residents are involved, including feeding, bathing, dressing, moving, and providing medication and other treatments. Therefore, it is important to educate older women on how to discourage violence against them and encourage them to actively participate in life and maintain their social support networks. This is especially true for those who live on lower incomes, have difficulty finding reliable transportation, and do not have someone to trust with the management of their money (Barnett, Buys, Lovie-Kitchin, Boulton-Lewis, Smith, and Heffernan, 2007).

Moreover, since immigration trends have contributed significantly to Canada's ethnocultural diversity in the aging sector of the population, the issue of elder abuse has to be studied in different cultural environments. It is estimated that approximately one-third of the country's older citizens were born outside of Canada (Wasylkewycz, 1993, in Podnieks, 2008). When examining elder abuse in Canadian ethnic communities, Bergin (1995) finds that, much like the circumstances that lead to elder abuse in the general population, financial and emotional dependency, socio-economic factors, dysfunctional family dynamics, and caregiver stress may lead to elder abuse, or its perpetuation, in ethnocultural communities. Added to those risk factors in immigrant families are language barriers, social isolation, and sociocultural factors. Often norms and values that are inconsistent with Canadian customs allow for the continuation of abuse into old age. For instance, issues of privacy, obligation, and unfamiliarity with formal services available to solve personal problems often prevent members of Asian families from seeking help (Yoshioka, Gilbert, El-Bassel, and Baig-Amin, 2003). Abused ethnocultural older people are unaware of their legal rights or about community resources. Unfortunately, the conditions of legal sponsorship, programs that reunify the family but reinforce elder dependence on the younger generations, may create circumstances that can lead to elder abuse.

When it comes to elder abuse in First Nations communities in Canada, the research is scarce. As already mentioned, there are overall higher rates of family violence in Aboriginal communities than in the non-Aboriginal population in Canada. Whether this holds true for the incidence and prevalence of elder abuse both on- and off-reserve remains to be confirmed (Dumont-Smith, 2002). A 1997 report by the Native Women's Association of Canada on Aboriginal elder abuse revealed that elderly Aboriginal women were abused due to financial reasons, lack of respect due to loss of traditional roles, lower level of education, and drug and alcohol problems of abusers (Dumont-Smith, 2002). More recently, a study on Aboriginal elders in the City of Toronto found that abuse is very common and is of various types, including economic and social marginalization, neglect, and lack of emotional support from family and other caregivers (Cyr, 2005). To prevent future abuse of Aboriginal elders and to provide resources for coping, more research needs to be done in this area.

Sibling Abuse The most common form of domestic violence is one that is considered natural, and therefore most acceptable in our society: between-sibling violence (Steinmetz, 1977). We often excuse violence between children by saying they "don't know better." For whatever reason, little research is done on sibling abuse. In general, the sibling relationship is less studied than the other spouse–spouse and parent–child relationships.

Same-Sex Violence Partner violence seems to be as prevalent in the gay and lesbian community as in the heterosexual community. In a sample of 499 ethnically diverse gay men, lesbians, bisexual, and transgendered people, physical violence was reported in 9 percent of current relationships and 32 percent of past relationships. One percent of participants had experienced forced sex in their current relationship and 9 percent in past

Elder Abuse in Canada

- Senior victims are more likely to be victimized by someone they know than by a stranger (Statistics Canada, 2006e).

- Senior victims of violence are most likely to report being victimized by an adult child or current or former spouse (Statistics Canada, 2006e).

- Senior female victims killed by a family member are most likely to be killed by their spouse (40 percent) or adult son (34 percent), while senior male homicide victims are most likely to be

killed by their adult son or stepson (61 percent) (Statistics Canada, 2006e).

- Older seniors (ages 85 and older) are less likely to report being victims of family violence compared to younger seniors (ages 75 to 84) and seniors ages 65 to 74 (Statistics Canada, 2006e).

- Common assault is the most commonly reported violent offence against seniors, followed by uttering threats and robbery (Statistics Canada, 2006e).

relationships. Emotional abuse was reported by 83 percent of the participants. Women reported higher frequencies than men of physical abuse, coercion, shame, threats, and use of children for control. Ethnic differences in physical abuse and coercion emerged. Higher income was correlated with increased threats, stalking, sexual, physical, and financial abuses (Turell, 2000).

In another study, 283 white gay men and lesbians, ages 18 to 79, reported on their experiences both as victims and perpetrators of relationship violence by completing a modified version of the Conflict Tactics Scale. Almost half (47.5 percent) of the lesbians and 29.7 percent of the gays reported being victims of abuse. Thirty-eight percent of lesbians reported having perpetrated abuse, compared with 21.8 percent for gay men (Waldner-Haugrud, Gratch, and Magruder, 1997).

Internalized homophobia is a strong predictive factor for gay and lesbian partner violence. Other factors include violence in the family of origin, substance abuse, and dependency conflicts (West, 1998). As with heterosexuals, poor communication and social skills make it harder to solve problems peacefully, and thus make violence more likely (McClennen, 2005).

McClennen (2005) found *power imbalance* to be a significant factor in violence in lesbian and gay couples. However, violence can occur in egalitarian couples too, as found in a study done on 52 psychologically abusive gay male couples (Landolt and Dutton, 1997). This may be because of other causes: for example, low self-esteem, secrecy due to not coming out, and lack of social support.

Same-sex violence challenges feminist theory on domestic violence. If patriarchal values and gender difference lead to partner violence, then why is it equally high among same-sex couples? Domestic violence theories that integrate a sociopolitical and psychological analysis of battering are better able to explain same-sex domestic violence (Klinger, 1995; Letellier, 1994) by focusing on power as something that is only *partly* predicted by gender.

Violence against Women in the Context of Poverty

Violence against women is widespread and occurs in all segments of society. However, rates of intimate partner violence are particularly high among low-income and homeless women both in Canada and the United States (Bassuk, Dawson, and Huntington, 2006; Morrow, Hankivsky, and Varcoe, 2004; Purvin, 2007). Among them, less educated, younger women with weaker social networks are even more likely to experience severe and recurring violence (Frias and Angel, 2007).

Seeming commitment to an abusive partner is strongest among women who have limited economic alternatives and are more heavily invested in their relationships. Thus, women with little education—and therefore little chance of achieving economic independence—and women with preschool children are more likely to stay. With practical help, these women could achieve economic independence and sever their ties with an abusive partner. Economic dependence on the partner or spouse, limited welfare assistance, and access to resources for coping with short-term and long-term effects of poverty restrict the available options.

Moreover, an interesting finding that calls for further research into this issue is the presence of significant ethnic variation among low-income women. Frias and Angel (2007) found that Hispanic women report the lowest lifetime rates of partner abuse than non-Hispanic white or African American women, and they also face lower risks of the initiation of abuse. In contrast, Hispanic and African American women are more likely than non-Hispanic white women to remain in an abusive relationship (Frias and Angel, 2007). Therefore, when it comes to intimate partner violence, we need to be wary of generalizations based on race, ethnicity, or income and realize that there are important differences in women's experience of domestic violence.

Effects of Violence

We know all too little about the thoughts and feelings of people involved in domestic violence. The victims of violence are less likely than average to verbalize their thoughts and feelings. In particular, female victims are much less aware of their emotional states and express many fewer positive feelings than the average adult woman (for a general review of this topic, see Jones, Hughes, and Unterstaller, 2001). This lack of emotional expression is likely an effect we spoke of earlier, called *post-traumatic stress disorder* (PTSD).

More than four in five battered women meet the criteria for a diagnosis of PTSD, as do two in three verbally abused women (Kemp, Green, and Hovanitz, 1995). Compared with other battered women, those with PTSD have been the victims of more physical abuse, more verbal abuse, more injuries, a greater sense of threat, and more forced sex. Besides the battery itself, other factors contributing to PTSD are the experience of other distressing life events and a lack of sensed social support.

Though not all violent events produce PTSD, battered women are three times as likely to suffer from PTSD as are women who are maritally distressed but have not suffered battering. Women showing symptoms of PTSD—whether battered or not—are more likely to report having experienced childhood sexual abuse. They also report more previous traumas than women without PTSD.

Though little research has been done on the linkage between spousal abuse and PTSD, much research has documented other symptoms of domestic violence that are similar to symptoms of PTSD. For example, women subject to violence or forced sex have more fear of future assaults than other women (DeMaris and Swinford, 1996).

Abused women typically have lower self-esteem and less faith in their own efficacy than non-abused women. Another common result of domestic violence is depression. As physical abuse increases in severity, so does the woman's depression (Orava, McLeod, and Sharpe, 1996). At a domestic violence shelter, more than four women in five are at least mildly depressed, and more than half remain depressed for six months or more after leaving the abusive home. Feelings of powerlessness, repeated abuse, and inadequate social support all contribute to persisting depression (Campbell, Sullivan, and Davidson, 1995).

Social and economic factors also conspire to make women fear their vulnerable and dependent condition. Typically, battered women live in "coercively controlling" environments and experience powerlessness and economic dependency (Forte, Franks, and Forte, 1996). To hide domestic conflict, abusive husbands often try to isolate their spouses, so that they also suffer from social isolation (Lempert, 1996).

Jacobson, Gottman, Gortner, Berns, and Shortt (1996) find that only 38 percent of couples separate or divorce in the two years following an early assessment of severe husband-to-wife violence. Why do women remain in abusive relationships? Some have been taught to forgive and forget, and feel they ought to help their spouses be better people and support them through stresses. Also, abuse that is coercively controlling creates feelings of powerlessness and hopelessness (Aguilar and Nunez Nightingale, 1994). Often women fear increased abuse, for themselves or their children, if they try to leave; blackmail and threats are not uncommon. Women may have few resources and believe they have nowhere to go. Some feel they deserve the abuse. Episodes of leaving or thinking about leaving are embedded in cycles of abuse. Commonly, after an abusive episode, the perpetrator apologizes, showers the victim with gifts and affection, and promises it won't happen again. Abused wives are inclined to think it's the last time and the abusive husband has changed and didn't mean to be violent. Added to this is social pressure to be in a relationship: the common view that marriage is for better or for worse, and that one ought to stick it out because marriage and family is the bedrock of society. Preoccupation with the relationship is associated with more frequent previous separations from the relationship, continuing emotional involvement with the partner after separation, and more frequent sexual contact with the partner (Henderson, Bartholomew, and Dutton, 1997). Interestingly, women with high degrees of physical disabilities may also find it hard to leave a violent relationship. Hassouneh-Phillips and McNeff (2005) found that women with high degrees of physical impairments were more likely to feel they were unattractive and sexually inadequate than other women with mild impairments. Low self-esteem and a strong desire to be partnered, especially with non-disabled men, increased the likelihood that disabled women would enter and stay in abuse relationships over time (Hassouneh-Phillips and McNeff, 2005).

Moreover, battered women often lose the ability to decide about their relationship in their own best interest. However, some research (for example, Campbell, Miller, and Cardwell, 1994) rejects a "learned helplessness" model for most women experiencing abuse. These researchers believe that most abused women just need practical help and advice to be able to break with their past. They argue for supporting battered women seen in the health-care and social services systems, so they can more easily decide the status of their relationship.

Witnessing Violence

Children also suffer from domestic violence, possibly even more than adults (Engle, Castle, and Menon, 1996). Witnessing violence between one's parents harms children's emotional and behavioural development (Kolbo, Blakely, and Engleman, 1996). Effects include aggression, delinquency, feelings of anxiety and depression, lowered self-worth, and poor academic performance.

Parent–child violence is also common in families where parent–parent violence occurs. Both are significant predictors of adolescent behaviour problems (O'Keefe, 1996). Exposure to physical abuse produces open hostility in children and a tendency to flare up in anger without a specific provocation. (Exposure to *emotional* abuse is more likely to produce shame, hostility, and anger, both expressed and unexpressed.) Often, the outcomes of domestic violence are gender-specific. Females tend to internalize their emotions, reporting higher levels of shame and guilt. Males are more likely to lash out or drink to excess.

Witnessing interparental violence is associated with more depression and post-traumatic stress disorder (PTSD) symptomology, even when controlling for demographic variables, quality of parent-child relationships, personal victimization, and other life stressors. PTSD symptoms and depression increase with the frequency of incidents witnessed but not with the severity of the violence. These results contribute to the growing body of research that stresses the importance of treating exposure to interparental violence as a risk factor for youth.

Factors that influence the effects of witnessing violence include whether the child was also abused, child gender and age, and time since last exposure to violence (Edleson, 1999). Among college undergraduates, witnessing marital violence is associated with other family mental health risks, childhood physical and sexual abuse, and adult physical assaults by strangers (Feerick and Haugaard, 1999).

Like battered women, battered children show signs of post-traumatic stress disorder (Wind and Silvern, 1994). Motta (1994) suggests that a rise in family violence, violence within schools, and various other stressors are leading to the characteristic PTSD symptoms increasingly noted among children.

A reported one-quarter to one-third of all female children suffer *sexual abuse* before their 18th birthday, and at least one-half of all women with severe mental illness admit such events. An even higher percentage of mentally ill homeless women have a history of childhood victimization (Rosenberg, Drake, and Mueser, 1996). Among adolescent psychiatric patients, family dysfunction and trauma are more marked in those who have been sexually abused (Wherry, Jeffrey, Jolly, Aruffo, Gillette, Vaught, and Methony, 1994). Sexual abuse, parental assault, and kidnapping experiences are especially strong predictors of depression and PTSD-related symptoms in 10- to 16-year-olds studied over a long period (Boney-McCoy and Finkelhor, 1996). Parental substance abuse, family conflict, and exposure to both child and adult abuse set in motion a vicious circle that predicts substance abuse and violence in later life (Sheridan, 1995).

In short, a **cycle of abuse** exists—a tendency for abused girls and daughters of abused mothers to become abused women and for male children of abusive fathers to become abusive fathers themselves. The connection between childhood abuse and adult abuse may lie in interpersonal functioning. Children who grow up in abusive families do not learn how to conduct their lives, or their marriages, in non-abusive ways, or how to prevent the escalation of violence or abuse (Weaver and Clum, 1996).

CONCLUDING REMARKS

We can learn a great deal from research about the best ways to intervene to solve problems of family stress and violence. First, we learn that violence is a major factor causing women to leave their marriages and children to leave their parents' home. Second, programs that try to address abuse directly—such as civil restraining orders, treatment programs for batterers, and policies requiring compulsory arrest and no dropped charges—are not usually effective in solving the problem of domestic violence (Davis and Smith, 1995). By contrast, treatments aimed at reducing alcohol and drug abuse may make a long-term difference to the likelihood of future violence (O'Farrell and Murphy, 1995; Brannen and Rubin, 1996).

Third, we must actively address problems like stress and violence. If we want to reduce family stresses, we must create a society that is family friendly, with increased social support and practical help to working parents with small children. Fourth, research shows us that the health and social service professions are, sadly, far behind the times. Fifth, research shows us that personal lives, and families, are increasingly diverse. For example, because of language, cultural, and immigration issues, recently arrived immigrant and refugee women have needs that differ markedly from most battered women in the general population (Huisman, 1996). Along similar lines, lesbians are less likely than heterosexual women to use traditional battered women services that were designed for male–female relationships. Gay men face similar problems.

In the end, however, we must recognize there will be no major decline in the violence against family members until societies reduce the stresses on family members and increase the personal value of all people—especially children, women, older adults, the poor, immigrants, and sexual minorities. Societies must also reject the cultural justifications for domestic violence and deprive violent people of opportunities to hide or repeat their behaviour. Ending domestic violence must be a societal project, no less complex than dealing with unemployment, illiteracy, AIDS, or any of a dozen other recognized social problems.

CHAPTER SUMMARY

We have discussed two realities—stress and violence—that reveal the dark side of close relations. Stress, like the other family problems we discussed in the previous chapter, is a normal part of family life. We may have trouble coping with it, but stress can never be removed from our lives.

Common causes of family stress fall into at least four categories: major upheavals, such as wars and natural disasters; major life transitions, such as the birth of a child or divorce; chronic stresses, such as chronic illnesses, drug abuse, or unemployment; and occasional stresses, such as a car accident or the flu.

Violence is a potential outcome of family stress. Domestic violence is widespread throughout society and diverse in nature. Family violence can take the form of physical, emotional, or psychological abuse. Stress does not always lead to violence, nor does violence always result from stress alone. However, stress is a common antecedent of violent behaviour and often mediates between violence and social conditions such as poverty and unemployment.

As we have seen, the experience of abuse in childhood or adulthood predicts more violence. Partner violence is also often associated with violence against children in the household. Although the perpetrators of violence are often men, women also abuse their male partners, but the motivation of the violence is different for each sex. Other types of violence include child abuse and elder abuse, which arise from attempts by the caregiver to control behaviour they find problematic. We have also seen how certain populations in society such as immigrants, Aboriginals, and the poor are particularly vulnerable to various forms of abuse. More importantly, by exploring the violence within these groups, it has become obvious that particular groups face unique dangers and factors that lead to and perpetuate violence.

Lastly, the effects of domestic violence are severe and widespread. They include depression, post-traumatic stress disorder, social isolation, and economic dependency. Children exposed to abuse are more likely to become abusers themselves, perpetuating the cycle of violence.

Key Terms

ABCX family crisis model A model of stress in which *A*, which represents the stressor event, interacts with *B*, the family's crisis-meeting resources, and with *C*, the family's interpretation of the event, to produce *X*, the crisis.

acculturative stress Stress originating from the challenges involved in adapting to a new society.

battered-child syndrome Physical injury due to abuse by parents or caregivers.

conflict tactics scales An instrument developed by Murray Straus to measure the extent of domestic violence based on frequency and severity of incidents.

cycle of abuse A tendency for family violence to repeat itself from one generation to the next, as abused girls and daughters of abused mothers grow up to become abused women, and abused boys or sons of abusive fathers grow up to become abusive husbands or fathers.

crisis episodes Significant events that are likely to lead to seeking help from professionals, changing caregiving conditions, and precipitating decision making.

domestic violence Family violence; violence against any member of the household, including a child, spouse, parent, or sibling.

elder abuse Physical violence, psychological cruelty, or neglect directed at an older person, usually by a caregiving family member.

intimate-partner violence Physical abuse between the members of a couple. It may be reciprocal ("common couple violence") or directed by one partner against the other, and may occur between cohabiters as well as legally married couples.

status inconsistency Lack of congruence between the various indicators of social class, such as education and occupation, or wealth and prestige.

stressor Something that causes stress; a challenge or threat.

Critical Thinking Questions

1. Why are some populations in society (for instance, single mothers, low-income families) especially vulnerable to chronic stress? Is their vulnerability based on larger structural problems inherent to their populations or rather due to a lack of coping resources?

2. Some have argued that family members, especially women, can obtain a high degree of satisfaction from caregiving. What are some positive aspects of caregiving for the caregiver? What changes can be made within the family to make caregiving a more positive experience?

3. Why is being an immigrant so stressful? Recalling changes to immigrant status in Canada mentioned in Chapter 2, further discuss the gendered implications between men and women in the family and how these changes can lead to violence.

4. Does the view of the elderly as burdensome and unproductive members of society make them more susceptible to abuse? Or are other factors more important in determining their vulnerability to violence?

5. Speculate why some children who are abused by their parents do not grow up to be abusers themselves, while others do.

6. Recalling information from previous chapters on Aboriginal communities in Canada, further account for the prevalence of family violence and familial fragmentation in this population. What changes can be made in Canadian policy to produce healthier Aboriginal families?

7. This chapter has mentioned many reasons why battered women stay in abusive relationships. What do you think is one of the most important reasons why women do not leave violent situations (for instance, financial, children, low self-esteem, and so on)?

8. Both men and women commit acts of intimate partner violence. However, men and women commit acts of abuse in different ways. How do men and women differ in the way they commit intimate partner violence and the reasons behind their actions? Why might these differences exist?

Weblinks

Shelternet.ca
www.shelternet.ca
This site provides a wide range of information about abuse offered in a variety of languages, including a comprehensive listing of women's shelters across the country and information specifically geared for kids and teenagers suffering from abuse.

Ontario Women's Justice Network
www.owjn.org
This site offers legal information related to violence against women, specifically on justice and legal issues

regarding rural, immigrant, transgender, and impoverished women.

Canadian Mental Health Association
www.cmha.ca
This site provides a wide range of information on mental health issues in Canada, including resources to better understand and prevent stress and violence.

Native Women's Association of Canada
www.nwac-hq.org
This site provides important resources for Aboriginal women in Canada, including a violence prevention kit that helps

female Aboriginal youth recognize and leave abusive relationships at www.nwac-hq.org/en/yvptoolkit.html.

Canadian Research Institute for the Advancement of Women
www.criaw-icref.ca
This site provides excellent and comprehensive information on the issues facing rural, immigrant, and low-income women.

Canadian Network for the Prevention of Elder Abuse
www.cnpea.ca
This wonderful source of information on elder abuse in English and French provides information on policy and practice for elderly issues in Canada, along with helpful links and resources to learn more about elder abuse prevention.

Changing Ways
www.changingways.on.ca
This site provides a variety of information on ways that men can stop violence against women, including important links to hotlines that offer 24-hour support to men, women, and children who suffer from abuse, along with information for both men and women on identifying and changing their abusive ways.

Ontario Women's Directorate
www.citizenship.gov.on.ca
This site provides specific information on women's legal, wellness, and child issues, along with resources for young women about sexual harassment and equality issues.

Chapter 9
Divorce and Ending Relationships
Trends, Myths, Children, and Ex-Spouses

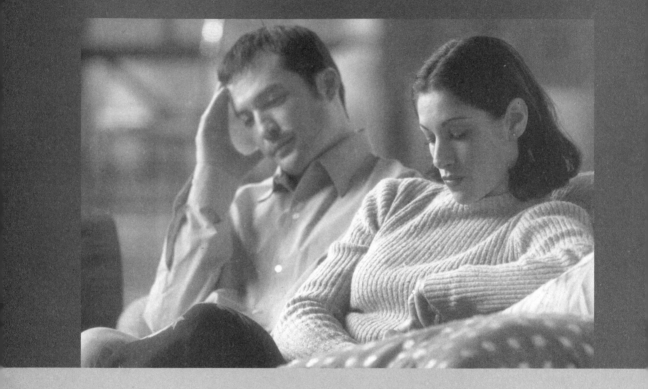

Chapter Outline

Divorce is sometimes hard to understand. The factors leading to divorce are complex, as are the consequences for the individuals involved and for society. Adding another challenge is that close couple relations have changed so much recently, as we saw in Chapter 4, with the growing popularity of cohabitation. Cohabiting relationships that end are not counted as divorces. So, the greater the numbers of couples who cohabit, the lower the divorce rate will fall. Adding even more complexity, divorce rates are sometimes misleading, as we shall soon see. So, in this instance like many others, the numbers don't speak for themselves.

It is often said that about one-half of all marriages end in divorce. That's scary, if people think that their own marriage stands only a 50-percent chance of surviving. However, this figure may be misleading, as different methods of measurement will lead to different statistical outcomes and sociological conclusions.

DIVORCE RATES

To explain why divorce rates are misleading at times, we must explain what the various indicators of divorce mean. There are several ways to compute divorce rates, and meanings depend very much on the method of calculation. The *crude divorce rate,* for example, is calculated as the number of divorces in a given year (say, 2010) divided by the mid-year population in 2010, multiplied by 100 000 (see Figure 9.1 for illustration).

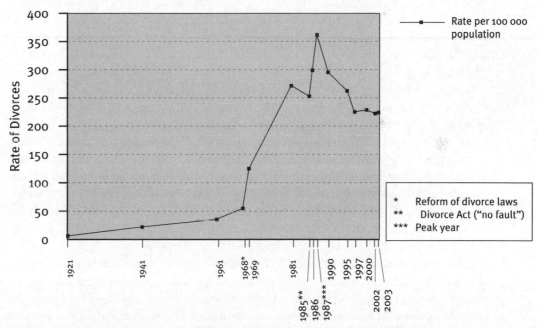

Figure 9.1 Divorce rate per 100 000 population in Canada, 1921–2003

Source: Data from Anne-Marie Ambert. 2005. Divorce: Facts, causes and consequences. The Vanier Institute of the Family. Data retrieved December 9, 2005, from www.vifamily.ca/library/cft/divorce_05.html.

This yields low rates because the denominator includes everyone in the population, many of whom are not at all at risk of divorce since they are children, single, or already divorced.

By contrast, another measure of divorce is based on the number of marriages in a given year. Here, the number of *divorces* in 2010 is divided by the number of *marriages* in 2010. This overestimates divorce risk and lends itself to attention-catching statements (for example, "One-half of all current marriages will end in divorce") that titillate but do not inform us. Those married in 2010 are *not* those at risk of divorce in 2010! As well, if the number of marriages in any given year goes down, as it has in the past decade in Canada, and the numbers of divorces stays the same, it may appear as if the risk of divorce is going up when it is not. As you can see, this way of calculating divorce rate and risk is very misleading. It can be a "false fact" reported as if true and then interpreted by couples as a risk to them. This is inappropriate and needlessly frightening.

Better measures of divorce risk, though too rarely provided for public discussion, consider the population at risk of a divorce, and *only* that population. Thus, the population at risk of a divorce in 2010 are those (and only those) who are married at the beginning of 2010 *and earlier*. This estimate can be improved by standardizing for age and other social characteristics that are known to influence people's inclination to divorce. Since older people divorce less than younger people do, for example, we would do well to compute divorce rates on a "standard population" with the same supposed age structure at two points in time. Only in this way would we know whether divorce-proneness was increasing or whether changes in population makeup (such as population aging or immigration of more young people) were causing the *appearance* of more divorce-proneness.

Another approach is to calculate a rolling divorce rate, which measures the number of people in the population ever divorced as a fraction of the population ever married. This method has advantages and disadvantages. One disadvantage is that this method is biased by cohort and period. Large cohorts (or generations) of people (like the baby boom generation) have an especially large effect on this kind of estimate.

The most refined method of measurement gives the closest approximation for the divorce rate in a lifetime. It looks at couples who married 30 years ago and what proportion of that population has since divorced. Since couples rarely divorce after 30 years of marriage (Ambert, 2005b), the actual divorce rate is significantly lower than the widely quoted "half of all marriages." According to the latest data, the number of Canadian marriages that end before the 30th anniversary is just over one-third (Clark and Crompton, 2006). However, this method is not widely used.

One final measure, which to our knowledge is never used in official data, calculates the number of adult years lived outside marriage. If our purpose in computing divorce rates were to gauge people's desire to be married and stay married, nothing would show the societal rejection of marriage more than a continuous decline in the time people spent being married. Similarly, increases in person-years spent cohabiting could also be viewed as a rejection of traditional marriage. However, the goal of computing divorce rates is not only to measure the societal rejection of marriage. Divorce rates also help sociologists make and test theories about the factors that contribute to the survival and breakdown of marriages. In turn, this helps us understand something about the conditions that make for better and worse family functioning.

An interesting illustration of the advantage of organizing survey data in original ways to answer sociological questions comes from Canadian sociologists Clark and Crompton (2006). The authors analyzed data from the 2001 General Social Survey (GSS) to find out whether people face differential risks of divorce after their first, second, and third marriages. Figure 9.2 presents their breakdown of the data. Looking at divorce in this way, we first see that most ever-married Canadians (89 percent) only marry once (Clark and Crompton, 2006: 24). Second, 69 percent of ever-married people remain with their first spouse, and people who do this, on average, remain married for 23.5 years. Only about 23 percent of people dissolve their first marriage after an average of 11 years together (Clark and Crompton, 2006: 23).

A lot more could be said about the challenges of divorce rates. Demographers spend a great deal of time perfecting these measures, and those who watch rates, like the readers of this book as well as policy makers, should be careful to know what is being measured and how. Generally, the best rate is one that correctly measures the risks of experiencing something such as divorce. It is wise never to rely on a rate without knowing what

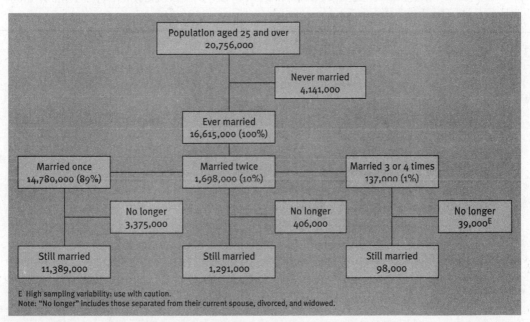

E High sampling variability: use with caution.
Note: "No longer" includes those separated from their current spouse, divorced, and widowed.

Figure 9.2 Risk of marriage dissolution after first, second, and third marriages

Source: Warren Clark and Susan Crompton. 2006. Till death do us part? The risk of first and second marriage dissolution. Ottawa: Statistics Canada. Catalogue no. 11-008. *Canadian Social Trends:* p. 24.

question you are trying to answer; equally, never accept a rate as valid unless you know how it was created and what it shows.

DIVORCE AND SOCIETY

Many questions involving divorce need answering, as divorce affects many people. As we shall se, divorce solves some problems and creates others: problems between people and their children, parents, siblings, and friends.

Sociologists hope to gain insights from research on divorce about the nature of social bonding, the effects of economy and culture on personal relations, and the causes and effects of divorce. At the micro-level, sociologists try to understand why individual couples divorce. To do this, they examine family dynamics and interaction patterns, the expectations people have about married life, who they choose to marry and why, and people's subjective assessments of available alternative mates. They also examine the effects on divorcing spouses, their children, and other family members. Then, they consider how people may individually work to reduce the harmful effects of divorce.

At the macro-level, sociologists debate how to measure divorce, how to measure "a marriage or relationship breakdown," and how to measure the link between relationship breakdown and legal divorce. Often relationships break down long before divorce occurs, so separation may be a better indicator than divorce of marital problems. As we have noted, with dramatic increases in cohabitation, divorce rates are no longer reliable indicators of relationship breakdown. However, even in the past, they may not have been good indicators. And today's higher rates of cohabitation may lead to even higher rates of divorce in future—since cohabiters who then marry are more likely to divorce (Le Bourdais, Neil, and Turcotte, 2000). However, higher cohabitation rates can also lead to lower divorce rates, since cohabiters are not at risk for legal divorce.

Macrosociologists have examined the social, cultural, economic, and political forces that shape marriage. Their goal has been to find out what accounts for the long-term increase in divorce rates over much of the twentieth century. To find out, they examine such large-scale processes as industrialization and urbanization, the increasing participation of women in the labour force, and changes in the societal norms regulating marriage and family life. They also study the macro-level effects of high divorce rates on family and social life, parenting, and the distribution of income.

Despite high divorce rates, the family is still the most important and most fundamental institution in society, as we have argued in earlier chapters. Therefore, it is understandable that some may interpret high divorce rates as a sign of societal breakdown. This interpretation, favoured by political conservatives today, began with the work of nineteenth-century sociologist Émile Durkheim in works like *Suicide* and *The Division of Labor in Society*. Political conservatives are also more likely to see an increase in divorce rates as proof of the decreasing value of marriage in our society today. However, some have argued the opposite: namely, that we value "good" marriages more than ever (Houston, 2004). Today, we expect more of marriage than merely housekeeping and reproduction, for example.

So, we are more likely today to hold off marrying or leave relationships in which we find ourselves unhappy.

Conservative sociologists, sometimes called "marriage promoters," also note that, even today, high divorce rates are associated with high suicide rates, suggesting the divorce rate reflects distress or disorganization in the general population (see Popenoe, 1996, for example). Positive correlations between divorce rates, suicide rates, and alcohol consumption per capita suggest a broad-based social characteristic—a **social pathology**, as early sociologists would have called it—that produces stress-related behaviours.

However, liberal sociologists deny that divorce rates necessarily show **social disorganization** (see Smart and Neale, 1999; Stacey, 1996, for example). Divorce may not hamper a healthy family and social life if clear social norms specify what is to happen to the husband, wife, and children after a divorce. In societies that handle divorce well, such as Sweden, children continue to live with their kin, often with their mother and her relatives. For this and other reasons, they may suffer less from the separation of their parents than North American children, for example. In Sweden, divorce produces fewer stress-related outcomes. And there are examples of smooth divorce arrangements in our own society. For example, the transition is easier when fathers remain involved with their children after divorce, or even become more involved (Smart and Neale, 1999).

People in our society have trouble thinking about divorce in a calm, dispassionate way, sometimes viewing it in dramatic terms, as evidence of a "pathology" or "societal breakdown." There may be two explanations for this way of thinking. First, divorce is both a personal (emotional) and religious (or ideological) matter. Leaders from many different religions argue that marriage is sacred and should not be dissolved. Politics also enter the debate, with socially conservative politicians and journalists debating more liberal people about the meaning of divorce and how societies ought to respond.

Second, we often have trouble remaining calm and dispassionate about divorce because we never prepare for divorce as we do for other major adult life experiences like education, employment, and marriage. Most young people, for example, say that they expect *never* to divorce (Vanier Institute of the Family, 2002). Although the odds slightly favour marriages lasting, many marriages do not. Yet people organize their lives and societal roles around the belief that long-term marriage is the most reasonable expectation. Some beliefs about marriage and divorce have not changed much in centuries, though historical and cross-national data show us that divorce practices surely have!

Separation and Divorce in the Immigrant Population

In general, marriage (as opposed to other intimate unions) is more common, and divorce is less common, in non-Western countries. There are exceptions such as Russia, where both marriage and divorce rates are high (Katz, 2000), but the previous statement applies to most countries from which immigrants come to Canada. This is because marriage is highly valued in traditional cultures. In these societies, women are often denied the right to divorce their mate, on religious grounds, or they are permitted to do so but stigmatized afterward (see Ayyub, 2000, for an outline of divorce in the South Asian Muslim population). Immigrating to countries like Canada where the opportunity to divorce is more readily accessible gives many women the chance to exercise this choice that was unavailable before.

However, research shows that divorce is still not as common among immigrants as it is among native-born members of the host country. This is largely because of persisting traditional views of the process which are mostly negative (Jaaber and Dasgupta, 2003). For example, some women view separation and divorce as a deliberate act of disobedience to their husband and an embarrassment to their family.

Chang (2003), who studied differences in reported reasons for divorce among Korean immigrant and white non-immigrant women, found that most immigrants divorced for clear reasons. These included their ex-husband's use of violence, severe financial problems, or other highly negative circumstances. By contrast, white non-immigrant women based their reasoning on vaguer concerns like lack of emotional fulfillment. These different explanations reflect different cultural justifications for divorce..

No wonder immigrant women are clear and cautious: immigrant women who do decide to divorce are at a higher risk of violence by their spouse than are native-born women in Canada (Spiwak and Brownridge, 2005). This increased risk is related to various factors: male dominance in patriarchical cultures, the financial dependence of women, and disagreement over various migration decisions (Spiwak and Brownridge, 2005; Morash, Bui, Zhang, and Holtfreter, 2007; and Katz, 2000).

A HISTORICAL, CROSS-NATIONAL OVERVIEW OF DIVORCE

In industrial societies, divorce rates hit a peak in the second half of the twentieth century. This peak occurred because of changes in the social, economic, and legal institutions that shape family life and individual expectations of marriage. Divorce is nothing new, however, nor is it limited to Western industrial societies (see Phillips, 1988). What follows is a thumbnail sketch of the relevant sociohistorical processes.

Social Changes

In pre-industrial times, as we discuss in Chapter 2, most families were rural, land-based, self-sufficient units. They produced most of what they needed to feed, clothe, and house their own members. The division of labour was simple. Tasks and responsibilities were allocated according to age and gender. *Social differentiation* beyond that was slight, except for royalty and the aristocracies in some parts of the world.

With the onset of the Industrial Revolution about two hundred years ago (mid-nineteenth century in Canada), however, the modern Western family lost its main economic function. Most production moved out of the household and into factories and (later) offices. Individual family members still worked to support themselves and their families; however, the family itself was not the basic social unit of production any more. Work and family were no longer the same thing, and a sense of family separate from work began to emerge. These changes affected the strength of family ties and the family's ability to control its members. People's lives became more individuated and governed by market forces.

In the last hundred years, other functions of the family, such as the education and training of the young, increasingly have become the responsibility of the state. In Canada, compulsory education was the state response to unruly youth of the early industrial period. The interest was less in educating children than in controlling them. The state grew larger, taking responsibility for more of our lives—health, education, welfare. This meant the family was no longer the only source of personal security. Of course, that period of state expansion is now at an end. With increasing job and policy insecurity (in pensions, social assistance, and so on), families may once again be becoming a crucial source of security for individuals (McDaniel, 2002).

To be sure, the family was always, and is still, important. Especially today, it is only by pooling their members' incomes that many families keep themselves out of poverty and off social assistance. Immigrant family members, in particular, pool their resources to achieve upward mobility.

Nonetheless, since the second half of the twentieth century, the family has been much less necessary for educational and other social purposes. As a result, people may invest less of themselves in the family. And the looser their ties become, the easier it is to sever them when problems arise or attractive alternatives beckon. So, divorce rates rise (South, Trent and Shen, 2001). Figure 9.3 shows the trends in marital status of Canadians

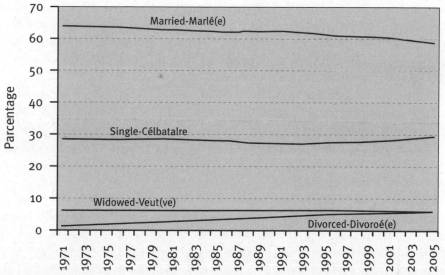

Figure 9.3 Population changes in marital status from 1971 to 2005 in Canada

Source: Statistics Canada. 2006. *Annual Demographic Statistics, 2005.* Ottawa: Statistics Canada. Catalogue no. 91-213. 8.

at the end of the twentieth century. Since 1971, the proportion of married people continued slowly to fall, while the proportion of divorced, cohabiting, and single people rose. By 2005, divorced people comprised 5.9 percent of the population aged 15 years and older compared to only 1.7 percent in 1975 (Statistics Canada, 2006a: 9). Also signalling the changed evaluation of family life, "the proportion of single people has been rising steadily since 1991 (27.1 percent), and by July 1, 2005, it had reached 29.3 percent" (Statistics Canada, 2006a: 8).

By this historical reckoning, higher divorce rates are the result of a change in the ties that bind family members to one another. Where family ties once rested on life-and-death economic dependence and co-dependence, today they rest more often on fragile emotions of love and liking. Since emotional ties are by their nature more fickle than ties of economic dependence, we more easily sever them. However, not every couple that falls out of love gets a divorce, since divorce is a legal process and not a social or emotional one. Some couples, as we shall see, may not wish to end their marriages publicly at all. Others do.

Legal Changes

To understand divorce as a legal process, we must understand the laws governing divorce and how they have changed. Divorce laws in Canada and other Western countries have gradually loosened over the past two centuries. For example, during the colonial period in North America, divorce was illegal in the southern United States and Quebec. It was granted elsewhere only under narrowly defined circumstances such as adultery or after seven years of desertion. Even then, it was nearly impossible to get a divorce granted. Until the mid-twentieth century, Canadian law required an Act of Parliament for each divorce to be granted (Snell, 1983). Not surprisingly, divorces were granted most often to well-to-do and influential people. Before the 1968 Divorce Act (which accepted separation as a legitimate ground for divorce), most marriages "dissolved by taking other options, such as separation, desertion, or maintaining an 'empty shell' relationship by minimizing communication between partners" (McVey, 2008: 190).

There was a strong sense in the early 1900s in Canada that divorce was a moral and political issue, with bad implications for the country. Snell (1983: 113) quotes E.A. Lancaster, the Conservative Member of Parliament for Lincoln, Ontario, 1900–1916: "Where will this country come to in twenty-five years if we are going to grant divorces because some woman has been disappointed in regard to her husband . . . The whole social fabric of the country would go to pieces."

Increasingly over the twentieth century, North American governments granted divorces on ever-widening grounds, such as marital cruelty, marital rape, sodomy, bestiality, homosexuality, and adultery. As divorce laws become more lenient, there was an accompanying rise in divorce rates. A turning point occurred in the late 1960s and early 1970s with the introduction of **no-fault divorce** laws in Canada and some jurisdictions in the United States. In Canada, the 1968 Divorce Act first enlarged the "fault grounds" under which a divorce could be granted, but also allowed divorce without accusations of wrongdoing in the case of "marital breakdown," which required three years of living apart, or five if both spouses did not agree to divorce.

The 1985 Divorce Act considers marriage breakdown to be the only ground for divorce, though the older grounds such as adultery or cruelty are considered evidence of breakdown. It is no longer necessary for one spouse or the other to accept moral blame for the breakdown of the marriage. This change in approach reflects a gradual societal redefinition of divorce.

No longer does divorce have to be a stigmatizing process where one party is held responsible under the law. On the contrary, we now may be more likely to look critically at marriages that survive even though they are emotionally dead. These are marriages that we now think could end, freeing their participants to find emotional fulfillment in another union.

No-fault divorce laws implicitly define marriages in which couples are "incompatible" or have "irreconcilable differences" as grounds for divorce. Divorce, according to no-fault laws, then, could end marriages that are "irretrievably broken." The grounds for no-fault divorce are not inherently adversarial; they are based almost entirely on the loss of emotional connections. In earlier times, many marriages may have broken down emotionally or may never have been emotionally secure in the first place. It is only recently the legal system has come to view this as reason enough to end a marriage.

In December 2002, the Government of Canada announced a new approach to divorce in Canada (Douglas, 2006).

The purpose of proposed changes to the 1985 Divorce Act was, according to then Minister of Justice Martin Cauchon, to focus on children's needs primarily. Bill C-22, an

Major Canadian Divorce Statistics

- The divorced population remained the fastest-growing group in 2004–2005 (3.4 percent). However, its rate of growth was lower than the average rate of 5.2 percent seen in the 1990s (Statistics Canada, 2006a: 9).

- More than one-third of marriages in Canada will end in divorce before the 30th wedding anniversary (Clark and Crompton, 2006).

- Men between the ages of 20 and 64 are six times as likely to suffer from depression if they were divorced or separated than if they stayed married. For women, the figure is 3.5 times as likely for the divorced or separated (Rotermann, 2007).

- Forty-three percent of women who have undergone a marital breakup (divorce or separation) had a substantial decrease in household income, while 15 percent of separated or divorced men had a financial decline (Rotermann, 2007).

- In 1951, divorce accounted for only 3 percent of lone parents, but the proportion of divorced lone parents has since increased tenfold, to 31 percent, in 2001 (Beaujot and Ravanera, 2008).

- Among seniors (age 65 and older), the proportion of divorced people tripled from 1.7 percent in 1981 to 5.1 percent in 2001 (Turcotte and Schellenberg, 2006: 139).

Act to amend the Divorce Act, et al., would have replaced the terms "custody" and "access" in the Divorce Act with "parental responsibility" and "contact." It also would have provided courts with a new list of factors to apply to decisions surrounding the post-separation parenting of children whose parents divorce (Douglas, 2006). Regrettably, the bill made no headway.

However, on May 1, 2006, amended Federal Child Support Guidelines came into force, which clarified the term "extraordinary expenses" to respond to judicial disagreement over the significance of the term. The guidelines also provided for education-related and extracurricular-activity extraordinary expenses to be added to child support amounts payable. They also included new tables for setting child support levels, which reflected changes in tax structures in the provinces (Douglas, 2006).

CAUSES OF DIVORCE

In the discussion that follows, we speak of "causes," but we might as well use the words **determinants** or **predictors**. Many supposed causes of divorce intertwine with other causes. Their distinct, separate influence is hard to discover. The most we can say with certainty is that these are predictors—correlates that typically precede divorce and influence its likelihood in sometimes complicated ways.

Although underplayed in sociological discussion about the "cause" of divorce, a couple's emotional interaction and personal characteristics, such as being naturally more caring, compromising, or compassionate, can also play a role in marriages and subsequent divorces. This means that although Chapter 5 stressed the importance of communication for the success of relationships, *knowing* how to communicate or problem solve may be still be inadequate if the marriage is not founded on mutual respect and admiration (Houston, 2004: 955). For instance, happy couples are more likely to have individual characteristics that make them more even-tempered and warm-hearted. They are also more likely to show good will toward their partners and therefore are more likely to work through any differences (Houston, 2004: 952).

Moreover, a couple's emotional climate and personal characteristics may clash from the beginning. Most people (wrongly) believe that unhappy marriages began as happy relationships, and that conflicts developed during the marriage that were unknown before. On the contrary, Houston found that most unhappy marriages fell short of happiness from the onset of the marriage (2004: 952). So, the reasons for divorce are complicated by the emotional climate of a marriage and the interplay of individual characteristics as well.

We also distinguish among three levels of causal explanation: the micro-, macro-, and meso-levels. By **micro-level** causes, we mean something close to the lived experience of people who divorce: attitudes, perceptions, sentiments, beliefs, and the like. We include the experiences of rejection, infidelity, and marital dissatisfaction in this category. By **macro-level** causes, we mean societal changes like social integration, women's involvement in the workforce, and changes in divorce laws.

Finally, middle-range or **meso-level** causes of divorce are, typically, demographic predictors—that is, characteristics of people who are at a high risk of divorce. In this area, it is unclear whether these characteristics are causes, determinants, or merely predictors. For example, people who marry at an early age, or after only a short relationship, run an especially high risk of divorce, due to the stress, conflict, and dissatisfaction that arise when two immature strangers try to work out a life together.

Precisely what we call the "cause" in the situation will vary from one analyst to another. Let us begin with the microsociological causes of divorce. They are the easiest causes to understand intuitively. However, they may not be the major factors leading to divorce—or, at least, predicting them.

Microsociological Causes

We commonly cite two kinds of microsociological "reasons." The first are grounds that people use when they file for divorce. These "grounds" may have value in a court of law, but sociologists find them largely unrevealing. We learn more from the personal accounts of individuals who have undergone divorce. They tell us a lot about the state of mind of the divorcing people, and the ways they make sense to themselves of what has happened. However, people often do not understand the reasons for their own behaviour. As well, "(b)ecause these studies only include divorced respondents, they can tell us little about the extent to which these factors predict divorce" (White, 1990).

The second kind of microsociological reasons people cite to explain divorce typically describes the dynamics of the marriage relationship. As we said in Chapter 5, the quality of a relationship largely determines the stability of a marriage. Marriages likely to end in divorce have a typical profile. Usually, they are characterized by poor communication and poor conflict-resolution skills as well as a lack of commitment to the spouse and/or to the institution of marriage. The spouses may have few shared values and interests, and there is often a perceived inequity between spouses, and limited respect, love, and affection on the part of one or both spouses. These are overall average traits and will not characterize each situation. We can imagine people in such relationships wanting and getting a divorce. However, because these are common problems of relationships, they are not good predictors. Even those on the inside of the relationship often cannot make that prediction.

Consider, instead, some life course (demographic) variables that make certain people more divorce-prone than others. These are better than microsociological variables at identifying conditions that produce tensions and unhappiness—which, in turn, increase the likelihood of divorce. Even if they do not seem to explain divorce as well, they are better at predicting it.

Mesosociological Causes

Not everyone who marries gets divorced. In fact, the majority stay married. Moreover, the probability of divorce is spread unevenly throughout the population. Thus, to understand the causes of divorce we must look at who gets divorced.

Major life course and demographic variables correlated with a high divorce risk include young age at marriage, cohabitation before marriage, second or subsequent marriage, parental divorce, premarital pregnancy and/or child-bearing, childlessness—or conversely having a large number of children—early stage of marriage, urban residence, residence in British Columbia or Alberta (or in Quebec), absence of religious belief or affiliation, and low socio-economic status.

Age at Marriage Young age at marriage is probably the strongest predictor of divorce in the first five years of marriage (Ambert, 2002). Risks are especially high for people who marry in their teens. Various explanations for this have been ventured: young people lack the emotional maturity needed for marriage; and they have ill-founded expectations of what married life holds in store. They are more likely to become disappointed and disillusioned with marriage, especially when they come upon plentiful alternatives to their current spouse (South, Trent, and Shen, 2001). As well, early marriage tends to reduce educational achievement. Young marriers divorce more often because they have less education, therefore a lower income, and fewer communication skills—which, in turn, can result in more marital conflict.

Ironically, though young marriers in our own society have high rates of divorce, young-marrying societies, in which the average age at marriage is low, have low rates of divorce. Typically, countries with low average ages of marriage have other features—for example, high rates of child-bearing, strongly institutionalized religion, extended families, and restrictive divorce laws—that keep the divorce rates low for people of all ages. Latin American and Islamic societies share these features, as do some cultures in Africa and Asia.

Cohabitation Cohabitation before marriage has, as we've said in earlier chapters, also been correlated with a higher risk of divorce. However, this fact needs careful interpretation. Societal and family pressures may push cohabiting people into marriage before they are ready, even if they are unsuited for marriage or for each other. Cohabitation, by hastening marriage, may increase the risk of separation and divorce (Ambert, 2002). On the other hand, couples in happy cohabiting relationships who succumb to societal pressures to marry may find their relationship changed by the social policies that shape expectations about wives and husbands and supposedly encourage stability. Couples, in other words, may not be separating as much from each other as from the socially scripted roles and expectations that legal marriage entails. Much has been learned about this from gay and lesbian couples, some of whom saw the reality that they could not legally marry (in most jurisdictions) as strengthening their relationships (see Lehr, 1999). In other words, couples are creating their own ways to be couples rather than working to fit into legally prescribed roles and obligations. Of course, that has now changed with the legalization of gay and lesbian marriage in Canada in 2005 and in a number of other countries.

Still another possible explanation for this finding is **adverse selectivity**—that is, that the people who choose to cohabit are different from those who choose to marry without first cohabiting. However, as more people—and more varied people—cohabit, cohabitation may no longer predict a high risk of divorce. Therefore, cohabitation as a predictor variable for divorce risk is likely on the way out of sociological theories, although not all sociologists agree.

Second Marriages Other things being equal, second marriages are more likely than first marriages to end in divorce. The risk in Canada is estimated to be about 10 percent higher than in first marriages (Ambert, 2002; 2005b). The probability that third marriages will end in divorce is higher still. (As well, remarriages that end in divorce end more quickly than first marriages.) Yet people still get married after a divorce. Approximately, 70 percent of men and 58 percent of women in Canada (excluding Quebec) marry again following separation. Remarriages are also more common among immigrants than among Canadian-born citizens (Ambert, 2005b).

This finding defies our common sense. One would expect remarriages—like cohabiting relationships—to have a lower divorce rate. People who had already gone through one divorce would, we imagine, be more careful choosing their next mate. They would try harder to make their marriage work, to avoid the problems and costs associated with divorce. Some, in fact, do just this. When a second marriage endures, it often outlasts the first (Ambert, 2002; 2005b). Moreover, when remarriages work out, it is typically because the remarried people are older than average. Older people are less likely to divorce. Young people who remarry are more likely to divorce than older people who remarry.

Another viable explanation is that people who have already been married choose cohabitation as a substitute to marriage the second time around. For these adults, cohabitation is a union in itself, one that will not end in marriage and that has a similar level of commitment as marriage (Ambert, 2005). In this case, older cohabiters experience higher levels of happiness and stability than younger ones (King and Scott, 2005). Despite their success, these relationships are not counted as remarriages and as such do nothing to decrease the perceived overall risk of divorce in second marriages.

Adverse selectivity may *again* be the explanation for the higher divorce tendency in second and third marriages. People who get a first divorce may be more willing to get a second. They may more readily see divorce as a solution to marital problems.

A competing theory argues that the stresses and strains of a remarriage are greater than those of first marriages are. Second marriages may bring "baggage" from the first marriage/divorce, the (difficult) integration of stepchildren into reconstituted families, or the challenges of ongoing interactions with ex-spouses. Furthermore, fewer norms guide second marriages, although that is changing with their greater frequency. This makes remarriages more challenging. Both theories are compelling. We need more research to decide which explanation is better or whether both sets of factors come into play, with other factors still not well understood.

Parental Divorce People whose parents divorced are also more likely to divorce. They also have a greater tendency not to marry. However, the mechanism that transmits this inheritance is unclear. Perhaps people whose parents divorced are less likely to believe that marriages can last. That makes them more likely to opt for divorce when things get

Myths about Divorce

Families where children live with their biological mothers are more stable across all situations.

- When a resident stepfather is present, the family is less stable than a family where the child is living with his/her biological father and a resident stepmother (Ambert, 2005b).

Higher divorce rates among children are a result of the conflict they saw in their families.

- This is not always true. Higher divorce risks also occur among adult children where their divorced parents had low levels of conflict. A sense of less commitment to each other may have been passed on to the children (Ambert, 2005b).

Step-parents have little connection with step-children.

- Many children enjoy the presence of a step-parent and benefit from the affection. Where stepfamilies endure, young adults are strongly attached to the reconstructed family (Ambert, 2005b).

With divorce, spouses are not concerned with what the ex-partner thinks.

- Perceptions of a former spouse can still have a powerful impact. Ex-wives' approval of the quality of fathering plays a role in how satisfied divorced fathers are (Cohen and Finzi-Dottan, 2005).

People with lower socio-economic status are least able to afford to leave their marriage and thus have lower risk of marital dissolution.

- People with less than high school education at the time of their first marriage face a 38 percent greater risk of divorce than those who completed high school. University graduates, on the other hand, are at 16 percent less risk for marital dissolution, suggesting that people with higher social status are happier and less likely to divorce (Clark and Crompton, 2006: 24).

Second marriages are more likely to end in divorce than first marriages.

- In reality, remarriages made after the age of 40 are more stable than first marriages, due to the partners' increased maturity. For example, the risk for marital dissolution of Canadians who remarried in their 40s is half that of those who were younger than 30 (Clark and Crompton, 2006: 25).

tough. They may have married before they were ready, out of fear that they would be alone (like their parents). They may have married before they understood what marriage was all about, because their parents' marriage did not last long enough for them to find out. On the other hand, they may be the victims of optimism. This does not mean, however, that if your parents are divorced your risks of divorce are automatically high. They are not. Many children of divorced parents marry well and live happily.

One Canadian study (Corak and Heisz, 1999) compares children whose parents divorced with those who lost a parent to death. They find, interestingly, that children who lose a parent to death have the same likelihood of marrying and of divorcing as anyone else.

The correlation of parental divorce with heightened divorce risk may be due again to adverse selectivity. People whose parents divorced were once a small minority. Today, they are not. Their parents' divorce stigmatizes them less and leaves them less ignorant about the variety of possible adaptations to marital conflict. They know that people survive divorce, and that many people are better for doing so. If this explanation is so, we might expect that more people will have "learned how to divorce" from their parents. However, demographically speaking, as the average age of the population increases, and as older people remarry less often and cohabit more often, we may see a decline in divorce.

Child-bearing, Before and After Marriage Evidence documenting the relationship between premarital child-bearing and the likelihood of divorce is overwhelming. For people who marry after having a child, the risk of divorce is high. Couples who marry after discovering that they are expecting a child may marry under extreme pressure to legitimate the birth of their child. This is not the best motivation to marry. The good news is that shotgun weddings are less common than they used to be.

The relationship between the birth of children within marriage and the likelihood of divorce is strong but not straightforward. Couples who end up divorcing tend to have no children or have fewer on average than those who stay married (Ambert, 2002). The reasons may be unrelated to child-bearing; it may be that most divorces occur within the early years of marriage. It is also likely that people who have no children will see themselves as freer to divorce than couples with children. Again, adverse selectivity is operating here.

However, children are quickly becoming less of a deterrent to divorce. The number of children affected by divorce and the fraction of divorces involving children have increased in recent years. Today, couples are less likely to stay together for the children.

Stage of Marriage Duration of marriage is strongly negatively correlated with a propensity to divorce. That said, the lowest risk of divorce is in the first year of marriage (Statistics Canada, 2002a). The rate follows an inverted-U shape that is skewed toward the left. Before the first anniversary, divorce occurs in less than one in every 1000 marriages. After the first anniversary, the rate goes up to 4.3, and then jumps to 18.0 the following year. The peak occurs at around the third and the fourth year, with 25.0 and 25.7 divorces respectively. The curve goes down slowly each year after the fourth anniversary (Statistics Canada, 2004a). After 15 years of marriage, couples are unlikely to divorce. The explanation is that the more time and energy people invest in their marriage, the higher the costs of abandoning the marriage and starting a new life. Couples are more aware of being badly matched early in the marriage since the factors responsible for divorce (for example, emotional satisfaction) carry more weight in the early years. As well, people think when a mistake has been made, it should be changed before it is too late. After about three years, relationships stabilize and many partners adjust.

On the other hand, the longer a marriage goes on, the older the spouses tend to be, and the more likely they are to have grown up with cultural values in which marriage had much greater normative pull than it does today. We must wait another few decades before we find out the strength of this **cohort effect**—something that influences everyone of roughly the same age.

Place of Residence People living in urban centres are much more likely to divorce than people in rural areas. On the one hand, these findings reflect a higher probability of divorce under the demands and stresses of urban life. However, in part these statistics also reflect adverse selectivity—specifically, the tendency for rural people to migrate to urban areas before, during, or after a divorce, or for younger people to migrate to cities for work or education and find themselves marrying there. A family farm or a rural small town can be a difficult place for divorced people, especially divorced women.

The effect of urban living is sometimes confounded by the divorce-increasing role of migration. When we control for many possible explanatory factors, rates of union instability are strongly related to recent and lifetime migration experience. The weaker socialties of some migrants appear to provide less social support for their unions and fewer barriers to union disruption. At the same time, many immigrants come from cultures with strong family sanctions for lasting marriages. An alternative explanation is that when immigrants from countries in which marriage is seen primarily as a practical arrangement come to Canada and encounter the expectation that marriage should be based on passion and companionship, they look at their own marriage from a different point of view and may become dissatisfied. A third possibility is that selectivity explains the finding. People who take the initiative of moving to a new country are risk takers, willing to confront challenges and make changes in their lives. They may be more willing to consider divorce than the more cautious people who stay behind. Alternatively, they may experience greater stresses, which can cause even firmly based marriages trouble.

Religion Finally, the ethnic and religious composition of the population has something to do with the patterns of divorce. The risk of divorce is lower for foreign-born Canadians. Interestingly, the risk of divorce is no higher in Quebec, where cohabitation is much more common than it is in other provinces. Wu (2000) notes that the risk of divorce is lower among Catholics and Protestants than among those with other or no religious affiliation. The more religious people are, the less likely they will be to opt for divorce, even if they are unhappy in their marriages. Religious affiliation also plays a part. Couples in which the spouses belong to different religions are more likely to divorce than couples who belong to the same religion. Couples in which neither spouse has a religious affiliation tend to have even higher rates of divorce (Goode, 1993: 320).

Related to this is the overall **secularization** of societies such as Canada. With the massive move away from religion as a dominant social institution have come new norms. Among these, individual choice and liberalization of sexual beliefs and behaviours loom large. Marriage has become, for many, an individual choice rather than a covenant taken before God. Even couples who marry in churches tend to believe less in the religious covenant aspect now. Divorce, then, is seen more as a choice rather than the breaking of a larger spiritual commitment.

Socio-Economic Status Class, or **socio-economic status** (SES), is strongly correlated with probability of divorce. The divorce rate increases as one moves down the socio-economic ladder. Study after study confirms that, whatever the index of socio-economic status used—income, occupation, or education—we observe an inverse correlation between SES and divorce rates.

This correlation may be explained by the higher level of financial insecurities that poor people face. Economic stresses produce marital stresses. Moreover, the poor have less (economically) to lose from divorce and less to gain from staying married. Their material investment in marriage may be lower, so divorce "costs" them less. However, differences in divorce rates by socio-economic status tend to be decreasing. This is in part a function of an increase in the divorce rate among middle- and upper-class people.

Goode (1993) suggests that this change is the result of a shift in the strongest variable in this pattern: the discrepancy between the husband's and the wife's incomes. Women with employment and incomes similar to their husbands' can afford to divorce. This explanation assumes that women are more likely to want out than men. The more economically independent women become, the more likely they will be to leave their marriages when they want. Along similar lines, some argue that marriage, though seemingly about love or emotional union, is still a way for women to gain economically. Women's desires for marriage work reflect their economic needs for support and wish to avoid poverty, according to this reasoning. Of course, to confirm this hypothesis, we would have to look further at who initiates separation or files for divorce, and why.

An unexpected finding is the opposite link between class and divorce for women and men. Data show that the higher a man's income, the less likely he is to divorce. On the other hand, the higher a woman's income, the more likely she is to divorce (Wu and Schimmele, 2005b). The latter suggests that marriage represents economic dependence for women, though not for men. However, this theory doesn't explain why men are reluctant to divorce if they earn a high income.

On this topic, the findings are confusing. Some research finds that increases in wives' socio-economic status and labour-force participation increase the probability of marriage disruption. For example, Wu (2000) finds that for women, having a job outside the home or being in school is associated with higher rates of divorce. When the wife's work status is higher than her husband's, the relationship often becomes unstable (Tzeng and Mare, 1995). However, other research finds no support for this hypothesis. Most research finds that marital happiness and well-being increase as women's income increases. This happiness, in turn, decreases the likelihood of divorce (Rogers and DeBoer, 2001).

Couples with more education and a stronger attachment to the workforce generally have more stable marriages. In addition, these couples are most likely to be egalitarian. Given the importance of work in stabilizing marriage, it is no surprise that unemployed people have higher divorce risks than employed people. The receipt of family-support income also increases the likelihood a married woman will become divorced (Hoffman and Duncan, 1995; Davies and Denton, 2001). This does not mean that social transfers cause marital instability, but only that economic and other instabilities may be correlated.

Macrosociological Causes

It should be clear by now that although the decision to divorce is one made by an individual couple, the decision is influenced strongly by large processes in the structure of society over which people have little, if any, control.

The institution of the family has changed a great deal over the past two centuries. The ties of authority and economic dependence that bind family members together have weakened considerably. In addition, the legal structure forcing people to remain together has loosened, making divorce an attainable option for many people. Other important macro-level determinants of divorce include wars and migrations, economic cycles, gender roles, social integration, and cultural values. We will look at each of these factors in turn.

Economic Cycles People are less likely to divorce during recessionary periods than during periods of economic prosperity. People feel freer to strike out on their own when economic opportunities exist. They are more wary of leaving a familiar home or relationship, even if it is unpleasant, in times of economic uncertainty.

Moreover, divorce is costly. It requires establishing separate households, dividing the property, and establishing specific terms for the support of children. These requirements tax most people's financial resources even during prosperity and often become prohibitive in bad times. Great financial hardship may draw together some couples who might otherwise become isolated from each other. If this happens, the effect is short-lived. Although divorce rates drop during depressions, they rise rapidly when the depression ends.

On the other hand, according to White's (1990: 905) review of the sociological literature on divorce, "(t)he most sophisticated analysis of American time series data . . . finds that the effect of prosperity is to reduce divorce." Although prosperity may make divorce more feasible, the *benefits* of prosperity outweigh this effect on personal relationships (South, 1985). Thus, divorce rates may fall because financial security adds stability to personal relationships. At the least, the evidence on this is inconclusive.

Gender Expectations The evidence regarding the influence of gender expectations is difficult to interpret. Researchers have examined two hypotheses. First, when social structures allow women more economic independence from men and families, women have more freedom to divorce (Hetherington and Kelly, 2002; Popenoe, 1996; Stacey, 1996). Second, a growing similarity of women's and men's lives and roles may produce less marital cohesion than complementary, reinforcing roles do. Both of these imply that the more women become financially secure, the higher the divorce rate will be.

Evidence suggests the most satisfying marriages (for both spouses) are those in which gender roles are egalitarian, men are sensitive and nurturing, and husbands and wives share equally in making the decisions that affect their lives (Stacey, 1996). Antill and Cotton (1987) studied 108 couples and found that when both spouses are high on "feminine" characteristics such as nurturance, sensitivity, and gentleness, couples are happier than when one or both spouses is low on this cluster of characteristics. **"Femininity"** of both wives and husbands is positively associated with a smooth marital adjustment

(Kalin and Lloyd, 1985). The explanation is that many of these qualities and characteristics are conducive to good interpersonal relationships. Relationships that both spouses view as equitable have the best marital adjustment. The greater the perceived inequity, the poorer the marital adjustment, and thus the higher the risks of divorce.

The nature of the relationship between gender expectations and divorce-proneness is unclear. Historical and cross-cultural research is addressing the issues of (1) whether divorce rates and rates of female participation in paid work are intrinsically related; (2) whether the observed relationship is a passing effect of the tension between changing social expectations and lagging societal understandings of these changes; and (3) whether the divorce rate is as high as in countries that have had a longer history of female participation in the labour force.

Cultural Values and Social Integration Since the 1960s, the cultural value placed on marriage has been declining. Many scholars argue that formal marriage has lost much of its normative support. This means it is no longer something that one *ought* to do, but is more a matter of personal choice or preference. Distinctions between marital and nonmarital child-bearing, between marriage and cohabitation, have lost their normative force. Marriage and divorce are seen as formalities, or sets of family options. Today, it is argued, we invest less, or at least differently, in family commitments, whether to parents, spouses, or children.

Another macro-level determinant of divorce is a society's degree of **social integration**. The higher the social integration, the lower the divorce rate. In a stable, highly integrated community, consensus on social rules is strong and rule breakers are punished. This happens especially when the rules broken bear on social institutions as central to the community life as "the family." The highly integrated community typically supports various "pro-family" ideals bearing on marriage, premarital or extramarital sexuality, or child obedience. By getting a divorce, people risk incurring social stigma for flouting social norms and tearing the social fabric of the community. In these highly integrated communities, this is scary stuff and a definite deterrent.

EFFECTS OF DIVORCE

Divorce, like the breakup of any important relationship, is messy and painful. Most couples decide to divorce only reluctantly over a long period. For most of them, considerable trauma is involved. A minority experiences some discrimination and may be, for a time, almost without friends. Some, notably women, suffer serious economic deprivation.

In such a high conflict time, outside intervention may become necessary to reduce the risk of harmful and potentially long-standing escalations. This is especially important when children are involved in a separation. The parents must make decisions about the children, child support, maintenance, and the division of marital assets, and must negotiate liabilities. Family therapists or marriage counsellors can provide short-term or continuing support and insight to couples going through separation.

Table 9.1 Coping with Divorce: Family Therapy and Mediation

	Therapy	Mediation
Definition	A branch of psychotherapy where a therapist intervenes to resolve mental health, behavioural, and relationship concerns and considers each person's unique family, cultural, and social context.	A process in which people use direct, assisted talks to resolve the issues between them. Negotiations and decisions are made by clients themselves.
Goal	Enhance family functioning and thus disrupt potential intergenerational transmission of problems such as family violence or substance abuse.	In divorce, it addresses parenting schedules and decision making for the children, child support, maintenance, and the division of marital assets and liabilities.
Involves both parties	Sometimes.	Always.
Goal oriented	Varies.	Always defined.
Insight	Used by therapist and elicited from client.	Used by mediator to frame and resolve issue.
Historical approach to problem	Sometimes the past is used to understand the problem.	The past is used to discover examples of solutions.
Feelings	Respected and often worked through.	Respected and acknowledged.
Use a resource model	Often.	Always.
Genograms	Multigenerational.	Focus on relevant parties.

Source: Adapted from Table 1 in Elana Katz. 2007. A family therapy perspective on mediation. *Family Process* 46(1): 96.

More recently, mediation has gained popularity among family therapists. The main purpose of mediation is not to counselor discuss with clients what they should do. Rather, the emphasis is on drawing "on the resources and knowledge of its participants to allow for creative solutions to the needs of the families who engage in this process" (Katz, 2007: 106). In other words, the role of the mediator is to promote an effective discussion between family members, who, in the process, will discover the unique resources they have available and come up with solutions on their own. Table 9.1 summarizes the main differences and similarities between traditional family therapy and mediation.

Effects on Both Spouses

One of the major effects of divorce is economic: for men and women, but especially women, incomes decrease. Economic distress is a large contributor to generalized psychological distress and to social-policy challenges (Davies, McMullin, and Avison with Cassidy, 2001).

However, economic distress is only one aspect of divorce and its aftermath. The other side is the emotional stress of interpersonal conflict. This begins well before the divorce, and may reach its peak then. In the years immediately preceding divorce, people experience higher-than-usual levels of distress. However, conflict does not end with divorce. The effects of divorce on the divorcing adults, both material and emotional, can be surprisingly long-lasting for some (Mastekaasa, 1995).

Former spouses often disagree on the involvement of non-custodial parents in co-parenting. An overwhelming majority of residential parents feel they have problems with the issue of visitation rights. A smaller but still large percentage of non-residential parents do too. In addition, these problems do not go away quickly. For residential parents, visitation problems are connected to feelings of hurt and anger about the divorce. They are also connected with concerns about the ex-spouse's parenting abilities, child support, and sometimes about abuse of the child. In some countries, there is less conflict over custody as custody arrangements are less variable.

After divorce, most parents find themselves unprepared for the new challenges they face and the inadequacy of counselling and support services. Separated parents often choose, or are forced, to make decisions that conflict with each other's wishes and beliefs. Further, children can play to parental conflicts and parents' desire to be the favoured parent. Custodial parents often fail to realize the impact of conflicts on the other parent. Even in the best post-divorce circumstances, many factors challenge a parent's efforts to maintain closeness with their children. For one, a study by Yarosh, Chew, and Abod (2009) found that parents and children faced communication challenges when children were away from the residential parent's home and visiting at the other parental house. Children found it difficult to carry on conversations about activities they did at the other parent's home and found phone conversations awkward. It was also difficult for them to think of meaningful topics for discussion. Ex-spouses were also hesitant to call their child while visiting for fear they would interrupt the flow of activities at the other house. Remarriage or a new partnership also added further complexity to interactions between ex-spouses (Weiss, 1996).

Remarriage is associated with less frequent co-parental interaction, less reported parenting support from the former spouse, and more negative attitudes about the other parent for both women and men. For men, remarriage predicts lower levels of parenting satisfaction and involvement in children's activities (Christensen and Retting, 1995).

Non-custodial fatherhood has increased due to trends in divorce and births outside of unions. The standard divorce—the mother with custody, the father with child-support responsibilities and visiting rights—is the reality in most cases involving longer duration marriages, higher male income, and younger children. Access to the children is seen as essential to some, but not all non-custodial parents and visiting is important to the quality of the subsequent father–child relationship. Access and child support are complementary, and joint custody tends to improve support compliance. Most mothers are willing to allow visitation even if the father does not pay child support, thus acknowledging the importance of father–child relationships (Laakso, 2004).

International Findings about Divorce

- As in Western societies, educational level in Japan is associated with divorce risk, which is lower among mothers with a university degree (Raymo, Iwasawa, and Bumpass, 2004). Divorced mothers in Japan have full custody of children. The parent without custody typically has no access to the child and is out of the child's life (Morely, n.d.).

- Russia has one of the world's highest divorce rates. Divorced Russian women with children have little likelihood of remarrying. One major reason for this is the shortage of men. Workers' mortality rates are high. There are a significantly higher proportion of women in their 30s than there are men (Nesterov, 2004).

- Though divorce is allowed, it is not widely practised in India. Where most marriages are arranged, women gain their social status from their husbands. When divorce occurs, the wife moves out. Her social connections break down too, as she is discouraged from befriending men and from socializing with married couples. The worry is that a divorced woman might be a marriage wrecker (Sonawat, 2001).

- Political and cultural resistance to divorce is strong in Italian society, where traditional family is deeply rooted. Italy has the lowest divorce rate in Europe, with Ireland, at 0.73 per 1000 population in 2003 (*United Nations Demographic Yearbook 2003*). Yet, separations occur, suggesting that unhappy married couples remain separated rather than take legal steps to divorce (De Rose, 2001).

- Divorce in China is rare, only 10 percent to 15 percent of the population. Society and neighbourhood groups become mediators when marriages fail, often preventing divorce. Divorced Chinese women are more likely to remarry than men and remarry sooner (Dong, Wang, and Ollendick, 2002).

- In the Netherlands, adults who chose to remarry after a divorce are younger on average (42–47 years) than those who choose living apart together (59–64 years) (De Jong Gierveld, 2004).

Divorce has a variety of effects on fathers, and on their children. For example, it affects non-custodial fathers' views of their parental role. Common themes among non-custodial fathers include divorce-related emotional distress; dissatisfaction with custody, visitation, and child support arrangements; perception of divorce proceedings as unfair; and ongoing conflicts with former spouses (Dudley, 1996). The father can view himself as a victim of his spouse. Moreover, his disempowerment, loss of legal custody, and relegation to the role of an economic provider has a profound impact on his masculine identity (Mandell, 1995). Fathers often have limited contact with their children after divorce, and this contact decreases over time. They are more likely to see preschool-age children every week than school-age children (Stephens, 1996).

Why do so many fathers have reduced contact and visitation? Researchers offer many explanations. One is that non-residential fathers feel less competent and less satisfied in the role of father. Typically, fathers of all kinds who identify strongly with the role of father are more frequently involved with their children. Non-residential fathers identify less strongly with the role (Minton and Pasley, 1996). Overall, fathers who do not want contact with their children are more apt to have been less involved with child rearing, to feel indifferent about their children, or to have been in an abusive or violent relationship (Smart and Neale, 1999; Greif, 1995).

In contrast to many non-custodial fathers, nine men studied by Arendell (1995) have developed strategies more congruent with their aim to parent their children actively. Their accounts and actions are child-centred. Each of these men has established, with their former wives, some type of parenting partnership. They actively seek to create "best case scenarios" post-divorce and become absorbed with family relationships. Unlike most divorced fathers, these men are satisfied, even pleased with their parenting. Simultaneously, they see themselves as defying the norms of masculinity. Thus, self-confidence and uncertainty coexist for these innovative fathers.

Some enticing research from a study of post-divorce parenting in the United Kingdom (Smart and Neale, 1999) finds that a significant proportion of post-divorce fathers become *more* involved than they were when they were married. Their reason is fascinating. The dads say that when they were married, their fathering was limited to earning money to support the family. They didn't feel as if they had to do anything more. Once they were divorced, however, they had to be involved with their kids to maintain contact with them since their physical presence in the home was no longer an option. They therefore worked out ways to be involved and responsible fathers to their kids for the first time.

Effects on Women

This section emphasizes the adverse effects of divorce. However, we will begin by acknowledging that divorce may also have benefits. For example, divorced mothers whose marriages were difficult, and sometimes abusive, are typically relieved that their marriages are over. However, even among those who are happy to be out of a bad or intolerable relationship, a majority expresses concern about the conditions they face after divorce. They tend to be angry about diminished opportunities and their perceived second-class treatment (Kurz, 1995).

Because women and men have different experiences after a divorce, they behave differently. For example, separated men are six times as likely as married men to commit suicide, especially in the younger age groups (Barrett and Turner, 2005). However, separated women do not have much higher suicide rates than married women. After divorce, both male and female suicide rates rise. Thus, as Durkheim said, marriage protects both sexes, but it does so differently. Women with more children have lower suicide rates than women with fewer children, for example. It is possible that their child-rearing responsibilities protect women against suicide. This protection erodes as their children become independent.

Divorce depresses both women and men. However, women undergoing divorce show greater increases in rates of depression. Men whose marriages are breaking up typically show higher rates of alcohol problems but not of distress (Wu and Hart, 2002). Women report more distress but not more alcohol problems. These findings support the idea that men externalize their problems in response to circumstances that lead women to internalize. Women also show more symptoms of distress before the separation, whereas men display more symptoms after the final separation. In short, men and women respond to the stresses of divorce differently. Therefore, researchers must measure men's and women's well-being differently and therapists must help them in ways appropriate to the problems they face.

After divorce, women suffer a decline in their standard of living. A classic American study by Lenore Weitzman (1985) estimated a decline of 73 percent in women's standard of living, compared to a 42-percent decline for men in the first year after divorce. (For comparable Canadian data, see Finnie, 1993, which will be discussed below. For more recent American data, see Arditti, 1997. For a re-analysis of Weitzman's data and less dramatic findings, see Peterson, 1996.) This drop in living standard occurs even among less advantaged subgroups, such as African American and Hispanic low-income adults. Most young minority men fare poorly after divorce in absolute economic terms. However, young minority women fare even worse, a disparity that stems, either directly or indirectly, from women's roles as primary child caretakers (Smock, 1994).

Finnie's (1993) Canadian research also demonstrates that both men's and women's income drops as a result of divorce, but women's income drops twice as much, on average. Men tend to recover lost income more quickly than women in the aftermath of divorce. As well, since men have higher income, they are less likely to be poor (Ambert, 2005b). Thus, divorce is much more likely to plunge divorced women into poverty, and keep them there for longer. This is especially true if they have children for whom they are solely or largely responsible.

Also, women get custody of the children, which means that fewer dollars have to support a lot more people. And women with children may have taken time out of paid employment to have or stay with the children while they are young, thus reducing their years of income and work experience. Low income is the cause of higher levels of life strains reported by separated women, according to a six-year longitudinal study (Nelson, 1994). On the other hand, some researchers find that "fathers are better off after divorce, for they can now spend most of their money on one person, themselves . . ." (Goode, 1993: 166). Some divorced fathers dutifully provide child support, however, for their children after divorce, and researchers like Finnie (1993) find that those fathers' incomes drop, though not as much as women's.

Women's economic disadvantage after divorce is largely due to the traditional practice of investing male human capital in the wage labour market and female human capital in the family and home. The latter greatly disadvantages women after divorce, when women are likely to receive inadequate compensation for time spent out of the wage labour market. Even women with almost the same educational background as men are at a disadvantage.

The impact of divorce is often lifelong; the healing process takes time. Healing is influenced by such variables as age of mother and child, potential for remarriage, coping skills, social networks, and income changes. Having a steady, satisfying job is associated with higher self-esteem and lower distress among divorced women. A good job provides meaning, social interaction and support, productivity, positive distraction, and income. Spirituality helps some women. Others change their behaviour to reduce stress. They may take up exercise or otherwise focus on nurturing a healthy body; they may take classes or take up hobbies to improve their mental well-being; they may revamp their personal appearance to give themselves a boost. (For more on this theme, see Wallerstein and Blakelee, 1990.) We will discuss more about life after divorce in Chapter 11 when we consider fresh family starts.

Effects on Children

Traditionally, many couples avoided divorce and stayed together "for the sake of the children." Their concern was, in some respects, justifiable. Divorce may have harmful effects for the children involved. However, research shows repeatedly that the effects of divorce on children as well as on parents depend very much on what is happening in the family before divorce and the quality of family relationships during and after the divorce (Amato and Booth, 1996; Amato, Loomis, and Booth, 1995; Smart and Neale, 1999; Stacey, 1996). If the family is violent or family relationships are abusive and hostile, for example, then divorce might provide relief.

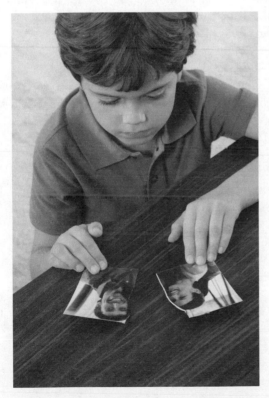

Children who have witnessed divorce show higher levels of depression, anxiety, and loneliness. Some children may even blame themselves for the result, and may have particular difficulty in adjusting to new circumstances.

Hetherington and Kelly (2002) suggest that the negative long-term effects of divorce on children may have become so exaggerated that it has become a self-fulfilling prophecy. For example, children of divorced parents can display poorer social and psychological adjustment than children from non-divorced homes (Kunz, 1992: 352).

But if schools, counsellors, and parents are taught to look for these outcomes, that could account, in part, for why they find them more often. When the children grow up, they are much more likely than those from intact families to think their own marriages may be in trouble. Were there other differences in these children prior to divorce? Are their subsequent expectations about their own marriages a result of childhood experience or of much-hyped research showing negative outcomes?

Research (Statistics Canada, 2005f) finds that the tension and turmoil leading up to the divorce are more harmful to children's mental health than the divorce itself. If most of the damage is done to children who live in families where there is constant fighting, then staying together, especially for the sake of the children, may not be the wisest choice.

Children of divorced parents show higher levels of depression and lower levels of self-esteem than children from intact families. They have more symptoms of anxiety and loneliness, more depressed moods, more suicidal thoughts, and more suicide attempts than children from intact families. In particular, children with irrational beliefs and feelings about divorce are most likely to develop behavioural and psychological problems (Skitka and Frazier, 1995). Some children, for example, believe they caused the divorce. This shows the need for counselling that puts the divorce in perspective. Children who blame themselves for their parents' problems seem to have particular difficulty adjusting.

Parental divorce can increase the risk of adolescent depression in two ways. First, it may be a source of many secondary problems and stresses that cause depression. Second, it can alter youths' reactions to these stresses, sometimes increasing the depressive effects. Economic hardships, a common outcome of divorce for children, also increase the risk of depression, thus accounting for the greater vulnerability of youths in single-parent families to depression (Amato and Sobolewski, 2001; Aseltine, 1996). That these factors go together makes it challenging for researchers to sort out the independent effects of divorce per se.

On the other hand, separation and divorce can improve family functioning (Statistics Canada, 2005f), especially if custody rules are clear and agreed upon, civility is maintained, and peaceful order is beneficial to both parents. Mothers with joint custody report lower levels of parenting stress and better co-parental relations than sole-custody mothers. But, joint custody is known to be more probable as well as more workable for couples that get along better in the first place and put their children's interests above their own (Smart and Neale, 1999). This produces a happier set of parents, which will no doubt lead to better parenting.

Other things being equal, marriage or living in a stable, long-term relationship is better for children than divorce. Children living in single-mother families with no parental conflict, and with much contact with the non-residential father, still have lower levels of well-being than children who live in two-parent families without parental conflict. However, the well-being of children living in peaceful single-mother families is higher than that of children living in two-parent families with much parental conflict. The degree of parental conflict after divorce is more important for the well-being of children than contact with the departed father. That is to say, it is better for the children of divorce if the father doesn't come around if parental arguments break out when he does (Dronkers, 1996).

Beyond the effects on thinking and feeling, divorce is correlated with variations in children's behaviour. So, for example, in a family that is not abusive, divorce can be related to deterioration in children's school performance; increased proneness to crime, suicide, and out of-wedlock births; lesser adult work performance; and likelihood of the children themselves becoming divorced later in life (Galston, 1996). The experience of divorce may weaken trust in people and institutions, and impede the capacity to form stable, enduring relationships.

Parental divorce and remarriage have strong effects on children's attitudes toward premarital sex, cohabitation, marriage, and divorce, even after controlling for parental attitudes (Axinn and Thornton, 1993). Thus, children do not merely replicate their parents' values and attitudes toward non-marital sex, marriage, and divorce but develop an approach that incorporates their lived experience. Kozuch and Cooney (1995) note, however, that results from studies using parental marital status to predict young adults' attitudes have been inconsistent. In their own survey of young adults from a variety of backgrounds, parental marital status predicted only two of five attitudes toward marriage and family. By contrast, level of parental disagreement predicted four of the five.

Children of divorce typically marry earlier, are more likely to cohabit, achieve less economically, and hold more pro-divorce attitudes. All these factors account for some intergenerational transmission of divorce. However, holding these constant, behaviour problems play the largest part in this transmission of divorce. Children witnessing their parents' divorce are more likely than other children to learn behaviours that interfere with the maintenance of stable intimate relationships (Amato, 1996)—for example, to learn how conflict works but not how co-operation works.

Divorce is associated with less formal schooling, possibly because young people with divorced parents may have less financial support for college from their family. The support they receive is much more likely to come from their custodial than non-custodial parent (Grissett and Furr, 1994). Thus, the lower educational and occupational attainment of children of divorce is more likely associated with reduced financial support than with a loss of confidence in higher education.

Despite these seemingly grim findings, recent research does not support the fear that divorce will inevitably produce problem behaviour. Neither exposure to parental divorce nor exposure to parental conflict affects the quality of attachment to adult intimates, nor the quality of parenting (Tayler, Parker, and Roy, 1995). Adolescence and early adulthood may present many challenges—more to women than to men. Coming from a divorced family may contribute to those pressures. However, coming from a divorced family does not, in the end, diminish an individual's ability to cope with new challenges (Dunlop and Burns, 1995).

Causes and Effects of Divorce

- In general, marriage is less likely to result in divorce for people who marry in their 30s or later, who did not live common-law before the wedding, have children, attend religious services, are university educated, and believe that marriage is important if they are to be happy (Clark and Crompton, 2006).

- According to data from the 2005 National Population Health Survey (NPHS), men and women who go through a divorce have a higher risk of being depressed in the two years following the end of the relationship. The risk is especially great for divorced men, who are six times more likely to be depressed than those who remained married (Rotermann, 2007).

- Problems in the realm of work and household labour as well as emotional and psychological relationship problems have become more important motives for a divorce, especially for women. This is consistent with the increase in emancipatory attitudes in the past decades (de Graaf and Kalmijn, 2006).

- Senior women who are divorced are more likely to live in low income than senior women who are widowed, and with the rising elderly population, more senior women are at risk for entering poverty in the future (Turcotte and Schellenberg, 2006).

- Changes in father–child contact are more closely linked to the mother's subsequent re-marriage than to the father's. Non-resident fathers reduce frequency of visits when their children acquire a stepfather, but they are not significantly reduced after the birth of a child in the father's new union (Juby, Billette, Laplante, and Le Bourdais, 2007).

- Divorce is associated with an increased level of anxiety and depression in children. However, child anti-social behaviour decreases when marriages in highly dysfunctional families are dissolved (Strohschein, 2005).

Relations with Parents

Since divorce often results in the departure of the biological father from the family, father–child relationships are often most affected. In a study by Dunn, Cheng, O'Connor, and Bridges (2004), positive relationships between children and non-resident fathers were correlated with ongoing contact between child and father, the quality of the mother–child relationship, and the frequency of contact between the mother and her former partner. Increasingly, children and fathers do preserve a continuing relationship after the divorce. However, on average, adolescents in divorced families get less advice from their fathers and feel less satisfied with paternal support. Adolescents from intact families say they have more positive emotional relationships with their fathers than do adolescents from divorced or remarried families. Adolescents who live with both parents fight their fathers to achieve independence. However, this can be a good thing, related to the development of more self-esteem and a stronger ego identity (McCurdy and Scherman, 1996).

Amato and Booth (1996) used data from a 12-year longitudinal study of marital instability to examine the effects of divorce on parent–child relationships. The quality of the parents' marriage has both direct and indirect implications for later parent–child affection. Problems in the parent–child relationship before divorce, and low quality in the parents' marriage when children were (on average) 10 years old, led to low parental affection for the children when they were (on average) 18 years old. Divorce continued to undermine affection between fathers and children, although not between mothers and children. Thus, when there is a long history of turbulence and indifference, the break in a father–child relationship may predate divorce. Departure may reduce the child's access to his or her father. However, those fathers who maintain contact remain important people in their children's lives and an important source of support in times of stress (Munsch, Woodward, and Darling, 1995; Smart and Neale, 1999).

As we have seen in previous chapters, there is a substantial amount of research on the lives of single mothers and the difficulties they face raising children. There is much less literature on father involvement in child rearing following a parental split. Edin, Tach, and Mincy (2009) use data from the Fragile Families and Child Wellbeing Study and from interviews with 150 unmarried fathers to understand contemporary non-marital father involvement. The authors find that "father involvement drops sharply after the parents' relationships end, especially when they enter subsequent relationships and have children with new partners" (Edin et al., 2009: 149).

As seen in Figure 9.4, father involvement is important not only for the welfare of the child(ren) involved but also because it affects the outcome of important deliberations about child custody and family reunification. For various reasons, unknown father cases rarely result in parent–child reunification, for several reasons. Mothers who are unable or

Figure 9.4 Discharge outcome by level of non-resident father involvement

Source: More about the Dads: Exploring Associations between Nonresident Father Involvement and Child Welfare Case Outcomes. 2008. Prepared for U.S. Department of Health and Human Services et al. Washington, D.C. http://aspe.hhs.gov/hsp/08/moreaboutdads/.

unwilling to identify their child's likely father may have other characteristics that are related to the likelihood of an adoption outcome. The uncertainty about a father's identity may point to a broader family dysfunction, for example. And, if an initial placement with a relative works out well, the caseworker may be reluctant to seek contact even with an identified father.

Compared with those who grew up in two-parent families, the adult children of divorced parents perceive their relationships with both mothers and fathers to be of lower quality. The quality is two or three times lower for fathers than for mothers. Usually, memories of parental conflict or other family problems can explain the effect of parental divorce on relationship quality. Adult children of divorce also have much less current contact with their parents than adults from two-parent families (Webster and Herzog, 1995). Children evaluate their relationships with mothers more positively than those with fathers. They evaluate pre-separation relationships more positively than post-separation relationships, with some recovery after the passage of time. A positive relationship with one parent contributes negatively to the evaluation of the other parent after separation, suggesting that separation typically polarizes loyalties (Hoffman and Ledford, 1995).

Stepfamilies Stepfamilies, often formed by the remarriage of biological parents after their divorce, are multiparent families that may give children as many as two full sets of parents (and siblings), and four sets of grandparents. The presence of loving parents and grandparents can be a real plus for a child, under the right circumstances. However, stepfamilies can pose problems too, for a variety of reasons. People form them after divorce, and marital conflict precedes the divorce. So, there are problems to solve—bad feelings between the former spouses—even before the new families begin. These feelings can affect the relationship between children and the step-parent. Portrie and Hill (2005) found that a mother's conflicts with the former spouse have negative effects on children and their stepfathers.

Chiefly, however, the problems associated with stepfamilies are due to the number and rapidity of changes a child must make. This is especially true if the remarriage occurs within a few years of the divorce.

Adapting to new parent(s) and potentially more siblings may cause confusion and stress for the child. Even a child who likes his or her new siblings may feel in competition with near-strangers for the affection of his or her parent.

Moreover, remarriages are problematic if they create an unstable environment for the child. As we have seen, remarriages have a higher failure rate than first marriages. Research also shows that changes in parenting can significantly hurt a child. These changes increase the likelihood that a child will suffer poor grades, poor health, low self-esteem, drug abuse, peer rejection, and lower self-reported well-being. At the extreme, a succession of divorces and remarriages presents an unstable environment, especially since expectations change with each new parent. We'll talk more about remarriage and stepfamilies in Chapter 11.

In sum, for children, parents, and other relatives, divorce, like other major life events, can be stressful. However, we must be careful not to exaggerate the extent or permanence of harm done. With divorce, the stresses include economic hardship, parental adjustment, interpersonal conflict, or parental loss. Developing resources and protections can reduce the negative effect of these stressors. Higher levels of coping resources support a greater optimism about the future, fewer financial problems, more confidence in parenting ability, and a more satisfactory relationship with the former spouse (O'Leary, Franzoni, and Brack, 1996).

Factors that reduce the adverse effect of divorce on children include a strong and clear sense that both parents still love them, an understanding that they are not to blame for the divorce, and regular visits with the non-custodial parent. Involved and caring parents can produce a good child adjustment to divorce. Parental distance, on the other hand, is likely to produce maladjustment. Parental conflict, as we have said so often, has a bad effect in both intact and divorced families (Weiner, Harlow, Adams, and Grebstein, 1995).

The impact of divorce on children varies enormously, depending on many factors, including the responsiveness of parents, schools, and community adults. Overall, young adults are optimistic about marriage, and their parents' divorce has not had a large impact on their attitudes toward marriage and divorce (Landis-Kleine, Foley, Nall, Padgett, and Walters-Palmer, 1995).

Though divorce may sometimes cause problems, it sometimes also solves problems. Divorce spares many children serious problems. It may even bring benefits. People whose parents divorced during their adolescent years display a much higher level of moral development than those whose parents did not divorce (Kogos and Snarey, 1995). Underlying the development of moral judgment is an increased perspective-taking, necessary for children of divorce who witness differences in opinions between their parents.

Effects on the Elderly

We have seen that today's older generation has more diverse family networks than previous generations. For example, older people today are more likely than previous cohorts to have experienced divorce. So it is important to understand how trends in family life and partnership dissolution may affect future support and care for older adults, given that their social networks are largely composed of family members (Askham, Ferring, and Lamura, 2007).

On the one hand, there is the belief the experience of divorce weakens family ties, thereby reducing family support. There is evidence that divorce can have negative effects on support at older ages (Curran, McLanahan, and Knab, 2003; Kalmijn, 2007; Shapiro, 2003). It has been suggested that older people who have gone through divorce experience decreased contact and relationship quality with adult children as well as perceived support from children when compared with those in intact marriages (Curran et al., 2003; Kalmijn, 2007). Further, a Canadian study has shown that divorce followed by remarriage among older couples is accompanied by decreased support from networks of friends (Schlesinger and Schlesinger, 2009).

On the other hand, it has been suggested that the deleterious effects of partnership dissolution for support in later life may be disappearing (Thornton and Young-DeMarco, 2001). For instance, Glaser, Stuchbury, Tomassini, and Aksham (2008) found that partnership dissolution did not have a detrimental association with late-life support. In fact, separated older parents (age 70 and older) were significantly more likely to receive help from their adult children than married older parents. The authors also found that the level of family support increased with increasing age and the health needs of the older person, regardless of family history (Glaser et al., 2008). Thus, a changing notion of the definition of "family," a greater acceptance of divorce, and an increasing tolerance of different family forms could be contributing to the stability of intergenerational support relationships.

CONCLUDING REMARKS

As we have seen, divorce is both a micro- and a macro-level phenomenon, with both micro- and macro-level effects. Little synthesis between macro- and micro-level analyses has been achieved. We are still far from having a comprehensive theory that predicts who will divorce and why.

The past 25 years have not fulfilled legislators' objectives in adopting no-fault divorce. There is no improved family life, no expanded choice and happiness, at least in the eyes of critics (see, for example, Stanton, 1996). Some have remarked on how the combined effect of increased divorce rates and increasing levels of unwed child-bearing have ensured that more than half the children born in the 1980s will be raised in single-parent homes for all or part of their lives. The decline of marriage has also led to paternal disinvestments in children. Allegedly, unmarried men are less likely to support children financially. Increased maternal earning capacity or improved public investment has not compensated for the decline in paternal support (Whitehead, 1996).

The conservative approach to the problems of divorce, teen pregnancy, suicide, violence, and substance abuse is to blame the emerging culture of tolerance and the expanded welfare state, contending that they undermine the benefits of self-reliance and community standards. The conservative definition of family values is too narrow. However, the perspective rightly emphasizes the role of the family in child-rearing education.

Liberals do recognize that increased unemployment, rising competition, and the need for dual-earner households have threatened the family. However, they overemphasize the extent to which government services can replace effective family bonds (Giele, 1996). Among socially conservative people, strategies to encourage the reinstitutionalization of the family would include restricting the legal benefits of family life and of marriage. These would begin with tighter controls on entry into marriage, more difficulties in leaving a marriage through divorce, and legally defining marriage as a moral duty between partners, rather than a personal contractual decision (Schneider, 1996).

Though it is not the job of sociologists to favour one side or the other, it is part of our responsibility to collect and examine data that would support one side or another. Here, sociology has an important role to play in the process by which a democratic society makes the policies and laws that govern family life.

The evidence shows us that divorce is correlated with unhappiness and trouble. The question is, does divorce cause the unhappiness and trouble or does unhappiness and trouble cause divorce? Further, does divorce prolong unhappiness and trouble or cut it mercifully short? While it is foolhardy to generalize about all divorces, there is no evidence to show that divorce is the cause of most family-related unhappiness. Though it is true that people benefit from stable family lives when those families are functioning well, it is also true that people suffer from family lives when those families are functioning badly.

For better or worse, it is up to the participants to decide whether their family life is functioning well or badly. Outsiders' impressions count for little. Remember, as we have pointed out so often throughout this book, what counts is a person's opinion. If the people involved think the family is working well, then to all intents and purposes, it is. If not, and efforts to correct the situation don't work, then divorce makes good sense—for the sake of the children as well as the spouses themselves. After all, a child can get good parenting without father and mother living together. On the other hand, conditions of stress, violence, unhappiness, and depression make good parenting almost impossible. We must assume, and probably can assume, that most parents take these factors into account when they decide to stay together or divorce. This being so, the conservative viewpoint on divorce has little to offer us.

CHAPTER SUMMARY

In this chapter we looked at the rise in divorce experienced since the middle of the twentieth century in most industrial societies. As social scientists, we look at the nature of social bonding, and our discussions on divorce cover not only some of the reasons behind increased divorce rates. We also examine the effects this increase has had on individuals and society as a whole. Although these trends show a dramatic change in family structure and the functions the family plays in our lives, research has shown that our beliefs and attitudes about the role of the family have not kept pace. This makes the task of assessing the real impacts of divorce a bit more difficult, yet all the more needed.

Historically, divorce has worried social scientists and policy makers alike. This concern has grown with the increase of divorce

rates worldwide. Social, legal, and cultural changes have all played a part in developing these trends.

Generally, causes of divorce should more accurately be called predictors, since it is easier to note relationships between variables than to pin down a cause-and-effect relationship. Factors influencing the likelihood of divorce are found at the micro-, meso-, and macro-levels. Micro-level factors include poor communication, poor conflict-resolution skills, lack of commitment, lack of shared interests, and perceived inequity. Meso-level factors include age, marital duration, location, religiosity, class, and race. Macro-level factors include war, economic cycles, and cultural values.

The effects of divorce were then considered. Divorce is a time of distress for spouses and children. Both men and women suffer a decline in standard of living, but men's incomes drop less and rebound faster. This effect is especially important for women, since they are most commonly the prime caregivers of the children after a divorce. Typically, fathers gradually disengage from children, though some do remain closely involved in parenting. Children are distressed immediately after a divorce but gradually adjust. Finally, with a growing senior population in Canada, it is important to understand the trends and effects of separation and divorce in this population, especially how this affects intergenerational relationships in families.

The harmful effects of divorce are often talked about. Yet it is important to recognize that many of the harmful effects observed stem not from divorce per se but from poor family interactions prior to, during, and after the divorce. Hence, it may be important and helpful for families to seek professional help during this emotionally stressful time. Family therapy and mediation are just two examples of options available for people going through separation and divorce.

We concluded with a look at some popular political viewpoints on divorce. There is a movement urging legal and policy changes to discourage divorce, in an attempt to alleviate some of the social burdens that divorce produces. We find many of the proposed solutions incomplete and ineffective because of the narrow interpretations of the problem, which labels divorce as the culprit rather than poor family interactions.

Key Terms

adverse selectivity A tendency for people who choose to engage in a given behaviour to be, by nature of the kind of people they are, also at risk for a given outcome; selectivity may create the appearance of cause-and-effect relationships where they do not exist.

cohort effect The accumulated experience of going through life in the same set of years. For example, people born in the period 1924–1928 experienced World War II as teenagers and the postwar economic boom as young marrieds, and may have certain views or attitudes in common because of these experiences.

determinant A factor that contributes to an outcome (such as divorce) without necessarily being the direct or principal cause.

femininity A cluster of characteristics, such as nurturance, sensitivity, and gentleness, traditionally considered natural to women but that can be found in men or women.

macro-level The broad level of examining a social phenomenon, focusing on changes that affect society as a whole.

meso-level A middle range at which a social phenomenon may be examined, focusing on

demographics—the characteristics of the people affected.

micro-level The smallest level at which a social phenomenon may be examined, the level of interactions between individuals and effects on individuals.

no-fault divorce Divorce granted because of marital breakdown rather than of specific wrongdoing (for example, adultery) on the part of one spouse or the other.

predictor A characteristic that is correlated with and precedes an outcome but may not be a direct cause.

secularization A move away from religion as an organizing principle of society.

social disorganization A breakdown of societal functioning.

social integration The state of societies that are closely knit and stable, in which people hold similar world views and there is a strong consensus on social rules.

social pathology A broad-based distress or disorganization within society.

socio-economic status Class; standing in society in terms of income, education, and prestige.

Critical Thinking Questions

1. In this chapter, you have learned the importance of understanding the variation in divorce rates. Formulate a sociological research question on the topic of divorce and propose how you would gather and analyze the data on divorce rates.

2. Using what you have learned from this chapter, discuss how changes in the legal aspects of divorce may make it difficult to study the history of family breakdown and analyze statistical data.

3. What is the relationship between the micro-level and macro-level reasons for divorce?

4. Discuss possible interventions that would lessen the negative impacts of divorce. For each approach, specify whether it addresses the micro-level, meso-level, or macro-level causes of divorce.

5. Discuss the possible advantages and disadvantages of "no-fault" divorce laws for individual families and for society.

6. Men are more likely than women to experience depression two years following a separation or divorce. Suggest possible reasons for this observation.

7. Discuss effective ways that stepfamilies can organize themselves to reduce conflict and stress.

8. The population of older adults in Canada is undoubtedly growing in size. Can you think how this trend may contribute to novel challenges faced by families or the society at large, when either the parents or grandparents divorce?

Weblinks

Service Canada: Getting Divorced
www.servicecanada.gc.ca/eng/lifeevents/divorce.shtml
This site provides a list of links and information to help understand the legal issues and the process of divorce in Canada.

Ontario Association for Marriage & Family Therapy
www.oamft.on.ca
This site is a resource for marriage and family therapists, as well as for the public interested in finding a therapist in Ontario or finding out about the profession in general.

Canadian Divorce Laws
www.canadiandivorcelaws.com
This site is a guide to the legal situation in Canada, written by a lawyer. It provides access to a library of articles on issues such as child support, child custody, spousal support, property division, divorce procedure, and more.

Ministry of the Attorney General—Family Law
www.attorneygeneral.jus.gov.on.ca/english/family
This site provides the public with comprehensive information about family law, the family court system, and legislation in Ontario.

Shared Custody: Increasing Benefits and Reducing Strains
http://extension.oregonstate.edu/catalog/html/ec/ec1443
An article prepared by Sue Doescher and Jan Hare, extension child development and parent education specialists from Oregon State University.

Stepfamily Network
www.stepfamily.net
This online forum and social networking site supports stepfamilies through sharing and discussion.

Organisation for Economic Co-operation and Development and (OECD) Family Database
www.oecd.org/els/social/family/database
This OECD database includes cross-national information on family outcomes and policies as categorized under four broad headings: the structure of families, the labour market position of families, public policies for families and children, and child outcomes.

Families Change
www.familieschange.ca
This site, developed by the Province of British Columbia, provides easy-to-understand pamphlets and information about separation and divorce for kids, teens, and adults.

Chapter 10
Family Transitions and Innovations
Second Families, Empty Nests, Cluttered Nests, and New Kinds of Families

Chapter Outline

Transitions into parenthood are perplexing and momentous events in one's life and in the life cycle of families. Transitions to different family situations can be just as challenging and momentous. The term "transition" can mean a happy shift to a new family life. Yet some transitions are not fresh starts, but stale starts, or redoing the old start without much that is new. Some transitions prove impossible. Family transitions can involve reinventing close relations, customizing social ideals to best fit one's particular needs and situation.

In the previous chapter we explored the many challenges posed by family dissolution. In this chapter, we focus on life *after* separation, divorce, or widowhood. We also examine what is possible and what we can learn from the multiple ways in which people make transitions from one kind of family to another as they experience family dissolution, as they age, and as they invent new ways to be familial.

FAMILY TRANSITIONS IN THE PAST

We often think of family transitions as a recent phenomenon. In reality, making fresh starts is nothing new, as we saw in Chapter 2. With the massive flows of refugees and immigrants out of strife-torn and, in some cases, poverty-stricken Europe throughout the first half of the twentieth century, many people started families afresh in North America. Immigrants and refugees from Europe are still coming, as strife recurs, and have been joined by people from Africa, Asia, Latin America, and the Caribbean who are fleeing an old life or seeking new opportunities in Canada, Australia, and the United States.

Fresh family starts were more characteristic of families in the past than we sometimes acknowledge today. The higher mortality rates of the past often meant that families often experienced the death of one or both spouses/parents while the children were still young, creating the possibility or the need for fresh family starts. Remarriage after the death of one's first spouse was frequent, as were step-parents, adoption, and fostering of children. In some ways, widows in the past were similar to single mothers today in the economic vulnerability they and their children faced and in the social challenges they posed (Gordon and McLanahan, 1991).

Nor did marriage failure and divorce begin only recently, as discussed in Chapter 2.

WHAT IS A FAMILY TRANSITION?

A family transition can be a step filled with hope and dreams for a wonderful shared future. The strength of this hope is evidenced in social research, which shows that most young people expect never to be divorced. This may be indicative of their sense of commitment to a lifelong relationship, but their hopeful expectations may blind them to the known risks of divorce. A fresh start at family can be any happy young couple on the brink of establishing themselves as a couple, whether married or cohabiting, whether gay/lesbian or heterosexual.

In this chapter we discuss second or subsequent starts at families or familial relationships. The processes through which transitions come about are various. It can be a flight from violence in a family of origin or a conjugal family/relationship, an escape from an abusive practice sanctioned by the prevailing culture, a mutually agreed upon separation or divorce, a death, or myriad other family changes over the life course. It can be a rediscovery of one's roots and a new basis on which to found and maintain a family, or even a discovery of cultural roots in a new setting or country. It can involve a personal reinvention of family to meet one's particular needs.

Family changes, transitions, and innovations are possible when things do not work out as planned, expected, or hoped for the first time around. Fresh family starts can begin reluctantly as one's idealism about family is tarnished by family dissolution. In this way, new families reflect change, both individual and social, as well as personal learning and adaptation. It is an adventure to explore the complex ways in which people make families afresh and the new ways for people to have close relations.

One of the themes in this book is that families are immensely varied. Perhaps at no point is this clearer than when families make transitions or innovations. The multiple pathways of transition include the shrinking of family to its smallest unit, a single-person household with non-household-based families, or to a parent with a child. It can also involve non-residential parenting and the development of intricate and large extended-kin or non-kin networks. Another theme highlighted in this book is that *family processes* rather than *family types* provide the rewarding focus of family studies. In considering family transitions and innovations, we observe families and individuals actively engaging in family as a process, in designing families anew, in negotiating family, and in striking bargains with former family members on how to endure as family. Our emphasis is on family dynamics, where lies the active development of new solutions to family challenges.

Multiple Family Starts

In today's world of long life expectancies and rapidly changing families, people may expect to make not one but multiple family transitions over the course of their lives. Think of those who marry or live together after having lived alone or as an adult in the parental home. They have already experienced two kinds of transitions: first, the new ways of being family when they became adults and continued to live with their parents and, second, marriage. And the family transitions are likely to continue throughout their lives, with possible separation, divorce, cohabitation, perhaps remarriage, then possibly widowhood, and maybe another later-life relationship or marriage.

Within each of these family states, phases can mark other kinds of transitions: into parenthood, into or out of working parenthood, from being in a two-earner to a one-earner (or no-earner) family, to grandparenthood, step-parenthood, and so on. In families today, diversity is now the norm, with almost endless possibilities. The **SNAF** (standard North American family) no longer exists.

Living Solo

Many people who experience the end of a marriage or committed relationship become single before becoming any other kind of family. Some may move directly from one relationship to another. And some stay single with no intimate relationship as part of their lives. Living solo is an option growing in popularity. The 2006 Census of Canada reveals a 57.5 percent growth in one-person households since 1981 (Statistics Canada, 2007a). The largest proportion living alone occurred among those aged 65 and older; 37 percent of women in this age group lived alone in 2006 compared with 33.7 percent in 1981. For men aged 65 and older, 16 percent lived alone in 2006. For both senior women and men, the proportion living alone increases with advancing years. Significant proportions of those aged 30 to 44 (10.1 percent) also lived alone, a substantial increase from previous censuses (Statistics Canada, 2007a).

Is singlehood an aspect of family life? Some might respond that a single person living alone is not a family. True enough, but a single person is not necessarily without a family. Most of us have families even if we live alone, live separated from our spouses or partners, or are simply between relationships. Family is not equivalent to household. Families and close relations can and do exist, and even thrive, across households.

She versus He on Marriage

HER VIEWS

A man in love is incomplete until he has married. Then he's finished.

—Zsa Zsa Gabor

Any intelligent woman who reads the marriage contract, and then goes into it, deserves all the consequences.

—Isadora Duncan

Before marriage, a girl has to make love to a man to hold him. After marriage, she has to hold him to make love to him.

—Marilyn Monroe

Being divorced is like being hit by a Mack truck. If you live through it, you start looking very carefully to the right and to the left.

—Jean Kerr

A wedding is just like a funeral except that you get to smell your own flowers.

—Grace Hansen

HIS VIEWS

All marriages are happy. It's the living together afterward that causes all the trouble.

—Raymond Hull

A good marriage would be between a blind wife and a deaf husband.

—Michel de Montaigne (also attributed to Honoré de Balzac)

A journey is like marriage. The certain way to be wrong is to think you control it.

—John Steinbeck

A man marries to have a home, but also because he doesn't want to be bothered with sex and all that sort of thing.

—W. Somerset Maugham

A man may be a fool and not know it, but not if he is married.

—H.L. Mencken

Source: www.brainyquote.com/quotes/topics/topic_marriage.html.

Findings from a national survey in Canada (McDaniel, 1994) reveal that a majority of adult children living away from home live within relatively close distances of family. Visiting between parents, particularly mothers, and adult children is frequent, as is contact by phone, letter, or e-mail. Among siblings, there is even more regular contact.

For some, living alone is a transitional stage to a new committed relationship. We will discuss that in a moment. For increasing numbers of North Americans, however, living alone is a life choice, a preference, or better than other alternatives. The diversity of solo living, however, prevents us from making any solidly based generalizations about it.

Lone-Parent Families

Marital or relationship dissolution can be the start of lone parenthood, but it is not the only pathway. There has also been growth in the numbers of people having children without being in a committed couple relationship. This, as we have seen in Chapter 3, can occur in a variety of ways. One of those, the deliberate seeking of parenthood on one's own, through biological parenting or adoption, will be considered in the next section as a kind of family innovation. Here, we will focus on the more common pathway to lone parenthood, as a result of marriage or relationship breakdown.

Before discussing lone parenthood as a family transition, it is important to shed some light on the perplexing problem of defining lone parents. Typically, estimates of the number of lone parents are based on a one-time sample, such as a census or a survey, and are looked at from the viewpoint of adults. The research question typically asked is: What proportion of adults at this moment are living in lone-parent families? Three problems, at least, are apparent in this approach.

The first is that it often remains unknown whether the parents surveyed are indeed living on their own or are cohabiting. For example, common-law families are rapidly increasing in number. Between 2001 and 2006, the number of common-law families grew by 19 percent (Statistics Canada, 2007b: 39). By 2006, the percentage of children aged 15 and younger who lived with lone parents reached 18.3 percent (Statistics Canada, 2007b: 39).

Second, without considering lone parenthood from a life course perspective, it is not possible to see it as a process rather than a state, to see how the experience affects adults and children, and to distinguish between transitional and permanent arrangements. Third, and importantly, examining single parenthood in terms of adult relationships tends to overlook the ways lone parenthood affects children. In Canada, the percentage of children aged 15 and younger who lived with lone parents was 12.4 percent in 1986, 16.0 percent in 1996, and 18.3 percent in 2006 (Statistics Canada, 2007b: 39)—a steady increase in the number of children growing up in single-parent households. Women make up the overwhelming majority (80 percent) of lone parents in Canada and are also the most economically disadvantaged families in the country.

Lone parenthood has increased dramatically in North America in recent decades. This pace of change is not seen, however, in other Western countries (Baker, 1995). In the United States in 2004, 23 percent of all families were single-mother families (ChildStats.gov, 2005). The overwhelming majority of lone parents in both Canada and the United States are mothers, although the fastest-growing family type in Canada over the 1990 to 2000 decade has been lone-father families (Sauve, 2002: 3). Between 2001 and 2006, lone-father households increased by 15 percent compared with only a 6 percent jump in those headed by women in Canada (Statistics Canada, 2007b). The United States has also seen a growth in single-father families, with the proportion increasing from 2 percent in 1980 to 5 percent in 2004 (ChildStats.gov, 2005).

The incidence of poverty remains high among lone parents, particularly lone mothers. In 2002, the national median income for lone-parent families was $28 100 (Statistics Canada, 2004f). In Canada in 2002, 51.6 percent of lone-mother families were below the low-income cutoffs, making these families the group with the highest incidence of family poverty in Canada (Canadian Feminist Alliance for International Action, 2005). This compares with a poverty rate of 7.4 percent among husband–wife families with children younger than age 18 living at home (Statistics Canada, 2002h: 5). Dooley (1993) found that poverty among lone-mother families is most resistant to remedy (Dooley, 1993: 117). The good-news part of this story is that low income among lone-mother families dropped by 10 percent from 1999 to 2000 in Canada, and among two-parent families with children by 2.6 percent (Statistics Canada, 2002h: 5). Lone mothers in the 1990 to 2000 decade experienced the highest increase in employment and are now more likely to be employed than are wives without children (Sauve, 2002: 3–4).

But the news on lone mothers in poverty is not all good. Among lone mothers still in poverty, the depth of their poverty may have increased. Affordable housing shortages over the past decade have posed big problems. "Among the surging number of single mothers who have taken refuge in temporary shelters [recently] are an entirely new class of homeless—formerly secure career women," notes Gadd (1997: D1).

Many women with dependent children tumble into poverty when their marriage or union ends. This occurs for a number of interconnected reasons. Marriage, in our society, is still a presumed economic alliance between a man who can earn more and a woman who is economically subordinate or dependent while devoting herself to child-bearing and child rearing (Townsend, 2002). It is part of what Townsend calls "the package deal" of marriage. When the marriage ends, women find (as noted in Chapter 9) that the initial disparity in income and potential income has widened. As well, a woman with young dependent children and perhaps fewer work skills, less training or education, and sole responsibility for children may not seem like a good prospect to an employer. And on separation, the considerable benefits of having the combined incomes of two earners no longer exist.

With the added challenge of finding affordable housing, lone mothers can quickly become poor, and tend to remain so, with disadvantages both for themselves and for their children (McDaniel, 1993). Not surprisingly, the consequences to men of divorce are seldom as financially bleak.

As discussed in Chapter 6, children in lone-parent families are known to suffer both directly from the disadvantage of their family situations—particularly poverty—and from society, which stigmatizes them and expects less from them. The two forces work together to create lower achievement prospects that tend to become self-fulfilling. These factors, though powerful, are not deterministic. Many children from lone-parent families achieve at high levels indeed, among them Barack Obama and Barbara Streisand, to cite but two world famous examples. Nonetheless, making opportunities for children from lone-parent families is often not easy for the mothers, the children themselves, or society.

The positive experiences of living in a lone-parent family, for both mothers and their children, are not to be discounted. Among other things, they may learn the value of interdependence, invention and innovation, self-reliance, and mutual interdependency, and may learn to value women in a world that too often fails to do so (Collins, 1991; Ferri, 1993). Children from deprived situations where love persists can learn to persevere, to aim high in their expectations, and to deny themselves for future gain.

Latchkey children, children who are regularly left for some part of the day without adult supervision, epitomize both the best and the worst of resilience. Not all latchkey children are from lone-parent families. Many are from two-income families where no one is home when they return from school each day. Both good and bad consequences are found for latchkey children in one study (Leung, Robson, Cho, and Lim, 1996). Benefits include learning to be independent and responsible, as well as acquiring useful skills such as how to start dinner for the family or how to grocery shop. Among the drawbacks are loneliness, fear, boredom, underachievement in school, and perhaps an increased likelihood of drug or alcohol abuse.

Lone parenthood after divorce or separation is a family transition plagued with perils, as we saw in the previous chapter. Not the least of the challenges is the stigma, both social and economic. It does not help that poverty and economic insecurity are generally associated with lone motherhood, but there is more to the stigma than economic deprivation and its labels. The negative attribution may start with the social sense of women's inadequacies as women and as mothers, and then move to the threat, both social and economic, that women having children without men pose to the society.

One transition to lone motherhood, not as often considered, is when the marriage or relationship ends because the husband "comes out" as gay. This is a more frequent occurrence than might be imagined, particularly with the societal encouragement of the recent past to deny same-sex attractions and marry anyway. Few marriage partners expect a change in sexual identity in their partners when they marry. Self-help groups for women married to gay men can provide support and reassure women that they are not alone in their experiences.

In one study, French (1991) finds that some couples agree to stay together after the "coming out," while others separate but maintain active parental involvement with the children. French points out how becoming a lone parent can be a means of problem solving for women in this situation. She further reveals that sexuality, like family, is not static and given, but a process sometimes worked through in family as the means to new identities and lifestyles. Interestingly, French's study shows that as the men came to grips with their gay identities, their interest in maintaining their father roles continued, sometimes even intensifying. The study reveals that family is indeed a process and that husbandhood and fatherhood need not be synonymous, and need not be only heterosexual roles.

Lone mothers in the United States, and increasingly in Canada, have become the targets for cutbacks to social assistance (welfare in the U.S.) and vicious public labels. They are variously termed slothful, manipulative, inadequate mothers, irresponsible women, and selfish takers of public monies. Some are even labelled as women who use their sexuality and reproduction to get public subsidies. That little of this has any basis in fact does not seem to matter. It has a reality of its own in belief systems that favour more and deeper cuts to social assistance and so-called incentives to lone mothers to work outside the home, even if there are no jobs and few child-care options for them. The campaigns against lone mothers also have a clear basis in efforts to preserve the nuclear family against other family forms.

Lone-parent families have posed perplexing problems for policy makers because of their persistent poverty. Many countries, including Canada and the United States, have had policies that explicitly or implicitly treat women and children as the responsibilities of husbands and fathers (Baker, 1995: 13). Only when this fails do states believe they must act, reluctantly and under pressure. State family policies have ranged from providing incentives to lone mothers to parent full-time, as in the Netherlands, to offering incentives for them to work in the paid labour force, as in Sweden and Australia (Baker, 1995), to apprehending children at risk in Aboriginal families (Castellano, 2002). Generally, policies in European countries are more generous to lone-parent families, as a result of greater gender equality in the workforce and more accessible and affordable childcare support for working mothers (Crompton and Lyonette, 2006). This, in turn, enables parents to maintain a work–life balance.

Behind social policies oriented to lone-parent families are three models. The first is the *private family approach*, characterized by the United Kingdom and the United States, where family is believed to be a private institution that ought to look after itself, with the state stepping in only on a casualty basis (Lesemann and Nicol, 1994: 117). This contrasts with the *family-oriented model* (France and Quebec), which sees the government as having a public interest in families. The third is the *state-based model* (Sweden), which sees state intervention as important not to help families but to promote socio-economic participation as fully as possible. Canada is caught between these models, using a little of each in its approach to policies for lone parents.

Much attention has been devoted to moving lone mothers away from social assistance. An interesting and innovative Canadian study of 150 single mothers on social assistance found that lone mothers on social assistance in Canada are actively involved in an extensive range of social and economic strategies to exit social assistance. They are realistic and hopeful about the possibilities but feel that they could benefit from useful supports and information. Indeed, the main predictors of successful exits are social supports, including information, and the women's aspirations (Gorlick and Pomfret, 1993).

- In Japan, a large proportion (25 percent) of divorced women aged 35 to 39 reside with their parents after divorce (Raymo, Iwasawa, and Bumpass, 2004).

- In China, due to concerns for their children's well-being, some parents refrain from remarriage after a divorce. Having custody of children is seen to be a disadvantage in seeking marriage. Some parents forfeit their rights to their children in order to remarry (Dong, Wang, and Ollendick, 2002).

- The sentiment in favour of marriage appears to be stronger in the United States than in other developed countries. The share of American adults who are likely to marry is higher, but so is the share likely to divorce. American children are also more likely to live in single-parent families at some time in their childhood (Cherlin, 2005).

- In Denmark, Iceland, and Sweden, a women who gets married for the first time is on average older than 30 years of age (Whiteford, 2009).

- Greece, Italy, Spain, and Mexico have relatively few lone parents and relatively low joblessness. It is possible that family values are more conservative and lone parenthood is less socially acceptable. Also, welfare supports for lone parents and jobless families is extremely limited, if available at all, which may deter people from dissolving their union (Whiteford, 2009).

- Across the Organisation for Economic Cooperation and Development (OECD) countries, the mean age of women at first marriage is now higher than the mean age of women at first childbirth (Whiteford, 2009).

A study of women on social assistance in Niagara Falls, Canada, provides a different understanding of poverty from the perspective of those who are poor. The participants described life on social assistance alike to "living under a giant microscope" (Collins, 2005: 22), where the perception of constant surveillance translates into feelings of guilt about "every little" purchase or action and also means the loss of many freedoms. "Freedom to spend, freedom to have a good time, freedom to voice an opinion, freedom to work and freedom to make sensible decisions ('sometimes have to go against good budgeting sense to follow the rules') are all identified" as sacrifices that must be made in order to live on social assistance. For these families, the successful exit out of poverty is impeded by their loss of autonomy, lowered self-esteem, and the cyclical nature of stress and money shortage (Collins, 2005).

Seeking Parenthood on One's Own

The largest growth in child-bearing outside of marriage or cohabiting relationships is occurring among women in their late 20s and early 30s (Ram, 1990: 33). Rates of non-marital child-bearing, however, have increased for most age groups. The exception has been births to teens, which in Canada has been falling (Dryburgh, 2001). The teen pregnancy rate in the United States is also decreasing, but remains about double that of the Canadian rate (Dryburgh, 2001: 2).

If mature women are having births without being in couple relationships, several factors could be at work. There could be accidental pregnancies, as there always are. More women who accidentally become pregnant now choose to keep and raise their babies instead of giving them up for adoption. This is a deliberate choice in favour of motherhood, even if the conception itself may not have been planned. There is also evidence that some women are seeking motherhood on their own without the traditional step of marriage or being in a committed relationship.

Few studies have looked at unmarried lone mothers, women who *begin* single parenthood without being married or in a union at all. One study (Clark, 1993) finds that the social and economic costs of unmarried single motherhood are evident 10 years after the first child is born. Although there are no effects on likelihood of marrying, the risks of poverty are greater than for married mothers (Dryburgh, 2001). As well, there is lessened opportunity to pursue education, thus further disadvantaging the unmarried mothers. As the children grow, however, the initial discrepancies between unmarried and married mothers decrease. The woman's age at first unmarried motherhood matters greatly: the younger one is, the greater the disadvantage and the less likely one is to catch up later on. Children born to younger unattached mothers do less well in school and in IQ tests than other children.

In deliberately seeking motherhood on one's own, options exist today that did not exist previously. We introduced some of these options in the scenarios in Chapter 3. With the stigma lessened of having a child outside marriage, it may not be surprising that some women are going for it. This may be a generation of women who have been taught to get what they aim for in life, rather than waiting for all their dreams to fall into place by luck or chance. Some are successful, educated, thoughtful career women who know their own minds. Others may have become infertile earlier in their lives, but not given up their dreams of motherhood. Options now include the new reproductive technologies of **artificial insemination** and **in vitro fertilization**, informal means to access sperm for conception, private adoptions, and foreign adoptions.

Let's look first at adoption, although in reality women often look at adoption only after considering the option of giving birth to a baby. Not long ago, adoption was carefully controlled by churches and the government. For good or for bad, it was thought that adoptive parents should be married and matched in religion, region, and ethnicity/race as much as possible to the adopted child. This left out single women, single men, cohabiting couples, and lesbians and gays. It also often left out the non-religious. Adoption has opened up considerably in recent years, most notably in private adoptions whereby the birth mother (or parents) can know and sometimes select the adoptive family for the baby/child. More single people have been able to adopt children too, although the waiting lists are lengthy and the screening tight and sometimes judgmental about lifestyle.

A new option that has opened things up for couples and single women wishing to adopt—and some single men too—has been foreign adoptions. These occur for numerous reasons. One is that strife and disruption in various world regions have created unwanted babies and children, either as war orphans or as a result of policies such as the forbidding of birth control and abortion in Romania a few years ago. The one-child policy in China has led to numbers of babies, primarily girls, being adopted by Canadians and others, as many Chinese choose, for cultural reasons, to have a boy if they can have only one child (Dorow, 2002). There is concern that some babies or children may be taken from their parents for the lucrative foreign adoption market, or brought into the world for the purposes of the adoption market. It is not fully known whether this occurs and, if so, to what extent.

The opening up of foreign adoption has meant that more Canadians and Americans can adopt who do not meet, or do not wish to meet, the requirements of domestic adoption agencies. International adoption is costly and time-consuming, with lengthy screening and often frustrating international negotiations, but it is possible for a small minority of people to become the adoptive parent of a child born elsewhere.

The new reproductive technologies have also opened possibilities for single people, and to some extent gay men and lesbians. For example, artificial insemination has been used for a long time. It has not been so routinely discussed until recently, however. Surrogate motherhood can be found in the Old Testament but has lately become more popular in North America. In 2004, Canadian legislation made surrogate motherhood for pay illegal. In vitro fertilization, or test-tube conception, has a low success rate but has been used to help women and couples conceive if one or both has fertility problems. These technologies have created new families and challenged the bases on which nuclear families have traditionally been built.

Changing families and reproductive technologies have also led to new types of fatherhood. Eichler (1997: 72) notes that there are now nine kinds of fathers:

- biological, social, exclusive, full fathers
- non-biological but social, exclusive, full fathers
- biological but not social fathers
- biological, social, exclusive, partial fathers (where the father is non-custodial)
- biological, social, non-exclusive (where the mother has a new partner), partial fathers
- non-biological but social, exclusive, partial fathers
- non-biological but social, non-exclusive, partial fathers
- gay co-fathers, non-biological, social, non-exclusive fathers
- post-mortem biological fathers (where the man's sperm is taken for impregnation after his death)

Not much is known about men seeking fatherhood outside marriage or committed relationships. Some gay men who are single, as well as some in committed relationships, have been pushing for the option of adoption in several provinces in Canada. It is not known how many men, on their own, are seeking fatherhood. It might be anticipated, however, that as men's self-images with respect to families and fatherhood change, more men might seek to have children outside of marriage or a committed relationship. It also might be predicted that, even with contemporary social changes, fewer men than women would deliberately seek single parenthood (Townsend, 2002). Practices such as surrogate motherhood (whereby a woman agrees to conceive and gestate a baby for a fee), where available, are more readily accessible to men, given their greater average purchasing powers. (Paid surrogate motherhood is illegal in Canada.)

PARENTING WITHOUT LIVING TOGETHER

When spouses separate, divorce, or part ways, the important question arises of who will assume responsibilities for the children in the new families that emerge. Custody decisions are often amicable and made by the couple without resort to the courts, but also can be the basis for immensely heated emotions, nasty court battles, and highly charged policy forums. The latter have been seen in Canada with the 1998 Senate committee hearings on divorce and custody. Successful fresh starts following divorce or separation can depend on custody arrangements being satisfactory for all family members involved. Custody involves the children's entire well-being, including day-to-day care, control, and protection, instilling of values, and future opportunities. Custody issues can relate to, and overlap with, issues of access to children by the non-custodial parent as well as issues of child support.

Joint custody (also called co-parenting) is rapidly increasing in both Canada and the United States. Many think (Drakich, 1993; Eichler, 1997, for example), however, that it is unlikely to work successfully except in those cases where the marriage breakdown was amicable. Joint custody requires negotiations in good faith by both partners, and the capacity of each to have the best interests of the children at heart. It has clear benefits in good situations, but can create problems too. For instance, the child(ren) can continue to be socially parented by both parents, which can help their development and their adjustment to the disruption of the separation and divorce. However, if the mother and father have different standards of living (as they often do), the kids may blame one or the other for the relative deprivation the child endures in that household. If Mom and Dad live in different regions, there can be a lot of travel back and forth, creating a sense of rootlessness for the child. And if the child has regular contact with both parents but the parents don't coordinate their parental roles well, the child can play one parent against the other. A major challenge for divorced families is that there is no clear model for non-residential parenting. The relation of parenting to custody issues is, in part, what makes custody such a political hot button, particularly for men's rights groups.

REMARRIAGE OR COHABITATION

Most divorced people remarry (Baker, 1996, Richardson, 2001) or form a new union. As mentioned in the previous chapter, in Canada, excluding Quebec, approximately 70 percent of men and 58 percent of women marry again following divorce (Ambert, 2005b). Remarriage of divorced people is so common now that some see it as normative. Called "conjugal succession" or "recycling the family" (Richardson, 2001: 231), it seems here to stay.

In the United States, more people marry, more divorce, and more remarry than in Canada (Richardson, 2001; Statistics Canada, 2002a). Although still popular, the overall rate of remarriage has declined a little in Canada recently, corresponding with the lower marriage rate. In fact, in 2006, more than half of divorced Canadians did not have intentions to remarry (see Figure 10.1). One explanation for that is that people were choosing cohabitation over remarriage.

When cohabitation is taken into account, the number of fresh starts may be even higher. It is difficult to determine levels of cohabitation, since, unlike marriage, cohabitation has no clear start and finish date. Language is also elusive: these unions may be described as common law, living together, trial marriage, **POSSLQ** or **PSSSLQ**, in French as **"union libre,"** or by slang terms such as "shacking up." Whether these terms connote similar kinds of living arrangements is far from clear. No matter how definitions are spelled out on surveys and census forms, people's own self- and social definitions of what is and is not cohabitation come into play in their responses In 2006, about 30 percent of divorced people were living in common-law unions. Further, data shows that intentions to remarry decrease with age (Beaupre, 2008). The trend is toward a preference for common-law unions after the dissolution, reflecting an overall increase in this form of union.

More divorced men than women remarry (see Figure 10.1(b)), and the likelihood of remarrying following divorce is reduced if one has children, particularly for women. Children limit the time available for searching for a marriage partner and may also deter potential partners. It seems that men may be uncomfortable with taking on the stepfather role or are unwilling to provide financially for someone else's child (Goldscheider, Kaufman, and Sassler, 2009).

But regardless of the form, most people do enter a new intimate partnership. More than anything else, the extent of new unions after divorce underlines people's desire to have committed, emotionally involving relationships. Divorce rates would mark a decline in family only if most divorced people stayed single.

Less is known about remarriage after widowhood, but generally it is less common than remarriage after divorce (Connidis, 2001: 108). In large part, this may simply be that divorce tends to occur earlier in life than widowhood. One Canadian study (Wu, 1995), using event history analysis, has found that men are almost twice as likely to remarry as women, with particularly high rates for high-income men. This is not surprising given that women tend to outlive men. Men who are widowed would have a larger pool of potential mates than women who are widowed. Prospects for remarriage of widows and widowers have dropped recently, particularly for young widowers (Nault and Belanger, 1996: 11). The drop was less for young widows. Nault and Belanger (1996: 13) conclude, "The chances of widowed persons remarrying are consequently much lower, in particular for women who at older ages find themselves facing a marriage market strongly slanted against them."

Second marriages, as we noted in Chapter 9, have a higher risk of divorce than do first marriages. The reasons for this could be many. When couples marry or form a committed relationship, they begin a process of "social construction of marriage," by which they create together their own shared traditions and memories. Over time, they create

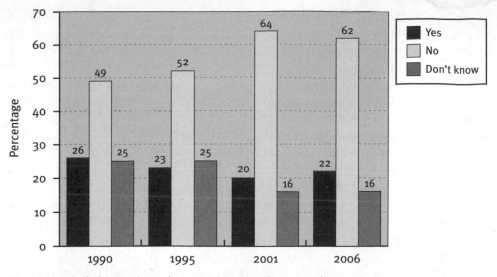

(a) More than half of divorced Canadians stated that they do not intend to remarry.

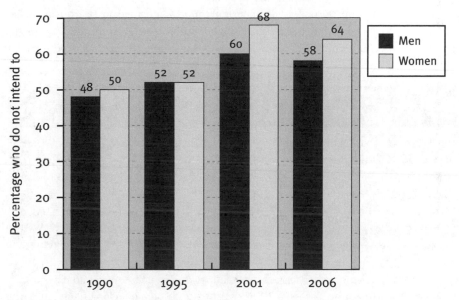

(b) Men are more likely than women to remarry.

Figure 10.1 Changes in intentions to remarry among divorced Canadians

Source: Pascale Beaupre. 2008. I do . . . Take two? Changes in intentions to remarry among divorced Canadians during the past 20 years. *The General Social Survey: Matter of Fact no. 5.* Ottawa: Statistics Canada. Catalogue no. 89-630-X.

together a shared new definition of themselves in relation to the world around them. When a marriage ends, this social construction of self-identity in relation to marriage becomes shaky but it is not forgotten.

In remarrying, new and different social constructions must be developed through negotiation of new social roles and divisions of labour. The shadow of the past relationship always provides implicit comparisons. Since the former relationship is in the past, memories of it can be either overly rosy or overly bleak, with no reality checks. Both types of memories can have implications for the present relationship and make it more challenging to maintain. When children are involved, the increased number of relationships and the need to maintain an ongoing relationship with the ex-spouse can make remarriage even more challenging.

Little is known about the extent to which obligations to extended family members remain after divorce and remarriage. One of the few studies that has looked at this finds that the divorce of either younger or older generations in families tends to magnify the gendered nature of family responsibilities (Connidis, 2001). Contacts with extended family members continue but are maintained more by women than by men. Another study finds that among 190 women and 93 men who divorced and remarried, most feel that they are obligated to help family members in need, if possible (Coleman, Ganong, and Cable, 1997). They perceive their obligations to the younger generation as stronger than those to elders.

The majority of couples succeed in meeting the challenges of a second marriage (Richardson, 2001). What works is, not surprisingly, similar to what works in a successful first marriage: good communication, realistic expectations, honesty, and a shared sense of

Family Transition Trends

- In 2005, almost one-third (31 percent) of children between the ages of 10 to 17 experienced the separation of their parents (Robinson, 2009).

- In 2006, married-couple families made up 69 percent of all families in Canada, while common-law and lone parents each represented 16 percent of all families (Statistics Canada, 2007b).

- Between 2001 and 2006, the number of male-headed lone-parent families increased by 15 percent compared with 6 percent among those headed by women. However, lone mothers still make up 80 percent of lone parents in Canada (Statistics Canada, 2007b).

- In 2006, 44 percent of all young adults aged 20 to 29 lived with their parents, up from 41 percent in 2001 and 32 percent in 1986 (Statistics Canada, 2007b).

- Senior men are much more likely to live with a spouse. This was the most common type of living arrangement for senior men aged 85 and older (38 percent), while it was the least frequent for senior women of the same age (7 percent) (Turcotte and Schellenberg, 2006).

- Cohabiting couples that experience an increase in earnings have greater odds of subsequent marriage. Cohabiting couples who become poor, on the other hand, are associated with a 37 percent decrease in marriage likelihood (Gibson-Davis, 2009).

humour. Meyerstein (1997) suggests that advance preparation is highly useful in a good second marriage. It helps to recognize that a second marriage is not the same as a first, and that the first marriage cannot be repressed and forgotten but should be mined for lessons learned. Beyond these sensible approaches, the couple needs to work to develop the marital relationship and to establish and maintain the new loyalties to each other (Kheshgi-Genovese and Genovese, 1997).

The transitions and innovations of immigrant families is an understudied field in sociology. What is known is that immigrants are more likely to remarry than are non-immigrants, most likely due to a preference for marriage in their culture, as well as other factors such as financial dependency (Berger, 2000). However, King (2007) recently found that children from immigrant families are significantly less close to their stepmothers than are non-immigrant children, although the reasons are unclear. Perhaps immigrant children also hold cultural values regarding sustained marriage and may therefore negatively view remarriage and their father's new spouse.

The Challenges of Blended/Stepfamilies

Blended families are remarried or cohabiting families in which one or both partners brings children into the new relationship (Statistics Canada, 2002a: 6). The terminology of blended families is as challenging as that for cohabiting couples. The terms "blended" or "reconstituted" make new families sound almost strange, in contrast to "regular" families. One suggestion is the term **"binuclear family"** (Church, 1996: 83), which also has drawbacks.

Making second families is not easy or straightforward. Even the language is perplexing: What should a child call step-parents? How should a child refer to the children of the step-parent? There is also the contemporary reality of biological fathers and mothers who are often a continuing part of the child's life. The child may make comparisons between the two "mothers" or "fathers," or play one against the other, or deny that the step-parent is really a parent after all. Step-parents, too, may make comparisons, experience self-doubts about their parenting, or find that the necessary ongoing relationship with the absent parent is challenging.

With the trend toward joint custody—or co-parenting responsibilities—children may be shuffled back and forth between the homes of parents (Ackerman, 1996). This can create a sense of rootlessness and possibly insecurity. It can also make for a mad rush as children fit in living in different homes along with all the many other demands of childhood (school, sports, music lessons, often language or religious classes, and so on). Children can also resent that one stepsibling gets to go off for what may appear as a holiday for a period while he or she cannot. Or the child may resent the presence of a stepsibling in what they consider "their" domain (Richardson, 2001: 233).

A particular challenge of life in blended families is the sharing of children at special family events, such as Christmas, Chanukah, or Ramadan. Children we may think of as ours are away at the other parent's place for some holidays, which creates the need for regular negotiations and close collaboration among the various parents and their other family members. Some parents, too, may deeply feel the absence of their children at important family times.

Family research is helpful in identifying what works successfully in blended families. A popular research strategy is to compare second families with so-called "intact" families. This research design has its problems, in that the two kinds of families may not be comparable. Using intact families as an implicit standard may lead to inappropriate and prejudicial comparisons. Members of blended families may have been through family disruption and, for good or bad, have learned strategies for dealing with problems, while intact families may not have had such lessons. In addition, while first families may follow the examples of their own families of origin, blended or stepfamilies may be breaking new territory, making up the rules as they live through experiences.

Nonetheless, the findings of what works well bear sharing. A significant predictor of success is the degree of focus on the children themselves. Another important factor is the consensus on parenting between the new spouse and the child's parent (Saintjacques, 1995). Preparation for the step-parent role is also important. Accept the reality that both the new spouse and stepchildren had a previous family life that did not, and never can, include the step-parent (Richardson, 2001: 232). Step-parents also need to recognize that they ultimately have limited control over whether the child(ren) accept them. Trying too hard can be a mistake.

Step-parenting can be stressful, and stepmothering is more challenging than step-fathering (Morrison and Thompson-Guppy with Bell, 1986). We all seem to have a vivid image of the wicked stepmother from fairy tales. In addition, women have traditionally borne the major responsibilities for child care and child rearing, meaning more contact with stepchildren and more points at which to encounter tender feelings on both sides.

Two forces draw lone parents to remarry, according to Collins (1991): first, there is the desire to escape from the "cheerless life" of the lone parent; and second, "the widespread view in Western societies that the nuclear family is the proper setting in which to bring up children" (Collins, 1991: 159), or what Church (1996: 87) refers to as filling the "kin vacuum." Recognition in the light of day that lone parenthood has distinct advantages, and that the nuclear family is not all that it is deemed to be for children or for anyone else, gets crowded out by the power of ideological beliefs that "order" must be restored to what is seen as a deviant family form. In deciding whether to make the transition to step-parenthood or blended family, lone mothers must balance the roles of mother and woman, and are influenced by the "herd" notion that marriage or being part of a couple relationship must be good because most people do it.

Research with 105 stepmothers in Canada (Church, 1996) finds that stepmothers define family in more fluid terms than members of other kinds of family. They do not see household and family as directly equivalent. And roles, including gender roles in family, are seen as more flexible. Church concludes that step-parents may not want to try to be parents to their stepchildren immediately but rather wait and see what new family relationships emerge.

From the child's viewpoint, there may be a need to establish new relationships with the step-parent, and perhaps with stepsiblings, but also with both the custodial and non-custodial parent, as all the relationships adjust to the new family arrangement. The development and ultimate success of these relationships depend on conceptions of who is family and who is not. Shared parenting can produce a broader and sometimes more accepting view of what family is, and can be. Where there is a distinct difference in socio-economic status between the homes of the two parents, there can be ambivalence and even guilt, which can cause the child to wonder about families and gender, but can also expand the child's horizons.

Discontinuity of relationships between children in blended families and their grandparents has not been the subject of much research. It is, however, of growing policy and legal importance as grandparents increasingly assert rights to access. Studies show that

Famous Quotes on Marriage

Marriage is the triumph of imagination over intelligence. Second marriage is the triumph of hope over experience.

—Oscar Wilde

A successful marriage requires falling in love many times, always with the same person.

—Mignon McLaughlin

As to marriage or celibacy, let a man take the course he will. He will be sure to repent.

—Socrates

When people get married because they think it's a long-time love affair, they'll be divorced very soon, because all love affairs end in disappointment. But marriage is a recognition of a spiritual identity.

Joseph Campbell

I have yet to hear a man ask for advice on how to combine marriage and a career.

—Gloria Steinhem

Sir, if you were my husband, I would poison your drink.

—Lady Astor to Winston Churchill

Madam, if you were my wife, I would drink it.

—Churchill's reply

I've sometimes thought of marrying, and then I've thought again.

—Noel Coward, 1956

Men marry women with the hope they will never change. Women marry men with the hope they will change. Invariably they are both disappointed.

—Albert Einstein

After marriage, husband and wife become two sides of a coin; they just can't face each other, but still they stay together.

—Hemant Joshi

Bigamy is having one wife too many. Monogamy is the same.

—Oscar Wilde

Love is blind, marriage is the eye-opener.

—Pauline Thomason

By all means, marry. If you get a good wife, you'll become happy; if you get a bad one, you'll become a philosopher.

—Socrates

I was married by a judge. I should have asked for a jury.

—Groucho Marx

Source: www.etni.org.il/quotes/marriage.htm.

grandparents (mostly paternal grandparents) are most at risk of losing contact with their grandchildren (Kruk, 1995; Ahrons and Tanner, 2003). Low rates of contact occur when the grandparent is related to the children's non-resident parent, or when the children live with a step-parent (Lussier, Deater-Deckard, Dunn, and Davies, 2002). The primary mediators in ongoing grandparent/grandchild relationships are the daughters-in-law. Disrupted contact is found to have adverse consequences for the grandparents. The consequences for grandchildren are less known. Yet a continuous relationship with grandparents can be of benefit, particularly when the grandparents themselves have a stable relationship. They can set positive examples and serve as a source of stability (Milan and Hamm, 2003).

WIDOWHOOD

Widowhood is an expectable life event. Given the difference between men's and women's life expectancies, a woman who marries or establishes a lasting relationship can realistically anticipate that she will be left a widow. The good news, however, is that widowhood is occurring later than it used to (Connidis, 2001: 93; Moore and Rosenberg, 1997: 31). In Canada, almost 80 percent of women aged 85 and older are widowed, while even at age 70 to 74, 40 percent are widowed. In contrast, 39.5 percent of men aged 85 and older are married, compared to only 7.2 percent of women the same age.

Older women, mainly widows, are much more likely than men to change their living arrangements late in life. Usually, these changes are related to health status, but they also relate to family. A man with health problems more often has a built-in caregiver at home, his wife, while a woman with health problems, even at the same age, is less likely to have that benefit. Hence, she is more likely to move in with relatives or into an institution.

Myths abound about widows. Mainly they are seen as sad and depressed. Depression does strike some, and at times it is debilitating. But it is not the only reality for widows. Eighteen months or so after the spouse's death, most widows are ready to start life over for themselves (Gee and Kimball, 1987: 90). Most often this means reaching out to friends, siblings, adult children, and others such as clergy or even lawyers. Some develop active new hobbies or interests. Contact with their peers seems to provide the most satisfaction for widows. Some even note that this is the first time that they have felt independent and that they enjoy it (Connidis, 2001: 96).

The death of a long-term partner for gay and lesbian couples poses different problems. The sense of loss may be similar, but the lack of institutionalized acceptance of gay and lesbian relationships may make for less strong support (Connidis, 2001: 96). On top of this challenge is the prevalence of AIDS among gay men, the stigma involved, and the reality that more bereaved partners will be left behind. There can also be losses of others in the gay network, intensifying the sense of loss and grief.

FAMILY TRANSITIONS IN MID- AND LATER LIFE

Most research on family transitions focuses on people younger than age 50. But with increasing life expectancy and divorce likelihood, the proportions of those older than age 65 who are divorced has risen. In 2001, approximately 6 percent of both men and women aged 65 and older in Canada were divorced, compared with 1 percent for both in 1971 (Statistics Canada, 2002j). People older than 50 remarry with increasing frequency and establish new cohabiting families as well. In Canada, a relatively small percentage of older people remarry or enter their senior years remarried. However, among those divorced or widowed at younger ages, a majority of men and a substantial minority of women eventually remarry (Connidis, 2001: 111).

Some older couples who are alone after widowhood or divorce may choose to cohabit but keep separate households in order to maintain continuity in their living arrangements and to avoid fuss by their offspring about loyalties and inheritance (Borell and Karlsson, 2002). An unusual study in France (Caradec, 1997: 65) of conjugal arrangements among those age 60 and older finds "a great diversity of conjugal lifestyles: some couples live together in marriage, some outside marriage (showing that cohabitation is not reserved for the young in age), and others have adopted more novel forms of union, intermittent or alternating cohabitation." Borell and Karlsson (2002) find similar innovative living arrangements among older people in Sweden.

Another family transition found in later life may be when grandparents take on a custodial or a near-parental role of their grandchildren. This transition can be extremely stressful for both grandparents and grandchildren. Most grandparents become caregivers of their grandchildren during a divorce, teen pregnancy, drug abuse, health concerns, or incarceration of parents. Grandparents may resent the fact that in their later years they must once again deal with parenting young children, but also may have the added stress of dealing with the problems of their own children as well (Lumpkin, 2008: 358). Lumpkin found that grandparents who serve as primary or near-custodial parents experienced more stress, more financial problems, poor physical health, limitations on activities, and depression (Lumpkin, 2008: 359). More research is needed as custodial and near-custodial grandparents become part of a bigger trend for dual-income families and grandparents who are healthier, more independent, and living longer.

Living apart together (LAT) is not only for high-powered couples but also for those who wish companionship without the traditional arrangement of sharing a home full-time. When LAT relationships were discussed in a large family sociology class by one of your authors (McDaniel) in fall 2002, several students mentioned that one of their parents had arrangements with a partner similar to those found in France and Sweden by researchers. And the students thought that these were happy and clever ways to be a couple. LATs may catch on as the university-age generation ages.

This may suggest two things: first, as Caradec (1997: 65) argues, an **intergenerational contagion** whereby non-marital unions have become diffused from young to old; and second, the need for different people—in this case, people at different stages in the life course—to customize relationships to fit their particular needs. Available statistical data routinely collected by censuses, vital statistics, or social surveys may not truly capture the immense diversity possible in family living arrangements.

GAY/LESBIAN FAMILIES

There have always been gay fathers and lesbian mothers; in the past, those who have become parents in a heterosexual marriage or relationship usually then come out as gay or lesbian. What is newer is gay and lesbian *families*, increasingly accepted by society (Mofina, 2003), with policy entitlements and protections under family law. Gay and lesbian couples more often now decide to have children together and raise them as a family unit. Gay and lesbian couples that form after the end of a heterosexual relationship or marriage are also living as a family with the children of one or both partners. At present in Canada, a majority of gay/lesbian families with children had these children with a heterosexual ex-spouse (Ambert, 2005c). However, more gay/lesbian couples are deciding to have children through adoption or donor insemination. Lesbian couples deciding to give birth to a child must negotiate which one will become pregnant and then agree on the process. This necessitates closeness in talking openly about their feelings and innermost desires and longings. Here, we will discuss gay and lesbian parents raising children in families, however they formed, as well as gay and lesbian couples in committed relationships.

Diversity among gay and lesbian families exists as well. Whether they are publicly open about their relationship is a significant step.

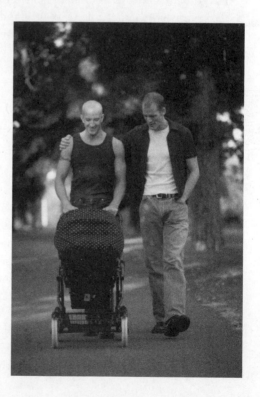

The significance of these new kinds of families cannot be underestimated. They are transforming the ways families are measured, as witnessed by the change in definition of family for the 2001 Census of Canada to include same-sex common-law unions (Statistics Canada, 2002c). And family laws and policies of Canada, as well as workplace policies, have largely been widened to include same-sex families.

Same-sex families have transformed thinking about families theoretically. An entirely new way to theorize close relations, *queer theory*, has grown out of this line of inquiry. Identities, relationships, even politics are seen as less fixed and more social (Lehr, 1999). Queer theory takes theoretical thinking in sociology beyond notions of roles and fixed identities in families and society. It argues that we *perform* gender, like a concert by Michael Jackson or Madonna, on a social stage, and in doing so, we change ourselves and society (Walters, 1999: 250). This gives both power and insight to people and to family theorists and researchers. In this way, same-sex families are really an engine of both social and sociological change, and a way to see how the two are linked.

Diversity exists among gay and lesbian families, as among all families. With respect to gay and lesbian families, there are several added dimensions. One is whether they are "out" as a family, or, in other words, open about their relationship with all they know and meet. Miller (2003: 104), in describing his own gay family, says:

> The family I live in as a father is also the family I live out in as a gay man. I call it an "out family" for three reasons: its openness to homosexual membership; its opposition to heterosexist conformity (the prejudicial assumption of heterosexuality as normal and proper); and its overtness within the contemporary lesbian and gay movement. . . . Mine is a family that opens out, steps out, and stands out. It opens out to people traditionally excluded from the charmed circle of Home; it steps out beyond the police and policed borders of the Normal; and it stands out as a clear new possibility on the horizon of what used to be called . . . the Just Society (Miller, 2003: 104).

Not all gay and lesbian families are "out" in this or any other sense. Some, particularly older couples, still remain cloaked in secrecy, out of fear for the children or themselves (Connidis, 2001).

Lesbian families with children have been seen as a contradiction: women having children without heterosexual relations. Or they are seen as threats: women without the need for men. Lesbian mothers became more visible in the 1970s and 1980s, according to Epstein (1996: 109), because they chose to claim their identities as both mothers and lesbians. She notes, with sadness, that the claiming often occurred in courtrooms in custody hearings, where lesbians were typically defined as unfit mothers. Recall the example of "Ms. T," discussed in Chapter 6, who was denied foster children despite years of successful foster parenting. The risk of losing custody of their children still gives lesbian mothers a strong motivation to conceal their orientation.

Same-gender families are becoming more of a cultural norm, and from a rural perspective, they tend to be more normative than within an urban context. Bell's paper discusses the symbolism of "farm boys" and "wild men" and homosexual relationships in an agricultural setting (2000). He mentions that the focus has been on the urban context as the prime site for sexual identity exploration and community formation; however, the rural context has also been eroticized in much media and film (Bell, 2000). The author suggests that the countryside seems to be a way to become a man, and that the natural environment causes homosexuality to take on a slant closer to nature rather than "against" it (Bell, 2000: 559).

Gay and lesbian families offer innovative models of family in several fundamental ways, according to family research. First, both gay and lesbian families may provide important developmental learning for children in the possibilities of resisting confining gender-role expectations (Epstein, 1996: 111).

Second, lesbians can teach daughters, in particular, how not to compete with other women but to bond with them to work together. Third, both gay men and lesbians force a questioning of the assumptions and values of heterosexist nuclear families. Fourth, gay families raise vital questions about the presumptions we make about masculinity in families and in society. And fifth, gay and lesbian families are an effective force of change in family policies.

The challenges involve rethinking what families are, what spouses are and do, and what parenting is. These are profoundly important sociological endeavours at reconceptualizing families. It was, in large part, this sort of rethinking that has led, in recent years, away from defining family by form and instead defining families broadly on the basis of processes: what families *do* rather than what they *are*.

Gay and lesbian families, not being structured hierarchically by gender, do not have the same divisions of labour by gender that many heterosexual families have. They are chosen families, characterized by fluid boundaries, new roles, and little institutionalized symbolism. They can be creative in making families and in devising new ways to be familial. Although this may be seen as a positive aspect of same-sex relationships, the absence of gender roles can make for complications when deciding to raise a family. A study on lesbian families by Fiona Nelson (1996) found that one of the problems associated with same-sex families was societies reluctant to see this as a real family, which in turn made it difficult for the lesbian parents to feel like a true family (Nelson, 1996, in Fox: 442). The women in Nelson's study found that many places did not offer family admission rates or discounts to lesbian families (Nelson, 1996, in Fox: 453). Furthermore, while the gay community may be a strong network of support for couples, the study found that there was a frequent lack of understanding within the lesbian community because of the relatively recent practice of lesbian couples deciding to start a family, and so the couples often felt that their friends did not understand what it meant to have a child and how this changed life (Nelson, 1996, in Fox: 452).

Furthermore, Epstein (1996) refers to parenting roles in lesbian couples being based on personality attributes rather than gender, so one parent is the funny one, or the hardliner, or the one pushing academics. One of Epstein's (1996: 119) respondents puts it well: "We're not modelling male–female power dynamics, we're modelling women doing everything that needs to be done in order to maintain life."

Yet, there are tensions in lesbian and gay families, emanating in part from the lingering lack of acceptance and the absence of blueprints on how to be.

Relationships in which gender forms no part of the household or the domestic division of labour may be described as **post-gender families**. This kind of relationship raises important questions about gender and about the social concept of "coupledom." Oerton (1997) explores these issues among lesbian couples in an article she evocatively entitles "Queer Housewives?" Her conclusion is that gendering processes may so intertwine with all domestic labour and all that we are in families that inventing family without these processes is challenging, but not impossible. She argues that creative new solutions to family processes, particularly divisions of labour, might be found in closer study of lesbian and gay couples. Risman (1998) argues that some of these new solutions can be found among heterosexual couples as well.

Risman and Johnson-Sumerford (1998) examine heterosexual "post-gender" marriages in which the partners share equally in paid and unpaid family work without regard for gender. They find that there are four pathways to such relationships: a dual-career household, a dual-nurturer relationship, a post-traditional relationship, and external forces that open relationships to egalitarianism. Egalitarianism is likely to affect both the power balance and the emotional quality of the relationship, Risman and Johnson-Sumerford suggest, for the good.

Major Findings about Family Transition

- Second union formation occurs faster following the disruption of a first union among cohabiters than among the divorced (Wu and Schimmele, 2005a).

- Non-marital child-bearing is adversely associated with the ability to marry economically attractive men and maintain long-term marital unions (Graefe and Lichter, 2008).

- Young adults are more likely to leave home at an earlier age (younger than 21 years) if they grow up in a non-traditional family, have more than two siblings, have a Canadian-born mother, did not attend religious services during adolescence, live in a region outside Quebec and grow up in a smaller town (population less than 5000) (Beaupre, Turcotte, and Milan, 2006a).

- Preschool children have a stabilizing effect on parental partnership, whether married or cohabiting, but the effect is weak for older children. Although pregnancy precipitates marriage among cohabiters, the odds of marriage decline to pre-pregnancy levels following the birth (Steele, Kallis, Goldstein, and Joshi, 2005).

- Older couples fare better when they are both retired. Married seniors, where both spouses are working or are looking for work, report the lowest relationship quality (Chalmers and Milan, 2005).

- In 2006, there were just over 45 000 same-sex couples in Canada, up 33 percent from 2001. Of those, 17 percent were married couples (Statistics Canada, 2007b).

Gay and lesbian parents often create a network of fictive kin or "chosen" family (friends, former partners, and willing relatives) for social and emotional support as well as to offer their children suitable adult role models of the other sex. This support system may be gay or lesbian or may not (Oswald, 2002). Gay and lesbian parents also have access to mainstream community organizations that are supportive of same-sex families.

It seems that from an urban standpoint, many organizations and support groups exist for gay and lesbian residents. However, what about those living in more geographically isolated areas? McCarthy touches upon rural lesbianism in her paper, discussing the challenges lesbians face in a non-urban environment due to a lack of reference groups and social arenas for mutual discussion and/or sharing of experiences (2000). This hinders their social group identity, which in turn may cascade into psychological problems. Unfortunately, research done on rural life usually omits gay and lesbian residents, and, in McCarthy's study, data illustrates that rural lesbians initially felt isolated and uncertain of social identity development (2000). Women require an outlet to showcase their iden-tity, network with others, and alleviate the tension present within the rural community, where they are alleviating the tension through friends and other sources (McCarthy, 2000).

While there is insufficient research, it can be presumed that gay and lesbian families follow daily routines much like those of heterosexual families (Nelson, 1996). All children need love and supervision. They all need to be sheltered, fed, taken to school, and so on. As well, the family life cycle is similar for both same-sex and opposite-sex-parent families: children arrive, grow up, go through stages, and parenting continues accordingly (Ambert, 2005c).

TRANSITIONS OUT OF PARENTING: EMPTY NESTS

Even without marital dissolution, transitions in family occur. Many families experience the empty nest, and increasing numbers of others may wish to. An empty nest occurs when all the children grow up and move away.

When the children do decide to leave the parental home, it is usually a significant event for their parents as well. For many parents, the move is accompanied by feelings of relief, pride in having fulfilled their parental role, and joy at seeing their children successfully transitioning toward greater independence. For the young adults, "the first departure is a symbolic marker as they make the transition from youth to adulthood" (Beaupre et al., 2006a).

In the past, getting a secure job and getting married to start a family were the two main reasons why people born between 1932 and 1946 left their parental home. Today, on the other hand, most young adults move out voluntarily to pursue educational or employment opportunities or simply in order to gain independence from their parents (Beaupre et al., 2006a). However, research consistently shows that children who leave home for these reasons are "more likely to boomerang than those who leave to marry and set up their own conjugal household" (Beaupre et al., 2006a:10).

Young adults are more likely to leave the parental home when they live in stepfamilies than when they live in either lone-parent or two-parent biological families (Beaupre et al., 2006a). This raises the important question of long-term implications for social inequalities (Mitchell, 1994). If some young adults increase their disadvantage by leaving the family home earlier than others, then the ultimate outcome could be widening social inequalities. If combined with early pregnancies, early family starts, or leaving school to support oneself, the long-term consequences are magnified. This is especially true for young people who find themselves in unstable family situations or who have to cope with difficult relationships in the family. Interestingly, women who live with a stepfamily have a much higher probability (57 percent risk) of leaving home before the age of 18 as compared with men (30 percent risk) (Mitchell, 1994: 11).

Retired seniors are another large and rapidly growing group in Canadian society. According to a Statistics Canada report entitled *A Portrait of Seniors in Canada*, the number of seniors living in Canada is predicted to rise from 4.2 million to 9.8 million between 2005 and 2036 (Turcotte and Schellenberg, 2006). Figure 10.2 provides a breakdown of living arrangements of seniors by sex and age group in 2001.

The overwhelming majority of seniors in Canada live either alone or with a spouse. So, empty nests are a reality for most Canadians. A minority of older adults feel that there is no one, or only one person, on whom they could rely for help (Moore and Rosenberg, with McGuinness, 1997: 47). Most, however, rely on a number of friends and family, both close and far. In fact, apart from spouses, close friends are often the main source of emotional support for older individuals (Turcotte and Schellenberg, 2006). Family networks are more geographically dispersed than are friends, so in essence family and friends may be reversed as older adults build family-like relationships with networks of friends.

SANDWICHED FAMILIES AND CLUTTERED NESTS

Recently, there has been a shift in living arrangements and family lives that in some ways constitutes a new kind of family. It takes two forms. One is the return to the family home of adult children, as well as the presence of adult children who have never left. This has become a very prevalent living arrangement. In fact, some researchers argue that "[i]t is now commonly understood that midlife parenthood often comprises prolonged periods of coresidence with grown adults" (Mitchell, 1998: 2). The other is older parents living with middle-aged children (Rosenthal, Martin-Matthews, and Matthews, 1996).

People in midlife who live with or have responsibilities for both the young and the old are sometimes called the "sandwich generation." It is rare for three or more generations to share living quarters, but it is far from rare for them to be dependent on each other in a variety of ways, even when they maintain separate households. Some view refilled nests as a crisis for middle-aged people struggling to work, care for older parents, and look after themselves, their homes, and their communities.

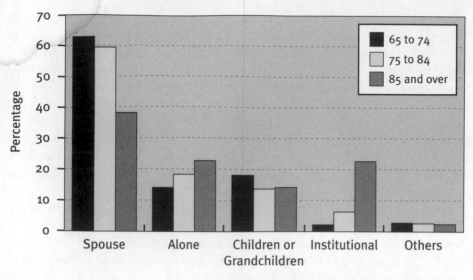

(a) Senior men by age group: The majority of 65- to 84-year-old men live either with a spouse or alone, while those 85 years and older live mostly alone or in an institution.

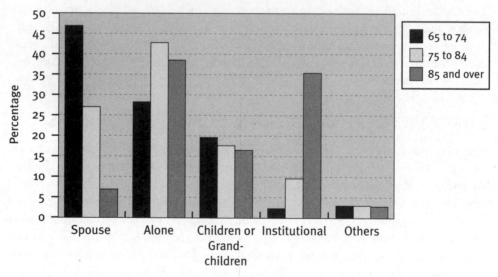

(b) Senior women by age group: The majority of 65- to 74-year-old women live either with a spouse or alone. Women are more likely than men to live alone or in an institution at a younger age.

Figure 10.2 Living arrangements of seniors, 2001

Source: Data from Martin Turcotte and Grant Schellenberg. 2006. *A Portrait of Seniors in Canada.* Ottawa: Statistics Canada. Catalogue no. 89-519-XIE: p. 191.

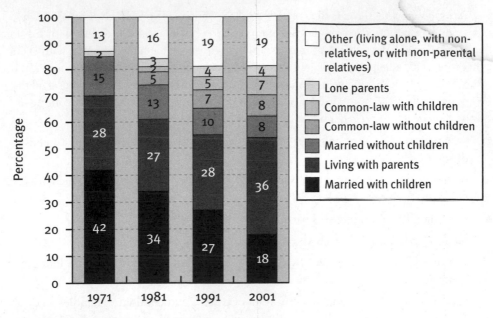

Note: Common-law unions were not identified in the 1971 Census.

Figure 10.3 Living arrangements of young adults aged 18 to 34 have changed between 1971 and 2001

Source: Warren Clark. 2007. Delayed transitions of young adults. *Canadian Social Trends.* Ottawa: Statistics Canada. Catalogue no. 11-008. Retrieved June 9, 2009, from www.statcan.gc.ca/pub/11-008-x/2007004/10311-eng.htm.

Children are still growing up, but they are moving away with less and less frequency, as can be seen in Figure 10.3. In fact, data from the 2006 Census shows that 60.3 percent of young adults aged 20 to 24 were living with parents, up from 49.3 percent in 1986 (Statistics Canada, 2007b: 40). Even older young adults, between the ages of 25 and 29, are increasingly staying home; in 2006, just over a quarter (26 percent) of them lived with parents, a substantial increase from 15.6 percent in 1986. This, suggests Statistics Canada, is one reason for the overall decline in the proportion of households headed by people younger than age 30 in Canada.

According to Beaupre et al. (2006a: 9), most of the increase took place in "the early 1980s and early 1990s, years during which Canada endured two of the most severe labour recessions since the 1930s." Together with the fact that today's young people are more highly educated and attend school for more years than their parents did (Clark, 2007), it makes sense financially to remain at home. As Clark points out, "the transitions of today's young adults are both delayed and elongated: delayed, because young adults take more time to complete their first major transition (leaving school), thus postponing all subsequent transitions; and elongated, because each subsequent transition takes longer to complete and stretches the process from their late teens to their early 30s" (2007: 14).

Another growing trend is the emergence of the "**boomerang kid**," a young adult who, after living away from the parental home for a period of time, returns to live with his or her parents. In the past, this was a rare event, but it has become more common with each generation. For example, only 1 in 10 early baby boomers born between 1947 and 1951 returned home within five years of first leaving, but 3 in 10 **Generation X** young adults (born between 1972 and 1976) do so today (Beaupre et al., 2006b). According to Statistics Canada, factors that explain this trend include:

- growing acceptance of common-law relationships, which are more likely to end in dissolution than marriage

- higher numbers of young adults pursuing post-secondary education, which leaves graduates with heavy student debts

- financial difficulties incurred with losing jobs

- reduced social stigma attached to living with parents

- wanting a higher standard of living that is not financially feasible when living on your own

- the emergence of new and different roles of parents and children in families, and

- needing a parent's emotional support during the stressful transition to adulthood and independence (Beaupre et al., 2006b: 28)

The common perception seems to be that young people are layabouts sponging off parents. Research by Mitchell (1998) shows that this is an incorrect presumption. Generations living together in families provide mutual support and generally get along well. Middle generations receive valued companionship and the satisfaction of facilitating their child's transition into adulthood.

For their part, adult children receive a number of valuable services, such as free or low-cost housing, food, perhaps access to a car. In other research (Mitchell and Gee, 1996a), even marital satisfaction is unaffected by the presence at home of adult children, provided the kids do not leave and return home multiple times.

In terms of social policy, it seems that the family home is becoming a kind of safety net for youth who cannot establish themselves in independent residences (Mitchell and Gee, 1996b). Some researchers call this transition stage in young adulthood as "semi-autonomous living," where the home is a refuge from financial and emotional difficulties (Beaupre et al., 2006b). Families that cannot afford, in economic or social terms, to take adult children into their homes may be forced to cut the net for their children. In times of sharp reductions in social transfers, this may force the young people to seek low-wage employment rather than education or training in order to support themselves. "Not being able to return to the security and comforts of home could have a devastating effect on the lives of young adults who are not psychologically prepared to be launched as adults" (Mitchell and Gee, 1996b: 68).

With respect to older relatives living with those in midlife, the issues are remarkably similar. In 2002, approximately 27 percent of Canadians in midlife are in the sandwich

Six Myths about the Sandwich Generation

People in sandwich generation situations are extremely stressed due to the added duties, and finding balance is challenging.

- According to the 2002 Statistics Canada General Social Survey, a large proportion of people (82 percent) who worked at the same time as providing care for their child(ren) and their parents were generally satisfied with the balance they had achieved (Williams, 2005).

Most children who have experienced a disruption in their family structure are unhappy.

- It is true that a disruption can cause unhappiness; however, the majority of children (72 percent) who experience family disruption remain happy or find ways of being happy. Yet, 92 percent of children who had lived with both of their parents until age 15 felt that they had a very happy childhood (Williams, 2001).

It is mainly women who provide care both to young and old.

- Though more women (32 percent) provide care to both their parents and their children, the portion of men who are "sandwiched" is not that far behind (25 percent) (Williams, 2005).

When grandparents live with the family, financial stress on the family increases.

- Grandparents are sometimes financial contributors. In multigenerational households where the middle generation is a couple, 16 percent of the grandparents were primary financial providers. And when the middle generation was a lone parent, 50 percent of grandparents were financial supporters (Milan and Hamm, 2003).

Living Apart Together (LAT) occurs mostly among the young.

- A significant portion (44 percent) of LAT occurs among people age 30 and older: 19 percent are in their 30s, 14 percent in their 40s, and 11 percent are aged 50 and older (Milan and Peters, 2003).

Adult children with children of their own increase contact with their parents after a marital disruption because they need support.

- Interestingly, marital status has no significant impact on the frequency of contact of adult children with their parents (Townsend-Batten, 2002).

generation (Williams, 2005). This proportion is likely to grow for a number of reasons. First, population aging will mean more older family members. It is projected that by 2026, one in five Canadians will be 65 years or older. Second, the pattern of low fertility rates means there will be fewer adults available to take care of seniors in the future (Williams, 2005). And lastly, today's adults are delaying forming unions and parenthood. All three trends together mean more situations where older family members require care while young children are still at home.

Finally, reductions in Canadian health-care services mean those who are hospitalized return home "quicker and sicker." This often means, for seniors, temporary or permanent reliance on their adult children. Nevertheless, older parents living in the home are not always a burden on the family, rather, they can be an asset, even financially (see "Six Myths about the Sandwich Generation").

NEW KINDS OF CLOSE RELATIONS

In addition to the types of relationships already discussed, other forms of family are emerging. The definition of a family is becoming more fluid and dependent on circumstances. For example, a crisis, such as a life-threatening illness, can challenge one's idea of family and precipitate new kinds of close relations. When people living with HIV/AIDS were asked who or what they considered to be family, the results were surprising (Wong-Wylie and Doherty-Poirier, 1997).

For this group, family as process was paramount. To be considered family, an individual must have a *reciprocal relationship* with the respondent, and must be *accepting, supportive*, a source of *health and wellness resources*, and an *inspirational influence*. What kinds of people met these criteria for the respondents? They listed seven categories of people as comprising their created families (not every respondent had family from each category): families of origin, health-care professionals, friends, other people with HIV/AIDS, deceased friends, family caregivers, and valued material objects.

Some specific examples fill in the human faces and the diversity of created family. One man saw his family as large and diverse. His closest family consisted of his partner (male), his daughter and his partner's daughter, and his 10 good friends, both male and female (two of whom were deceased). Beyond that, family to him was members of the HIV/AIDS society, his parents and their siblings and friends, numbering 13 in all, and then his grandparents on both sides, three of whom were also deceased. Another respondent saw her in-laws as being as important to her as her husband and father. Her many friends, both gay and straight (four of whom also had HIV/AIDS), were also part of her created family.

Another included his physician in his self-defined family in an equal place with his wife and son. In his case, all but one of the friends included in his family definition also had HIV/AIDS. Significantly, he specifically excluded some members of his blood family, such as his mother, from his family definition. Yet another defined his family as consisting of computers, bridge, his ex-partner, and the "gay world" writ large, only incidentally noting his mother, brother, and sister.

These findings emphasize the limitations of assuming we know what family is. We all possess the power to define family for ourselves. Most importantly, this study shows that family, however we define it, is becoming more rather than less important. This is a point we have made throughout this book in a variety of ways, and with numerous examples.

It need not take the crisis of HIV/AIDS for us to create new kinds of families. Many of us create families for ourselves—in a new land, in situations where we have lost our families through war or time, when we have irresolvable disputes with families, or when our memories of our families of origin are too horrid to forgive. In these cases, and endless others, we make families of our friends, neighbours, communities, those with whom we share something important, and even our pets, plants, work, computers, and sporting equipment.

CONCLUDING REMARKS

We have explored multiple and varied transitions and innovations in family in this chapter. With family being placed increasingly into the realm of ideology and politics, it sometimes seems as if different approaches to family are in competition for our hearts. The transitions and new kinds of close relations discussed here are not the full list of possible ways that family life changes and that we change family for ourselves. Nor are they arranged like a smorgasbord for us to choose what we like best. For most of us, the kinds of families we live in choose us. Sometimes, as the old phrase has it, life happens. We do not necessarily make informed and deliberate choices about the ends of marriages or relationships. Sometimes the choice is not ours, but our partner's or spouse's. Sometimes we flee from violence or an intolerable situation to something unknown but safer.

Within our various kinds of families, however, we do make choices. We engage in and develop processes that define us as families. We try to do our best within the opportunities and constraints society offers. It is these choices, not the shape our families take, that matter most to our happiness and the happiness of our children.

In the contest over which kind of family is preferable, we can lose track of the reality that all of us in families are sharing and caring for each other. The similarities in daily family living far outweigh the differences.

CHAPTER SUMMARY

This chapter discusses transitions to different family situations of many sorts: singlehood, one-parent families, second relationships or remarriage, stepfamilies, empty nests, and the invention of new kinds of families. Some transitions can bring new ways to behave and to live in close relations, or fresh starts. Others could better be called stale starts, since they merely lead to a repetition of old patterns and of old relational problems.

Family transitions and new families are not new phenomena in human society. With large-scale immigration and high death rates in the past in North America, many single-parent families and orphans existed.

The perils of some transitions in family, such as to single parenthood, include high risks of poverty for single mothers and their children after separation and divorce. Similar risks exist

for women who choose to have children on their own without partners, a phenomenon growing in popularity. Adoption of children from other countries can have perils as well: the children face the cultural challenges of adapting to the new family's customs and the lingering effects of trauma experienced in early childhood.

Becoming a parent without a partner as a deliberate choice is a new kind of family, one which makes for multiple kinds of parenthood and families. Parenting arrangements on separation and divorce also create new kinds of parents, most notably in shared parenting situations in which a non-residential parent is involved in active parenting. The good news here is that families can extend beyond the walls of a household.

Remarriage is more common for men than for women; for both, the risks of divorce are higher with a second marriage. Social pressures toward remarriage are sometimes more ideological than material; people want to be like other couples in society and to avoid stigma. Cohabitation after divorce is growing as the family of choice in Canada, particularly in Quebec.

Blended families are increasing in Canada and pose challenges to the ways we think of families. As the number of relationships both within and outside the household multiply, new vocabularies must be invented.

We learn that not all family transitions are choices. Some people flee from abuse, or from culturally sanctioned violence into new lives, in the process creating new families.

Living solo is a growing option for many people who maintain close family ties but not in their own households. Counter to this is the sandwich family, which involves both youth and older parents living together with the middle generation, or cluttered nests, a variant on this theme where youth either never leave the family home or return home to live.

With aging, families change and family transitions are made. Changing times have enabled post-gender families to develop and some same-sex families to live more openly.

Key Terms

artificial insemination A process of introducing semen into a woman's body without sexual intercourse; can be a medical process but may not be.

binuclear family A term used to describe a blended family, or a family where the spouses each bring children and non-residential parents into a new family.

blended family Typically describing a family comprising two previously married spouses, with children, who marry each other and bring their children together in a new family.

boomerang kid A young adult that returns to the parental home after a period of living independently.

generation X According to Statistics Canada, this is the cohort born between 1967 and 1976.

in vitro fertilization Commonly known as test-tube fertilization; conception that occurs by bringing together ova and sperm in medical procedures.

intergenerational contagion A process by which trends that begin in one generation may be adopted by other generations. An example is cohabitation, which was mostly a youthful phenomenon but has now been adopted by people of all generations.

latchkey children Children who are regularly left for some part of the day without adult supervision.

POSSLQ Person of the opposite sex sharing living quarters.

post-gender families Families in which the division of labour is not based on gender.

PSSSLQ Person of the same sex sharing living quarters.

SNAF Standard North American family—mother, father, two kids, and usually a dog or a cat.

union libre Widely used term for common-law union in Quebec.

Critical Thinking Questions

1. Discuss how immigration can produce new ways to be family. In your opinion, is change only limited to immigrant groups?

2. Not only are lone mothers the most economically disadvantaged, but their poverty is also the most resistant to remedy. Create a cause-and-effect flowchart to illustrate the factors involved in the perpetuation of poverty among single mothers.

3. In this chapter, three social policy approaches to lone-parent families were discussed: the private family model, the family-oriented

model, and the state-based model. Discuss which approach(es) Canadian policy makers should adopt in light of the recent trends and changes in family life.

4. Choose a family transition mentioned in the chapter. Discuss the broader societal factors and the family characteristics that influence the timing and ease of the transition.

5. Discuss how demographic changes in Canada can affect family life and transitions.

6. What role does technology play in accommo-dating or hindering the family transitions and innovations discussed in this chapter?

7. In this chapter we learned that young adults are more likely than in the past to remain in the parental home longer and to "boomerang" back. Thinking about the issues they involve, what kinds of policies can the government introduce to enable young adults to successfully transition into adulthood and independence?

8. Provide a working definition of "family" that would encompass the various transitions and innovations that were discussed in this chapter.

Weblinks

The Future of Children
www.futureofchildren.org
This collaborative research undertaking by Princeton University and the Brookings Institution seeks to promote effective policies and programs for children. This site is a great resource for research publications that focus on policy changes.

Families in Transition (FIS)
www.fsatoronto.com/programs/families.html
This Family Service Toronto branch provides specialized services for separating, divorcing, and remarrying families that focus on supporting children.

Empty Nest Moms
http://emptynestmoms.com
An on-line support group for single mothers facing the challenges associated with their children moving out or heading to college or university.

Lesbian & Gay Parenting
www.apa.org/pi/parent.html
This on-line publication by the American Psychological Association contains highlights of research findings on lesbian mothers, gay fathers, and their children, an annotated bibliography, and additional resources.

Transition Magazine
www.vifamily.ca/library/transition/transition.html
An on-line publication from the Vanier Institute of the Family in Canada that provides up-to-date information on the trends in family life and policy affecting Canadians.

TroubledWith
www.troubledwith.com
TroubledWith.com is a collection of articles, resources, and referrals organized by topic around family issues and concerns.

National Stepfamily Resource Center
www.stepfamilies.info
This site provides information, resources, and support for stepfamily members. Topics include counselling, finances, co-parenting, co-grandparenting, and more.

Chapter 11
A Glimpse into the Future
Where Do Families Go from Here?

Chapter Outline

In this chapter, we wonder what the future will bring. Methodically studying and predicting the future has important practical value, as thinking about the future in useful ways can help avoid the mistakes people made in the past. This is not to say that we can hope to predict the future perfectly. A record of many inaccurate past predictions shows that we cannot do so. Besides, no matter how good our predictions may be, we could never prepare completely. However, where social organization is concerned, preparing is always better than being taken by surprise.

Our close relations—especially our family relations—are intricate, varied, and always changing. We will end this book by addressing the likely changes to family life in the future, and the forces—especially technological forces—behind those changes.

Some family problems of the present will likely persist and new problems will emerge. A future family without problems is unthinkable, if only because we humans continue to create new problems as we go along. Like much else in the past hundred years, the problems of the future will probably involve science and technology, travel and communication, war and intergroup conflict. Since we will likely continue to live in a global society, humanity's problems will be progressively global in scope. Though human health is continually improving, concerns about health will continue to grow. Medical technology will continue to improve, but new illnesses will also develop.

Most important, since we rely on information and technology more and more, our problems will be increasingly concerned with information flow, the abuse of technology, and the malfunctioning of technology. Our ability to solve family problems—and, in this way, to improve society—will need better social science.

FAMILY LIFE IN THE TWENTY-FIRST CENTURY

The pace of technological change in the last decade has been daunting to even the most technologically aware people. Many social theorists think technological changes bring about social changes (for example, Castells, 1996). In their theories, the presumed impacts of technological changes and innovations on societies, social institutions, and individuals result in various ethnic, cultural, and social concerns. People and societies are always having to react to, adjust to, or repair a change caused by technology. This is only partly true. While technology does influence culture, it alone does not drive the process of social change; a society's search for change does. Social change is the co-production of economic and political imperatives, social values, and technical and social inventions.

One of the most fundamental understandings to emerge from the new sociology of technology is that technology is more than hard wires and virtual buttons. Technologies have not transformed us or our families' communications. Instead, we use the technologies because social life in families has changed so much that, for many, direct communication is not as possible as it once was. The technological boom itself is created more by the demands of a changing society than by any inherent aspect of the technologies themselves (Brown and Lauder, 2001; McDaniel, 2000).

Yet this technological explosion is changing families in multifaceted ways. Reproductive technologies that allow clinically infertile people to become parents raise many questions. Equally challenging are questions posed by medical technology that extends lives and close relations for longer than ever before.

Other concerns arise from the cultural effects of technology. For example, routines such as family dinners—an important part of identity development—are becoming less common with the use of microwave ovens and prepared, fast, or frozen foods to ease the time pressure so many families experience today. Rather than sharing time together, family members may eat alone, standing in the kitchen, before racing off to the next activity.

Electronic technologies have helped some individuals to jump off the so-called hamster wheel and set their own hours at home, away from the hubbub of commutes, office gossip, and the nine-to-five regime. It might be many years before we will learn what outcomes such changes will have for families.

Today, new technologies offer families new ways to start and prolong close relations, but they also pose new challenges to our relationships. In this chapter, we focus on new information technology as one example.

Just as earlier social inventions—the development of cities, factories, automobiles, telephones, and television—changed families in earlier times, information technologies—especially the computer, e-mail, and cyberspace—have already changed and will continue to change families within our own lifetimes. We cannot tell precisely how much or in what ways these technologies will affect family life.

However, it is already obvious that computers and other new information technology (IT) affect families in several ways (Hughes, Ebata, and Dollahite 1999). First, IT affects the culture as a whole and, thus, affects families indirectly. Second, IT affects the ways family members communicate with one another. Since communication is a central aspect of family life, new communication technology can change family lives greatly. Third, IT is a means of teaching and providing therapy, giving people unequalled access to information and advice about family life.

FAMILIES IN THE CONNECTED SOCIETY

Today, any discussion of close relations must consider *virtual communities*, especially close relations that exist in cyberspace. These relations are characterized by rare face-to-face contact and regular electronic contact. Because of the country's vast geography, Canada's researchers have always been at the forefront of theorizing about long-distance communication technology. As a nation of vast distances and sparse population, Canada has always relied on transport and communication technology to make social organization possible.

As such, Canada has been a "connected" nation for many years, with usage rates of basic telephone, internet, and cable services among the highest in the world (see Figure 11.1 for information about current internet use).

A few simple statistics tell the tale. In 2006, more than 99 percent of Canadian households had landline or mobile telephone service, almost 80 percent owned a computer, and nearly 70 percent had home internet access (Statistics Canada, 2008b). These numbers are significantly higher than in previous years and continue to increase quickly, reflecting the willingness of Canadians to remain connected in virtual communities. Table 11.1 paints the picture of the rapid evolution of connectivity.

As a result, ever-speedier delivery of information, goods, and services has become a social fixation. Beepers, cell phones, PDAs, smart phones, and laptops connect ever more people, making them continuously available. As for the effects of being "wired," the jury is still out—some argue that electronic connectedness makes censorship and information management possible on a scale never before imagined. Others argue that connectedness weakens elite control over information and enables ordinary people to air their political, social, and cultural views more freely.

So how does internet use affect social relations? Researchers disagree about the overall effect of IT on family and community life. On the one hand, the new connectedness may intrude on family life, disturbing family rituals and cohesion. Early research highlighted the tendency of computers and other IT to isolate families, individuate family members—separate them from one another in individual activities—and even produce addictive behaviour. For instance, Nie and Hillygus (2002) found that frequent internet use is associated with less time spent with family and friends, and on social activities in general, as well as increased depression and loneliness.

On the other hand, increased connectedness makes it easier to contact friends, neighbours, acquaintances, spouses, children, parents, and siblings. This is exactly what the authors of a three-year study by University of Toronto sociologists Barry Wellman and Keith Hampton (1999) found. Wellman and Hampton surveyed residents moving into and living in a community they nicknamed Netville.

Residents varied from beginner to expert in their degree of computer and internet experience. Of the 109 homes in Netville, 64 were connected to the local network. The researchers found that residents with access to the high-speed local network recognize, talk, and visit with many more of their neighbours than do residents without this technology. Access to the local computer network introduces new methods of communication and increases communication with friends and relatives, and with neighbours. A neighbourhood e-mail list increases in-person socializing, as residents organize parties, barbecues, and other local events on-line. Wired residents also have more contact and exchange more help with friends and relatives living *outside* their neighbourhood. Far from destroying social life, Wellman and Hampton found that virtual relations improve it.

Reinforcing the positive effects of virtual relations on social life, a separate study by the Media Awareness Network, *Young Canadians in a Wired World*, concludes that "a wired kid is a social kid" (Moscovitch, 2007). The study finds that the internet is a crucial part

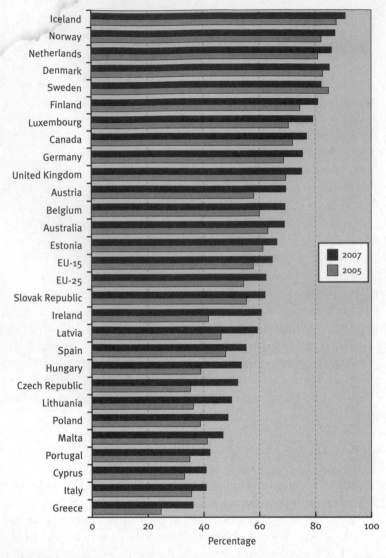

Note: Data refer to individuals aged 16 to 74. For Canada, 2005 refers to individuals aged 18 to 74 and 2007 refers to individuals aged 16 to 74. For Australia, 2005 refers to individuals aged 18 or older for the reference period 2004 to 2005, and 2007 refers to individuals aged 15 or older for the period 2006 to 2007. The EU-15 and EU-25 values refer to European Union 15-country and 25-country aggregate averages, respectively.

Data sources: Eurostat, *Community Survey on ICT Usage in Households and by Individuals,* 2005 and 2007; Statistics Canada, *Canadian Internet Use Survey,* 2005 and 2007; and Australian Bureau of Statistics, *Multi-Purpose Household Survey,* 2004 to 2005 and 2006 to 2007.

Figure 11.1 Internet use by individuals from any location, by country, 2005 and 2007

Source: Statistics Canada. 2009. *Innovation Analysis Bulletin.* Catalogue no. 88-003-X, vol. 11, no. 1, www.statcan.gc.ca/pub/88-003-x/2009001/article/10816/c-g/c-g001-eng.htm.

Table 11.1 Diversity of Methods for Connecting in Canada

Connections by type	1999	2000	2001	2002	2003
Fixed telephone lines[1]	19,806,248	20,347,014	20,805,058	20,300,831	20,067,563
Mobile telephony[1]	6,911,038	8,726,636	10,648,824	11,872,050	13,227,851
Residential Internet access[2]	3,367,000	4,324,000	5,706,000	6,547,000	7,013,000
Dial-up[2]	2,785,000	2,969,000	3,149,000	3,020,000	2,500,000
High speed[2]	582,000	1,355,000	2,558,000	3,527,000	4,513,000
Cable TV[3]	8,019,000	7,983,000	7,848,000	7,623,000	7,573,000
Satellite and wireless cable TV[3]	554,000	967,000	1,609,000	2,019,000	2,204,000
Total	**38,657,286**	**42,347,650**	**46,616,882**	**48,361,881**	**50,085,414**
Connections by type per 100 person					
Fixed telephone lines	65.1	66.3	67.1	64.7	63.4
Mobile telephony	22.7	28.4	34.3	37.8	41.8
Residential Internet access	11.1	14.1	18.4	20.9	22.2
Dial-up	9.2	9.7	10.2	9.6	7.9
High speed	1.9	4.4	8.2	11.2	14.3
Cable TV	26.4	26.0	25.3	24.3	23.9
Satellite and wireless cable TV	1.8	3.2	5.2	6.4	7.0
Total	**127.1**	**138.0**	**150.3**	**154.2**	**158.2**

1. Statistics Canada, *Annual Survey of Telecommunications.*
2. CRTC, *Status of Competition in Canadian Telecommunications Markets,* November 2004.
3. Statistics Canada and the CRTC, *Annual Return for Broadcasting Distribution Licensees.*

Sources: Statistics Canada. 2005. Table 1: Connections by Type. *Innovation Analysis Bulletin.* Catalogue no. 88 003 XIE. Vol. 7, No. 2. p. 13, www.statcan.gc.ca/pub/88-003-x/88-003-x2005002-eng.pdf.

of adolescents' social environment, allowing them to connect with friends, explore social roles, learn about their interests, and express themselves. Overall, for most adolescents, the internet contributes to increasing their confidence about making friends. Most new friends, however, still come from schools, sports, and parties (Moscovitch, 2007). Thus, the internet works as a social lubricant for adolescents, allowing them to engage in and strengthen their real-world networks.

So, overall, communication technologies have had different effects on social life and will continue to have unpredictable effects, at least for a while.

Information technology is becoming more and more necessary from an academic standpoint. In 2005, more than one-quarter of adult Canadians—an estimated 6.4 million— used the internet for education, training, or school work (McKeown and Underhill, 2005).

Table 11.2 Purpose of Internet Use, 2005

Province	Education Users	Other Users	Non Users
		Percent	
Newfoundland and Labrador	20	30	50
Prince Edward Island	24	33	43
Nova Scotia	28	37	36
New Brunswick	20	34	46
Quebec	21	37	42
Ontario	32	38	30
Manitoba	28	35	37
Saskatchewan	26	37	37
Alberta	30	38	32
British Columbia	29	38	33

Source: Statistics Canada. 2005. *Canadian Internet Use Survey.* www.statcan.gc.ca/pub/81-004-x/2007004/10375-eng.htm.

Table 11.2 shows the number of Canadians who use the internet for educational purposes by province. Despite its growing popularity, IT access varies in different regions for different people. Looker and Thiessen (2003) analyze the difference between urban and rural dwellings, and access to information technology within residential neighbourhoods as well as schools. Gender, socio-economic status, and location play a major role in access to IT. This study illustrates that despite being less likely to have access to computers at home, the use and competency levels of rural youth are not compromised because of increased use of computers at school (Looker and Thiessen, 2003). Also, female youth and youth from families with low parental education have a lesser chance of accessing a computer in the home. Interestingly, the data show that rural schools have been able to provide resources for students who may not have access at home, and therefore 60 percent of youth (rural) versus 40 percent (urban) first learned to use IT for academic purposes. On the contrary, rural schools have less educational software and use less specialized software (Looker and Thiessen, 2003). Addressing this issue through strategies for fund allocation for rural institutions may improve educational prospects for students.

Adding to the growing debate about information technology, Bowers, Vasquez, and Roaf (2000) have examined the use of computers in First Nations reservation schools across North America. While educators, linguists, and tribal leaders have highlighted the positive aspects of allowing Aboriginal youth to access computers in schools, others are less sure. On the one hand, computer access in schools will allow First Nations youth to engage in various forms of networking, increase their employment opportunities, and allow them to learn more about their cultural traditions (Bowers et al., 2000). Conversely, computer use can be seen as culture-transforming technology and may negatively contribute to First Nations people's sense of identity by exposing them to the dominant Western culture and challenging their local values, knowledge, and traditions (Bowers et al., 2000). The need for teachers to educate their students on the appropriate and inappropriate uses of information technology is crucial for First Nations youth to gain the benefits of computer access while avoiding the negative outcomes of culture loss.

Intimacy and Technology

The effects of technology on intimacy depend on the *type* of close relationship.

Haythornthwaite (Haythornthwaite, Kazmer, Robins, and Showmaker, 2000; Haythornthwaite 2001a, 2001b) has shown that among strongly tied (that is, closely related) people, easy, cheap technologies such as e-mail do not replace traditional communication media, for example, face-to-face meetings or telephone calls. Closely related communicators use new as well as old technologies and communicate often. More frequent, and more varied, communication strengthens a relationship. By contrast, weakly tied communicators rely on one medium and are less motivated to explore new technologies. Their relationships remain distant as a result.

Connectedness has a huge impact on people's lives. In a post-industrial, information-based economy, connectedness affects people's employability—their chance of getting a good job or any job at all. Indirectly, this has an impact on family life, since as we have stressed in other chapters, the demands of work (including schoolwork) always influence the quality of close relations. Canadians' unequal access to on-line computer use, and their unequal computer literacy, may affect people's educational and occupational attainment and, indirectly, the class structure.

We cannot predict how quickly the differences in technology access will shrink. In the end, the computer may provide traditionally disadvantaged and isolated people with new opportunities to improve their social condition. This will improve family life, as well as change the face of work and community life. However, we are far from seeing this happen yet.

Technology and Family Development

Changes in technology that simplify contact among family and friends are likely to contribute to the quality and cohesion of relationships. Over the last 150 years, changes in communications and transport technologies have made contact among kin and friends, whether they live near one another or great distances apart, less expensive, faster, and easier. As e-mail and internet use spreads, geographic constraints on social relationships continue to lessen.

The spread of easy communication shrinks distances, and we can expect this shrinking of distances to continue. Yet, despite the constant changes in the technological context of social relationships, most social theory continues to assume that people will form and preserve close relationships mainly through face-to-face interaction (Adams, 1998). It was not until recently that people could travel or communicate often enough with people who lived at a distance to form a relationship with them. So, researchers who studied close relations focused on people who were geographically as well as emotionally close. Psychologists who studied interpersonal attraction, for example, focused on the importance of visual cues: how physical appearance plays a role in attraction, and what gestures and facial expressions people use to show involvement (see Short, Williams, and Christie, 1976). In the internet age, we need a new inventory of the ways people signal their characteristics, preferences, and qualities.

Comparing Communication Technologies

One strategy for studying the future of close relations and technology is to examine how technology has affected close relations in the past. New technologies rapidly cross traditional social barriers and achieve wide adoption (Fischer, 1992). Let us review the history of two recent communication technologies: the telephone and e-mail.

The Telephone Social histories of the telephone (Pool, 1977; Fischer, 1992) show that, from the beginning, telephones were used mainly for long-distance calling. Commercial interests advertised the telephone as a means to link family and friends; women were shown using it for "kin-keeping."

The telephone allowed people to express their views in their own voice, it was simple to use and, once the private line replaced the party line, as private as face-to-face communication. As a result, the telephone was adopted by everyone and widely used to preserve close relations, even at a distance. People quickly became dependent on this new communication instrument.

Yet surprisingly, the effects of the telephone on social life have been modest. There is no systematic evidence that the telephone has changed close relations. At most, the telephone has helped them by keeping people in touch between face-to-face meetings.

Note that the telephone—like other forms of communication—has had both positive and negative effects on close relations. Applewhite and Segal (1990) studied the ways peacekeeping troops in the Sinai (in Israel) use telephones on the frontlines. Talking to parents and spouses preserves social support systems while on duty. However, a large minority report feeling sad after a phone call, or angry about being in the Sinai, or anxious after receiving disturbing news from home. Yet, given the opportunity, people use telephones and other communication technology, all of which have the capacity to make them happy, anxious, or sad.

Along similar lines, a study of the U.S. military (Pincus, House, Christenson, and Adler, 2004) finds that many spouses are frustrated with the unidirectional phone contact initiated only by the soldier, making them feel "trapped" at home waiting for a call. And when soldiers call home and no one answers, they may feel forgotten, which can lead to anger and resentment—especially if this occurs frequently. "Now that Internet and e-mail are widely available," the study notes, "spouses report feeling much more in control as they can initiate communication and do not have to stay waiting by the phone. Another advantage of e-mail, for both Soldier and spouse, is the ability to be more thoughtful about what is said and to 'filter out' intense emotions that may be unnecessarily disturbing. This is not to say that military couples should 'lie' to protect each other, but rather it helps to recognize that the direct support available from one's mate is limited during the deployment."

E-mail The advantages of e-mail are sometimes similar to those of the telephone. E-mail is even cheaper than telephone communication and much cheaper than long-distance travel. It allows people to avoid being seen by the message recipient, yet it creates "symbolic proximity."

Like the telephone, e-mail allows escape from continued contact if that is desired. It gives one time to think and reflect. E-mail is not as interruptive as the telephone, nor is it dependent on both people being available at the same time. Unlike the telephone, e-mail is strictly a print medium. However, e-mail carries a variety of dangers of its own. Faceless anonymity poses the risk of indiscretion, misunderstanding, and misquoting. The shield of visual and vocal anonymity may encourage blunt disclosure and self-misrepresentation. On the other hand, some studies have found that the greater self-disclosure made possible by this shield outweighs any negative outcomes.

The lack of temporal and spatial boundaries frees relationships and makes new ones possible. This also makes relationships with on-line communicators possible for people formerly prevented from socializing—for example, people housebound by illness or child care. However, the community feeling gained from cyber relations is often illusory. At this point, we have no idea what net effect e-mail will have on close relations.

Communication Technology and the Family Cycle

What effect will newer technologies—the internet, direct communication that combines sight and sound—have on family life? Research on the topic is just beginning; so far, the most plentiful information concerns parental fears about children's safety on-line.

However, an existing theory can be used to consider the likely effects of innovations. Adams and Stevenson (2002) look at technology from the viewpoint of family development theory.

Research regarding the effects of communication technologies on family life is ongoing. With decreasing privacy, on-line safety is of most concern at this time.

The basic premise of this theory is that families continuously change with changes in social expectations, environmental constraints, and the demands of family members (for example, biological, psychological, and social needs). As families change and restructure, they engage in *developmental tasks*, or activities that prepare them for coming stages.

Traditional "stages" include marriage without children, marriage with various-aged children (for example, infant, preschool, school-age, adolescent, young adult), marriage with children who live outside the household, grandparenting, and marriage in late life. White (1998) has expanded these traditional stages to include divorce and remarriage, stages that people previously classified as "non-normative," or not widely accepted, but are now considered normative. Also, the growth of cohabitation and the rise of child-bearing as a "discretionary option" have increased the variety of family lives (Rowland, 1991). With so many different kinds of family experiences, it makes no sense to speak of "the average family." Family development theory allows researchers to organize family experiences, issues, and opportunities into specific categories while recognizing the dynamic nature of stage progression.

The primary research question offered by family development theory is, How does technology influence family change over time? Specifically, how does the use of on-line communication influence the norms and roles of family members? How do families use technology in the developmental tasks that contribute to stage transitions? In what ways is the use of technology different across various stages of development? Does technology affect or contribute to the experience of *off time*, or non-normative stage transitions? Finally, how does family development differ in families with continuous access to technology and in families without such access? Note that we could pose parallel questions about the development of friendship groups or networks—indeed, any networks of close relations.

Home use of the computer will likely affect some stages more than others. For example, it could harm "early marriages"—newly formed couples and couples with no children or young children—more than long-established post-retirement relationships. Usually, families with preschool children need to invest much time in preserving cohesion and solving new problems. They cannot afford to devote much time to computing (unless it is work-related and unavoidable), or parenting and marital quality could suffer.

Busy working couples in settled, loving relationships might rely on communication technologies to keep in touch with each other. Communication technologies also allow parents to keep in touch with their children when they go to college or university. Increasingly, e-mail can be an important means of staying in touch with relatives in different parts of the world, as well as with aging parents. Text messaging, instant messaging, and Skype (and similar software used to make voice calls over the internet) are other means people use to stay in touch with distant relatives.

Communication Technology and the Forming of Relationships

As mentioned earlier, technology not only helps maintain relationships, it may also help create them. While dates and romantic relationships were traditionally initiated via face-to-face interaction, recently people have started launching romantic relationships using short message service (SMS) text messaging, a form of computer-mediated communication (CMC) enabled by cell phones. In a study examining the preferred channel of communication in romantic relationships, O'Sullivan (2000) found that initiators who wish to preserve a certain impression that could be threatened by their relationship partner have a preference for computer-mediated communication channels over face-to-face communication. A different study that investigated how sex differences influence the choice of channel of communication suggests that males and females differ in their pattern of preference for communication channels in making the first move. Females are more likely to make the first move using text messaging. The results also show that women initiate more first moves through text messaging than by telephone calls (Byrne and Findlay, 2004). The increasing popularity of text messaging by cell phone in recent years may, therefore, contribute to changes in dating scripts in the near future.

Currently, on-line dating is also experiencing an incredible boom. Most on-line daters seek long-term partners and list the advantages of internet dating as convenience, privacy and confidentiality, and the opportunity to meet people they would otherwise never meet (Brym and Lenton, 2001). On-line romantic relationships are thus rapidly becoming commonplace for most parts of the population. Despite being scarce, the research on the extent of involvement of older adults in internet dating reveals that older adults do use the internet to meet potential romantic partners. A Canadian study (Brym and Lenton, 2001), for instance, found that 1.6 percent of on-line daters were aged 60 and older, and a number of on-line dating sites now cater exclusively to clientele age 50 and older.

The on-line relationships of the older adults reflect those of their younger counterparts. For instance, Malta (2007) found that older Australian adults (ages 61 to 85) develop intimate, meaningful, and long-lasting relationships on-line. Further, for a majority the relationships become sexual very quickly, in all cases at the first face-to-face meeting; and for some of the participants, cybersex is an integral part of their relationship. Such results illustrate that the desire for love and intimacy remains very important regardless of age.

It is too early to tell the long-term outcomes of relationships formed through internet dating. Given the expanded possibility of meeting people, the types of relationships formed will be more diverse. Future research will need to address several questions: Are these relationships more prone to breakups and divorces? Will spouses feel insecure or suspicious that their partner might be meeting someone else on-line? Will parents who met on-line have different attitudes to their children's dating? Will they be more open to internet use by their children?

Cyberspace offers people unparalleled opportunities to meet and grow emotionally close to total strangers who may be at a great distance (Merkle and Richardson, 2000). Nearness and physical attraction are key in starting a conventional relationship. However, physical attraction plays a less immediate part in the plunge into intimate, sometimes highly sexualized, and self-disclosing cyber-relationships. Many people report adopting bogus names and identities for their interactions. Deception is part of the fun of cyberspace, a type of social gaming.

A sense of distance and seeming anonymity reduces the anxiety people feel about showing their feelings or fears in face-to-face relationships. Usually, people reveal themselves fully only in the deepest and most intimate relationships—typically in those relationships that have survived a test of time. However, in computer-mediated relationships (CMRs), people come to know each other intimately much more quickly than they do in face-to-face relationships. This rapid intimacy may pose a threat to established relationships. Collins (1999) asks, "Should we regard cyber sexual affairs as a species of adultery, an impermissible form of sexual betrayal, and cyber-romances as a comparable species of emotional infidelity?" Computer-mediated relationships, by largely erasing the sexual aspect of betrayal and stressing the emotional aspect, may redefine how our culture thinks about fidelity.

By now, many of us know people who met their mates, or left their spouses, because of cyber-romance. In her classic work on divorce, Diane Vaughan (1985) stresses that a key stage in the breakdown of a marriage is the establishment, by one partner, of an alternate social world. Fantasy worlds sometimes become real worlds, and cyber-romances reveal (for some) defects in a marital relationship that they had not previously noticed or preferred to ignore. Their partners feel betrayed by internet intimacy because they feel that all intimacy must remain within the boundaries of the marital relationship. However, for some, cybersex or on-line affairs may not be considered a form of infidelity. Some have suggested that couples may feel a sense of betrayal by a partner's internet relationship. However, a study by Whitty and Quigley (2008) discovered that cybersex or falling in love on-line may not yet be considered the most upsetting infidelity. In fact, they found that not everyone in their sample was convinced cybersex or on-line relationships were considered real infidelity, although they did consider them transgressions away from the relationship (Whitty and Quigley, 2008: 465). It seems that cyber relationships and infidelities are something that more couples will be dealing with in the future and will need to set up acceptable rules for on-line relationships and friendships. Also, family therapists need to recognize that computer-mediated entry into rapid emotional intimacy may be a risk to any relationship where one or both partners are dissatisfied.

Cyberspace allows various forms of sexual stimulation without the complications involved with buying porn from book/video stores, prostitutes, and street exhibitionism and voyeurism (Schneider, 2003). Pornography can be purchased easily, inexpensively, and privately in one's own home. In extreme cases, the activities change from mere browsing to sharing in cybersex with on-line chat partners. The on-line infidelity sometimes turns into real-life infidelity for seriously involved users. Schneider's study showed that cybersex can be addictive, affecting the relationship with real-life partners. As the user spends less time with the real-life spouse, cybersex can be a major contributor to separation and divorce.

Technology for Family Caregiving

Cyberspace is not only a place for meeting and mating with strangers, or keeping in touch with family and friends. It is also a storehouse of useful information for people with problems. Increasingly, people look to cyberspace for the answers to questions about health, jobs, and family relations. In recent years, researchers have paid particular attention to the possible uses of the telephone and internet as means of delivering social support to caregivers. Researchers provided taped informational lectures over the telephone for some subjects and a peer telephone network for others. After three months, caregivers in *both* programs showed less psychological distress, more perception that they were receiving social support, and more satisfaction with the support they were receiving. However, after six months, the gains had levelled off or declined; caregiver burden and social conflict increased again (Goodman, 1990).

Some health professionals have set up telephone support groups for AIDS caregivers. Use of the telephone gives people a sense of confidentiality not always possible in face-to-face groups. It also supports people who are isolated because of the stigma associated with HIV/AIDS and the lack of support networks in their communities (Wiener, Heilman, and Battles, 1998). In one program, caregivers in semi-structured groups made eight conference calls to exchange information about resources and coping strategies. Participants reported feeling satisfied with the group experience (Meier, Galinsky, and Rounds, 1995). They felt less isolated and more personally effective, but their sense of social support and coping did not improve (Rounds, Galinsky, and Despard, 1995).

The internet can also be a source of support for caregivers. Computer-mediated groups eliminate time and distance barriers and limits on group size; they increase variety and diversity of support, anonymity, pre- and post-group support, opportunity for expression through written communication, and potential training experiences for group leaders (Finn, 1995). Furthermore, the internet can have positive effects on caregiver well-being through various support programs. For instance, a study that set to evaluate the efficacy of a multimedia support program delivered over the internet to employed family caregivers of persons with dementia found that 30 days post-exposure participants displayed more positive perceptions of caregiving (Beauchamp et al., 2005). The caregivers also showed significant improvements in depression, anxiety, and the level and frequency of stress and caregiver strain. Such interactive multimedia interventions delivered over the internet thus have the potential to provide low-cost, effective social support for caregivers. And today, family caregiver support is much needed, as elder care is becoming a central part of many people's lives.

Potential disadvantages of going on-line include the chance of destructive interactions, a lack of clear and accountable leadership, limited access to non-computer-using populations, and a lack of research about benefits and user satisfaction (Finn, 1996; Finn and Lavitt, 1994).

Much information relevant to family life is available through the internet, especially on parenting and human development (Elliott, 1999). Fewer sites are to be found in areas such as family resource management. In time, people will fill these gaps. Since men use the internet disproportionately, parenting sites may help fathers increase their role in their children's development (Morris, Dollahite, and Hawkins, 1999).

The internet also has a role to play in family therapy, especially in treating families that are isolated or whose members are geographically separated. It is also a valuable source of information on travel, leisure activities, health, and other areas of interest for older adults, who are the fastest-growing group of internet users (Silver, 2001). Figure 11.2 shows the different areas of information that attract older surfers to the internet.

Use of computer monitoring can allow older adults who need care to live by themselves—a preference of many disabled adults, as revealed in a survey by the American Association of Retired People (SPRY Foundation, 2004). The report also shows that older adults want to choose who will provide necessary care. Web sites provide health-care information for specific conditions to help them make informed decisions on the care they receive, who provides it, and the costs involved.

Computerization can provide people with illnesses with quick feedback on how their condition is affected by their compliance with medication, exercise, and diet. This type of information can lighten the burden on family members who act as caregivers

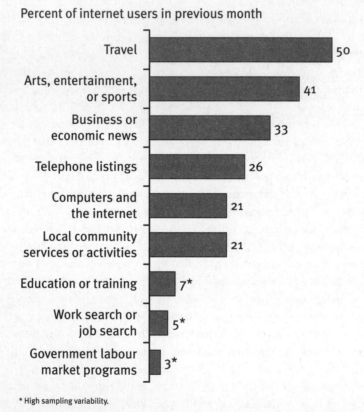

Percent of internet users in previous month

* High sampling variability.

Figure 11.2 Information that attracts older surfers to the internet

Source: Cynthia Silver. 2003. Older surfers. *Canadian Social Trends.* Ottawa: Statistics Canada. www.statcan.gc.ca/pub/11-008-x/11-008-x2001003-eng.pdf.

- Although the young are the most avid users of information and communications technology, little difference exists between young and middle-aged adults in Canada with respect to internet use. As of 2003, 29.4 percent of young Canadians aged 16 to 25 used computers and the internet at home for 10 to 30 hours per month, compared to 29.1 percent of people aged 36 to 45 (Middleton and Leith, 2007).

- Of the younger users (ages 16 to 25), nearly half (44.1 percent) use the internet to search for employment opportunities in a typical month. Interestingly, 43.6 percent of young Canadians who were already employed searched for additional employment opportunities on-line (Middleton and Leith, 2007).

- The proportion of surfers aged 16 to 25 who download music in Canada (73.5 percent) is almost double the proportion of those in their late 20s or 30s, and almost six times the proportion of those older than age 50 (Middleton and Leith, 2007).

- Instant messaging programs found on the internet are especially popular among the young, a reflection of a generation that more and more wants to "reach" and "be reached" with immediacy (Middleton and Leith, 2007).

- Older surfers are more likely to search for certain types of information through the internet, including government and health information (Middleton and Leith, 2007).

and, at the same time, help older adults retain the sense of autonomy so important to well-being.

Electronic bulletin boards can play a similar role, helping caregivers at home to develop problem-solving skills and providing counselling to prevent physical, emotional, and social crises (Bucher, Houts, Mezy, and Maguth Nezy, 1996).

THE NEW REPRODUCTIVE TECHNOLOGIES

New reproductive technologies make it possible to separate fertilization from child-bearing and parenting. In this way, they have the potential to revolutionize family life. Often, however, technologies are used to advance traditional goals by traditional social means—through families, kinship networks, communities, churches, schools, and other ways.

Research by Maureen Baker (2002) illustrates this point. Many cultures link heritage and status to "biological" children—children who are genetically related to their parents. So, in most parts of the world, "blood ties" are central to kinship. As a result, infertility causes people great anxiety, self-doubt, and depression, especially in societies that consider having children equivalent to entering normal adulthood. There, fertility clinics increasingly offer hope.

More low-fertility couples can now reproduce. This helps to perpetuate the ideal of the "normal" family with biological children and reinforces the social pressure on all couples to reproduce. Couples who have struggled unsuccessfully to bear children tend to focus especially strongly on the traditional aspects of family life. For example, many women who have undergone successful fertility treatment want to stay home from work to care for their child after spending so much time and effort trying to reproduce. Rather than challenging traditional views of family, these new technologies appear merely to reinforce them. The wish to create a "normal" and socially accepted family unit remains strong in modern societies.

This finding supports our argument that, at most, technology is a co-producer of social change. Often, technology is merely the handmaiden of human ambitions, however forward or backward they may be. If technology is to be understood in terms of social values and social organization, changes in family life must also be understood in those terms. As shorthand, we can think of recent changes in family life as a growth of *individualization*.

THE GROWTH OF INDIVIDUALIZATION

With industrialism and post-industrialism came a package of changes that had the net effect of allowing people to lead more separate yet interdependent lives. This has had a major impact on family life. Let us focus on one aspect of this change—what we call the *individualization* of people's lives (Jones, Marsden, and Tepperman, 1990; Beck-Gernsheim, 1983; Schultz, 1983; Herlyn and Vogel, 1989). With individualization, there is more variety, fluidity, and idiosyncrasy in all the major demographic processes: in migration, marriage, divorce, child-bearing, family decision making, and the relation of work life and family life. We expect people to be self-sufficient actors in their economic, household, leisure, and intimate relationships.

Individualization of social roles means the empowerment of women through higher levels of formal education and more participation in the paid labour force. The rise of a service economy creates more employment opportunities for women and thus speeds up this process. Any growth in jobs that free people from family dependency and control increases the variety, fluidity, and idiosyncrasy of people's private lives. Nevertheless, they still need and want the emotional attachments of family life.

Why, given the choice, do most North Americans still value and want marriage and children? Repeatedly, these activities have changed form and resurfaced. Family life, whatever its form, is driven more by emotional needs than by rational considerations. At the same time, people continue to show signs of wanting to increase their happiness by choosing their own destinies—with or without families. When people are able to choose their own lives—for example, their mate, their living arrangement, or the number of children they will bear—they exercise this choice. This produces heightened satisfaction—at least, at the time of the decision—but also social changes.

More choice also produces more confusion and ambivalence about how, and when, to limit choice. Do we tolerate or celebrate the marriages of same-sex couples? Support or oppose birth control awareness among teenagers? Allow abortion after the occurrence of sexual abuse or violent sexual assault but not in other cases when women seek it?

The outcome of struggles for and against change in family life is hard to predict. However, it seems likely that anything that (1) slows the growth of opportunities after an earlier growth, (2) increases the individualization of lives faster than the creation of new cultural meanings and norms, or (3) otherwise produces uncertainty and confusion (for example, a war or environmental disaster) will increase support for a backward-looking mythology of the family.

How do people cope with the ambivalence and confusion of intimacy and close relations these days? Typically, they develop new social forms and invent new lifestyles to deal with the doubts they face. Solutions to the problem of uncertainty include both formal and informal changes. *Formal* changes include laws and policies such as new legislation to define marriage and its rights and duties, to support gender equity and affirmative action for women, to improve daycare, and to encourage fertility control. *Informal* changes include efforts people make in their own lives to negotiate new social roles and norms. For example, people work out new ways of disciplining the children of their spouse's first marriage, interacting with their mother's new boyfriend, or getting to know a co-worker's same-sex spouse.

Trends in Canadian Internet Use

- Internet use can take time away from other activities. For instance, more than 25 percent of Canadian internet users spend less time watching television once they start using the internet, 15 percent of internet users take time away from reading, 11 percent from sleeping, 11 percent from doing leisure activities at home, and 10 percent from doing household chores (Dryburgh, 2001).

- Conversely, internet use can improve interaction with family and friends. For example, some Canadians report that their communications with friends (5 percent) and family (3 percent) increased as a result of their using the internet (Dryburgh, 2001).

- Canada is a wired nation. Currently, it ranks as the second most wired of all OECD countries (after South Korea) for high-speed access (Statistics Canada, 2005h).

- Cell phone subscriptions increased from 98,000 in 1987 to more than 18 million by the end of 2006. Currently, there are almost as many wireless phones as landlines in Canada (Moscovitch, 2007).

- In Canada, long-distance calling increased as a proportion of total calling, with long-distance minutes almost tripling from almost 20 billion in 1995 to 56 billion in 2002 (Sciadas, 2006).

- Although information and communications technology (ICT) prices decreased significantly between 1997 and 2003, average Canadian household spending on all ICT (including telephones and television) increased from $2118 to $2780 during that time (Sciadas, 2006).

- Almost 7 million Canadians aged 18 and older placed an order on-line in 2005, while more than 9 million logged on to browse or, in other words, to do some "window shopping." The people who made an on-line purchase represented about 41 percent of all adults who used the internet in 2005 (Statistics Canada 2005h).

A NEW CULTURE OF INTIMATE LIFE

Out of all these efforts a new culture of intimate life emerges. Social and cultural changes, in turn, bring pressure for further changes by government and business. For example, the growth in part-time work, work sharing, and workplace child care all reflect, in part, new ideas about the necessary relationship between work and family life.

In turn these changes further increase choice, confusion, and cultural change, so the cycle of family change continues. With few exceptions, this cycle works similarly in all societies. Bearing that in mind, what kinds of families are likely to result from this continuing process of individualization? At least four main kinds of nuclear family are likely to appear, which differ along two main dimensions: (1) role separability and (2) personal interchangeability (Jones et al., 1990).

Role separability in families refers to the separation of being a spouse from being a parent. Many North American households are made up of cohabiting couples with children, or reconstituted or blended families, where spouses may or may not parent one another's children. A second dimension, **personal interchangeability**, refers to the choice of a spouse based on his or her ability to fill certain roles rather than for the individual's unique characteristics. People who marry for love choose a mate for his or her unique characteristics. People who marry for instrumental reasons are more interested in a mate who is a good provider, or who can produce healthy offspring. Personal interchangeability is well suited to societies with high rates of mortality. By contrast, purely romantic marriages are unpredictable and unstable.

Now we can cross-classify nuclear families along these two dimensions. Doing so yields four possibilities: we call them the (1) corporate, (2) collected, (3) concatenated, and (4) cyclical family.

Inseparable family roles and personal interchangeability characterize the **corporate family**. In this kind of family people can come and go without changing the essential structure of the family. The husband serves as father to the younger generation in the household—children, apprentices, and household servants—and the wife serves as mother, whoever the natural parents of these children may be.

It is only in a society dominated by this kind of family that people can think and speak of "the family" as a well-defined social institution. The state protects the institution of "the family." In culture and by law, "the family" has social importance, enjoys its own resources, and commands its members' loyalties. This kind of family underlines its members' duty to the group. As Sacks (1991) says, such families exist because of choices people do *not* make: To be a child is to accept the authority of parents one did not choose. To be a parent is to accept responsibility for a future one may not live to see (Sacks, 1991: 56–7).

This kind of family is best suited to a theocratic, undifferentiated social structure. There, the state, the law, and religion are closely tied together and lean the same way on family matters. In societies where the corporate family dominates, competing models of life—for example, notions that individuals have rights and liberties—and competing institutions (like the secular school) hold little sway. The "corporate family" existed among the nineteenth- and early twentieth-century European and North American middle classes. It is a patriarchal family in which a double standard prevails and in which men are dominant. Today, the corporate family—once the dominant model in Western societies—has lost its support in law and public opinion, at least in Canada. In the more religious United States, such a patriarchal model of the family still prevails in traditional circles, despite the mass culture's commitment to romantic choice. An attempt to combine the two notions of marriage is evident in the popular HBO series about polygamy in Utah, *Big Love*.

By contrast, separable roles and interchangeable performers characterize the **collected family**. It is similar to Duberman's (1975) "reconstituted" family, which follows the remarriage of partners who have children from previous unions. Like the corporate family, the collected family needs family members to conform to traditional notions of husband, wife, father, mother, and child. However, given the complexities of remarriage, family members concede the impossibility of compelling mates to be both good spouses *and* good parents to the resident children.

In these families, it is not the family as a whole but the unit roles that are the locus of loyalty, meaning, and resources. Children are allowed to feel close to their mother, for example, without feeling obliged to love her intimate partner or call him "Daddy." Societies like our own—with growing numbers of reconstituted families—are beginning to recognize the odd character and special needs of collected families. For example, the state increasingly delivers benefits to partners *or* parents *or* children, not to the "family head" of earlier days. In this system, one cannot assume the family has a "head," or even that the traditional idea of "family head" has any meaning today.

The Census of Canada long ago changed from referring to "head of household" to calling one person in the household—whoever the person filling in the Census chooses— "Person 1." In 1988, the Canadian government began to send out family allowance cheques made payable to the custodial parent of a child, typically the mother. This change recognized the important difference between a corporate family and a collected family. Not surprisingly, people who live in, or idealize, corporate families oppose this change. After all, it concedes that corporate families are becoming less common. Opponents argue that accepting this change makes families normatively less important to people's lives than they once were.

A third kind of family, the **concatenated family**, is exactly opposite to the corporate family, since separable roles and unique performers characterize it. From the outside, the concatenated family looks like a chance event, a slow collision of individuals in time and space. The concatenated family is nothing more than a household at a particular moment. Here, family members vest meanings, loyalties, and resources in particular individuals, not roles. Families exist only through sharing these meanings and resources. As a result, family members must constantly affirm and renegotiate the bases for this sharing.

Here, the meaning of *intimate partner* or *parent* is no longer certain. Occasionally definitions will mesh for long periods. In any event we cannot assume, in these families, that members will have a permanent commitment to "the family" or even to their current partner and children. The concatenated family is an extreme version of radical individualism. It assumes that people ought to have continuous, unlimited free choice in their living arrangements. This freedom is subject only to the legal protection of minors from the results of a family breakdown and the protection of all family members from household violence. Supporters of this family type see family life as a lifestyle or individual choice—so far as the adults are concerned, a supermarket for intimate relations.

In this system, mating is motivated by considerations of the spouse's unique characteristics, which may not continue to allure. Child-bearing is motivated by a biological drive to reproduce or by self-expression—a form of psychic consumption of children for personal pleasure. Under these conditions, marital dissolutions will likely be frequent. Not surprisingly, this family system creates many potential kinship connections—for example, many sets of grandparents (Gross, 1987). However, more mothers than fathers will remain with their children in case of a divorce. So in practice, concatenated families (with children) are more matrifocal. Women and children remain in the household, while men come and go. In North America and Europe, concatenated families are still far from the average.

Like the corporate family, the **cyclical (or recycled) family** features traditional (inseparable) roles. Still, unlike the corporate family, there is no interchangeability in the cyclical one. Each is a "return engagement" occurring *because of* the unique relationship of the members. This return engagement may be a second marriage of the same people, which is rare but occurs. More often, it is a second parenthood, during which people are called on to parent their now-adult children (occasionally called "boomerang kids") a second time.

For example, in Canada since 1981 the percentages of men and women between the ages of 20 to 34 living with parents have risen significantly. The result is a complex household that *looks* like a corporate family but has none of the predictability or normative power of that older arrangement. Many reasons account for the return of adult children: unemployment, inadequate income for accommodation, or the need for extra education or babysitting help. Unique family situations result from an interaction between the reasons for return and the expectations of the children and parents.

We can wonder whether the change from corporate families to collected, concatenated, and cyclical families is as certain as it seems. Some wishful thinkers want (and some policy makers encourage) mothers of preschool children to leave the workforce and devote their adult lives to family. If they did, family incomes would drop significantly. For illustration, in 2000 women contributed 35.6 percent to the total household income in the United States (Boushey, 2009) and 42 percent in Canada in 2008 (Statistics Canada, 2009). Even after considering the costs that they would not incur, such as daycare and other work-related expenses, families would still suffer a net loss of income. The loss would be greatest for those dual-income families in which the wife earns more than the husband—25.3 percent of dual-earner families in the United States (Selvin, 2007) and 29 percent in Canada (Statistics Canada, 2006i). However, there are no signs suggesting a return to old, restrictive family forms—at least not in Canada.

LIKELY CHANGES IN THE FUTURE

When Canadians discuss family today, they talk about two things. They stress that families, and what happens with families, matter to them. They also talk about the diversity of families today in comparison to the past. The diversity to which most people refer is a range of family forms, defined by legal and living arrangements of spouses and whether children are present. So, we hear about married couples with or without children, common-law or cohabiting couples with or without children, female- or male-headed single-parent families, adoptive families, foster families, empty nesters, gay or lesbian families, and the list goes on. At times the impression might be that a smorgasbord of choices about how to live in families exists.

Viewing diverse families only as varied structures may be deceptive in other ways. We may overlook or underestimate diversity *within* various family forms, suggesting that families are more uniform than they are. The term "family" itself may be too restrictive, ignoring everyone to whom we are not related by conventional notions of blood or marriage. This restrictive idea of family, which suggests a clear distinction between family and friends, takes away from us other ways to care for those we like. For example, we may parcel out our love and caring cautiously, thinking that family has a monopoly on caring. Yet, as discussed in Chapter 10, people may define many different kinds of people as family (McDaniel, 1994).

Major Findings about Families

- In 2003, 30 percent of women primary breadwinners had a university degree compared with 21 percent of secondary-earner wives and 25 percent of primary-earner husbands. Moreover, more than one-third of primary-earner wives had more education than their husbands (Statistics Canada, 2006i).

- Canada is one of the developed countries with the lowest rates of communication between young people and their parents, with fewer than 50 percent of Canadian teens talking with their parents on a regular basis (Bernard, 2008).

- Family meals are most common in Italy (93.8 percent), France (90.4 percent), and Switzerland (89.9 percent). Canada lags behind with only 72 percent of Canadian 15-year-olds saying they sit down with their parents to eat the main meal of the day "several times a week" (Bernard, 2008).

- In Canada, the 2001 census revealed that 15 percent of households headed by lesbian couples had children versus 3 percent among male same-sex households (Ambert, 2005c).

- Forty-four percent of Canadians feel that their work has a negative impact on their family and interferes with the amount of time they spend with their children (Duxbury and Higgins, 2003).

- Employees with a serious work–family conflict miss an average of 13.2 days of work a year versus 5.9 days missed for those without a conflict. This results in financial losses of $2.7 billion a year in direct costs and $10 billion in indirect costs in Canada (Barette, 2009).

People are inventing new ways to be family. **Other-mothering** is one such family innovation, which allows extended relations or friends to mother children and moves beyond the nuclear, biological family. Other-mothering is

> . . . revolutionary in American society because it takes place in opposition to the ideas that parents, especially mothers, should be the only child rearers . . . This kind of shared responsibility for child care can only happen in small community settings where people know and trust one another. It cannot happen in those settings if parents regard their children as their 'property,' their possession (hooks, 1984: 144).

The Vanier Institute of the Family (2004) lists the "top 10 trends for Canadian families," as follows:

1. Fewer couples are getting legally married.
2. More couples are breaking up.
3. Families are getting smaller.
4. Children experience more transitions as parents change their marital status.
5. Canadians are satisfied with life.
6. Family violence [continues to be] under-reported.
7. Multiple-earner families [have become] the norm.
8. Women [continue to do] most of the juggling involved in balancing work and home.
9. [Socio-economic] inequality [between families] is worsening.
10. The future will have more aging families.

Not all of these items are truly "trends." For example, items 5, 6, 7, and 8 make no statement about change over time, so they are not trends. However, the other items identify continuing changes—trends—in Canadian family life that we have discussed in this book.

As social scientists and as citizens, we have several ways of responding to these stated trends. First, we can continue to watch the data and report whether these trends are continuing. Second, we can make and test theories about the reasons for these trends. Third, we can propose and evaluate social policies that will increase the benefits and decrease the harms associated with these trends. Fourth, we can lead public discussions about the ways we can promote the trends we favour and slow down the trends we dislike.

We have argued throughout this book that inevitably more people will cohabit and divorce and bear fewer children (items 1–3 on p. 334), and by implication that children will experience more transitions as parents change their relationships (item 4). Not only are these trends universal in industrial societies, they are unlikely to reverse themselves and they result from the growth of human freedom—a quality most of us would want to promote. Also, families and populations will continue to age (item 10); this is a sure result of the decline in child-bearing.

It is hard to imagine social conditions that would lead Canadians to return to low rates of cohabitation or divorce or to high birth rates. It is therefore important for us to think about the problems these conditions create, and the ways we can reduce the associated harm. Consider, for example, the changes associated with the rise to dominance of the multiple-earner family, a family form that is likely to become even more common in the future.

Dual-Income Families

Dual-income families are important carriers of family change. As discussed earlier, the proportion of women with families who work outside the home has grown steadily. This pattern is not likely to change. The economy needs the wages and skills of women too much, and governments need the taxes women contribute. Career and job commitments may lead to postponed weddings and to more commuting relationships in the future. Women may delay child-bearing, but the emotional value placed on children will still mean that most couples will have children at some point.

In years to come, life with children and two incomes will continue to challenge both work and family for both men and women. With changes in the global marketplace, men's work may not be as privileged as it was in the past, when men were viewed as *primary* family providers. Women increasingly are taking on the role of provider, even where a man is present, as men's work becomes more precarious and insecure. More husbands may follow their spouses' career or job opportunities. This means changes in the roles and expectations of spouses and in the ways children come to see what mothers and fathers are and do.

Refilled Nests

For a time it was the common pattern that children grew up and left the family home when they could make their own way in the world. However, as discussed in Chapter 10, couples who thought that their children had grown up and "flown away" soon experience a **refilled nest** with adult children who are returning to school (or have never left school), having trouble finding or keeping jobs, getting separated or divorced, or even having children of their own (Boyd and Pryor, 1989).

The future may be, then, like the past: some families live in refilled nests only out of necessity and see themselves as merely pooling housing and resources to survive. Others, however, may see huge creative possibilities in refilled nests—grandparents providing child care while parents work; sharing housework among more family members; reducing environmental problems by having fewer accommodations; developing new ways of intergenerational caring for elders. In her book, *The Boomerang Age*, Canadian sociologist Barbara Mitchell notes that today's young people often move through a larger variety of family-related roles, statuses, and living arrangements.

Mitchell also notes that public issues such as globalization, the decline of the welfare state, and various forms of social inequality affect the circumstances of young adulthood, resulting in an increased need for social policy reforms related to education, housing, child care, and gender equality. However, increased individualization in the pursuit of social goals makes the problems associated with boomerang kids almost unavoidable, for we are unlikely to see a permanent return to the traditional, extended family.

Nominal and Virtual Families

In the future, we are also likely to see an increase in the number of non-standard "virtual" families, and increased confusion about how these families should be treated, relative to what we are calling "nominal" families. *Nominal families* are those empowered (by law) to care for their members—in particular, for children, older adults, and people with disabilities or severe illnesses. *Virtual families* do the actual work of caring for these family members. To be sure, in many households, virtual families *are* nominal families—that is, the working family unit coincides in structure with the legal definition of family. But as domestic arrangements continue to diversify, family responsibilities are increasingly being taken up by a broad and non-traditional range of caregivers. Virtual families may include grandparents, aunts, uncles, cousins, friends, and even neighbours.

To understand the difference, consider Kay, a 24-year-old university student. Kay lived in Toronto for the last seven years with her younger brother, her mother's mother, Bea, and Bea's second husband, Harold. Kay's younger sister, Jo, lives in a group home in Oshawa; she attends school only sporadically and periodically gets into trouble with the law. Bea has refused to let her come home, because Jo has stolen money from Bea in the past to buy drugs. Kay's estranged mother, a drug addict, lived in Sudbury until last spring, when she died of a drug overdose. Kay has met her father only once, though he lives in Toronto with a wife and young children. Kay is emotionally closest to her grandmother, her sister, and an aunt—her mother's sister—who lives in Ottawa. Kay has recently moved to Montreal, where she will live with a close friend from high school and attend a different university. Question: Who are the members of Kay's "family"? Answer: It's hard to say.

Canadian policy makers tend to think in terms of nominal families. Virtual families, in contrast, reflect the true diversity of our nation's family landscape. Only after we have adequately defined "families" can we study the formation and dissolution of "families." With virtual families, this may mean studying the formation and dissolution of intimate, long-lived support groups or support networks—networks of kin and friends that care for Canada's children, older adults, and people with disabilities or severe illnesses.

How does this notion of nominal versus virtual family connect with shifting patterns of family structure, formation, and dissolution, and what are the policy implications? Take, as an example, the issue of custody rights following divorce. In most jurisdictions, when a couple divorces, only they—as heads of a nominal family—have automatic rights to child custody and access. Yet in Canada's increasingly diverse family landscape, new partners, grandparents, uncles and aunts, friends, older siblings, fictive kin, and others— potential members of a virtual family—may play at least as big a role as one or both biological parents in caring for those children. While current legal and social policies assign to parents the default right to these children, other people who have accepted responsibility for them may be refused rights to custody or access.

The policy challenges, then, are to recognize the limits of traditional legal and social definitions in capturing the modern diversity of family structures; to better document the practical and often inventive networks of caregiving that families create to promote their own well-being; and to ensure that social programs and services are delivered with these realities of Canadian family life in mind.

There are a great many things we need to learn about virtual and nominal families in Canada. For example,

- What is the (empirical) *overlap* between nominal families and virtual families in Canada today? For example, what proportion of families is both nominal and virtual? How does this overlap (or congruence) vary regionally, and by various groupings (age, ethnicity, and so on)? If we don't know, how could we find out (since this pattern identifies the most vulnerable families)?

- *How well do people do* in virtual families, compared with people in nominal families? Are we right to assume that people in well-functioning virtual families (whether or not these families are also nominal) are the happiest and healthiest Canadians? If we don't know, how could we find it out?

- What factors affect the *well-being of people in virtual families*? In particular, are virtual families hampered by not enough income or not enough rights to perform their family-like roles? If we don't know, how could we find it out?

- What factors affect the *formation, maintenance, and dissolution of virtual families*? What factors influence members of these families to continue supporting one another? And, for virtual families, what defines "formation," and what defines "dissolution"? If we don't know, how could we find out?

- How are virtual families—their formation, dissolution, and well-being affected by any of the following *trends*: increases in cohabitation; immigration; poverty and unemployment, especially among the young (for example, boomerang generation); globalization and increased LAT; improved new communications technology for holding family together at a distance; in-home work; young mothers working outside the home; increased longevity; prolonged survival of people with disabilities or severe illness; same-sex union formation; individualization of women's lives? What effects do these trends have on family problems, such as domestic violence? If we don't know, how could we find out?

The Future of Immigrant Families

Previous chapters have noted that Canada faces a future of increased immigration and interaction between cultures from all over the world. Simultaneously, the country will witness further modifications to family forms. According to Bourne and Rose (2001), these are two of the most important transformations already occurring in Canadian society. We can foresee increased diversity in metropolitan areas as well as shifts in social attitudes regarding work and gender relations (Bourne and Rose, 2001: 107). These changes will occur in combination with each other to change both the future of immigrant families and of our country. No doubt, they will affect the variety of family lives in this country.

Diversity Across the Life Cycle

However, immigration is not the only source of increased variety. The trend toward diversity in close relations across the life cycle reveals a clear pattern of individualization of family life. People live longer now than ever before. In the lifetime allotted to each of us, we can—and likely will—live in many kinds of families. This is true even if our family lives are stable and secure. Children grow up and leave home eventually—even if it takes them a longer time to do so! Couples find themselves in different family situations by living year after year. The longer we live, the more family diversity we will face. The life-cycle perspective offers a different view of diversity and one well worth considering, if for no other reason than to promote tolerance of other ways of being close in families.

Policy Challenges

Societies are not especially good at guessing the challenges that will face them in a few years. Growing family inequalities pose a major policy challenge today.

Between 1990 and 2000, the richest 20 percent saw their incomes increase by 10 percent, while incomes remained stagnant for the poorest 20 percent (Statistics Canada, 2005g). The result is increasing family income inequality in Canada, a trend obvious since 1980. Using data from the terminated Survey of Consumer Finances (SCF) and its replacement, the Survey of Labour and Income Dynamics (SLID), Picot and Myles (2004) report a 6 percent increase in the inequality in incomes of Canadian families between 1990 and 2000. That said, income inequality has always been greater in Canada than it is in Europe, though lower than in the United States.

The most recent available statistics, for 2008, show a Gini index (measuring the inequality of family incomes) of 32.1 in Canada compared with 45.0—more than a third higher—in the United States (CIA World Factbook, 2008).

This inequality, of course, is not evenly spread around the population. Statistics Canada reports that a few Canadian groups are especially subject to long-term or persistent economic deprivation: "Persistent low income tends to be concentrated among five groups: single parents, recent immigrants, people with work disabilities, unattached people aged between 45 and 64, and Aboriginal people" (Statistics Canada, 2005g).

Myths and Facts about Internet Use

Older adults are not technologically adept, so they use the internet less often than people in other age groups.

- Individuals in their late 50s and early 60s use the internet for many of the same purposes as individuals in younger age groups. For example, at least 85 percent of internet users in all age groups use the internet for e-mail. Similarly, internet users aged 56 to 65 are as likely as younger users to search for health or government information. In contrast, internet users aged 56 to 65 are less likely than their younger counterparts to use the internet to do their banking, to purchase goods or services, to download music, or to participate in chat groups or on-line discussions. The majority of older users (73 percent) feel that their computer skills meet their current needs (Turcotte and Schellenberg, 2007).

Due to increasing use of e-mails and fax machines, regular mail is being sent less often than in the past, bringing mail delivery to an imminent demise.

- The volume of postal deliveries, both by the public and private sectors, has increased, despite the use of faxes, e-mails, and text messages. Canada Post's mail delivery continues to grow at a steady rate, although at a slower rate than in the 1990s (Sciadas, 2006).

ICTs and ICT-related activities, by replacing previous methods of doing things, can be considered time-saving technologies.

- Overall, ICTs have been found to add to co-tasking and to the loss of distinction between work and play. They also lead to the replacement of other activities for which a learning curve must be climbed. All this adds to a sense of being busier than before (Sciadas, 2006).

For young people, on-line relationships eventually turn into real-life relationships.

- Almost 60 percent of young people pretend to be someone else on-line and 79 percent say that they have never met an on-line acquaintance face-to-face (Moscovitch, 2007).

Traditionally, government support and tax policies have reduced family income inequalities. However, transfer payments did less in the 1990s to mitigate the market effects of income inequality than they did in the 1980s (Frenette, Green and Milligan, n.d.).

Will continuing declines in government support for low-income families further increase inequality? Research evidence suggests that this is a significant problem, not only for low-income families, but for all of society. In pioneering research, Wilkinson (1994) has shown that mortality rates and life expectancies in the industrialized world are more closely related to income inequality than to *per capita* income or *per capita* economic growth. Despite an overall increase in Canadian life expectancies, shorter life expectancies are found in poorer neighborhoods—and the poorer, the shorter (Statistics Canada, 2002k).

McDaniel (1998) shows how meanings given to relative deprivation filter through families. Poor children in wealthy societies feel bad about themselves and often blame their families. This has severe implications for their life chances and potential to contribute to society. Cheal (1996: xv) adds that two factors—the higher risks of being poor while a child and the shortage of government programs for low-income families with children—pose a huge cause for concern about future families. Poor children often grow up to be poor adults or adults whose early deprivation prevents them from catching up on growth, education, skills acquisition, or lost hope.

A second major policy challenge is child care, as discussed earlier. If mothers of young children continue to work for pay in the numbers they currently do, and if "mother work" remains mainly a woman's domain, some solutions to caring for children must be found. In the lengthy public deliberation on the pros and cons of daycare, children are not getting the care they need.

This issue is central to the future of families, since without some solution, couples may have little choice but to restrict their child-bearing even further or forgo parenthood altogether. All society would suffer as a result. Child care is also important to gender equality, since affordable child care makes it easier for women to contribute to society in ways equal to their talents and education.

Family policy challenges are complex and diverse but may be central to the future of families and of us all. We openly admit the centrality of families to our individual lives and happiness and to our collective future and yet we seem reluctant to meet the needs of families in developing creative solutions. Lesemann and Nicol (1994: 124) note that, "It is paradoxical that the family seems simultaneously to be recognized and supported by the government . . . and abandoned by it."

The authors of an analysis of data from the National Longitudinal Survey of Children and Youth (NLSCY) end with a "blueprint for a family-enabling society." The first recommendation is constructive collaboration among all levels of government, parents, teachers, and children themselves to set the conditions for improving outcomes for children. The Early Childhood Development (ECD) Accord between the provinces and the federal government in 2000 identified four areas of co-operation: promoting healthy pregnancy, birth and infancy; improving parenting and family supports; strengthening early childhood development, learning and care; and strengthening community supports.

The second is investment in human capital, based on lifelong learning. To achieve this, we need seamless and universal support for families, from conception to kindergarten. Older children, strongly influenced by classroom and school environments, need continuing educational and social supports to stay in school.

The third is social inclusion. Successful communities bolster outcomes for their least advantaged children. Finally, we need an increased capacity for program evaluation, overseeing, and research. We need to examine policies to see if they are making the intended difference.

The United Nations Convention on the Rights of the Child was confirmed by Canada in 1991. Respect for children is implicit in the research collected and in the conclusions of the NLSCY study. However, respect for children must be put into practice to build a family-enabling society and to have positive results for vulnerable children. Children must be viewed as having inherent rights as human beings. They must also be seen as individuals with a growing need for autonomy.

CONCLUDING REMARKS

Two views of history are directly useful for our glimpse into the future of families. First, there is the image of the present as the peak of progress; according to this view, the future advances in the same direction. A contrasting view, equally prevalent, is that we used to have, or be, something wonderful, but with time what was good slipped away and was replaced by a society with fewer clear values, more social problems, less stability, and less certainty.

We consider both views simplistic. We end this book with a call for modest optimism about the future of the family. In all likelihood, the future holds new and unforeseen problems that will challenge many families and their members—in addition to all the problems we can already expect.

So far, no one has found a technological fix for the kinds of organizational, interpersonal, and emotional problems that normally arise in ordinary family life—indeed, in all close relations. We do not foresee an easy solution to the problems of family life through genetic engineering, artificial intelligence, faster computers, smarter houses, better electrical appliances, or little white pills that can satisfy our human needs for love, meaning, belonging, attachment, and communication. However, families themselves will continue to largely meet these needs. And through continuing study we can hope to learn more about how healthy families work and how to help other families do the same.

CHAPTER SUMMARY

In this chapter, we mull over the future of close relations, beginning with a clear understanding that social prediction is far from a perfect science or art. Contesting visions of families in the future are considered.

We begin with an examination of the new communication technologies, virtual communities, and the role of families in the "connected society." We note that new technologies increase the reach of family life, instead of limiting it, as critics had feared. While it is difficult to predict the likely effects of cyberspace on family life, we note that two major communication technologies—telephone and e-mail—did not transform family life as drastically as people had expected. On the contrary, they allowed people to pursue their most cherished goals more efficiently.

The new communication technology poses problems with sexuality, specifically cybersex and the potential for on-line infidelity. Mating and dating on-line create new ethical issues and may force families to rethink what they mean by commitment in the face of extended sexual opportunities. The same technology that extends the reach of mating and dating also extends the reach of caregiving. So, just as technology lures people away from their families, it also allows them to pay closer attention to their family members' needs, if they wish.

The way technology will be used, and will affect society, depends on people's wishes and values. The new reproductive technologies also show the importance of human agency. Though these new technologies offer new opportunities and new ethical challenges, they are being used to further traditional pro-natalist agendas.

The most dramatic future changes to family life are extensions of a change that has been in process for centuries: the individualization of family life. More families are rethinking spousal and parental roles and shifting away from uniform corporate family structures to a wide variety of collected, concatenated, and cyclical family structures.

We have noted various trends in this chapter; for example, families continue to get smaller, children experience more transitions as parents change their marital status, family violence continues to be under-reported, multiple-earner families have become the norm, socio-economic inequality between families is worsening, and the future will have more aging families.

Dual-income families will continue to be important carriers of family change. In years to come, life with children and two incomes will continue to challenge both work and family for both men and women.

Family nests can refill readily when adult children bring their own children and possibly spouses back to the family home. The increase in boomerang families will place new demands on parents and children alike. In short, the longer we live, the more family diversity we will face.

Growing family inequalities pose a major policy challenge today. In the past 20 years, income inequalities have widened in Canada. The concern for the future is whether continuing declines in government support for low-income families will further increase family inequality in Canada. Family policy challenges are complex and diverse and their solution may be central to the future of families and of us all.

Key Terms

collected family A structure that requires family members to conform to traditional notions of husband, wife, father, mother, and child. However, given the complexities of remarriage, family members concede the impossibility of compelling mates to be both good spouses *and* good parents to the resident children.

concatenated family A family exactly opposite to the corporate family, characterized by separable roles and unique performers. The concatenated family is nothing more than a household at a particular moment in time.

corporate family A family in which people can come and go without changing the essential structure of the family. The husband serves as father to the younger generation in the household—children, apprentices and household servants—and the wife serves as mother, whoever the natural parents of these children may be.

cyclical (or recycled) family A family form featuring traditional (inseparable) roles, but no role interchangeability. Instead, the performances of its members are unique. Each is a "return engagement" occurring *because of* the unique relationship of the members.

other-mothering Close parental-type care by extended relations or friends.

personal interchangeability Choosing a spouse based on his or her ability to fill certain roles rather than for the individual's unique characteristics.

refilled nests Family homes to which adult children have returned, possibly bringing their own children and/or spouses.

role separability The separation of being a spouse from being a parent.

Critical Thinking Questions

1. The internet is a crucial part of children's social environment because it allows them to connect with friends, explore social roles, learn about their interests, and express themselves. Discuss.

2. Now that wireless technology makes it possible for us to always be reached and able to reach others, there's a growing expectation that this should be a right. What is the impact of always being connected to the world via one electronic medium or another on intimacy, with one's self or others?

3. Currently, in the workplace, at school, and even at home, people use e-mail and various other technologies to connect with people who may be at a desk next to theirs. In your opinion, is there a difference in using ICTs to maintain relations with people who are at a distance compared to people with whom we share a close environment?

4. Consider two stereotypes: firstly, that older adults don't do computers—and certainly not the internet—and, secondly, that older adults don't do sex—they are asexual. How do these stereotypes influence research and hence knowledge about computer-mediated

communication, the formation and maintenance of internet relationships, as well as the nature of on-line romantic relationships for older adults?

5. How do computer-mediated relationships (CMRs) compare to face-to-face relationships in terms of intimacy and gender roles? Are the dating scripts different for CMRs, in your opinion?

6. The feminization of labour has had and continues to have profound effects on the family dynamic. The percentage of women in the labour force in Canada rose from 33 percent in 1971 to more than 50 percent in 2008, and of this number, 69 percent are mothers with a child younger than three years old. What are some possible solutions for these women to balance work–family conflict, without risking a return to traditional family forms?

7. Why does one have to keep in mind the distinction between nominal versus virtual family and what are the policy implications?

8. Discuss the changes you think will happen to family life in the future.

Weblinks

Online Dating
www.onlinedating.org
This site provides reviews of different dating sites based on a number of criteria, including user base, user profile characteristics, reviews from other users, and fees.

Center for Genetics and Society: Assisted Reproduction
www.geneticsandsociety.org
The Center for Genetics and Society: Assisted Reproduction is a non-profit information and public affairs organization that endorses responsible uses and effective societal governance of the new human genetic and reproductive technologies. This site provides background information about

emerging reproductive technologies, and issues and policies surrounding them.

Center for Internet Addiction Recovery
www.netaddiction.com
This site provides information about internet addiction, including compulsive surfing, on-line affairs, and cybersex addiction. It also offers self-tests and treatment resources.

Caring Connections
www.caringinfo.org
This site is based on a national consumer and community engagement initiative to improve care at the end of life. It provides free resources and information to help people make decisions about end-of-life care and services before a crisis.

References

Abad, Neetu S., & Kennon M. Sheldon. 2008. Parental autonomy support and ethnic culture identification among second-generation immigrants. *Journal of Family Psychology* 22: 652–657.

Abbott, Douglas A., & Glenna Slater. 2000 Spring. Strengths and stresses of Omaha Indian families living on the reservation. *Great Plains Research* 10(1): 145–168.

Abe, Namiko. 2005. Getting married in Japan. *Japanese Language*. Retrieved November 4, 2005, from **http://japanese.about.com/library/weekly/aa080999.htm**.

Abu-Laban, Sharon McIrvin, & Susan A. McDaniel. 1998. Beauty, status and aging, pp. 78, 102. In Nancy Mandell (Ed.), *Feminist Issues: Race, Class and Sexuality* (2nd edition). Scarborough, ON: Prentice-Hall Allyn and Bacon.

Abu-Laban, Sharon, & Susan A. McDaniel. 2004. Aging women and standards of beauty. In Nancy Mandell (Ed.), *Feminist Issues: Race, Class and Sexuality* (4th edition). Toronto: Prentice-Hall.

Ackerman, Marc J. 1996. *Does Wednesday Mean Mom's House or Dad's? Parenting Together While Living Apart*. Toronto: Wiley & Sons.

Adams, Rebecca G. 1998. The demise of territorial determinism: Online friendships, pp. 153–162. In Rebecca G. Adams and Graham Allan (Eds.), *Placing Friendship in Context*. UK: Cambridge University Press.

Adams, Rebecca G., & Michelle Stevenson. 2002. A lifetime of relationships mediated by technology. In F. Lang and K.L. Fingerman (Eds.), *Growing Together: Personal Relationships Across the Lifespan*. New York: Cambridge University Press.

Aguilar, Rudy J., & Narina Nunez Nightingale. 1994 March. The impact of specific battering experiences on the self-esteem of abused women. *Journal of Family Violence* 9: 35–45.

Ahmad, Farah, Angela Shik, Reena Vanza, Angela M. Cheung, Usha George, & Donna E. Stewart. 2004. Voices of South Asian women: Immigration and mental health. *Women and Health* 40(4): 113–130.

Ahmadi, Khodabakhsh, & Fateme Hossein-abadi. 2009. Religiosity, marital satisfaction and child rearing. *Pastoral Psychology* 57: 211–21.

Ahrons, Constance R., & Jennifer L. Tanner. 2003. Adult children and their fathers: Relationship changes 20 years after parental divorce. *Family Relations* 52(4): 340–351.

Aida, Yukie, & Toni Falbo. 1991. Relationships between marital satisfaction, resources, and power strategies. *Sex Roles* 24(1–2): 43–56.

Alberta Justice. 2002. Alberta's Adult Interdependent Relationship Act and you. Retrieved August 5, 2005, from **www.justice.gov.ab.ca/home/default.aspx?id=3550**.

Alexander, Christopher. 1997. Factors contributing to the termination of long-term gay male relationships. *Journal of Gay & Lesbian Social Services* 7(1): 1–12.

Al-Krenawi, A., V. Slonim-Nevo, Y. Maymon, & S. Al-Krenawi. 2001. Psychological responses to blood vengeance about Arab adolescents. *Child Abuse & Neglect* 25(4).

Amato, Paul R. 1996 August. Explaining the intergenerational transmission of divorce. *Journal of Marriage and the Family* 58.

Amato, Paul R., & Alan Booth. 1996 May. A prospective study of divorce and parent–child relationships. *Journal of Marriage and the Family* 58: 356–365.

Amato, Paul R., & J.M. Sobolewski. 2001. The effects of divorce and marital discord on adult children's psychological well-being. *American Sociological Review* 66: 900–921.

Amato, Paul R., David R. Johnson, Alan Booth, & Stacy J. Rogers. 2003. Continuity and change in marital quality between 1980 and 2000. *Journal of Marriage and the Family* 65: 1–22.

Amato, Paul R., Laura Spencer Loomis, & Alan Booth. 1995. Parental divorce, marital conflict and offspring well-being during early adulthood. *Social Forces* 73(3): 895–915.

Ambert, Anne-Marie. 2002. Divorce: Facts, causes, and consequences. Ottawa: Vanier Institute of the Family.

Ambert, Anne-Marie. 2005a. Cohabitation and marriage: How are they related? Ottawa: Vanier Institute of the Family. Retrieved November 15, 2005, from **www.vifamily.ca/library/cft/cohabitation.html**.

Ambert, Anne-Marie. 2005b. Divorce: Facts, causes and consequences. Ottawa: Vanier Institute of the Family. Retrieved December 9, 2005, from **www.vifamily.ca/library/cft/divorce_05.html**.

Ambert, Anne-Marie. 2005c. Same-sex couples and same-sex-parent families: Relationships, parenting, and issues of marriage. Ottawa: Vanier Institute of the Family. Retrieved January 10, 2006, from **http://www.vifamily.ca/library/cft/samesex_05.html#FAMILIES**.

Ammar, Nawal H. 2007. Wife battery in Islam: A comprehensive understanding of interpretations. *Violence Against Women* 13: 516–26.

Amnesty International. 2004, June 2. Turkey: Women confronting family violence. Retrieved July 14, 2005, from **http://web.amnesty.org/library/Index/ENGEUR440132004?open&of=ENG-TUR**.

Amnesty International UK (n.d.). A global outrage: Global and UK statistics. Retrieved July 14, 2005, from **www.amnesty.org.uk/svaw/vaw/global.shtml**.

Andersson, B.E. 1996. Children's development related to day-care, type of family and other home factors. *European Child & Adolescent Psychiatry* 5, supplement 1, 73–75.

Andersson, Gunnar. 2004. Childbearing after migration: Fertility patterns of foreign-born women in Sweden. *International Migration Review* 38: 747–75.

Angus Reid Group. 1999. *Family Matters: A Look at Issues Concerning Families and Raising Children in Canada Today.* Toronto: Angus Reid Group.

Anstorp, Trine, & Kirsten Benum. 1988. Social network stimulation as preventive method among middle-aged women in a neighborhood in Oslo. *International Journal of Family Psychiatry* 6(2): 177–187.

Anthony, E.J. 1970. The impact of mental and physical illness on family life. *American Journal of Psychiatry* 127: 138–145.

Antill, John K., & Sandra Cotton. 1987. Self disclosure between husbands and wives: Its relation to sex roles and marital happiness. *Australian Journal of Psychology* 39(1): 11–24.

Antonucci, T., & Akiyama, A. 1995. Convoys of social relationships: Family and friendships within a life span context, pp. 355–371. In R. Blieszner & V.H. Bedford (Eds.), *Handbook of Aging and the Family* (4th edition). Westport, CT: Greenwood Press.

Applbaum, Kalman. 1995 Winter. Marriage with the proper stranger: Arranged marriages in metropolitan Japan, *Ethnology* 34: 37–51.

Apple, R.D., & J. Coleman. 2003. As members of the social whole: A history of social reform as a focus of home economics, 1895–1910. *Family and Consumer Sciences Research Journal*, 32(2): 104–126.

Applewhite, Larry W., & David R. Segal. 1990 Fall. Telephone use by peacekeeping troops in the Sinai. *Armed Forces and Society* 17(1): 117–126.

Arditti, Joyce A. 1997. Women, divorce, and economic risk. *Family and Conciliation Courts Review* 35(1).

Arendell, Terry J. 1995. *Fathers in Divorce: Best Case Scenarios.* American Sociological Association.

Ariss, Rachel. 2007. Intimacy, commitment, and family formation, pp. 44–63. In David Cheal (Ed.), *Canadian Families Today: New Perspectives.* Toronto: Oxford University Press.

Armitage, Susan H. 1979 April. Household work and childrearing on the frontier: The oral history record. *Sociology and Social Research* 63(3): 467–474.

Armstrong, Pat, & Hugh Armstrong. 1985 Summer. Political economy and the household: Rejecting separate spheres. *Studies in Political Economy* 17: 167–177.

Armstrong, Pat, & Hugh Armstrong. 1994. *The Double Ghetto: Canadian Women and Their Segregated Work* (3rd edition). Toronto: McClelland & Stewart.

Aseltine, Robert H. Jr. 1996 June. Pathways linking parental divorce with adolescent depression. *Journal of Health and Social Behavior* 37.

Askham, J., Ferring, D., & Lamura, G. 2007. Personal relationships in later life, pp. 186–208. In J. Bond, S. Peace, F. Dittmann-Kohli, and G.J. Westerhof (Eds.), *Ageing in Society.* Sage, London.

Ataca, B., & J.W. Berry. 2002. Psychological, sociocultural and martial adaptation of Turkish immigrant couples in Canada. *International Journal of Psychology* 37: 13–26.

Attree, Pamela. 2005. Parenting support in the context of poverty: A meta-synthesis of the qualitative evidence. *Health & Social Care in the Community* 13(4): 330–337.

Avison, William R., Jennifer Ali, & David Walters. 2007. Family structure, stress, and psychological distress: A demonstration of the impact of differential exposure. *Journal of Health and Social Behavior* 48(3): 301–317.

Axinn, William G., & Arland Thornton. 1993. Mothers, children, and cohabitation: The intergenerational effects of attitudes and behavior. *American Sociological Review* 58(2): 233–246.

Ayyub, Ruksana. 2000. Domestic violence in the South Asian Muslim immigrant population in the United States. *Journal of Social Distress & the Homeless* 9: 237–48.

Baines, C.T., P.M. Evans, & S.M. Neysmith. 1998. Women's caring: Work expanding, state contracting, pp. 3–22. In C.T. Baines, P.M. Evans, & S.M. Neysmith (Eds.), *Feminist Perspectives on Social Welfare.* Oxford University Press, Toronto.

Baker, Maureen, & Donna Lero. 1996. Division of labour: Paid work and family structure, pp. 78–103. In Maureen Baker (Ed.), *Families: Changing Trends in Canada* (3rd edition). Toronto: McGraw-Hill Ryerson.

Baker, Maureen. 1995. *Canadian Family Policies: Cross-National Comparisons.* Toronto: University of Toronto Press.

Baker, Maureen. 1996. Introduction to family studies: Cultural variations and family trends, pp. 3–34. In Maureen Baker (Ed.), *Families: Changing Trends in Canada* (3rd edition). Toronto: McGraw-Hill Ryerson.

Baker, Maureen. 2001. *Families: Labour and Love, Family Diversity in a Changing World.* Vancouver: University of British Columbia Press.

Baker, Maureen. 2002. *Medically Assisted Fertility, Gender and the Future of Family Life.* International Sociology Association Paper, Brisbane, July 7–13, 2001.

Baker, Maureen. 2005a. Definitions, cultural variations and demographic trends. In Maureen Baker (Ed.), *Families: Changing Trends in Canada* (5th edition). Toronto: McGraw-Hill Ryerson.

Baker, Maureen. 2005b. Families, the state and family policies, pp. 259–276. In Maureen Baker (Ed.), *Families: Changing Trends in Canada* (5th edition). Toronto: McGraw-Hill Ryerson.

Balakrishnan, T.R., Evelyne Lapierre-Adamcyk, & Karol J. Krotki. 1993. *Family and Childbearing in Canada: A Demographic Analysis.* Toronto: University of Toronto Press.

Barbeau, Carole. 2001. Work-related child-care centres in Canada—2001. Retrieved May 22, 2005, from Human Resources Development Canada Labour Program: **www.hrsdc.gc.ca/en/lp/spila/wlb/pdf/child_care_en.pdf**.

Barer, M.L., R.G. Evans, & C. Hertzman. 1995. Avalanche or glacier? Health care and demographic rhetoric. *Canadian Journal on Aging* 14(2): 193–224.

Barette, J. 2009. Work/family balance: What do we really know? *Contemporary Family Trends.* Ottawa: Vanier Institute of the Family. Retrieved June 11, 2009, from **www.vifamily.ca/library/cft/barrette/work_family_balance.pdf**.

Barnett, Karen, Laurie Buys, Jan Lovie-Kitchin, Gillian Boulton-Lewis, Dianne Smith, & Maree Heffernan. 2007. Older women's fears of violence: The need for interventions that enable active ageing. *Journal of Women & Aging* 19(3–4): 179–193.

Barnett, Mark A., Steven W. Quackenbush, & Christina S. Sinisi. 1996. Factors affecting children's, adolescents', and young adults' perceptions of parental discipline. *Journal of Genetic Psychology* 157(4): 411–424.

Barnett, Ola W., Tomas E. Martinez, & Mae Keyson. 1996 June. The relationship between violence, social support, and self-blame in battered women. *Journal of Interpersonal Violence* 11: 221–233.

Barraket, Jo, & Millsom S. Henry-waring. 2008. Getting it on(line): Sociological perspectives on e-dating. *Journal of Sociology* 44: 149–65.

Barrett, Anne E., & R. Jay Turner. 2005. Family structure and mental health: The mediating effects of socioeconomic status, family process, and social stress. *Journal of Health and Social Behavior* 46(2): 156–169.

Barrett, Michele, & Mary McIntosh. 1980. *The Anti-Social Family*. London: Verso.

Basavarajappa, K.G. 1998. Living arrangements and residential overcrowding among older immigrants in Canada. *Asian Pacific Migration Journal* 7(4): 409–432.

Bassuk, Ellen, Ree Dawson, & Nicholas Huntington. 2006. Intimate partner violence in extremely poor women: Longitudinal patterns and risk markers. *Journal of Family Violence* 21(6): 387–399.

Bastida, Elena. 2001. Kinship ties of Mexican migrant women on the United States/Mexico border. *Journal of Comparative Family Studies* 32: 549–69.

Beauchamp, N., A.B. Irvine, J. Seeley, & B. Johnson. 2005. Worksite-based internet multimedia program for family caregivers of persons with dementia. *The Gerontologist* 45(6): 793–801.

Beaujot, Rod. 2000. *Earning and Caring in Canadian Families*. Peterborough, Ontario: Broadview Press.

Beaujot, Roderic, & Zenaida Ravanera. 2008. Family change and implications for family solidarity and social cohesion. *Canadian Studies in Population* 35(1): 73–101.

Beaupre, Pascale, Pierre Turcotte, & Anne Milan. 2006a. When is junior moving out? Transitions from the parental home to independence. *Canadian Social Trends*. Ottawa: Statistics Canada. Catalogue no. 11-008: 9–15.

Beaupre, Pascale, Pierre Turcotte, & Anne Milan. 2006b. Junior comes back home: Trends and predictors of returning to the parental home. *Canadian Social Trends*. Ottawa: Statistics Canada. Catalogue no. 11-008: 28–34.

Beaupre, Pascale. 2008. I do . . . Take two? Changes in intentions to remarry among divorced Canadians during the past 20 years. *The General Social Survey: Matter of Fact no. 5*. Ottawa: Statistics Canada. Catalogue no. 89-630-X.

Beck-Gernsheim, Elisabeth. 1983. From living for others to a life of one's own: Structural changes in women's lives. *Soziale Welt* 34(3): 307–340.

Beeby, Dean. 2006. End polygamy ban, report urges Ottawa. *Globe and Mail*, January 13. Retrieved January 14, 2006, from **www.theglobeandmail.com/servlet/Article=News/TPStory/LAC/20060113/POLYGAMY13/TPNational/?query=polygamy**.

Behnke, Andrew O., Brent A. Taylor, & Taylor Ruben Parra-Cardona. 2008. I hardly understand English, but . . . : Mexican origin fathers describe their commitment as fathers despite the challenges of immigration. *Journal of Comparative Family Studies* 39: 187–205.

Belgrave, Faye Z., Barbara Van Oss Marin, & Donald B. Chambers. 2000. Cultural, contextual, and interpersonal predictors of risky sexual attitudes among urban African American girls in early adolescence. *Cultural Diversity & Ethnic Minority Psychology* 6(3): 309–322.

Bell, David. 2000. Farm boys and wild men: Rurality, masculinity, and homosexuality. *Rural Sociology* 65(4): 547–561.

Belsky, J., S. Woodworth, & K. Crnic. 1996. Troubled family interaction during toddlerhood. *Development and Psychopathology* 8: 477–495.

Benjamin, W., Ann C. Crouter, Stephanie T. Lanza., & Martha J. Cox. 2008. Paternal work characteristics and father-infant interactions in low-income, rural families. *Journal of Marriage and Family* 70(3): 640–653.

Bennett, Neil G., Ann K. Blanc, & David E. Bloom. 1988. Commitment and the modern union: Assessing the link between premarital cohabitation and subsequent marital stability. *American Sociological Review* 53: 127–138.

Bennun, Ian. 1997. Systemic marital therapy with one partner: A reconsideration of theory, research and practice. *Sexual and Marital Therapy* 12(1).

Berger, R.M. 1990. Passing: The impact on the quality of same-sex couple relationships. *Social Work* 35: 328–332.

Berger, Roni. 2000. When remarriage and immigration coincide: The experience of Russian immigrant stepfamilies. *Journal of Ethnic & Cultural Diversity in Social Work* 9: 75–96.

Bergin, B. 1995. *Elder Abuse in Ethnocultural Communities: An Exploratory Study with Suggestions for Intervention and Prevention*. Ottawa, ON: Canadian Association of Social Workers.

Bernard, Jessie. 1973. *The Future of Marriage*. New York: Bantam.

Bernard, R., & Petipas J. 2008. Rediscovering the family meal. *Contemporary Family Trends*. Ottawa: Vanier Institute of the Family. Retrieved June 12, 2009, from **www.vifamily.ca/library/cft/food/food_eng.pdf**.

Bersamin, M.M, D.A. Fisher, S. Walker, D.L. Hill, & J.W. Grube. 2007. Defining virginity and abstinence: Adolescents' interpretations of sexual behaviours. *Journal of Adolescent Health* 41: 182–188.

Betts Adams, K. 2006. The transition to caregiving: The experience of family members embarking on the dementia caregiving career. *Journal of Gerontological Social Work*, 47(3/4): 3–29.

Beyer, Sylvia. 1995. Maternal employment and children's academic achievement: Parenting styles as mediating variable. *Developmental Review* 15(2): 212–253.

Bianchi, S.M., & L.M. Casper. 2000. American families. *Population Bulletin: Washington* 55(Part 4).

Bibby, Reginald. 2001. Canada's teens: A national reading on family life. *Transition Magazine* 31(3). Ottawa: Vanier Institute of the Family. Retrieved August 15, 2002, from **www.vifamily.ca**.

Bibby, Reginald. 2004. *The Future Families Project: A Survey of Canadian Hopes and Dreams*. Ottawa: Vanier Institute of the Family. Retrieved from **www.vifamily.ca/library/future/future_toc.html**.

Biggs, Simon, Chris Phillipson, & Paul Kingston. 1995. *Elder Abuse in Perspective*. Taylor & Francis.

BioPortfolio. 2006. Retrieved from **www.bioportfolio.com/cgi-bin/acatalog/info_996.html**.

Bird, Chloe E., & Michelle Rogers. 1998. *Parenting and Depression: The Impact of the Division of Labor within Couples and Perceptions of Equity*. Society for the Study of Social Problems (SSSP).

Birenbaum-Carmeli, Daphna. 1998. Reproductive partners: Doctor-woman relations in Israeli and Canadian IVF contexts, pp. 75–92. In Nancy Scheper-Hughes and Carolyn Sargent (Eds.), *Small Mall Wars: The Cultural Politics of Childhood*. Berkeley: University of California Press.

Birman, Dina, & Tina Taylor-Ritzler. 2007. Acculturation and psychological distress among adolescent immigrants from the former soviet union: Exploring the mediating effect of family relationships. *Cultural Diversity & Ethnic Minority Psychology* 13: 337–46.

Blackmon, Amy Dixon. 2000. Empathy in marriage: Implications for marital satisfaction and depression. *Dissertation Abstracts International: Section B: The Sciences and Engineering* 61(5-B), 2746.

Blanchet, T. Bangladesh girls sold as wives in north India. 2005. *Indian Journal of Gender Studies* 12: 305–44.

Blando, J.A. 2001. Twice hidden: Older gay and lesbian couples, friends, and intimacy. *Generations* 25(2): 87–89.

Boies, S.C. 2002. University students' uses of and reactions to online sexual information and entertainment: Links to online and offline sexual behaviour. *Canadian Journal of Human Sexuality* 11: 77–89.

Bolovan, I., & S.P. Bolovan. 2008. From tradition to modernization: Church and the Transylvanian Romanian family in the modern era. *Journal for the Study of Religions and Ideologies* 7: 107–33.

Boney-McCoy, Sue, & David Finkelhor. 1996 December. Is youth victimization related to trauma symptoms and depression after controlling for prior symptoms and family relationships? A longitudinal, prospective study. *Journal of Consulting and Clinical Psychology* 64: 1406–1416.

Borell, Klas, & Sofie Ghazanfareeon Karlsson. 2002. Reconceptualising intimacy and ageing: Living apart together. Paper presented at International Symposium, *Reconceptualising Gender and Ageing*, Centre for Research on Ageing and Gender, University of Surrey, 25–27 June.

Bourne, Larry S., & Damaris Rose. 2001. The changing face of Canada: The uneven geographies of population and social change. *The Canadian Geographer* 45 (2001): 105–19.

Boushey, H. 2009. Infographic: The importance of women breadwinners. Washington, D.C.: Center for American Progress. Retrieved June 11, 2009, from **www.americanprogress.org/issues/2009/04/women_breadwinners.html**.

Bowers, C.A, Miguel Vasquez, & Mary Roaf. 2000. Native people and the challenge of computers: Reservation schools, individualism and consumerism. *American Indian Quarterly* 24(2): 182–199.

Bowlby, J. 1969. *Attachment and Loss: Vol. 1. Attachment*. New York: Basic Books.

Boyce, Cheryl A., & Andrew J. Fuligni. 2007. Issues for developmental research among racial/ethnic minority and immigrant families. *Research in Human Development. Special Issue: Social context, cultural processes and mental health across the life span among ethnically diverse populations* 4: 1–17.

Boyce, William, Maryanne Doherty, Christian Fortin, & David MacKinnon. 2003. Canadian youth, sexual health and HIV/AIDS study: Factors influencing knowledge, attitudes and behaviours. Ottawa: Council of Ministers of Education, Canada. Retrieved November 4, 2004, from **www.cmec.ca/publications/aids/CYSHIAS_2002_EN.pdf**.

Boyd, Monica, & Anne Li. 2003. May–December: Canadians in age-discrepant relationships. *Canadian Social Trends* 70: 29–33.

Boyd, Monica, & Edward T. Pryor. 1989. The cluttered nest: The living arrangements of young adult Canadians. *Canadian Journal of Sociology* 14(4): 461–477.

Boyd, Monica, & Elizabeth Grieco. 2003. Women and migration: Incorporating gender into international migration theory. Retrieved September 12, 2008, from **www.migrationinformation.org/issues_mar03.cfm**.

Bradbury, Bettina. 1984. Pigs, cows and boarders: Non-wage forms of survival among Montreal families, 1861–1891. *Labour/Le Travail* 14: 9–46.

Bradbury, Bettina. 2001. Social, economic, and cultural origins of contemporary families, pp. 69–95. In Maureen Baker (Ed.), *Families: Changing Trends in Canada* (4th edition). Toronto: McGraw-Hill Ryerson.

Brannen, Stephen J., & Allen Rubin. 1996. Comparing the effectiveness of gender-specific and couples groups in a court-mandated spouse abuse treatment program. *Research on Social Work Practice* 6(4): 405–424.

Brinkerhoff, Merlin B., & Eugen Lupri. 1988. Interspousal violence. *Canadian Journal of Sociology* 13(4): 407–434.

Brison, Robert J., William Pickett, Richard L. Berg, James Linneman, Jamie Zentner, & Barbara Marlenga. 2006. Fatal agricultural injuries in preschool children: Risks, injury patterns and strategies for prevention. *Canadian Medical Association Journal* 174(12): 1723–1726.

Bronstein, Phyllis, Paula Duncan, & Adele D'Ari. 1996 October. Family and parenting behaviors predicting middle school adjustment: A longitudinal study. *Family Relations* 45: 415–426.

Bronte-Tinkew, Jacinta, Kristin A. Moore, Randolph C. Capps, & Jonathan Zaff. 2006. The influence of father involvement on youth risk behaviors among adolescents: A comparison of native-born and immigrant families. *Social Science Research* 35: 181–209.

Brotman, S. 1998. The incidence of poverty among seniors in Canada: Exploring the impact of gender, ethnicity and race. *Canadian Journal on Aging* 17(2): 166–185.

Broude, Gwen J. 1996 Fall. The realities of daycare. *Public Interest* 125: 95–105.

Brown, S.L., J.R. Bulanda, & G.R. Lee. 2005. The significance of nonmarital cohabitation: Marital status and mental health benefits among middle-aged and older adults. *The Journal of Gerontology: Social Sciences* 60B: S21–S29.

Brown, Jennifer S.H. 1980. *Strangers in Blood: Fur Trade Company Families in Indian Country*. Vancouver: University of British Columbia Press.

Brown, Jennifer S.H., 1992. A Cree nurse in the cradle of Methodism: Little Mary and the Egerton R. Young family at Norway House and Berens River, pp. 93–110. In Bettina Bradbury (Ed.), *Canadian Family History: Selected Readings*. Toronto: Copp Clark Pitman.

Brown, Phillip, & Hugh Lauder. 2001. *Capitalism and Social Progress: The Future of Society in a Global Economy*, pp. xvi, 338. Basingstoke, Hampshire; New York: Palgrave.

Brown, Susan L. 2004. Moving from cohabitation to marriage: Effects on relationship quality. *Social Science Research 33*: 1–19.

Brownridge, Douglas A. 2008. Understanding the elevated risk of partner violence against Aboriginal women: A comparison of two nationally representative surveys in Canada. *Journal of Family Violence 23*: 353–367.

Brownridge, Douglas A., & Shiva S. Halli. 2002. Understanding male partner violence against cohabiting and married women: An empirical investigation with a synthesized model. *Journal of Family Violence 17*(4): 341–361.

Bruhn, J.G. 1977. Effects of chronic illness on the family. *Journal of Family Practice 4*: 1057–1067.

Brumer, Anita. 2008. Gender relations in family-farm agriculture and rural-urban migration in Brazil. *Latin American Perspectives 35*: 11–28.

Bryant, H.D., A. Billingsley, & G.A. Kerry. 1963. Physical abuse of children: An agency study. *Child Welfare 42*: 125–130.

Brym, Robert J., & Rhonda L. Lenton. 2001. *Love Online: A Report on Digital Dating in Canada*. www.msn.ca. Retrieved June 14, 2009, from **www.nelson.com/nelson/harcourt/sociology/newsociety3e/loveonline.pdf**.

Bucher, Julia A., Peter S. Houts, Arthur M. Nezu, & Christine Maguth Nezu. 1996 January. The prepared family caregiver: A problem-solving approach to family caregiver education. *Patient Education & Counseling 27*(1), 63–73.

Buddington, Steve A. 2002. Acculturation, psychological adjustment (stress, depression, self-Esteem) and the academic achievement of Jamaican immigrant college students. *International Social Work 45*: 447–64.

Bui, Hoan N., & Merry Morash. 2007. Social capital, human capital, and reaching out for help with domestic violence: A case study of women in a Vietnamese-American community. *Criminal Justice Studies: A Critical Journal of Crime, Law and Society 20*: 375–90.

Buki, Lydia P., Tsung-Chieh Ma, Robert D. Strom, & Shirley K. Strom. 2003. Chinese immigrant mothers of adolescents: Self-perceptions of acculturation effects on parenting. *Cultural Diversity & Ethnic Minority Psychology 9*: 127–40.

Bumpass, Larry, & Hsien-Hen Lu. 2000. Trends in cohabitation and implications for children's family contexts in the United States. *Population Studies 54*(1): 29–41.

Bumpus, Matthew F., Ann C. Crouter, & Susan M. McHale. 1999 May. Work demands of dual-earner couples: Implications for parents' knowledge about children's daily lives in middle childhood. *Marriage and the Family 61*(2): 465–475.

Bumpus, Matthew Franklin. 2001 February. Mechanisms linking work-to-family spillover and parents' knowledge of their children's daily lives. *Dissertation Abstracts International, A: The Humanities and Social Sciences 61*(8), 3368–A.

Burholt Vanessa, & Clare G. Wenger. 1998 September. Differences over time in older people's relationships with children and siblings. *Ageing and Society 18*(5): 537–562.

Busby, Dean M. 1991. Violence in the family, pp. 335–385. In Stephen J. Bahr (Ed.), *Family Research: A Sixty-Year Review, 1930–1990, Volume 1*. New York: Lexington Books, Maxwell Macmillan International.

Byrne, R., and Findlay, B. 2004. Preference for SMS versus telephone calls in initiating romantic relationships. *Australian Journal of Emerging Technologies and Society 2*(1): 48–61.

Caldwell, John C., P.H. Reddy, & Pat Caldwell. 1984. The determinants of family structure in rural south India. *Journal of Marriage and the Family 46*(1): 215–229.

Calliste, Agnes. 2001. Black families in Canada: Exploring the interconnections of race, class and gender, pp. 401–419. In Bonnie J. Fox (Ed.) *Family Patterns, Gender Relations* (2nd edition). Toronto: Oxford University Press.

Campbell, Jacquelyn C., Paul Miller, & Mary M. Cardwell. 1994 June. Relationship status of battered women over time. *Journal of Family Violence 9*: 99–111.

Campbell, Rebecca, Cris Sullivan, & William S. Davidson. 1995 June. Women who use domestic violence shelters: Changes in depression over time. *Psychology of Women Quarterly 19*: 237–255.

Canada, Department of Justice. 2003. *Abuse Is Wrong in Any Language*. Ottawa: Dept of Justice Canada. Catalogue no. J2-131/1995E.

Canada, Department of Justice. 2005a. Dating violence: A fact sheet from the Department of Justice Canada. Family Violence. Retrieved November 4, 2005, from **http://canada.justice.gc.ca/en/ps/fm/datingfs.html#head2**.

Canada, Department of Justice. 2005b. Civil marriage and the legal recognition of same-sex unions. Retrieved January 13, 2006, from **www.canada.justice.gc.ca/en/fs/ssm/index.html**.

Canada, Department of National Defence. 2006. Retrieved February 25, 2006, from **www.forces.gc.ca/site/operations/current_ops_e.asp**.

Canadian Centre for Policy Alternatives. 2004. Medicare still on life support: Health care accord flawed by poor accountability and enforcement. Retrieved April 18, 2006, from **www.policyalternatives.ca/index.cfm?act=news&do=Article&call=983&pA=BB736455**.

Canadian Feminist Alliance for International Action. 2005. Women's civil and political rights in Canada 2005. Retrieved January 10, 2006, from **www.fafia-afai.org/images/pdf/CanadaICCPR2005_Oct.pdf**.

Cannon, Bethany. 1999 December. Marriage and cohabitation: A comparison of adult attachment style and quality between the two types of relationships. *Dissertation Abstracts International B: The Sciences & Engineering 60*(5–B), 2332.

Caradec, Vincent. 1997. Forms of conjugal life among the young elderly. *Population: An English Selection 9*: 47–74.

Carolan, M. 1999. Contemporary Muslim women and the family. In H. McAdoo (Ed.), *Family Ethnicity: Strength in Diversity*. Newbury Park, CA: Sage, 213–221.

Carr, D. 2004. The desire to date and remarry among older widows and widowers. *Journal of Marriage and Family 66*(4): 1051–1068.

Carr, Deborah. 1996. Two paths to self-employment? Women's and men's self-employment in the United States, 1980. *Work and Occupations* 23(1): 26–53.

Carstensen, Laura L., John M. Gottman, & Robert W. Levenson. 1995 March. Emotional behavior in long-term marriage. *Psychology and Aging* 10.

Cashdan, Elizabeth. 1993. Attracting mates: Effects of paternal investment on mate attraction strategies. *Ethology and Sociobiology* 14(1): 1–23.

Castellano, Marlene Brant. 2002. *Aboriginal Family Trends: Extended Families, Nuclear Families, Families of the Heart.* Ottawa: Vanier Institute of the Family. Accessed December 30, 2002, from **www.vifamily.ca**.

Castells, Manuel. 1996 March. The net and the self: Working notes for a critical theory of the informational society. *Critique of Anthropology* 16(1): 9–38.

Caughy, Margaret O'Brien, Saundra Murray Nettles, & Patricia J. O'Campo. 2008. The effect of residential neighbourhood on child behavior problems in first grade. *American Journal of Psychology* 42: 39–50.

Cavan, R., & K.R. Ranck. 1938. *The Family and the Depression.* Chicago: University of Chicago Press.

CBC News Online. 2005 June 29. The Supreme Court and same-sex marriage. Retrieved from **www.cbc.ca/news/background/samesexrights/**.

CBC News Online. 2008. Retrieved from **www.cbc.ca/news/background/census/mixed-marriages.html**.

CBS News Online. 2003 September 2. Rape debate in Japan. Retrieved November 4, 2005, from **www.cbsnews.com/stories/2003/09/02/world/main571280.shtml**.

Central Intelligence Agency. 2008. Distribution of family income. Gini index 2008 country ranks. *CIA World Factbook.* Washington, D.C.: Central Intelligence Agency, Office of Public Affairs. Retrieved from **www.cia.gov/library/publications/the-world-factbook/rankorder/2172rank.html**.

Cha, Heung Bong. 2004. Public policy on aging in Korea. *Geriatrics and Gerontology International* 4: 45–48.

Chalmers, Lee, & Anne Milan. 2005. Marital satisfaction during the retirement years. *Canadian Social Trends.* Ottawa: Statistics Canada. Catalogue no. 11-008.

Chang, Janet. 2003. Self-reported reasons for divorce and correlates of psychological well-being among divorced Korean immigrant women. *Journal of Divorce & Remarriage* 40: 111–28.

Chant, Sylvia. 2000 December. Men in crisis? Reflections on masculinities, work and family in North-West Costa Rica. *European Journal of Development Research* 12(2): 199–218.

Chappell, Neena L., & Margaret Penning. 1996 January. Behavioural problems and distress among caregivers of people with dementia. *Ageing and Society* 16(1): 57–73.

Cheah, Charissa S.L., & Valery Chirkov. 2008. Parents' personal and cultural beliefs regarding young children. *Journal of Cross-Cultural Psychology* 39(4): 402–423.

Cheal, David. 1991. *Family and the State of Theory.* Toronto: University of Toronto Press.

Cheal, David. 1996. *New Poverty: Families in Postmodern Society.* Westport, CT: Greenwood Press.

Cheal, David. 1997. *Hidden in the Household: Poverty and Dependence at Different ages.* Paper presented at the Conference, Intergenerational Equity in Canada, 20–21 February. Statistics Canada, Ottawa.

Cheal, David. 2002. *Sociology and Family Life.* London: Palgrave.

Cherlin, Andrew J. 2005. American marriage in early twenty-first century. *Marriage and Child Wellbeing* 15(2).

Cheung, Maria. 2008. Resilience of older immigrant couples: Long-term marital satisfaction as a protective factor. *Journal of Couple & Relationship Therapy* 7: 19–38.

ChildStats.gov. 2005. America's children: Key national indicators of well-being 2005. Retrieved January 10, 2006, from **http://childstats.ed.gov/americaschildren/pop6.asp**.

Choi, Alfred, & Jeffrey L. Edleson. 1996. Social disapproval of wife assaults: A national survey of Singapore. *Journal of Comparative Family Studies* 27(1): 73–88.

Christensen, Donna-Hendrickson, & Kathryn D. Rettig. 1995. The relationship of remarriage to post-divorce co-parenting. *Journal of Divorce and Remarriage* 24: 1–2.

Church, Elizabeth. 1996. Kinship and stepfamilies, pp. 81–106. In Marion Lynn (Ed.), *Voices: Essays on Canadian Families.* Scarborough, ON: Nelson.

Clark, Susan M. 1993. Support needs of the Canadian single parent family, pp. 223–238. In Joe Hudson & Burt Galaway (Eds.), *Single Parent Families: Perspectives on Research and Policy.* Toronto: Thompson.

Clark, Warren, & Susan Crompton. 2006. Till death do us part? The risk of first and second marriage dissolution. *Canadian Social Trends.* Ottawa: Statistics Canada. Catalogue no. 11-008: 23–32.

Clark, Warren. 2007. Delayed transitions of young adults. *Canadian Social Trends.* Ottawa: Statistics Canada. Catalogue no. 11-008. Retrieved June 9, 2009, from **www.statcan.gc.ca/pub/11-008-x/2007004/10311-eng.htm**.

Clifford, Janice Elizabeth. 1998 February. The effects of single-mother families on adult children's marital stability. *Dissertation Abstracts International, A: The Humanities and Social Sciences* 58(8), 3320–A.

Cohan, Catherine L., & Stacey Kleinbaum. 2002. Toward a greater understanding of the cohabitation effect: Premarital cohabitation and marital communication. *Journal of Marriage and Family* 64(1): 180–192.

Cohen, Orna, & Ricky Finzi-Dottan. March 2005. Parent-child relationships during the divorce process: From attachment theory and intergenerational perspective. *Contemporary Family Therapy* 27(1): 81–99.

Cohen, Philip N. 1998. Replacing housework in the service economy: Gender, class, and race-ethnicity in service spending. *Gender & Society* 12(2): 219–231.

Coleman, Jean U., & Sandra M. Stith. 1997 June. Nursing students' attitudes toward victims of domestic violence as predicted by selected individual and relationship variables. *Journal of Family Violence* 12: 113–138.

Coleman, Marilyn, Lawrence Ganong, & Susan M. Cable. 1997 February. Beliefs about women's intergenerational family obligations to provide support before and after divorce and remarriage. *Journal of Marriage and the Family* 59: 165–176.

Collins, Louise. 1999 Summer. Emotional adultery: Cybersex and commitment. *Social Theory and Practice* 25(2): 243–270.

Collins, Randall. 1985. *Sociology of Marriage and the Family: Gender, Love, and Property.* Chicago: Nelson-Hall.

Collins, Stephanie Baker. 2005. An understanding of poverty from those who are poor. *Action Research* 3(1): 9–31.

Collins, Stephen. 1991. The transition from lone-parent family to step-family, pp. 156–175. In Michael Hardy & Graham Crow (Eds.), *Lone Parenthood: Coping with Constraints and Making Opportunities in Single-Parent Families*. Toronto: University of Toronto Press.

Coltrane, Scott. 1998. *Gender and Families*. Thousand Oaks, California: Pine Forge Press.

Comeau, Tammy Duerden, & Anton L. Allahar. 2001. Forming Canada's ethnoracial identity: Psychiatry and the history of immigration practices. *Identity* 1: 143–60.

Connidis, Ingrid Arnet. 2001. *Family Ties and Aging*. Thousand Oaks, CA: Sage.

Cooksey, Elizabeth C., Elizabeth G. Menaghan, & Susan M. Jekielek. 1997. Life course effects of work and family circumstances on children. *Social Forces* 76(2): 637–667.

Coontz, Stephanie. 1997. Working with what we've got: The strengths and vulnerabilities of today's families, pp. 157–171. In Stephanie Coontz, *The Way We Really Are*. New York: Basic Books.

Coontz, Stephanie. 2005. *Marriage, a History: From Obedience to Intimacy, or How Love Conquered Marriage*. New York: Viking.

Corak, Miles, & Andrew Heisz. 1999. *Death and Divorce: The Long-Term Consequences of Parental Loss on Adolescents*. Analytical Studies Branch Research Paper Series. Ottawa: Statistics Canada. Catalogue no. 11F0019MIE999135.

Couch, Danielle, & Pranee Liamputtong. 2008. Online dating and mating: The use of the internet to meet sexual partners. *Qualitative Health Research* 18: 268–279.

Courts, N.F., A.N. Newton, & L.J. McNeal. 2005. Husbands and wives living with multiple sclerosis. *Journal of Neuroscience Nursing* 37(1): 20–27.

Cowan, Ruth Schwartz. 1979 January. From Virginia Dare to Virginia Slims: Women and technology in American life. *Technology and Culture* 20(1): 51–63.

Cox, Christine E. 2000. *The Contributions of Grandmothers to Perceived Competence in Young Children*. Southern Sociological Society (SSS).

Cox, Martha, J., & Jeanne Brooks-Gunn (Eds.). *Conflict and Cohesion in Families: Causes and Consequences*. Mahwah, NJ: Lawrence Erlbaum.

Creel, Liz. 2005. Domestic violence: An ongoing threat to women in Latin America and the Caribbean. Population Reference Bureau. Retrieved July 12, 2005, from www.prb.org/Template.cfm?Section=PRB&template=/ContentManagement/ContentDisplay.cfm&ContentID=4744.

Crohan, Susan E. 1996 November. Marital quality and conflict across the transition to parenthood in African American and white couples. *Journal of Marriage and the Family 58*.

Crompton, Rosemary, & Clare Lyonette. 2006. Work–life "balance" in Europe. *Acta Sociologica* 49(4): 379–393.

Cronk, Lee, & Dunham Bria. 2007. Amounts spent on engagement rings reflect aspects of male and female. *Human Nature* 18(4): 329–333.

Cross, Gary, & Richard Szostak. 1995. Women and work before the factory, pp. 37–51. In Gary Cross & Richard Szostak (Eds.), *Technology and American Society: A History*. Englewood Cliffs, NJ: Prentice Hall.

Crossley, Thomas F., & Lori J. Curtis. 2006. Child poverty in Canada. *Review of Income and Wealth* 52(2): 237–260.

Cullen, Jennifer C., Leslie B. Hammer, Margaret B. Neal., & Robert R. Sinclair. 2009. Development of a typology of dual-earner couples caring for children and aging parents. *Journal of Family Issues* 30(4): 458–483.

Cunningham, M., & A. Thornton. 2004. *The Influence of Parents' and Childrens' Union Transitions on Attitudes toward Cohabitation*. Annual meeting of the Population Association of America.

Curran, Melissa, Nancy Hazen, Deborah Jacobvitz, & Amy Feldman. 2005. Representations of early family relationships predict marital maintenance during the transition to parenthood. *Journal of Family Psychology* 19(2): 189–197.

Curran, S., McLanahan, S., & Knab, J. 2003. Does remarriage expand perceptions of kinship support among the elderly? *Social Science Research 32*(2): 171–190.

Curtis, Kristen Taylor, & Christopher G. Ellison. 2002. Religious heterogamy and marital conflict: Findings from the national survey of families and households. *Journal of Family Issues* 23(4): 551–576.

Cyr, R., 2005. Breaking the cycle of violence: Preventing violence against seniors in the Aboriginal community. Retrieved May 20, 2009, from www.web.net/~ocsco/downloads/abuse_of_aboriginal_seniors.pdf.

Dahinten, V. Susan, & J. Douglas Willms. 2002. The effects of adolescent child-bearing on children's outcomes, pp. 243–258. In J. Douglas Willms (Ed.), *Vulnerable Children: Findings from Canada's National Longitudinal Survey of Children and Youth*. Edmonton: University of Alberta Press, and Ottawa: Human Resources Development Canada, Applied Research Branch.

Dahinten, V. Susan, Jennifer D. Shapka., & J. Douglas Willms. 2007. Adolescent children of adolescent mothers: The impact of family functioning on trajectories of development. *Journal Youth and Adolescence* 36: 195–212.

Dakin, John, & Richard Wampler. 2008. Money doesn't buy happiness, but it helps: Marital satisfaction, psychological distress, and demographic differences between low- and middle-income clinic couples. *American Journal of Family Therapy* 36(4): 300–311.

Daley, Suzanne. 1999 October 14. France gives legal status to unmarried couples. *New York Times*.

Darvishpour, Mehrdad. 2002. Immigrant women challenge the role of men: How the changing power relationship within Iranian families in Sweden intensifies family conflicts after immigration. *Journal of Comparative Family Studies 33*: 271–96.

Dasgupta, Shamita Das. 1998. Gender roles and cultural continuity in the Asian Indian immigrant community in the U.S. *Sex Roles* 38(11–12): 953–974.

Davidson, Kate, Sara Arber, & Jay Ginn. 2000. Gendered meanings of care work within late life marital relationships. *Canadian Journal on Aging* 19(4): 536–553.

Davidson, Kate. 2001. Late life widowhood, selfishness and new partnership choices: A gendered perspective. *Ageing and Society* 21(3): 297–317.

Davies, Lorraine, & Patricia Jane Carrier. 1998. The importance of power relations for the division of household labour. *Canadian Journal of Sociology* 23(4).

Davies, Lorraine, Julie Ann McMullin, William R. Avison, with Gale L. Cassidy. 2001. *Social Policy, Gender*

Inequality and Poverty. Ottawa: Status of Women Canada.

Davies, Sharon, & Margaret Denton. 2001. *The Economic Well-Being of Older Women Who Become Divorced or Separated in Mid and Later Life.* Social and Economic Dimensions of an Aging Population Research Papers, Number 66. Hamilton, ON: McMaster University.

Davis, Phillip W. 1996. Threats of corporal punishment as verbal aggression: A naturalistic study. *Child Abuse and Neglect* 20(4): 289–304.

Davis, Robert C., & Barbara Smith. 1995 October. Domestic violence reforms: Empty promises or fulfilled expectations? *Crime and Delinquency* 41: 541–552.

Deal, James E., Karen Smith Wampler, & Charles F. Halverson Jr. 1992 December. The importance of similarity in the marital relationship. *Family Process* 31(4): 369–382.

Dearing, Eric. 2004. The developmental implications of restrictive and supportive parenting across neighborhoods and ethnicities: Exceptions are the rule. *Applied Developmental Psychology* 25: 555–575.

DeBoer, Danelle D. 2002 December. The effect of infertility on individual well-being. *Dissertation Abstracts International, A: The Humanities and Social Sciences* 62(6), 2249–A.

De Graaf, Paul M., & Matthijs Kalmijn. 2006. Divorce motives in a period of rising divorce. *Journal of Family Issues* 27(4): 483–505.

Deimling, Gary T., Noelker, Linda S., & Aloen L. Townsend. 1989. *A Comparative Analysis of Family Caregivers' Health and Well-Being.* North Central Sociological Association (NCSA).

De Jong Gierveld, Jenny. 2004. Remarriage, unmarried cohabitation, living apart together: Partner relationships following bereavement or divorce. *Journal of Marriage and the Family* 66(1): 236–243.

DeKeseredy, Walter S., & Katharine D. Kelly. 1995. Sexual abuse in Canadian university and college dating relationships: The contribution of male peer support. *Journal of Family Violence* 10(1): 41–53.

DeLamater, J., & M. Sill. 2005. Sexual desire in later life. *Journal of Sex Research* 42: 138–149.

DeLongis, Anita, & Darrin R. Lehman. 1989 March. The usefulness of a structured diary approach in studying marital relationships. *Journal of Family Psychology* 2(3): 337–343.

DeMaris, Alfred, & Steven Swinford. 1996 January. Female victims of spousal violence: Factors influencing their level of fearfulness. *Family Relations* 45: 98–106.

DeMaris, Alfred. 2007. The role of inequity in marital disruption. *Journal of Social and Personal Relationships* 24(2): 177–195.

De Rose, Alessandra. 2001. Separation and divorce: Effect on family structures and life conditions. *Labour* 14(1): 145–160.

De Valk, Helga A.G., & Aart C. Liefbroer. 2007. Parental influence on union formation preferences among Turkish, Moroccan, and Dutch adolescents in the Netherlands. *Journal of Cross-Cultural Psychology* 38: 487–505.

De Wolff, Alice. 2004. Working and having a life in Canada: a ten year review, pp. 1–19. In *Bargaining for work and life.* Retrieved May 27, 2005, from **http://ofl.ca/index.php/library/index_in/C41/.**

Dickason, Olive. 2002. *Canada's First Nations: A History of Founding Peoples from Earliest Times.* Don Mills, ON: Oxford University Press.

Diez-Bbolanos, A.M., & Perez Rodrigues. 1989 July. Effects of inequality on the female's marital adjustment and satisfaction. *Revista de Psicologia General y Aplicada* 42(3): 395–401.

Ding, Shijun. 2004. The rural elderly support in China and Thailand. *Geriatrics and Gerontology International* 4: 56–59.

Dinkmeyer, Don, & Robert Sherman. 1989 March–June. Brief Adlerian family therapy. *Individual Psychology: Journal of Adlerian Theory, Research & Practice. Special Issue: Varieties of Brief Therapy* 45(1–2): 148–158.

Divale, William, & Albert Seda. 2001. Modernization as changes in cultural complexity: New cross-cultural measurements. *Cross-Cultural Research* 35: 127–53.

Dong, Qi, Yanping Wang, & Thomas H. Ollendick. 2002. Consequences of divorce on the adjustment of children in China. *Journal of Clinical Child and Adolescent Psychology* 31(1): 101–110.

Dooley, Martin. 1993. Recent changes in the economic welfare of lone mother families in Canada: The roles of market work, earnings and transfers, pp. 115–132. In Joe Hudson & Burt Galaway (Eds.), *Single Parent Families: Perspectives on Research and Policy.* Toronto: Thompson.

Doosje, Bertjan, Krystyna Rojahn, & Agneta Fischer. 1999. Partner preference as a function of gender, age, political orientation and level of education. *Sex Roles* 40(1–2): 45–60.

Dorow, Sara. 2002. China R us? Care, consumption and transnationally adopted children. In D. Cook, (Ed.), *Symbolic Childhood.* New York: Peter Lang.

Douglas, Kristen. 2006. *Divorce Law in Canada.* Ottawa: Government of Canada, Law and Government Division. Retrieved from **www.parl.gc.ca/information/library/PRBpubs/963-e.html.**

Doust, Janet L. 2008. Two English immigrant families in Australia in the 19th century. *The History of the Family* 13: 2–25.

Drakich, Janice. 1993. In whose best interest? The politics of joint custody, pp. 331–341. In Bonnie Fox (Ed.), *Family Patterns, Gender Relations.* Toronto: Oxford University Press.

Dronkers, Jaap. 1996. *The Effects of Parental Conflicts and Divorce on the Average Well-Being of Pupils in Secondary Education.* American Sociological Association.

Dryburgh, H. 2001. Changing our ways: Why and how Canadians use the internet. Retrieved June 11, 2009, from **www.statcan.gc.ca/bsolc/olc-cel/olccel?lang=eng&catno=56F0006X.**

Dryburgh, Heather. 2001. Teenage pregnancy. *Health Reports* 12(1): 1–9. Ottawa: Statistics Canada. Catalogue no. 82–003.

Dua, Enakshi. 1999. Beyond diversity: Exploring the ways in which the discourse of race has shaped the institution of the nuclear family, pp. 237–260. In Enaskshi Dua (Ed.), *Scratching the Surface: Canadian Anti-Racist Feminist Thought.* Toronto: Women's Press.

Duberman, Lucile. 1975. *The Reconstituted Family: A Study of Remarried Couples and their Children.* Chicago: Nelson-Hall Publishers.

Dudley, James R. 1996. Noncustodial fathers speak about their parental role. *Family and Conciliation Courts Review* 34(3).

Duffey, T.H., H.R. Wooten, & C.A. Lumadue. 2004. The effect of dream sharing on marital intimacy and satisfaction. *Journal of Couple & Relationship Therapy* 3: 53–68.

Duffy, Anne, & Nancy Mandell. 2001. The growth in poverty and social inequality: Losing faith in social justice, pp. 77–114. In Dan Glenday & Ann Duffy (Eds.), *Canadian Society: Meeting the Challenges of the Twenty-First Century*. Toronto: Oxford University Press.

Dumont-Smith, C. 2002. Aboriginal elder abuse in Canada. Retrieved May 20, 2009, from **www.ahf.ca/pages/download/28_37**.

Dunlop, Rosemary, and Ailsa Burns. 1995. The sleeper effect: Myth or reality? *Journal of Marriage and the Family* 57(2): 375–386.

Dunne, Gillian A. 1997. *Lesbian Lifestyles: Women, Work and the Politics of Sexuality*. Toronto: University of Toronto.

Dunne, Gillian A. 2001. Opting into motherhood: Lesbians blurring the boundaries and transforming the meaning of parenthood and kinship. *Gender and Society* 14(1): 11–35.

Duong Tran, Quang, Serge Lee, & Sokley Khoi. 1996 December. Ethnic and gender differences in parental expectations and life stress. *Child and Adolescent Social Work Journal* 13: 515–526.

Durkheim, Émile. 1951. *Suicide, étude de sociologie*. (English Title) *Suicide: A Study in Sociology*. Translated by John A. Spaulding and George Simpson. Glencoe, Ill: Free Press.

Dush, Claire M. Kamp, & Paul R. Amato. 2005. Consequences of relationship status and quality for subjective well-being. *Journal of Social and Personal Relationships* 22(5): 607–627.

Duxbury, L., & Higgins, C., 2003. *Work–Life Conflict in Canada in the New Millennium: A Status Report*. Ottawa: Healthy Communities Division, Health Canada.

Duxbury, Linda Elizabeth, Christopher Alan Higgins, & D. Roland Thomas. 1996. Work and family environments and the adoption of computer-supported supplemental work-at-home. *Journal of Vocational Behavior* 49(1): 1–23.

Dwairy, Marwan, & Kariman E. Menshar. 2006. Parenting style, individuation, and mental health of Egyptian adolescents. *Journal of Adolescence* 29: 103–117.

Eastwick, Paul W. & Eli J. Finkel. 2008. Sex differences in mate preferences revisited: Do people know what they initially desire in a romantic partner? *Journal of Personality and Social Psychology* 94(2): 245–264.

Eaton, Linda Carole. 2000 August. A study of the correlation between the coming-out process and the first long-term homosexual relationship between gay males. *Dissertation Abstracts International, A: The Humanities and Social Sciences* 61(2): 782–A-783–A.

Echtelt, Patricia Van, Arie Glebbeek, Suzan Lewis, & Siegwart Lindenberg. Post-Fordist work: A man's world? Gender and working overtime in the Netherlands. *Gender & Society* 23(2): 188–214.

Edelman, M.A., & B.L. Menz. 1996. Selected comparisons and implications of a national rural and urban survey on health care access, demographics, and policy issues. *Journal of Rural Health* 12: 197–205.

Edin, Kathryn, & Joanna M. Reed. 2005. Why don't they just get married? Barriers to marriage among the disadvantaged. *The Future of the Children* 15(2): 117–137.

Edin, Kathryn, Laura Tach, & Ronald Mincy. 2009. Claiming fatherhood: Race and the dynamics of paternal involvement among unmarried men. *The ANNALS of the American Academy of Political and Social Science* 162(1): 149–177.

Edleson, Jeffrey L. 1999 August. Children's witnessing of adult domestic violence. *Journal of Interpersonal Violence* 14(8): 839–870.

Edmonds, P., B. Vivat, R. Burman, E. Silber, & I.J. Higginson. 2007. Loss and change: experiences of people severely affected by multiple sclerosis. *Palliative Medicine* 21: 101–107.

Eells, Laura Workman, & Kathleen O'Flaherty. 1996. Gender perceptual differences in relation to marital problems. *Journal of Divorce and Remarriage* 25(2).

Eichler, Margrit. 1997. *Family Shifts: Families, Policies and Gender Equality*. Toronto: Oxford University Press.

Eichler, Margrit. 2001. Biases in family literature, pp. 51–66. In Maureen Baker (Ed.), *Families: Changing Trends in Canada* (4th edition). Toronto: McGraw-Hill Ryerson.

Eisikovits, Rivka A. 2000. Gender differences in cross-cultural adaptation styles of immigrant youths from the former U.S.S.R. in Israel. *Youth and Society* 31: 310–31.

Elder, Glen H. Jr. 1992. Models of the life course. *Contemporary Sociology* 21: 632–635.

Elder, Glen H. Jr., Monica Kirkpatrick Johnson, & Robert Crosnoe. 2004. The emergence and development of life course theory, pp. 3–19. In Jeylan T. Mortimer and Michael J. Shanahan (Eds.), *Handbook of the Life Course*. New York: Kluwer.

Elgar, Frank J., Christine Arlett, & Renee Groves. 2003. Stress, coping, and behavioural problems among rural and urban adolescents. *Journal of Adolescence* 26(5): 574–585.

Elgar, Frank J., John Knight, Graham J. Worrall, & Gregory Sherman. 2003. Attachment characteristics and behavioural problems in rural and urban juvenile delinquents. *Child Psychiatry and Human Development* 34(1): 35–48.

El-Ghannam, Ashraf R. 2001. Modernisation in Arab societies: The theoretical and analytical view. *International Journal of Sociology and Social Policy* 21: 88–131.

Elliot, M. 1999. Classifying family life education on the World Wide Web. *Family Relations* 48: 7–13.

Ellison, Nicole B. 1999 Fall. Social impacts: New perspectives on telework. *Social Science Computer Review* 17(3): 338–356.

Emanuels-Zuurveen, Lineke, & Paul M.G. Emmelkamp. 1997. Spouse aided therapy with depressed patients. *Behavior Modification* 21(1).

Emmers-Sommer, Tara M. 2003. Couple relationships, pp. 327–332. In James J. Ponzettie, Jr. (Ed.), *International Encyclopedia of Marriage and Family* (2nd edition), Vol. 1. New York: Macmillan Reference USA.

Engels, Frederick. [1884]1972. *The Origin of the Family, Private Property and the State*. New York: Pathfinder.

Engle, Patrice L., Sarah Castle, & Purnima Menon. 1996. Child development: Vulnerability and resilience. *Social Science and Medicine* 43(5): 621–635.

Epstein, Rachel. 1996. Lesbian families, pp. 107–130. In Marion Lynn (Ed.), *Voices: Essays on Canadian Families*. Toronto: Nelson Canada.

Ermisch, John. 2008. Origins of social immobility and inequality: Parenting and early child development. *National Institute Economic Review* 205: 62–71.

Esping-Andersen, G. 1999. *Social Foundations of Post Industrial Economics*. Oxford University Press, New York.

Espiritu, Yen Le. 2001. "We don't sleep around like white girls do": Family, culture, and gender in Filipina American lives. *Signs* 26(2): 415–440.

Estrada, Ana Ulloa, & Julianne M. Holmes. 1999 April–June. Couples' perceptions of effective and ineffective ingredients of marital therapy. *Journal of Sex & Marital Therapy* 25(2): 151–162.

Ezra, Marni, & Melissa Deckman. 1996 March–April. Balancing work and family responsibilities: Flextime and child care in the federal government. *Public Administration Review* 56: 174–179.

Farhood, Laila, Huda Zurayk, Monique Chaya, Fadia Saadeh, Garbis Meshefedjian, & Thuraya Sidani. 1993. The impact of war on the physical and mental health of the family: The Lebanese experience. *Social Science and Medicine* 36(12): 1555–1567.

Fast, Janet E., Norah C. Keating, Leslie Oakes, & Deanna L. Williamson. 1997. *Conceptualizing and Operationalizing the Costs of Informal Elder Care*. NHRDP Project No. 6609–1963–55. Ottawa: National Health Research and Development Program, Health Canada.

Fawcett, Matthew. 1990. Taking the middle path: Recent Swedish legislation grants minimal property rights to unmarried cohabitants. *Family Law Quarterly* 24: 179–202.

Feerick, Margaret M., & Jeffrey J. Haugaard. 1999 December. Long-term effects of witnessing marital violence for women: The contribution of childhood physical and sexual abuse. *Journal of Family Violence* 14(4): 377–398.

Feingold, Alan. 1995. Physical appearance and gender: Sociobiological and sociocultural perspectives, review of Linda A. Jackson. *Archives of Sexual Behavior* 24(5): 580–581.

Feldman, Shirley S., Lawrence Fisher, & Laura Seitel. 1997. The effect of parents' marital satisfaction on young adults' adaptation: A longitudinal study. *Journal of Research on Adolescence* 7(1): 55–80.

Ferri, Elsa. 1993. Socialization experiences of children in lone parent families: Evidence from the British National Child Development Study, pp. 281–290. In Joe Hudson & Burt Galaway (Eds.), *Single Parent Families: Perspectives on Research and Policy*. Toronto: Thompson.

Fincham, Frank D., & Steven R.H. Beach. 2006. Relationship satisfaction, pp. 579–594. In Anita L. Vangelisti and Daniel Perlman (Eds.), *The Cambridge Handbook of Personal Relationships*. New York: Cambridge University Press.

Fineman, Martha Albertson, & Roxanne Mykitiuk (Eds.) 1994. *The Public Nature of Private Violence: The Discovery of Domestic Abuse*. New York, NY: Routledge.

Fingerson, Laura. 2000. *Do Parents' Opinions Matter? Family Processes and Adolescent Sexual Behavior*. Paper presented to the American Sociological Association (ASA).

Finn, Jerry, & Melissa Lavitt. 1994. Computer-based self-help groups for sexual abuse survivors. *Social Work with Groups* 17(1–2): 21–46.

Finn, Jerry. 1996. Computer-based self-help groups: On-line recovery for addictions. *Computers in Human Services* 13(1): 21–41.

Finnie, Ross. 1993. Women, men, and the economic consequences of divorce: Evidence from Canadian longitudinal data. *Canadian Review of Sociology and Anthropology* 30(2): 205–241.

Firestone, Juanita M., Linda C. Lambert, & William A. Vega. 1999 June. Intimate violence among women of Mexican origin: Correlates of abuse. *Journal of Gender, Culture, and Health* 4(2): 119–134.

Fischer, Claude S. 1992. *America Calling: A Social History of the Telephone to 1940*. Berkeley, CA: University of California Press.

Fisher, H. 1992. *Anatomy of Love: A Natural History of Mating, Marriage and Why We Stray*. New York: Fawcett.

Fisher, S., A. Allan, & M.M. Allan. 2004. Exploratory study to examine the impact of television reports of prison escapes on fear of crime, operationalised as state anxiety. *Australian Journal of Psychology* 56(3): 181–190.

Fiske, Jo-Anne, & Rose Johnny. 1996. The Neduten family: Yesterday and today, pp. 225–241. In Marion Lynn (Ed.), *Voices: Essays on Canadian Families*. Toronto: Nelson.

Fisman, Raymond, & Sheena Iyengar. 2008. Racial preferences in dating. *Review of Economic Studies* 75: 117–132.

Fitzgerald, B. 1999. Children of lesbian and gay parents: A review of the literature. *Marriage and Family Review* 29(1): 57–76.

Flandrin, J-L. 1979. *Families in Former Times: Kinship, Household and Sexuality in Early Modern France*. Cambridge: Cambridge University Press.

Fleras, Augie, & Jean Leonard Elliott. 2003. *Unequal Relations: An Introduction to Race and Ethnic Dynamics in Canada* (4th edition). Toronto: Prentice Hall.

Follette, William C., Neil S. Jacobson, Dirk Revenstorf, Donald H. Baucom, Kurt Hahlweg, & Gayla Margolin. 2000 June. Variability in outcome and clinical significance of behavioral marital therapy: A reanalysis of outcome data. *Prevention & Treatment* 3: unpaged.

Forsdick Martz, Diane J. 2006. *Canadian Farm Women and Their Families: Restructuring, Work and Decision Making* [Dissertation].

Forsyth, Craig, & Robert Gramling. 1998. Socio-economic factors affecting the rise of commuter marriage. *International Journal of the Sociology of the Family* 28(2): 93–106.

Forte, James A., David D. Franks, & Janett A. Forte. 1996 January. Asymmetrical role-taking: Comparing battered women. *Social Work* 41: 59–73.

Forthofer, Melinda S., Howard J. Markman, & Martha Cox. 1996 August. Associations between marital distress and work loss in a national sample. *Journal of Marriage and the Family* 58.

Foshee, Vangie A., Katherine J. Karriker-Jaffe, Heathe Luz McNaughton Reyes, Susan T. Ennett, Chirayath Suchindran, Karl E. Bauman, & Thad S. Benefield. 2008. *Journal of Adolescent Health* 42: 596–604.

Fox, Bonnie J. 1993. The rise and fall of the breadwinner-homemaker family, pp. 147–157. In Bonnie J. Fox (Ed.), *Family Patterns, Gender Relations*. Toronto: Oxford University Press.

Fox, Bonnie J. 2001. The formative years: How parenthood creates gender. *La Revue Canadienne de Sociologie et d'Anthropologie/The Canadian Review of Sociology and Anthropology* 38(4): 373–390.

Fox, Bonnie J., & Meg Luxton. 2001. Conceptualizing family, pp. 22–33. In Bonnie J. Fox (Ed.), *Family Patterns, Gender Relations* (2nd edition). Toronto: Oxford University Press.

Fox, Greer Litton, & Dudley Chancey. 1998 November. Sources of economic distress: Individual and family outcomes. *Journal of Family Issues* 19(6): 725–749.

Fredriksen, Karen. 1996. Gender differences in employment and the informal care of adults. *Journal of Women & Aging* 8(2): 35–53.

Freiband, David M. 1996. The fulfillment of marital ideals: A study of marital satisfaction and personal well-being. *Dissertation Abstracts International: Section B: The Sciences and Engineering* 56(12-B), 7092.

Freidenberg, Judith, & Muriel Hammer. 1998 Spring. Social networks and health care: The case of elderly Latinos in East Harlem. *Urban Anthropology* 27(1): 49–85.

French, Maggie. 1991. Becoming a lone parent, pp. 126–142. In Michael Hardy & Graham Crow (Eds.), *Lone Parenthood: Coping with Constraints and Making Opportunities in Single-Parent Families*. Toronto: University of Toronto Press.

Frenette, Marc, David A. Green, & Kevin Milligan. n.d. The tale of the tails: Revisiting recent trends in Canadian after-tax income inequality using Census data. Retrieved April 24, 2006, from **www.econ.ubc.ca/kevinmil/research/centax6.6.pdf**.

Frias, Sonia M., & Ronald J. Angel. 2007. Stability and change in the experience of partner violence among low-income women. *Social Science Quarterly* 88(5): 1281–1306.

Frideres, J.S. 2007. Building bridges: Aboriginal, immigrant, and visible minority families in the twenty-first century, pp. 195–212. In David Cheal (Ed.), *Canadian Families Today: New Perspectives*. Toronto: Oxford University Press.

Fu, Xuanning. 2008. Interracial marriage and family socio-economic well-being: Equal status exchange or caste status exchange? *Social Science Journal* 45: 132–155.

Fuller-Thomson, E. 2005. Canadian First Nations grandparents raising grandchildren: A portrait in resilience. *International Journal of Aging and Human Development* 60(4): 331–342.

Gadd, Jane. 1997. The drift to the bottom. *Globe and Mail*, 21 June: D1, D2.

Galambos, Nancy L., & Heather A. Sears. 1998 November. Adolescents' perceptions of parents' work and adolescents' work values in two-earner families. *Journal of Early Adolescence* 18(4): 397–420.

Galston, William A. 1996. Braking divorce for the sake of children, The American Enterprise 7 (May/June). *Globe and Mail*, 2000, 49.

Ganong-Coleman, Lawrence H. 1998 Fall. Attitudes regarding filial responsibilities to help elderly divorced parents and stepparents. *Journal of Aging Studies* 12(3): 271–290.

Ganster, Daniel C., & Bart Victor. 1988 March. The impact of social support on mental and physical health. *British Journal of Medical Psychology* 61(1): 17–36.

Gartner, Rosemary, Myrna Dawson, & Maria Crawford. 2001 (1998). Women killing: Intimate femicide in Ontario, 1974–1994. In Bonnie J. Fox (Ed.), *Family Patterns, Gender Patterns* (2nd edition). Toronto: Oxford University Press, 473–490.

Gaunt, Ruth. 2006. Couple similarity and marital satisfaction: Are similar spouses happier? *Journal of Personality* 74(5): 1401–1420.

Gazso, Amber, & Susan McDaniel. 2009. *The Risky Business of Being a Lone Mother on Income Support in Canada and the U.S.* Paper presented at the Pacific Sociological Association meetings, San Diego, April 2009.

Gee, Ellen M. 1986. The life course of Canadian women: An historical and demographic analysis. *Social Indicators Research* 18: 263–283.

Gee, Ellen M., & Meredith M. Kimball. 1987. *Women and Aging*. Toronto: Butterworths.

Gelles, R., & D. Loseke (Eds.). 1993. *Current Controversies on Family Violence*. Newbury Park, CA: Sage.

Gelles, Richard J. 1994 Spring. Introduction: Part of a special issue on family violence. *Journal of Comparative Family Studies* 25: 1–6.

Ghimire, Dirgha J., William G. Axinn, Scott T. Yabiku, & Arland Thornton. 2006. Social change, premarital nonfamily experience, and spouse choice in an arranged marriage society. *American Journal of Sociology* 111: 1181–1218.

Gibbs, Jennifer L., Nicole B. Ellison, & Rebecca D. Heino. 2006. Self-presentation in online personals: The role of anticipated future interaction, self-disclosure, and perceived success in internet dating. *Communication Research* 33: 152–77.

Gibson-Davis, Christina M. 2009. Money, marriage, and children: Testing the financial expectations and family formation theory. *Journal of Marriage and Family* 71(1): 146–160.

Giddens, Anthony. 1992. *The Transformation of Intimacy: Sexuality, Love, and Eroticism in Modern Societies*. Cambridge: Polity Press.

Giele, Janet Zollinger. 1996. Decline of family: Conservative, liberal and feminist views. In David Popenoe, Jean Bethke Elshtain, and David Blankenhorn (Eds.), *Promises to Keep: Decline and Renewal of Marriage in America*. Lanham, MD: Rowman and Littlefield Publishers, Inc.

Gilliam, C.M., & A.M. Steffen. 2006. The relationship between caregiving self-efficacy and depressive symptoms in dementia family caregivers. *Aging and Mental Health* 10(2): 79–86(8).

Gillian, A.D. 2001. The lady vanishes? Reflections on the experiences of married and divorced non-heterosexual fathers. *Sociological Research Online* 6(3). Retrieved May 25, 2009, from **www.socresonline.org.uk/6/3/dunne.html**.

Gim Chung, R.H. 2001. Gender, ethnicity, and acculturation in intergenerational conflict of Asian American college students. *Cultural Diversity and Ethnic Minority Psychology* 7: 376–386.

Gladstone, J.W. 1995. The marital perceptions of elderly persons living or having a spouse living in a long-term care institution in Canada. *The Gerontologist* 35(1): 52–60.

Glaser, K., R. Stuchbury, C. Tomassini, & J. Askham. 2008. The long-term consequences of partnership dissolution for support in later life in the United Kingdom. *Ageing & Society* 28(3): 329–351.

Glass, Jennifer, & Tetsushi Fujimoto. 1995. Employer characteristics and the provision of family responsive policies. *Work and Occupations* 22(4): 380–411.

Glick, Susan. 1997 April. Examining the relationship between perceived emotional expressiveness and marital adjustment. *Dissertation Abstracts International: Section B: The Sciences & Engineering* 57(10–B), 6648.

Godard, J. 2007. PACS seven years on: Is it moving towards marriage? *International Journal of Law, Policy and the Family* 21(3): 310–321.

Goldscheider, Frances, Gayle Kaufman, & Sharon Sassler. 2009. Navigating the "new" marriage market: How attitudes toward partner characteristics shape union formation. *Journal of Family Issues* 30(6): 719–737.

Goldstein, Marion Z. 1990. The role of mutual support groups and family therapy for caregivers of demented elderly. *Journal of Geriatric Psychiatry* 23(2): 117–128.

Goode, William. 1993. *World Changes in Divorce Patterns*. New Haven: Yale University Press.

Goodman, Catherine. 1990 November. Evaluation of a model self-help telephone program: Impact on natural networks. *Social Work* 35(6): 556–562.

Goossens, Frits A., Geertruud Ottenhoff, & Willem Koops. 1991. Day care and social outcomes in middle childhood: A retrospective study. *Journal of Reproductive and Infant Psychology* 9(2–3): 137–150.

Gordon, Linda, & Sara McLanahan. 1991. Single parenthood in 1900. *Journal of Family History* 16(2): 97–116.

Gordon, Sarah A. 2004. Boundless possibilities: Home sewing and the meanings of women's domestic work in the United States, 1890–1930. *Journal of Women's History* 16(2): 68–91.

Gorlick, Carolyne A., & D. Alan Pomfret. 1993. Hope and circumstance: Single mothers exiting social assistance, pp. 253–270. In Joe Hudson & Burt Galaway (Eds.), *Single Parent Families: Perspectives on Research and Policy*. Toronto: Thompson.

Gott, M., & S. Hinchliff. 2003. How important is sex in later life? The views of older people. *Social Science and Medicine* 56: 117–28.

Gottlieb, B.H. (Ed.). 1981. *Social Networks and Social Support*. Beverly Hills, CA: Sage.

Gottlieb, Benjamin H. 1985 Spring. Social networks and social support: An overview of research, practice, and policy implications. *Health Education Quarterly* 12(1): 5–22.

Gottman, John M., with Nan Silver. 1999. *The Seven Principles for Making Marriage Work*. New York: Random House.

Gottman, John Mordechai. 1995. *Why Marriages Succeed or Fail: And How You Can Make Yours Last*. New York: Fireside Books, 1995.

Government of Canada. 2005. News Release, 18 April. Retrieved November 30, 2005, from **www.cic.gc.ca/english/press/05/0511-e.html**.

Grable, John E., Sonya Britt, & Joyce Cantrell. 2007. An exploratory study of the role financial satisfaction has on the thought of subsequent divorce. *Family and Consumer Sciences Research Journal* 36: 130–50.

Graefe, Deborah Roempke, & Daniel T. Lichter. 2007. When unwed mothers marry: The marital and cohabiting partners of midlife women. *Journal of Family Issues* 28(5): 595–622.

Graefe, Deborah Roempke, & Daniel T. Lichter. 2008. Marriage patterns among unwed mothers: Before and after PRWORA. *Journal of Policy Analysis and Management* 27(3): 479–497.

Graham, Carolyn W., Judith L. Fischer, Duane Crawford, Jacki Fitzpatrick, & Kristan Bina. 2000 October. Parental status, social support, and marital adjustment. *Journal of Family Issues* 21(7): 888–905.

Grahame, Kamini M. 2006. Shifting arrangements: Indo-Trinidadian women, globalization, and the restructuring of family life. *Sociological Spectrum* 26: 425–52.

Grant, Bruce. 2005. The traffic in brides. *American Anthropologist* 107: 687–89.

Gray-Little, Bernadette, Donald H. Baucom, & Sherry L. Hamby. 1996. Marital power, marital adjustment and therapy outcomes. *Journal of Family Psychology* 10(3).

Greaves, Kathleen Marie. 2001 May. The social construction of sexual interaction in heterosexual relationships: A qualitative analysis. *Dissertation Abstracts International, A: The Humanities and Social Sciences* 61(11), 4565-A-4566-A.

Green, Alan G., & David Green. 2004. The goals of Canada's immigration policy: A historical perspective. *Canadian Journal of Urban Research* 13: 102–39.

Green, R.J., P.L. Williams, C.S. Johnson, & I. Blum. 2008. Can Canadian seniors on public pensions afford a nutritious fiet? *Canadian Journal on Aging* 27(1): 69–79.

Greenland, K., & R. Brown. 2005. Acculturation and contact in Japanese students studying in the United Kingdom. *Journal of Social Psychology*, 145: 373–389.

Greif, Geoffrey L. 1995. When divorced fathers want no contact with their children: A preliminary analysis. *Journal of Divorce and Remarriage* 23(1–2).

Grimm-Thomas, Karen, & Maureen Perry-Jenkins. 1994 April. All in a day's work: Job experiences, self-esteem, and fathering in working class families. *Family Relations* 43: 174–181.

Gringeri, Christina. 1995. Flexibility, the family ethic, and rural home-based work. *Affilia* 10(1): 70–86.

Grissett, Barbara, & Allen L. Furr. 1994. Effects of parental divorce on children's financial support for college. *Journal of Divorce and Remarriage* 22(1–2).

Gross, Penny. 1987. Defining post-divorce remarriage families: A typology based on the subjective perceptions of children. *Journal of Divorce* 10(1, 2): 205–217.

Groves, Melissa, & Diane Horm-Wingerd. 1991. Commuter marriages: Personal, family and career issues. *Sociology and Social Research* 75(4): 212–217.

Gruber, James E., & Susan Fineran. 2007. The impact of bullying and sexual harassment on middle and high school girls. *Violence Against Women* 13(6): 627–643.

Gündüz-Hoşgör, Ayse, & Jeroen Smits. 2008. Variation in labor market participation of married women in Turkey. *Women's Studies International Forum* 31: 104–17.

Guttman, Joseph. 1993. *Divorce in Psychosocial Perspective: Theory and Research*. Hillsdale, NJ: Lawrence Erlbaum Associates.

Haas, Stephen M., & Laura Stafford. 1998 December. An initial examination of maintenance behaviors in gay and lesbian relationships. *Journal of Social and Personal Relationships* 15(6): 846–855.

Hadas, Doron, Gila Markovitzky, & Miri Sarid. 2008. Spousal violence among immigrants from the former Soviet Union—general population and welfare recipients. *Journal of Family Violence* 23: 549–55.

Hadjistavrolous, Thomas, & Myles Genet. 1994. The underestimation of the role of physical attractiveness in dating preferences: Ignorance or taboo? *Canadian Journal of Behavioural Science* 26(2): 298.

Hagan, John, & Bill McCarthy. 1998. *Mean Street: Youth, Crimes and Homelessness*. Cambridge, MA: Cambridge University Press.

Haimes, Erica, & Kate Weiner. 2000 July. "Everybody's got a dad . . . ": Issues for lesbian families in the management of donor insemination. *Sociology of Health and Illness* 22(4): 477–499.

Handrahan, Lori. 2004. Hunting for women: Bride-kidnapping in Kyrgyzstan. *International Feminist Journal of Politics* 6: 207–33.

Hannah, Mo Teresa, Wade Luquet, & Joan McCormick. 1997 Spring. COMPASS as a measure of the efficacy of couples therapy. *American Journal of Family Therapy* 25.

Hareven, Tamara K. 1991 Spring. The home and the family in historical perspective. *Social Research* 58(1): 253–285.

Harris, Colette. 2006. Bride kidnapping in Kyrgyzstan. *Slavic Review* 65: 153–54.

Harris, Marvin. 1997. *Culture, People, Nature: An Introduction to General Anthropology* (7th edition). New York: Longman.

Harrison, Kelley A., Gina S. Richman, & Glenda L. Vittimberga. 2000 March. Parental stress in grandparents versus parents raising children with behavior problems. *Journal of Family Issues* 21(2): 262–270.

Hartos, Jessica L., & Thomas G. Power. 2000 September. Relations among single mothers' awareness of their adolescents' stressors, maternal monitoring, mother-adolescent comunication, and adolescent adjustment. *Journal of Adolescent Research* 15(5): 546–563.

Hassebrauck, Manfred. 1996. Relationship concepts and relationship satisfaction: The importance of real and perceived similarity in couples. *Zeitschrift für Sozialpsychologie* 27(3), 183–192.

Hassouneh-Phillips, Dena, & Elizabeth McNeff. 2005. I thought I was less worthy: Low sexual and body esteem and increased vulnerability to intimate partner abuse in women with physical disabilities. *Sexuality and Disability* 23(4): 227–240.

Haythornthwaite, Caroline, M.M. Kazmer, J. Robins, & S. Showmaker. 2000. Community development among distance learners: Temporal and technological dimensions. *Journal of Computer-Mediated Communication* 6(1).

Haythornthwaite, Caroline. 2001a. January. *Tie Strength and the Impact of New Media*. Proceedings of the 24th Hawaii International Conference of System Sciences.

Haythornthwaite, Caroline. 2001b. November. Introduction: The Internet in everyday life. *American Behavorial Scientist* 45(3): 363–382.

Heaphy, B., A.K.T. Yip, & D. Thompson. 2004. Ageing in a non-heterosexual context. *Ageing and Society* 24(6): 881–902.

Heather, Barbara, Lynn Skillen, Jennifer Young, & Theresa Vladicka. 2005. Women's gendered identities and the restructuring of rural Alberta. *Sociologia Ruralis* 45(1–2): 86–97.

Heimdal, Kristen R., & Sharon K. Houseknecht. 2003. Cohabiting and married couples' income organization: Approaches in Sweden and the United States. *Journal of Marriage and Family* 65(3): 525–538.

Heitritter, Dianne Lynn. 1999 November. Meanings of family strength voiced by Somali immigrants: Reaching an inductive understanding. *Dissertation Abstracts International, A: The Humanities and Social Sciences* 60(5), 1782–A-1783–A.

Helbig, Sylvia, Thomas Lampert, Michael Klose, & Frank Jacobi. 2006. Is parenthood associated with mental health? Findings from an epidemiological community survey. *Social Psychiatry and Psychiatric Epidemiology* 41(11): 889–96.

Henderson, A.J.Z., K. Bartholomew, & D.G. Dutton. 1997. He loves me; he loves me not: Attachment and separation resolution of abused women. *Journal of Family Violence* 12 (June): 169–191.

Henningsen, David Dryden, Mary Braz, & Elaine Davies. 2008. Why do we flirt?: Flirting motivations and sex differences in working and social contexts. *Journal of Business Communication* 45.4: 483–502.

Henry, Ryan G., & Richard B. Miller. 2004. Marital problems occurring in midlife: Implications for couples therapy. *American Journal of Family Therapy* 32: 405–417.

Hequembourg, A.L. 2007. Becoming lesbian mothers. *Journal of Homosexuality* 53(3): 153–180.

Herlyn, Ingrid, & Ulrike Vogel. 1989 July. Individualization: A new perspective on the life situation of women. *Zeitschrift fur Sozialisationsforschung und Erziehungssoziologie* 9(3): 162–178.

Hetherington, E. Mavis, & John Kelly. 2002. *For Better or for Worse: Divorce Reconsidered*. New York: W. W. Norton.

Higgins, Chris, & Linda Duxbury. 2002. The 2001 national work-life conflict study: Report one. Retrieved May 25, 2005, from Public Health Agency of Canada: **www.phacaspc.gc.ca/publicat/work-travail/report1/**.

Higgins, Daryl J., & Marita P. McCabe. 1994. The relationship of child sexual abuse and family violence to adult adjustment: Toward an integrated risk-sequelae model. *Journal of Sex Research* 31(4): 255–266.

Hill, R. 1949. *Families Under Stress: Adjustment to the Crises of War Separation and Reunion*. New York: Harper and Bros.

Hiotakis, Samantha. 2005. An investigation of familial variables associated with marital satisfaction. *Dissertation Abstracts International: Section B: The Sciences and Engineering* 66(5-B), 2877.

Hochschild, A. 2001 (1997). The third shift. In Bonnie J. Fox (Ed.), *Family Patterns, Gender Relations* (2nd edition). Toronto: Oxford University Press, 338–51.

Hochschild, Arlie Russell. 1997. *The Time Bind: When Work Becomes Home and Home Becomes Work*. New York: Metropolitan Books.

Hoem, Britta, & Jan M. Hoem. 1988 September. The Swedish family: Aspects of contemporary developments. *Journal of Family Issues* 9(3): 397–424.

Hofferth, Sandra L. 1996. Effects of public and private policies on working after childbirth. *Work and Occupations* 23(4): 378–404.

Hoffman, Charles D., & Debra K. Ledford. 1995. Adult children of divorce: Relationships with their mothers and fathers prior to, following parental separation, and currently. *Journal of Divorce and Remarriage 24*(3–4).

Hoffman, Martin L. 1979. Development of moral thought, feeling, and behavior. *American Psychologist 34*(10): 958–966.

Hoffman, Saul, & Greg Duncan. 1995 Winter. The effect of incomes, wages and AFDC benefits in marital disruption. *Journal of Human Resources 30*.

Holtzworth-Munroe, Amy, Jennifer Waltz, Neil S. Jacobson, Valerie Monaco, Peter A. Fehrenbach, & John M. Gottman. 1992. Recruiting nonviolent men as control subjects for research on marital violence: How easily can it be done? *Violence and Victims 7*(1): 79–88.

Hook, Jennifer L. 2006. Care in context: Men's unpaid work in 20 countries, 1965–2003. *American Sociological Review 71*: 639–660.

hooks, bell. 1984. *Feminist Theory: From Margin to Centre.* Boston: South End Press.

Horowitz, Allan V., Julie McLaughlin, & Helene Raskin White. 1998. How the negative and positive aspects of partner relationships affect the mental health of young married people. *Journal of Health and Social Behavior 39*(2): 124–136.

Houston, Ted L. 2004. The case for promoting marriage: The devil is in the details. *Journal of Marriage and Family 66*(4): 943–958.

Howell, Nancy, with Patricia Albanese & Kwaku Obosu-Mensah. 2001. Ethnic families, pp. 116–142. In Maureen Baker (Ed.), *Families: Changing Trends in Canada* (4th edition). Toronto: McGraw-Hill Ryerson.

Huang, Frederick Y., & Salman Akhtar. 2005. Immigrant sex: The transport of affection and sensuality across cultures. *American Journal of Psychoanalysis 65*: 179–88.

Huang, I-Chiao. 1991. Family stress and coping, pp. 289–334. In Stephen J. Bahr (Ed.), *Family Research: A Sixty-Year Review, 1930–1990, Volume 1*. New York: Lexington Books, Maxwell Macmillan International.

Huck, Barbara. 2001 February/March. Love in another world. *The Beaver: Canada's History Magazine*: 12–19.

Hughes, R., A.T. Ebata, & D. Dollahite. 1999. Introduction: Family life in the information age. *Family Relations 48*: 5–6.

Huisman, Kimberly A. 1996. Wife battering in Asian American communities: Identifying the service needs of an overlooked segment of the U.S. population. *Violence Against Women 2*(3): 260–283.

Human Resources and Skills Development Canada. 2005a. Addressing work-life balance in Canada. Retrieved May 27, 2005, from **www.hrsdc.gc.ca/asp/gateway.asp?hr=/en/lp/spila/wlb/awlbc/01table_of_contents.shtml&hs=wnc**.

Human Resources and Skills Development Canada. 2005b. Work-related child-care centres in Canada–2001. Retrieved May 27, 2005, from **www.hrsdc.gc.ca/asp/gateway.asp?hr=/en/lp/spila/wlb/wrccc/02table of_contents.shtml&hs=wnc**.

Humphreys, Terry, & Ed Herold. 2007. Sexual consent in heterosexual relationships: Development of a new measure. *Sex Roles 57*: 305–15.

Huston, Ted L., & Heidi Melz. 2004. The case for (promoting) marriage: The devil is in the details. *Journal of Marriage and Family 66*(4): 943–958.

Hwang, Wei-Chin. 2006. Acculturative family distancing: Theory, research, and clinical practice. *Psychotherapy: Theory, Research, Practice, Training 43* (2006): 397–409.

Hyman, Ilene, Sepali Guruge, & Robin Mason. 2008. The impact of migration on marital relationships: A study of Ethiopian immigrants in Toronto. *Journal of Comparative Family Studies 39*: 149–63.

Hynie, Michaela, Richard N. Lalonde, & Nam Lee. 2006. Parent-child value transmission among Chinese immigrants to North America: The case of traditional mate preferences. *Cultural Diversity and Ethnic Minority Psychology 12*: 230–44.

Illig, Diane S. 1999 October. Instrument development for assessing the task allocation by lesbian and gay couples with regard to household and familial tasks. *Dissertation Abstracts International, A: The Humanities and Social Sciences 60*(4), 1347–A.

Jaaber, R., & S. Das Dasgupta. 2003. Assessing social risks of battered women. *Praxis International 10:* 14. Available at **www.praxisinternational.org/library_frame.html** under "Library: Advocacy."

Jackson, Stevi. 1992. Towards a historical sociology of housework: A materialist feminist analysis. *Women's Studies International Forum 15*(2): 153–172.

Jacobson, Bert H., Steven G. Aldana et al. 1996 September–October. The relationship between perceived stress and self-reported illness-related absenteeism. *American Journal of Health Promotion 11*(1): 54–61.

Jacobson, N.S., J.M. Gottman, E. Gortner, S. Berns, & J.W. Shortt. 1996. Psychological factors in the longitudinal course of battering: When do the couples split up? When does the abuse decrease? *Violence and Victims 11*: 371–392.

Jacoby, A.P., & J.D. Williams. 1985. Effects of premarital sexual standards and behavior on dating and marriage desirability. *Journal of Marriage and the Family 47*: 1059–1065.

Jaffe, Dena H., Orly Manor, Zvi Eisenbach, & Yehuda D. Neumark. 2007. The protective effect of marriage on mortality in a dynamic society. *Annals of Epidemiology, 17*(7): 540–547.

Jain, D., S. Sanon, L. Sadowski, & W. Hunter. 2004. Violence against women in India: Evidence from rural Maharashtra, India. *Rural and Remote Health 4*, article number 304.

Jambunathan, Saigeetha, Diane C. Burts, & Sarah Pierce. 2000. Comparisons of parenting attitudes among five ethnic groups in the United States. *Journal of Comparative Family Studies 31*: 395–406.

Jamieson, Lynn. 1999. Intimacy transformed? A critical look at "the pure relationship." *Sociology 33*(3): 477–494.

Jeffrey, Kirk. 1975. Marriage, career, and feminine ideology in nineteenth-century America: Reconstructing the marital experience of Lydia Maria Child, 1828–1874. *Feminist Studies 2:* 2–3, 113–130.

Jepson, Lisa K., & Christopher A. Jepson. 2002. An empirical analysis of the matching patterns of same-sex and opposite-sex couples. *Demography 39*(3): 435–453.

Jin, Xiaochun, Morris Eagle, & Marianne Yoshioka. 2007. Early exposure to violence in the family of origin and positive attitudes towards marital violence: Chinese immigrant male batterers vs. controls. *Journal of Family Violence 22*: 211–22.

Johnson, Susan, and Jay Lebow. 2000. The "coming of age" of couple therapy: A decade in review. *Journal of Marital and Family Therapy* 26(1): 23–38.

Johnston, C. 2008. The PACS and (post-)queer citizenship in contemporary republican France. *Sexualities* 11(6): 688–705.

Jones, Charles L., Lorna Marsden, & Lorne Tepperman. 1990. *Lives of Their Own: The Individualization of Women's Lives*. Toronto: Oxford University Press.

Jones, Elise F., Jacqueline Darroch Forrest, Noreen Goldman, Stanley Henshaw, Richard Lincoln, Jeannie Rosoff, Charles F. Westoff, & Deidre Wulf. 1993. *Teenage Pregnancy in Industrialized Countries*. New Haven: Yale University Press.

Jones, Loring, Margaret Hughes, & Ulrike Unerstaller. 2001. Post-traumatic stress disorder (PTSD) in victims of domestic violence: A Review of the research. *Trauma, Violence and Abuse* 2(2): 99–199.

Jordan, Karen M., & Robert H. Deluty. 2000. Social support, coming out, and relationship satisfaction in lesbian couples. *Journal of Lesbian Studies* 4(1): 145–164.

Juby, Heather, Celine Le Bourdais, & Nicole Marcil-Gratton. 2005. Sharing roles, sharing custody? Couples' characteristics and children's living arrangements at separation. *Journal of Marriage and the Family* 67: 157–172.

Juby, Heather, Jean-Michel Billette, Benoit Laplante, & Celine Le Bourdais. 2007. Nonresident fathers and children. *Journal of Marriage and Family* 28(9): 1220–1245.

Judge, Sharon Lesar. 1998 July. Parental coping strategies and strengths in families of young children with disabilities. *Family Relations* 47(3): 263–268.

Kahana, Eva, Boaz Kahana, & Jennifer Kinney. 1982. Coping among vulnerable elders, pp. 64–85. In Zev Harel, Phyllis Ehrlich et al. (Eds.), *The Vulnerable Aged: People, Services, and Policies*. New York: Springer Publishing Co.

Kalin, Rudolf, & Carol A. Lloyd. 1985. Sex-role identity, sex-role ideology and marital adjustment. *International Journal of Women's Studies* 8(1): 32–39.

Kallivayalil, Diya. 2007. Feminist therapy: Its use and implications for South Asian immigrant survivors of domestic violence. *Women & Therapy* 30: 109–27.

Kalmijn, M. 2007. Gender differences in the effects of divorce, widowhood, and remarriage on intergenerational support: does marriage protect fathers? *Social Forces* 86(3): 1079–104.

Kalmijn, Matthijs. 1991. Shifting boundaries: Trends in religious and educational homogamy. *American Sociological Review* 56(6): 786–800.

Kalmijn, Matthijs. 1993. Spouse selection among the children of European immigrants: A comparison of marriage cohorts in the 1960 Census. *International Migration Review* 27(1): 51–78.

Kalnins, Ilze V., M. Pamela Churchill, & Grace E. Terry. 1980. Concurrent stresses in families with a leukemic child. *Journal of Pediatric Psychology* 5(1): 81–92.

Karasek, Robert, & Tores Theorell. 1990. *Healthy Work: Stress, Productivity, and the Reconstruction of Working Life*. New York: Basic Books.

Karlsson, S.G., & K. Borell. 2002. Intimacy and autonomy, gender and ageing: Living apart together. *Ageing International* 7(4): 11–26.

Karney, Benjamin R., & Thomas N. Bradbury. 1995. Assessing longitudinal change in marriage: An introduction to the analysis of growth curves. *Journal of Marriage and the Family* 57(4): 1091–1108.

Karriker-Jaffe, Katherine J., et al. 2008. The development of aggression during adolescence: Sex differences in trajectories of physical and social aggression among youth in rural areas. *Journal of Abnormal Child Psychology* 36: 1227–1236.

Kashyap, Lina. 2004. The impact of modernization on Indian families: The counselling challenge. *International Journal for the Advancement of Counselling* 26: 341–50.

Katz, Elana. 2007. A family therapy perspective on mediation. *Family Process* 46(1): 93–107.

Katz, Jennifer, & Laura Myhr. 2008. Perceived conflict patterns and relationship quality associated with verbal sexual coercion by male dating partners. *Journal of Interpersonal Violence* 23.6: 798–814.

Katz, Jennifer, & Vanessa Tirone. 2009. Women's sexual compliance with male dating partners: Associations with investment in ideal womanhood and romantic well-being. *Sex Roles* 60(5–6): 347–356.

Katz, Jennifer, Ileana Arias, Steven R.H. Beach, Gene Brody, & Paul Roman. 1995. Excuses, excuses: Accounting for the effects of partner violence on marital satisfaction and stability. *Violence and Victims* 10(4).

Katz, Ruth. 2000. Attitudes of new immigrant and veteran-resident Israeli divorced mothers toward single motherhood. *International Migration* 38: 83–97.

Keating, Norah, Janet Fast, Judith Frederick (Statistics Canada), Kelly Cranswick (Statistics Canada), & Cathryn Perrier. 1999. *Eldercare in Canada: Context, Content and Consequences*. Ottawa: Statistics Canada, Housing, Family and Social Statistics Division.

Kellogg, Nancy D., Thomas J. Hoffman, & Elizabeth R. Taylor. 1999 Summer. Early sexual experiences among pregnant and parenting adolescents. *Adolescence* 34(134): 293–303.

Kemp, Anita, Bonnie L. Green, & Christine Hovanitz. 1995 March. Incidence and correlates of post-traumatic stress disorder in battered women: Shelter and community samples. *Journal of Interpersonal Violence* 10: 43–55.

Kemp, C.L., & M. Denton. 2003. The allocation of responsibility for later life: Canadian reflections on the roles of individuals, government, employers and families. *Ageing & Society* 23: 737–760.

Kempe, C.H., F.N. Silverman, B.F. Steele, W. Droegmueller, & H.K. Silver. 1962. The battered-child syndrome. *Journal of the American Medical Association* 181: 17–24.

Kennedy, M.A., & B.B. Gorzalka. 2002. Asian and non-Asian attitudes toward rape, sexual harassment, and sexuality. *Sex Roles* 46: 227–38.

Kerr, Don, & Roderic Beaujot. 2003. Child poverty and family structure in Canada, 1981–1997. *Journal of Comparative Family Studies* 34(3): 321–335.

Kerr, Don, Melissa Moyser, & Roderic Beaujot. 2006. Marriage and cohabitation: demographic and socio-economic differences in Quebec and Canada. *Canadian Studies in Population* 33(1): 83–117.

Kesner, John E., & Patrick C. McKenry. 2001 March–April. Single parenthood and social competence in children of color. *Families in Society* 82(2): 136–144.

Keyfitz, Nathan. 1988. On the wholesomeness of marriage. In L. Tepperman & J. Curtis (Eds.), *Readings in Sociology: An Introduction*. Toronto: McGraw-Hill Ryerson.

Kheshgi-Genovese, Zareena, & Thomas A. Genovese. 1997. Developing the spousal relationship within stepfamilies. *Families in Society: The Journal of Contemporary Human Services* 78(3): 255–271.

Kiecolt-Glaser, Janice K., & Tamara L. Newton. 2001. Marriage and health: His and hers. *Psychological Bulletin* 127(4): 472–500.

Kiko-Net (2002). White Paper on the Internet in Japan. Retrieved July 28, 2005, from **www.kiko-net.com/ Foreigners/White_Paper/White_Paper.php?year= 2002#PersonalService**.

Kim-Goh, Mikyong, & Jon Baello. 2008. Attitudes toward domestic violence in Korean and Vietnamese immigrant communities: Implications for human services. *Journal of Family Violence* 23: 647–54.

King, Rosalind Berkowitz, & Kathleen Mullan Harris. 2007. Romantic relationships among immigrant adolescents. *International Migration Review* 41: 344–70.

King, V. 2007. When children have two mothers: Relationships with nonresident mothers, stepmothers, and fathers. *Journal of Marriage and the Family* 69: 1178–1193.

King, V., & M.E. Scott. 2005. A comparison of cohabiting relationships among older and younger adults. *Journal of Marriage and Family* 67: 271–285.

Kinnunen, Ulla, Jan Gerris, & Ad Vermulst. 1996 October. Work experiences and family functioning among employed fathers with children of school age. *Family Relations* 45: 449–455.

Kirchler, Erich. 1989 March. Everyday life experiences at home: An interaction diary approach to assess marital relationships. *Journal of Family Psychology* 2(3): 311–336.

Kissane, Rebecca Joyce, & Richard Krebs. 2007. Assessing welfare reform, over a decade later. *Sociology Compass* 1–2: 789–813.

Kleban, Morton H., Elaine M. Brody, Claire B. Schoonover, & Christine Hoffman. 1989 May. Family help to the elderly: perceptions of sons-in-law regarding parent care. *Journal of Marriage and the Family* 51(2): 303–312.

Klein, David M., & James M. White. 1996. *Family Theories: An Introduction*. Thousand Oaks, California: Sage.

Klinger, Rochelle L. 1995. Gay violence. *Journal of Gay & Lesbian Psychotherapy* 2(3): 119–134.

Kluwer, Esther S., & Jose Heesink, & Evert Van de Vliert. 1996 November. Marital conflict about the division of household labor and paid work. *Journal of Marriage and the Family* 58.

Knee, Raymond C., Cynthia Lonsbary, Amy Canevello, & Heather Patrick. 2005. Self-determination and conflict in romantic relationships. *Journal of Personality and Social Psychology* 89: 997–1009.

Knox, David, Marty Zusman, & Andrea McNeely. 2008. University student beliefs about sex: Men vs. women. *College Student Journal* 42(1): 181–185.

Knox, David. 2005. *Choices in Relationships: Introduction to Marriage and Family* (with Infotrac). Belmont: Thomson Wadsworth. Retrieved November 4, 2005, through Google Print Publisher Program.

Kobayashi, A. 1992. The Japanese-Canadian redress settlement and its implications for "race relations." *Canadian Ethnic Studies* 24(1): 1–19.

Kogos, Jennifer L., & John Snarey. 1995. Parental divorce and the moral development of adolescents. *Journal of Divorce and Remarriage* 23(3–4).

Kohen, Dafna, Clyde Hertzman, & J. Douglas Willms. 2002. The importance of quality child care, pp. 261–276. In J. Douglas Willms (Ed.), *Vulnerable Children: Findings from Canada's National Longitudinal Survey of Children and Youth*. Edmonton: University of Alberta Press, and Ottawa: Human Resources Development Canada, Applied Research Branch.

Kohli, M., M. Rein, A. Guillemard, & H. Van Gunsteren. 1991. *Time for Retirement: Comparative Studies of Early Exit from the Labour Force*. Cambridge: Cambridge University Press.

Kohli, Martin. 1986. Social organization and subjective construction of life course, pp. 271–292. In A.B. Sorenson, F.E. Weinhert, & L.R. Sharrod (Eds.), *Human Development and the Life Course*. Hillsdale, CA: Erlbaum.

Kolbo, Jerome R., Eleanor H. Blakely, & David Engleman. 1996 June. Children who witness domestic violence: A review of empirical literature. *Journal of Interpersonal Violence* 11: 281–293.

Koskinen, S., K. Joutsenniemi, T. Martelin, & P. Martikainen. 2007. Mortality differences according to living arrangements. *International Journal of Epidemiology* 36: 1255–1264.

Kozuch, Patricia, & Teresa M. Cooney. 1995. Young adults' marital and family attitudes: The role of recent parental divorce, and family and parental conflict. *Journal of Divorce and Remarriage* 23(3–4).

Kruger, Helga, & Rene Levy. 2001. Linking life courses, work and the family: Theorizing a not so visible nexus between women and men. *Canadian Journal of Sociology* 26(4): 145–166.

Kruk, E. 1995. Grandparent grandchild contact loss: Findings from a study of grandparent rights members. *Canadian Journal on Aging* 14(4): 737–754.

Kumar, Pramod, & Jayshree Dhyani. 1996. Marital adjustment: A study of some related factors. *Indian Journal of Clinical Psychology* 23(2): 112–116.

Kunz, J. 1992. The effects of divorce on children. In S.J. Bahr (Ed.), *Family Research: A Sixty-Year Review, 1930–1990, Volume 2*. New York: Lexington Books, pp. 325–376.

Kunz, Jennifer, & Stephen J. Bahr. 1996. A profile of parental homicide against children. *Journal of Family Violence* 11(4): 347–362.

Kurz, Demie. 1995. *For Richer or For Poorer: Mothers Confront Divorce*. New York: Routledge.

La Rose, Lauren. CBC News In Depth. 2008 April 2. Census: Mixed-race taboo drops away. Retrieved April 15, 2009, from **www.cbc.ca/news/background/census/ mixed-marriages.html**.

Laakso, Janice. 2004, Spring. Key determinants of mothers' decisions to allow visits with non-custodial fathers. *Fathering*.

Lademann, A. 1980. The neurologically handicapped child. *Scandinavian Journal of Audiology* 10 (suppl.): 23–26.

Laermans, Rudi, & Carine Meulders, 1998. Washing practices, cleanliness and social identity. A historical-sociological interpretation in the light of the private/public distinction [original title: Waspraktijk, properheid en sociale identiteit. Een historisch-sociologische interpretatie in het licht van het onderscheid prive/publick]. *Tijdschrift voor Sociologie* 19(3): 281–299.

Lai, D., & Leonenko, W. 2007. Correlates of living alone among single elderly Chinese immigrants in Canada. *International Journal of Aging and Human Development* 65(2): 121–148.

Lai, D.W.L. 2005. Cultural factors and preferred living arrangements of aging Chinese Canadians. *Journal of Housing for the Elderly* 19(2): 71–86.

Lampard, Richard. 2007. Couples' places of meeting in late 20th century Britain: Class, continuity and change. *European Sociological Review* 23.3: 357–371.

Landis, Dana, Noni K. Gaylord-Harden, Sara L. Malinowski, Kathryn E. Grant, Russel A. Carleton, & Rebecca E. Ford. 2007. Urban adolescent stress and hopelessness. *Journal of Adolescence* 30(6): 1051–1070.

Landis-Kleine, Cathy, Linda Foley, Loretta Nall, Patricia Padgett; & Leslie Walters-Palmer. 1995. Attitudes toward marriage and divorce held by young adults. *Journal of Divorce & Remarriage* 23(3&4): 63–74.

Landolt, Monica A., & Donald G. Dutton. 1997 September. Power and personality: An analysis of gay male intimate abuse. *Sex Roles* 37(5–6): 335–359.

Landry, Yves. 1992. Les filles duroi au xvie siècle: Orphelines en France. *Pioniéres au Canada*. Montreal: Lemeac.

Lapierre-Adamcyk, Evelyne. 1987 May. *Mariage et politique de la famille*. Paper presented at the Association des Demographiques du Québec, Ottawa.

Larcombe, E.S. 1978. A handicapped child means a handicapped family. *Journal of the Royal College of General Practice* 28: 46–52.

LaRossa, Ralph. 2004. The culture of fatherhood in the fifties: A closer look. *Journal of Family History* 29(1): 47–70.

Larson, Jeffrey H., Stephan M. Wilson, & Rochelle Beley. 1994 April. The impact of job insecurity on marital and family relations. *Family Relations* 43: 138–143.

Larson, Reed W., & Sally Gillman. 1999 February. Transmission of emotions in the daily interactions of single-mother families. *Journal of Marriage and the Family* 61(1): 21–37.

Lau, Anna S., David T. Takeuchi, & Margarita Alegria. 2006. Parent-to-child aggression among Asian American parents: Culture, context, and vulnerability. *Journal of Marriage and Family* 68: 1261–275.

Lauer, Robert H., Jeanette C. Lauer, & Sarah T. Kerr. 1990. The long-term marriage: Perceptions of stability and satisfaction. *International Journal of Aging and Human Development* 31(3): 189–195.

Laumann, E.O, J.H. Gagnon, R.T. Michael, & S. Michaels. 1994. *The Social Organization of Sexuality: Sexual Practices in the United States*. Chicago: University of Chicago Press.

Lavoie, F., M. Hebert, R. Tremblay, F. Vitaro, L. Vezina, & P. McDuff. 2002. History of family dysfunction and perpetration of dating violence by adolescent boys: A longitudinal study. *Journal of Adolescent Health* 30: 375–383.

Lavoie, Francine, Line Robitaille, & Martine Herbert. 2000. Teen dating relationships and aggression: An exploratory study. *Violence Against Women* 6: 6.

Lawrence, Erika, Alexia D. Rothman, Rebecca J. Cobb, Michael T. Rothman, & Thomas Bradbury. 2008. Marital satisfaction across the transition to parenthood. *Journal of Family Psychology* 22(1): 41–50.

Le Bourdais, Celine, & Nicole Marcil-Gratton. 1994. Quebec's pro-active approach to family policy, pp. 103–116. In Maureen Baker (Ed.), *Canada's Changing Families: Challenges to Public Policy*. Ottawa: Vanier Institute of the Family.

Le Bourdais, Celine, & Nicole Marcil-Gratton. 1996. Family transformations across the Canadian/American border: When the laggard becomes the leader. *Journal of Comparative Family Studies* 27(3): 415–436.

Le Bourdais, Celine, G. Neil, & Pierre Turcotte. 2000. The changing face of conjugal relationships. *Canadian Social Trends* 56: 14–17.

Le Bourdais, Celine, Evelyne Lapierre-Adamcyk, & Philippe Pacaut. 2004. Changes in conjugal life in Canada: Is cohabitation progressively replacing marriage? *Journal of Marriage and the Family* 66: 929–942.

Légaré, Jacques, Laurent Martel, Leroy O. Stone, & Hubert Denis. 2000. *Living Arrangements of Older Persons in Canada: Effects on Their Socio-Economic Conditions*. UN Economic Commission for Europe [ECE]: Geneva, Switzerland. United Nations Population Fund [UNFPA]: New York, New York.

Lehr, Valerie. 1999. *Queer Family Values: Debunking the Myth of the Nuclear Family*. Philadelphia: Temple University Press.

Leiter, Michael P., & Marie-Josette Durup. 1996. Work, home, and in-between: A longitudinal study of spillover. *Journal of Applied and Behavioural Science* 32(1): 29–47.

Lempert, Lora Bex. 1996. Language obstacles in the narratives of abused women. *Mid-American Review of Sociology* 19(1–2): 15–32.

Lesemann, Frederic, & Roger Nicol. 1994. Family policy: International comparisons, pp. 117–125. In Maureen Baker (Ed.), *Canada's Changing Families: Challenges to Public Policy*. Ottawa: Vanier Institute of the Family.

Lester, David. 2003. The regional correlates of suicide in Canada: Changes over time. *Archives of Suicide Research* 7: 145–148.

Letellier, Patrick. 1994 Summer. Gay and bisexual male domestic violence victimization: Challenges to feminist theory and responses to violence. *Violence and Victims* 9(2): 95–106.

Leung, A.K.C., W.L.M. Robson, H. Cho, & S.H.N. Lim. 1996. Latchkey children. *Journal of the Royal Society of Health* 116(6): 356–359.

Lever, Janet, Christian Grov, Tracy Royce, & Brian Joseph Gillespie. 2008. Searching for love in all the "write" places: Exploring internet personals use by sexual orientation, gender, and age. *International Journal of Sexual Health* 20.4: 233–246.

Levin, Irene. 2004. Living apart together: A new family form. *Current Sociology* 52(2): 223–240.

Levy, D.M. 1945. The War and Family Life: Report for the War Emergency Committee, 1944. Reprinted in *American Journal of Orthopsychiatry* 15: 140–152.

Li, P.S. 1996. *The Making of Post-war Canada*. Toronto: Oxford University Press.

Lichter, D.T., & Z. Qian. 2008. Serial cohabitation and the marital life course. *Journal of Marriage and Family* 70(4): 861–878.

Lichter, D.T., Z. Qian, & L. Mellott. 2006. Marriage or dissolution? Union transitions among poor cohabiting women. *Demography* 43: 223–240.

Lichter, Daniel T., & Julie H. Carmalt. 2009. Religion and marital quality among low-income couples. *Social Science Research* 38: 168–187.

Liebkind, Karmela. 1993. Self-reported ethnic identity, depression, and anxiety among young Vietnamese refugees and their parents. *Journal of Refugee Studies* 6(1): 25–39.

Lipman, Ellen L., David R. Offord, Martin D. Dooley, & Martin H. Boyle. 2002. Children's outcomes in differing types of single-parent families, pp. 229–242. In J. Douglas Willms (Ed.), *Vulnerable Children: Findings from Canada's National Longitudinal Survey of Children and Youth*. Edmonton: University of Alberta Press, and Ottawa: Human Resources Development Canada, Applied Research Branch.

Liu, J.H., S.H. Ng, A. Weatherall, & C. Loong. 2000. Filial piety, acculturation, and intergenerational communication among New Zealand Chinese. *Basic & Applied Social Psychology* 22: 213–223.

Lleras, Christy. 2008. Employment, work conditions, and the home environment in single-mother families. *Journal of Family Issues* 29(10): 1268–1297.

Lloyd, Eva. 2008. The interface between childcare, family support and child poverty strategies under New Labour: Tensions and contradictions. *Social Policy & Society* 7(4): 479–494.

Logan, John Allen, Peter Hoff, & Michael Newton. 2008. Two-sided estimation of mate preferences for similarities in age, education, and religion. *Journal of the American Statistical Association* 103.482: 559.

Looker, Diane E., & Victor Thiessen. 2003. Beyond the digital divide in Canadian schools: From access to competency in the use of information technology. *Social Science Computer Review* 21(4): 475–490.

Lu, Luo, Shu-Fang Kao, Cary L. Cooper, Tammy D. Allen, Laurent M. Lapierre, Michael O'Driscoll, Steven A.Y. Poelmans, Juan I. Sanchez., & Paul E. Spector. 2009. Work resources, work-to-family conflict, and its consequences: A Taiwanese-British cross-cultural comparison. *International Journal of Stress Management* 16(1): 25–44.

Lugo-Gil, Julieta, & Catherine S. Tamis-LeMonda. 2008. Family resources and parenting quality. Links to children's cognitive development across the first 3 years. *Child Development* 79(4): 1065–1085.

Lumpkin, James R. 2008. Grandparents in a parental or near-parental role: Sources of stress and coping mechanisms. *Journal of Family Issues* 29(3): 357–372.

Luo, Shanhong, & Eva C. Klohnen. 2005. Assortive mating and marital quality in newlyweds: A couple-centered approach. *Journal of Personality and Social Psychology* 88(2): 304–326.

Lupri, Eugen. 1993. Spousal violence: Wife abuse across the life course. *Zeitschrift fnr Sozialisationforschung und Erziehungssoziologie* 13(3): 232–257.

Lussier, Gretchen, Kirby Deater-Deckard, Judy Dunn, & Lisa Davies. 2002. Support across two generations: Children's closeness to grandparents following parental divorce and remarriage. *Journal of Family Psychology* 16(3): 363–376.

Luster, Tom, Harry Perlstadt, & Marvin McKinney. 1996 July. The effects of a family support program and other factors on the home environments provided by adolescent mothers. *Family Relations* 45: 255–264.

Luxton, Meg (Ed.). 1997. *Feminism and Families: Critical Policies and Changing Practices*. Halifax: Fernwood.

Luxton, Meg. 2001. Conceptualizing "families": Theoretical frameworks and family research, pp. 28–50. In Maureen Baker (Ed.), *Families: Changing Trends in Canada* (4th edition). Toronto: McGraw-Hill Ryerson.

Lye, Diane N., & Timothy J. Biblarz. 1993. The effects of attitudes toward family life and gender roles on marital satisfaction. *Journal of Family Issues* 14(2): 157–188.

Lynn, Marion. 2003. Single-parent families, pp. 6–54. In Marion Lynn (Ed.), *Voices: Essays on Canadian Families* (2nd edition). Toronto: Thomson Nelson.

Macmillan, R.I., & R. Gartner. 1999. When she brings home the bacon: Labour force participation and spousal violence against women. *Journal of Marriage and the Family* 61: 947–958.

Madathil, Jayamala, & James M. Benshoff. 2008. Importance of marital characteristics and marital satisfaction: A comparison of Asian Indians in arranged marriages and Americans in marriages of choice. *The Family Journal* 16: 222–230.

Malta, S. 2007. Love actually! Older adults and their romantic internet relationships. *Australian Journal of Emerging Technologies and Society* 5(2): 84–102.

Man, Guida. 2001. From Hong Kong to Canada: Immigration and the changing family lives of middle-class women from Hong Kong, pp. 420–438. In Bonnie J. Fox (Ed.), *Family Patterns, Gender Divisions* (2nd edition). Toronto: Oxford University Press.

Mandell, Deena. 1995. Fathers who don't pay child support: Hearing their voices. *Journal of Divorce and Remarriage* 23(1–2).

Manning, W.D., M.A. Longmore, & P.C. Giordano. 2007. The changing institution of marriage: Adolescents' expectations to cohabit and to marry. *Journal of Marriage and Family* 69(3): 559–575.

Manning, W.D., P.J. Smock, & D. Majumdar. 2004. The relative stability of cohabiting and marital unions for children. *Population Research and Policy Review* 23: 135–159.

Manning, Wendy D. 2004. Children and the stability of cohabiting couples. *Journal of Marriage and the Family* 66(3): 674–689.

Marano, Hara-Estroff. 1997 March–April. Love lesson: Six new moves to improve your relationship. *Psychology Today* 30.

March, James G., & Herbert A. Simon. 1958. *Organizations*. New York: Wiley.

Marcil-Gratton, Nicole, Céline Le Bourdais, & Évelyne Lapierre-Adamcyk. 2000 Autumn. The implications of parents' conjugal histories for children. *Isuma* 1(2): 32–40.

Marcil-Gratton, Nicole. 1993. Growing up with a single parent: A transitional experience? Some demographic measurements, pp. 73–90. In Joe Hudson and Burt Galaway (Eds.), *Single Parent Families: Perspectives on Research and Policy*. Toronto: Thompson Educational Publishing.

Marshall, Katherine. 2009. The family work week. *Statistics Canada Perspectives*. Ottawa: Statistics Canada. Catalogue no. 75-001-X. Retrieved from **www.statcan.gc.ca/pub/75-001-x/75-001-x2009104-eng.htm**.

Martel, Laurent, & Jacques Légaré. 2001. Avec ou sans famille proche à la vieillesse : une description du réseau de soutien informel des personnes âgées selon la présence du conjoint et des enfants. *Cahiers québécois de démographie* 30(1): 89–114.

Martz, Diane J. Forsdick. 2007. Canadian farm women and their families: Restructuring, work and decision making. *Dissertation Abstracts International, A: The Humanities and Social Sciences*. 67(10): 3932.

Mason, Mary Ann, Arlene Skolnick, & Stephen D. Sugarman (Eds.). 2003. *All Our Families: New Policies for a New Century* (2nd edition). New York: Oxford University Press.

Mason, Robin. 2003. Listening to lone mothers: Paid work, family life, and childcare in Canada. *Journal of Children & Poverty* 9(1): 41–54.

Mastekaasa, Arne. 1995. Divorce and subjective distress: Panel evidence. *European Sociological Review* 11(2).

Matthews, Lisa S., Rand D. Conger, & K.A.S. Wickrama. 1996. Work-family conflict and marital quality: Mediating processes. *Social Psychology Quarterly* 59(1): 62–79.

Matthey, Stephen, Bryanne Barnett, Judy Ungerer, & Brent Waters. 2000. Paternal and maternal depressed mood during the transition to parenthood. *Journal of Affective Disorders* 60(2), 75–85.

Mattingly, Marybeth J., & Robert N. Bozick. 2001. *Children Raised by Same-Sex Couples: Much Ado about Nothing.* Southern Sociological Society (SSS).

Mauno, Saijo, & Ulla Kinnunen. 1999 August. Job insecurity and well-being: A longitudinal study among male and female employees in Finland. *Community, Work & Family* 2(2): 147–171.

McCabe, M. 2006. A longitudinal study of coping strategies and quality of life among people with multiple sclerosis. *Journal of Clinical Psychology in Medical Settings* 13: 369–379.

McCabe, Marita P. 1999. The interrelationship between intimacy, relationship functioning, and sexuality among men and women in committed relationships. *Canadian Journal of Human Sexuality*, 8(1): 31–38.

McCarroll, Linda Diane. 2000 August. Family Rituals: Promoting the ethnic identity of preschoolers. *Dissertation Abstracts International, A: The Humanities and Social Sciences* 61(2), 783–A.

McCarthy, Linda. 2000. Poppies in a wheat field: Exploring the lives of rural lesbians. *Journal of Homosexuality* 39(1): 75–94.

McClennen, Joan C. 2005. Domestic violence between same-gender partners: Recent findings and future research. *Journal of Interpersonal Violence* 20(2): 149–154.

McCloskey, Laura A. 1996 August. Socio-economic and coercive power within the family. *Gender and Society*: 449–463.

McCormack, Arlene, Ann Wolbert Burgess, & Peter Gaccione. 1986. Influence of family structure and financial stability on physical and sexual abuse among a runaway population. *International Journal of Sociology of the Family* 16(2): 251–262.

McCurdy, Susan J., & Avraham Scherman. 1996. Effects of family structure on the adolescent separation-individuation process. *Adolescence* 31(122).

McDaniel, S.A. 1997. Serial employment and skinny government: Reforming caring and sharing among generations. *Canadian Journal on Aging* 16(3): 465–84.

McDaniel, S.A. 2005. The family lives of the middle-aged and elderly in Canada. In Maureen Baker (Ed.), *Families: Changing Trends in Canada* (5th edition). Toronto: McGraw-Hill Ryerson, 181–199.

McDaniel, Susan A. 1994. *Family and Friends 1990: General Social Survey Analysis Series*. Ottawa: Statistics Canada, Minister of Supply and Services. Catalogue No. 11-612E, No. 9, ISBN 0-660-15354-8.

McDaniel, Susan A. 1996a. The family lives of the middle-aged and elderly in Canada, pp. 195–211. In Maureen Baker (Ed.), *Families: Changing Trends in Canada* (3rd edition). Toronto: McGraw-Hill Ryerson.

McDaniel, Susan A. 1996b. Toward a synthesis of feminist and demographic perspectives on fertility. *The Sociological Quarterly* 37(1): 83–104.

McDaniel, Susan A. 1998. Towards healthy families, pp. 3–42. In *National Forum on Health, Determinants of Health: Settings and Issue, Vol. 3.* Ste.-Foy, Quebec: Editions Multimodes.

McDaniel, Susan A. 1999. Untangling love and domination: Challenges of home care for the elderly in a reconstructing Canada. *Journal of Canadian Studies* 34(3): 191–213.

McDaniel, Susan A. 2000. Capturing the elusive social impacts of technology: Towards a research agenda, pp. 109–121. In John de la Mothe and Gilles Paquet (Eds.), *Information, Innovation, and Impacts.* One of a series on Economics of Science, Technology, and Innovation, from Kluwer Academic Publishers.

McDaniel, Susan A. 2001. "Born at the right time": Gendered generations and webs of entitlement and responsibility. *Canadian Journal of Sociology* 26(2): 193–214.

McDaniel, Susan A. 2002. Women's changing relations to the state and citizenship: Caring and intergenerational relations in globalizing western democracies. *Canadian Review of Sociology and Anthropology* 39(2): 1–26.

McDaniel, Susan A., & Robert Lewis. 1998. Did they or didn't they? Intergenerational supports in families past: A case study of Brigus, Newfoundland, 1920–1945, pp. 475–497. In Lori Chambers & Edgar-Andre Montigny (Eds.), *Family Matters: Papers in Post-Confederation Canadian Family History.* Toronto: Canadian Scholars Press.

McDaniel, Susan A., & van Roosmalen, Erica. 1991. Sexual harassment in Canadian academe: Explorations of power and privilege. *Atlantis: A Women's Studies Journal* 17(1): 1–19.

McElroy, Ann. 1975. Canadian arctic modernization and change in female Inuit role identification. *American Ethnologist* 2(4): 662–686.

McGlone, J. 1980. Sex differences in human brain asymmetry: A critical survey. *The Behavioral and Brain Sciences* 3: 215–223.

McKeown, Larry, & Cathy Underhill. 2005. Learning online: Factors associated with use of the Internet for education purposes. *Education Matters.* Ottawa: Statistics Canada. Catalogue no. 81-004-XIE. Retrieved from **www.statcan.gc.ca/pub/81-004-x/2007004/10375-eng.htm**.

McLanahan, Sara, & Julia Adams. 1987. Parenthood and psychological well-being. *Annual Review of Sociology* 13: 237–257.

McLanahan, Sara, & Julia Adams. 1989. The effects of children on adults' psychological well-being: 1957–1976. *Social Forces* 68.

McLanahan, Sara. 2009. Fragile families and the reproduction of poverty. *The Annals of the American Academy* 621: 111–131.

McLean, Lorna. 2004. To become part of us: Ethnicity, race, literacy and the Canadian Immigration Act of 1919. *Canadian Ethnic Studies/Etudes Ethniques au Canada* 35: 1–28.

McMahon, Martha. 1995. *Engendering Motherhood: Identity and Self-Transformation in Women's Lives*. New York: Guilford.

McMullin, Julie Ann, & Victor W. Marshall. 1996 Fall. Family, friends, stress, and well-being: Does childlessness make a difference? *Canadian Journal on Aging/La Revue Canadienne du Vieillissement* 15(3): 355–373.

McVey, Wayne W. Jr. 2008. Is separation still an important component of marital dissolution? *Canadian Studies in Population* 35(1): 187–205.

Meier, Andrea, Maeda J. Galinsky, & Kathleen A. Rounds. 1995. Telephone support groups for caregivers of persons with AIDS. Social Work with Groups. *Special Groups: Current Perspectives on Theory and Practice* 18(1): 99–108.

Melby, Janet N., Shu-Ann Fang, K.A.S. Wickrama, Rand D. Conger, & Katherine J. Conger. 2008. Adolescent family experiences and educational attainment during early adulthood. *Developmental Psychology* 44(6): 1519–1536.

Merkle, Erich R., & Rhonda A. Richardson. 2000 April. Digital dating and virtual relating: Conceptualizing computer-mediated romantic relationships. *Family Relations* 49(2): 187–192.

Merrill, Lex L., Linda K. Hervig, & Joel S. Milner. 1996. Childhood parenting experiences, intimate partner conflict resolution, and adult risk for child physical abuse. *Child Abuse and Neglect* 20(11): 1049–1065.

Metz, Michael E., & Norman Epstein. 2002. Assessing the role of relationship conflict in sexual dysfunction. *Journal of Sex & Marital Therapy* 28: 139–64.

Meyerstein, Israela. 1997. The problem box ritual: Helping families prepare for remarriage. *Journal of Family Psychotherapy* 8(1): 61–65.

Miall, Charlene E., & Karen March. 2005a. Open adoption as a family form: Community assessments and social support. *Journal of Family Issues* 26(3): 380–410.

Miall, Charlene E., & Karen March. 2005b. Social support for changes in adoption practice: Gay adoption, open adoption, birth reunions, and the release of confidential identifying information. *Families in Society* 86(1): 83–92.

Middleton, Catherine, & Jordan Leith. 2007. *Intensity of Internet Use in Canada: Exploring Canadians' Engagement with the Internet*. Paper for the Statistics Canada 2007 Socio-Economic Conference. Retrieved from www.broadbandresearch.ca/ourresearch/middleton_leith_STC2007.pdf.

Milan, Anne, & Alice Peters. 2003. Couples living apart. Statistics Canada: Canadian Social Trends. Retrieved June 4, 2005, from http://64.233.161.104/search?q=cache:bB5S6r-666QJ:www.statcan.ca/english/studies/11-008/feature/star2003069000s2a02.pdf+living+apart+together,+canada&hl=en

Milan, Anne, & Brian Hamm. 2003 Winter. Across the generations: Grandparents and grandchildren. *Canadian Social Trends*: 2–7. Retrieved January 11, 2006, from http://dsp-psd.pwgsc.gc.ca/Collection-R/Statcan/11-008-XIE/0030311-008-XIE.pdf.

Milan, Anne, & Brian Hamm. 2004 Summer. Mixed unions. *Canadian Social Trends*: 1–8. Statistics Canada Catalogue no. 11-008.

Mileham, Beatriz Lia Avila. 2007. Online infidelity in Internet chat rooms: An ethnographic exploration. *Computers in Human Behavior* 23(1): 11–31.

Milikian, Levon H., & S. Al-Easa Juhaina. 1981. Oil and social change in the Gulf. *Journal of Arab Affairs* 1(1): 79–98.

Millar, Nancy. 1999. *Once Upon a Wedding*. Calgary: Bayeaux Arts.

Millar, Paul, & Anne H. Gauthier. 2002. What were they thinking? The development of child support guidelines in Canada. *Canadian Journal of Law and Society* 17(1): 139–162.

Millar, Wayne, & Surinder Wadhera. 1997. A perspective on Canadian teenage births, 1992–1994: Older men and younger women? *Canadian Journal of Public Health* 88: 333–336.

Miller, David, & P. Gillies. 1996. Is there life after work? Experiences of HIV and oncology health staff. *AIDS Care* 8(2): 167–182.

Miller, James. 2003. Out family values. In Marion Lynn (Ed.). *Voices: Essays on Canadian Families*. Scarborough, ON: Thomson.

Miller, Kim S., Rex Forehand, & Beth A. Kotchick. 1999. Adolescent sexual behavior in two ethnic minority samples: The role of family variables. *Journal of Marriage and the Family* 61(1): 85–98.

Mills, T.L., Z. Gomez-Smith, & J.M. De Leon. 2005. Skipped generation families: Sources of psychological distress among grandmothers of grandchildren who live in homes where neither parent is present. *Marriage & Family Review* 37(1–2): 191–212.

Mincieli, L., J. Manlove, M. McGarrett, K. Moore, & S. Ryan. 2007. *The relationship context of births outside of marriage: The rise of cohabitation* (Child Trends Research Brief No. 2007-13). Washington, D.C.: Child Trends. Retrieved May 20, 2009, from www.childtrends.org/Files//Child_Trends-2007_05_14_RB_OutsideBirths.pdf.

Minton, Carmelle, & Kay Pasley. 1996. Fathers' parenting role identity and father involvement: A comparison of nondivorced and divorced, nonresident fathers. *Journal of Family Issues* 17(1).

Mintz, Steven. 2006. Housework in Late 19th Century America, on Digital History.com. Retrieved July 19, 2006, from www.digitalhistory.uh.edu/historyonline/housework.cfm.

Mirdal, Gretty M. 2006. Stress and distress in migration: Twenty years after1. *The International Migration Review* 40: 375–89.

Misra, Joya, Stephanie Moller, & Michelle J. Budig. 2007. Work-family policies and poverty for partnered and single women in Europe and North America. *Gender & Society* 21(6): 804–827.

Mistry, Rashmita S., Edward D. Lowe, Aprile D. Benner, & Nina Chien. 2008. Expanding the family economic stress model: insights from a mixed-methods approach. *Journal of Marriage and Family* 70(1): 196–210.

Mitchell, Barbara A., & Ellen M. Gee. 1996a. Boomerang kids and midlife parental marital satisfaction. *Family Relations* 45: 442–448.

Mitchell, Barbara A., & Ellen M. Gee. 1996b. Young adults returning home: Implications for social policy, pp. 61–71. In Burt Galaway & Joe Hudson (Eds.), *Youth in Transition: Perspectives on Research and Policy*. Toronto: Thompson Educational Publishing.

Mitchell, Barbara. 1998. *The Refilled Nest: Recent Canadian Trends and Their Implications*. Paper presented at the 9th Annual John K. Friesen Conference, The Overselling of Population Aging, Simon Fraser University, 14–15 May 1998.

Mitchell, Barbara. 2005. *The Boomerang Age: Transitions to Adulthood in Families*. Somerset, NJ: Transactions Books.

Mofina, Rick. 2003. Gay families no longer rejected. *Edmonton Journal*, 3 January: A5.

Molassiotis, A., O.B.A. Van Den Akker, & B.J. Broughton. 1997 February. Perceived social support, family environment and psychosocial recovery in bone marrow transplant long-term survivors. *Social Science & Medicine* 44(3): 317–325.

Moncher, Frank J. 1995 September. Social isolation and child-abuse risk. *Families in Society* 76: 421–433.

Mongeau, P.A., & C.M. Carey. 1996. Who's wooing whom: An experimental investigation of date initiation and expectancy violation. *Western Journal of Communication* 60(3): 195–213.

Montgomery, James C. 2003. The issues shared by professionals living and working in rural communities in British Columbia. *Canadian Journal of Rural Medicine* 8(4): 255–260.

Monzo, Lilia D., & Robert Rueda. 2006. A sociocultural perspective on acculturation: Latino immigrant families negotiating diverse discipline practices. *Education and Urban Society* 38: 188–203.

Mooney-Somers, F., & S. Golombok. 2000. Children of lesbian mothers: From the 1970s to the new millennium. *Sexual and Relationship Therapy* 15(2): 121–126.

Moore Lappé, Frances. 1985. *What to Do After You Turn Off the TV? Fresh Ideas for Enjoying Family Time*. New York: Ballantine Books.

Moore, Dahlia. 1995. Role conflict: Not only for women? A comparative analysis of 5 nations. *International Journal of Comparative Sociology* 36(1–2): 17–35.

Moore, Eric G., & Mark W. Rosenberg, with Donald McGuiness. 1997. *Growing Old in Canada: Demographic and Geographic Perspectives*. Toronto & Ottawa: Nelson & Statistics Canada. Catalogue no. 96-321-MPE, no. 1.

Moorman, S.M., A. Boodi, & K.L Fingerman. 2006. Women's romantic relationships after widowhood. *Journal of Family Issues* 27(9): 1281–1304.

Morash, Merry, Hoan Bui, Yan Zhang, & Kristy Holtfreter. 2007. Risk factors for abusive relationships. *Violence Against Women* 13: 653–675.

Morely, Jeremy D. n.d. *Japanese Family Law—or The Lack Thereof!* Retrieved on December 9, 2005, from **www.international-divorce.com/d-japan.htm**.

Morgan, Debra G., Karen M. Semchuk, Norma J. Stewart, & Carl D'Arcy. 2002. Rural families caring for a relative with dementia: Barriers to use of formal service. *Social Science and Medicine* 55(7): 1129–1142.

Morgan, Maggie. 1996. Jam making, Cuthbert rabbit and cakes: Redefining domestic labour in the Women's Institute, 1915–60. *Rural History* 7(2): 207–219.

Morris, S.R., D.C. Dollahite, & A.J. Hawkins, 1999. A qualitative evaluation of the theoretical and ethical foundations and practical implications of father education sites on the World Wide Web. *Family Relations* 48: 23–30.

Morrison, Kati, & Airdrie Thompson-Guppy, with Patricia Bell. 1986. *Stepmothers: Exploring the Myth*. Ottawa: Canadian Council on Social Development.

Morrow, Marina, Olena Hankivsky, & Colleen Varcoe. 2004. Women and violence: The effects of dismantling the welfare state. *Critical Social Policy* 24(3): 358–384.

Morton, Suzanne. 1992. The June bride as the working-class bride: Getting married in a Halifax working-class neighbourhood in the 1920s, pp. 360–379. In Bettina Bradbury (Ed.), *Canadian Family History: Selected Readings*. Toronto: Copp Clark Pitman.

Moscovitch, A. 2007. *Good Servant, Bad Master? Electronic Media and the Family*. Ottawa: Vanier Institute of the Family. Retrieved June 13, 2009, from **www.vifamily.ca/library/cft/media07.html**.

Mossakowki, Krysia N. 2008. Dissecting the influence of race, ethnicity, and socioeconomic status on mental health in young adulthood. *Research on Aging* 30(6): 649–671.

Motiejunaite, Akvile, & Zhanna Kravchenko. 2008. Family policy, employment and gender-role attitudes: A comparative analysis of Russia and Sweden. *Journal of European Social Policy* 18(1): 38–49.

Motohashi, S. 1978. A record of a mother of a handicapped child. *Japanese Journal of Nursing* 42: 968–970.

Motta, Robert W. 1994. Identification of characteristics and causes of childhood post-traumatic stress disorder. *Psychology in the Schools* 31(1): 49–56.

Moustgaard, H., & Martikainen, P. 2009. Nonmarital cohabitation among older Finnish men and women: Socioeconomic characteristics and forms of union dissolution. *Journal of Gerontology: Social Sciences*. 10.1093/geronb/gbp024. Retrieved May 13, 2009, from **http://psychsocgerontology.oxfordjournals.org/cgi/reprint/gbp024v1**.

Muncer, Steven, Roger Burrows, Nicholas Pleace, Brian Loader, & Sarah Nettleton. 2000. Births, deaths, sex and marriage . . . but very few presents? A case study of social support in cyberspace. *Critical Public Health* 10(1): 1–18.

Munsch, Joyce, John Woodward, & Nancy Darling. 1995. Children's perceptions of their relationship with coresiding and non-coresiding fathers. *Journal of Divorce and Remarriage* 23(1–2).

Murdock, George. 1949. *Social Structure*. New York: MacMillan.

Murphy, Christopher M., Shannon-Lee Meyer, Daniel K. O'Leary. 1994. Dependency characteristics of partner assaultive men. *Journal of Abnormal Psychology* 103(4): 729–735.

Myers, Jane E., Jayamala Madathil, & Lynne R. Tingle. 2005. Marriage satisfaction and wellness in India and the United States: A preliminary comparison of arranged marriages and marriages of choice. *Journal of Counseling & Development* 83(2): 183–190.

Myers, Scott M. 2006. Religious homogamy and marital quality: Historical and generational patterns, 1980–1997. *Journal of Marriage and Family* 68(2): 292–304.

Myers, Scott M., & Alan Booth. 1996. Men's retirement and marital quality. *Journal of Family Issues* 17(3).

Myles, John, & Feng Hou. 2004. Changing colours: Spatial assimilation and new racial minority immigrants. *Canadian Journal of Sociology* 29: 29–58.

Naiman, Sandy. 2005, June 7. Marriage: Take the plunge . . . or run away? Retrieved June 6, 2005, from www.canoe.ca/LifewiseHeartLove01/0110_marriage_sun.html.

Nakhaie, M.R. 1995. Housework in Canada: The national picture. *Journal of Comparative Family Studies* 26(3): 409–425.

National Child Benefit. 2009. NCB: A unique partnership of the Government of Canada, provinces and territories and First Nations. Retrieved April 19, 2009, from www.nationalchildbenefit.ca/eng/06/ncb.shtml.

Nault, Francois, & Alain Belanger. 1996. *The Decline in Marriage in Canada, 1981–1991*. Ottawa: Statistics Canada. Catalogue no. 84–536-XPB.

Naumann, Pamela D., et al. 2007. My grandfather would roll over in his grave: Family farming and tree plantations on farmland. *Rural Sociology* 72(1): 111–135.

Nelson, F. 2001 (1996). "Lesbian Families." In Bonnie J. Fox (Ed.), *Family Patterns, Gender Relations* (2nd edition). Toronto: Oxford University Press, 441–457.

Nelson, Fiona. 1996. *Lesbian Motherhood: An Exploration of Canadian Lesbian Families*. Toronto: University of Toronto Press.

Nelson, Geoffrey. 1994 January. Emotional well-being of separated and married women: Long-term follow-up study. *American Journal of Orthopsychiatry* 64.

Nesterov, Andrey. 2004, June 25. Eighty percent of marriages in Russia end up in divorce. Pravda, 25 June. Retrieved December 9, 2005, from http://english.pravda.ru/main/18/90/359/13194_divorce.html.

Newell, Lloyd David. 1999 October. A qualitative analysis of family rituals and traditions. *Dissertation Abstracts International, A: The Humanities and Social Sciences* 60(4), 1348–A.

Ng, Kok-mun, Johnben Teik-cheok Loy, Clinton G. Gudmunson, & Winnee Cheong. 2009. Gender differences in marital and life satisfaction among Chinese Malaysians. *Sex Roles* 60: 33–43.

Niaz, U. 2003. Violence against women in South Asian countries. *Archives of Women's Mental Health* [Wien] 6: 173–84.

Nie, Norman H., & D. Sunshine Hillygus. 2002. The impact of Internet use on sociability: Time-diary findings. *IT & Society,* 1(1): 1–20.

Nielsen, Mark R. 2002. Are all marriages the same? Marital satisfaction of middle-class couples. *Dissertation Abstracts International, A: The Humanities and Social Sciences* 63(11), 4108–A-4109–A.

Nielsen//Net Ratings. 2005. 21st century dating: The way it is. Retrieved November 4, 2005, from www.netratings.com/pr/pr_050802_uk.pdf.

Nielsen//NetRatings. July 2005. Online Dating Survey, UK: MegaPanelo.

Nissimi, Hilda. 2007. From Mashhad to New York: Family and gender roles in the Mashhadi immigrant community. *American Jewish History* 93: 303–28.

Nobes, Gavin, & Marjorie Smith. 2002 April. Family structure and the physical punishment of children. *Journal of Family Issues* 23(3): 349–373.

Noel, Melanie, Carole Peterson, & Beulah Jesso. 2008. The relationship of parenting stress and child temperament to language development among economically disadvantaged preschoolers. *Journal of Child Language* 35(4): 823–843.

Noller, Patricia. 1996. What is this thing called love? Defining the love that supports marriage and family. *Personal Relationships* 3(1): 97–115.

Nova Scotia Advisory Council on the Status of Women. 2000, March. Unpaid work: Some selected statistics. Retrieved May 25, 2005, from www.gov.ns.ca/staw/unpaidw.htm.

O'Donohue, William, & Julie L. Crouch. 1996 January. Marital therapy and gender-linked factors in communication. *Journal of Marital and Family Therapy* 22.

O'Farrell, Timothy J., & Christopher M. Murphy. 1995 April. Marital violence before and after alcoholism treatment. *Journal of Consulting and Clinical Psychology* 63: 256–262.

O'Keefe, M. 1998. Factors mediating the link between witnessing interparental violence and dating violence. *Journal of Family Violence* 13: 39–57.

O'Keefe, Maura. 1996. The differential effects of family violence on adolescent adjustment. *Child and Adolescent Social Work Journal* 13(1): 51–68.

O'Keefe, Maura. 1997 March. Incarcerated battered women: A comparison of battered women who killed their abusers and those incarcerated for other offenses. *Journal of Family Violence* 12(1): 1–19.

O'Leary, Micky, Janet Franzoni, & Gregory Brack. 1996. Divorcing parents: Factors related to coping and adjustment. *Journal of Divorce and Remarriage* 25(3–4): 85–103.

O'Sullivan, P.B. 2000. What you don't know won't hurt me: Impression management functions of communication channels in relationships. *Human Communication Research* 26: 403–431.

Oakley, Ann. [1974]1985. *The Sociology of Housework*. London: Martin Robertson. Reprinted with new Introduction. Oxford: Basil Blackwell.

Oerton, Sarah. 1997. Queer housewives? Some problems in theorising the division of domestic labour in lesbian and gay households. *Women's Studies International Forum* 20(3): 421–430.

Oerton, Sarah. 1998. Reclaiming the "housewife"? Lesbians and household work. *Journal of Lesbian Studies* 2(4): 69–83.

O'Hara, Patricia. 1998. *Partners in Production? Women, Farm and Family in Ireland*. CI, New York: Berghahn Books.

Oliver, Mary Beth, & Constantine Sedikides. 1992. Effects of sexual permissiveness on desirability of partner as a function of low and high commitment to relationship. *Social Psychology Quarterly* 55: 321.

Ontario Association for Marriage and Family Therapy (1996). Marriage and family therapy fact sheet. Retrieved June 7, 2005, from www.oamft.on.ca/about.htm.

Orava, Tammy A., Peter J. McLeod, & Donald Sharpe. 1996 June. Perceptions of control, depressive symptomatology, and self-esteem of women in transition from abusive relationships. *Journal of Family Violence* 11: 167–186.

Orbuch, T.L., J. House, R.P. Mero, & P.F. Webster. 1996. Marital quality over the life course. *Social Psychology Quarterly* 9(2): 162–171.

Orodenker, Sylvia Z. 1990 February. Family caregiving in a changing society: The effects of employment on caregiver stress. *Family & Community Health* 12(4): 58–70.

Oropesa, R.S., & Nancy S. Landale. 2004. The future of marriage and hispanics. *Journal of Marriage and Family* 66: 901–20.

Oswald, Ramona Faith. 2002. Resilience within the family networks of lesbians and gay men: Intentionality and redefinition. *Journal of Marriage and the Family* 64(2): 374.

Overstreet, Stacy, & Shawnee Braun. 2000 April. Exposure to community violence and post-traumatic stress symptoms: Mediating factors. *American Journal of Orthopsychiatry* 70(2): 263–271.

Owen, Michelle K. 2001. "Family" as a site of contestation: Queering the normal or normalizing the queer? pp. 86–102. In Terry Goldie (Ed.), *In Queer Country: Gay and Lesbian Studies in the Canadian Context.* Vancouver: Arsenal Pulp Press.

Paden, Shelley, & Cheryl Buehler. 1995. Coping with the dual-income lifestyle. *Journal of Marriage and the Family* 57: 101–110.

Pagnini, Deanna, & S. Philip Morgan. 1990. Intermarriage and social distance among U.S. immigrants at the turn of the century. *American Journal of Sociology* 96: 405–432.

Pandy, Shanta, & Jeoung–hee Kim. 2008. Path to poverty alleviation: Marriage or postsecondary education? *Journal of Family and Economic Issues* 29: 166–184.

Parr, Joy (Ed.). 1990. *Childhood and Family in Canadian History.* Toronto: McClelland & Stewart.

Paulson, Sharon E. 1996 April. Maternal employment and adolescent achievement revisited: An ecological perspective. *Family Relations* 45: 201–208.

Pecchioni, Loretta L. 2001 April. Implicit decision-making in family caregiving. *Journal of Social and Personal Relationships* 18(2): 219–237.

Peiser, Nadine C., & Patrick C.L. Heaven. 1996 December. Family influences on self-reported delinquency among high school students. *Journal of Adolescence*: 557–568.

Penhale, Bridget. 1993. The abuse of elderly people: Considerations for practice. *British Journal of Social Work* 23(2): 95–112.

Peplau, Letitia Anne, & Adam W. Fingerhut. 2007. The close relationships of lesbian and gay men. *Annual Review of Psychology* 58: 405–424.

Perunovic, Mihailo, & John G. Holmes. 2008. Automatic accommodation: The role of personality. *Personal Relationships* 15: 57–70.

Pescosolido, Bernice A. 1996. Bringing the "community" into utilization models: How social networks link individuals to changing systems of care. *Research in the Sociology of Health Care,* 13(Part A): 171–197.

Pescosolido, Bernice A., Eric Wright, & William Patrick Sullivan. 1995. Communities of care: A theoretical perspective on case management models in mental health. *Advances in Medical Sociology* 6: 37–79.

Peterson, B.D., M. Pirritano, U. Christensen, & L. Schmidt. 2008. The impact of partner coping in couples experiencing infertility. *Human Reproduction* 23(5): 1128–37.

Pflieger, Jacqueline C., & Alexander T. Vazsonyi. 2006. Parenting processes and dating violence: The mediating role of self-esteem in low- and high-SES adolescents. *Journal of Adolescence* 29: 495–512.

Phillips, Lisa. 1995. The family in income tax policy. *Policy Options/Options Politiques* 16(10): 30–32.

Picot, Garnette, & John Myles. 2004. *Income Inequality and Low Income in Canada.* Retrieved March 20, 2006, from **policyresearch.gc.ca/page.asp?pagenm=v7n2_art_03**.

Pina, Darlene L., & Vern L. Bengston. 1995 June. Division of household labor and the well-being of retirement-aged wives. *The Gerontologist* 35.

Pincus, Simon H., Robert House, Joseph Christenson, & Lawrence E. Adler. 2004. The emotional cycle of deployment: A military family perspective. U.S. Army. Retrieved at **www.hooah4health.com/deployment Familymatters/emotionalcycle.htm**.

Plambech, Sine. 2005. "Mail order brides" in northwestern Jutland: Transnational marriages in the global care economy. *Dansk Sociologi* 16: 91–110.

Podnieks, E. 2008. Elder abuse: The Canadian experience. *Journal of elder abuse and neglect* 20(2): 126–150.

Pong, Suet-ling, Lingxin Hao, & Erica Gardner. 2005. The roles of parenting styles and social capital in the school performance of immigrant Asian and Hispanic adolescents. *Social Science Quarterly* 86: 928–950.

Pool, Ithiel de Sola (Ed.). 1977. *The Social Impact of the Telephone.* Cambridge, MS: MIT Press.

Popenoe, David. 1993. American family decline, 1960–1990: A review and appraisal. *Journal of Marriage and the Family* 55(3): 527–542.

Popenoe, David. 1996. Modern marriage: Revising the cultural script, pp. 247–270. In David Popenoe, Jean Bethke Elshtain, & David Blankenhorn (Eds.), *Promises to Keep: Decline and Renewal of Marriage in America.* Lanham, MD: Rowman and Littlefield Publishers, Inc.

Portelli, Christopher J. 2004. Economic analysis of same sex marriage. *Journal of Homosexuality* 47(1): 95–109.

Portrie, Torey, & Nicole R. Hill. 2005. Blended families: A critical review of the current research. *The Family Journal: Counseling and Therapy for Couples and Families* 12(4): 445–451.

Prentice, Susan. 2007. Less access, worse quality: New evidence about poor children and regulated child care in Canada. *Journal of Children & Poverty* 13(1): 57–73.

Pruissen, Catherine M. 2006. Reducing illness in child care. The Resource Centre; Child Care Online. Retrieved April 18, 2006, from **www.childcare.net/ library/reduceillness.shtml**.

Purvin, Diane. 2007. At the crossroads and in the crosshairs: Social welfare policy and low-income-income women's vulnerability to domestic violence. *Social Problems* 54(2): 188–210.

Quach, Andrew S., & Elaine A. Anderson. 2008. Implications of China's open-door policy for families: A family impact analysis. *Journal of Family Issues* 29: 1089–103.

Quirk, Gregory J., & Leonel Casco. 1994. Stress disorders of families of the disappeared: A controlled study in Honduras. *Social Science and Medicine* 39(12): 1675–1679.

Rabin, Claire, & Giora Rahav. 1995. Differences and similarities between younger and older marriages across cultures: A comparison of American and Israeli retired nondistressed marriages. *American Journal of Family Therapy* 23(3).

Raffaelli, M., & L.L. Ontai. 2001. 16 years old and there are boys calling over to the house: An exploratory study of sexual socialization in Latino families. *Culture, Health, and Sexuality* 3: 295–310.

Raj, Aditya. 2004. The world in a city. *The Canadian Review of Sociology and Anthropology* 41: 85–86.

Ram, Bali. 1990. *New Trends in the Family: Demographic Facts and Features*. Ottawa: Statistics Canada. Catalogue no. 91–535E.

Ramsay, Guy M. 2000. The family and cultural identity in Aborigines and Torres Strait Islanders of Chinese ancestry: A rural-urban divide. *Journal of Family Studies* 6(2): 199–213.

Rankin, Elizabeth Anne DeSalvo. 1993. Stresses and rewards experienced by employed mothers. *Health Care for Women International* 14(6): 527–537.

Ravanera, Zenaida R., & Fernando Rajulton. 1996. Stability and crisis in the family life course—findings from the 1990 General Social Survey, Canada. *Canadian Studies in Population* 23(2): 165–184.

Ravanera, Zenaida R., Fernando Rajulton, & Thomas K. Burch. 1998. Early life transitions of Canadian women: A cohort analysis of timing, sequences, and variations. *European Journal of Population* 14(2): 179–204.

Ray, JoAnn. 1990. Interactional patterns and marital satisfaction among dual-career couples. *Journal of Independent Social Work* 4(3): 61–73.

Raymo, James M., Miho Iwasawa, & Larry Bumpass. 2004. Marital dissolution in Japan: Recent trends and patterns. *Demographic Research* 11: 396–419.

Read, Jen'nan Ghazal. 2004. Cultural influences on immigrant women's labor force participation: The Arab-American case. *International Migration Review* 38: 52–77.

Regnerus, Mark D. 2006. The parent-child relationship and opportunities for adolescents' first sex. *Journal of Family Issues* 27(2): 159–183.

Reimann, Renate. 1999. *Becoming Lesbian Mothers: Lesbian Couples' Transition to Parenthood*. American Sociological Association (ASA).

Reisner, Ellin. 2000 October. Work/family spillover: A qualitative study of public transportation operators. *Dissertation Abstracts International, A: The Humanities and Social Sciences* 61(4), 1637–A.

Reiter, Michael, Jaimie Krause, & Amber Stirlen. 2005. Intercouple dating on a college campus. *College Student Journal* 39.3: 449–455.

Remennick, Larissa. 2000 December. Childless in the land of imperative motherhood: Stigma and coping among infertile Israeli women. *Sex Roles* 43(11–12): 821–841.

Remennick, Larissa. 2005. Cross-cultural dating patterns on an Israeli campus: Why are Russian immigrant women more popular than men? *Journal of Social and Personal Relationships* 22: 435–54.

Remennick, Larissa. 2007. "Being a woman is different here": Changing perceptions of femininity and gender relations among former Soviet women living in Greater Boston. *Women's Studies International Forum* 30: 326–41.

Ren, Xinhua Steve. 1997 January. Marital status and quality of relationships: The impact on health perception. *Social Science and Medicine* 44(2): 241–249.

Renaud, Philip J. 2004. Adult interdependent partners and farm estate planning. *Ag-Succession Factsheet* (Alberta Ministry of Agriculture, Food, and Rural Development). Retrieved May 13, 2009, from www1.agric.gov.ab.ca/$department/deptdocs.nsf/all/agdex8649/$file/812-20.pdf?OpenElement.

Rhoades, G.K., S.M. Stanley, & H.J. Markman. 2009. Couples' reasons for cohabitation: Associations with individual well-being and relationship quality. *Journal of Family Issues* 30(2): 233–258.

Richard, Madeline. 1991. *Ethnic Groups and Marital Choices: Ethnic History and Marital Assimilation*. Vancouver: University of British Columbia Press.

Richardson, C. James. 2001. Divorce and remarriage. In Maureen Baker (Ed.), *Families: Changing Trends in Canada* (4th edition), pp. 206–237. Toronto: McGraw-Hill Ryerson.

Richer, Shawna. 2002, June 8. Abstinence, Inc., *Globe and Mail*.

Riches, Gordon, & Pamela Dawson. 1996. An intimate loneliness: Evaluating the impact of a child's death on parental self-identity and marital relationships. *Journal of Family Therapy* 18(1).

Richmond, Virginia P. 1995. Amount of communication in marital dyads as a function of dyad and individual marital satisfaction. *Communication Research Reports* 12(2): 152–159.

Rishi, W.R. 1970. *Marriages of the Orient*. Singapore: Chopmen.

Risman, Barbara J., & Danette Johnson-Sumerford. 1998. Doing it fairly: Study of postgender marriages. *Journal of Marriage and the Family* 60: 23–40.

Risman, Barbara. 1998. *Gender Vertigo: American Families in Transition*. New Haven: Yale University Press.

Rivières-Pigeon, Catherine des, Marie-Josèphe Saurel-Cubizolles, & Patrizia Romito. 2002. Division of domestic work and psychological distress 1 year after childbirth: A comparison between France, Quebec and Italy. *Journal of Community and Applied Social Psychology* 12: 397–409.

Roberts, Albert R. 1996 September. Battered women who kill: A comparative study of incarcerated participants with a community sample of battered women. *Journal of Family Violence* 11: 291–304.

Roberts, Glenda S. 2005. Balancing work and life: Whose work? whose life? whose balance? *Asian Perspective* 29(1): 175–211.

Roberts, Judy, Julia O'Sullivan, & Joan Howard. 2005. The roles of emerging and conventional technologies in serving children and adolescents with special needs in rural and northern communities. *Journal of Distance Education* 20(1): 84–103.

Robinson, Paul. 2009. Profile of child support beneficiaries. *Juristat* 29(1). Ottawa: Statistics Canada. Catalogue no. 85-002-X.

Rodrigues, James R., & Tricia L. Park. 1996. General and illness-specific adjustment to cancer: Relationship to marital status and marital quality. *Journal of Psychosomatic Research* 40(1).

Rogers, Stacy J., & Danelle D. DeBoer. 2001. Changes in wives' income: Effects on marital happiness, psychological well-being, and the risk of divorce. *Journal of Marriage and the Family* 63(2): 458–472.

Roschelle, Anne R. 2008. Welfare indignities: Homeless women, domestic violence, and welfare reform in San Francisco. *Gender Issues* 25(3): 193–209.

Rosen, Larry D., Nancy A. Cheever, Cheyenne Cummings, & Julie Felt. 2008. The impact of emotionality and self-disclosure on online dating versus traditional dating. *Computers in Human Behavior* 24: 2124–2157.

Rosenberg, Stanley D., Robert E. Drake, & Kim Mueser. 1996. New directions for treatment research on sequelae of sexual abuse in persons with severe mental illness. *Community Mental Health Journal* 32: 387–400.

Rosenthal, Carolyn J., & Pam Dawson. 1991. Wives of institutionalized elderly men: The first stage of the transition to quasi-widowhood. *Journal of Aging and Health* 3: 315–334.

Rosenthal, Carolyn J., Anne Martin-Matthews, & Sarah H. Matthews. 1996. Caught in the middle? Occupancy in multiple roles and help to parents in a national probability sample of Canadian adults. *Journal of Gerontology* 51B(6): S274–S283.

Rosenthal, Carolyn. 1985. Kinkeeping in the familial division of labor. *Journal of Marriage and the Family* 47: 965–974.

Ross, Susan M. 1996. Risk of physical abuse to children of spouse-abusing parents. *Child Abuse and Neglect* 20(7): 589–598.

Rotermann, M. 2007. Marital breakdown and subsequent depression. *Health Reports* 18(2): 33–44.

Rounds, Kathleen A., Maeda J. Galinsky, & Mathieu R. Despard. 1995 October. Evaluation of telephone support groups for persons with HIV disease. *Research on Social Work Practice, Special Issue: A Festschrift in Honor of Edwin J. Thomas*, Vol. 5(4): 442–459.

Rowland, D.T. 1991 Spring. Family diversity and the life cycle. *Journal of Comparative Family Studies* 22(1): 1–14.

Russell, Mary, Barbara Harris, & Annemarie Gockel. 2008. Parenting in poverty: Perspectives of high-risk parents. *Journal of Children and Poverty* 14(1): 83–98.

Rwampororo, Rosern Kobusingye. 2001 March. Social support: Its mediation of gendered patterns in work-family stress and health for dual-earner couples. *Dissertation Abstracts International, A: The Humanities and Social Sciences* 61(9), 3792-A-3793-A.

Ryan-Nicholls, Kimberley D., & John M. Haggarty. 2007. Collaborative mental health care in rural and isolated Canada. *Journal of Psychosocial Nursing* 45(12): 37–47.

Sabourin, Teresa Chandler. 1995. The role of negative reciprocity in spouse abuse: A relational control analysis. *Journal of Applied Communication Research* 23(4).

Sacks, Jonathan. 1991. The *Persistence of Faith: Religion, Morality and Society in a Secular Age*. The 1990 Reith Lectures. London: Weidenfeld and Nicolson.

Saewyc, Elizabeth M., Darlene Taylor, Yuko Homma, & Gina Ogilvie. 2008. Trends in sexual health and risk behaviours among adolescent students in British Columbia. *Canadian Journal of Human Sexuality* 17: 1–13.

Saintjacques, M.C. 1995. Role strain prediction in stepfamilies. *Journal of Divorce and Remarriage* 24(1–2): 51–72.

Salisbury, D.L. 1997. Retirement planning and personal responsibility: The changing shape of the three-legged stool. *Generations* 21(2): 23–26.

Salvadori, Marina, et al. 2008. Elevated blood pressure in relation to overweight and obesity among children in a rural Canadian community. *Paediatrics* 122(4): 821–827.

Sanchez, Laura, & Elizabeth Thomson. 1997. Becoming mothers and fathers: Parenthood, gender and the division of labour. *Gender and Society* 11(6): 747–772.

Sauve, Roger. 2002. *Job, Family and Stress among Husbands, Wives and Lone Parents 15–64 from 1990 to 2000*. Ottawa: Vanier Institute of the Family. Accessed December 30, 2002, at **www.vifamily.ca**.

Sauve, Roger. 2009. *Family Life and Work Life: An Uneasy Balance*. Ottawa: Vanier Institute of the Family. Retrieved from **www.canadiansocialresearch.net/work_life_balance.htm**.

Sayer, Liana C., Anne H. Gauthier, & Frank F. Furstenberg, Jr. 2004. Educational differences in parents' time with children: Cross-national variations. *Journal of Marriage and the Family* 66: 1152–1169.

Scanzoni, John. 2000. *Designing Families: The Search for Self and Community in the Information Age*. Thousand Oaks, CA: Pine Forge Press.

Scanzoni, John. 2001. From the normal family to alternate families to the quest for diversity with interdependence. *Journal of Family Issues* 22(6): 688–710.

Scaramella, Laura V., Tricia K. Neppl, Lenna L. Ontai, & Rand D. Conger. 2008. Consequences of socioeconomic disadvantage across three generations: parenting behavior and child externalizing problems. *Journal of Family Psychology* 22(5): 725–733.

Schlesinger, R.A., and B. Schlesinger. 2009. Canadian-Jewish seniors: Marriage/cohabitation after age 65. *Journal of Gerontological Social Work* 52(1): 32–47.

Schneider, Carl E. 1996. The law and the stability of marriage: The family as a social institution, pp. 187–213. In David Popenoe, Jean Bethke Elshtain, & David Blankenhorn (Eds.), *Promises to Keep: Decline and Renewal of Marriage in America*. Lanham, MD: Rowman and Littlefield Publishers, Inc.

Schneider, Jennifer P. 2003. The impact of compulsive cybersex behaviours on the family. *Sexual and Relational Therapy* 18(3): 329–354.

Schultz, Wolfgang. 1983. From the institution of the family to differentiated relationships between men, women, and children: On structural changes of marriage and the family. *Soziale-Welt* 34(4): 401–419.

Schulz, Marc S., Carolyn Pape Cowan, & Philip A. Cowan. 2006. Promoting healthy beginnings: A randomized controlled trial of a preventive intervention to preserve marital quality during the transition to parenthood. *Journal of Consulting and Clinical Psychology* 74(1): 20–31.

Schwartz, Christine, & Robert Mare. 2005. Trends in educational assortative marriage from 1940 to 2003. *Demography* 42.4: 621–646.

Schwartz, Jonathan P., Michael Waldo, & David Daniel. 2005. Gender-role conflict and self-esteem: Factors associated with partner abuse in court-referred men. *Psychology of Men & Masculinity* 6(2): 109–113.

Schwartz, Pepper, & Virginia Rutter. 1998. *The Gender of Sexuality*. Thousand Oaks, California: Pine Forge Press.

Sciadas, G. 2006. Our lives in digital times. *Connectedness Series* 14: 5–23. Retrieved June 11, 2009, from **www.statcan.gc.ca/pub/56f0004m/56f0004m2006014-eng.pdf**.

Scott, Katherine. 1996. *The Progress of Canada's Children*. Ottawa: Canadian Council on Social Development.

Selvin, M. 2007. More wives becoming primary breadwinners. *Los Angeles Times*. Retrieved June 12, 2009, from **http://www.mcall.com/business/yourmoney/sns-yourmoney-0211pay,0,7399103.story**.

Senn, C.Y., S. Desmarais, N. Verberg, & E. Wood. 2000. Predicting coercive sexual behavior across the lifespan in a random sample of Canadian men. *Journal of Social and Personal Relationships* 17: 95–113.

Serewicz, Mary, Claire Morr, & Elaine Gale. 2008. First-date scripts: Gender roles, context, and relationship. *Sex Roles* 58(3–4): 149–164.

Serran, Geris, & Philip Firestone. 2004. Intimate partner homicide: A review of the male proprietariness and the self-defense theories. *Aggression and Violent Behavior*, 9: 1–15.

Sev'er, Aysan. 1990. Mate selection patterns of men and women in personal advertisements. *Atlantis: A Women's Studies Journal* 15(2): 70–76.

Shackelford, T.K., & J. Mouzos. 2005. Partner killing by men in cohabiting and marital relationships: A comparative, cross-national analysis of data from Australia and the United States. *Journal of Interpersonal Violence* 10: 1310–1324.

Shadish, William R., Kevin Ragsdale, & Renata R. Glaser. 1995. The efficacy and effectiveness of marital and family therapy: A perspective from meta-analysis. *Journal of Marital and Family Therapy* 21(4).

Shapiro, A. 2003. Later-life divorce and parent-adult child contact and proximity. *Journal of Family Issues* 24(2): 264–85.

Shaver, Sheila, & Jonathan Bradshaw. 1995. The recognition of wifely labour by welfare states. *Social Policy and Administration* 29(1): 10–25.

Shek, Daniel T.L. 1995 June. Gender differences in marital quality and well-being in Chinese married adults. *Sex Roles 32*.

Sheldon, Kennon. 2007. Gender differences in preferences for singles ads that proclaim extrinsic versus intrinsic values. *Sex Roles* 57(1–2): 119–129.

Sheridan, Michael J. 1995. A proposed intergenerational model of substance abuse, family functioning, and abuse/neglect. *Child Abuse and Neglect* 19(May): 519–530.

Shi, Liping. 2000 February. The communication structure of intercultural married couples and their marital satisfaction. *Soshioroji* 44(3): 57–73.

Short, J., E. Williams, & B. Christie. 1976. *The Social Psychology of Telecommunications*. London; New York: Wiley.

Silver, Cynthia. 2001. Older surfers. *Canadian Social Trends*. Retrieved June 11, 2009, from **www.statcan.gc.ca/pub/11-008-x/11-008-x2001003-eng.pdf**.

Silver, Hilary, & Frances Goldscheider. 1994 June. Flexible work and housework: Work and family constraints on women's domestic labor. *Social Forces* 72: 1103–1119.

Simon, R.W. 1995. Gender, multiple roles, role meaning, and mental health. *Journal of Health and Social Behaviour* 36: 182–194.

Simpson, Jeffry A., W. Steven Rholes, Lorne Campbell, Sisi Tran, & Carol L. Wilson. 2003. Adult attachment, the transition to parenthood, and depressive symptoms. *Journal of Personality and Social Psychology* 84(6): 1172–1187.

Sims-Gould, J., A. Martin-Matthews, Monique A.M. Gignac. 2008. Episodic crises in the provision of care to elderly relatives. *Journal of Applied Gerontology* 27(2): 123–140.

Singer, Merrill C., Pamela I. Erickson, Louise Badiane, Rosemary Diaz, Dugeidy Ortiz, Traci Abraham, & Anna Marie Nicolaysen. 2006. Syndemics, sex and the city: Understanding sexually transmitted diseases in social and cultural context. *Social Science & Medicine* 63: 2010–2021.

Sitrin, Allison Gayle. 2001 September. The impact of the quality of marital adaptation on prenatal maternal representations and postnatal satisfaction with social support. *Dissertation Abstracts International: Section B: The Sciences & Engineering* 62(3–B), 1599.

Skinner, Kevin B., Stephen J. Bahr, D. Russell Crane, & R.A. Call Vaughn. 2002. Cohabitation, marriage, and remarriage: A comparison of relationship quality over time. *Journal of Family Issues* 23(1): 74–90.

Skitka, Linda, & Michele Frazier. 1995. Ameliorating the effects of parental divorce: Do small group interventions work? *Journal of Divorce and Remarriage* 24(3–4).

Skultety, K.M. 2007. Addressing issues of dexuality with older couples. *Generations* 31(3): 31–37.

Smart, Carol, & Bren Neale. 1999. *Family Fragments?* Cambridge, UK: Polity Press.

Smith, Andrea. 2008. Transnationalism and the immigrant: Continuity or paradigm shift? *Identities: Global Studies in Culture and Power* 15: 462–481.

Smith, Jane E., V. Waldorf, & D. Trembath. 1990. Single white male looking for thin, very attractive. . . . *Sex Roles* 23(11–12): 675–683.

Smith, Richard B., & Robert A. Brown. 1997. The impact of social support on gay male couples. *Journal of Homosexuality* 33(2): 39–61.

Smithers, John, & Paul Johnson. 2004. The dynamics of family farming in North Huron County, Ontario. Part I: Development trajectories. *The Canadian Geographer* 48(2): 191–208.

Smithers, John, Paul Johnson, & Alun Joseph. 2004. The dynamics of family farming in North Huron County, Ontario. Part II: Farm-community interactions. *The Canadian Geographer* 48(2): 209–224.

Smock, P., P. Huang, W. Manning, & C. Bergstrom. 2006. *Heterosexual Cohabitation in the United States: Motives for Living Together among Men and Women*. Working Paper. Ohio: Center for Family and Demographic Research.

Smock, Pamela J. 1994 September. Gender and the short-run economic consequences of marital disruption. *Social Forces 73*.

Snell, James G. 1983. The white life for two: The defence of marriage and sexual morality in Canada, 1890–1914. *Histoire sociale/Social History* 16(31): 111–128.

Sommer, Dion. 1992. A child's place in society: New challenges for the family and day care. *Children and Society* 6(4): 317–335.

Sonawat, Reeta. 2001. Understanding families in India: A reflection of societal changes. *Psicologia: Teoria e Pesquisa* 17(2): 177–186.

Song, Jung Ah, Betsy M. Bergen, & Walter Schumm. 1995. Sexual satisfaction among Korean-American couples in the Midwestern United States. *Journal of Sex and Marital Therapy* 21(3).

South, S.J., K. Trent, and Y. Shen. 2001. Changing partners: Toward a macrostructural opportunity theory of marital dissolution. *Journal of Marriage and the Family* 63: 743–754.

South, Scott. 1985. Economic conditions and the divorce rate: A time-series analysis of the children. *Journal of Marriage and the Family* 47(1): 31–42.

Spanking poll backs ruling. 2004, February 1. *Winnipeg Sun*.

Spiegel, Hans M.L., & Donna C. Futterman. 2009. Adolescents and HIV: Prevention and clinical care. *Current HIV/AIDS Reports* 6(2): 100–107.

Spillane-Grieco, Eileen. 1984. Characteristics of a helpful relationship: A study of empathic understanding and positive regard between runaways and their parents. *Adolescence* 19(73): 63–75.

Spiwak, Rae, & Douglas A. Brownridge. 2005. Separated women's risk for violence: An analysis of the Canadian situation. *Journal of Divorce and Remarriage* 43: 105–17.

SPRY Foundation (2004). Computer-based technology and caregiving of older adults: What's new, what's next. Retrieved July 28, 2005, from **www.spry.org/new_publications/CBTCOA_English.pdf**.

Srinivasan, S. 2001. Being Indian, being American: A balancing act or a creative blend? *Journal of Human Behavior in the Social Environment* 3: 135–158.

Stacey, J., & Biblarz, T. 2001. (How) Does the sexual orientation of parents matter? *American Sociological Review* 66: 159–183.

Stacey, Judith. 1990. *Brave New Families*. New York: Basic Books.

Stacey, Judith. 1996. *In the Name of the Family: Rethinking Family Values in the Postmodern Age*. Boston: Beacon.

Stacey, William A., Lonnie R. Hazlewood, & Anson D. Shupe. 1994. *The Violent Couple*. Westport, CN: Praeger.

Stack, C. 2001 (1974). Swapping: What goes round comes round. In Bonnie J. Fox (Ed.), *Family Patterns, Gender Relations* (2nd edition). Toronto: Oxford University Press, 393–400.

Stafford, Laura, Susan L. Kline, & Caroline T. Rankin. 2004. Married individuals, cohabiters, and cohabiters who marry: A longitudinal study of relational and individual well-being. *Journal of Social and Personal Relationships* 21(2): 231–248.

Stanley, S.M., G.K. Rhoades., & H.J. Markman. 2006. Sliding versus deciding: Inertia and the premarital cohabitation effect. *Family Relations* 55(4): 499–509.

Stanton, Glenn T. 1996 May–June. The counterrevolution against easy divorce: New rumbling in the states. *The American Enterprise* 7.

Statistics Canada. 1993. Violence against women survey. *The Daily*, 18 November.

Statistics Canada. 1996a. *Life Events: How Families Change, Labour and Income Dynamics* 5(1). Ottawa: Statistics Canada.

Statistics Canada. 1996b. Dual-earner families. *The Daily*, 6 June.

Statistics Canada. 1997c. *Income Distributions by Size in Canada, 1996*. Ottawa: Statistics Canada. Catalogue no. 13–207–XPB.

Statistics Canada. 1998b. Marriages and Divorces, 1996. *The Daily*, 29 January.

Statistics Canada. 2001a. Marriages. *The Daily*, Thursday, 15 November.

Statistics Canada. 2002a. Changing conjugal life in Canada. *The Daily*, 11 July. Retrieved December 9, 2005, from **www.statcan.ca/Daily/English/020711/d020711a.htm**.

Statistics Canada. 2002b. 2001 Census: Profile of Canadian families and households: Diversification continues. Census release 22 October 2002, **www.statcan.ca**.

Statistics Canada. 2002c. *General Social Survey–Cycle 15: Family History*. Ottawa: Statistics Canada. Catalogue no. 89–575–XIE. Retrieved July 11, 2002, from **www.statcan.ca**.

Statistics Canada. 2002d. Divorces, 1999 and 2000. *The Daily*, 2 December.

Statistics Canada. 2002e. *The Daily*, 26 September. Retrieved April 25, 2006, from **www.statcan.ca/Daily/English/020926/d020926c.htm**.

Statistics Canada. 2002f. *2001 Census of Canada: Profile of Canadian Families and Households: Diversification Continues*. Ottawa: Statistics Canada. Catalogue no. 96F0030XIE2001003. Retrieved October 22, 2002, from www. statcan.ca.

Statistics Canada. 2002g. 2001 Census: Marital status, common-law status, families, dwellings and households. *The Daily*, October 22. Retrieved from **www.statcan.gc.ca/daily-quotidien/021022/dq021022a-eng.htm**.

Statistics Canada. 2002h. Family income, 2000. *The Daily*, 30 October.

Statistics Canada. 2002i, November 6. 2001 Census. Retrieved May 13, 2005, from **www12.statcan.ca/english/census01/Products/Analytic/companion/fam/canada.cfm**.

Statistics Canada. 2002j. *2001 Census of Canada*. Legal marital status, age and sex, Canada. Retrieved January 12, 2006, from **www12.statcan.ca/english/census01/products/standard/themes/RetrieveProductTable.cfm?Temporal=2001&PID=55525&APATH=3&GID=355313&METH=1&PTYPE=55496&THEME=38&FOCUS=0&AID=0&PLACENAME=0&PROVINCE=0&SEARCH=0&GC=0&GK=0&VID=0&FL=0&RL=0&FREE=0**.

Statistics Canada. 2002k. Impact of income on mortality in urban Canada. *The Daily*, 26 September. Retrieved July 28, 2005, from **www.statcan.ca/Daily/English/020926/d020926a.htm**.

Statistics Canada. 2002l. Changing conjugal life in Canada. *General Social Survey*. Retrieved May 13, 2009, from **www.statcan.gc.ca/pub/89-576-x/89-576-x2001001-eng.pdf**.

Statistics Canada. 2002m. Profile of Canadian families and households: Diversification continues. Retrieved May 24, 2009, from **www12.statcan.ca/english/census01/Products/Analytic/companion/fam/pdf/96F0030XIE2001003.pdf**.

Statistics Canada. 2003a, February 24. 2001 Census: Where Canadians work and how they get there: Work at home stable while working outside the country increases. Retrieved May 27, 2004, from **www12.statcan.ca/english/census01/Products/Analytic/companion/pow/home.cfm**.

Statistics Canada. 2003b. Couples living apart. *Canadian Social Trends*. Retrieved May 13, 2009, from **www.statcan.gc.ca/pub/11-008-x/2003001/article/6552-eng.pdf**.

Statistics Canada. 2004a. Divorces. *The Daily*, 4 May. Retrieved August 5, 2005, from **www.statcan.ca/Daily/English/040504/d040504a.htm**.

Statistics Canada. 2004b. Births. *The Daily*, 19 April. Retrieved October 16, 2005, from **www.statcan.ca/Daily/English/040419/d040419b.htm**.

Statistics Canada. 2004c. 2001 Census: Profile of Canadian families and households. Retrieved November 30, 2005, from **www12.statcan.ca/english/census01/Products/Analytic/companion/fam/canada.cfm#same_sex_common_law**.

Statistics Canada. 2004d. 2001 Census: Profile of Canadian families and households. Retrieved November 30, 2005, from **www12.statcan.ca/english/census01/Products/Analytic/companion/fam/canada.cfm#children**.

Statistics Canada. 2004e. June 28. 2001 Census: Families and household profile–Canada. Retrieved May 27, from 2005, **www12.statcan.ca/english/census01/Products/Analytic/companion/fam/canada.cfm#seniors**.

Statistics Canada. 2004f. Family Income. *The Daily*, 26 May. Retrieved January 12, 2006, from **www.statcan.ca/Daily/English/040526/d040526d.htm**.

Statistics Canada. 2005a. Births. *The Daily*, 12 July. Retrieved October 16, 2005, from **www.statcan.ca/Daily/English/050712/d050712a.htm**.

Statistics Canada. 2005b. Canada's Aboriginal population in 2017. *The Daily*, 28 June. Retrieved October 16, 2005, from **www.statcan.ca/Daily/English/050628/d050628d.htm**.

Statistics Canada. 2005c. *Family Violence in Canada: A Statistical Profile*. Ottawa: Statistics Canada. Catalogue no. 85-224-XIE.

Statistics Canada. 2005d. Study: Mature singles who don't expect to marry. *The Daily*, 7 June. Retrieved November 18, 2005, from **www.statcan.ca/Daily/English/050607/d050607a.htm**.

Statistics Canada. 2005e. *The Daily*, 7 February. Retrieved from **www.statcan.ca/Daily/English/050207/d050207b.htm**.

Statistics Canada. 2005f. Divorce and the mental health of children. *The Daily*, 13 December. Retrieved December 14, 2005, from **www.statcan.ca/Daily/English/050309/d050309b.htm**.

Statistics Canada. 2005g. Trends in income inequality in Canada from an international perspective. *The Daily*, 10 February. Retrieved July 28, 2005, from **www.statcan.ca/Daily/English/050210/d050210c.htm**.

Statistics Canada. 2005h. E-commerce: Shopping on the internet. *The Daily*, 1 November. Retrieved from **www.statcan.gc.ca/daily-quotidien/061101/dq061101a-eng.htm**.

Statistics Canada. 2006a. *Annual Demographic Statistics, 2005*. Ottawa: Statistics Canada. Catalogue no. 91-213.

Statistics Canada. 2006b. *Canada's Changing Labour Force*. Ottawa: Statistics Canada. Catalogue no. 97-559-X.

Statistics Canada. 2006c. *The Daily*, 7 March. Retrieved April 18, 2006, from **www.statcan.ca/Daily/English/060307/d060307a.htm**.

Statistics Canada. 2006d. *The Daily*, 30 March. Retrieved from **www.statcan.ca/Daily/English/060330/d060330a.htm**.

Statistics Canada. 2006e. *Family Violence in Canada: A Statistical Profile*. Ottawa: Statistics Canada. Catalogue no. 85-224-X.

Statistics Canada. 2006f. The Internet experience of younger and older Canadians. *Information Analysis Bulletin* 8(1): 8–10.

Statistics Canada. 2006g. Survey of 2005 household expenditures. *The Daily*, 12 December. Retrieved **www.statcan.ca/Daily/English/061212/d061212b.htm**.

Statistics Canada. 2006h. *Telecommunication Statistics*. Retrieved June 11, 2009, from **www.statcan.ca/Daily/English/070514/d070514d.htm**.

Statistics Canada. 2006i. Wives as primary breadwinners. *The Daily*, 23 August. Retrieved from **www.statcan.gc.ca/daily-quotidien/060823/dq060823b-eng.htm**

Statistics Canada. 2007a. 2006 Census: Families, marital status, households and dwelling characteristics. *The Daily*, 12 September. Retrieved May 13, 2009, from **www.statcan.gc.ca/daily-quotidien/070912/dq070912a-eng.htm**.

Statistics Canada. 2007b. Census snapshot of Canada: Families. *Canadian Social Trends*. Ottawa: Statistics Canada. Catalogue no. 11-008: 39–40.

Statistics Canada. 2007c. *Family Portrait: Continuity and Change in Canadian Families and Households in 2006*. Ottawa: Statistics Canada. Catalogue no. 97-553-XIE.

Statistics Canada. 2007d. *Labour*. Ottawa: Statistics Canada. Retrieved from **www41.statcan.ca/2007/2621/ceb2621_000_e.htm**.

Statistics Canada. 2007e. Marriages. *The Daily*, 17 January. Retrieved May 13, 2009, from **www.statcan.gc.ca/daily-quotidien/070117/dq070117a-eng.htm**.

Statistics Canada. 2008a. Births. *The Daily*, 26 September. Retrieved from **www.hc-sc.gc.ca/sr-sr/pubs/hpr-rpms/bull/2005-10-chang-fertilit/intro-eng.php**.

Statistics Canada. 2008b. *Information and Communications Technology*. Retrieved June 13, 2009, from **www41.statcan.gc.ca/2008/2256/ceb2256_000-eng.htm**.

Statistics Canada. 2008c. Life after teen motherhood, *The Daily*, 23 March.

Statistics Canada. 2009. *Study: Hours and Earnings of Dual-Earner Couples*. Retrieved June 13, 2009, from **www.statcan.gc.ca/daily-quotidien/090424/dq090424beng.htm**.

Steele, Fiona, Constantinos Kallis, Harvey Goldstein, & Heather Joshi. 2005. The relationship between childbearing and transitions from marriage and cohabitation in Britain. *Demography* 42(4): 647–673.

Steinberg, Laurence, Susie D. Lamborn, Nancy Darling, Nina S. Mounts, & Sanford M. Dornbusch. 1994. Over-time changes in adjustment and competence among adolescents from authoritative, authoritarian, indulgent, and neglectful families. *Child Development* 65(5): 754–770.

Steinhauer et al. 1984 March. The process model of family functioning. *Canadian Journal of Psychiatry* 29: 77–88.

Steinhauer, Paul D., Jack Santa-Barbara, & H. Skinner. 1984. The process model of family functioning. *The Canadian Journal of Psychiatry/La Revue canadienne de psychiatrie* 29(2): 77–88.

Steinmetz, S.K. 1977. *The Cycle of Violence: Assertive, Aggressive, and Abusive Family Interaction*. New York: Praeger.

Stephens, Linda S. 1996. Will Johnny see Daddy this week? An empirical test of three theoretical perspectives of post-divorce contact. *Journal of Family Issues 12*(4).

Stern, Susan B., & Carolyn A. Smith. 1995. Family processes and delinquency in an ecological context. *Social Service Review 69*(4): 703–731.

Stiffman, Arlene Rubin. 1989a. Physical and sexual abuse in runaway youths. *Child Abuse and Neglect 13*(3): 417–426.

Stohs, Joanne Hovan. 1995. Predictors of conflict over the household division of labor among women employed full-time. *Sex Roles 33*(3–4).

Stop Violence Against Women. 2003, September 10. Prevalence of domestic violence. Retrieved on July 14, 2005, from **www.stopvaw.org/Prevalence_of_Domestic_Violence.html**.

Story, Nathan T., Cynthia A. Berg, Timothy W. Smith, Ryan Beveridge, Nancy J. M. Henry, & Gale Pearce. 2007. Age, marital satisfaction, and optimism as predictors of positive sentiment override in middle-aged and older married couples. *Psychology and Aging 22*: 719–27.

Strasser, Susan M. 1978. The business of housekeeping: The ideology of the household at the turn of the twentieth century. *The Insurgent Sociologist 8*(2–3): 147–163.

Strasser, Susan. 2006. Housework, on Answers.com. Retrieved July 19, 2006, from **www.answers.com/topic/housework**.

Straus, M. 1992. Family violence. In Edgar F. Borgatta & Marie L. Borgatta (Eds.), *Encyclopedia of Sociology, Vol. 2*. New York: Macmillan Publishing Co.

Straus, Murray A. 1996. *Identifying Offenders in Criminal Justice Research on Domestic Assault*. Beverley Hills, CA: Sage Publications.

Strohnschein, Lisa. 2005. Parental divorce and child mental health trajectories. *Journal of Marriage and Family 67*(5): 1286–1300.

Strong-Boag, Veronica. 2000. Long time coming: The century of the Canadian child? *Journal of Canadian Studies 35*(1): 124–261.

Stutzer, Alois, & Bruno S. Frey. 2006. Does marriage make people happy, or do happy people get married? *Journal of Socio-Economics 35*(2): 326–347.

Sudarkasa, N. 2001 (1997). African-American families and family values. In Bonnie J. Fox (Ed.), *Family Patterns, Gender Relations* (2nd edition). Toronto: Oxford University Press, 377–392.

Sugiman, P. 1983. Socialization and cultural duality among aging Japanese Canadians. *Canadian Ethnic Studies 15*(3): 17–35.

Sugiman, P., & H.K. Nishio. 1983. Socialization and cultural duality among aging Japanese Canadians. *Canadian Ethnic Studies 15*(3): 17–35.

Suitor, Jill J., & Karl Pillemer. 1988 November. Explaining intergenerational conflict when adult children and elderly parents live together. *Journal of Marriage and the Family 50*(4): 1037–1047.

Sulman, Joanne, Carolyn J. Rosenthal, Victor W. Marshall, & Joanne Daciuk. 1996. Elderly patients in the acute care hospital: Factors associated with long stay and its impact on patients and families. *Journal of Gerontological Social Work 25*(3–4): 33–52.

Sun, S.H. 2008. "Not just a business transaction": The logic and limits of grandparental childcare assistance in Taiwan. *Childhood 15*(2): 203–224.

Sunahara, A.G. 1981. *The Politics of Racism: The Uprooting of Japanese Canadians during the Second World War*. Toronto: James Lorimer & Company.

Sussman, D., & S. Bonnell. 2006. Wives as primary breadwinners. *Perspectives on Labour and Income 7*(8). Retrieved June 10, 2009, from **www.statcan.gc.ca/pub/75-001-x/10806/9291-eng.htm**.

Sutherns, Rebecca, & Ivy Lynn Bourgeault. 2008. Accessing maternity care in rural Canada: There's more to the story than distance to the doctor. *Health Care for Women International 29*: 863–883.

Sutherns, Rebecca, Marilou McPhedran, & Margaret Haworth-Brockman (Eds). 2004. *Summary Report: Rural, Remote and Northern Women's Health: Policy and Research Directions*. Winnipeg: Centres of Excellence for Women's Health.

Suzuki, Kenji. 2008. Politics of the falling birthrate in Japan. *Japanese Journal of Political Science 9*(2): 161–182.

Swahn, Monica, Thomas Simon, Ileana Arias, & Robert Bossarte. 2008. Measuring sex differences in violence, victimization and perpetration. *Journal of Interpersonal Violence 23.8*: 1120–1138.

Sydie, Rosalind A. 1987. *Natural Women, Cultured Men: A Feminist Perspective on Sociological Theory*. Toronto: Methuen.

Tang, T.N., & K. Oatley. 2002. *Transitions and Engagement of Life Roles among Chinese Immigrant Women*. American Psychological Association Annual Convention.

Taniguchi, Hiromi. 1999. The timing of childbearing and women's wages. *Journal of Marriage and the Family 61*(4), 1008–1019.

Tannen, Deborah. 1993. *Gender and Conversational Interaction*. New York: Oxford University Press.

Tayler, Lyn, Gordon Parker, & Kay Roy. 1995. Parental divorce and its effects on the quality of intimate relationships in adulthood. *Journal of Divorce and Remarriage 24*(3–4).

Taylor, B.J., & M. Donnelly. 2006. Professional perspectives on decision making about the long-term care of older people. *British Journal of Social Work 36*: 807–826.

Teachman, Jay D., & Karen A. Polonko. 1990. Cohabitation and marital stability in the United States. *Social Forces 69*(1): 207–220.

Teare, John F., Karen Authier, & Roger Peterson. 1994. Differential patterns of post-shelter placement as a function of problem type and severity. *Journal of Child and Family Studies 3*(1): 7–22.

Tennstedt, Sharon L., & John B. McKinlay. 1987. *Predictors of Informal Care: The Role of Social Network Characteristics*. American Sociological Association (ASA).

Ternikar, Farha Bano. 2004. Revisioning the ethnic family: An analysis of marriage patterns among Hindu, Muslim, and Christian South Asian immigrants. *Dissertation Abstracts International, 65*(8), 3176–A-3177–A. (UMI No. 3143927).

Thomas, Linda Thiede, & Daniel C. Ganster. 1995 February. Impact of family-supportive work variables on work-family conflict and strain: A control perspective. *Journal of Applied Psychology* 80: 6–15.

Thomas, Madhavappallil, & Jong Baek Choi. 2006. Acculturative stress and social support among Korean and Indian immigrant adolescents in the United States. *Journal of Sociology and Social Welfare* 33: 123–43.

Thomas, Tania N. 1995. Acculturative stress in the adjustment of immigrant families. *Journal of Social Distress and the Homeless* 4(2): 131–142.

Thompson, L.W., J.N. Breckenridge, D. Gallagher, & J Peterson. 1984. Effects of bereavement on self-perceptions of physical health in elderly widows and widowers. *Journal of Gerontology* 39(3), 309–314.

Thompson, Suzanne C., Louis J. Medvene, & Debra Freedman. 1995. Caregiving in the close relationship of cardiac patients: Exchange, power and attribution perspectives on caregiver resentment. *Personal Relationships* 2(2).

Thomson, Elizabeth Jean, & Min Li. 1992. Family Structure and Children's Kin. Madison: University of Wisconsin Center for Demography and Ecology.

Thornton, A., & L. Young-DeMarco. 2001. Four decades of trends in attitudes toward family issues in the United States. *Journal of Marriage and the Family* 63(4): 1009–1037.

Tingey, Holly, Gary Kiger, & Pamela J. Riley. 1996. Juggling multiple roles: Perceptions of working mothers. *Social Science Journal* 33(2): 183–191.

Tjaden, P., & N. Thoennes. 2000. *Prevalence, Incidence, and Consequences of Violence Against Women: Findings from the National Violence Against Women Survey*. Research Report. Washington, D.C., and Atlanta, G.A.: U.S. Department of Justice, National Institute of Justice, and U.S. Department of Health and Human Services, Centers for Disease Control and Prevention.

Todd, Sheri. 2004. *Improving Work-Life Balance: What Are Other Countries Doing?* Retrieved May 22, 2005, from Human Resources and Skills Development Canada & Labour Program: **www.hrsdc.gc.ca/en/lp/spila/ wlb/pdf/improving-work-life-balance.pdf**.

Townsend, John Marshall. 1990. Effects of partners' physical attractiveness and socio-economic status on sexuality and partner selection. *Archives of Sexual Behaviour* 19(2): 149–164.

Townsend, Nicholas W. 2002. *The Package Deal: Marriage, Work and Fatherhood in Men's Lives*. Philadelphia: Temple University Press.

Townsend-Batten, Barbara. 2002 Spring. Staying in touch: Contact between adults and their parents. *Canadian Social Trends* 64: 9–12. Retrieved January 12, 2006, from **http://dsp-psd.pwgsc.gc.ca/Collection-R/Statcan/ 11-008-XIE/0040111-008-XIE.pdf**.

Trudel, Gilles, Lyne Landry, & Yvette Larose. 1997. Low sexual desire: The role of anxiety, depression and marital adjustment. *Sexual and Marital Therapy* 12(1).

Tucker, M. Belinda, & Claudia Mitchell-Kernan. 1995. *The Decline in Marriage among African Americans: Causes, Consequences, and Policy Implications*. New York: Russell Sage Foundation.

Turcotte, Martin, & Grant Schellenberg. 2006. *A Portrait of Seniors in Canada*. Ottawa: Statistics Canada. Catalogue no. 89-519-XIE.

Turnbull, Annmarie. 1994. An isolated missionary: The domestic subjects teacher in England, 1870–1914. *Women's History Review* 3(1): 81–100.

Turell, Susan C. 2000. A descriptive analysis of same-sex relationship violence for a diverse sample. *Journal of Family Violence* 13: 281–293.

Twenge, Jean M., W. Keith Campbell, & Craig A. Foster. 2003. Parenthood and marital satisfaction: A meta-analytic review. *Journal of Marriage and the Family* 65: 574–583.

Tzeng, Jessie M. 2000. Ethnically heterogamous marriages: The case of Asian Canadians. *Journal of Comparative Family Studies* 31(3): 321–337.

Tzeng, Jessie, & Robert Mare. 1995 December. Labor market and socioeconomic effects on marital stability. *Social Science Research* 24.

United Nations Demographic Yearbook 2003. Table 25: Divorces and Crude Divorce Rate by Urban/Rural Residence. Retrieved January 12, 2006, from **http:// unstats.un.org/unsd/demographic/products/dyb/ dyb2.htm**.

United Nations Secretariat. 2003, May. Partnership and reproductive behaviour in low-fertility countries. ESA/P/WP.177. Retrieved November 30, 2005, from **www.un.org/esa/population/publications/ reprobehavior/partrepro.pdf**.

United Nations, Department of Economic and Social Affairs, Population Division. 2004. World Contraceptive Use 2003. Retrieved April 26, 2006, from **www.un.org/esa/ population/publications/contraceptive2003/ wcu2003.htm**.

United Nations. 1991. *Building the Smallest Democracy at the Heart of Society*. Vienna: United Nations International Year of the Family Secretariat.

Usita, P.M., S.S. Hall, & J.C. Davis. 2004. Role of ambiguity in family caregiving. *Journal of Applied Gerontology*, 23: 20–39.

Uskul, Ayse, Richard Lalonde, & Lynda Cheng. 2007. Dating among Chinese and European Canadians: The roles of culture, gender, and mainstream cultural identity. *Journal of Social and Personal Relationships* 24.6: 891.

Utz, R.L., E.B. Reidy, D. Carr, R. Nesse, & C. Wortman. 2004. The daily consequences of widowhood: The role of gender and intergenerational transfers on subsequent housework performance. *Journal of Family Issues* 25(5): 683–712.

Vaijayanthimala, K., K. Bharati Kumari, & Bharati Panda. 2004. Socio-economic heterogamy and marital satisfaction. *Journal of Human Ecology* 15(1): 9–11.

Valdivia, Corinne, & Jere Gilles. 2001. Gender and resource management: Households and groups, strategies and transitions. *Agriculture and Human Values* 18(1): 5–9.

Valens, E.G. 1975. *The Other Side of the Mountain*. New York: Warner Books.

Van de Vijver, & J.R. Fons. 2007. Cultural and gender differences in gender-role beliefs, sharing household task and child-care responsibilities, and well-being among immigrants and majority members in he Netherlands. *Sex Roles* 57: 813–24.

Van Kirk, Sylvia. 1980. *"Many Tender Ties": Women in Fur-Trade Society, 1670–1870*. Winnipeg: Watson & Dwyer.

Van Kirk, Sylvia. 1992. The custom of the country: An examination of fur trade marriage practices, pp. 67–92. In Bettina Bradbury (Ed.), *Canadian Family History: Selected Readings*. Toronto: Copp Clark Pitman.

Van Riper, Marcia. 2007. Families of children with Down syndrome: Responding to a "change in plans" with resilience. *Journal of Pediatric Nursing* 22(22): 116–128.

Vanier Institute of the Family. 1994. *Profiling Canada's Families*. Ottawa: Vanier Institute of the Family.

Vanier Institute of the Family. 2000. *Family Facts*. Retrieved May 12, 2005, from **www.vifamily.ca/library/facts/facts.html**.

Vanier Institute of the Family. 2002. *Profiling Canada's Families II*. Ottawa: Vanier Institute of the Family.

Vanier Institute of the Family. 2004. *Profiling Canada's Families III*. Ottawa: Vanier Institute of the Family.

Vansteenwegen, Alfons. 1996a. Individual and relational changes seven years after couples therapy. *Journal of Couples Therapy* 6(1–2).

Vansteenwegen, Alfons. 1996b. Who benefits from couple therapy? A comparison of successful and unsuccessful couples. *Journal of Sex and Marital Therapy* 22(1).

Vansteenwegen, Alfons. 1998 April–June. Divorce after couple therapy: An overlooked perspective of outcome research. *Journal of Sex & Marital Therapy* 24(2): 123–130.

Varela, Enrique R., Juan Jose Sanchez-Sosa, Angelica Riveros, Eric M. Vernberg, Montserrat Mitchell, & Joanna Mashunkashey. 2004. Parenting style of Mexican, Mexican American, and caucasian-non-Hispanic families: Social context and cultural influences. *Journal of Family Psychology* 18: 651–57.

Vaughan, Diane. 1985. *Uncoupling: Turning Points in Intimate Relationships*. New York: Oxford University Press.

Verberg, N., E. Wood, S. Desmarais, & C. Senn. Gender differences in survey respondents' written definitions of date rape. 2000. *Canadian Journal of Human Sexuality* 9: 181–90.

Vergun, Pamela Bea, Sanford M. Dornbusch, & Laurence Steinberg. 1996. *"Come All of You Turn to and Help One Another": Authoritative Parenting, Community Orientation, and Deviance Among High School Students*. American Sociological Association paper.

Vinokur, Amiran D., Richard H. Price, & Robert D. Caplan. 1996. Hard times and hurtful partners: How financial strain affects depression and relationship satisfaction of unemployed persons and their spouses. *Journal of Personality and Social Psychology* 71.

Vitaliano, Peter P., James M. Scanlan, Jianping Zhang, Margaret Savage, Irl Hirsch, & Ilene Siegler. 2002. A path model of chronic stress, the metabolic syndrome, and coronary heart disease. *Psychosomatic Medicine* 64: 418–435.

Wadsby, Marie, & Gunilla Sydsjoe. 2001 December. From pregnancy to parenthood: A study of couples' relationship. *Frangraviditet till foeraeldraskap: En studie av parrelationen. Nordisk Psykologi* 53(4): 275–288.

Wainwright, Jennifer L., Stephen T. Russell, & Charlotte J. Patterson. 2004. Psychosocial adjustment, school outcomes, and romantic relationships of adolescents with same-sex parents. *Child Development* 75(6): 1886–1898.

Waite, Linda J. 1999. Reviewed work: *Marriage in Men's Lives* by Steven L. Nock. *American Journal of Sociology* 105(3): 866–868.

Waite, Linda J. 2000. The family as a social organization: Key ideas for the twenty-first century, *Contemporary Sociology* 29(3): 463–469.

Walczynski, Pamela Theresa. 1998 April. Power, personality, and conflictual interaction: An exploration of demand/withdraw interaction in same-sex and cross-sex couples. *Dissertation Abstracts International: Section B: The Sciences & Engineering* 58(10–B), 5660.

Waldner-Haugrud, Lisa K., Linda Vaden Gratch, Brian Magruder. 1997 Summer. Victimization and perpetration rates of violence in gay and lesbian relationships: Gender issues explored. *Violence and Victims* 12(2): 173–184.

Wallace, Jean E. 1997 April. It's about time: A study of hours worked and work spillover among law firm lawyers. *Journal of Vocational Behavior* 50(2): 227–248.

Waller, Maureen R., & Sara S. McLanahan. 2005. His and her marriage expectations: Determinants and consequences. *Journal of Marriage and the Family* 67(1): 53–67.

Wallerstein, J., & S. Blakelee. 1990. *Second Chances: Men, Women, and Children a Decade After Divorce*. New York: Ticknor and Fields.

Wallerstein, Judith S. 1996 April. The psychological tasks of marriage: Part 2. *American Journal of Orthopsychiatry* 66.

Wallerstein, Judith S., & Julia M. Lewis. 2004. The unexpected legacy of divorce: Report of a 25-year study. *Psychoanalytic Psychology* 21(3): 353–370.

Walters, Karina L., & Jane M. Simoni. 1999 August. Trauma, substance use, and HIV risk among urban American Indian women. *Cultural Diversity & Ethnic Minority Psychology* 5(3): 236–248.

Walters, Suzanna Danuta. 1999. Sex, text and context: (In)between feminism and cultural studies. In Myra Marx Ferree, Judith Lorber, and Beth B. Hess (Eds.), *Revisioning Gender*. Thousand Oaks, CA: Sage.

Walton-Roberts, Margaret. 2003. Transnational geographies: Indian immigration to Canada. *Canadian Geographer* 47: 235–50.

Warren, Jennifer A., & Phyllis J. Johnson. 1995 April. The impact of workplace support on work-family role strain. *Family Relations* 44: 163–169.

Wasylkewycz, M.N. 1993. The elder abuse resource centre, a coordinated community response to elder abuse: One Canadian perspective. *Journal of Elder Abuse and Neglect* 5(4): 21–33.

Wathen, C. Nadine, & Roma H. Harris. 2007. "I try to take care of it myself": How rural women search for health information. *Qualitative Health Research* 17(5): 639–651.

Watts, Charlotte, & Susannah Mayhew. 2004. Reproductive health services and intimate partner violence: Shaping a pragmatic response in sub-Saharan Africa. *International Family Planning Perspectives* 30(4): 207–213.

Weaver, Terri L., & George A. Clum. 1996. Interpersonal violence: Expanding the search for long-term sequelae within a sample of battered women. *Journal of Traumatic Stress* 9(4): 783–803.

Webster, Pamela S., & Regula A. Herzog. 1995 January. Effects of parental divorce and memories of family problems on relationships between adult children and their parents. *Journal of Gerontology, Series B: Psychological Sciences and Social Sciences* 50B.

Weil, Jennifer M., & Hwayun H. Lee. 2004. Cultural considerations in understanding family violence among Asian American Pacific Islander families. *Journal of Community Health Nursing* 21(4): 717–227.

Weiner, Jennifer, Lisa Harlow, Jerome Adams, & L. Grebstein. 1995. Psychological adjustment of college students from families of divorce. *Journal of Divorce and Remarriage* 23(3–4): 75–95.

Weinfeld, Morton. 2001. *Like Everyone Else … but Different: The Paradoxical Success of Canadian Jews.* Toronto: McClelland and Stewart.

Weiss, Robert S. 1996. Parenting from separate households, pp. 215–230. In David Popenoe, Jean Bethke Elshtain, & David Blankenhorn (Eds.), *Promises to Keep: Decline and Renewal of Marriage in America.* Lanham, MD: Rowman and Littlefield Publishers, Inc.

Weitzman, Lenore. 1985. *The Divorce Revolution: The Unexpected Social and Economic Effects for Women and Children in America.* New York: Free Press.

Wellman, Barry, & Keith Hampton. 1999 November. Living networked on and offline. *Contemporary Sociology* 28(6): 648–654.

West, Carolyn M. 1998. Leaving a second closet: Outing partner violence in same-sex couples, pp. 163–183. In Jana L. Jasinski, & Linda M. Williams (Eds.), *Partner Violence: A Comprehensive Review of 20 Years of Research.* Thousand Oaks, CA: Sage.

Wharton, Amy S., & Rebecca J. Erickson. 1995. The consequences of caring: Exploring the links between women's job and family emotion work. *Sociological Quarterly* 36(2): 273–296.

Wheaton, Blair. 1999. The nature of stressors. In Allan V. Horwitz and Teresa L. Scheid (Eds.), *A Handbook for the Study of Mental Health.* New York: Cambridge University Press, 176–197.

Wherry, Jeffrey N., John B. Jolly, John F. Aruffo, Greg Gillette, Lela Vaught, & Rebecca Methony. 1994. Family trauma and dysfunction in sexually abused female adolescent psychiatric and control groups. *Journal of Child Sexual Abuse* 3(1): 53–65.

Whisman, Mark A., & Neil S. Jacobson. 1989. Depression, marital satisfaction, and marital and personality measures of sex roles. *Journal of Marital and Family Therapy* 15(2): 177–186.

White, James M. 1998. The normative interpretation of life course event histories. *Marriage and Family Review* 27(3–4): 211–235.

White, Lynn. 1990. Determinants of divorce: A review of research in the eighties. *Journal of Marriage and the Family* 52(4): 904–912.

Whiteford, Peter. 2009. *Family Joblessness in Australia.* Australia: Document prepared for the Social Inclusion Unit, Department of the Prime Minister and Cabinet. Retrieved June 2, 2009, from **http://74.125.113.132/ search?q=cache:FdSvSrx4KPwJ:www.socialinclusion. gov.au/Documents/Family%2520Joblessness%2520in %2520Australia2%2520(3).rtf+lone+parenthood+ international+data&cd=12&hl=en&ct=clnk&gl=ca& client=firefox-a.**

Whitehead, Barbara Dafoe, & David Popenoe. 2001. Who wants to marry a soul mate? New survey findings on young adults' attitudes about love and marriage. In *The State of Our Unions: The Social Health of Marriage in America.* Retrieved June 6, 2005, from **http://marriage. rutgers.edu./Publications/SOOU/TEXTSOOU2001. htm.**

Whitehead, Barbara Dafoe. 1996. The decline of marriage as the social basis of childbearing, pp. 3–14. In David Popenoe, Jean Bethke Elshtain, & David Blankenhorn (Eds.), *Promises to Keep: Decline and Renewal of Marriage in America.* Lanham, MD: Rowman and Littlefield Publishers, Inc.

Whitty, Monica T., & Laura-Lee Quigley. 2008. Emotional and sexual infidelity offline and in cyberspace. *Journal of Marital and Family Therapy* 34(4): 461–468.

Wiener, Lori S., Nancy Heilman, & Haven B. Battles. 1998. Public disclosure of HIV: Psychosocial considerations for children, pp. 193–217. In Valerian J. Derlega, & Anita P. Barbee (Eds.) *HIV and Social Interaction.* Thousand Oaks, CA: Sage.

Wienke, Chris, & Gretchen J. Hill. 2009. Does the "marriage benefit" extend to partners in gay and lesbian relationships? *Journal of Family Issues* 30(2): 259–289.

Wiersma, Uco J. 1994 February. A taxonomy of behavioral strategies for coping with work-home conflict. *Human Relations* 47: 211–221.

Wight, Daniel, Lisa Williamson, & Marion Henderson. 2006. Parental influences on young people's sexual behaviour: a longitudinal analysis. *Journal of Adolescence* 29: 473–494.

Wilkinson, Richard G. 1994. From material scarcity to social disadvantage. Daedalus: *Journal of the American Academy of Arts and Sciences* 123(4): 61–77.

Williams, Cara. 2005 Summer. The sandwich generation. *Canadian Social Trends* 77: 16–21. Retrieved January 10, 2006, from **http://dsp-psd.pwgsc.gc.ca/Collection-R/Statcan/11-008-XIE/0010511-008-XIE.pdf.**

Williams, John D., & Arthur P. Jacoby. 1989. The effects of premarital heterosexual and homosexual experience on dating and marriage desirability. *Journal of Marriage and the Family* 51(2): 489–497.

Williams, L., M. Kabamalan, & N. Ogena. 2007. Cohabitation in the Philippines: Attitudes and behaviors among young women and men. *Journal of Marriage and Family* 69(5): 1244–1256.

Williams, Rhys H., & Gira Vashi. 2007. Hijab and American Muslim women: Creating the space for autonomous selves. *Sociology of Religion* 68: 269–87.

Williamson, Deanna L., & Fiona Salkie. 2005. Welfare reforms in Canada: implications for the well-being of pre-school children in poverty. *Journal of Children & Poverty* 11(1): 55–76.

Willms, J. Douglas (Ed.). 2002. *Vulnerable Children: Findings from Canada's Longitudinal Survey of Children and Youth.* Edmonton: University of Alberta Press.

Wills, C. 2001. Women, domesticity and the family: Recent feminist work in Irish cultural studies. *Cultural Studies* 15: 33–57.

Wilson, Paul A., Stephen T. Moore, Dana S. Rubin, & Pamela K. Bartels. 1990. Informal caregivers of the chronically ill and their social support: A pilot study. *Journal of Gerontological Social Work* 15(1–2): 155–170

Wilson, S.J. 1996. *Women, Families and Work* (4th edition). Toronto: McGraw-Hill Ryerson.

Wilson, Sue J. 2005. Partnering, cohabitation and marriage, pp. 145–162. In Maureen Baker (Ed.), *Families: Changing Trends in Canada* (5th edition). Toronto: McGraw Hill Ryerson.

Winch, Robert F. 1962. *The Modern Family.* New York: Holt.

Wind, Tiffany-Weissmann, & Louise Silvern. 1994 May. Parenting and family stress as mediators of the long-term effects of child abuse. *Child Abuse and Neglect 18:* 439–453.

Winfield, Idee, & Beth Rushing. 2005. Bridging the border between work and family: The effects of supervisor-employee similarity. *Sociological Inquiry 75*(1): 55–80.

Wong, Yin-Ling, Irene Wong, & Irving Piliavin. 2001. Stressors, resources, and distress among homeless persons: A longitudinal analysis. *Social Science & Medicine 52:* 1029–1042.

Wong-Wylie, Gina, & Marianne Doherty-Poirier. 1997. *Created Families: Perspectives From Persons Living with HIV/AIDS.* Paper presented at the Canadian Home Economics Association, Victoria, B.C.

Wright, Eric Reaney. 1994 August. Caring for those who "can't": Gender, network structure, and the burden of caring for people with mental illness. *Dissertation Abstracts International, A: The Humanities and Social Sciences 55*(2), 380–A.

Wu, Zheng, & Christoph M. Schimmele. 2005a. Repartnering after first union disruption. *Journal of Marriage and the Family 67*(1): 157–172.

Wu, Zheng, & Christoph Schimmele. 2005b. Divorce and Repartnering, pp. 202–228. In Maureen Baker (Ed.), *Families: Changing Trends in Canada* (5th edition). Toronto: McGraw-Hill Ryerson.

Wu, Zheng, & R. Hart. 2002. The effects of marital and non-marital union transition on health. *Journal of Marriage and the Family 64:* 420–432.

Wu, Zheng, & T.R. Balakrishnan. 1995. The dissolution of premarital cohabitation in Canada. *Demography 32:* 521–532.

Wu, Zheng. 1995. Remarriage after widowhood: A marital history study of older Canadians. *Canadian Journal on Aging 14*(4): 719–736.

Wu, Zheng. 2000. *Cohabitation: An Alternative Form of Family Living.* Don Mills, ON: Oxford University Press.

Wylie, Mary Lou. 2000. Halving it all: How equally shared parenting works. *Gender & Society 14*(3): 485–487.

Xiaohe, Xu, & Martin King Whyte. 1990. Love matches and arranged marriages. *Journal of Marriage and the Family 52*(3): 709–722.

Xu, Anqi, Xiaolin Xie, Wenli Liu, Yan Xia, & Dalin Liu. 2007. Asia: Chinese family strengths and resiliency. *Marriage & Family Review 41*(1–2): 143–164.

Yaffee, Jennifer Beth. 2003. The role of perceived attitude similarity in relationship satisfaction among heterosexual and lesbian couples. *Dissertation Abstracts International: Section B: The Sciences and Engineering 63*(12-B), 6148.

Yarosh, Svetlana, Yee Chieh "Denise" Chew, & Gregory D. Abowd. 2009. Supporting parent-child communication in divorced families. *International Journal of Human-Computer Studies 67:* 192–203.

Yeh, H.-C., F. Lorenz, K.A.S. Wickrama, R.D. Conger, & G.H. Elder. 2006. Relationships among sexual satisfaction, marital quality, and marital instability at midlife. *Journal of Family Psychology 20:* 339–343.

Yick, Alice G. 2001. Feminist theory and status inconsistency theory: Application to domestic violence in Chinese immigrant families. *Violence Against Women 7:* 545–62.

Yick, Alice G., & Jody Oomen-Early. 2008. A 16-year examination of domestic violence among Asians and Asian Americans in the empirical knowledge base: A content analysis. *Journal of Interpersonal Violence 23:* 1075–094.

York, Glyn Y. 1987 Summer. Religious-based denial in the NICU: Implications for social work. *Social Work in Health Care 12*(4): 31–45.

Yoshioka, M.R., L. Gilbert, N. El-Bassel, & M. Baig-Amin. 2003. Social support and disclosure of abuse: Comparing South Asian, African American, and Hispanic battered women. *Journal of Family Violence 18*(3): 171–180.

Young, C., & Boyd, S. 2006. Losing the feminist voice? Debates on the legal recognition of same sex partnerships in Canada. *Feminist Legal Studies 14*(2): 213–240.

Yousif, Ahmed F. 1994. Family values, social adjustment and problems of identity: The Canadian experience. *Journal Institution of Muslim Minority Affairs 15.1:* 108–120.

Zachariah, Rachel. 1996. Predictors of psychological well-being of women during pregnancy; replication and extension. *Journal of Social Behavior and Personality 11*(1).

Zhan, Gao. 1998 June. The sojourning life as problematic: Marital crises of chinese students who are studying in the U.S. *Dissertation Abstracts International, A: The Humanities and Social Sciences 58*(12), 4825–A.

Zhang, S.Y., & S.L. Kline. 2009. Can I make my own decision? A cross-cultural study of perceived social network influence in mate selection. *Journal of Cross-Cultural Psychology 40:* 3–23.

Zhenchao, Qian, & Daniel T. Lichter. 2007. Social boundaries and marital assimilation: Interpreting trends in racial and ethnic intermarriage. *American Sociological Review 72:* 68–94.

Zhou, Min, & Carl L. Bankston III. 2001. Family pressure and the education experience of the daughters of Vietnamese refugees. *International Migration 39*(4): 133–151.

Zick, Cathleen D., & Jane L. McCullough. 1991 April. Trends in married couples' time use: Evidence from 1977–78 and 1987–88. *Sex Roles 24 (7–8):* 459–487.

Photo Credits

Chapter 1 p. 1: © Masterfile; p. 15: Retrofile/agefotostock

Chapter 2 p. 28: Glenbow Archives NA659-2; p. 37: Jupiter

Chapter 3 p. 61: Jupiter; p. 79: Andresr/Dreamstime/Getstock

Chapter 4 p. 92: Jupiter; p. 113: © Masterfile

Chapter 5 p. 122: Jupiter; p. 155: © Masterfile

Chapter 6 p. 159: Tetra/BSIP; p. 166 : John Prescott/Istock

Chapter 7 p. 193: Jupiter; p. 207: Getty

Chapter 8 p. 230: Real Life/Getty Images; p. 245: Getty

Chapter 9 p. 268: Bruce Ayres/Getty Images; p. 293: Jupiter

Chapter 10 p. 304: © Masterfile; p. 324: © Peter M. Fisher/CORBIS

Chapter 11 p. 338: Veer; p. 347: © Brooke Fasani/CORBIS

Index